The

BOOKER T. WASHINGTON

Papers

The BOOKER T. WASHINGTON *Papers*

VOLUME 9

1906–8

Louis R. Harlan
and
Raymond W. Smock
EDITORS

Nan E. Woodruff
ASSISTANT EDITOR

University of Illinois Press
URBANA · CHICAGO · LONDON

The Booker T. Washington *Papers*
is supported by
The National Endowment for the Humanities
The National Historical Publications and Records Commission
The University of Maryland

MANUFACTURED IN THE UNITED STATES OF AMERICA

Library of Congress Cataloging in Publication Data

Washington, Booker Taliaferro, 1856–1915.
The Booker T. Washington papers.

Vol. 9 edited by L. R. Harlan and R. W. Smock;
Nan E. Woodruff, assistant editor.
Includes bibliographies.
CONTENTS: v. 1. The autobiographical writings.
—v. 2. 1860–89.–[etc.]—v. 9. 1906–08.
1. Washington, Booker Taliaferro, 1856–1915.
2. Afro-Americans—History—1863–1877—Sources.
3. Afro-Americans—History—1877–1964—Sources.
4. Afro-Americans—Correspondence. I. Harlan,
Louis R. II. Smock, Raymond W.
E185.97.W274 301.45'19'6073024 75–186345
ISBN 0–252–00771–9 (v. 9)

To the Memory of
Charles William Anderson

CONTENTS

INTRODUCTION

BOOKER T. WASHINGTON always gave the impression of being on top of events and of controlling the course of Afro-American affairs because of his quick pragmatic response to changing situations. The major events shaping the destiny of black Americans in the early twentieth century, however, were out of Washington's control or significant influence. In common with other blacks, he could only adjust to the gathering storm of white racial aggression in the South, symbolized by the Atlanta race riot in 1906; the decline of Republican and federal alliance with black rights, dramatized by President Roosevelt's dishonorable discharge of black regular troops allegedly involved in the Brownsville affray; and the spread of virulent white racism to the North, illustrated by a race riot in Lincoln's home town of Springfield, Illinois. Washington never openly acknowledged that these events were signs of the inadequacy of his program or his leadership, and continued his public course of moderation and optimism. Privately, however, he redoubled his efforts to silence his black critics, to influence white opinion, to build his personal political machine, and to strengthen Tuskegee Institute as a model of black self-reliance.

Washington continued to use spies to infiltrate the ranks of his critics, employing Richard T. Greener at the second meeting of the Niagara Movement, the Wood Detective Agency to seek embarrassing personal information about Monroe Trotter's family, and Melvin J. Chisum to gather information on the Brooklyn branch of the Niagara Movement, which he passed on to Washington at clandestine meetings on a park bench. Though the evidence is not conclusive, Washington also probably focused the light of unfavorable publicity on the interracial Cosmopolitan Club of New York in 1908 as he later did in 1911.

In this period also Washington greatly increased his control of the black press. He acquired part-ownership of the New York *Age*, the leading black weekly of the time, but repeatedly denied publicly and privately any ownership of newspapers. He and his secretary Emmett Scott directed in detail the editorial, news, and business management of the *Age*. Other newspapers in Washington and Chicago also fell under his influence. When J. Max Barber, anti-Bookerite editor of the *Voice of the Negro*, fled to Chicago after the Atlanta Riot, Washington and his lieutenants began systematic efforts to hound Barber into failure and succeeded in driving him out of careers in editing and teaching. Barber finally escaped Washington's wrath by becoming a dentist.

Washington's continued efforts to control black public life were manifested in this period by his private efforts to control the actions of two fraternal orders of which he was not a member. He was successful in keeping one of his supporters as editor of the *Odd Fellows' Journal*, but after heated debate the Prince Hall Masons withdrew their invitation to Washington to be the orator on the occasion of their centennial celebration. To improve his relations with black colleges and to move them more into line with his own educational ideas, he became a trustee of Howard University and secured Carnegie libraries for Fisk University, Alabama State College in Montgomery, and Atlanta Baptist College.

Washington did his best privately to prevent and then to delay the Brownsville dismissal, but after it became clear that Roosevelt's mind was made up, he defended the President and Secretary of War William Howard Taft, not so much in this particular decision but in their general policies. He endorsed Taft early in the campaign of 1908 as Roosevelt's chosen successor, and successfully used the anti-Brownsville utterances of his own critics as a means of putting them in political disfavor and of moving his own lieutenants into their places. Washington and Emmett Scott also tried to use the occasion to improve the lot of blacks in the military system. They were successful in securing an order to replace white bandmasters with black ones in the bands of black regiments, but failed in a more ambitious campaign to balance the dismissed black infantry troops by the creation of a black artillery regiment.

On September 28, two days after the Atlanta race riot, Washington traveled to the city to aid its besieged black leaders and to cooperate with white moderates. The restoration of law and order was accompanied by interracial efforts to achieve a long-range improvement of race relations. Washington gave these efforts an overoptimistic endorsement, urged blacks to control their own lawbreakers, and supported liquor prohibition as a deterrent to black crime.

In the presidential campaign of 1908, Washington's faction struggled with a combination of lily-white Republicans and anti-Brownsville black Republicans for control of the party in Alabama and Louisiana, and carried this fight to the national convention, where he sought to influence the Negro rights and suffrage planks, secure positions for his lieutenants as speakers and campaign workers, and influence Taft's utterances on racial themes.

A commission from Liberia appeared in Washington, D.C., in 1908 to plead with the United States to rescue the small African nation from capitulation to its European creditors and colonial neighbors. Washington played a crucial role as their sponsor, introducing them to the President and Secretary of State and arranging for an American commission to go to Liberia and report on its condition in 1909. At the end of 1908, both the trustees of Tuskegee and President-elect Taft decided that Washington should not be a member of the American commission, but he was to continue to influence its course and American policy toward Liberia.

Tuskegee Institute, now past its twenty-fifth year, underwent little change in these years. In 1906 the Jesup Wagon began its ministry of agricultural reform in the countryside around the school, and in the same year Washington arranged with Seaman A. Knapp of the U.S. Department of Agriculture and with the General Education Board to furnish agricultural demonstration agents for black farmers in the South. After a flurry of efforts by local whites to end the tax-exempt status of Tuskegee Institute, on the ground that its sale of the products of its farms and shops was unfairly competing with private enterprises, an auditor appointed by the governor gave the school a favorable report, and the tax bill was killed. Ever the politician, Washington later interceded with President Roosevelt in behalf of the auditor's son, a Naval Academy cadet dismissed for obscene language.

When Robert C. Ogden resigned as chairman of the Tuskegee trustees in 1907, his place was taken by Seth Low, president of Columbia University, whose emphasis was on rationalizing the educational process and rendering the farms and industries more efficient. Several faculty crises illustrated the decline of Washington's paternal control over the personal lives of faculty members. When G. David Houston, a young Harvard graduate, took another job without giving what Washington considered adequate notice, Washington hounded him in his new job and even went so far as to use Houston's letters to his pastor, purloined from the pastor's desk, to force his apology. When Ruth Anna Fisher, a young Oberlin graduate, refused to "dovetail" the industrial work into her English classes or to teach Sunday school, Washington summarily dismissed her. It was the Edgar J. Penney scandal, however, that presented the principal of Tuskegee with one of his worst dilemmas. The dean of Phelps Hall Bible Training School was accused by a girl student of sexual advances. Though the student was alleged to be promiscuous herself, and though it was a matter simply of her word against Penney's, Washington decided to dismiss Penney for the good of the institution, without passing judgment on his guilt or innocence. Washington perhaps justified this course to himself pragmatically and as a policy of leniency, since Penney had been similarly accused but exonerated some years earlier. To those at Atlanta University, Penney's alma mater, where he served as a trustee, however, Washington's decision seemed specious and unfair. President Horace Bumstead of Atlanta wrote Washington a sharp rebuke, which elicited a rather lame reply.

Washington found many opportunities to encourage the liberalization of white attitudes. The early history of the Jeanes Fund, which he helped to found, is outlined in the letters between Washington and James H. Dillard, the first secretary of the Jeanes Fund. Through agents in the national capital he employed ex-Senator Henry W. Blair to lobby first for and then against the Warner-Foraker amendment to the Hepburn railroad-rate bill. This amendment would have required equal facilities but would have indirectly sanctioned separate facilities on interstate carriers. Washington hastily switched stands on the issue when he learned that Trotter and Du Bois were going to oppose it. After the Atlanta Riot, when Ray Stannard Baker did the research for his articles and book, *Following the Color Line,* Washington not only discussed the subject with him at length but orchestrated his other interviews and bombarded him with advice and criticism. Among the highlights of Washington's public utterances were his address to the theology school of Vanderbilt University, his speaking tour of Mississippi in 1908 in behalf of better schools for blacks, and his candid expression of male chauvinism in a statement on woman suffrage. Privately, he enlisted the support of southern paternalist lawyers, Attorney General Charles Bonaparte, and northern liberals in the case of Alonzo Bailey, a peonage victim. The U.S. Supreme Court decision in this case outlawed peonage in Alabama.

These years were rather uneventful in Washington's personal and family life. He visited his birthplace at Hale's Ford, Virginia. In 1907 for the first time he shifted his summer headquarters from Boston to New York, and rented a house on the beach on Long Island. His daughter Portia returned from her music studies in Germany, and soon thereafter married W. Sidney Pittman, a Tuskegee graduate and an architect.

The editors thank Clarence A. Bacote for permission to publish letters of his father, Samuel W. Bacote. Arthur P. Dudden informed us of the Joseph Fels letter of October 12, 1907. We are grateful to J. Kenneth Morris for calling to our attention an error in Volume 4, which we correct on the Errata page of this volume.

The staff of the Booker T. Washington Papers has made invaluable contributions to this volume, and the editors acknowledge and appreciate the work of Sadie M. Harlan, Denise P. Moore, Judy A. Reardon, Susan M. Valenza, and Linda E. Waskey. Geraldine McTigue was away on a fellowship during the preparation of this volume but returned to the staff in time for proofreading.

The National Endowment for the Humanities, the National Historical Publications and Records Commission, and the University of Maryland have given this project their generous support, and we are grateful for it.

ERRATA

VOLUME 4, p. 433, Judge George W. Kelley was a white man, originally of South Braintree, Mass. He moved to Rockland, Mass., in 1896, where he lived until his death in 1926. Beginning in 1883, he was justice of the second district of Plymouth. He was chairman of the board of trustees of the Voorhees Normal and Industrial School for many years.

VOLUME 8, p. 145, the endnote of the Article on Black Labor in the South should read: "PD Con. 956 BTW Papers DLC." The version that appeared in the Atlanta *Constitution*, Nov. 27, 1904, 9, had another headline and varied slightly from the pamphlet version in capitalization and punctuation.

SYMBOLS AND ABBREVIATIONS

STANDARD ABBREVIATIONS for dates, months, and states are used by the editors only in footnotes and endnotes; textual abbreviations are reproduced as found.

DOCUMENT SYMBOLS

1. A – autograph; written in author's hand
   H – handwritten by other than signator
   P – printed
   T – typed
2. C – postcard
   D – document
   E – endorsement
   L – letter
   M – manuscript
   W – wire (telegram)
3. c – carbon
   d – draft
   f – fragment
   p – letterpress
   t – transcript or copy made at much later date
4. I – initialed by author
   r – representation; signed or initialed in author's name
   S – signed by author

Among the more common endnote abbreviations are: ALS – autograph letter, signed by author; TLpI – typed letter, letterpress copy, initialed by author.

REPOSITORY SYMBOLS

Symbols used for repositories are the standard ones used in *Symbols of American Libraries in the National Union Catalog of the Library of Congress,* 10th ed. (Washington, D.C., 1969).

A-Ar	Alabama Department of Archives and History, Montgomery, Ala.
ATT	Tuskegee Institute, Tuskegee, Ala.
CtY	Yale University, New Haven, Conn.
DHU	Howard University, Washington, D.C.
DLC	Library of Congress, Washington, D.C.
DNA	National Archives, Washington, D.C.
MH	Harvard University, Cambridge, Mass.
MWA	American Antiquarian Society, Worcester, Mass.
MeB	Bowdoin College, Brunswick, Me.
NN	New York Public Library, NYC.
NNC	Columbia University, NYC.
NN-Sc	Schomburg Collection, New York Public Library, NYC.
OO	Oberlin College, Oberlin, Ohio
ViHaI	Hampton Institute, Hampton, Va.

OTHER ABBREVIATIONS

BTW	Booker T. Washington
Con.	Container
NNBL	National Negro Business League
RG	Record Group
Ser.	Series

Documents, 1906–8

From Emmett Jay Scott

Tuskegee Institute, Alabama. May 3, 1906

Dear Mr. Washington: There is something very interesting about the Voice of the Negro which I am sending you today. In the first part of the magazine Barber tries to damn everything as far as he can with faint praise. In an editorial, however, in the last part of the magazine Dr. Bowen unstintedly praises everything. A curious publication from that point of view. Yours truly,

E. J. Scott

TLS Con. 566 BTW Papers DLC.

From Kelly Miller

Washington, D.C., May 6, 1906

My Dear Dr Washington: Since seeing you here in Washington, Sen Blair has recovered his health and has been very active in our matter. He has had frequent conferences with Sen Foraker, Hopkins[1] and others as to the wisest plan of procedure. Some time ago Sen Foraker introduced an amendment providing equal accommodation for all inter-state passengers. This of course we could not sanction; for that would be merely the legal enactment of conditions which it is claimed now exist. Upon our insistence Sen. B. prepared the form of an amendment which goes "the whole hog" and demands that inter-state carriers shall make no discrimination in the choice of accommodations on part of inter-state passengers on account of race color or previous condition. Senator Hopkins has consented to feel the pulse of the senate on this measure, and will introduce it if he finds for it a decent support among his colleagues. So you may imagine it was quite a task to find any one who would even consider it for a moment.

We feel that more has already been accomplished than we set out to do. The original purpose was to keep a sharp eye on things so as to see that no negative legislation was put through on this line. While we are not sanguine enough to hope for affirmative action on the proposed amendment, still we are assured that it will put the enemy on the defensive and thus deprive him of his offensive opportunity.

What about the other installment of counsel fee. It has been intimated to us that it would be acceptable at this time. Yours truly,

Kelly Miller

I trust that you received the Taft pamphlet which I sent you in care of the Stevens House, New York.

K M

ALS Con. 328 BTW Papers DLC.

[1] Albert Jarvis Hopkins (1846–1922) was a Republican congressman from Illinois from 1885 to 1903 and U.S. senator from 1903 to 1909.

To Kelly Miller

[Tuskegee, Ala., ca. May 8, 1906]

My dear Prof. Miller: Your kind letter has been received.

I appreciate all that has been done, but think it wiser for us to wait until the end, or near the end of Congress, before asking any additional payment.

Certainly we want to be sure we are out of the woods. Very truly yours,

Booker T. Washington

TLpS Con. 328 BTW Papers DLC.

From William Burns Paterson

Montgomery, Ala., May 9, 1906

Dear Sir: I claim that Mr Carnegie in your presence after you introduced me to him, promised me:

1. To give me $10,000 for a School Library.

2. To add $5000 to this to make it a Public Library for the colored citizens of Montgomery if the city council appropriated $500 annually for the support of the same.

I claim that the two propositions were separate and distinct from each other. Mr Bertram does not understand it so.

I called your attention to this before, and you promised to see Mr Bertram and set him straight. As he still claims that I am mistaken, I ask you to write him at once as to what Mr Carnegie said. At your suggestion I wrote the propositions down at the time and know I am not mistaken. I write to you in this matter, as you are the only one who can endorse my statement.

My Board of Trustees has appropriated $1000 annually for the support of the Library, and the alumni and citizens will give another $1000 but Mr Bertram still insists on an appropriation from the City. Yrs Very truly,

W. B. Paterson

ALS Con. 331 BTW Papers DLC.

To William Burns Paterson

[Tuskegee, Ala., ca. May 11, 1906]

Dear Sir: I have received your letter of recent date bearing upon Mr. Carnegie's proposition for a library for your school. I would state that I cannot attempt to remember in detail just now what Mr. Carnegie said to you or said to me. I do remember, however, that I introduced you both to Mr. Bertram and Mr. Carnegie and that both expressed a willingness and, in fact, a wish to grant your request for a library. I also recall that either Mr. Bertram or Mr. Carnegie, or perhaps both, expressed the further wish that the building might be used for both school and city purposes and that the city of Montgomery might bear a part of the expense of maintenance, but all this is past history. If you are now convinced that the city council will not contribute anything towards the maintenance of the library and if the board of trustees will put in some definite shape their proposition to give a certain sum annually towards the maintenance, I will be willing to aid you in all the way[s] I can to get Mr. Carnegie to carry out that suggestion. I do not believe — this is of course purely confidential and personal — that Mr. Carnegie would place much stress upon the promise of your graduates to give a certain sum annually. I happen to know that he is constantly besieged with similar propositions, but he sticks to the plan as a rule, of considering only propositions from some official responsible body of persons such as a city council. In promising to take this matter up with Mr. Bertram again, I hope you will appreciate the fact that there is almost never a day that I do not receive a letter from somebody urging me to put some kind of proposition before Mr. Carnegie, and usually the request is to get him to change some condition which he has laid down for the disposal of his money. Of course to 99 out of 100 of these requests I have to say no, because if I were to write Mr. Carnegie or Mr. Bertram every time it is suggested I should make myself a nuisance and have no influence with either of them. In taking you into the presence of Mr. Carnegie and Mr. Bertram, I did something that I have not done except in two other cases during my whole acquaintance with Mr. Carnegie, but since you and I were neighbors I thought it my duty to act as I did.

I think the main thing now is to let Mr. Bertram understand that there is no hope, if you are sure of it, of help from the city council, and the next best thing is to get the $10,000 without considering the council. Yours truly,

Booker T. Washington

P.S. — If you will allow me to express a personal wish in this matter, it would be in the direction of hoping that the library building might be so located that it could be used by both the citizens and school whether the town council helps or not.

B. T. W.

TLpS Con. 331 BTW Papers DLC.

To Thetus Willrette Sims[1]

[Tuskegee, Ala.] May 12, 1906

Dear Sir: In reply to your letter of April 20, let me say that it has been my custom to write and speak of the members of my race as

Negroes, and when using the term Negro as a race designation, to employ the capital "N." To the majority of the people among whom we live, I believe this is customary and what is termed in the rhetorics "good usage." That being so, I am not disposed to quarrel with the use of the word on grounds either of logic or science.

It has long seemed to some of our people, however, that the members of my race have been so long in this country and have become so closely identified with it in all their interests and aspirations that they should be given a political rather than a racial designation and be called Afro-Americans. On the ground of logic and of science this latter title is, perhaps, as good a designation as could be devised. But the fact is — and in this I think you will agree with me — the language is not made by either scientists or logicians. Rightly or wrongly all classes have called us Negroes. We cannot escape from that name if we would. To cast it off now would be to separate us, to a certain extent, from our history and deprive us of much of the inspiration we now have to struggle on and upward. It is to our credit, not to our shame, that we have risen so rapidly, more rapidly than most other peoples, from savage ancestors, through slavery, to civilization. For my part, I believe the memory of these facts should be preserved in our name and tradition as it is preserved in the color of our faces. I do not think my people should be ashamed of their history nor of any name that people choose, in good faith, to give them. Yours truly,

Booker T. Washington

TLpS Con. 382 BTW Papers DLC. The letter was published in U.S. Congress, House, *Congressional Record*, 59th Cong., 1st sess., 1906, 40, pt. 10, App., 83.

1 Thetus Willrette Sims (1852–1939) of Tennessee served in the U.S. House of Representatives from 1897 to 1921. His letter of April 20, 1906, stated that he had moved in the Committee on Education to substitute the word "negro" for "colored race," on the ground that the latter was not sufficiently descriptive, in a bill providing for appointments to the D.C. Board of Education. Some members of the committee argued that use of the word "negro" was offensive, but he replied that he had only "the kindliest feeling for the negroes of South, North or elsewhere." Both letters were reprinted in the New York *Evening Post*, May 19, 1906, 5. BTW's letter and the varying opinions of many prominent blacks and whites were published in the New York *Tribune*, June 10, 1906, sec. 5, 2.

To Neal L. Anderson

[Tuskegee, Ala.] May 12, 1906

My dear Sir: One of the matters which I want to take up with you when I see you I will try to put briefly in writing.

First, I wish to call your attention to the marked portion of my annual report to our Board of Trustees which I enclose. My main effort, in connection with other schools, for a number of years has been to get the masses of the colored people to the point where they would see the value of industrial training, that is, where the public sentiment among the colored people would sustain and support it. I think we have reached that point.

Now, to come more directly to the point. I want to get your opinion concerning the wisdom of our establishing in Montgomery a small department for doing the kind of work that I have outlined in my report. It would be my plan to establish the institution in a small, modest way and to say little or nothing about it in the public press until it had demonstrated what could be accomplished. It would be my wish to have it run during the three summer months, and if there was a probability of its succeeding I would try to push it all through the year, but I think the three summer months would demonstrate whether the plan would succeed.

Now in suggesting this, I realize fully that it would be invading Professor Paterson's territory, but it would not be my plan to try to reach the same class of people that he has in his cooking school or that we have in our cooking school here. The work wants to be taken nearer to the masses of the people and nearer to the interests of the white people than either of us is now doing. It will be my plan to get hold of the colored women who are actually at work at present in the kitchens and dining rooms in Montgomery and to have them spend an hour or more, either in the afternoon or at night, in receiving lessons in proper methods of preparing and serving food, and also in the matter of cleanliness and system in reference to their work. Of course, in this connection emphasis will be laid upon the matter of keeping their promises in the way of contracts and of doing honest, good, careful work, in short it would be a training school for servants, something that does not exist now in any part of the South so far as I know. Now, unless such an effort were to receive the hearty cooperation of the people of Montgomery of both races, the plan could not be carried out. I think I can control the colored people if the white people will cooperate and if Professor Paterson will not feel that we are interfering with his work. I am to see him within a few days and will go over the matter more fully with him in a way to get his hearty cooperation.

Let me add further that on a small scale I have been doing this very thing in the town of Tuskegee for several years, and many of the heads of families have cooperated in the matter. We are hoping to enlarge and perfect this work in the town of Tuskegee during the summer so that in the future it will mean more than it has in the past.

This, in brief, is one of the things I want to consult you about.

Enclosed I send you copy of a letter which I have just received from Professor Paterson, also copy of my reply. Yours truly,

Booker T. Washington

Also, special effort would be made to impress upon the colored women the fact that in proportion as they made themselves more useful, they would receive higher wages.

TLpS Con. 310 BTW Papers DLC.

To William Dorsey Jelks

[Tuskegee, Ala.] May 17, 1906

Dear Sir: I have just found time to read with some care the address which you delivered before the Methodist General Conference at Birmingham, and I want to let you know how very much I appreciate the strong words which you spoke on that occasion and how grateful I am to you for doing so.[1] Yours truly,

Booker T. Washington

TLpS Con. 324 BTW Papers DLC.

1 Jelks spoke out against mob violence and lynching in the South, and urged the assembled ministers to preach against lawlessness. Birmingham *Age-Herald*, May 4, 1906, 1, 8.

To Richard Theodore Greener

[Tuskegee, Ala.] May 18, 1906

PERSONAL

My dear Mr. Greener: I was very glad to receive your telegram yesterday.[1]

I beg to thank you for your goodness in notifying me of your article, and especially glad to learn that all of the statements which have been circulated regarding you are entirely false, and that you have easily refuted them.

I beg to suggest that you arrange for a very frank talk with Secretary Root, and go over the whole matter with him.

I hope to have opportunity of meeting you sometime when I am in the North. Very truly yours,

Booker T. Washington

TLpS Con. 3 BTW Papers DLC.

[1] Greener wired that he had just arrived in Washington, D.C., and was surprised at the slanderous reports circulating about his conduct in Vladivostok. He said he could refute the charges, and that he had the endorsement of the Americans in Vladivostok. (May 16, 1906, Con. 3, BTW Papers, DLC.) A few days later Greener wrote BTW a long letter in defense of his service in Russia. The charges of misconduct and lack of sobriety, Greener explained, were brought against him by a State Department official "*who was never within a thousand miles* of my consulate and who attributes to me the facts of another person of the same name." Greener expected vindication in this case of mistaken identity and hoped to get a promotion and appointment to another office. (May 21, 1906, Con. 33, BTW Papers, DLC; see also Blakely, "Richard T. Greener," 305–21.)

From William Dorsey Jelks

Montgomery [ca. May 18, 1906]

My Dear Sir: I am striving all the time, with all my might, for advancing the cause of law and order in this state. I am succeeding in a fair measure & yet there is much uncovered ground. Truly

Wm. D. Jelks

ALS Con. 324 BTW Papers DLC.

From Andrew B. Humphrey

New York, N.Y. May 20th 1906

Senator Warners[1] rate bill amendment nationalizes Jim Crow Cars. Opportunity of your life to benefit your race by defeating it. Will you join league in effort to defeat it in house conference. Answer care republican Club.

A. B. Humphrey, Secy

HWSr Con. 3 BTW Papers DLC.

[1] William Warner (1840–1916) was a Republican member of the U.S. House of Representatives from Missouri from 1885 to 1889 and U.S. senator from 1905 to 1911.

To Andrew B. Humphrey

[Tuskegee, Ala.] May 22, 1906

Personal

My dear Sir: I have your telegram of May 20th this morning.

I write to say that as I understand it, the various organs of the Republican Club, and the colored people of Boston and Washington as well as of Chicago, have been behind Senator Foraker's effort in the matter of the amendment which was defeated, and which was subsequently re-introduced by Senator Warner and passed.

I regret to say that I had not seen Senator Warner's amendment, and of course could not intelligently proceed without having it before me.

Let me add, that the Committee of Twelve has a committee in Washington composed of Mr. Miller, and Mr. Grimke, with funds, and with some one employed to guard the interests of the race on this particular subject, and I have communicated your telegram to them.

They being on the ground, of course, I think will know better how to handle the situation than any one from a distance. Very truly yours,

Booker T. Washington

TLpS Con. 3 BTW Papers DLC. A carbon is in the Archibald H. Grimké Papers, DHU.

From Kelly Miller

Washington, D.C. May 22 1906

My Dear Dr Washington: The Warner-Foraker Amendment providing equal accommodations for passengers paying like fare has passed the Senate and now goes to Conference. Mr Grimke and myself regard this provision as obnoxious in that it gives implied national sanction to local jim-crow laws. The matter of equal accommodation is no more than the several Southern States now provide. Should this provision be imbedded in the law, the rail road companies in the North could separate the races without, and indeed inspite of state enactment. I do not see a single feature of good in the amendment. The colored people in the jim-crow states have already the provision requiring equal accommodations, which, strange to say, they rarely invoke. The nation at large has shown quite fully its inability or indisposition to deal effectually with Southern conditions against local sentiment.

We have been using all of our influence to have this enactment withdrawn in conference. If this can be done, as now seems likely, the rate bill will leave us where it found us, and while it will not advance, it will not prejudice our cause.

Perhaps I ought to say that Sen. B.[1] has been very active in our behalf. He tried his best to get some senator to introduce an affirmative amendment guaranteeing passengers against discrimination on account of race or color, but no such senator could be found. Sen B does not agree with us as to the wisdom of having the Warner-Foraker amendment withdrawn. He does not see that it can be interpreted or construed into national sanction of jim crow laws. In this judgment however I find myself in most strenuous disagreement. However we are both satisfied with the interest and energy with which he has pressed the matter and feel sure that he has fully earned the stipulated fee. There is nothing further left for him to do in the case. He is always ready however to put us in touch with parties whom we think it well to see.

I will be out of town for some time and beg that you forward balance of counsel fee through Mr Grimke and also whatever further suggestions you care to make in the matter. Yours truly

Kelly Miller

ALS Con. 33 BTW Papers DLC.

[1] Henry W. Blair.

From Archibald Henry Grimké

Washington, May 25/06

Dear Mr. Washington: Yours of the 22d inst. with enclosures was duly recd & contents carefully noted. Both Kelly Miller & myself have done what we could do to get the Warner amendment out of the Railway Rate Bill. Other bodies of colored men have also been active in the matter, and I think that it will be eliminated in the Conference Committee of the two houses of Congress in deference to the wishes of the colored people. Kelly Miller has left the city to be gone about a month & so I am here alone. Ex Sen. Blair will be glad to get the other $150. for his services at the earliest possible convenience to the Committee of Twelve. Very truly yours,

Archibald H. Grimké

ALS Con. 3 BTW Papers DLC.

To Robert Curtis Ogden

[Tuskegee, Ala.] May 28, 1906

Dear Mr. Ogden: Replying to yours of May 21 I would state that in order to be absolutely sure of retaining Mr. Taylor's services, in my opinion I am sure we will have to add four or five hundred dollars to his present salary.[1] The Oklahoma people are very insistent and very tempting in their offers. As I have told Mr. Peabody, I should consider it a far-reaching calamity for us to lose Mr. Taylor at Tuskegee. Yours very truly,

Booker T. Washington

TLpS Con. 602 BTW Papers DLC.

[1] Ogden replied: "You are authorized to add four hundred dollars to salary as suggested." (May 31, 1906, Con. 602, BTW Papers, DLC.)

To Samuel Laing Williams

[Tuskegee, Ala.] May 28, 1906

Personal

Dear Mr. Williams: I write to say that all during the session of the Congress I have had two colored and one white friend on guard at Washington, who have been very carefully looking into such amendments as were made to the rate bill. This white friend is Senator Blair who has access to the floor of the Senate and who has kept out of the bill so far any legislation against us. He will continue until the session ends.

With reference to the other matter to which you refer in another communication, I am really somewhat at a loss as to how to proceed. We have, as you know, the President's statement that in case you declined Bahia that something equally as good would be provided, but I have approached him as you know, so many times, and while I do not hesitate to render any service I can, I yet am wondering now just how I can again seek to draw his attention to the matter. I wonder if there is any way you can have the Illinois senators help out? Yours very truly,

Booker T. Washington

TLpS Con. 34 BTW Papers DLC.

An Account of the Twenty-fifth Anniversary of Tuskegee Institute by Jesse Max Barber

May, 1906

The Twenty-fifth Anniversary of the founding of Tuskegee Institute marks an epoch and emphasizes an idea. This is a commercial age, and Tuskegee is the most striking instance of the regnancy of industrialism. A curve is determined by finding the points through which it moves. Even so the significant movements of human progress and regress are determined by knowing the points through which forward and backward movements actually proceed. Tuskegee is a point on the curve in the great sweep of American history. This is the era of the "Captains of Industry." It is an era when economic culture is more potent than mental and spiritual culture, and Tuskegee is its thermometer. Few events in human history are so startling and significant as this sudden, mushroom-like upgrowth of an idea. The noblest and best impulses of a democracy, such as social justice, civic and political equality and brotherly sympathy have lost power over the minds of men. There has been a general revolution in American thought on the Negro question. The desire to maintain a real democracy crumbles. The old and ancient doctrines of equality have fallen into desuetude. The country has swung around to the side of a respectable aristocracy. The one great tendency which gradually evolves itself out of the wreck and chaos of old ideals is the tendency towards a sordid utilitarianism. This came out in all the principal addresses at the Anniversary. The speakers argued that in as much as we were living in the presence of great forces of capital and labor, and in as much as the age is worshiping the gold and silver deities we jingle in our pockets, then the sensible thing for us to do in order to be rated as a great people is to join in the mad race for the current coin of greatness — money — and overtake it. So much for the moral awryness of the times. But this great Anniversary has a significance wholly apart from its emphasis of the industrial idea. It was of magnitudinous import from a political standpoint. It brought together the millionaires, the educators and the politicians, the three classes which run this country; and they all joined in the praise of Booker Washington and pledged him their support. They claimed that we are coming to the end of a mistaken policy and that Mr. Washington is responsible therefor. Therefore, they plead for him to have enormous and unshackled power. Thus, this Anniversary, revealing, as it did, the fact that we have not only the massing of great wealth in the hands of one man for the propagation of an idea, but also the unprecedented concentration of all the political power and destiny of a race in the hands of a single man — signifies the fact that Mr. Washington's well-known political ideas regarding the Negro are going to prevail. Of course the magnificently disciplined student body was [an] inspiration to all visitors; the music of the choir was, as Andrew Carnegie said, "heavenly"; the exhibits, evidently prepared with the utmost care, were bedazzling; and the vast sweep of the plant was almost overawing. That was the purpose of the Anniversary. It was designed to emphasize the Tuskegee idea and to advertise Mr. Washington. As such, it was a glorious success.

TUSKEGEE'S REMARKABLE GROWTH

Tuskegee has, as it were, sprung up in a night. She has not moved along on her upward journey with tranquil and stately tread like the great educational institutions of the world. Rather she has fairly galloped along with noise and shouting. Twenty-five years is a very short period in which to build either a school or a community with the dimensions of Tuskegee. The school was opened July 4, 1881, with one teacher and thirty pupils. Today there are 2,100 people in the community, 1,600 of whom are students and 156 of whom are teachers. The school started in a dilapidated old church, and even that was not owned by the Institute. Today the plant includes 2,300 acres of land with 83 buildings. The present property of the school is valued at $831,895, and the endowment fund is in the neighborhood of $2,000,000. Eight hundred and eighty-eight persons hold diplomas from the school and the courses at Tuskegee include 37 distinct industries. Aside from the regular school work, much good is being done among the farmers, ministers and mothers around the town. The 6,000 men who have taken partial or complete courses in the school are doing much to ameliorate economic conditions and to promote and conserve economic progress among our people. It would be unjust to claim that no general good had been accomplished by the school. Tuskegee is a blessing to the black belt of Alabama, and, by developing habits of thrift in the people, by creating a healthy sentiment against the death-traps in unsanitary one-room log cabins and by creating within the people a desire for economic independence, Tuskegee has done much good, and yet has the opportunity to lift from the weight of human woe an almost incalculable degree of poignant and pathetic misery. Any opposition to Dr. Washington is unreasonable which is based merely upon dislike for industrial schools. It is true that the buildings are poor and crude for the most part; but then they were built by the students and serve their purpose as advertisements. It is true that the graduates of Tuskegee are not so well fitted to be teachers and leaders as they are to be ordinarily intelligent and independent citizens. But the majority of us must have that as our ambition after all. We try to define the attitude of those who criticise Mr. Washington in the following note.

Booker Washington

Tuskegee is the creation of Dr. Washington and takes its form and absorbs its spirit from its distinguished founder. Therefore, when we speak of either the accomplishments or the failures of Tuskegee, we give the credit to Mr. Washington. Mr. Washington is not a man whom we reverence without reservation. He does not clasp hands across the ages with such strong men as Cavour, Alfred the Great and Frederick the Great. Nevertheless, he has a strong personality and is a man of unusual force and power. He has risen from slavery and up through the heat of a vital struggle to the place where he is one of the foremost figures of the times. This man has really started a movement and led captive a nation. Any man who is able to eject prejudice and establish a basis of sympathy between the races possesses some of the elements of greatness and deserves credit. Whatever fault may be found with Washington — and there are a few specks on his dazzling career — cannot obscure the fact that he has achieved a tremendous task. Ordinary men are not in possession of the superb organizing ability and business acumen of this man. At Tuskegee "the tall, the wise and the reverend heads" were all bowing to a Negro. Washington is a man of magnificent poise, else his head would be turned amidst all the tumult of demonstrative loyalty. We pay him the tribute of our admiration. But all of this glory cannot veil the weakness of some of Mr. Washington's positions. It was said once that "nearly all origins are tainted." That may account for any taint of hyprocrisy and deception we see about Tuskegee. Mr. Washington has made grave mistakes in his public policy. Mr. Washington's injudicious admirers who indulge in absurd rhapsodies, mere undiscriminating eulogies over him will not be pleased that we have said this. Nevertheless, this criticism is made with knowledge and discretion. At Tuskegee the spectacular side is overdone. The Anniversary was like a great fair and we would venture the assertion that many weeks were required in doing nothing but getting the show in order. While Mr. Washington himself appears to be simplicity personified, still he is behind and over the whole school as its great head and general. While it is true that he has advanced beyond the position he took up twenty years ago, still he insists that our problem is economic, that the Negro's chief need is wealth and that for the present we do not need to concern ourselves about civic and political rights and duties. Here lies the essential antagonism between the two schools of thinkers on the race problem. The men who criticise Mr. Washington agree that economic culture is good, that poverty is a drawback, that thrifty habits made wildernesses blossom and that general industrial and agrarian prosperity is desirable. But they do not yield mere material prosperity the right to hold the sceptre. High ideals will, in the end, have more to do with the ultimate ethological condition of the race, will aid us more in our fight against sodden environment or hereditary sins than any amount of wealth. The things which sustain and elevate character are higher in the hierarchy of forces, more exalted than the things which we can handle. The principles of right and justice are fundamental and not subsidiary. Food and raiment are not the most important elements in human progress. Rather the march of human progress is characterized by the language evolved, the literature created and the historical events humanity has figured in. If a race makes wealth the chief object of its life, in the pursuit of it, the higher moral and intellectual faculties are left uncultivated; the formation of character is neglected; and the purpose of existence, the simultaneous development of those qualities and faculties to the utmost degree of which they are capable, is altogether lost sight of. The various faculties of man demand the widest variety of vocation in order to promote the expansion of the individual character and to develop the race. While Mr. Washington has of late thrown in a parenthetical expression about higher education, his main influence has been on the other side and he has at times poked fun at the college-bred Negro. How far a word from Mr. Washington goes! He has laid a spell on the imagination of the American people, so that his words, instead of being lighter than the words of Eliot and Hadley are tinctured with a greater gravity.

The Place for Mr. Washington

Thus it is plain that upon one thing, we are all agreed: Tuskegee is a useful institution. Mr. Washington, as its head, is an eminently useful citizen. His admirers claim for him that he has the capacity to conceive and the courage to execute a comprehensive policy of racial development. On the other hand, it seems true that while he is a man of profound political ability, being more adroit than the man who was bred in the school of politics, he does not seem to possess sound political ideas. Probably, however, his most fatal blunder was his decrying at the very beginning the work the higher schools were doing. Without the colleges Tuskegee herself could not exist. Suppress these higher institutions and you might have a people without noble ambition, without high personal morality — without all of those noble qualities which confer nobility upon men and greatness upon nations. Mr. Washington surely could not wish it, but it is true that his preachments have almost paralyzed the higher schools for the Negro. Mr. Washington might not have so desired, but the truth is that the South has used his public speeches effectively to convince the North that what the Negro wanted was not political and civic equality but industrial opportunity. The white man is a vain animal. He loves flattery. He loves to be told that his race is a race of lords. He loves to be entreated and looked up to as high and mighty. He loves to think that the whole earth lays hushed beneath the shadow of his gigantic power. Mr. Washington is a great student of human nature. He has won his way up largely by his cajolery. Now that he has won by his exceedingly smart diplomatic strokes, he is not to be scoffed at lightly. All of us must concede him a place in the shaping of the destinies of the Negro. Great good may come out of Tuskegee, as has come out of and redeemed other human errors and wanderings. Then, what place can Mr. Washington fill to the satisfaction of all the intelligent forces of the race? Surely, not that of a political leader; certainly not that of advisor to the President for the Negro, whether openly or secretly. Assuredly not that of supervisor of education for the Negro race in America. He is more useful as a leader in promoting the economic efficiency of the race; and then his work would be done best as a group-worker. Instead of frittering away his strength looking into every three and six penny affair that pertains to the Negro, he ought to give himself to the work which he has so nobly founded. The black belt of Alabama needs him more than any other section of the country.

Principal Addresses

We cannot so much as mention all of the speeches upon this great occasion. Men and women from all the principal avenues of life were on the program. There were educators, financiers, journalists, churchmen and statesmen. This is one of the greatest benefits derived from the Anniversary: it brought together many of the leading thinkers and workers of the country, North and South, who ventilated their opinions on the race question. A great deal has been accomplished when free speech can be had in the South, when the men of all sections, white and black, can come and discuss the problems of the country without danger of insult or personal injury. Scarcely any other school in the whole country could have brought together a more notable group of men. The names of Lyman Abbott of the New York Outlook, Oswald Garrison Villard of the New York Evening Post, Presidents H. B. Frissell of Hampton, Eliot of Harvard, Wiggins of the University of the South, and Abercrombie of the University of Alabama, William Lloyd Garrison, son of the famous abolitionist, Robert Ogden, Andrew Carnegie, Bishop Grant and Secretary Taft but convey to the reader an idea of the personnel of the gathering. There were many significant addresses made during the days of the Anniversary. To the writer, most of the speeches made by the colored speakers were light and school-boyish. They did not seem to venture out from the shore of mere praise for Mr. Washington. Seldom did one launch out into the deep to discuss the real vital problems of the day. Probably it should be said of Mr. W. J. Edwards, of Snow Hill, Ala., that he did make a splendid address in which he showed a disposition to break away from the dreary drip of doleful declamation about the greatness of Booker T. Washington and to tell the truth about conditions in the South. The speech of Principal Washington was really a new speech. There was about it a fine show of exalted emotion characteristic of statesmen and scholars. After reviewing the history of Tuskegee Mr. Washington entered upon a discussion of civil and political conditions in the South. In a way he rebuked the country for its political treachery to the Negro, sounding a warning note to the effect that free government was losing ground thereby; pointed out the impossibility of a community rising while at the same time trying to keep down an integral part of itself; rebuked the mob and declared that he desired that the Negro have free scope to develop himself to the limit. Of course, he still sticks to his original doctrine, that the fundamental industries are the birthright of the race, but, on the whole, the address was a hint to the world that the man had come to think more of the finer and higher things in life than he did in days gone by. The addresses of Revs. E. C. Morris and S. G. Atkins were unfortunate in that they introduced denominationalism into a meeting that was altogether non-sectarian. One discussed the contribution of the Baptists to racial uplift, while the other spoke of what the A.M.E. Zion Church had done along the same line. The Negro is already too violently denominational when it comes to the place where we need unity of action from a racial standpoint. Such addresses are out of place anywhere save in a denominational gathering. Of course, the speakers were not responsible, only so far as they were willing to lend themselves to the occasion in any way the program committee saw fit to use them. A strong, manly address was made by President Wiggins of the University of the South at Sewanee, Tenn. As a white man, he took the position that a Negro had a right to citizenship both through the Constitution and through the labor of his strong right arm. Bishop Galloway is an orator of the old Southern school. His address was replete with fine flights of eloquence and rich, rounded periods. The good Bishop is one of the first and most liberal men in the whole South. He said that "sections and races should be forgotten" in this great upward struggle, that the Southern demagogue who stirred up race hate "writes day by day a social and national tragedy," and he put himself squarely on the side of liberty, justice and equal opportunity for all the races. President Eliot of Harvard suggested something alien to the Constitution. He thought that the national government would do well to appropriate large amounts of money for colored industrial schools. The Negroes, as citizens of this country, cannot expect such special legislation nor do they want it. Such legislation would superimpose upon the country something utterly unknown to the Constitution: class legislation. Probably the most vivid and dramatic feature of the whole Anniversary was the ten-minute address of William Lloyd Garrison, son of the famous abolitionist by the same name. President Abercrombie of the University of Alabama, had just made a typical Southern white man's speech. He defended the South in all of its prejudices, declared the enfranchisement of the slave to be a colossal blunder and said that the Negro could only rise in proportion to the way in which he got along with his white neighbors. Mr. Washington paused in the execution of the program at the conclusion of Abercrombie's speech long enough to introduce Mr. Garrison, who was seated in the audience. Garrison, venerable and white-bearded, simply arose and bowed to the deafening applause of the audience. But the audience was insistent and continued its applause until Mr. Garrison went to the stage. In a ten-minute address delivered in a low but vibrant and penetrating voice, he repudiated Abercrombie. He declared that class distinctions were invidious and perversive of democratic principles; that he was a member of the human race as well as the white race, and therefore wanted to see all men treated justly; he said that this talk about the enfranchisement of the Negro being a blunder was the veriest nonsense, for, said he, "the way to teach a man to vote is to put a ballot in his hand." The audience was swept by this manly address and fairly broke loose in thunderous hand-clapping and shouting as at no other time during the whole Anniversary.

Secretary Taft and Mr. Carnegie

But if Mr. Garrison's address was the most dramatic, Secretary of War William Taft's was by far the most significant. The speech was important as defining the policy to which the administration has committed itself regarding the Negro, for the big Secretary of War declared that he brought a message from the President and the Cabinet. The speech was one of the few clear declarations of policy on political conditions in the South which has emanated from men high in authority. The speeches of most of the government authorities on this question, from Roosevelt down, have been marked by no spirited policy. Rather they have been full of soft, purring, patronizingly charitable phrases and platitudes. Mr. Taft was frank. The very frankness of his speech with its fluent phrases made the address fall pleasantly upon the listening ear. It seemed so full of liberality as it came trippingly from his great, persuasive tongue. The Secretary casts a spell upon his hearers while he talks, but when his speech is critically examined in cold print, it will at once be observed that it has no moral bottom to it. Mr. Taft took for his text the "Three War Amendments." He declared that the Thirteenth and Fourteenth Amendments were right and just and that they must be enforced. From the Fourteenth Amendment he branched out into an extensive discussion of the history of the Negro in the field of politics and education. He said that the many movements for securing Negro education were not best adapted to the Negro's needs. He declared that "the only hope of the Negro race was economic independence" and paid a great tribute to Booker T. Washington for leading out along this line of "least popular resistance." He declared that we were "a people not fit to enjoy or maintain the higher education" as "primary and industrial education" was our chief need. Returning to the Fifteenth Amendment Mr. Taft assumed that the reports that it had been violated were true, but said that the situation was by no means hopeless for the Negro. He thought that we ought to acquiesce in the discriminatory laws and look forward to the day when we would be able to return to the polls because of our educational and property qualifications. Mr. Taft took the position that "the very desire to avoid fraudulent methods which were wont to overcome the colored vote in the South itself indicates a turn for the better." Here lies a double delusion. In the first place time will destroy the dream and expose the fallacy that prejudice against the Negro will abate as he rises. The ballot is the most powerful weapon against race prejudice. There was not near as much of it when the Negro had the ballot as there is today. Then disfranchisement certainly does not indicate a turn for the better, as Mr. Taft maintains. To make stealing legal and public does not indicate a more healthy morality; and although the operations of a thief are artistic, that is no reason why the police should not guard the people. Disfranchisement indicates a distinct lowering of the moral tone of the South. Heretofore, this section was not bold enough and strong enough in its deviltry to flaunt it before the world as law. Certainly in this instance Mr. Taft pandered to dishonesty. Why are we to maintain a bland indifference to our political interests? Why is not such advice given to the offscourings of Europe's destitution who come to America? Is the democracy a failure and are the principles of equality to be found only in the poetry of politics? In declaring that our only hope is economic independence, Mr. Taft overlooks the most insistent warning of all history, and that is that any people who grow materially rich while remaining spiritually poor sow the seeds of their own decay and dissolution. Mr. Taft's speech is important, not only as a message from Roosevelt but also because Mr. Taft is slated to a seat on the bench of the Supreme Court or the candidacy for the Presidency under the Republican party. Mr. Carnegie's speech was important as coming from one of the richest men of the world. He enunciated a sound principle when he declared that the degradation of one race was the degradation of all. He too, paid a magnificent tribute to Mr. Washington, pronouncing him as the best "climber" the world has ever seen. His tribute to Negro music in general and the Tuskegee choir in particular was well deserved. Probably the old plantation melodies were never better rendered.

Voice of the Negro, 3 (May 1906), 315–22.

To Archibald Henry Grimké

Tuskegee Institute, Alabama. June 2, 1906

Dear Mr. Grimke: I am sorry that many duties have prevented earlier answer to your favor of May 25th.

My own opinion is that the best we can hope to do is to keep anything referring to us out of the rate bill instead of seeking to get any affirmative legislation.

I do not find myself in agreement with you and Mr. Miller as to paying the final $150 to Senator Blair at this time. This will be an unusual proceeding. We have already paid him the retainer fee, and the balance of course, will be paid when the bill is finally disposed of. I am sure he will agree with this point of view.

I have been watching with very great care the contest going on in Washington for the elimination of the Warner amendment. Yours truly,

Booker T. Washington

TLS Archibald H. Grimké Papers DHU. A press copy is in Con. 3, BTW Papers, DLC.

Henry A. Rucker to Emmett Jay Scott

Atlanta, Ga., June 2, 1906

Dear Mr. Scott: Your letter informing me of Mr. Washington's wishes is at hand.[1] I very much appreciate the trust he imposes and nothing would delight me more than to accept and accompany you, on what, I am sure, will be a most enjoyable trip.

But as Mr. Davis is included in the party it will be impossible to get together the class of people Mr. Washington would like to have on the trip. Such people will not associate with him and will forego any pleasure or opportunity rather than do so. This has been emphasized more in the last two weeks, since his article concerning mulattoes, than ever before and I think you should know of this feeling.

The man is void of social standing, and knowing this, our best people, the ones I should like to see with Mr. Washington and the company proposed, will have no social intercourse with him.

I regret that this is true and only wish that you and Mr. Washington had known it in time.

Of course it is not only agreeable to have Mr. Washington with us but we are always especially glad to have him and he is always welcome whether his coming is heralded or not.

Likewise yourself.

Best wishes to all. Sincerely yours,

H. A. Rucker

TLS Con. 332 BTW Papers DLC.

[1] Scott had written Rucker explaining that BTW was inviting to Tuskegee fourteen of his Atlanta supporters, including Rucker and Benjamin J. Davis, the dark-skinned editor of the Atlanta *Independent,* on a special railroad coach. (June 1, 1906, Con. 332, BTW Papers, DLC.)

Emmett Jay Scott to John Anderson Lankford

[Tuskegee, Ala.] June 4, 1906

See A. H. Grimke at once. Get full account work done by him and Miller in reference to Warner amendment and have it published in Bee for this week. Will be responsible for expenses.

E. J. S.

TWpIr Con. 3 BTW Papers DLC.

To Melvin Jack Chisum

[Tuskegee, Ala.] June 5, 1906

Dear Mr. Chisum: Please keep up with the matter you have been watching. I send you herewith five dollars on account. Yours truly,

Booker T. Washington

TLpS Con. 318 BTW Papers DLC.

Emmett Jay Scott to Richard W. Thompson

[Tuskegee, Ala.] June 5, 1906

Confidential
Kelly Miller and Archibald Grimke representing committee of twelve handled fight against Warner Amendment. Give them full credit this week's Freeman and other papers.

E. J. S.

TWpIr Con. 34 BTW Papers DLC.

From James Weldon Johnson

Puerto Cabello, Venezuela June 6th 1906

My dear Dr. Washington: After a long but very interesting journey I am at last in Puerto Cabello. The trip down here, in many respects, was more interesting than my trip to Europe last summer; the curious field for the study of questions of race and color made it so.

Our first stop was at San Juan; I strolled about that quaint old town for two days, and there caught the first glimpse of the great and intricate color scheme of humanity that is being worked out in this part of the world. I found that in spite of American occupation and domination, prejudice, based solely on race and color, had made very little headway there. Among the people, from the pure whites — who are, by the way, very scarce — to those showing the slightest mixture, I could discover no distinct lines of division. I could not make myself sure of the exact status of the pure blacks, because my stay was too short, and there was no one whom I could question confidentially. I called on the mayor and the president of the City Council, and was treated very cordially by them; they are both men of color.

Our next stop was at Curacao, a curious little Dutch town, so thrifty and clean that it looks as though it might have been taken up bodily from Holland, and set down on this rocky island in the Caribbean. In Curacao I found colored men—sure enough colored men—in every kind of work and business, laborers, storekeepers, tailors, watchmakers, in short they seemed to be taking a hand in everything going on. I stayed in Curacao only a couple of hours so had no chance to form any kind of estimate as to social conditions.

My first sight of Venezuela was very discouraging; it was the town of La Guaira. But I shall not stop to describe La Guaira nor the wonderful ride from there to Caracas, the city in the clouds; nor shall I describe Caracas, the capital of Venezuela, the one-storied Paris of South America; you can get it much better in the guide-books. I stayed three days in Caracas. I reached there on the eve of the national holiday which corresponds to our Fourth of July; and so had an opportunity to form some impressions of the ways and means of Venezuelan politics. I shan't give you those impressions, it is not expedient. I first paid my respects to our minister then strolled about watching the crowds. I heard music in the plaza by the National Band, a really excellent band, and was much interested to note that fully a third of the fifty odd members were colored.

I was lucky enough to strike the opening night of the opera season; and so had a chance to see Caracas society out in full force. The theater is a rather nice one, and the opera was well sung by an Italian company, but I was, of course, more interested in the people. After the second act I followed the crowd up to the Grand Saloon, and there I found the President[1] holding an informal levee. The ladies and gentlemen were in evening dress just as they would be at the opera in New York; and I judged that many of the ladies' gowns came from Paris. And the ladies! some of them were women of remarkable beauty, they ran the whole range of colors from seal brown to lily white; and on the whole one could say as Abraham did of Sarah, "They were fair to look upon."

But that was not all; when I saw in the President's suite, and mingling among the crowd, colored colonels, and generals, and major-generals, clad in crimson and gold, with gold handled swords clinking at their sides, and silver spurs clinking at their heels, using another biblical quotation, I felt like exclaiming with the prophet, "Lord, mine eyes have seen thy salvation, let now thy servant depart in peace." But in all seriousness, I must say that the sight gave me a sort of thrill I never felt before. You know in Europe we are not shut out, but everything we see is white, and we can't feel, somehow, that we are a part of the procession; but I felt that night that I, too, was in it.

I had no intention of stringing this letter out to such length, I shall be thoughtful enough not to bore you just now with any account of Puerto Cabello and my work.[2] But this subject and its setting was so interesting to me I somehow felt it would not be much less so to you. There is floating around through my mind in a hazy way an article, or a pamphlet, or something of that sort on the "Black freedmen of North and South America."

I hope you are quite well. I am in good health in spite of the heat. You will please remember me kindly to Mrs. Washington, I think she may remember who I am. Yours very truly,

James W. Johnson
American Consulate,
Puerto Cabello, Venezuela

TLS Con. 324 BTW Papers DLC.

[1] Cipriano Castro (1858?–1924) led an insurrection against President Ignacio Andrade in 1899 and became military dictator of Venezuela. He was elected president in 1902 and was deposed by revolution in 1908.

[2] In another letter to BTW, Johnson described his daily work and social conditions in the Puerto Cabello community, where Indians and pure blacks constituted the lower class, but where many Indians and blacks as well as whites and light-skinned persons of mixed descent held high position. (Aug. 30, 1906, Con. 324, BTW Papers, DLC.)

Emmett Jay Scott to A. N. Johnson

[Tuskegee, Ala.] June 7, 1906

Personal and Confidential

Dear Mr. Johnson: I wonder if you would not like to publish this week in your paper a kind of editorial urging colored men throughout the state of Alabama to register during the months of July and August when the books are open. Those that do not register within that time of course will not have opportunity to do so for another long season. You can urge them to present themselves for registration at all places where the books are open.

If you can write a letter to the editors of all the colored papers in Alabama calling attention to this matter and asking them to reproduce your editorial or some similar one, I think good will be accomplished. Yours truly,

E. J. Scott

TLpS Con. 3 BTW Papers DLC.

From Melvin Jack Chisum

New York, N.Y. June 11th, 1906

Dear Dr. Washington: Allow me to acknowledge receipt of yours of the 5th inst. In reply, I beg to advise that I was in Brooklyn yesterday (Sunday) with a crowd of Niagara Movement men. They do not know the date as yet. As soon as they do, I will also.

They are working like beavers to get up a crowd to go to the convention and are complaining because Mr Du Bois will not decide the date. I thank you very much for the check. Yours faithfully,

Chisum

P.S. Rev. Miller:[1] Has a list to be signed by all who intend going to the Convention. I was requested to sign it yesterday, but did not. Do you wish me to go? Is it best?

ALS Con. 2 BTW Papers DLC.

[1] George Frazier Miller (1864–1943), educated at Howard University, General Theological Seminary, and New York University, was rector of St. Augustine's Church (Protestant Episcopal) in Brooklyn, N.Y., from 1896 to 1943. A leading black radical, Miller was a member of the Niagara Movement, president of the National Equal Rights League, and in 1918 ran for Congress on the Socialist ticket. He also served on the NAACP's committee which met with Woodrow Wilson to protest the court-martial of black troops in the wake of the Houston Riot in 1917.

From Nelson Edward Henry

China Ala. June 12, 1906

Dear Principal It gives me pleasure to occasionally inform you of how I am getting on with my work. Owing to the fact that I started to teaching here four years ago under a tree with five pupils. With nothing but an ignorant and superstitious community to deal with and only a strong determination to settle and help them help themselves. I feel that much has been accomplished. Instead of a three months school as when we started, it runs 7 seven months each year. It has grown from one teacher to four. The people are gradually becoming more interested in our School. But are too poor to help much. Many of them own land but have been shiftless having to mortgage their crops every year for food supplies. In connection with our regular school work we hold a monthly farmer's conference with the farmers teaching them to raise more food supplies and also hold a monthly mother's meeting. Through these meetings much good is accomplished. The people are growing more corn, peas, peanuts, sugar cane, potatoes and garden vegetables than ever. Some of the articles which we had on exhibition at the Anniversary at Tuskegee we had in our closing exercises here and attracted the attention of the people. During last term there were many hopeful signs of progress. Our sewing class was larger and better and also our class in agriculture, made up of both sexes, did more practicle work. The white citizens of the community manifested more interest in the school this term than before. Mr. J. E. Witherington Post Master and merchant of China has helped us much. We are very much in need of money to build a dormitory for boys which will cost $1000 besides labor. $800 for teacher's salaries, clothing new or second hand; and bed-clothing. If we can keep the School running there will be much good done. The school is located 8 miles from the rail-road in a district where my people have been neglected. And a good school very much needed. Yours for education

N. E. Henry

ALS Con. 885 BTW Papers DLC.

From Melvin Jack Chisum

New York, N.Y. June 16th 1906

Dear Dr. Washington: The Niagara Movement people have about-faced. Their convention will be at Harpers Ferry, W.Va. and will begin Wednesday morning August 15th and adjourn Saturday night Aug 18th.

I attended a meeting last night in Brooklyn where I learned this. That much and that much only is *settled*. Another meeting Wednesday night next. The enclosed blanks are being sent to all who have registered their names with them and their various local secretaries.

I am almost sure I will be able to attend the secret conferences at the Convention, if you desire me to go please notify me. Your obedient servant,

Chisum

ALS Con. 2 BTW Papers DLC.

To Melvin Jack Chisum

[Tuskegee, Ala.] June 19, 1906

My dear Mr. Chisum: I thank you very much for the valuable information contained in your last two communications.

I am writing to say that I shall be in New York at the Stevens House between the 25th and the first of July, and I should like to have a conference with you, we can then determine what is the best course for you to pursue. Yours truly,

Booker T. Washington

TLpS Con. 2 BTW Papers DLC.

To Lucia True Ames Mead[1]

[Tuskegee, Ala.] June 19, 1906

My dear Mrs. Mead: I regret to be so tardy in replying to your letter of June 10, but I was not at home when it came.

In reply, I would state that Mr. Ransom's case is a very sad one.[2]

I think, however, that nothing is to be gained by not being perfectly frank. I have known Mr. Ransom, or known of him, for a number of years. For some time he was pastor of a church in Cleveland, and went from there to Chicago where he remained for a good many years, and from there to New Bedford, and from New Bedford to Boston. In each one of these places Mr. Ransom in some way got the reputation for drinking whiskey to excess or in plain words, getting drunk. It is no secret among colored people who are in position to know that he had to leave Chicago largely because of this unfortunate habit. My secretary has recently told me that a man who was with him in Europe some years ago states that he got so beastly intoxicated that he had to be carried aboard the ship on his return passage.

Judging by what I know of conditions in the South, I would state that traveling over the road that Mr. Ransom was using and acting in a way not to attract attention, that is by being sober and quiet, I do not believe that the mere fact of his riding in a Pullman car would have caused him any trouble. Colored people constantly ride in Pullman cars in the South, and while there are cases where they are disturbed, such cases are not common. Only day before yesterday a colored man rode with me from Louisville, Ky., through Kentucky, Tennessee and into Alabama in a Pullman car and there was not the slightest indication of disturbance or violence.

In regard to Councill's actions at Normal, the school where he went to deliver an address, I cannot do better than to enclose you the statement of the principal and the statement of Mr. Charles Stewart, a newspaper correspondent. I have no reason to doubt that both of these statements are true. I place especial emphasis on what Charles Stewart says; he is a man rather mild and modest in such matters and would be the last to make a damaging statement regarding anyone, his disposition is to yield to the temptation of exaggerating one's virtues rather than his vices.

I confess that I do not blame Ransom so much for the unfortunate predicament in which he is at present as I do the officers, and I mean by that the Bishops, of his church who knowing his weakness placed him in such a responsible and conspicuous position as he now holds in Boston.

If I can further serve, please be kind enough to command me. Yours very truly,

Booker T. Washington

TLpS Con. 328 BTW Papers DLC.

[1] Lucia True Ames Mead (1856–1936), a student of Emerson, was a lecturer and writer on international arbitration and economic and social questions. Her husband was the editor and reformer Edwin Doak Mead.

[2] Reverdy C. Ransom was reported to have been drunk and unfit to deliver an address to students at William H. Councill's school at Normal, Ala., on May 27, 1906. Ransom denied that he was intoxicated when his train arrived in Huntsville, and attributed his disheveled condition to a beating he took when several white men objected to his traveling in the Pullman car. According to Ransom, his luggage, which contained many stickers from a recent European tour, attracted the attention of a white woman on the train who asked if he was a foreigner and if he could speak French. The light-skinned Ransom replied in French that he did not know the language well and went back to his reading. In the meantime, a pamphlet containing one of Ransom's speeches fell into the hands of several white passengers, who then accused Ransom of pretending to be a French count when in fact he was an ordinary "nigger." Ransom was then kicked and shoved into the Jim Crow car. Later, when he had been informed that the bullies had left the train, Ransom returned to the Pullman only to find his assailants were still there. He was cuffed and kicked back into the Jim Crow car and remained there, deprived of food, water, and sleep until the train reached Huntsville. Still dazed, he went straight to bed when he reached the school at Normal. A committee sent by W. H. Councill to investigate Ransom's condition, however, declared he was intoxicated. Ransom believed that they were afraid to have him speak because he was too outspoken for Councill's conservative school.

In June William M. Trotter held a meeting in Faneuil Hall to protest Ransom's treatment and blamed BTW's policies for the worsening racial conditions that led to the incident. (Mobile *Weekly News*, June 16, 1906; Boston *Herald*, June 11, 1906; New York *Age*, June 28, 1906, Clippings, Con. 1043, BTW Papers, DLC.)

To Timothy Thomas Fortune

[Tuskegee, Ala.] June 19, 1906

My dear Mr. Fortune: As per my telegram to-day, I send you the enclosed marked statement from Councill and from Charles Stewart. I am especially anxious that you publish both of these statements. I have suggested a head line, but of course you can use it or not as you see fit. The scoundrels in Boston are trying to make

Ransom out a saint, and I see no reason for our lying down while the enemy is constantly at work. Yours truly,

Booker T. Washington

[*Enclosure*]

We think the time has come when a plain, frank word should be spoken regarding the case of Dr. Ransom of Boston. It is a well known fact that The Age has no love for Prof. Councill, but nevertheless we think that the truth should be stated. There is no need of our trying to disguise the fact, however unpleasant it may be, that for over a dozen years wherever Dr. Ransom has gone, he has unfortunately achieved a reputation for getting intoxicated. He had this reputation in Cleveland, in Chicago, in New Bedford, and now it has followed him to Boston. There is not a single bishop or general officer in the African Methodist church who does not believe that the charges of intoxication made by Professor Councill are true because it is well known among the members of the African Methodist church that Ransom has been guilty of intoxication wherever he has been to a disgraceful extent. The church should either get rid of such men or be brave enough to acknowledge his faults. It is a well known fact among many members of the African Methodist church that when Ransom went to Europe some years ago he was so intoxicated that he had literally to be carried aboard the ship. Let us face the facts and cease to indulge in hysterics. If we have made a wrong statement or done Mr. Ransom an injustice, he knows the courts are open for vindication.

TLpS Con. 32 BTW Papers DLC. The letter and enclosure were pressed on one sheet of paper.

To Perry C. Parks[1]

[Tuskegee, Ala.] June 19, 1906

Mr. Parks: There is considerable complaint from white people who live in this county and who come from a distance to sell various kinds of goods that they are not treated politely and considerately by you. The same complaint comes from teachers, and especially those in your department. Some of the white people in town refuse to go to the barn because they say that they fear they may lose their temper and get into trouble. I advise that you try in every way possible to try to cultivate a kindly disposition toward all with whom you come in contact.

[Booker T. Washington]

TLp Con. 567 BTW Papers DLC.

1 Perry C. Parks was superintendent of the Tuskegee Institute farm and a member of the executive council from 1904 to 1907. He left to take a position at Clark University in Atlanta as director of its agriculture department.

To Lucia True Ames Mead

Wilberforce, Ohio, June 21, 1906

Dear Mrs. Mead: In addition to what I said in my recent letter I wish to add that I have just completed a trip through the states of Alabama, Tennessee and Kentucky in a Pullman car, and during that time seven colored people were in the same car, yet there was no disorder or disturbance of any kind at any time. It is often a fact that Pullman car authorities try to prevent colored people from buying tickets or from entering the car, but it is very seldom that after they once get in that there is any trouble. Very truly yours,

[Booker T. Washington]

TLc Con. 328 BTW Papers DLC.

From Portia Marshall Washington

[Berlin, Germany] June 27. 06

My dear Papa: This is a letter of business. I am going to leave here July first for London and I shall go to one of Cook's Hotels and use their coupons until I find a good Pension. I shall rest a good while and then prehaps take a little trip to Scotland visiting Edinburgh and Ayr.

You have sent me 70 dollars for July — I shall pay my debts here which will be about thirty dollars, and my ticket to London second class, costs me 18 dollars. I got fifty dollars from the Kolonial Komitee so that I shall be secure until the first of August. You can then use American Express Co. Checks in sending me money. Seventy dollars or eighty is enough I think per month. The people with whom I lived in London last summer were very expensive. I shall visit Mr. Taylor and the Unwins.

I take my final examination tomorrow of Prof. Krause.[1] I shall write you what he says. The weather here is frightfully warm and it is so hard to practice.

I do wish you would come to Berlin in September. Lots of love — From yours

Portia

My address in London is American Express Co.

ALS Con. 17 BTW Papers DLC.

[1] Martin Krause (1853–1918), a follower of Franz Liszt, was a German pianist and pedagogue who taught at Leipzig, Dresden, and at Stern's Conservatory in Berlin.

From Portia Marshall Washington

Berlin, June 29—06

My dear father: This is probably my last letter to you before I leave Berlin. I thought you would be interested to know how successful I was in my examination before Prof. Krause. He expressed himself as being very much satisfied with my work and the great progress I had made during the year. He said that my work showed that I had been very industrious. I was so frightfully nervous over this examination that now I really am completely run down. I took it yesterday (June 28th) and it was one of the hottest days I have ever known. I shall be so glad to get out of Berlin for a while and have a complete rest.

It is such a satisfaction for me to know that I have gained Prof.

Krause's confidence and respect for he is one of the greatest teachers now living and his pupils are the best in Berlin.

I have had many unpleasant experiences in this boarding this year but it is all good experience for me and I know human nature much better than ever before.

I am going to see a man this afternoon, who is to make the second translation of your book in German. His name is Herr Karl Axenfeld — you may hear from him. He sent for me to discuss the book with me. You should hear me speak German now. I understand the language perfectly and speak fairly well so they say.

Please write me. In care of the American Express Co. 3 — Waterloo Pl. London. I shall write you again when I get there. Much love From

Portia

ALS Con. 17 BTW Papers DLC.

To William L. Reed[1]

[Tuskegee, Ala.] June 30, 1906

Personal.

My dear Mr. Reed: I have received your kind letter of recent date,[2] but being away from my mail for several days I have been prevented from writing to you earlier. I appreciate fully what you say regarding your feeling toward me and others of the race there in Boston, and the kindly interest which prompts you to write me.

I do not think, however, that the most important element is that which concerns myself so much, as it is that which concerns the race there and the attitude in which the race in Boston is placed. They are being led on by a set of unprincipled and unscrupulous men and none of the other stamp seem to have the courage to speak out. It is, in my opinion, as the Boston letter in the Age of this week says that the race in Boston is being damaged by such leadership.

Before deciding definitely whether or not to accept your kind invitation, I should like to think the matter over and perhaps see you when in Boston. At any rate I could not decide to come there and speak to a miscellaneous audience, but if the representative element, to which you referred cared to give a dinner, making the price so low that the masses could attend I should consider the matter.

I wish to repeat so far as my own interests are concerned these people have done me all the harm they possibly can and their opposition and actions are of no importance, but their position and actions are of vital interest to the people of Boston. Very truly yours,

[Booker T. Washington]

TLc Con. 810 BTW Papers DLC.

[1] William L. Reed (1866–1943) held several public offices in Boston. In 1896 he was the first black man elected to the Massachusetts House of Representatives, a post he held for two terms. From 1898 to 1900 he was deputy collector of internal revenue, and from 1900 to 1902 he was deputy tax collector for Boston. For twenty-two years, beginning in 1902, Reed was a clerk and messenger in the executive department of the Massachusetts State House. In 1924 Governor Channing Cox appointed Reed to the position of executive secretary of the governor's council.

[2] Reed reported to BTW harsh criticisms of him by other blacks at a Faneuil Hall meeting on June 20. He urged BTW to come to Boston and answer "such wild, irresponsible utterances as we have to hear from day to day, now." (June 21, 1906, Con. 810, BTW Papers, DLC.)

Emmett Jay Scott to Richard W. Thompson

[Tuskegee, Ala.] July 2, 1906

Dear Mr. Thompson: The Afro-American Council was held in Louisville, Ky., as you may recall, the latter part of June and the first of July, three years ago. Trotter and his crowd were present and kicked up their usual furore. I got up for one of the evening papers, I do not recall which, a column of interviews with prominent colored men who were present at the meeting as to what they thought of Trotter and his gang; among others Morris joined in the general condemnation.

I am wondering if it will be possible for you to see the files of the evening papers for July 1, 2 or 3 and locate these interviews and secure for me as many copies of the paper as they will let you have. I should say that 10 would meet my needs. I should be satisfied with a fewer number, however, if you can do no better.

I have been thinking of printing Morris's opinion of Trotter and also his eulogy of the Doctor somewhere as showing just how these men change from position to position. Yours truly,

E. J. Scott

TLpS Con. 566 BTW Papers DLC.

From Emmett Jay Scott

[Tuskegee, Ala.] 7/7 [1906]

Mr. Washington: Here is Morris' own comment on Trotter & his gang at Louisville.[1] He wrote it with his own hand & in my presence!

Isn't he consistent?

E J Scott

ALS Con. 327 BTW Papers DLC.

[1] Enclosed was a typed extract from the Louisville *Evening Post,* July 3, 1903: "The Rev. Charles S. Morris, of New York, pastor of one of the leading churches of that place, said:

" 'Samson slew the Philistines with the jawbone of an ass. The little crowd from Boston has the same weapon, but doesn't know how to use it. Everybody knows it is the best fruit tree in the orchard that is pelted most with sticks and stones. The shallows may roar, but the great deeps of Negro manhood believe in Booker Washington and are proud to trust and follow him.' "

From Emmett Jay Scott

Tuskegee Institute, Alabama, July 9, 1906

Dear Mr. Washington: We have looked very thoroughly for the Chisum report. I recall its return by Harry Smith, but Miss Lloyd,[1] who is on the grounds, tells me that she does not remember its coming back to her. I have had the files very thoroughly looked through and it does not seem to be in them. I seem to have a vague impression that you told some one you wanted to carry this report with you to the North, and that was my reason for suggesting that perhaps Mr. Cox might have it. Yours truly,

E J Scott

TLS Con. 566 BTW Papers DLC.

[1] Penelope (Nellie) Belle Lloyd, a postgraduate student at Tuskegee Institute in 1902, was a filing clerk in the principal's office from 1903 to 1906.

From Melvin Jack Chisum

[New York City] Thursday July 12th 3:30 [1906]

Dear Dr. Washington: I sat in the park today from 12:45 to now and will be there near where we sat again tomorrow Friday at 1 sharp.

Brooklyn meeting Tuesday night amounted to a bit of cheap talk. Your obedient servant,

Chisum

ALS Con. 2 BTW Papers DLC.

To Charles Allmond Wickersham

[Tuskegee, Ala.] July 18, 1906

My dear Sir: I am writing you in regard to a matter about which I think you will not misunderstand me.

As you perhaps know, on the 29, 30 and 31st of August the National Negro Business League is to hold its annual meeting in Atlanta. This organization brings together a very large number of the most useful colored men and women throughout the country. We usually have from thirty to thirty five states represented. The meeting in Atlanta, I think, will be larger than any heretofore held.

My especial point in writing you is to see if some action can be taken by those in authority which will modify, during the days of the meeting of the Negro Business League, if possible, the rule now existing in the new depot which requires colored people to enter and leave the depot at a side door. I would not bring this matter to your attention except that I am quite sure it will be the cause of much bitterness and, I fear, friction. No matter how good-intentioned the visitor may be, the arrangements are such that persons who have not lived in Atlanta and learned by experience where to enter and leave would think of going to the side door.

I do not believe that there is any such arrangement in a depot anywhere in the Southern States or outside of them. So far as I know colored people can go into the main entrance at every depot in the United States, and it would be difficult to train them to act differently in Atlanta during these three days.

I am quite sure that it would require the services of a number of people constantly reminding the delegates where they must enter and leave.

If the rule is modified, I do not feel that the colored people would in any way make themselves offensive.

In Montgomery, as you know, while the colored people have their separate waiting room, they have the privilege of coming in the main entrance and waiting room, and I do not believe that they over-ride that privilege.

I hope that I have made myself clear and that in some way you can help me in this matter.[1]

I am in receipt of letters almost daily from colored people in various parts of the country asking about this provision. Of course it has been exaggerated to them in many cases. Yours very truly,

Booker T. Washington

TLpS Con. 338 BTW Papers DLC.

[1] Wickersham in reply described the "luxurious" separate accommodations for blacks and explained that there was no "General Main Entrance" but a "White Entrance" and a "Negro Entrance." "To prevent misunderstandings," he wrote, "we will have additional signs placed on the corner of Mitchell Street and the Plaza, pointing out the Main Colored Entrance." E. J. Scott remarked in a marginal notation: "Will do more harm than good!" (Aug. 3, 1906, BTW Papers, ATT.)

To Hollis Burke Frissell

Tuskegee Institute, Alabama. July 18, 1906

My dear Dr. Frissell: In connection with the Georgia meeting which I understand is to take place in August, I want to put before you and two or three others, as plainly as I can, the absolute necessity of our Northern friends taking a strong stand in reference to Negro country schools.

It is true that a great deal is being done in the way of improving the white public schools and there is little to complain of in the larger towns and cities so far as Negroes are concerned, but in the country districts I am quite sure that matters are going backward, and I am afraid that the Southern members of the various Boards do not put themselves on record in a straight and frank manner as much as they should.

I think investigation would show that extension of the school terms by extra taxation, which is now being done in Alabama, North Carolina and other states, means almost nothing so far as Negro schools are concerned.

I have it on good authority that in recent years Negro public schools in Coosa County, Alabama, for example, have been reduced from thirty to three. In many cases in Alabama teachers are being paid as little as Ten dollars per month. This of course means no school. I actually saw a contract made between a Negro teacher and a school official to the effect that he was to teach school at the rate of $1.60 per month.

I am sending this same letter to Mr. R. C. Ogden, Dr. Buttrick and Mr. Peabody. Yours very truly,

Booker T. Washington

TLS BTW Folder ViHaI. A press copy is in Con. 321, BTW Papers, DLC.

From George Mellen Prentiss King

So. Paris, Maine. July 18, 1906

Dear Mr. Washington: Can it be true that you will secure this aid for me, from the Carnegie Fund. The thought has set me to planning for the few years, that will take me to the sundown of my life.

Your letter found me here in my old home, where I learned to love the mountains and hills.

What rewards will be yours for all your kindness!

I hope you are to have a vacation—a change in your burdens, at least.

We shall be here until the middle of August. Very Truly yours

G. M. P. King

ALS Con. 325 BTW Papers DLC.

To Portia Marshall Washington

[Tuskegee, Ala.] July 19, 1906

My dear Portia: I hope that you are now well rested. One thing I want to caution you about, and that is that you do not break yourself down by sight-seeing. What you need is plenty of good, quiet rest, not running around.

I hope that you have seen the Chesnutts by this time.

The seventy dollars was sent you from New York several days ago, and I hope you received it in London.

The letter which you wrote me from Berlin just before you left was a very good and encouraging one. I am especially glad to know that you passed your examinations so creditably and that your professor was so well pleased with your work. It is very encouraging to know that you speak German so fluently.

Matters here are going quite well. I start North in a few days and shall be traveling during the greater part of the summer. Your papa,

B. T. W.

TLpI Con. 17 BTW Papers DLC.

From James R. Wood, Jr.[1]

Boston, July 19th 1906

My dear Mr. Washington: We received the following telegram from you this morning.

"Let me know at Manhattan Hotel, New York by Saturday in what way the wife of William Monroe Trotter, 3 Tremont St., Boston is employed, if in Domestic service state the nature of it and for whom she is working. Don't say for whom information is wanted."[2]

B. T. W.

Our Mr. Wood Jr. reports as follows:

I ascertained the following from a Boston directory.

William Monroe Trotter, Mortgages, 262 Washington St., Room 30, and pub. #3 Tremont Row, Room 19, house 74 Julian St., Dorchester.

Maude A. Trotter, Editor at #3 Tremont Row, Room 19, boards at 74 Julian St., Dorchester.

Virginia Trotter, widow of James M. house 74 Julian St., Dorchester.

I then went to #3 Tremont Row and ascertained that Room 19 is the office of "The Guardian" a weekly colored paper, that the editor is William Monroe Trotter, that his wife also works on the paper, she is at the office every day generally from 10:00 A.M. until 3:00 P.M. or 4:00 P.M. The other tenants informed me that Mrs. Trotter was thought to cut out clippings from other papers, etc., in fact did general office work, that she could not work outside anywhere else as she spent most of her time there. That Miss Maude A. Trotter was the sister of William Monroe Trotter, that she also was employed on "The Guardian" and was at Room 19, #3 Tremont Row every day, that William Monroe Trotter was not at Room 19 #3 Tremont Row a great deal leaving the business mostly to the woman.

I then made inquiries at 262 Washington St., (Journal Bldg) where William Monroe Trotter has a desk room. One of the gentlemen in Room 30 (a white man) informed me that Mr. Trotter came there very little, perhaps two or three times a week, that he was about town getting notes for his paper, that Mrs. Trotter was employed by her husband and did most of the work in the office at #3 Tremont Row, that she could be found there most any time during the day, that she was not employed anywhere else.

I did not deem it advisable to go to 74 Julian St., Dorchester to make any inquiries as it would excite suspicion.

There is no doubt but what Mrs. Trotter is at "The Guardian" office every day as the tenants at #3 Tremont Row know her well.

If you desire further information kindly advise us. I am, Yours respectfully,

J R Wood Jr.

TLS Con. 5 BTW Papers DLC.

[1] James R. Wood, Jr. (1880–1948) was superintendent of the James R. Wood Detective Agency in Boston, of which his father was the manager. He gained fame in the 1920s as a criminologist.

[2] A press copy of this wire, dated July 18, 1906, is in Con. 5, BTW Papers, DLC.

To Samuel Laing Williams

N Y [City] July 21 [190]6

Be at Palmer House noon Monday. Editor Conservator[1] seems friendly might be good idea to have frank talk.

B. T. W.

HWcIr Con. 34 BTW Papers DLC.

[1] D. Robert Wilkins.

To Emmett Jay Scott

[Chicago, Ill.] July 24, 1906

Dear Mr. Scott: I have just had a talk with a man in Chicago who is on the inside of affairs and knows everything concerning Hertel Jenkins & Co. He tells me that they have gone completely to the wall financially, that they have fallen out and do not speak. Jenkins has lost every dollar he had on The Voice of the Negro, and that together Hertel & Jenkins have lost over $20,000 in the venture. The Stock Company is only a bluff to deceive a few colored people to put money into nothing. It seems they have sold about $400 worth of stock for cash. The company was formed to let Hertel & Jenkins slide out easily and not have the Magazine die on their hands. He further said that Barbour and the others are getting no salary, and the whole thing is a miserable failure. The magazine made a mistake, so they realize, in fighting the forces in existence instead of cooperating with them.

I think you had better send out the League advertisements to the twelve papers at once. Send one to Mr. S. L. Williams for the Conservator. I will make arrangements with him to get it published. Very truly yours,

Booker T. Washington

TLS Con. 566 BTW Papers DLC. Written on Tuskegee Institute letterhead.

From Melvin Jack Chisum

New York, N.Y. July 27 [1906]

Dear Doctor: It is 2 in the morning, I have just returned from Brooklyn, where I have been visiting with the N. M. friends.

Aug 2d meeting has fallen through — Du Bois has informed Rev Miller that Morgan has a case in the Boston court that will preclude the possibility of his attending, while he himself (Du Bois) finds the trip will entail an extra expense, not justified by the returns up to date, which have fallen about $400.00 short of his (Du Bois) expectations.

I am nursing and encouraging the Morris situation as dexterously as I can. Enclosed are a couple of cuttings which I believe are interesting. Yours faithfully

Chisum

ALS Con. 2 BTW Papers DLC.

From Richard Theodore Greener

Storer College, Harper's Ferry, [W.Va.] July 31st, 1906

Private and Confidential

My dear friend: I have been here recuperating for a few days. Not that I need much vacation. I have had quite enough in the past six months. I am sorry McKinlay and I, missed you. There was much I had to talk about. Since, I am here, I learn of the approaching "Niagara" convention, to be held here. My intent has been to return here in any event. Now, I seem to see a chance to be present, as a spectator, and perchance have an opportunity to say a word, in reconcilement of apparently conflicting elements, which at the present time, of all others, ought to be completely in harmony, to be effective. Will you be north again before this Niagara meeting? If so, can you not let me know, in advance, so that we can have a private talk over the situation. I should consider it a privilege to have a chance to hold up your hands – did you really need it, or, at any rate, do some thing to reciprocate your consistent friendship of twenty-two years standing. There's nothing new in my matter. Durham has just sent me copy of a letter he has of his own volition addressed to the President. I am simply biding my time. The Republican party can scarcely afford to disgrace me, at my time of life. Hope you enjoyed your trip northward. Regards to all. Sincerely Yours,

R. T. Greener

I return to Washington, today. My address, #1940-11th St. N.W.

ALS Con. 322 BTW Papers DLC. Scott docketed the letter with the remark: "Here is a good chance to get a good friend into the inner portals of the Niagara meeting. He gives his Washington address in case you want to write him. He writes in grateful & sincere terms. E J Scott 8/2."

To Wallace Buttrick

[Traveling in Midwest][1] August 3, 1906

Dear Dr. Buttrick: The meeting referred to in my recent letter ought to have been, "The Lake George meeting."

Enclosed I am sending you a clipping from the white paper published in Tuskegee. You will be surprised and pleased to know that the white Farmer's Institute in company with about two hundred from Auburn came and held a session upon our grounds. For several years they have been coming in a body to inspect the school farm, but I had no idea they would get to the place to be brave enough to hold a session on our grounds and in our buildings and publish the fact to the world. Very truly yours,

[Booker T. Washington]

TLc Con. 32 BTW Papers DLC.

[1] The record of BTW's whereabouts during August 1906 is incomplete. When carbon copies rather than press copies of his correspondence appear in the files, they are an indication that he was away from Tuskegee. BTW was in Chicago in late July, and in early August he made several stops in Iowa, Kansas, and Nebraska before returning east to Bar Harbor, Me., on Aug. 14. He was in Tuskegee twice in the later part of August, and in between he traveled to Columbus, Ohio (Aug. 25). He ended the month in Atlanta, Ga., where he attended the annual convention of the NNBL.

To Kelly Miller

[Traveling in Midwest] Aug. 4, '06

Dear Mr. Miller: I have received your letter of recent date, and thank you for calling my attention to the different matters. I am glad that you and Mr. Grimke have written The Age in connection with the Warner Amendment. In fact the more I think of it the more I am convinced that the Warner Amendment would have been a good measure, and very helpful.

I was in New York several days ago, and had a long talk with Mr. Villard, regarding Mr. Ewings book, and he told me that after he had re-read the manuscript he was convinced that it was in no condition to publish, and that he returned the manuscript, asking him to revise it, but up to that time he had not heard from him, in regard to the publication of the book. I feel sure that unless it had the imprint of some reliable and well known Publisher the circulation would fall flat. If we could get some reliable Magazine or Publisher to father the Article the Committee of Twelve would then reprint the Article, and it would command better circulation, as the matter now stands I see nothing to do, but to await the further action of Mr. Ewing.

Thanking you for calling my attention to the census matter. I shall try to have the truth brought out fully.

When I see you again I want to have a further talk with you about the advisability of having another meeting in New York in December or January, such as we held sometime ago, but possibly composed of different people, say a leader from every national organization.

I am exceedingly glad you made your trip South. You can now speak with authority and from the inside.

Trusting that you are well, I am, Very truly yours,

[Booker T. Washington]

TLc Con. 328 BTW Papers DLC.

To Melvin Jack Chisum

[Traveling in Midwest] Aug. 4, '06

Dear Mr. Chisum: I am glad to get your letter of July 27th, and thank you for the information. I have been handicapped in communicating with you on account of not having your address. While in New York City several days ago I tried to communicate with you at different addresses given but could not locate you. I plan to be in New York about the 13th and shall hope to see you at the usual place at that time. Very Truly Yours,

[Booker T. Washington]

TLc Con. 2 BTW Papers DLC.

To Emmett Jay Scott

Sioux City Ia 8–7 [1906]

Find out from Calloway how much expended from Jeanes Funds for school houses. Answer send me to New York Copy of Agreement signed by Du Bois and others in New York also *Chisum* Report send Balance of Mail to New York.

B. T. W.

TWIr Con. 566 BTW Papers DLC.

To Richard Theodore Greener

Sioux City Ia Aug-7-[190]6

Letter received — Please meet me Hotel Manhattan New York Sunday night, twelfth, ten o'clock. At my expense. Treat this as private and confidential. Answer Sioux City, Iowa.

Booker T. Washington

HWcSr Con. 322 BTW Papers DLC.

To Francis Jackson Garrison

[Omaha, Neb.] August 8, 1906

My dear Mr. Garrison: Prof. Kelly Miller has let me see your letter of June 4th. He has been South for several weeks and that accounts for the delay.

I was in New York several days ago, and had a long talk with Mr. Villard and he told me that he had returned the manuscript to Mr. Ewing suggesting that he revise it, but up to that time he had not heard from him.

In regard to the Committee of Twelve publishing the manuscript, I am convinced that the circulation would fall flat unless some reliable and well known firm of publishers, or magazine, would first publish the article. In that case the Committee could have it reprinted, then circulated, as we did in the case of the article of Carl Schurz. Our Committee circulated about ten or twelve thousand of that article throughout the South.

This reminds me to ask have you read the speech of the Hon. Walter H. Fleming,[1] which he delivered before the University of Georgia? It is, in my judgement, one of the finest expressions, from a Southern white man, that I have ever read. Very truly yours,

Booker T. Washington

TLS James Weldon Johnson Collection CtY. Written on Tuskegee Institute letterhead. A carbon is in Con. 322, BTW Papers, DLC.

1 William Henry Fleming (1856–1944), a former superintendent of public schools of Augusta and Richmond County, Ga., was a Democratic member of the U.S. House of Representatives from 1897 to 1903. After an unsuccessful bid for a fourth term, he returned to his law practice in Augusta.

Fleming's speech at Athens, June 19, 1906, appeared in pamphlet form as *Slavery and the Race Problem in the South, with Special Reference to the State of Georgia* (Boston: Dana Estes & Co., [1906]). Fleming argued that the question of who was responsible for slavery should be laid to rest, since both North and South were partners in the traffic of slaves. He approved of the Reconstruction amendments to the Constitution while recognizing that they were harsh measures at the time. Using census statistics, Fleming argued that fears of black domination were groundless. All this suggested to Fleming "that the white people of the South, and especially the state of Georgia, can now proceed to work out their racial problem on lines of justice to the negro, without imperilling white supremacy." Fleming contended that white supremacy was the "first and absolutely essential factor in any working hypothesis at the South." He tempered his views by opposing race prejudice and those "whose stock in trade is 'hating the nigger.'" He condemned disfranchisement, pointing out that political rights could be granted to blacks without raising the question of social equality, and that white supremacy could be maintained through the party primary system and the cumulative poll tax.

From Emmett Jay Scott

[Tuskegee, Ala.] August 8, '06

Dear Mr. Washington: I send you herewith summary of the first meeting – the Conference – out of which grew the Committee of Twelve. In it you will find the statement signed by all of those who were present, including, of course, Du Bois. The original must be in the hands of Mr. H. M. Brown[e] or Kelly Miller who was the first Secretary. In addition *also* I am sending you the recommendations submitted by Du Bois for the government of the body, & a newspaper report of the organization of the Niagara Movement. *These are the only copies of each of these documents*, & I hope they will come back in *good* shape for our records. I send the things not asked for with the thought that you may find them useful.

E J Scott

ALS Con. 566 BTW Papers DLC.

To Charles Allmond Wickersham

[Atchison, Kan.] August 9, 1906

Dear Sir: I have your letter of August 3rd and thank you for the information and explanation which it contained. I hope you understand quite fully that my only reason for writing was to prevent a misunderstanding or friction at the depot. I anticipate no trouble from our Southern delegates, but I feared there were others who might honestly not understand conditions and get into trouble.

While on this matter let me say that I have heard many expressions from prominent people in Atlanta and elsewhere to the effect that they were highly pleased with the unusual facilities for eating, toilets, etc. which are provided. Further, I wish to let you know how deeply grateful we are for the accommodations which you have provided on the Atlanta and West Point Road. The main complaint made, however, was about the matter of which I wrote you.

I want to make one suggestion and that is, I do not think it will be wise to put up any more signs around the corner of Mitchell street and the Plaza, in regard to the entrance for colored people. My object in suggesting this is to prevent a certain element of colored newspaper editors taking the matter up and scattering it over the country. I will get in touch with Howell,[1] and I think by the proper instruction to the local committee, which will meet the delegates, we can help to prevent friction.

I have not seen the notices to which you refer, in the Richmond papers, but I suppose it is from some competing road.

Enclosed I send you copy of letters written to Chicago and New York, from which points most of our Northern delegation will come. Very truly yours,

[Booker T. Washington]

TLc BTW Papers ATT.

[1] Clark Howell.

From Emmett Jay Scott

Tuskegee Institute, Alabama. August 9, 1906

Dear Mr. Washington: When you wired me from New York July 7 and 8 for the Chisum report I wired you and wrote you as per the attached.

Since receiving your telegram from Sioux City I have made another attempt to locate it for you, but without success. Since it went to Harry Smith at Cleveland we seem to have lost it altogether. I am very sorry that this should be so, but I have exhausted every possible resource in trying to look for it. Yours truly,

E J Scott

TLS Con. 566 BTW Papers DLC.

From Robert Curtis Ogden

New York August 10th, 1906

Dear Mr. Washington: In some recent letters there was reference to an approaching educational meeting in Georgia, which after some consideration I conclude is a type-writer's error and that the meeting of the Southern Education Board at Lake George, was intended.

The Board convened at Mr. Peabody's house and remained in session about four days. In the course of our deliberations, the question of negro education was taken up with a deeper interest and more vigorous discussion than ever before and certain plans were formulated to secure valuable information and to inspire useful influences. We are already securing important data as to the amount actually expended upon negro schools that we may compare such disbursements with public appropriations and test the accuracy of the large claims made for public expenditure in the South upon the education of the negro. Our Southern members are greatly interested in the results that it is hoped and expected will be secured from this inquiry.[1]

I desire again to express my very deep regret that I am prevented from responding to your request for Lake Mohonk. Very truly yours,

Robert C Ogden

TLS Con. 991 BTW Papers DLC.

1 Ogden characteristically overstated the southern members' commitment to Negro education. (Harlan, *Separate and Unequal*, 97.)

From Richard Theodore Greener

Chicago Ills 8/11 1906

Both telegrams recd — Think best not to see you before the meeting — Letter will reach me here until Tuesday morning.

Greener

HWSr Con. 322 BTW Papers DLC.

To Richard Theodore Greener

[Traveling in Midwest] August 11, 1906

Personal

My dear Prof. Greener: I have just received your telegram. There are some facts which I wanted to put before you before that meeting, but I suppose it will do just as well to see you afterward.

You will find, in the last analysis, that the whole object of the Niagara Movement is to defeat and oppose every thing I do. I have done all I could to work in harmony with Du Bois, but he has permitted Trotter and others to fool him into the idea that he was some sort of a leader, consequently he has fritt[er]ed away his time in agitation when he could succeed as a scientist or soc[i]ologist.

I hope that you will spare no pains to get on the inside of everything. I appreciate very much the spirit and object of your letter of a few days ago, and I shall trust your judgement. Very truly yours,

[Booker T. Washington]

TLc Con. 322 BTW Papers DLC.

From Henry A. Rucker

[Atlanta, Ga.] 8/11/06

Dear Mr. Washington – The Wickersham letter is here enclosed. I think he should be advised against placing any signs.

His threat will amount to nothing. He knows of activity against the Terminals discriminations, which I believe he could adjust if he were so inclined, [to move?]. I know no other means of reaching these people or at any rate of making them smart, than to touch their coffers.

Such things together with a few local disgruntled critics among our own people are making efforts for the meeting somewhat difficult of accomplishment. But the work is going measurably well in spite of this.

Mrs Rucker writes Mr Scott by even mail. Yours

Rucker

ALS BTW Papers ATT.

From Samuel Laing Williams

Chicago 8/12/1906

My Dear Dr Washington Your two letters of the 3rd and 4th inst containing enclosures which I return herewith were duly received. In reading both of these letters I cannot but feel some what fearful lest you become somewhat discouraged in the presence of so many evidences of reaction. It requires no ordinary soul in these times to stand erect and look straight ahead with confidence that right must come through error and wrong doings. I would regard it as a calamaty to our progress if you and others with you became discouraged by the seeming increase of criticism and lying by our own people. You are everlastingly right, and what you stand and contend for is bound to prevail unless the world and everything good in it comes to an end. I am satisfied that there is no use in attempting to conciliate this crowd of indignation-people. I met Bently on the cars last night and he began on me at once about the great harm you are doing to the cause of negro advancement. He became quite impatient with me because I showed him specific instances in which he and his kind had grossly misrepresented you in doing and saying certain things which you never did and never said. They are disappointed and fume just as soon as you show them that the things that they have been taking as true are false. They are like a criminal lawyer who is paid to make out a case. I doubt if there can be found in the country an organization of men at the foundation of which there is so much false assumption untruth and disappointed hopes as in these Niagara folks.

A friend of mine who has been getting some advertisements for the Conservator tells me that he is compelled to keep the papers from being seen by these advertisers on account of its silly and lying misrepresentations of you and your work. He told Wilkins the other day that advertisers without exception admire you and your work and will not stand for his unrelenting abuse.

I am in a position to say that Wilkins is not followed by the readers of his paper. His head man and printer is against him in the matter and told me so. But he is a hard headed conceited mean spirited Bourbon. He has many more enemies in this town than you have, and his enemies increase in the proportion that your friends increase.

I hope you will be able to come here in response to the Press Club invitation. I think this is the "psychological moment" to bring people to their sober senses.

The Presidents message as to us is satisfactory to me. The one or two lapses of error are amply made up in the generous sweep of his plea for even handed justice to both races. Bently kicks on the presidents reference to Education. I suppose he wants a Harvard college in each county of the black belt. He dispises the word "industrial." "It is degrading dont you know!" Even at this late day with all the evidence within his reach I find him and his kind still of the opinion that your students work but dont learn! But as I said before the real truth is not agreeable to them. If they were men seriously engaged in the actual, everyday and really interesting work of solving the real and not imaginary problem they would take less notice of the passing evidence of human measures. Sincerely yours,

S. Laing Williams

ALS Con. 34 BTW Papers DLC.

To Frederick Randolph Moore

[aboard] Train Aug. 16 [1906]

Find out exactly how many went to Harper's Ferry from Greater New York and Wire me Tuskegee.

B. T. W.

HWcIr Con. 33 BTW Papers DLC.

From Frederick Randolph Moore

Brooklyn N.Y. [Aug.] 17 [1906]

My information not more than two Miller and Waller[1] Thompson couldn't borrow money. Morris nor Wibecan did not go.

Fred R Moore

TWSr Con. 33 BTW Papers DLC.

[1] Owen Meredith Waller (1868–1939), a graduate of New York Theological Seminary (1892) and Howard University Medical School (1903), was rector of St. Luke's Protestant Episcopal Church in Washington, D.C., from 1896 to 1904. At the time of the founding of the NAACP Waller was residing in Brooklyn. He was a member of the Committee of Forty in 1909, and was on the first executive committee of the NAACP in 1910. He was active in the anti-lynching campaign and opposed segregated military camps during World War I. He was also a member of the Cosmopolitan Club and the American Negro Academy.

To William Estabrook Chancellor[1]

[Tuskegee, Ala.] August 20, 1906

Personal

My dear Sir: I am doing that which I very rarely consent to do and that is, without solicitation from you, writing a letter of endorsement of one of our workers. Mr. Roscoe Conkling Bruce is, I understand, desirous of obtaining a position of responsibility in the city of Washington in the colored Public Schools.[2] Mr. Bruce has been at the head of the Academic Department of this institution for four years and has rendered high and efficient service. It will be a matter of regret and loss to have him leave us but he naturally looks upon such a change as being a promotion and we feel, in view of this, that we cannot consistently oppose his making the change.

I can give you no better idea of the efficiency of Mr. Bruce's work than to enclose a pamphlet containing copies of letters from Superintendents of Education who visited us some years ago inspecting the work done under Mr. Bruce.

If you desire any further information I should be glad to supply it as far as I can.

I am writing this letter with some hesitation as I would not like to do anything that would appear in the light of meddling in local conditions. Yours truly,

Booker T. Washington

TLpS Con. 316 BTW Papers DLC.

[1] William Estabrook Chancellor (b. 1867) was superintendent of schools in Washington, D.C., from 1906 to 1908.

[2] Bruce had sent BTW two letters asking for a recommendation to Chancellor. He wrote that he had heard that W. E. B. Du Bois was also being considered for the post. (Aug. 8, 1906, Con. 872, and Aug. 19, 1906, Con. 564, BTW Papers, DLC.)

To Kelly Miller

[Tuskegee, Ala.] August 20, 1906

My dear Prof. Miller: That was a very good set of resolutions which you wrote for the Young People's Congress. I have heard no one say that you wrote them, but your ear marks are all through them. I think, however, that you lean just a little in the direction of what is termed "higher" education. Perhaps, however, I am a little sensitive on that point.

My main object in writing you at this time, is to urge you to accept Bishop Walter's invitation to attend the Afro-American Council in New York, and that you begin soon to draw up a pointed and strong set of resolutions for that meeting. I shall be willing to be responsible for the pay in connection with your doing the work.[1] An element to be taken into consideration in such resolutions is the fact that our people throughout the country just now are committing a terrible amount of crime, more than they have done for a long time, and we cannot do our duty by the race unless we recognize this, as well as to condemn lawlessness on the other side. Yours truly,

Booker T. Washington

TLpS Con. 328 BTW Papers DLC.

[1] Miller replied that he would "undertake preparation of resolutions as suggested." (Aug. 23, 1906, Con. 328, BTW Papers, DLC.)

From Richard Theodore Greener

Washington, D.C., August 23rd, 1906

My dear friend: I am sorry circumstances prevented me from meeting you, when I was at Chicago. I am confident you saw the prudence of my course.

The details, as well as some points of mutual interest, I hope to have a chance to go over with you either at Atlanta, or while *en route* there.

I have never visited that city and at Mack's[1] suggestion, think your League meeting, a good reason. Mack and I expected to see you, yesterday; but I did not know of your telegram until too late. We all go to Harper's Ferry tomorrow. Mack has had a *sciatica* touch, which has kept him house bound for a week, and today Mrs. Mack, is not at all well. I send this by chance to the Manhattan Hotel, New York City.

I had supposed "the Manhattan" at Coney island was your *habitat*; but assume Mack knows. If possible I should be glad to join you on your trip South. A telegram or letter will reach me at Storer College, Harpers Ferry until Monday 26th August.

Hoping you are well, despite this hot and enervating spell. I am, Sincerely Yours,

R. T. Greener

ALS Con. 322 BTW Papers DLC.

[1] Whitefield McKinlay.

To Frederick Randolph Moore

Columbus O. Aug. 25 [190]6

Fear that Fortune is drinking. If he goes to Atlanta keep close hold on him and see he does not stir up trouble on way or in Atlanta. Might be wise to persuade him to let Stokes go in his place. Do not mention my name in talking to him.

B. T. W.

HWcIr BTW Papers ATT.

To Richard Le Roy Stokes

[Tuskegee, Ala.] August 27, 1906

Dear Mr. Stokes: I think the policy that the Age has pursued during the last three or four months has driven the Niagara people to the point where they see that they cannot afford any more to let the public understand that their organization is opposing me. This is shown by the fact that none of the speakers made reference to me and there was less direct reference in their resolutions. Since we have accomplished this much, the next policy to pursue is to ignore the whole organization as much as possible. Without the use of my name, it is impossible for them to keep themselves before the public very long. Yours very truly,

Booker T. Washington

TLpS Con. 261 BTW Papers DLC.

An Account of a Speech before the National Negro Business League

Atlanta, Ga., August 30, 1906

LAW-BREAKING NEGROES WORST MENACE TO RACE

Booker Washington in Address to Business League Says South Is Best Place for Blacks Who Will Work

That the worst enemies of the negro race are those negroes who commit crimes, which are followed by lynching, and that the south is after all the best place for black men who are willing to work, was the keynote of the address of Booker T. Washington to the National Negro Business League last night. He said in part:

"It is well that the National Negro Business League holds this session right here in the heart of the south where the great body of our people live, and where their salvation is to be worked out. This organization does not undertake to concern itself with all the interests of the race, for there are other organizations that deal with the political, religious and educational interests of our people.

"From the first, and I hope this meeting will prove no exception, the National Negro Business League has steadfastly held to the policy of stimulating the activities of our people in the direction of agriculture, industrial and business enterprises. It is the policy of this organization to hold up before the race its advantages, rather than its disadvantages, its successes, rather than its failures, to call the attention of the world to the efforts of our friends, rather than to those of our enemies.

"We believe that while the world may pity a crying, whining race, it seldom respects it. In a word, the National Negro Business League, while not overlooking or justifying injustice or wrong or failing to recognize the value of other methods seeking to reach the same end, feels that the race can make progress and secure the greatest protection by its efforts in progressive, constructive directions, by constantly presenting to the world tangible, and visible evidences of our worth as a race. We believe that the influence of one great success in really accomplishing something that the world respects will go furthest in promoting our interests. Let constructive progress be the dominant note among us in every section of America. An inch of progress is worth more than a yard of fault-finding. The races that have grown strong and useful have not done so by depending upon finding fault with others, but by presenting to the world evidences of the progress in agriculture, industrial and business life, as well as through religious, educational and civic growth.

South Best for the Negro

"Right here in Georgia we have abundant evidence that the negro, in spite of difficulties, is learning this lesson at a rapid rate. It is safe to say that the negro in Georgia owns at least $20,000,000 worth of taxable property, and that our people in other sections of the south have made almost equal progress. Within the past year I have inspected and studied the conditions and progress of our people in the northern and western states as I have never done before, and I have no hesitation in reaffirming my former opinion that the southern states offer the best permanent abode for the masses of our people. While many individuals may find prosperity outside of the south, and have the right to make the effort, yet laying the foundation for growth in life essentials, which this organization seeks first of all to promote, I know no section of this country where our people are making more progress, and where the future is more full of promise than right here in the south. In thus expressing myself, I do not overlook the fact that we have a large number of negroes in the north and west whose success is in the highest degree creditable, nor do I overlook those things in the south, which often discourage many of our people.

"In connection with our future here in the south I do not share the fear that immigration will retard or prevent our progress. The millions of unoccupied and unused acres in the south have yet to be used by someone, and the present scarcity of all forms of labor upon which business prosperity in a large measure rests, cannot always remain unsatisfied. A few thousand, strong, sturdy, thrifty foreigners in each county will go far toward quickening our energy and sharpening our wits, by bringing their healthy competition, which is very much needed in many sections of the south. Our salvation is to be found not in our ability to keep another race out of territory, but in our learning to get as much out of the soil, out of the occupations, or business, as any other race can get out of theirs.

"The more I study our conditions and needs, the more I am convinced that there is no surer road by which we can reach civic, moral, educational, and religious development than by laying the foundation in the ownership and cultivation of the soil, the saving of money, commercial growth, and the skillful, conscientious performance of any duty with which we are entrusted. This policy does not mean the limiting or circumscribing of the activities or ambitions of the race. Progress through this method means the exercise of patience, faith, courage and eternal vigilance; but there is no escape from it. It is the road that all nations have traveled, which have gotten upon their feet.

"There is much that the brave, intelligent, patriotic white men of America can do for us; there is much that we can do for ourselves. The executive authorities should see to it that every law is enforced, regardless of race or color, that the weak are protected against injustice from the strong. We have examples in several southern states that this is being done in an encouraging degree. Without this encouragement and protection of the law it is not possible for the negro to succeed as a laborer, or in any line of business.

DUTY OF THE NEGRO

"On the negro's part we have a duty. Our leaders should see to it that the criminal negro is gotten rid of whenever possible. Making all allowances for mistakes, injustice and the influence of racial prejudice, I have no hesitation in saying that one of the elements in our present situation that gives me most concern is the large number of crimes that are being committed by members of our race. The negro is committing too much crime north and south. We should see to it, as far as our influence extends, that crimes are fewer in number; otherwise the race will permanently suffer. The crime of lynching everywhere and at all times should be condemned, and those who commit crimes of any nature should be condemned. Our southland today has no greater enemy to business progress than lynchers and those who provoke lynching.

"In this same connection let us bear in mind that every man, white or black, who takes the law into his hands to lynch or burn or shoot human beings supposed to be, or guilty of crime is insulting the executive, judicial and lawmaking bodies of the state in which he resides. Lawlessness in one direction will inevitably lead to lawlessness in other directions. This is the experience of the whole civilized world.

"In this connection let us consider the classes of negroes that do not commit crime and are seldom charged with crime. They are those who own homes, who are tax-payers, who have a trade or other regular occupation; they are those who are in professional service; those who have received education, and such business men and women as those who compose this organization.

"I think I would be safe in saying that no graduate of Clark University, Atlanta Baptist College, Atlanta University, Morris Brown College or Spelman Seminary has been arrested for any crime in Atlanta during the last twelve months.

"In this we have a strong, practical demonstration right here at home in favor of education of the classes of our citizenship. Ignorance will always mean crime, and crime will mean an unwieldy burden fastened about the neck of the south. The only safety for both races is in the direction of education, industry and high character.

"I have named the classes that do not commit crime. Which is the class that is guilty, as a rule, of criminal action? They are the loafers, the drunkards and gamblers, men for the main part without permanent employment, who own no homes, who have no bank account, who glide from one community to another without interest in any one spot. One of the practical courses that men such as those who compose this business league, our leaders in the pulpit and every sphere of life, should pursue is to try to get hold of the floating class of our people and see to it that their lives are so changed as to make them cease to disgrace our race and disturb our civilization. We cannot be too frank or too strong in discussing the harm that the committing of crime is doing to our race. Let us stand up straight and speak out and act in no uncertain terms in this direction. Let us do our part, and then let us call upon the whites to do their part.

"Let us never grow discouraged as a race. Right here in the south there are more things upon which the races agree, than upon which they disagree. Let us not be so much absorbed in our grievances that we fail to remember our successes and opportunities.

"In the southern states the negro has organized and is now conducting thirty-three banks. He has in the United States over one hundred drug stores. Almost every town and city in the south has its negro grocery store and other places of business. There is practically no section of the south where the negro farmer, mechanic, merchant and banker cannot find encouragement, opportunity and prosperity. In this respect let us not overlook the fact that many similar opportunities are at our door.

"At a very conservative figure the negro is now paying taxes upon over $300,000,000 worth of property and I suppose the negro imitates other races in not always paying taxes upon all of his belongings.

"What we have accomplished in the past, in the face of many difficulties is a guarantee of what we can attain to in the future.

"Finally, let us cultivate a spirit of racial pride. Let us learn to be as proud of our race as the Frenchman, German, the Japanese, or the Italian is of his. The race that has faith and pride in itself will eventually win the respect, the confidence and cooperation of the rest of the world."

Atlanta *Constitution,* Aug. 30, 1906, 4. A typescript version is in BTW Papers, ATT. The speech was delivered on the evening of Aug. 29, 1906.

To Lyman Abbott

[Tuskegee, Ala.] Sept. 2, 1906

Personal

My dear Dr. Abbott: Enclosed I send you a copy of the platform of the National Negro Business League and a copy of the address which I delivered before that body. These two utterances I am convinced by experience and talk with the masses of our people, represent their views of the subjects discussed.

In the last issue of the Outlook I fear you gave too much serious attention to Dr. Du Bois and his movement.[1] I have watched it closely from the beginning. All told I do not believe there are more than two or three hundred colored people of any prominence or influence who are inclined to follow such folly as he is the leader of. The actual attendance at the Harpers Ferry meeting was less than 50. There were at least 600 delegates present at our Atlanta meeting. Yours truly,

Booker T. Washington

TLpS BTW Papers ATT.

[1] *Outlook,* 84 (Sept. 1, 1906), 3–4. The magazine presented the platform of the Niagara Movement and described it as "the more assertive spirit of the negro race, under the leadership of Dr. Du Bois." At the same time, the *Outlook* stated that it preferred "the more industrial and more pacific spirit" represented by BTW and Tuskegee Institute.

James A. Cobb to Emmett Jay Scott

Washington, D.C. September 3, 1906

Dear Mr. Scott: The school question is warmer now than ever, Du Bois is turning heaven and earth to be appointed assistant superintendent. I suppose you have seen some of the Washington papers, if so, you have seen where Montgomery's[1] position is very precarious at present; the friends of Du Bois are trying to oust him and place Du Bois in his place. Mrs. Terrell came home Saturday night and hasn't slept any since. Judge and I have been at work on the matter. Will write you later. Very sincerely yours,

James A. Cobb

TLS Con. 32 BTW Papers DLC.

1 W. S. Montgomery.

To William Estabrook Chancellor

[Tuskegee, Ala.] September 4 [1906]

Dear Dr. Chancellor: I shall be very glad indeed if you decide to appoint Mr. Bruce to a Supervisorship. I feel quite sure that he will perform the service well and satisfactorily as he has ability of a high order.

I hope at some time to have the privilege of meeting you in a personal way. Yours truly,

Booker T. Washington

TLpS Con. 872 BTW Papers DLC.

To Richard Carroll[1]

[Tuskegee, Ala.] September 5, 1906

Personal

My dear Mr. Carroll: I have your kind letter of September 1st and you do not know how very grateful [I am] indeed for your kind and generous expressions regarding me. I am glad you see the conditions in their true light.

The little crowd who are opposing me are seeking, in the first place, notoriety, and in the second place they are very largely actuated by motives of jealousy. They seem to want to do something but hardly know what to do nor how to do it. The effect of the resolutions passed at Harper's Ferry was most hurtful, and practically every newspaper in the country has condemned them. As your own letter suggests this crowd is hurting the race instead of helping it.

Enclosed I send you two copies of the address which I delivered in Atlanta last week. I have many evidences to show that this address has accomplished some good.

I have just asked Mr. Scott to put your paper on the exchange list of the Tuskegee Student. Yours very truly,

Booker T. Washington

TLpS Con. 333 BTW Papers DLC.

[1] Richard Carroll, born in slavery during the Civil War, was a prominent Baptist minister in Columbia, S.C., who was sometimes compared with BTW. One historian called him "black Carolina's nearest counterpart to Washington." (Newby, *Black Carolinians*, 169.) From 1899 to 1906 Carroll ran a home for black youths on a 226-acre farm he acquired with the help of white philanthropists. He was also instrumental in the movement to establish a state reformatory for blacks in 1900. He published his own newspaper, *The Southern Ploughman*, which was an organ for his racial philosophy based on self-help and economic advancement similar to that of BTW, although on some issues he was more conservative than the Tuskegean. In 1907 Carroll organized an annual race conference that brought together leading black and white Carolinians. (Newby, *Black Carolinians*, 168–84.)

To Oswald Garrison Villard

Tuskegee Institute, Alabama, September 6, 1906

Personal

My dear Mr. Villard: I am taking the first opportunity I can seize to thank you for permitting Miss Ovington[1] to report our proceedings in Atlanta for your paper. Aside from accomplishing good, in my opinion, for the whole race, I am quite sure it was very fortunate that we went to Atlanta at the special time that we did. When I got there I found the feeling between the races intensely strong, almost to the breaking point. In addition to the bitterness stirred up by the Hoke Smith campaign, several outrages had recently been committed by colored people on white women in Atlanta and in that county which added to the bitterness. In one case an English woman who had not been in this country very long, was most brutally treated; one of her eyes was put out, her nose destroyed and several limbs broken so that she will be maimed for life. This, with several minor outrages, added to the feeling. One of the afternoon papers was advocating openly the formation of a Ku Klux Klan, another had offered a thousand dollars for the lynching of a colored man guilty of one of these crimes. My first action was to go directly to the managing editor of each of the four newspapers in Atlanta and talk the situation over frankly with them, and in every case I was received with cordiality, and all expressed the feeling that they needed help. The result was that under the circumstances I think the papers gave us reasonably good attention, but the good that we did was not evidenced so much in the local newspaper reports as by the expression of individuals which we heard from many quarters. The result was that one of the bitterest afternoon newspapers gave us [more] space than any other Atlanta newspaper, and had several editorials of an encouraging character. The last day that we were in Atlanta, the protest contained in the Journal against the formation of a Ku Klux Klan was circulated and printed. I have had numerous letters from colored people since the meeting was over, thanking us for coming to Atlanta, and expressing the feeling of relief because of the changed situation. Yours very truly,

Booker T. Washington

TLS Oswald Garrison Villard Papers MH.

[1] Mary White Ovington (1865–1951) was an officer of the NAACP throughout its first forty years. Born into a prosperous Unitarian family in Brooklyn Heights, N.Y., she became a socialist while a student at Radcliffe, and from 1895 to 1903 was head of the Greenpoint Settlement of the Pratt Institute Neighborship Association. Turning to journalism for the *Outlook* and the New York *Evening Post* and to an increasing interest in the Negro, she moved into a black model tenement, founded the Cosmopolitan Club for social relations between the races in 1906, and wrote *Half a Man: The Status of the Negro in New York* (1911). Though sympathetic with the social work at Tuskegee, she early identified herself with W. E. B. Du Bois and the Niagara Movement, and in 1909 she was one of the founders of the NAACP. Serving

over the years as secretary, treasurer, branch director, and chairman of the board of the NAACP, Ovington found that one of her principal duties was making peace between the factions, and particularly between Du Bois and O. G. Villard. The author of a number of books on racial themes, she is perhaps best known for *The Walls Came Tumbling Down* (1947), part autobiography and part a history of the NAACP.

From Charles William Eliot

Asticou, Me., Sept. 7, 1906

Dear Mr. Washington: I find that there have remained in my mind, as results of my visit to Tuskegee last April, a few ideas about the Institution which I think perhaps might yield some fruit if communicated to you. So I venture to set them down as follows.

(1) It seemed to me doubtful whether Tuskegee offered any adequate training for the profession of the ministry. Is it best for the Institution to spend money and force in providing an inadequate training for that profession?

(2) I felt much doubt about the training Tuskegee is able to offer for nurses. The training of nurses has been well developed in our Northern cities within the last twenty-five years, but everywhere, so far as I know, access to large hospitals is felt to be indispensable to a satisfactory training. And the instruction in natural and medical science which forms the basis of the clinical training in nursing is given by experts of high quality. Ought Tuskegee to offer any training for nurses when it is visibly incapable of providing the best training?

(3) I felt some anxiety concerning the expansion of the agricultural and mechanical equipment at Tuskegee. It is very easy at any educational institution to let the expenditures on the plant absorb too large a proportion of the total income. At Harvard University this is a danger which has to be incessantly guarded against. You have at Tuskegee a large acreage and many buildings. Do these things absorb too large a proportion of your income?

(4) I felt some concern lest at Tuskegee the manual labor side had an excessive development as compared with the mental labor side, or in other words, lest industrial training should unduly impair academic training. Is it not important that the graduates of

Tuskegee should have acquired not only a trade or an art, but the power to read and cipher intelligently, and a taste for reading? Otherwise the isolated negro farmer or mechanic will not prove to be capable of progress. The world changes so fast nowadays that the man or woman who does not read will be left behind, no matter what the calling. The academic side of Tuskegee ought therefore to give all its graduates a competent mental equipment, and especially to implant the purpose to improve continually.

(5) I would suggest that you get onto your Board of Trustees a few white men of mark who are not over thirty-five to forty years old, either Northerners or Southerners. Tuskegee has had large support from a generation which is going off the stage. It should now enlist the support of a much younger generation.

(6) My experience in Cambridge leads me to think that a serviceable addition to your equipment would be a chemical fire engine. You have always ready a considerable force of active young men who could bring a chemical fire engine very quickly to a fire. At the beginning of a fire the chemical engine is far the most effective means of defense, and it does little injury to the contents of a building. It is always ready, and being comparatively light, can be drawn quickly to the point of danger. The little fire which I witnessed in Tuskegee would have been extinguished in thirty seconds by a chemical engine.

I have been glad to hear within a few days that Mr. Bruce is likely to go to a good position in Washington. A few years' experience there will make him a more valuable man later for Tuskegee or some other educational institution for negroes.

I am, with great regard, Very truly yours,

Charles W. Eliot

TLS Con. 321 BTW Papers DLC.

SEPTEMBER · 1906

An Account of a Speech in New York

September 21, 1906

WASHINGTON ADVISES NEGROES

NOT TO ENCOURAGE SO MUCH TALK ABOUT THE EQUALITY OF THE RACES

Booker T. Washington made an address last evening in the Mount Olivet Baptist Church, in West Fifty-third street, under the auspices of the committee for improving the industrial condition of negroes in New York. Despite the extreme heat and sultriness the church was crowded.

Mr. Washington advised the members of his race, who constituted the bulk of the audience, not to encourage so much talk about the equality of the races.

"Why," said the negro educator, "if a sandwich is refused a colored man at a railroad station restaurant, it gets more space in the newspapers of our race than if that same colored man had successfully founded a bank. I don't say the sandwich ought to have been refused him. Probably it oughtn't, but it is a mere incident in the progress of our race. Don't hold up such untoward incidents to dishearten our boys and girls."

Mr. Washington said that the negro race, while it needed mental discipline, needed all the hand training it could get, because its wants increased as its education progressed. The race needed constantly better houses, clothing and surroundings, and if it couldn't get them there would be much misery.

"And the black man doesn't always find the door of employment so open in the North as it is in the South," he added. "There are plenty of ways to spend money here, and not so many in which to earn it. We must teach our young people to save their money. We must cease to have the reputation of a spending, thriftless and poverty stricken race.

"It is vitally necessary for the progress of our race that we become creators of enterprise and not depend on the goodwill and the energy of other races. One of our greatest obstacles is that most other races associate the color of our faces with poverty. We are known as a poverty stricken race. We must profit by the example of the Italian and the German immigrant, who land here unable to speak a word of our tongue. But they work hard and they save, and many of them wind up by becoming bank presidents and directors and the controllers of great industrial enterprises."

Mrs. Mary Schenck Woolman,[1] William Jay Schieffelin and William Lewis Bulkley also made talks.

New York *Sun*, Sept. 21, 1906, 8.

[1] Mary Schenck Woolman (b. 1860), a specialist in home economics, was instructor of domestic arts at Teachers College, Columbia University, from 1902 to 1910. She was organizer and director of the Manhattan Trade School for Girls, President of the Women's Educational and Industrial Union, and a writer and lecturer on various social and economic subjects. In 1911 she was chairman of the committee to organize the Camp Fire Girls. From 1912 to 1914 she was head of the household economics department at Simmons College in Boston.

To the Editor of the New York *World*

New York, Sept. 25 [1906]

BOOKER T. WASHINGTON ADVISES
COLORED RACE NOT TO RETALIATE

HE URGES THE BEST WHITE PEOPLE
AND THE BEST COLORED PEOPLE TO
MEET IN COUNCIL AND ENDEAVOR TO
STOP DISORDER

To the Editor of The World: As a rule I never discuss the matter of mob violence except when I am in the South, but in this case I make an exception.

In answer to your request, I will state that in my address in Atlanta to the National Negro Business League, a few days ago, I spoke plainly against the crime of assaulting women and of resorting to lynching and mob law as a remedy for any evil. I feel the present situation[1] too deeply to give any extended utterance at this time, except to say that I would strongly urge that the best white people and the best colored people come together in council and use their united efforts to stop the present disorder.

I would especially urge the colored people in Atlanta and elsewhere to exercise self-control and not make the fatal mistake of attempting to retaliate, but to rely upon the efforts of the proper authorities to bring order and security out of confusion. If they do this they will have the sympathy of good people the world over.

Let me repeat that wherever I have met them, without exception, I have found the leading colored people as much opposed to crime as the leading white people; but what is needed now is to get the best element of both races together and try to change the present deplorable condition of affairs. We of both races must learn that the inflexible enforcement of the laws against all criminals is indispensable, and in this I will do my utmost to have my race co-operate.

The Atlanta outbreak should not discourage our people, but should teach a lesson from which all can profit. And we should bear in mind also that while there is disorder in one community there is peace and harmony in thousands of others. As a colored man I cannot refrain from expressing a feeling of very deep grief on account of the death of so many innocent men of both races because of the deeds of a few despicable criminals.

Booker T. Washington

New York *World*, Sept. 26, 1906, 3. The item appeared also in the New York *Times* on the same date.

[1] On Sept. 22, 1906, a five-day race riot began in Atlanta that resulted in the deaths of at least ten black persons and one white, and there were many physical injuries and property losses among blacks. The race riot followed the race-baiting gubernatorial primary contest between Hoke Smith and Clark Howell, in which the victorious Smith promised disfranchisement of black voters and enlisted the vitriolic racism of Tom Watson in his behalf. The racial tension in Atlanta was evident when the NNBL met in the city in August, and the sensational Atlanta newspapers exacerbated white fear and hostility with news and rumors of black rape day after day.

On the night of Sept. 22 a white mob gathered to raid the "Decatur Street dives" of the black business section, ignored pleas to disperse by the mayor and police commissioner, and began to attack black persons as well as black restaurants and saloons. Rioters congregated at streetcar stops to seize and beat the black passengers. Many blacks fled the city, but others resisted or took sanctuary on the campuses of the black colleges, and black self-defense near Clark University held the white mob in check.

The Atlanta police not only were ineffective in maintaining order, but probably prolonged the riot by disarming blacks and deputizing 200 aggressive whites. Eventually the state militia entered the city and restored order. President Roosevelt rejected all suggestions of federal intervention in the riot, including Clark Howell's request for a federal commission of investigation. (Crowe, "Racial Massacre in Atlanta," 150–73.)

BTW went to Atlanta, arriving on the evening of Sept. 28, to aid in interracial efforts to restore order and to prevent future outbreaks of racial violence.

To John Wesley Edward Bowen

[New York City] September 26, 1906

My dear Dr. Bowen: I must pause a moment at least to write and say that the whole nation sympathizes with you on the account of your trying ordeals through which you have been passing. No one, who knows you, believes you would do a wrong or rash thing; we all love you and believe in you.

I believe good in the end will result from the present trials, through which, we as a race, are passing. The leaders there deserve the greatest credit for the wisdom, self-control and patient endurance which they have exhibited.

Believe me, Sincerely yours,

[Booker T. Washington]

TLc Con. 316 BTW Papers DLC.

From Oswald Garrison Villard

New York September 27th, 1906

Dear Mr. Washington, The enclosed dispatch came for you this morning. I replied as follows: "Mr. Kennan[1] should start within ten days or two weeks if possible." I shall keep you posted as to the outcome, and hope you will approve that I set a limit of two weeks upon the starting. Sincerely yours,

Oswald Garrison Villard

P.S. Since writing the above the head of the Pinkerton Agency has been in to inquire whether we did not think we could get a Secret Service man to do the work. I told him I did not see on what ground we could base such a request of the Government. Yesterday he was very doubtful whether Mr. Pinkerton would consent to be mixed up in the affair. Today he says that they will give us a man or men if we want them, but he is so lukewarm and doubtful about the matter that I question very much whether we had better trust ourselves to them. What do you think? I think in any case it would be well to talk over the matter with Mr. Kennan, as we can get hold of a detective in three days time. If you think I have given Mr. Kennan too much lee-way, please wire me on receipt of this and I will telegraph him, cutting down the time.

TLS Con. 34 BTW Papers DLC.

[1] George Kennan (1845–1924), author, lecturer, and investigative reporter, was a former Associated Press manager in Washington, D.C., who wrote for the *Outlook* and *McClure's Magazine*. His most notable work was *Siberia and the Exile System* (2 vols., 1891). Because of other commitments he was unable to serve Villard and BTW in investigating the Atlanta Riot.

To Oswald Garrison Villard

Atlanta, Ga., September 29, 1906

Personal.

My dear Mr. Villard: I sent you a brief telegram this morning regarding conditions here. I have been getting in touch with all parties and I am convinced that the city and state officials are in deep earnest to stop mob violence at any cost and I do not believe there will be any more trouble. I have spent the day seeing people as well as the leaders in the city and have been trying to help and encourage our people in every way possible, and I think, accomplished some good.

The joint conference this afternoon will be between ten of the best white men in the city, appointed by a mass meeting, and twenty colored men of the same class and I believe much permanent good will result.

The treatment which some of our people received during the last few days would be hard to describe, but on the whole they are bearing up bravely. Very truly yours,

Booker T. Washington

TLS Oswald Garrison Villard Papers MH. A carbon is in Con. 34, BTW Papers, DLC.

To the Editor of the Houston *Texas Freeman*

Atlanta, Ga., Sept. 29, 1906

Editor Texas Freeman: I have just spent some time upon the grounds of Clark University and Gammon Theological Seminary, with President Crogman and Dr. Bowen. I have also looked very thoroughly into conditions so far as our people are concerned, and I have no hesitancy in advising the students of Clark and Gammon to return as speedily as possible to these two institutions, and since getting into direct touch with the presidents of these two institutions I am convinced that new students as well as old ones will find themselves perfectly safe on the grounds and in the city of Atlanta as well. The dangerous period, I am sure, has passed. During the last few days President Crogman and Dr. Bowen have passed through severe trials for these two institutions and for the race, but they have stood manfully and courageously at their posts. When the true history of the Atlanta disturbance is written it will be shown that no two individuals acted more heroically and deserve greater credit than is true of President Crogman and Dr. Bowen. They have done their duty, now let the race do its duty by supporting and encouraging them.

It would prove of great value just now to these great and grand men for the race to crowd these two institutions with students as speedily as possible, and I very much hope this will be done.

Booker T. Washington

Houston *Texas Freeman*, Nov. 9, 1906 Clipping Con. 1045 BTW Papers DLC.

To Wallace Buttrick

[Tuskegee, Ala.] September 30, 1906

Personal

My dear Dr. Buttrick: I have just returned from Atlanta where I have been spending a part of two days getting into touch with the situation and trying to be of what assistance I could in straightening matters out.

One or two elements in the situation stand out rather prominently in my mind.

First, the honest people in Atlanta made no concealment of the fact that the number of assaults on women was exaggerated three or four fold.

Secondly, I am convinced that the whole of Atlanta now feels thoroughly ashamed of itself for what has happened. I have never, in all my experience, seen the leading men, including the highest officials of a great city, at the mourner's bench to the extent that these people are. Yesterday, at the request of the whites, twenty leading colored people met ten leading white people at the Colored Young Men's Christian Association, and for two hours there was a frank, heart to heart talk. The colored people did not mince their words; they told the whites in no uncertain terms the way the colored people had been grievously injured. The whites were equally frank; they acknowledged their sins of omission and commission, and promised in most sincere terms amends for the future; in fact, their one dominant plea was to know what the colored people wanted. Their committee was headed by Captain English[1] who is in a way the most prominent man in Atlanta. The colored people told the others that if the whites were to have saloons they were to have saloons too, if the whites were to go on the Negro must go on, and so on to the end. And the white people took it seemingly all right and agreed to the justice of the colored people's contention. The best outcome, however, I think, of the joint meeting was the appointing of a permanent cooperating committee of ten of each race. This, I think, is going to accomplish good work. I feel very sure that Atlanta is deeply in earnest in its determination to blot out lawlessness in that city. One is just as safe in Atlanta at present as in New York.

I wish I had time to tell you of some of the heroic deeds performed by the colored and white people. There is much that has not gotten in print that is creditable to the white people, while of course there is much that is disgraceful and discreditable. For example, there was a decent colored family living on a street where there was no other family of the same race. The mob went for that family at once. As soon as the mob assembled, the white neighbors clustered around the house of this one colored man and his family and told the mob that in order to disturb the Negro family they would have to pass over their dead bodies, and of course the mob dispersed. There were more than half a dozen equally heroic examples. Both Dr. Bowen and Dr. Crogman stood by their posts heroically.

The main thing now is to keep the colored people from becoming discouraged. All of us should bend our efforts as far as possible in that direction. At present many of the best element feel like pulling out and leaving Atlanta.

I hope you will read to-day's New York World which gives a reasonably fair account of the riot, except I do not believe with the writer that the labor question is at the bottom of the trouble. Neither of our races in the South has reached the point where it is willing to fight for the opportunity of working. Most of us want to let the other fellow do all the work he is willing to do without let or hindrance. The editorial in the World is also worth reading.

Of course all this is confidential. Yours truly,

Booker T. Washington

TLpS Con. 32 BTW Papers DLC.

[1] James Warren English (1837–1925), a former captain in the Confederate Army, was the owner of a brick company and a banker in Atlanta. English was active in Atlanta politics beginning in the 1870s and served as mayor from 1881 to 1883. During the Atlanta Riot he was head of the police commission. At the outset of the riot he tried to calm the mob but was shouted down as a "nigger lover." (Crowe, "Racial Massacre in Atlanta," 155.)

To Henry Hugh Proctor

[Tuskegee, Ala.] Oct. 1, 1906

Dear Mr. Proctor: I suppose you have learned by this time that B's[1] name was not exposed through the treachery of the World, but he was foolish enough to send a telegram to the World requesting that his name not be used in the article, and the Atlanta people got hold of the facts through the telegraph office. Yours truly,

Booker T. Washington

TLpS Con. 331 BTW Papers DLC.

[1] Jesse Max Barber.

To Oswald Garrison Villard

Tuskegee Institute, Alabama. October 1, 1906

Personal

My dear Mr. Villard: I have received your telegram, also your letter. Since nothing can be decided at present concerning Mr. Kennan, I think it wise, perhaps, to let the whole matter remain in abeyance until I go to New York again. I am planning to be there to speak at the Afro-American Council on the 11th of this month, and, according to Mr. Kennan's letter, that will be ample time.

I confess that I was surprised at the attitude which the Pinkerton people assumed regarding the Atlanta matter, and the fact that they impressed you in the same way convinces me that it would not be well to have them take the case. I do not quite understand them in this matter. I have worked with them in other matters and they have shown a great deal of interest.

One other point while writing. Let me say that it is not safe for you to send me telegrams bearing upon Atlanta conditions. When in Atlanta a few days ago, I found that one of our leading colored men in that city had gotten into serious trouble through a telegram sent to New York by the telegraph authorities revealing the nature of his message. Yours truly,

Booker T. Washington

TLS Oswald Garrison Villard Papers MH. A press copy is in Con. 34, BTW Papers, DLC.

To the Editor of the New York *Age*[1]

Atlanta, Ga. Oct. 1 [1906]

Editor New York Age: Your correspondent notes that it was generally telegraphed throughout the country that Mr. Price, the postmaster at South Atlanta, was arrested during the recent riot here. This is a mistake. Mr. Price, fearing that his life was in danger from the mob, asked the officials to put him in the jail for safe keeping, and he remained in prison several days at his own request. He is now out, having been released when he requested that it be done.

There is a rumor to the effect that Mr. J. Max Barber, the editor of the Voice of the Negro, has left Atlanta because of some threats against him. Mr. Barber's best friends in this city very much hope that the rumor is not true, and that he is not going to desert the people at this time. There is little doubt but that threats have been made against Mr. Barber because it is stated that he wrote an article for a certain New York paper that reflected on the uprightness of the white people, but threats have been made against dozens of other leading Afro-Americans in Atlanta and they have stood their ground and have faced in some cases death and in other cases they have been led very near death's door. We all will be disappointed in Mr. Barber's bravery and sense of loyalty to the race if he deserts us in this trying hour. What is needed just now is for the intelligent men to stand up and set a good example for the others. If Mr. Barber however, does leave us and go North, we very much hope that he will not follow the example of so many others, that is, after fleeing himself, spend his time in giving advice to the Negro from a long distance how he should conduct himself in the South.

Notwithstanding the effect of the recent riots, the colleges and universities in this city are opening with a reasonably good attendance, and the heads of these institutions say that within a few days the number of students will be very nearly up to normal. President Hope, of the Atlanta Baptist College, President Bumstead of Atlanta University, as well as the heads of Spelman and Clark and Gammon and Morris Brown inform your correspondent that they are not discouraged, but are going to plan to do the best year's work in the history of these grand institutions.

[Booker T. Washington]

TLp Con. 330 BTW Papers DLC.

[1] By dating this at Atlanta and not signing it, BTW or E. J. Scott intended to keep the authorship secret.

From Henry Hugh Proctor

Atlanta, Ga. October 1, 1906

My Dear Mr. Washington: I was very glad you came to us in our trouble, and your presence and counsel were an inspiration when we most needed it. I regretted I did not get to see you before you left. In the preliminary gathering of colored men when I suggested that you were in the city some one objected to having any one present except Atlanta people. I did not push the matter, and it was not mentioned after the white committee came. I regret that you could not have been with us, as I am sure it would have been helpful to all. But you will be glad to know we had a good meeting. An even finer spirit was manifest in that than in the previous meeting. We got together finely. A permanent committee of ten colored men was appointed to co-operate with the committee of the ten white men, with the consent and approval of the white committee.

Yesterday afternoon a large mass meeting was held at the Wheat St. Baptist Church at which a number of white men spoke, and a better feeling is being engendered between the races. The city is quiet and no more trouble is apprehended. I believe a better city is to spring forth.

Thanking you for your coming, I am Very truly yours,

H. H. Proctor

TLS Con. 331 BTW Papers DLC.

To Francis Jackson Garrison

Tuskegee Institute, Alabama. October 2, 1906

Personal

My dear Mr. Garrison: I have just returned from Atlanta where I have been spending a part of two days in looking into conditions and trying to be of what assistance I could.

My special purpose in writing you, however, is to call your attention to an article published in the Sunday New York World and also an editorial in the same issue. On the whole, I think it contains perhaps the most correct account of the Atlanta disgrace of anything that has been published. I do not, however, agree with the writer that the question of labor had anything to do with the riot. We have not yet reached the point where either race is so very anxious to work in the South that it is willing to risk its life for the opportunity to labor. I think we are going to get to the point, however, in the future, where the economic element is going to play an important part; for that reason it will be seen in the future that an element of the white people in the South will be more opposed to industrial and technical education than to the higher education.

There were many unspeakably cruel acts perpetrated in Atlanta during the riot; on the other hand, there were some brave, fine things done by colored people and by a few of the white people in behalf of the lives of the Negro race, but so far as handling the immediate trouble is concerned, I think all agree that the police authorities were criminally negligent and, in fact, in many cases sided with the rioters.

While I was in the city, a joint meeting was held at the invitation of the whites, composed of ten of the strongest white and twenty of the best colored people, to discuss conditions and form plans for the future. Everything is now quiet and I believe will remain so for a long time. It was very interesting to see how plainly and frankly the colored representatives at the joint meeting spoke to the whites concerning the rights of the colored people. The colored representatives told the whites plainly that they would be satisfied with nothing in the way of injustice, but if the white people were to have saloons the colored people must have saloons, that if the colored people were disarmed the white people must be disarmed, and so on through.

It has been a very trying period for all of us, and we hope that the end has come. Yours very truly,

Booker T. Washington

TLS Francis Jackson Garrison Papers NN-Sc. A press copy is in Con. 322, BTW Papers, DLC.

To James Warren English

[Tuskegee, Ala.] October 2, 1906

My dear Sir: I do not remember that I have met you in a personal way, but I spent a part of two days in Atlanta last week and I am writing to say that you do not know how grateful our people there are to you for what you are doing in the direction of encouraging and helping them; they seem to have implicit faith in you, and all feel that through your guidance and leadership conditions are going to be much more satisfactory in Atlanta for both races than they have been in the past.[1] Yours truly,

Booker T. Washington

TLpS Con. 321 BTW Papers DLC.

1 BTW also wrote to Clark Howell, thanking him for his "practical, timely" editorials in the aftermath of the Atlanta Riot. (Oct. 4, 1906, Con. 885, BTW Papers, DLC.)

To Robert Heberton Terrell

[Tuskegee, Ala.] October 4, 1906

Confidential. Hope can see way clear send Dancy care Colored Odd Fellows meeting Richmond at once, pressing telegram suggesting friends report he is working with Morris of Chicago in opposition to interests we represent. Urge him stand by Asbury and others our friends.

W.

TWpIr Con. 336 BTW Papers DLC.

To Christopher James Perry[1]

[Tuskegee, Ala.] October 5, 1906

Personal Not to be printed.

My dear Mr. Perry: I have read the editorial in your issue of September 29 bearing upon the President and what you think his relations to the Atlanta riot should have been. I think in spirit and in utterance you unintentionally do the President an injustice, and on account of my friendship with you I am taking the liberty of personally writing you.

There is a limitation to what the President can do in connection with local and state affairs. The President, as the head of the nation, can deal with the heads of other countries, but the whole constitution and genius of our government place the states and local communities in control of local criminal matters, and the President has no right to interfere. Each state within a given sphere is supreme within itself. So much for the legal side of the matter.

Now as to the wisdom of the President's interfering in such riots as we had at Atlanta. Those of us who live in the heart of the South are more and more convinced that our security and our rights are in an increasing degree dependent upon the forming of a right local public sentiment; that is to say, in proportion as we can get the leading classes of Southern white people to shoulder the responsibility of the protection of the Negro, we shall go further in securing protection than by depending upon some outside force.

For example, though they were tardy in doing so, and were inexcusably to blame during the riots, the state and local authorities finally awoke to the situation in Atlanta and took the mob in hand and thoroughly controlled it. This awakening of local public conscience has brought a security to the Negro and a closeness of relations between the whites and the best class of colored in that city to an extent that hardly prevails in any other part of the South today. If the President had made a move to call troops into Georgia or into Atlanta to control affairs, both the state and city officials would have said, "Alright, we shall be hands off. The National Government is going to be responsible, therefore it must assume the whole responsibility." This would have meant that for a few hours, or while the troops were on the grounds, the Negroes would have been safe, but when they were removed the Negroes would have been in a worse condition than they were before. I am sure that our good President has spoken out so often and so bravely against lynching and rioting that no one can question where his heart is in all such matters, and no one can question his disposition to speak and act whenever speech and action are wise. Yours truly,

Booker T. Washington

TLpS Con. 330 BTW Papers DLC. A signed copy is in the Theodore Roosevelt Papers, DLC.

[1] Christopher James Perry (1859?–1921) was founder and editor of the Philadelphia *Tribune* beginning in 1884. He served on the Philadelphia City Council from 1897 to 1905, and later was president of the National Negro Press Association.

A Sunday Evening Talk

[Tuskegee, Ala.] October 7, 1906

THE KINGDOM OF GOD

When we hear of The Kingdom of Heaven, we at once get the impression that it is a place that is very beautiful, that is very grand, a place where there is always happiness, and we get the impression further, that it is a place where one would like to live always. Now, you will perhaps remember the passage in the Bible which refers to the location of the Kingdom of God; it says, the Kingdom of Heaven is within. I do not quote exactly, but the sense of the passage is, the Kingdom of Heaven is right within us.

It is true, very often, that the most beautiful things are the things that attract the attention of the average individual the least; the things that to the average man are most common are to the trained eye of the cultured and educated individual the things that are most valuable and beautiful. One of the most interesting books that ever I read, was one that described the beauty in a common, ordinary mud puddle. A woman studied the common, ordinary mud puddle in order that she might find how much there was in Nature that was beautiful; how much there was in that mud puddle that was worth knowing about. You would be surprised to know how interesting the book was. If you ever come across it, I hope very much that you will read it. You will find it filled with interesting pictures and beautiful thoughts concerning how much beauty there is in Nature. If you will get into the habit of going into the forest about you once in a while, or rather the woods, as you have no forest about you, you will see for yourself some of the beauty of Nature. And that reminds me, that I never see Mr. Carver with a bunch of sticks, weeds, or branches, but that I remember that we have one man here on the grounds who sees all that is beautiful in the things about us. The same is true of rocks. It is worth while for every person to grow into the habit of finding all that is good, all that is beautiful in the things with which he comes into contact right about his door.

I have often spoken to you about a lecture that Russell Converse[1] has delivered about seven hundred times, and the title is "Acres of Diamonds," the beautiful things that are right about your feet, that you are coming into contact with every day and don't rightly appreciate.

Now we often think of the Kingdom of God as being a thousand miles away; above the sun, above the moon, above the stars, above the clouds, anywhere, just so it is miles and miles away. The Kingdom must be so very far away. That is a wrong idea of the Kingdom of God. The Bible says the Kingdom is right within us. That brings to my mind that I want to help you to make up your minds to get to the point, as soon as possible, where you can have that power of self-control which will enable you to make the place, hereafter, wherever you are, the most beautiful and the happiest place there is in existence. If this cannot be done, then the teaching of the Bible is not true. You can make within yourselves a little Kingdom, where every minute of the day will be happiness.

The average individual has the idea, and often expresses it, that he would be happier somewhere else; that happiness is always existing in some other surroundings. We often hear people speak of "Good old times" fifty, sixty, or one hundred years ago—never anything good in the present-day generation. There never was a period when there were so many good boys and girls as today. They get into the habit of speaking of the good old times. Whenever I come into contact with him, I at once grow suspicious of the person who is lamenting that he would be happy if he were somewhere else, fifty or one hundred miles away, somewhere, where there was enjoyment. I repeat, whenever I hear an individual making those kind of remarks, I grow suspicious of that individual, and nine cases out of ten, it shows the state of mind that man or woman is in.

Whenever we come into contact with a student who is always unhappy, always grieving, always complaining, always fault-finding, there is never anything right, the atmosphere in which he is living is not right. The Kingdom of God is right within us, and we can make ourselves control our conversations so that we shall have an atmosphere of brightness, of luxury and courage; so that we can make those who come into contact with us feel they are in a place almost holy, and they will depart from us feeling that they are helped, made stronger, and happier. We want you to cultivate the habit of controlling circumstances and even make the atmosphere in which you breathe, in which you live happy. And last of all, make up your minds to make your lives as pleasant as possible. Now remember that we have within our power, every day of the week, every minute of the week, we have it within our power to have a little kingdom within ourselves. At our tables, in our bedrooms, on the grounds, at home, no matter where we are, we have it within our power to have a little kingdom in which we are living, and a kingdom that is living within us.

Many of you this year are going to be tempted to leave, to give up in despair because, probably, you will find some of your fellow-students about you dressing well, in correct style, and in some cases, wearing expensive clothing and with all the luxuries of dress. Unless you are able to control the atmosphere of happiness and contentment, to which I have referred, you will find that you will soon become unhappy. Don't let the thought of poverty drive you from school. If you find that you lack in dress and comfort do not grow into the mood of discontentment and decide that you are not going to make that Kingdom of God.

Now I want every student to make up his mind that under all circumstances you will have the Kingdom of God within you. I want each student, who sits before me tonight, to make up your mind that you are going to finish the course of training that you have started upon, that you will allow none of these circumstances to dishearten you; that you are going to master whatever you undertake.

Let me repeat in conclusion, that I hope every one here will go out with the resolution that on tomorrow morning you will try to have a little Kingdom of God really existing within yourself.

Tuskegee Student, 18 (Oct. 13, 1906), 1.

1 Russell Herman Conwell.

From Francis Jackson Garrison

Lexington, [Mass.] Oct. 7, 1906

My dear Mr. Washington: I thank you heartily for your letter of the 2nd inst. concerning your recent visit to Atlanta, & take much heart from what you tell me of the joint council of white & colored citizens, & of the frankness & plainness of speech of the latter. But how much barbarity there is yet! Here are Mobile & Macon continuing the lynching outrages. Hon. Wm. H. Fleming of Augusta writes my nephew that he intends to write an article on the Atlanta riot & "endeavor to diagnose the case & suggest at least a general line of hopeful treatment." I wrote to Joel Chandler Harris the other day & begged him to come out & express himself, but I have had no response, & fear I shall have none, although, according to the press report, a stone or bullet fired by the rioters pierced his front door.

I did not happen to see the N.Y. World article & must look it up. I wish that a true account of the riot could be written, with the brave & manly deeds of blacks & whites fairly set forth. I am thankful that you always see the silver lining to every cloud! Yours faithfully,

Francis J. Garrison

I am sorry you have lost Bruce from Tuskegee.

ALS Con. 322 BTW Papers DLC.

From Samuel Laing Williams

Chicago 7/10/1906

My Dear Mr. Washington Max Barber is here and is to locate "Voice of the Negro" on Ills soil. He claims to be a refugee from Atlanta. He claims that he was sent for by a Banker who is owner of the "Atlanta News," and was told that if he was the author of the New York World article signed by a "Colored Citizen," he had better leave town, and he left as fast as he could and he never stopped until he reached Chicago.

He and Dr Bentley called on Mrs Wool[le]y[1] to day and she was very much worried by what he said concerning you. He represented to Mrs Wool[le]y that your Business League address was a part of the cause of the riot! and that an Editor of one of the papers of Atlanta dictated that portion of your address relating to crime among Negroes. I took it upon myself to deny the charge with all possible emphasis. I told her I would write to you and ask you about it although the matter was too absurd.

If you can furnish me with a copy of your Atlanta Speech I can use it to advantage.

I note your going to Atlanta in the midst of the anarchy down there. It was an exceedingly courageous thing for you to do and, like thousands of others I thank you for this exhibition of that sort of courage which counts in trying affairs.

I would like very much to have you write me something in reference to these charges and insinuations of Barber because they can be used now to good effect. Sincerely yours

S Laing Williams

ALS Con. 34 BTW Papers DLC.

[1] Celia Parker Woolley.

From Theodore Roosevelt

The White House, Washington. October 8, 1906

My dear Mr. Washington: I thank you for sending me the copy of that letter.[1] I had not seen the article in the Tribune. I wonder if the foolish writer has taken the trouble to learn that I had absolutely *no* authority under the circumstances to send troops to Atlanta. I suppose the Tribune editor is a colored man, is he not?

I thank you for your excellent letter. Sincerely yours,

Theodore Roosevelt

TLS Con. 7 BTW Papers DLC.

[1] See BTW to C. J. Perry, Oct. 5, 1906, above.

From Charles Waddell Chesnutt

Cleveland, October 9, 1906

My dear Dr. Washington: I am in receipt of your letter and telegram from Tuskegee, calling my attention to the meeting of the Committee of Twelve at the Stevens House on October 12th. This is one of the meetings at which I should very much like to be present, and I regret exceedingly that I am tangled up here in a lawsuit which absolutely demands my presence during the whole of this week and very probably into the middle of next week; it is of a nature which does not permit of a substitute and I am therefore compelled to forego the privilege of attending the meeting.

I wish also to acknowledge your brief note calling my attention to the issue of the New York World, containing a review of the Atlanta horror. I read with great interest Mr. H. G. Wells' article in Harper's Weekly on the "Tragedy of Color," and I think you will agree that my views and those of Mr. Wells are very much the same. I do not believe it possible for two races to subsist side by side without intermingling; experience has demonstrated this fact and there will be more experience along that line. Another thing of which I am firmly convinced, in view of recent events, is that no system which excludes the Negro or any other class from the use of the ballot and leaves this potent instrument in the hands of the people who are alien to him in sympathy and interest, can have any healthy effect in improving his condition. No subterfuge of equal qualifications and just application to black and white alike of disfranchising provisions, can overcome the solemn fact which is brought home every day by reading the newspapers that these state constitutions leave the Negro absolutely at the mercy of the white man.

I have never been able to see how any man with the interest of his people at heart could favor those abominations. I know that your heart is all right, but I think your very wise head is wrong on that proposition, and I should regard it as a much more hopeful day for the Negro in this country when you cease to defend them. There is no hope for the Negro except in equality before the law, and I suspect that hope will be deferred for many a day in the Southern States. At the same time I think nothing is lost and everything gained by insisting upon the principle. A man weakens his position immensely when he takes any attitude which justifies or excuses his oppressor.

I notice a great deal has been said by colored people about the Atlanta matter. And of course I have not failed to observe that those best qualified to speak, and whose utterances would carry most weight, have not been in a position to express themselves fully. I appreciate the difficulty of their situation. And so far as the mere matter of speech is concerned, discretion on the part of people who live and work in the South is imperative. I observe that a Georgia editor was expelled from that State for saying a few truthful things about the Jim Crow law in Savannah. After all, the Northern press, with a surprising unanimity and vigor, has said the things which ought to have been said, much to the chagrin of the South, much to our satisfaction and I trust much to the enlightenment of Northern readers.

Negro leaders for some time to come are likely to lead a somewhat strenuous existence. They have my sympathy and will have any small support & cooperation that I can contribute.

With best wishes for a successful meeting of the Committee and of the Council, at which you will doubtless be present to exercise a wise and restraining influence, I remain Sincerely yours,

Chas. W. Chesnutt

P.S. I presume you have been reading the "Autobiography of a Southerner" in the Atlantic. I don't know who wrote it (tho I presume you do). It is great stuff, & shows a real insight into Southern conditions.

C. W. C.

TLS Con. 317 BTW Papers DLC. Postscript in Chesnutt's hand.

From Melvin Jack Chisum

New York Thursday 4:30 pm October 11–06

Dear Doctor Washington: I have *Chase* in leash. Questions are to be asked you tonight. I will, I think, succeed in stopping them. I shall see Mr. Moore and get him to talk to the Captain of the Police and get plain clothes men. *I shall not tell Mr. Moore that I am informing you.* Faithfully yours

Chisum

ALS Con. 2 BTW Papers DLC.

Extracts from an Address Before the Afro-American Council[1]

New York, October 11 [1906]

PRINCIPAL WASHINGTON'S ADDRESS
CLOSES THE ANNUAL SESSION

In the season of disturbance and excitement, if others yield to the temptation of losing control of their judgment and give way to passion and prejudice, let us as a race teach the world that we have learned the great lesson of calmness and self-control, that we are determined to be governed by reason rather than by feeling. Our victories in the past have come to us through our ability to be calm and patient, often while enduring great wrong.

Again, I am most anxious, and I know that in this respect it is the sentiment of every conservative member of our race that our race everywhere bears the reputation of a law-abiding and law-respecting people. If others would break the law and trample it under foot, let us keep and respect it and teach our children to follow our example. In this connection I repeat what I have urged on a recent occasion, every iota of influence that we possess should be used to get rid of the criminal and loafing element of our people and then make decent law-abiding citizens.

To the members of my race who reside in the Northern States let me utter the caution that, in your enthusiastic desire to be of service to your brethren in the South, you do not make their path more thorny and difficult by rash and intemperate utterances. Before giving advice to the Negro in the South, the Negro in the North should be very sure that what he advises is that which he himself would be willing to take into the heart of the South and put into practice. Be careful not to assist in lighting a fire which you will have no ability to put out.

Some may think that the problems with which we are grappling will be better solved by inducing millions of our people to leave the South for residence in the North, but I warn you that instead of this being a solution it will but add to the complications of the problem. While condemning the giving of prominence to the work of the mob in the South, we should not fail to give due credit to those of the white race who stood manfully and courageously on the side of law and order during the recent trying times throughout which this section of our country has been passing. During the racial disturbances the country very seldom hears of the brave and heroic acts of a certain element of Southern white people, whose deeds are seldom heralded throughout the press.

The indiscriminate condemnation of all white people on the part of any member of our race is a suicidal and dangerous policy. We must learn to discriminate. We have strong friends both in the South and in the North, and we would emphasize and magnify the efforts of our friends more than that of those who wish us evil. I have said we must differentiate between white people in the South. We can not afford to class all as our enemies. The country must learn to differentiate between the people. We must frankly face the fact that the great body of our people are to dwell in the South, and any policy that does not seek to harmonize the two races and cement them is unwise and dangerous.

Creation—construction in the material, civic, educational, moral and religious world, is what makes races great. Any child can cry and fret, but it requires a full grown man to create—to construct. Let me implore you to teach the members of our race everywhere that they must become, in an increasing degree, creators of their own careers.

Tuskegee Student, 18 (Oct. 27, 1906), 3. A reprint of an Associated Press report.

[1] BTW's address was entitled "The Requirements of Citizenship." BTW persuaded a few whites, including Oswald Garrison Villard and John E. Milholland, to participate. Spurred by competition from the Niagara Movement, the Council meeting of 1906 was the largest gathering in the organization's history and had a more militant tone than usual, especially on the subjects of lynching and disfranchisement. It was, however, the last significant meeting of the organization, which had dissolved by 1908.

To Charles William Eliot

[Tuskegee, Ala.] Oct. 20, 1906

My dear President Eliot: You do not know how very much I appreciate the suggestions which you make in your letter of September 7 from Asticou, Maine. My delay in answering has been owing to the fact that I had not returned from the summer vacation when your letter first came, and owing to the further fact that I wanted to take a little time to consider carefully the various points which your letter discusses.

In regard to the first question, The Phelps Hall Bible Training School as we call it here. I would state if I had had a choice between spending the money in establishing the Bible Training School or in some other manner, I would not have favored the Bible Training School, but it was in that case as I suppose it is with you at Harvard sometimes, the persons who proposed its establishment had been among our constant and most generous donors in other directions and for this reason we could not quite see our way clear to not accede to their wishes to establish this Bible Training School. We have never made the attempt in it, however, to give theological or what might be termed professional training. Our aim has been to get hold of the man who preaches and works in the average plantation district of the South and better fit him for his work. With this in view, we have given instruction in the English Bible, methods of preparing sermons, and have laid especial emphasis upon practical methods of helping the people to improve their economic and moral life. A good many of the men who have finished this course are doing excellent work in these directions.

In regard to the nurse training, I cannot agree with your suggestion that it might be a mistake to maintain this work. Of course in this as in other directions, it is a question whether we shall do nothing because we cannot do the ideal thing. I do not know as you went into our hospital. We have a hospital of some size, and we are just now spending considerable in the enlargement of the hospital and making it more up-to-date. We have in the vicinity of Tuskegee just now three colored physicians and three white ones, all of whom use the hospital and help in our nurse training work. You, perhaps, cannot realize what a lack of trained nurses there is in the South. I can remember when we first undertook this work that there was no trained nurse within a radius of a hundred miles. The question is, whether we should turn out people who can partially relieve suffering, or wait until we, or some other institution, are in a position to turn out those who are much better equipped than our nurses now are. There is not a single hospital in Alabama where a colored woman can receive such training, and only one or two for whites. Almost without exception the Southern white doctors under whom these nurses work have given them praise for doing satisfactory work. Another important element in this situation is the fact that the nurses we send out from here are the only ones of our graduates who get into such close contact with a Southern white woman as to let her see the value of Negro education. I know numbers of cases where our nurses have gone into white families that have been prejudiced against Negro education and have been able in two or three weeks to change their ideas because of the gentleness, tact and conscientious service of the nurse. Enclosed I send a letter just received from our head nurse concerning one of our last year's graduates.

As to your third suggestion, I think that there is danger in the direction that you emphasize and that is the physical work, including the mechanical part of our plant, absorbing too much of our income and time, and I shall give immediate attention to that. We have already reorganized our course of training so that we are spending more time in strictly academic work than was true when you were here. The department of our industrial work which has given me the most concern has been the farm; that I am taking hold of in a rather radical manner, and while it is going to require some considerable outlay for the present, I believe that by close attention such as I am now giving, within a few years it will be put upon a more satisfactory basis and will not only be made to pay in a larger degree than it is now, but will prove much more educational.

In regard to your fifth suggestion about putting young men on our board of trustees, I heartily agree with you and shall urge that policy, also shall take up the matter of securing chemical fire engines.

I am going to take the liberty of putting all these suggestions before our Trustees at the proper time. I shall be very glad if you will write me fully and frankly upon any point of our work at any time. Yours very truly,

Booker T. Washington

TLpS Con. 321 BTW Papers DLC.

To Quincy Ewing

[Tuskegee, Ala.] October 22, 1906

My dear Sir: I am quite anxious to inaugurate a movement which will permit the leading colored people to get into such touch with the highest element of white people in the South as will enable the colored leaders to work in harmony with the wishes and general sentiment of the white race. I am going to urge this in every way possible through ministers and other leaders.

My especial point just now is to say that we have here at this institution nearly eighteen hundred teachers and students who exert a great influence over the masses of our people throughout the South, and I am planning to have half dozen of the strongest white men in the South come here and talk to them during the present year on such subjects as will prove helpful. I think it very important that the educated colored man be made to understand that he has strong friends among the Southern white people. At the same time he must realize that he has certain responsibilities in doing his duty in the direction of keeping these friends and of elevating and controlling his own race.

I am writing to ask you to be at one of these lectures. I am going to extend the same invitation to Bishop Wilmer[1] of Atlanta, Dr. Stakely[2] of Montgomery, Dr. White[3] of Atlanta, and men of this character.[4] We can pay your traveling expenses, and in addition a fee of fifty dollars for the lecture. We shall also be responsible for your entertainment at the hotel in the town of Tuskegee. Yours truly,

[Booker T. Washington]

TLp Con. 328 BTW Papers DLC.

1 Cary Breckenridge Wilmer (b. 1859) was a Protestant Episcopal clergyman who served as rector of St. Luke's Church in Atlanta beginning in 1900. Earlier (1891–98) he was superintendent of the Colored Orphan Asylum in Lynchburg, Va. Wilmer was a member of the National Child Labor Committee, and in the 1920s was active in the anti-lynching movement.

2 Charles Averett Stakely (d. 1937) was pastor of the First Baptist Church in Montgomery beginning in the late 1880s.

3 John Ellington White (1868–1931) was pastor of the Second Baptist Church in Atlanta from 1901 to 1916. From 1916 to 1927 he was president of Anderson College in South Carolina.

4 Invitations were also sent to Neal L. Anderson of Montgomery, Ala., J. W. E. Cox of Mobile, Ala., and John A. Rice of Montgomery.

From Richard Carroll

Columbia, S.C., October-22-06

My Dear Sir: Your letter received. I arrived home from Philadelphia, Pa., to-day. I am very sorry that you cannot furnish me with your cut. I wanted to write up my impressions of you and your speech at the National Negro Council in New York, which will be of interest to my readers. One-third of my readers are white people. What I say of men, I generally mean. You impressed me favorably. In fact, you made an indelible impression on my mind as a true man and one, that we should uphold rather than destroy.

I did not tell you that Mr. Granville Martin and I came near "having blows" in New York. He cursed me to my face and called me one of "Booker Washington's henchmen" and "an endorser of lynching." There would have been a fight; but a man (I think the editor of the Citizen) of Phila got between us. I simply told Mr. Martin that I had heard you twice and endorsed every word that you said and that, if Jesus Christ came down from Heaven and was permitted to speak, I believe that he would have said just what you said in Zion church to the colored men.

Just as soon as I can get away, I want to come to Tuskegee and see your work. I have been confined to this work here for eight years. My health improves with travelling and, as I have connected myself with Dr. S. G. Miller's work in Philadelphia, this will cause me to travel a great deal. I shall put some one in charge of my work here and continue to travel throughout the South and try to do some good. I am very anxious to see your Institution. I do not speak well of you to gain your favor or to get anything from you; but you really merit the endorsement of every good-thinking Negro in this country. I think that you are a very wise and safe man. If you have no cut of yourself with you, please tell me where I can get one. I want it for the November issue of the Southern Ploughman and want it at once.

I remain, Yours Very Respectfully,

Richard Carroll

TLS Con. 317 BTW Papers DLC.

From Clark Howell

Atlanta, Ga. Oct. 22d, 1906

Personal

Dear Sir: I have your favor of the 18th instant and in reply beg to say that the Constitution has, of course, no objection to your making use of the communications and editorials referred to in any way that you please.

Our country has a great problem in hand in settling this question properly and the most discouraging feature of it to me is that we do not seem to be making any progress in reaching a satisfactory understanding.

The situation seems to be growing worse instead of better. The daily papers are filled with reports of attempted rape in every part of the country and the apparent increase in this sort of thing is having an effect on the public mind which is manifesting itself by intensifying race prejudice not only in the South, but through the country.

One of the worst things that can possibly happen for the Negro race is taking place every day in the very dangerous advice being given by some Negroes and Negro newspapers of the North,[1] to which we call editorial attention this morning in commending your attitude on the subject.

It is a pity that your race as a whole should be made to suffer from the offense of its brutal and criminal element and yet that is the situation. The remedy must be in the conservative and law abiding element of your race following your effort to impress the public with the fact that the better element of your race is just as much opposed to protecting its criminal element as is the better element of the white race to the protection of its criminal element.

You have done good work on this line and can do more than any member of your race, and I especially commend your attitude in condemning the Northern hot heads and incendiaries who are endeavoring to incite the Negroes of the South to adopt a course which would provoke the very worst possible result that could happen to the race as a whole. Very truly yours,

Clark Howell

TLSr Copy Con. 323 BTW Papers DLC.

[1] BTW agreed with Howell on this point and forwarded the letter to Theodore Roosevelt with the comment: "One of the worst features of the situation is the talk indulged in by a few radical papers published in the North." (Oct. 23, 1906, BTW Papers, ATT.)

Samuel Laing Williams to Emmett Jay Scott

Chicago, Ill. 22/10/1906

My Dear Scott, I am [under] many obligations to you for your letter and Mr. Washington's address. I am going to use it and the facts recited in your letter where it will do the most good.

There is something devilish about the way Dr. Washington is being misrepresented by the Conservator. This thing seems to have been intensified by the presence of the "fleeing editor," I have not had a chance to have any talk with him. I had a talk with Dr. Hall[1] a few days ago. He tells me that he gave him directly to understand that his "Voice" will get slight support here if he is going to be influenced by the Guardian and the Conservator. I want you and Dr Washington [to] understand that the fulminations of the Conservator are not making any head way in fooling the solid common sense of the people, where-ever our friends get a chance there is a loyal uprising in vigorous protest. Two Sundays ago some of the Orators began an attack of misrepresentation. Instantly there was a splendid uprising by the Minister and the young people in an emp[h]atic protest. From 75 to 90 percent are with Dr W. with a firmness of loyalty that is simply splendid. I was at a meeting yesterday where the Niagara people gave a report of the Harpers Ferry meeting. The speakers were Bentley, Barber, Madden and Wilson.[2] They all protested that the aim of the "Movement" was in no way in opposition to Dr. Washington! Mrs. Wool[l]ey told me that she had become thoroughly sick of Du Bois. She calls his "litany"[3] was simply "sickening."

I am going to prepare a leaflet on the Atlanta affair to be published by the Frederick Douglass Center. I am anxious to know some thing of the real facts of these alleged assaults. The public mind in the North is becoming affected by these repeated charges that the Negro is a rapist. If you can give me any data on this subject, I can use it in a way that will do the most good. If you can give me any matter I wish you would do me the favor of letting me have it at the earliest time.

I am writing to Dr W by same mail. Sincerely yours,

S. Laing Williams

ALS Con. 34 BTW Papers DLC.

[1] George Cleveland Hall.

[2] Edward E. Wilson, a prominent black attorney in Chicago and an active opponent of accommodationism. He denounced separate schools and was one of the few black opponents of Julius Rosenwald's financing of segregated black YMCAs. (Spear, *Black Chicago*, 61–62, 85.)

[3] W. E. B. Du Bois, "Litany of Atlanta," *Independent*, 51 (Oct. 11, 1906), 856–58. This poem has been widely reprinted as an expression of black protest against white terrorism.

To Booker Taliaferro Washington, Jr.

[Tuskegee, Ala.] Oct. 24, 1906

My dear Booker: Davidson has just been examined in his Algebra, and he made a passing mark, one hundred, and I wonder if you are doing as well. Your papa,

B. T. W.

TLpI Con. 17 BTW Papers DLC.

To Whitefield McKinlay

[Tuskegee, Ala.] Oct. 25, 1906

Personal

My dear Mr. McKinlay: This is for your own eye and must not get out. The President is planning to take up the Southern riots in his message to Congress. I am to see him about the matter soon. Yours truly,

Booker T. Washington

TLpS Con. 327 BTW Papers DLC.

To Samuel Laing Williams

[Tuskegee, Ala.] October 25, 1906

My dear Mr. Williams: I really have been so busy lately that I have not kept up with the correspondence which I hear is appearing in one or two of the Niagara Movement papers. I understand that they are stating with continual emphasis that my speech at the League was prepared or suggested very largely by the white people in Atlanta. The fact is, my speech was sent out to the Associated Press before I even went to Atlanta, and it was not altered in a single line or sentence after I got there. I always prepare my speeches at least a week ahead, and not only that, but I go carefully over them with friends of the race with different points of view. For example, in the case of the interview that I sent out from New York during the Atlanta riots, an hour was spent in consultation with such men as Dr. Gilbert,[1] Mr. Oswald Garrison Villard, Mr. Fortune, Bishop Walters, and one or two others. The whole thing was thoroughly thrashed out, and after we thought it was in satisfactory form it was given to the press. I follow the same policy in reference to all of my public utterances. I get the views of radical and conservative elements. In the case of the Atlanta speech, I did not see Mr. John Temple Graves except for about two minutes. The fact is, he was leaving Atlanta for the Bryan reception in New York on the same train that took me into Atlanta; we met in the station, shook hands, and spoke for about two minutes. That is all there is to the story which I understand they are trying to spread. Yours very truly,

Booker T. Washington

TLpS Con. 34 BTW Papers DLC.

1 Presumably Matthew W. Gilbert.

Extracts from a Speech at the Alabama State Fair

[Montgomery, Ala. Oct. 27, 1906]

The negroes of Alabama are most grateful to Governor Jelks for consenting to be present and speak to us on this occasion. We honor Governor Jelks, and have faith in him, because ever since he has held his position, he has stood up for law and order and justice to all classes of citizens of Alabama.

I wish to express the thanks of my race to Mr. Vandiver,[1] the President, and the officials of the State Fair, for the opportunity which they have extended to us to show to the people of the State our progress as a people. We have made a beginning this year, and I feel quite sure that if there is opportunity afforded us that the negro exhibit will be even more creditable in the future than it has been during the present year.

I am quite sure that all sensible and conservative people of both races have made up their minds that the two races are to dwell here in Alabama, side by side, for all time to come. Since this is a fact, it naturally follows that the only sensible and wise course for any one to advocate is the policy which will keep the two races living together in harmony, friendship and peace, and everything, such as this Fair, that tends to encourage the best element of negroes and to show them that the white people of Alabama are willing to give them a chance to make progress and to show their progress to their fellows, goes a long ways in the direction of keeping our people happy, satisfied and encouraged.

I very much wish that those who doubt the two races living here together in peace and harmony and prosperity, might have the opportunity to come on these Fair grounds for the week, as I have done, and witness the sincere interest of thousands of white people in the negro race; I wish they might have seen the thousands of the two races on these grounds together, without a single instance of hostility or unkindness. I wish they might have heard the sincere expres[sions] . . .[2] made by the negroes of Alabama in moral, material and educational directions.

TWO CLASSES OF NEGROES

There are two classes of negroes, as every white man knows. The great majority of negroes in Alabama are peaceful, law-abiding citizens. Everyone knows hundreds of negroes in his county, who, in the matter of industry, in the matter of honesty, can be trusted to the limit, and I often think that a mistake is made when people speak broadly of the negro race as being lazy and immoral. What they really do mean in most cases is, that there is an element of the race that is lazy and immoral.

I hope, wherever it is possible, that in speaking of the race the worthy will be encouraged, as is being done at this Fair. The element that gives trouble is small as compared with the whole number. Nevertheless, the time has come when every minister, teacher and leader of every character, must face frankly the fact that the criminal element, however small, is working great damage to our race, and however difficult the task may be, we must in some way reach this criminal element and see to it that they cease to disturb our peace and bring trouble upon our communities. Those for the main part, who are guilty of crime are the loafers, the gamblers, the drunkards, those who carry concealed weapons, and those who are in the habit of lingering about dens. In every way possible, we must create a public sentiment in every community that will ostracise such characters and make them feel the weight of our condemnation to such a degree that these characters cannot exist in any community.

Again, we should let it thoroughly be understood that we condemn any man who lays unholy hands upon a woman. We want to make progress in this direction until it shall be known throughout the world that any man of our race guilty of this crime, can find no shelter or comfort in any one of our communities. We must let the municipal and county and state officials understand that no man guilty of crime will be concealed or encouraged by us, that we are just as ready to perform our duty in exposing those guilty of crime as any other member of the community and yet it should always be borne in mind that the negro has no official power in the punishment of crime, but he can, and should use his moral influence against it. If necessary and wherever the conditions make it necessary, law and order leagues should be organized among us to curb those who, by committing crime, disgrace us. Let us not for a single minute let the impression prevail that because a man is of our own race he can be concealed or encouraged in his criminal acts.

Plea for Education

In this connection let us consider the classes of negroes that do not commit crime. They are those who have homes, who are taxpayers, who have a trade or other regular employment; they are those who are in professional service; those who have received education.

In this we have a strong, practical demonstration right here in Alabama, in favor of the education of all classes of our citizenship. Ignorance will always mean crime, and will be an unwieldy burden fastened about the neck of the South. The only safety for both races is in the direction of education, industry and high-character. The country will never know how much it owes to the educated leaders of our race, nor of the wide influence they have exerted in the direction of peace and law and order.

Let us never grow discouraged as a race. Right here in the South, there are more things upon which the races agree, than upon which they disagree. Let us not be so much absorbed in our grievances that we fail to remember our successes and opportunities.

I am very anxious, again, that we get back to the old days when there was a closer touch between the best element of negroes and the best element of white people. I advise that every negro minister in Alabama omit no occasion, for example, to have the best white ministers and white leaders come into his pulpit and talk to his people; that whenever it is possible that the leaders of the two races in each community confer together concerning the law and order and peace and happiness of that community. Throughout the South I believe that the white race is realizing as never before that it is their duty not only to enlighten and civilize the heathen in Africa and China and other foreign lands, but it has a pressing duty right at its doors, to lift up, to Christianize, the black man that lives right by their side. In all these respects, just in proportion as an interest of this character is manifested in the upbuilding of the race, I believe that our people will repay such effort by proving themselves to be law-abiding, useful and industrious citizens.

Negro Needs Encouragement

Here in Alabama we cannot escape the fact that the negro needs the example, the encouragement, and the assistance of the white race. The white race needs the presence and the work of my race. Neither can get on without the other, but every time that there is an outbreak in any community, it injures the whole State financially, morally, and from every other point of view. In most parts of our State there is constant peace and the utmost friendship existing between the races, but the world does not hear of that as much as it hears of the few communities where there is trouble.

We want to get in motion an influence in every corner of the State that shall get rid of every idle man loafing about the street corners or in barrooms. There is plenty of work in this State for every man who desires to work, but no community can afford to support loafers. We should make it so uncomfortable, through the influence of public sentiment, for the loafer, that he cannot afford to tarry among us. The man who idles away his time, who roams through the community with no steady employment, who has no trade, who wanders from one plantation to the other, or from one town to the other, is the individual who in most cases is guilty of crime and disgraces the race.

Every man seen in idleness upon the streets is a bad advertisement for the race. Aside from the economic or money value of laboring, there is a moral side. The man who works and loves work, for its own sake, is the man who, I repeat, in nine cases out of ten, leads a moral and upright life. The idle man soon becomes the criminal, and the criminal is a burden to any community and a disgrace to our people.

ADVISES THRIFT

We should not only see to it that our people are industrious, that they do not throw away their time, but that their money, to invest it in homes, they are taught everywhere to save something that will remain with them, to keep it in banks. And let us come to have the reputation of being spend thrifts.[3]

Let the negro race throughout Alabama not feel discouraged. The best element of the white race in this State and in other Southern States, is determined to stand by us, to encourage us, to protect us; and we should do our part in upholding the hands of this better element.

Our people are making progress; progress in buying property, in securing homes, in learning to save money, in educating their children, in moral and religious growth. Immense progress is being made. We want to be sure, however, that this progress is not retarded or halted by reason of any unwise action on our part. Let us hold up our hands and go bravely and wisely forward, and our course will meet with the approval of all men whose good will is worth possessing.

Montgomery *Advertiser*, Oct. 28, 1906, 20.

[1] William Franklin Vandiver (1850–1908), a prominent Montgomery grocer and banker, was founder of the Alabama Agricultural Fair Association.

[2] Line dropped by newspaper.

[3] Paragraph garbled in original.

A Sunday Evening Talk

[Tuskegee, Ala.] October 28, 1906

In the Sunday Evening Service leaves from which we read Sunday to Sunday, these words you will find, "The earth is full of thy riches."

Now, the average reader passes over those words very lightly, without getting any practical meaning from them, but no one can keep his eyes open without being constantly convinced, without knowing that those words mean exactly what they say. One difference between a successful man and another who fails is that the first individual has learned to think practically of those words; the other has not.

The man who succeeds in life is the man who has learned to interpret the words of the Scriptures, however quoted, in a practical way. "The earth is full of thy riches." The man who believes that and actually looks for it, is the man who is going to succeed. The average individual gets the impression that that is simply put there to tickle the ears without having any practical meaning, but it is just as true as stated in the Bible, "The earth is full of thy riches." In getting the riches out of the earth there is no color line, no race line. One man has just as fair a chance to get those riches out of the earth as the other man; one race has even chance with other races to get the riches out of the earth.

Now I shall speak to you in that connection for a minute about the effort that has been made at Montgomery, Ala., during the past week at the State Agricultural Fair. Now what does holding a State Fair mean? What do all such expositions mean? They are meant to help people get all that there is out of the earth, and turn it into usefulness, into happiness, into morality, into spirituality. That is the object of all such enterprises as the one held during the past week at Montgomery. I think the instances in the South are few where our race has been given a better opportunity to show what they are able to do in getting riches out of the earth, than the opportunity provided for them in Montgomery during the past week.

In spite of all the differences that seem to be in the atmosphere, I am quite sure that of all people from Tuskegee who have had any connection with the Fair that they will agree with me when I say that notwithstanding the many thousand black and white people who attended the Fair, no one heard of a single act of unkindness. I do not think I am overestimating the matter when I say that perhaps ten thousand people passed through the Negro Building during the past week, and I am quite sure that no one heard a single whisper of unkindness. On the other hand, the persons in charge of the Negro Department were rather overwhelmed with words of congratulation and kindness by members of the white race. That should convince you that many of the white people of the South are better than you think; that after all there is something in human nature that gives encouragement to people who are trying to do their best to succeed. I have never been more convinced of that until the experience in Montgomery during the past week.

At these fairs an opportunity is given for the two races to come together, to look each other in the face, to see the things we, each, are trying to accomplish. The Negro Building, for a week, was the center of meeting for the interchange of views and ideas. All of this has gone far in establishing better relations between the two races. I hope all of you will try to make an opportunity to attend such expositions in the future. Many of the people who made exhibits have come into Alabama during the last ten years and have established throughout the State little kingdoms of their own. They have gone out into counties that we have scarcely heard of and have selected little spots of earth in the forests, some with a few dozen acres, some with a few thousand acres of land and have established little kingdoms for themselves. Many of these people have come from the West, from the North, from foreign countries, and from other places; have come and quietly taken hold of land, cultivated it, prospered. Of what do these kingdoms consist? In many cases, as were illustrated by these exhibits, the people began by raising pigs. I had no idea that such pigs and hogs were being raised in the South as were on exhibition at Montgomery. Many of these people have grown wealthy in a few years simply by raising pigs. They have gone out quite a distance from some large city, have planted themselves, and are living happily. There was one woman there who had an exhibit of live stock, and who took the first prize for live stock; she was ahead of all the white people. The average colored woman does not want to begin with live stock, or pigs, or poultry; she wants to begin by being a bookkeeper, a typewriter, a stenographer, or a music teacher. I believe, and earnestly, in all of that, but I want you to understand that the people who endure longest, who will get to the top and stay at the top, are those people who begin by selecting a little piece of land, and establish themselves; they are the people who after a while can sell land for which they paid a mere trifle for large sums of money; for this land always gets to be valuable in the course of time. Many of us like to go into a city and discuss what seat we shall sit on in the car, third from the front, or second from the back; discuss where we will walk on the street, what store we will patronize, or where we will drink soda-water. Now the man who is wise, goes out into the country, miles from any street car or soda fountain, and makes a kingdom for himself where he is master of all, and where he can say what shall take place and what shall not take place.

The question with you who are going out to be leaders is, are you going to be strong enough to leave the electric lights, and the telephones to go out into the country to establish something for yourselves. You have the same chance as other people throughout Alabama where you can go and establish these little kingdoms if you will. Don't be like the average individual who is so weak that, like these flies that cling about the electric lights, they hold on to the wire as long as they can, then drop to earth, useless, purposeless. There is no comparison between the opportunity afforded our people all through the South with what they find elsewhere. In these counties you will find numbers of these restrictions about which people spend their time in fretting. There is Mr. Isaiah T. Montgomery of Mound Bayou, Miss., who has been the Mayor and director of the town. The colored people there select their own Board of Aldermen and settle their own affairs. Mr. Montgomery, years ago, was strong enough to go out into the swamps and establish a city there for himself and his people, and what he has done other people can do.

Going back to the Fair at Montgomery: you would have been surprised at the garden and farm products that were exhibited by these people, this same class of people who have gone quietly out into the forests and established their own little kingdoms. One family, from Dallas County, had an exhibit with a woman in charge. They had everything that was necessary for existence that had been raised on their farm by the efforts of mother, father, brother and sister.

Now, in these days of freedom and independence, and success, we want to reach forward and succeed in larger ways than ever before. The question of color and of prejudice will, I am sure, in a large degree, melt away if we grasp these opportunities to make ourselves useful, if we fasten ourselves upon the soil, and prosper as other people are doing.

Tuskegee Student, 18 (Nov. 10, 1906), 1.

To Charles Waddell Chesnutt

[Tuskegee, Ala.] Oct. 29, 1906

Personal

My dear Mr. Chesnutt: I have time to take only a minute to answer one point in your letter. I very much fear that you place too much reliance upon the ballot to cure evils that we are at present suffering. The ballot is valuable and should not be surrendered. Every man who can do so should vote, but in this connection, how do you account for the Atlanta riot, the worst that we have had in forty years? That occurred in practically the only Southern state where the Negro has not been disfranchised by reason of constitutional enactment. Yours truly,

Booker T. Washington

TLpS Con. 317 BTW Papers DLC.

To Theodore Roosevelt

[New York City] November 2, 1906

Personal.

My dear Mr. President: The enclosed extract is taken from a letter written by Ex-Governor Candler (not Chandler) and was published in the Washington Post, September 1st, 1899. I think you are safe in using it.

Enclosed, I also send a marked copy of The Montgomery Advertiser, containing a recent address delivered in Montgomery in which I spoke out against Negro crimes, even more strongly than you have done.

If you possibly can avoid doing so, I very much hope you will not take definite action regarding the Negro soldiers in the Brownsville affair, until after your return from Panama. There is some information which I must put before you before you take final action.

I think that what you are trying to say regarding crime and education is going to accomplish a great deal of good. Very truly yours,

[Booker T. Washington]

TLc BTW Papers ATT.

From Whitefield McKinlay

Washington, D.C., 11/2/[190]6

Personal

Dr Mr Washington Imagine my surprise & mortification when approached by Dr Atwood[1] tonight & asked whether a secret conference was held at my house on Tuesday at 3 P.M. to go over the question of the Presdts message on lynching. When I disclaimed all knowledge of it, he then offered to bet $50.00 that he could name those present & tell what occurred. He came so near the facts that I concluded that some one leaked & it merely surpasses what so many of us painfully know that a colored man cant keep a secret.

I am utterly at a loss to know who is the guilty one. Atwood remarked that I ought to have known that a Negro cant keep a secret. Very truly

W McKinlay

How is the political outlook in N Y[?]

ALS Con. 327 BTW Papers DLC.

[1] Possibly Oliver Madison Atwood, a black Washington physician and pharmacist who graduated from the University of Michigan and Howard University. He died in 1916.

To Raymond Albert Patterson

New York City, November 3, 1906

Personal.

My dear Mr. Patterson: I have just had the opportunity to glance through your analysis of the Negro problem, and in a hasty glance of it, it seems to me that you attach too much importance to the small fraction of the race North of the Mason and Dixon Line. The majority of the ten millions of the Negro race live in the South, and I do not believe any such conditions, as your letter emphasizes, exist in the South. It is true that there is a large element of the class with such education as you describe which gives them the opportunity to be heard in the newspapers, conventions and what not; in a word they keep up a great deal of noise, and deceive the unsuspecting.

I have passed through several conditions, such as you have described, and I have learned not to suffer myself to become unduly alarmed or depressed. In the last analysis I find that the sober second thought of the race reasserts itself.

Even in Washington, if you will brush aside the many so called leaders, you will find the great masses all right. I mean the common, hard-working class, and that is the class to whom I give my greatest attention.

Some time while passing through Washington, I hope to see you and have a talk with you further on this subject. Very truly yours,

[Booker T. Washington]

TLc Con. 331 BTW Papers DLC.

From W. S. Jones

Devall[s] Bluff, Arkansas, Nov. 3, 1906

My dear Sir: I write to informed you, as least as you may think of it, you are the greatest present, or past enemy living or dead the race has ever had.

1st Your public utterances, at Memphis several years ago as to the negro being the meanest and worst race on earth.

2nd Your advice to the negro to stay out of politics, or not to vote.

3rd. Your advice to us not to retaliate when our fathers, mothers, brothers, and sisters are sleeping in an innocent and undeserved grave.

4th Your advice to us to give up our weapons and surrender to an angry mob.

5th Every natural secret the race possess, you have revealed.

6th When the President was advocating a "square deal," "All men up and no man down," "equal Political," and "business right to all," you through your public and private utterances advised him to stop.

7th Your telling the world that the race is only good for hewers of wood and drawers of water.

8th Your telling the race to remain where they are.

9th To always hold the second place as servants.

10th That we are incapable of everything, but bodily servants.

These are a *part* of the things as to why I say you are the greatest present or past enemy the race has ever had. As to the second accusation, no one knows better than you, that to peacefully defend life and property, help the best class of white people to defend theirs and put down the criminals of both races is to put the ballot untrample in the hands of the best intelligent citizens, white or black. You tell us not to retaliate, pray and wait. No-where in history, only one place in the Bible, where God ever fought a battle for his people and they were not the instruments.

There is no freedom, nor liberty sweet without the shedding of blood.

I dont mean to fight as a mass, but when the occasion presents itself as at Atlanta.

To give up your weapons means to die without resenting.

6th No one knows better than you that the Nation on promise from the Southern representatives has ceased to interfear with the race question, on promise that they would peacefully settle everything for all concern if let alone.

And you well know things have grown worse.

8th You know if a few thousands of us leave the South it will be better for those who stay.

9th Nothing can nor will curb the high ambition of the race, (intelligent).

10th You say we are incapable, when only one race on earth stands above us in intelligence (white).

If you cant say better things than you have said "hold thy peace." At the expense of the race you have exalted yourself, now "go back and sit down." I am, respectfully yours,

W. S. Jones

ALS Con. 324 BTW Papers DLC.

From Charles Waddell Chesnutt

Cleveland, November 3, 1906

My dear Dr. Washington: I beg to acknowledge receipt of your letter of recent date. I note what you say about the franchise in Georgia, and while the riot occurred in Georgia, it was not because the Negroes had exercised the franchise or made any less progress or developed any less strength than elsewhere, but because of a wicked and indefensible effort to disfranchise them.

I am quite aware that the Negro will not enjoy any large degree of liberty at the South until there has developed in that section a white party which is favorable to his enjoyment of the rights guaranteed by the Constitution of the United States. The rise of such men as Mr. Fleming indicates that this party, while small, is finding a voice. Surely no colored man can afford to demand less for his race than a white man is willing to concede, and as I read Mr. Fleming's pamphlet cursorily during a very busy week, he is willing to give them their rights under the Constitution. The scheme proposed in Georgia for the disfranchisement of the Negro is substantially that enacted in Alabama. This Mr. Fleming condemns. He uses this language: "Let us not in cowardice or want of faith needlessly sacrifice our higher ideals of private and public life." Manhood suffrage is an ideal, already attained in this country except where the reactionary Southern States have qualified it. Surely in a country where every one else votes and the suffrage is freely conceded to foreigners in a great many States, including I believe Alabama, as soon as they declare their intention of becoming citizens, it is not only a great lapse from the ideal, but the rankest sort of injustice that any different rule should be applied to so numerous and important a class of the population as the Negro constitutes in the South. I think a little more anti-Negro agitation in the South will very likely result in an effort at the North to see, for the welfare of the whole country, that the Thirteenth, Fourteenth and Fifteenth Amendments shall become not only the theoretical but the real law of the land. The practical difficulties I admit are enormous, but the value of equal citizenship is so great and so vital that it is worth whatever it may cost. Slavery was as deeply entrenched as race prejudice, yet it fell. And the sound of the trumpets you will remember shook down the walls of Jericho.

If I wanted to answer with the *argumentum ad hominem*, with reference to the Atlanta riot, I could point out the fact that the riot occurred only a few days after your splendid object lesson of the Negro's progress in business and the arts of peace. The fact of the matter is that this race problem involves all of the issues of life and must be attacked from many sides for a long time before it will approach anything like a peaceful solution. The American people will have to swallow the Negro, in punishment for their sins. Doubtless the dose is a bitter one, but there is no other way out. It only remains for all of us to make the process as little painful as possible to all concerned.

One of your agents, Mr. Powell,[1] has been operating around here for several weeks. I have shown him such small courtesies as I could during one of the busiest months of my life. And he tells me that he has been meeting with some encouragement.

I have read a review somewhere of a book which is described as a very vicious attack on Tuskegee. I trust that this false and reckless publication has not done you any injury.

I also beg to thank you on behalf of myself and Mrs. Chesnutt, for the handsome little volume, "Putting the Most into Life," which you were good enough to send us. We shall prize it very highly. Sincerely yours,

Chas. W. Chesnutt

TLS Con. 317 BTW Papers DLC.

[1] Clarence Alpheus Powell, an 1891 Tuskegee graduate, taught agriculture at Slater Industrial Academy in Winston-Salem, N.C., until he became a northern financial agent for Tuskegee Institute about 1906.

From Theodore Roosevelt

The White House, Washington. November 5, 1906

My dear Mr. Washington: I have your letter of the 2nd instant. I could not possibly refrain from acting as regards those colored soldiers. You can not have any information to give me privately to which I could pay heed, my dear Mr. Washington, because the information on which I act is that which came out in the investigation itself. Sincerely yours,

Theodore Roosevelt

TLSr Copy NN-Sc. Another copy is in BTW Papers, ATT.

To Charles William Anderson

[Tuskegee, Ala.] November 7, 1906

Personal and Confidential.
Dear Mr. Anderson: You will of course see by the papers this morning that our friend in Washington has carried out his determination which, as I told you, was in my opinion a great blunder. The whole course is all the more regrettable because of his waiting until just the day after election before putting the order into effect. I have done my full duty in the matter, however, as the enclosed

letter from him will show. He usually, however, comes out on top and I presume he will in this case, in the long run if not in the short run. Of course, you will not let the President's letter pass out of your hands. Yours truly,

Booker T. Washington

P.S. Of course I am at a disadvantage in that I must keep my lips closed. The enemy will, as usual, try to blame me for all of this. They can talk; I cannot, without being disloyal to our friend, who I mean to stand by throughout his administration.

TLpS Con. 249 BTW Papers DLC.

To Whitefield McKinlay

[Tuskegee, Ala.] Nov. 8, 1906

Personal

Dear Mr. McKinlay: I have not had time to write you since our conference at your house. I spent over an hour with the President in taking up in detail his message. He did not take all the medicine which we prescribed for him, but he did take a portion of it. He agreed to modify most of the objectionable expressions except those in the first paragraph; when I tackled him on that, he gritted his teeth and absolutely refused to budge a single inch. He did, however, preface what he had originally written with another introduction which will soften the first part of the message somewhat. He also added, I think, all of the quotations from Southern men which we suggested.

I very much hope that nothing concerning our conference will get to the public, as it will injure our chances for such opportunities in the future. Yours truly,

Booker T. Washington

P.S. He modified, as I have stated, most of the sentences to which we objected except the first part.

TLpS Con. 327 BTW Papers DLC.

To Oswald Garrison Villard

Tuskegee Institute, Alabama. November 9, 1906

My dear Mr. Villard: Mr. Baker[1] came here day before yesterday and is going to remain several days. We have just gone over the Atlanta situation thoroughly. He plans to remain South for sometime, but is going to be in New York immediately after Thanksgiving, and as I plan to be in New York about the same time I think we can arrange for a conference of the character that we discussed. He has spent about two weeks in Atlanta and has gathered some valuable information.

I asked him this morning if he could not do the work of making the investigation which we desire, if he would be willing to superintend it as his name would carry great weight. Of course, I told him that I had no power to decide the matter, but would have to wait until I saw you.

One interesting fact he has already gotten hold of, and that is, a young white lawyer by the name of Hopkins[2] in Atlanta has already made an investigation into the number of alleged criminal attacks and he finds that out of the eleven reported that only in three cases was there any rape. There were several other cases where an attempt was made.

Another fact gotten hold of is that not a single one of the persons killed was of the kind classed as loafers or vagrants.

He has already found out that many interesting occurrences have taken place, some of them rather encouraging, since the riot which have been kept out of the newspapers. Yours truly,

Booker T. Washington

TLS Oswald Garrison Villard Papers MH.

[1] Ray Stannard Baker (1870–1946) was one of the leading muckraker journalists of the Progressive era, writing chiefly for *McClure's* and *American Magazine,* and one of the few reform-minded whites of his day to take a sustained interest in the issue of racial discrimination. In 1904 he visited the scenes of four lynchings in Georgia, Alabama, Ohio, and Illinois, and wrote two muckraking articles on them. After the Atlanta Riot, Baker spent almost two years traveling and interviewing in the South and in the northern cities for a series of articles in the *American Magazine,* which later appeared in book form as *Following the Color Line* (1908). Baker interviewed persons as diverse as James K. Vardaman and W. E. B. Du Bois, but it was BTW whom he most freely consulted and who gave him lists of others to interview, and his work

reflected the Tuskegee influence more than that of BTW's militant critics, who might have been expected to be the allies of the muckraker. Though Baker joined the NAACP and gave addresses at several of its national conferences, his private journals revealed his essential agreement with BTW's "constructive" approach and his misgivings about black assertion of civil rights. A strong supporter of Woodrow Wilson, Baker spent the 1920s in writing an eight-volume biography of Wilson. (Semonche, *Baker*.)

2 Charles T. Hopkins, a prominent white Atlanta lawyer, played a part in the efforts to quiet the white mob during the Atlanta Riot, and he was one of a group who raised $4,423 to aid blacks injured by the mob. He became a member of a committee of ten prominent citizens that worked with public officials to restore order in the city. Out of the work of this group grew the Atlanta Civic League, which worked with black leaders to improve interracial relations. (Baker, *Following the Color Line*, 18–21.)

A Memorandum of Agreement between Tuskegee Institute and the General Education Board

[Tuskegee, Ala.] November 9th, 1906

1st. It is understood that a man to be selected by mutual agreement, shall be appointed to act as our agent in conducting Co-operative Demonstration Work (to be exclusively under our control) for one year from November 15th, 1906, the territory to be Macon County and possibly adjacent counties.

2nd. It is further understood that there shall be set aside from the appropriation made by the General Education Board of New York, for demonstration work in the South the sum of Five Hundred Dollars ($500.00) payable to the party employed in monthly installments pro rata for the time employed. Hence the full amount would not be used unless he worked the entire period of one year.

3rd. It is agreed that Thomas M. Campbell,[1] a graduate of the Tuskegee Normal and Industrial Institute, shall be assigned to the work at a salary of $840.00 per annum, or pro rata for the time employed and that all amounts allowed agent for salary and for general or traveling expenses (above this sum paid out of the General Education Board fund, as stated in Paragraph 2nd) shall be paid by the Tuskegee Normal and Industrial Institute.

4th. It is further understood that out of the funds assigned us by the General Education Board, we will expend $250.00 for valuable seeds to be distributed free to the Demonstration Farms in the territory worked by our Agent, as above appointed.

5th. In assigning Mr. Campbell to this work, it is understood that he will devote his entire time to it, and be under the immediate direction of our Department as outlined in our letter above referred to, it being, however, understood that the Jesup wagon will be operated by him also in this connection, as far as may be deemed advisable.

Booker T. Washington
Principal, for Tuskegee Normal
& Indl Inst.

S A Knapp[2]
Special agent in charge

TMS Con. 33 BTW Papers DLC. Enclosed in Knapp to BTW, Nov. 13, 1906.

[1] Thomas Monroe Campbell (b. 1883) graduated from Tuskegee Institute in 1906 and became the first black county agent in Alabama.

[2] Seaman Asahel Knapp (1833–1911) originated the idea of farmers' cooperative demonstration work in the South and headed the program for the General Education Board and the U.S. Department of Agriculture from 1902 to 1910.

To Oswald Garrison Villard

Tuskegee Institute, Alabama. November 10, 1906

Personal

My dear Mr. Villard: I have just read your editorial on punishing the colored troops. When I saw you in New York, I knew what was to take place, but the President bound me to absolute secrecy. I did my full duty in trying to persuade him from the course not only when I saw him, but wrote him strongly after reaching New York. I am not going to give up. As soon as he returns I expect to have a conference with him with a view of arranging some plan to do justice to innocent men. There is no law, human or divine, which justifies the punishment of an innocent man. I have the strongest faith in the President's honesty of intention, high mindedness of purpose, sincere unselfishness and courage, but I regret for these reasons all the more that this thing has occurred. Yours truly,

Booker T. Washington

TLS Oswald Garrison Villard Papers MH.

From Charles William Anderson

New York, N.Y., November 10th, 1906

(Personal)

My dear Doctor: I want to thank you for your good letter of the 7th instant, and to say, that I very much regret that our "friend" did not act upon your advice. It is the more to be regretted, because he seems to have pleased nobody by the act. Both the friendly and unfriendly newspapers hereabouts are criticising him severely. The Times, the Morning Sun, the Evening Sun, the Evening Post and the World have all had strong editorials on the subject. The World editorial of this morning is headed "executive lynch law," and maintains, he has acted just as the lynchers act, in punishing the innocent with the guilty. It goes on to say, that this historic regiment rendered as distinguished service as did the "Rough Riders," but of course, was not so widely advertised. The Evening Post had a column and a half editorial pointing to the gallantry of this regiment, and emphasizing the fact, that the action was taken on the recommendation of an officer of Southern birth. All papers here agree, that the action was inexplicable, in that it disgraces the colored non-commissioned officers, when it did not punish the white commissioned officers, who were directly responsible for the lack of discipline, which made the Brownsville riot possible. This is the tone of the press of this city.

Of course, the Milholland crowd are making the most of it, and are saying loudly, that if the order had been signed three days earlier, this state would have elected Hearst,[1] and other Northern states would have gone democratic. They are even threatening to hold a public indignation meeting. I am doing my best to prevent this, and hope to succeed.

Gilchrist Stewart, who has been on the road for the Constitutional League, is now at work in this city, trying to get some of the local Colored Republican Clubs to go over to the League. He is their organizer.

Governor Magoon[2] of Cuba seems to be drawing the color-line, if we are to credit newspaper reports. Gualberto Gomez,[3] the colored Cuban leader, is very much dissatisfied with Magoon, and the entire Liberal party are claiming, that he is filling the offices with the men who stood behind Palma.[4] They accuse him of reversing the attitude of Taft. All these things will form different counts in the indictment, which the enemy will make. However, let us hope for the best. Yours truly,

Charles W. Anderson

TLS Con. 32 BTW Papers DLC

1 William Randolph Hearst (1863–1951), the newspaper publisher, ran for governor of New York in 1906.

2 Charles Edward Magoon (1861–1920) was provisional governor of Cuba from 1906 to 1909 during the occupation by U.S. forces.

3 Juan Gualberto Gómez (1854–1933), the son of slaves in Cuba, was a champion of Cuban independence and the Negro race. During the U.S. occupation of Cuba from 1906 to 1909, Gómez, a leading member of the Liberal party, was an adviser to Governor Magoon and also served on a commission to revise Cuba's legal system.

4 Tomás Estrada Palma (1835–1908), first president of Cuba (1902–6).

From James A. Cobb

Washington, D.C. November 13, 1906

Dear Dr. Washington: Yours of the 8th inst. with inclosed to Mr. McKinlay, received, for which I thank you very much. I am very sorry that the President could not see his way clear to modify the first paragraph; as to my mind it was the most objectionable of all in the message. Personally, I think it better that he say nothing, if that portion of it remains. However, I think that you have accomplished a great deal in having him to change any expression detrimental to the Negro. I have long since come to the conclusion that the President has a very low estimate of the Negro; his recent act in regard to the colored soldiers forces that conclusion beyond debate in my mind. The way in which it was done, the order being issued on the day of the election, shows that he is capable of playing very low politics.

The colored people here are going to have a mass meeting Sunday to discuss the matter — I have been asked to take part in it — I shall be in New York Sunday, if here, I would not attend, as I do not believe in abusing the President; but I think all of the colored people should go slow on him hereafter.

I am happy to say that the news papers here in Washington, especially, the Post, don't agree with the President. Very truly yours,

[James A. Cobb]

P.S. Your admonition as to keeping secret our conference, is well taken.

TL Con. 32 BTW Papers DLC. Written on stationery of James A. Cobb.

To Ruth Anna Fisher

[Tuskegee, Ala.] Nov. 14, 1906

Miss Ruth Fisher: I am in receipt of a report from the Head of the Academic Department to the effect that you absolutely refuse to carry out his wishes in regard to correlating the academic and industrial work. Mr. Lee also informs me that he did not call this matter to my attention when you first refused because he wished to give you time in which to consider very carefully your attitude in the matter. Mr. Lee further informs me that, owing to your lack of experience in such work, he has, in addition to making the same kind of formal request that he has of other teachers, talked with you several times in a way that he has not done with other teachers with a view of trying to show you the mistake that you were making, but has not been successful in changing your attitude. Since the matter has been called to my attention by Mr. Lee, I have also waited for sometime before acting in the matter in order to be sure that no injustice was done you by hasty action. You will recall that, in addition to the direct request made of you by Mr. Lee in this regard, at the opening of the school year I explained fully what the plans and policy of the school are in regard to its method of instruction.

A portion of the exact language used by the Head of the Academic Department in making his report I quote: "Miss Fisher said that she was unwilling to cooperate with us in correlating our work and that we need not expect her to do so; she said I might so inform you."

We cannot change the policy of the school, nor can we permit you to be an exception to the rule followed by the majority of the other teachers, therefore I see nothing for me to do but ask that you hand in your resignation. I regret the necessity of this action exceedingly, because I feel that you could have rendered good service here had you undertaken the work in the proper spirit.

In addition to your refusal to cooperate in the work of the Academic Department, the head of the Sunday School Department[2] tells me that you absolutely refuse to have any part in Sunday School work. All this plainly shows that it is not wise for us to attempt to continue you here longer in the service of the school. We have no right to keep any one here unless she is heartily in sympathy with the spirit and methods of our work. Yours truly,

Booker T. Washington

I have directed our Treasurer to settle your account when you call upon him.

TLpS Con. 564 BTW Papers DLC.

[1] Ruth Anna Fisher (1886–1975), a member of a prominent black family in Lorain, Ohio, graduated from Oberlin College and began teaching in Tuskegee's academic department in September 1906. She quickly found herself at odds with Tuskegee's emphasis on industrial work and the requirement that she teach Sunday school. After BTW dismissed her she taught in the public schools of Lorain and Indianapolis, Ind., and later was head of English teaching at Manassas Industrial School in Virginia. She then moved to New York and worked for the YWCA. In 1920 she studied in London and there met J. Franklin Jameson, then director of the Carnegie Institution. Jameson hired her to copy manuscripts relating to American history in British repositories, which became her life work. She eventually supervised the entire London project. When Jameson became head of the Manuscripts Division of the Library of Congress, Fisher also began an association with that institution that lasted until her retirement in 1956. During the bombing of London during World War II, Fisher returned to the United States to process the documents she had gathered, returning to London in 1949. She was the center of an intellectual circle there which

included such persons as Harold Laski, H. G. Wells, Samuel F. Bemis, W. E. B. Du Bois, and Langston Hughes. In 1963 she participated in the March on Washington. (Render, "Afro-American Women.")

2 Possibly Edgar James Penney or another member of the staff of Phelps Hall Bible Training School.

To Portia Marshall Washington

[Tuskegee, Ala.] November 15, 1906

My dear Portia: I have received your letter, and have read it with a great deal of satisfaction and interest. I regret that my answer to yours must be so short, but the fact is, I am preparing to go to New York in a day or two, and I have to hurry matters.

I shall see that the American publications you desire are sent to you. I am exceedingly glad that you have gotten into a more satisfactory boarding place.

I think you will make a mistake if you will let your mind dwell too much upon American prejudice, or any other race prejudice. The thing is for one to get above such things. If one gets in the habit of continually thinking and talking about race prejudice, he soon gets to the point where he is fit for little that is worth doing. In the northern part of the United States, there are a number of colored people who make their lives miserable, because all their talk is about race prejudice.

I think it will be an excellent idea for you to put some time during the winter in the study of French.

Your mother has been making a little visit to Booker at Dummer Academy. He is making a good record in his studies. Davidson is not very strong this winter, but is managing to keep up with his studies.

Matters here go about as well as usual.

All desire to be remembered to you. Your father,

B. T. W.

TLpI Con. 17 BTW Papers DLC. Addressed to Berlin, Germany.

To Henry Churchill King[1]

Tuskegee Institute, Alabama. November 15, 1906

Personal

Dear President King: Enclosed I send you copy of a letter which I have with great regret just sent Miss Ruth Fisher. Perhaps you will remember her. She graduated last year. She is quite young and immature in many ways, and I have been quite patient with her, hoping that she would gradually fall into line and do good work, but I am disappointed. She seems to be bright intellectually, but otherwise is weak. She seems to lack moral earnestness. Especially am I disappointed with the fact that notwithstanding the deep religious spirit which seems to exist at Oberlin, Miss Fisher seems to have brought none of it with her here so far as her being willing to take hold and help the students in Sunday School and in other directions outside of the routine work. Yours truly,

Booker T. Washington

TLS OO.

1 Henry Churchill King (1858–1934), president of Oberlin College from 1902 to 1927.

To D. C. Fisher[1]

[Tuskegee, Ala.] November 16, 1906

My dear Sir: Owing to the youth and inexperience of your daughter, I am taking the liberty of sending you a copy of a letter which I have just been compelled to write her. I have been unusually lenient and patient in this case, but, of course, with your business experience you must realize that no institution can stand for a minute in the face of refusal to comply with its rules. Yours truly,

Booker T. Washington

TLpS Con. 321 BTW Papers DLC.

1 D. C. Fisher, a black realtor and owner of an ice house in Lorain, Ohio, was

the head of the most prominent black family in Lorain. He also served for a time as town clerk. Fisher was angered when BTW fired his daughter from a teaching position at Tuskegee. (See D. C. Fisher to BTW, Nov. 21, 1906, below.)

From Oswald Garrison Villard

New York Nov. 16, 1906

Dear Mr. Washington, I thank you sincerely for your recent letters in regard to the 25th Infantry outrage, and Mr. Baker's visit.

I have not yet been able to get hold of Mr. Clarkin,[1] and am waiting for further word from you.

In regard to the 25th Infantry, I can well believe that the awakening to the instability of Mr. Roosevelt has been a trying one for the colored people. I knew it must come sooner or later. He is as the shifting sands, and they must realize it. The outcry against this act is astounding. We have had many letters here, most of which we have printed, and most of which came from white regular army officers. It is really disgraceful, but it is in keeping with Mr. Roosevelt's whole treatment of the army. So far as his administration of it is concerned, I can prove to you that he has been the worst President we have had in 25 years. Sincerely yours,

Oswald Garrison Villard

TLS Con. 34 BTW Papers DLC.

[1] Franklin Clarkin (b. 1869), an editor of the New York *Evening Post,* was a war correspondent during the Spanish-American and Russo-Japanese wars. In 1914 he was the New York reporter for the Boston *Transcript.* Oswald Garrison Villard recommended Clarkin to do a study in depth of the Atlanta Riot, but the assignment was ultimately carried out by Ray Stannard Baker.

From Kelly Miller

Washington, D.C., Nov. 16th 1906

My dear Dr. Washington: Your favor came duly to hand this morning and contents noted with satisfaction.

Since I wrote you last I have been thinking deeply over the situation which it seems to me is about to be seriously complicated by the proposed treatment of the Negro as a criminal race in the President's forthcoming message. The more I think of it the more I am convinced of the lasting hurt that this utterance will do the race. The Negro is held up as a race of criminals and rapists, banded together to uphold one another in crime, with only occasional individual exceptions. No further justification would be needed by those who despitefully treat us. This utterance from the White House will do more to damn the Negro to everlasting infamy than all the maledictions of Tillman, Vardaman, Dixon and John Temple Graves. I cannot believe that the President intends to do this, but the evil effect will be the same whatever his intention might be. His message becomes a part of the documentary history of the nation. The Negro will thus be branded as a lecherous race, with the authority of the President of the United States. This will be the most serious official blow that the race has ever received.

Can you not bring him to see that he is about to inflict a great and lasting wrong upon a helpless and dependent race? His whole treatment of this issue is purposeless and without effective point, except a moral brand upon the Negro. It is a mere moral homily. There is no suggestion of remedy for the deplorable state of things, which comes within the scope of federal authority. There is lack of the true Rooseveltian ring. In the midst of our awful trials, will the President now say one helpful word? If, in all the circumstances, he does not deem it prudent to do this, will he at least refrain from giving aid and encouragement to those from whom we suffer most? The President's recent order dismissing the colored battalion has evoked the universal condemnation of the race. If upon the heels of this action he sends out this damaging statement, it will surely aggravate the bitter feeling already engendered.

It would seem that the President might be dissuaded from reasons of good policy, even if he fails to appreciate the inherent harmfulness of his statement. On a previous occasion, when he gave offense to the Negro race by discrediting the valor of the colored soldiers who saved his life, he was solicitous enough to remove the impression pending his election as governor of New York. The political phase of this question may prove serious and far reaching. Secretary Taft is his reputed choice for the Republican nomination in 1908. Did he tacitly consent to this action, or was he purposely shielded from responsibility with political prevision? Some colored voters are apt to think on these things. The President has now the opportunity, in some measure, to offset the effect of the hurt which the race feels over the treatment of these soldiers by saying in his message a word that shall be clear and strong, patriotic and Rooseveltian.

As the acknowledged spokesman for the race, you will be held responsible for the President's utterances in these matters. When Mr. Roosevelt requested you to act as his adviser and when you accepted that delicate responsibility, the world may be expected to believe that he is guided by the advice of his own seeking. This, I know, often works injustice to you, but is exactly the kind of injustice that all leaders must bear. In the minds of many you are held responsible for the dismissal of the colored soldiers, although few fair minded men could believe that you counseled it. You will allow Mr. Roosevelt to do you a great wrong if he sends forth this reproach against the Negro race, seemingly with the stamp of your approval.

Pardon me for writing so freely. I deeply appreciate the gravity of the situation. Yours truly,

Kelly Miller

TLS Con. 327 BTW Papers DLC.

An Item in the *Tuskegee Student*

Tuskegee Institute, Alabama, November 17, 1906

THE JESUP AGRICULTURAL WAGON

A SHORT DESCRIPTION OF THE WAGON WHICH HAS SO HELPED THE FARMERS OF MACON AND OTHER COUNTIES

The Jesup Agricultural Wagon for better farming started from the grounds of the Tuskegee Normal and Industrial Institute, on its mission of usefulness at the close of the last school term, May 24, 1906 under the guidance of Mr. George R. Bridgeforth[1] of the

Agricultural Department. The benefits of its work have been shown in many ways.

The Tuskegee Institute has always had for its object the reaching of the farming masses. The results of the Annual Negro Conferences, the Monthly Farmers' Institute, and other meetings held among the farmers have been so encouraging that the plan of reaching every man and every woman in the county in a practical and useful manner became imperative. An agricultural wagon was suggested to meet this demand. A good friend, Mr. Morris K. Jesup, of New York, gave the money to have a wagon made to suit the conditions, and to buy mules and harness. The wagon and harness were made at the school by students. Two large mules were purchased to pull the wagon.

The wagon carried on it daily for practical demonstrations among the farmers, a revolving churn, butter mold, diverse cultivator, planters, cotton chopper, plows, different kinds of fertilizers, seeds, feed stuffs, milk tester, cream separator with a number of charts and demonstrative material.

This wagon goes on the farms of the smallest and largest farmers of Macon County and adjoining counties. The needs of the individual farmers were studied and demonstrations made showing how each can improve the old clumsy methods used at present. Where a man is running one furrow he is shown how he can run seven by using a different plow, and with the same animal. Instead of a man taking his wife and two or more children to spread his manures and fertilizers, he is shown how he can take a fertilizer distributor and do the same work and do it in less time, thus allowing his wife and children to do something else. Women were shown the advantages of a revolving churn over the old dasher churn; the use of butter moulds to increase the value of their product by handling it more neatly, and putting it on the market in better condition. The garden plows were put into the hands of the women and they were shown how to raise good gardens without so much drudgery and loss of time. There are many people who would rather buy vegetables because it is so inconvenient to raise them. The wagon has helped the farmers to see the advantage of raising their own vegetables.

Each farmer's soils were studied in his fields; fertilizers and manures were recommended to suit his soils. Many farmers spend money for fertilizers because it is something they can buy without thinking of the manures they can make at home. Plant diseases, insects and remedies for the same are taken up at the farmer's home, with him and his family. Experience has proven that when a man alone is reached and his wife and children are not reached, it is most difficult for that man to make advancement; if the woman is reached and the man not, the same is true.

The feeding of farm animals, their care, the money to be made from poultry and from live stock, are often discussed. For a man to live in a country home, breathing fresh air, where all kinds of fruits and vegetables can be grown during many months of the year, and for him to board himself and family and stock from the stock yards of Chicago, and from the granaries of Minneapolis, will mean poverty and discomfort for him and his family, regardless of how much cotton he raises.

An exchange of products can be made at great profit. The Jesup Wagon lays great emphasis upon the raising and saving of all food supplies for home consumption. Cotton is emphasized as a surplus cash crop.

It is often found that while the people raise plenty, they waste much. As a rule they feed their stock improperly and too profusely, and by selling corn in the fall at forty cents per bushel, when the same corn will cost them one dollar the next spring. This common practice, an effort is being made to correct.

The wagon not only goes to the individual's farm, but often the operator inspects and advises with farmers concerning their best interests. After field demonstrations are given on the farms, a mass meeting is worked up in each settlement. All the farmers then come together and demonstrations are made. Some of the farmers that are succeeding are invited to speak.

They are asked to bring some of their finest products to the meeting. Crop reports are made, questions are asked and answered, and general enthusiasm is engendered. These meetings are held in open air at the end of some cotton patch, corn field, cross road, country store, or any place that is most central for all concerned. The children, women and men come. Old and young are eager to learn. White men owning large plantations often invite the operator to come on their farms and spend a day in giving instruction to their tenants.

This wagon in going through all parts of Macon and adjoining counties, reaches those who, in many cases, could not even visit the school.

Tuskegee Student, 18 (Nov. 17, 1906), 1. Probably written by Emmett Jay Scott.

[1] George Ruffin Bridgeforth (b. 1873) taught agriculture at Tuskegee beginning in 1902 and was assistant director of the agricultural experiment station until 1907, when he became director of the department of agricutural industries.

From Ray Stannard Baker

Atlanta Ga. Nov. 18 [1906]

My dear Mr. Washington: I have your letter. I am planning to see Senator Tillman on the 24th or the 27th at Chicago and to be in Michigan with my family on Thanksgiving day. I had not expected to reach New York until a week later: though I might plan to get there earlier. We are anxious to have our first article from down here in our February number, that article to be the interviews with you & with Senator Tillman, covering the ground pretty fully. In order to reach the February number I am to have this copy in about Dec. 5. Now, if I could have your comments on the Tillman propositions early this week, I could get the whole matter into shape to send to you or to show you when you are in New York. I shall, of course, wish to have you review the manuscript & proofs thoroughly, so that there will be no possibility of misquotation or misrepresentation.

I had hoped to get over to Mound Bayou this week, but I must now postpone it until next month. I hope to look into conditions here at Atlanta pretty fully & I find a good deal more to do, *to get at the facts,* than I had expected. It is astonishing, the diversity of evidence upon conditions that seem perfectly clear.

Have you seen the accounts of the trial & acquittal of the negro Glenn here in Atlanta?[1] Was there ever a better argument against lynching! Sincerely,

Ray Stannard Baker

ALS Con. 310 BTW Papers DLC.

[1] Joe Glenn, a prosperous black farmer, was arrested on a charge of rape and was

positively identified by the woman in the case. Atlanta attorney Charles T. Hopkins defended Glenn, who was acquitted. BTW saw this as a sign that law and order was replacing mob rule. See An Article in *Outlook*, Dec. 15, 1906, below.

From Raymond Albert Patterson

Washington, D.C. Nov. 18, 1906

CONFIDENTIAL

My dear Mr. Washington: I was very glad to get your letter regarding my rather hastily written article on the ever recurring negro problem. I may possibly say to you confidentially that I had chiefly in view a situation right here in the District of Columbia. The new Superintendent of Schools here is not the kind of man who ought to be in such a position. He is quite in sympathy with the colored representatives on the school board. Their point of view is exactly that to which I called attention. So true is this that they had under consideration the calling to Washington as Assistant Superintendent of Professor Du Bois. I have great regard for him and I think he is many generations ahead of his race, somewhat unfortunately for him and for the race. He is a wonderful man in his way, but I do not think his theories are good for the colored people. I know they are diametrically opposed to those you hold.

Of course it is quite true that only a few of the colored people are in the north while the many millions of them are in the south. Yet I think you will agree with me that the great bulk of the whites are in the north, and in the future some day it must be those whites who after all will solve this race problem for the country. The agitators, the politicians, the mere talkers among the colored people are those who make themselves known most commonly in the north. The colored man in the southern states today is not much of a free agent, as you have cause to know. He is surrounded by a distinctly unfriendly white population, for whatever they say of themselves, they fear the negro and they hate him in about equal proportions.

If anything is to be done in the future by the national administration for the uplifting of the negro, it will be done, in my judgment, by the sober pressure of public opinion in the wealthy and populous northern states. I believe as you do that the negro in the south as a race needs first of all an elementary education and then a knowledge of how to use his physical strength and his dawning mental strength to the best advantage. I believe you are going about it in the right way, and I am hoping that in the future the conscience of the nation will be aroused so that it will undertake to build not universities nor post graduate schools for the negro, but sensible manual training institutions, and enterprises such as that you have by your own great genius so skillfully organized and conducted.

It is unfortunately true that in the border states and in the northern states the influence of that section of the colored people which seeks to accomplish the uplifting of the race through the uncertain means of a classical education and by political methods is not generally exerted along the lines which you have laid down. This is unfortunate, as I say, but it is undeniably true. Whenever one talks to a colored lawyer, doctor, preacher, or other professional man, it is almost invariably found that they are wedded to the idea of universities and high schools for the colored people and are constantly mixing in politics in a way which seldom redounds to their credit. You do not have the same condition in your section because no negro is permitted to go into politics. The brutal supremacy of the white man is, I believe, the salvation of your own plan for the redemption of the negro. That is to say, if the negro in Alabama and Georgia were allowed to vote and to hold petty offices, and to participate in politics, you would not find such a large proportion who would be willing to undertake the drudgery of manual labor. The more ignorant the class the more likely they are to be misled, and to think that in partizan politics they can achieve social equality.

I thoroughly believe that if in the days to come the national government shall undertake a wise system of education for the negro in the south, based nearly upon the lines you have indicated in your own great work, the whole mass of the negro race in America will soon be uplifted a little bit, then more and more in geometrical progression. Once get the average raised from the immediate vicinity of downright ignorance and savagery and we will begin to see the solution of the problem. When the average begins to approach anywhere near that of the white man, the negro cannot possibly be kept out of his political rights any longer. Until that time comes, it is a terrible mistake for the agitator and the super-educated among the negroes to demand for the ignorant millions of their race the political or social rights to which they as individuals might fairly be entitled.

In what I have written hitherto I have been deeply impressed by your work. I am entirely in sympathy with it, and I shall always testify everywhere to the great benefit I believe you have been to the negro race and almost equally, of course, to the white race, to which you also belong. From time to time I have been disturbed by the apparent success of the people who are not in sympathy with your work. Just at present here in Washington they are, in my judgment, influencing the colored people of this city in the wrong direction. What I have written thus far has been designed, so far as haste would permit of any design, to discourage the growth of this dangerous sentiment and to promote respect among whites and blacks for the utilitarian ideas with which your name has been associated in such an honorable manner.

I am longing for a time when I may again devote myself to a new study of this great subject which has taken a wonderful hold upon me, but so many other duties have come in between that I do not know whether I shall ever be able to go over the ground again.

In any event it is hardly necessary for me to renew my expressions of appreciation for your work and for your suggestions from time to time, which I hope you will do me the honor to continue. Faithfully yours,

Raymond Patterson

TLS Con. 331 BTW Papers DLC.

To Kelly Miller

[Tuskegee, Ala.] November 19, 1906

Personal

My dear Professor Miller: I have your kind letter of November 16 and appreciate fully what you say in it. Of course, all of us could have discussed the President's Message in a little different light if we had had any idea of his intended action regarding the Negro troops. He did not mention the matter to me until I saw him that evening, and then told me that the matter had been decided. I tried to persuade him to take a different course but without success. When I reached New York and realized the seriousness of it I wrote him, and I enclose a copy of his reply.

I do not believe that the general effect of his message on rape and lynching is going to be as bad as you now fear it will. Of course there are going to be some persons who are going to read and ponder every word and every sentence in the Message, but they will be comparatively few. The great mass of people whom the Message is sought to reach and influence will simply, in my opinion, get the general effect of it, which is that he condemns crime of all character among all races. I think that is the sum total of what the President is trying to say, and I believe that will be the impression left upon the average man. Of course, you must bear in mind that he has for his object the saying of something that will help to make life and property for the Negro in the South safer, and in order to do this he has, in a measure, placed himself in touch with the Southern people. I am now simply presenting his side of the case. I believe that the Message, on the whole, is going to do good. At the same time I state now, as I stated in our little conference and to the President, there are certain features of it which I wish might have been changed, especially the first part of it. I wish also, that he had modified more than he did the part of the Message where he speaks about Negroes hunting down criminals, and also modified a little more the part where he refers to speedy trials. In all but those measures I got him to make modifications along the line of our advice.

In regard to getting him to make any change in his forthcoming Message, my greatest fear is that there will be no time for such change after his return from Panama. I very much fear that the Message now is in shape for distribution to the press.

I have written two letters lately to Secretary Taft, putting the whole situation before him. I have never seen a time when the whole race has been so stirred and hurt on a subject as it seems to be on this one.

As for anybody holding me responsible for any such action, I would state that in this case and in others, I simply fall back on the old doctrine, somewhat obsolete but nevertheless potent, that truth in the last analysis always asserts itself, and I confess that more and more I am finding myself having implicit faith in that doctrine.

The President or no one else has ever asked me to be his official adviser in regard to race matters. All matters outside of my immediate educational work, especially anything that bears upon politics is exceedingly distasteful to me. I have no inclination in that direction, but I have felt in the past, and feel now that no Negro should refuse to give whatever advice or information the President of the United States might seek of him. To fail to do so would be acting cowardly. This is the position that I have always taken. Of course, one acting in this capacity is always at a disadvantage in that he must keep his mouth closed every [so] often in the face of glaring falsehoods and in the face of wrong, but I repeat that my experience in life so far has taught me that if one is right and square, everything usually comes out all right. Yours sincerely,

Booker T. Washington

Of course you easily realize that the kind of persons who will accuse me of thus advising the President are for the most part, those who are afraid to come out and place the blame where it belongs, and therefore they act the hypocrite and coward. The same weakness of character would lead these men to twist matters in some other direction.

B. T. W.

TLpS Con. 327 BTW Papers DLC.

To William Dorsey Jelks

Tuskegee Institute, Alabama. November 19, 1906

Dear Sir: In your address to the colored people at the State Fair on October 27, you referred to the results of Negro education.[1]

In that connection I thought you might like to get in some definite form, information as to what students are doing in a single county who have attended the Tuskegee Institute for a longer or shorter time.

The enclosed list contains the names of practically all the students who have graduated from this institution, or who have attended this institution for any length of time, who are living in Montgomery County. I have selected Montgomery County for the reason that it is convenient for any one to investigate further if he wishes to.

My experience teaches me that an equally good showing can be made in almost any county of the state where there is any considerable number of our graduates and ex-students.

In your conversation with me, and in your addresses, I am bearing in mind that you often referred to the importance of colored students being taught to stick to the farm. I am thoroughly in sympathy with this idea, but we have not, as this investigation will show, been as successful in getting students to go on the farm as we should like. In the first place, Montgomery County contains one of our largest cities, and that naturally attracts a large proportion of students to that city. In the second place, the demand for mechanical and factory work is so tremendous and the inducements are so great, that many of our students are naturally attracted in those directions. A student finishing our course in bricklaying finds that he needs no capital except enough money to buy a trowel to begin work, while if he wants to begin farming he has to find some one to advance him money enough to live on while he is raising the crop. Aside from these difficulties, it has only been in recent years that we have been able to overcome the old prejudice existing among our people against giving any intelligent attention to the study of farming. We have a large and increasing number of students each year who are expecting to make farming their life work.

Our work is far from perfect, but we realize we can only make it more so by facing the facts and trying to remedy present weaknesses.

I think you will find that some who have attended this institution are not doing the work that we would like to have them do, but very few in any part of the state have gone to the bad, or are in the loafing or criminal class. Yours truly,

Booker T. Washington

P.S. — I find, too, it is more difficult to get definite information regarding people on the farm, as the expense of travel is great, and, of course, it is not like locating a person in the city where he has a definite number, etc.

B. T. W.

TLS William Dorsey Jelks Papers A-Ar. No enclosure found with letter.

[1] Jelks's speech, as reported in the Montgomery *Advertiser*, dealt only indirectly with black education. The speech had as its theme the importance of blacks and whites upholding the law. Jelks implied that when blacks could eliminate the large class of loafers and dishonest men of the race, racial problems would be largely solved. Jelks said: "We boast that we are cutting down our illiterates in this State. It would be better if we could boast that we are cutting down the number of those who violate the laws." (Montgomery *Advertiser*, Oct. 28, 1906, 19.) BTW heartily endorsed Jelks's remarks but said that the class of loafers was small. (See Extracts from a Speech at the Alabama State Fair, Oct. 27, 1906, above.)

To William Howard Taft

[Tuskegee, Ala.] November 20, 1906

Personal and Confidential

My dear Secretary Taft: Will you not tell me whether it is the intention of the War Department to enlist additional colored soldiers to take the place of the three companies which were dismissed?

I am also writing to say that I very much hope, by the time the President returns, some plan will have been thought out by which to do something that may change the feeling of the colored people now as a whole have regarding the dismissal of the three colored companies. I have never in all my experience with the race, experienced a time when the entire people have the feeling that they have now in regard to the administration. The race is not so much resentful or angry, perhaps, as it feels hurt and disappointed. I am not excusing or justifying this feeling, because I do not know the detailed facts upon which the action was based, but I am simply putting a condition before you. In considering it, it must be borne in mind that this order came at a time when the race was experiencing deep trial on account of the Atlanta riots and when there was much to discourage the race in the atmosphere. Yours truly,

[Booker T. Washington]

TL Copy Con. 5 BTW Papers DLC.

From D. C. Fisher

Lorain, Ohio, November 21 1906

Dear Sir: Yours of the 16th at hand. I should have answered before but for the fact that I have been absent from the city.

Your copy was absolutely unnecessary as I had already seen the original. I am surprised to think that you would try to ruin a young life. I can think of nothing so contemptible, so low, so mean, so unjust as that of any man asking for the resignation of and dismissing any of his employees without giving them a hearing. You say in your letter that all your information concerning my daughter was from hearsay. I myself have employed hundreds of men, with the most trust worthy foremen, but never did I discharge one without hearing his side of the affair.

You give as one of your reasons for asking my daughter to resign the fact that she refused to teach in Sunday-school. That is a thing unheard of in any institution. You had two years from the time you first began your correspondence with my daughter in which to tell her just what you expected of her. This you failed to do.

If these things were going on all along why did you not inform me at the time "owing to the youth and inexperience of my daughter" rather than to wait until you saw fit to ask her for her resignation?

I am very sorry indeed that my daughter ever went to Tuskegee. I think your action in this case very unwise as it will reflect upon both you and your school. Very truly yours,

D. C. Fisher

TLS Con. 321 BTW Papers DLC.

An Address in Memory of Carl Schurz

[Carnegie Hall, New York City, Nov. 21, 1906]

The details of the life and deeds of the late Honorable Carl Schurz are so well known as to call for no recital here. The most and least that can be done at this time is to emphasize the lessons to be gleaned from his life and call attention to the service rendered by him to the Indian and Negro races. My first acquaintance with Carl Schurz was gained when I was a student at the Hampton Institute in Virginia. He came to Hampton when Secretary of the Interior under President Hayes, to inspect the work of General Armstrong in the education of the Indians and to note the progress of the Negro students. During that visit his striking personality, which combined deep moral earnestness with strength of intellect, left in my mind an impression which has always remained with me, and which was deepened as I came to know Mr. Schurz better in later years. The impression made upon a poor student of another race — not long out of slavery — by the words and presence of this great soul, is something which I cannot easily describe. As he spoke to the Negro and Indian students on the day of his visit to Hampton, there was a note of deep sincerity and sympathy, which, with his frankness and insight into the real condition and needs of the two races, made us at once feel that a great and extraordinary man was speaking to us. He had a heart overflowing with sympathy for the two most unfavored races in America, because he himself had known what it meant to be oppressed and to struggle towards freedom against great odds. It is easier, however, from many points of view, to sympathize with a people or a race that has had an unfortunate start in life than it is to be frank and at the same time just — to say the word and do the thing which will permanently help, regardless for the moment of whether words or acts please or displease. As Mr. Schurz stood before the Hampton students, it was plain that he was a man who had been able to lift himself out of the poisoned atmosphere of racial as well as sectional prejudice. It was easy to see that here was a man who wanted to see absolute justice done to the Indian, the Negro, and to the Southern white man.

At the time when Mr. Schurz entered President Hayes's cabinet, it was a popular doctrine that "the only good Indian was the dead Indian." The belief had gained pretty general acceptance that the Indian was incapable of receiving a higher civilization. More than that, the Indian was being plundered of his lands, his rations, and was being used as the tool in a large degree to further the ends of unscrupulous schemers. It was easier to shoot an Indian than to civilize him. It has been easier to fight for freedom than work for the freedman. Easier to kick or down him than to lift him up. It was a period also when the Negro race was being plundered and deceived in reference to its vote. Not only this, when Mr. Schurz entered the Hayes cabinet, the Negro was being in a large degree used as the tool of demagogues, and at the same time many influences were at work to alienate the black and white races at the South, regardless of the permanent effect on either. Against all this Mr. Schurz threw the weight of his great name and forceful personality. Few men in private or public life did more than he to clear the atmosphere and put all sections of our country sanely and unselfishly at work for the highest welfare of the black and red races.

Mr. Schurz was among the first to see that if the Indian was to be permanently helped, he must be taught to become an independent and willing producer, rather than an irresponsible recipient of the bounty of the general government. Hence, he was among the first to encourage agricultural and other forms of industrial education for the Indians. He was among the first, both in his official capacity and as a private citizen, to aid General Armstrong at Hampton in his first attempt to give industrial training to the Indian in [a] systematic way and on a large scale. I have said that he saw clearly into the needs and conditions of my race and its relations to the white race. Time permits only three illustrations. One is found in his report to President Johnson in 1865. A second is an article printed in McClure's Magazine in 1903, under the title, "Can the South Solve the Race Problem?" A third instance of the sanity of his views was given some of us when a conference of the leaders of the Negro race was, a few months before his death, held in this building, to which our good friend, Mr. Andrew Carnegie, kindly brought him. None will forget how, for nearly an hour, he lifted us, as it were, into a new world, while there came from his lips such words of advice, caution, and encouragement as only he could speak.

But he has passed from earth. My race, the Indian race, American life as a whole are the poorer. There never was a time when such men were more needed than at present. My own belief is that one such character encourages and makes possible in time many other characters of like strength and helpfulness. I do not despair. One great life makes possible many great lives. We need at present, when the question of races is occupying the attention of the world as has seldom been done, as never before, it seems to me, men of clear, calm view, and with the courage of their convictions. I am not discouraged as to present conditions, nor as to the future. It is good to be permitted to live in an age when great, serious, and perplexing problems are to be solved. It is good to live in an age when unfortunate and backward races are to be helped, when great and fundamental questions are to be met and solved. For my part, I would find no interest in living in an age where there were no weak members of the human family to be helped, no wrongs to be righted. Men grow strong in proportion as they reach down to help others up. The farther down they reach in the assisting and encouraging of backward and unpopular races, the greater strength do they gather. All this is borne out in the character of the hero of this evening. Without oppression, without struggle, without the effort to grapple with great questions, such a great character could not have been produced. It required the white heat of trouble to forge such a man.

Because Carl Schurz lived, the Germans in America are stronger and greater. Because he lived, my race is the richer, more confident and encouraged. The Indian race and my race are proud that they had the privilege of claiming as their friend so great a man as Carl Schurz. The great are never ashamed to assist the unfortunate or the unfavored. The usefulness of a great man can no more be limited by race or color than by national boundaries. Because of the friendship of such a soul, every Negro can be the more proud of his race. For myself, I was never more proud of being a Negro than I am today. If I had the privilege of re-entering the world, and the Great Spirit should ask me to choose the color and the race with which to clothe my spirit and my purposes, I would answer, "Make me an American Negro."

Mr. Schurz never sought the popular side of any question, nor did he seek the popular race. One word embodied his whole philosophy of life — that word was Duty.

Because he lived, we shall live better, more nobly. His spirit is still moving among us, and will continue to strengthen, to guide, and to encourage us now and evermore.

Addresses in Memory of Carl Schurz (New York: Committee of the Carl Schurz Memorial, 1906), 38–41.

From William Howard Taft

Washington November 22, 1906

My dear Mr. Washington: It is the intention of the War Department to enlist additional colored soldiers at once to take the place of the three companies dismissed. The order of dismissal does not include all of the battalion, for there were some who were absent. Very sincerely yours,

Wm H Taft

TLS Con. 5 BTW Papers DLC.

From William Dorsey Jelks

Montgomery, [Ala.] November 22, 1906

My Dear Sir: I have your letter, together with the list which you enclosed me. It came to my desk by the same mail that brought me a letter from a gentleman out in the West. He wrote me that he had read my speech delivered on Negro Day at the Fair. He made some complimentary allusions to myself and the speech. He writes that he had your school on his list of charities, but he would like to know from me if I considered your work worthy of assistance. I am writing him by this mail and I am saying to him that I have no knowledge "of any teaching of the Tuskegee Institute that does not look towards the uplifting of his (Washington's) people. I have never read a sentence from one of his speeches or from his pen that would lead me to doubt his entire sincerity." I am also telling him that "the Institute has turned out many useful mechanics and many useful women," and I am further very candid with him in saying that the number of vagrants and crimes attributed to your race are larger in numbers than ever before and that an education in your school educates the boy away from the farm. I expressed regret at this. However, I may say to you that an education in the higher white schools is having the same effect. I quoted in my letter to this party part of your letter to me and enclosed him the list you made out to me, thinking it fair to him and to you, with the request that the list be returned to me. Some time soon I may take occasion to look into the lives and habits of your late students of this County.

I have heard nothing but praise for your speech on Negro Day. Truly yours,

Wm. D. Jelks

TLpS William Dorsey Jelks Papers A-Ar.

To Theodore Roosevelt

[New York City] November 26, 1906

My dear Mr. President: This letter will be handed you by Mr. Charles W. Anderson and Mr. Scott. It is very important that you grant them an interview as they wish to place some facts before you for consideration before you see any of the colored delegations that are likely to seek an interview regarding the colored troops.

Mr. Anderson has stood up in a manly way in regard to this matter which has created so much feeling and discussion throughout the country. Very truly yours,

[Booker T. Washington]

TLc BTW Papers ATT.

To Theodore Roosevelt

[New York City] November 26, 1906

Personal.

My dear Mr. President: I have asked our mutual friend, Mr. Charles W. Anderson, to lay before you the following points, to be considered, if possible, before you receive any of the colored delegations that are likely to seek an interview regarding the colored troops.

First: Of the present deep feeling that your order was given out at a time when the race was much disheartened and sore on the account of the Atlanta Riot.

Second: There is a deep feeling that some wholly innocent men are being punished.

Third: The fact that the order appeared on the night, after the election, created the impression that it was held up to secure the Negro vote.

Fourth: In case you make any modification of your order, I hope you will find some way to give credit to the friends of the administration, who have sought to help in the matter, and not let the enemies of the administration, who are seeking every means possible to destroy the influence of the administration, get full credit of it.

[Booker T. Washington]

TLcf BTW Papers ATT. Not found in Theodore Roosevelt Papers, DLC.

From Emmett Jay Scott

Washington D C Nov 27 1906

Interview most satisfactory dictated in our presence fine statement that if could have been dissuaded by any living being your and Andersons protest would have prevented action goes the limit in your and Andersons favor but will not change verdict.

E J S

HWIr Con. 566 BTW Papers DLC.

From Anonymous

Chicago Ills Novr 28th 1906

Prof. Booker T. Washington Time is getting on. The negro troops have been discharged without honor, and a lot of fool negroes have commenced to annoy and get in the way of their northern friends. Can't you see that the white people north and south are drawing closer every day on this race question. Now is the time for you to spring petitions from yourself & all the negro preachers who will join you in asking the President & Congress to provide several millions of acres of fine plateau land in the Paraguay country south of Brazil and 50 million dollars to carry negro emigrants there to found the *great Negro Republic of the future.* Catch up and send over there first of all the floating negroes without wives or homes who are mainly the perpetrators of outrages. Ship all the vagrant negroes out of the country at once and let us begin to have peace. If you can have the courage to state that 15th & 14th amendments—*and* all war time legislation is a dead letter so far as the negro is concerned & that it would be better that all of it be repealed and ask that it be repealed in order that the country may *get rid of the negro question* even if the very few negroes who now vote give up the franchise. The white men are not allowing the negroes to vote, they say they don't intend to let the negroes vote, and northern Republican papers are backing them up and public sentiment is drifting more strongly that way. Why not take the bull by the horns and sell out to best advantage securing a great big appropriation from U.S. Govt.

Very probably you could be the first President and give all the finely educated & wealthy negroes a show in a country of their own where they could prove to the world that the negro can produce a civilization superior to any in the world which I believe is quite possible if you worked on the lines you originally started on.

This country can well afford to pay $500,000,000 to accomplish the peaceful separation of the white and black races. This country can afford to secure for the *negro nation* by treaty as fine a national location as is in the world. Now is the time to ask for it and get it—get busy on this line and you will not regret it. Very Truly Yours

A Friend

ALSr Con. 34 BTW Papers DLC. Enclosed in BTW to S. L. Williams, Dec. 3, 1906, below.

From John Hope

Atlanta, Ga. Nov. 29, 1906

My Dear Mr. Washington: I received your letter of Nov. 21st some days ago, but the pamphlets did not come until some time afterwards. I thank you very much for the gift and shall distribute them among the students, the teachers have already been supplied with copies.

Mr. Carnegie's benevolence is unquestioned and I believe he has a very deep interest in our people especially, but I must say that I think he is very much misinformed about the educational situation in the south. I deem it a great pity that a man of his influence and power should be so far astray about the condition of a people in whom he is so thoroughly interested and for whom he is doing so much.

Thanking you again for your favor, I remain, Yours truly,

John Hope

P.S. You will see from the date that this letter has been lying on my desk for some time. In the meantime I have again read the address for fear of making a hasty judgment. I do still feel that Mr. Carnegie does not know, as he ought, the Negro Public School system of the South and the attitude of the ruling south to Negro Public Education. A great heart like Mr. Carnegie ought to know these things intimately. I know of no other Colored man to whom he would listen as to you. Permit me Mr. Washington, to say that this task falls on you.

TLS Con. 323 BTW Papers DLC. Postscript in Hope's hand.

From William Estabrook Chancellor

Montgomery, Ala. Nov. 29, 1906

Dear Dr. Washington, I hope and intend to take the train Saturday that leaves here at 9.15 a.m. and arrives at Chehaw at 10.33; I cannot learn here today just what connection is made with the Tuskegee Branch R. R.

I do not know whether you know anything as to my personal views anent the question of colored people. But I cite three personal items—(1) I took your R. C. Bruce on his merits and not under any pressure real or attempted. (2) I married a niece of Henry Ward Beecher and of Harriet Beecher Stowe. (3) Arthur Curtis[s] James,[1] whom I know that you know well, is an Amherst, '89 man, Alpha Delta Phi & so am I.

I intend to work out in the largest system of Negro schools in the world the best education that I can discover and organize in the face of Congressional dictation and District of Columbia agitation. I was one of the men who took part in the earliest work of organizing and operating Pratt Institute in Brooklyn.

But I am committed irrevocably to the proposition that education is a matter of universal principles, to be applied judiciously to individual cases, of course, but true always irrespective of sex, race, color and creeds.

In this tour, I am engaged in an investigation of two things: 1st. Why are the schools generally of the District of Columbia so inferior to those of the North? and 2nd. Why is there "a race question" in the District?

The explanation is to be found south of Mason and Dixon's line, not north of it.

I found several friends at Fisk. I hope that you at Tuskegee will adopt me. I hope also that you will allow me to stay several days. Believe me Faithfully yours,

Wm. E. Chancellor

ALS Con. 317 BTW Papers DLC.

[1] Arthur Curtiss James (b. 1867), a New York merchant and corporate executive, was a member and later chairman of the board of trustees of Hampton Institute.

To Edgar Gardner Murphy

[Tuskegee, Ala.] December 2, 1906

My dear Mr. Murphy: I thank you very much for your letter and the suggestions therein.

I wish I had time to tell you about a movement that has been slowly gathering force in Atlanta ever since the riot. In my opinion, it is the sanest, wisest and most helpful undertaking that has been put on foot by Southern white people to change present conditions. The effort is led by a young white lawyer, a native Georgian and a graduate of Williams College, seconded by ex-Governor Northen. The foundation stone of their organization, which already contains the names of several hundred of the best white people in Georgia and is later to have the names of 500 of the same element of the colored people, is justice to the Negro. I hope you will follow this movement. The most discouraging feature of it, however, is in the fact that notwithstanding the work is going on almost daily in Atlanta, the press outside of Atlanta, especially in the North, gives no attention to it. I have sent Mr. Villard clippings and I hope he will publish them. I shall hope to go to Atlanta next Sunday to speak in connection with it. Yours very truly,

Booker T. Washington

TLpS Con. 5 BTW Papers DLC.

To Samuel Laing Williams

[Tuskegee, Ala.] December 3, 1906

Personal

My dear Mr. Williams: The enclosed anonymous letter may mean very little, but I pass it on to you. It is one of many that I get. It is one of the straws that shows that the feeling between the Northern white people and the Southern white people is getting more akin all the time. You already know my position on the President's action. I very much fear that these frequent meetings held by these agitators is hurting us tremendously in the North, in fact I am sure they are. There are many sections of the North where the Negro as an individual or as a race is not thought of separate from the other portion of American citizenship except when the attention of the white people is called to it through these meetings. If our people would have a meeting once in a while for the purpose of starting a bank, insurance company or building a railroad or opening a coal mine, it would be far different, but practically every time the white man hears from the Negro in an organized capacity it is in connection with a meeting of condemnation or protest. I do not say that such meetings do not have their place, but the difficulty is that we hold them so often that they grow monotonous, tiresome and hurtful to a large class of people in the North. The sentiment of the white people in Boston has almost been completely changed within a few months by reason of this senseless agitation. Yours truly,

Booker T. Washington

TLpS Con. 34 BTW Papers DLC. Enclosed was the anonymous letter dated Nov. 28, 1906, above.

To Ralph Waldo Tyler

[Tuskegee, Ala.] December 5, 1906

Personal.

My dear Mr. Tyler: I agree with every word that you state in your letter of recent date. I did my best to persuade the President from taking the action which he did, but he seemed to feel that under all the circumstances he could not refrain from acting as he has done. I feel sure, however, that gradually he will reinstate all the men who had no knowledge of the outbreak. In the meantime it is a fact, as you state, that the matter has stirred up the Negro to a very high pitch of agitation.

I presume you have seen the publication sent out by the War Department. This, I think, gives the main facts. I think the President will make a statement covering the whole matter a little later on, at least that was his intention a few days ago. After he has made his statement, you will be in a position to pass judgment.

I agree with you thoroughly that there is great danger now that the race will get a backset among its friends in the North by these intemperate utterances at frequent indignation meetings. Of course, it was natural that some protest should be made, but I fear there is danger of too much of it. One thing the American people will not stand for any length of time, and that is abuse by any group of people of the President of the United States, and if our people make the mistake of going too far, there will be a reaction in the North among the people and newspapers who have stood by us. I am doing all I can to check the folly. I am writing Mr. Fortune on the subject to-day. Yours very truly,

Booker T. Washington

TLpS Con. 336 BTW Papers DLC.

A Christmas Greeting

Tuskegee Institute, Alabama, Dec 7, 1906

It is good to be permitted to live in an age when great, serious and perplexing problems are to be met and solved. For my part I would not care to live in an age when there was no weak part of the human family to be helped up and no wrongs to be righted.

Through struggle only are great men and useful races produced. Yours Sincerely,

Booker T. Washington

ALS Facsimile Seth Low Papers NNC.

A Facsimile of a Christmas Greeting

It is good to be permitted to live in an age when great, serious and perplexing problems are to be met and solved, for my part I would not care to live in an age when there was no weak part of the human family to be helped up and no wrongs to be righted, through struggle only are great men and useful races produced.

Yours Sincerely

Booker T. Washington

Tuskegee Institute
Dec 7, 1906 Alabama.

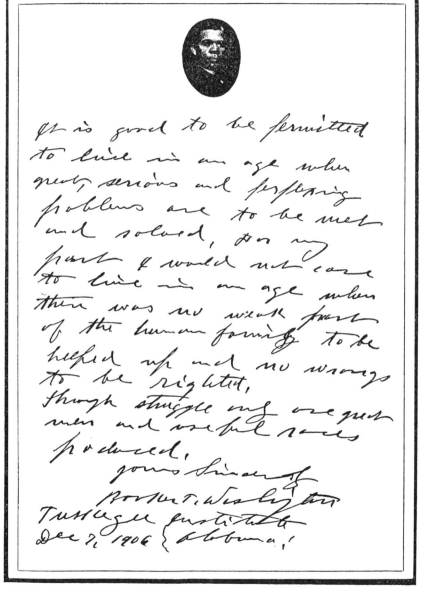

ALS Facsimile Robert C. Ogden Papers DLC.

To Herbert Edwin Lombard[1]

Tuskegee Institute, Alabama. December 8, 1906

My dear Sir: Several times when I have been in South Byfield to see my son, I have wanted to see you but have been prevented. I do not know exactly what contact you have with my boy, Booker T. Washington, Jr., but I am very anxious, if it is not asking too much, that you try to influence him in every way you can so as to help him deepen and broaden his religious belief and activity. I think he is at the age when he ought to be impressed very strongly in that direction. He is a very curious boy from several points of view, and you will have to be very careful how you approach him. For example, it would not help matters for him to get the idea that I suggested your approaching him. He is rather timid also. On the other hand, he likes to do things, especially when he is leading or made to feel that he is in the lead. I shall be very glad of any service you can render in this matter.

As I am away from home a great deal, any correspondence on this subject regarding him had better be addressed to Mrs. Washington.

I am planning to be in South Byfield for a few hours sometime during this month and shall hope to see you. Yours very truly,

Booker T. Washington

TLS MWA.

1 Herbert Edwin Lombard was pastor of the Byfield (Mass.) Parish Congregational Church in 1902. He was a member of the Dummer Academy board of trustees and taught English there from 1904 to 1906.

From Timothy Thomas Fortune

New York, December 8, 1906

Dear Mr. Washington: I forgot to state in my telegram to you last night, or to write you before about it, because I have been very busy all the last days of the week, because I [was] two people short in the office force, that I got rid of Mr. Stokes on Thursday last. He took the matter coolly, saying that he should have no trouble in making good. I gathered from what he said and what I have heard the past two days that it is highly probable that he and Stewart will start a newspaper in New York soon. It will not last, as neither of them has any business ability whatever, and I shall be surprised if you give Stokes a penny of assistance if he should start the paper. Leave him alone and I think he will soon peter out with the venture. He said he did not want to mix with the Constitutional League people, as he did not wish to offend you, and I left him in ignorance of the fact that he has already lost your confidence.

Poor Simmons[1] has not enough circulation to get the pound rates, and so has to put a one cent stamp on all of the papers he sends out, I am told.

I am sorry that the President did not let you blue pencil his message, as far as it relates to us, and all the more so as he has employed throughout the message your phraseology and often your idioms. His advice that Afro-Americans who know nothing of their criminals shall help to hunt them down and his adoption of the lynch law method of slaying the innocent with the guilty are vile propositions calculated to do us great injury. And his advice as to the type of education good for us will do the cause of industrial education no good whatever, in the estimation of Afro-Americans and especially those antagonistic to you, and as a general proposition to which you have subscribed the race needs the very sort of education that other Americans need.

The President has forfeited the confidence and good esteem of the Afro-American people and largely of the American people by the adoption of Southern ideas and methods in dealing with us, and Mr. Scott and I both think that you have gone as far with him as you can afford to. He has two years more as President, and you have the remainder of your life as the controlling genius of the Tuskegee Institute and leader of the Afro-American people, and your future will depend largely on how far you allow it to be understood that you are sponsor for what he says and does as far as the Afro-American people are concerned. I wish you would talk over this matter with Mr. Scott, as we have had a thorough talk about it, and I am sure you will find it hard to find two other men who will give you better advice in this matter and who will do it more sincerely.

We ran very short of money this week, as it was necessary to pay some of the old bills, and because the people who owe us always hold back payments in the holidays, so I am glad you will be here Thursday.

I am staying at Red Bank to-day and shall do my regular writing for next week between now and Monday. Yours sincerely,

T. Thos. Fortune

TLS Con. 32 BTW Papers DLC.

[1] Roscoe Conkling Simmons, a nephew of Margaret M. Washington, was editor of the *National Review*, a weekly black newspaper in New York.

Extracts from an Address in Atlanta, Georgia[1]

[Atlanta, Ga., Dec. 9, 1906]

I have been watching with the keenest interest everything that has taken place in Atlanta in the way of reconstruction or regeneration since the days of the riot, and I do not hesitate to say to the members of my race that the effort which is now being fathered and led by a group of the best white people in the city of Atlanta, in co-operation with a similar group of members of my own race, in my opinion, constitutes one of the most helpful, sane and promising efforts that have been made in any portion of the South to improve the relations of the races since the war.

I make this statement fully conscious of the scope of my words. In too large a degree, heretofore, the interests of the black man have been left wholly to negro leaders or wholly to teachers who have come from the North or West. The ministers and the conservative element among the white people have consciously or unconsciously drifted away from helping the negro and taking the interest in him that was true in former days. I do not believe that they have been conscious, for the most part, of doing this, but in some way the South grew into the idea of feeling that by some hit or miss manner the question of the negro would be taken care of by somebody at some time.

Another element in the situation which has prevented the

Southern white people from taking hold in a whole-souled way, as they are now doing in Atlanta, has been the scare of social equality; something existing somewhere that nobody exactly understands, but it was something that was always used on every occasion when Southern white men or women attempted to put forth genuine effort to help the black man.

Another element that has kept the two races from co-operating has been the constant threat of negro domination. I am in constant touch with all classes of my people, North and South, and I do not hesitate to say that the negro has no ambition to mingle socially with the white race, neither has he any ambition to dominate the white man in political matters. With these two points definitely understood, I see no reason why we cannot co-operate on the platform laid down by the league. What the negro is interested in far beyond any matter of social intermingling, far beyond the matter of racial or political domination, is that every individual black man, with his family, shall be absolutely sure that he will receive justice. Assure the negro that the same justice administered to the white man will be administered to him and we have the key to the solution of our whole racial problem. The scare of social equality, the scare of possible racial domination have kept many of the white people in the South from helping the negro. And I confess to you that the fear on the part of the negro that he will not receive justice and fair play at the hands of the white man has kept the negro leaders in many cases from attempting to co-operate with the white people in efforts to bring about a better civilization. Even in the case of this movement so magnificently led by prominent citizens, there are negro leaders in this city who are doubting, who are timid, who are fearful that after all the members of the league do not mean exactly what they say in relation to the black man receiving justice and fair play. To all such doubters, I want to say, I have not come here to speak today without careful examination into the situation. I have watched every move; I have read every word that has been uttered on the part of the leaders of this movement, and I do not hesitate to say that I have as much faith in their earnestness, in their sincerity, in their ability to help lift up the negro in a way that no other group of white men in any part of the country can do at the present time. I believe in their sincerity as much as I believe in the sincerity of any of our friends who live in

Boston, New York or Chicago and we shall prove recreant to our race if we do not heartily co-operate in every effort they are putting forward to bring better conditions in Atlanta and throughout the South.

I believe, further, that what is being done by the league and other organizations that have grown out of the Atlanta riot will not only serve a high purpose in the city of Atlanta and the state of Georgia, but I believe the movement will spread throughout the South, and I hope the leaders here will see to it that the influence of it is not confined to Atlanta or the state of Georgia.

Because of the uncertainty, because of the timidity, because of the distrust existing in the minds of the black people and white people, the South has not only suffered from a moral point of view, but our commercial interests have been held back because of distrust of one race on the part of the other. It is impossible to have good and efficient labor unless that labor is assured that in every avenue of life justice will be meted out to them and that after persons have worked hard and accumulated property they will not be driven away from their homes and property at great loss at the will of a mob.

I want to fittingly express the appreciation to race leaders in this city who have co-operated with the white men in Atlanta in perfecting and launching this movement. From now on let the league have the united and sympathetic help of every member of our race. Let those who doubt the efficacy of such a movement remember that certainly if we fail in this, the race will be in no worse condition than it has been. There are nine chances out of ten that it will succeed. If failure is the result, nothing will have been lost.

The fact is that we of both races in too large a degree have tried to go around our duty, have tried to go under it, or over it, but the time has come when frankly and squarely and honestly we have got to face our duty in this matter, face the responsibility that is before us and face the actual condition of the race right here in the South and then do what this condition demands.

The average white man in the South is just as much interested in the elevation of the black man as the white race in any other part of the country, but he has been timid and backward and uncertain in his method of exhibiting that interest and that friendship. This league furnishes a channel through which much interest can be shown in the future.

We of both races must thoroughly understand that there is an element of agitators among both races that is continually stirring up strife with no end in view to bettering of present conditions. They stir up strife simply for the purpose of attracting attention to themselves or for the purpose of securing some recognition or position. It is the duty of both races, it seems to me, to frown down on these characters who serve neither race to any good purpose.

In connection with this effort, however, it must be borne in mind that the negro is human and too much cannot be expected of him, but in proportion as you will place responsibility upon him he will respond to such responsibility. I wish that in every community and every locality where there is any considerable number of our people that in some manner the negro himself might feel a responsibility in the apprehending of the criminal classes. I wish that members of the race might be clothed, wherever possible, with some official responsibility in the bringing of the criminal classes to justice. The mere fact that such responsibility was placed upon the negro himself would give them an amount of interest in the welfare of the community which they do not now always feel, but that is a matter of detail which each community must work out for itself.

Atlanta *Georgian*, Dec. 18, 1906, 4.

[1] Delivered on Sunday, Dec. 9, 1906, a day set aside for sermons on law and order, at Friendship Baptist Church.

To James Kirkman Jackson[1]

Tuskegee Institute, Alabama. December 12, 1906

Dear Sir: If it is not asking too much and will not take too much of his valuable time, I am very anxious to have this man, Darius H. Henry,[2] see the Governor for a few minutes. The Governor is deeply interested in farming and he has often expressed the wish to me that educated colored men go back to the farm. This young man graduated at Tuskegee about sixteen years ago. He now owns 1100 acres of land right in the community where he lived before coming to Tuskegee. During the farming season he plows and works the land with his own hands. He has a ginnery on his farm, and a good house. He earns his living entirely by farming. There are many other cases like this one. Yours truly,

Booker T. Washington

TLS William Dorsey Jelks Papers A-Ar. A press copy is in Con. 324, BTW Papers, DLC.

[1] James Kirkman Jackson (b. 1862), a former Alabama Railroad Commission clerk, was private secretary to Alabama governor William Dorsey Jelks from 1901 to 1907.

[2] Darius H. Henry (b. 1866) graduated from Tuskegee Institute in 1890 and became a schoolteacher in Alabama and then Texas for seven years. While in Texas he also edited a newspaper, *The Watchman*. Returning to Alabama, Henry bought a large farm which had its own gin, gristmill, and sawmill. He was also active in the state Baptist association and was nominated, but not appointed, to fill the post of register of the U.S. Treasury when W. T. Vernon resigned.

From William Dorsey Jelks

Montgomery, [Ala.] December 12th, 1906

Dear Sir: I last night had the pleasure of reading your story in the "World's Work," which you were kind enough to send me, in reference to the teaching which is now being done by means of your "Jesup" wagon.[1] For sometime I have maintained that possibly a model farm in each thickly settled community was worth as much or more than a model school. I remember to have stated to some members of the Ogden party some years ago, that a large expenditure of capital could be profitably made in establishing small model farms; thus teaching a neighborhood ten or fifteen miles in diameter. Your "Jesup" wagon is on the same line. I congratulate you upon the work it is doing.

It grieves me daily to know that young men and young women attending our colleges and our larger schools of both colors, seem almost unanimously to have no inclination to return to the farm. I am sure it would be better if we had no larger schools, so far as the State is concerned, but depend upon high schools — very high —

in each county. A boy who gets his education upon his native heath will probably remain at home. Those who get their education away from home, will probably stay away; thus taking from the land its most intellectual and hopeful cultivators. This is only one view of it, however.

I do not remember that I acknowledged receipt of your list of students covering Barbour county. If I did not acknowledge its receipt, I do so now. I am acquainted with some of them, they are very respectable people. Yours very truly,

Wm D. Jelks

TLS Con. 324 BTW Papers DLC. A press copy is in the William Dorsey Jelks Papers, A-Ar.

[1] See below, December 1906.

Emmett Jay Scott to William Howard Taft

Tuskegee, Ala. December 12, 1906

My dear Sir: I beg to call to your attention the fact that years ago white men were enlisted and appointed chief musicians, and placed in charge of the colored regimental army bands. At that time there were no capable colored musicians available. The custom is still in force, although the cause has long since ceased to exist. The duties of chief musician have been satisfactorily performed by colored musicians in the absence of the chief musician in the regular army. The colored volunteer bands were led by colored chief musicians, one of which was promoted to the grade of second Lieutenant in recognition of his ability as a chief musician and his efficiency as a soldier. The enlistment of white men for the position of chief musician in colored bands "closes the door of opportunity" and promotion to that grade to the best colored talent in the service, and makes it harder to enlist desirable civilian musicians.

In view of the foregoing, I beg to ask that here after "for the good of the service" enlistments for the colored regiments will be kept strictly within the ruling of Section 1104, Revised Statutes of the United States 2nd Ed. 1876, dated 28th July, 1866: "The enlisted men of the two regiments of cavalry shall be colored men." The same pertains to the Infantry.

I shall further suggest that the white chief musicians now in the colored bands be transferred to white bands in the service of the United States Army. Yours respectfully,

Emmett J. Scott

TLSr Copy Con. 5 BTW Papers DLC.

[1] Taft ordered that whenever possible chief musicians of black regiments should be black. The Indianapolis *Freeman* reproduced the exchange of correspondence between Scott and Taft, and praised Scott for opening a new "door of opportunity" for blacks in the military. (Indianapolis *Freeman*, Feb. 23, 1907, 8.)

To John Hope

[Tuskegee, Ala.] December 13, 1906

Dear Mr. Hope: I have your letter of recent date, and I thank you for writing me.

In regard to Mr. Carnegie, I would say that he is a very curious proposition. He gets ideas into his head in his own way, and when they once get there, it is very hard to get them out. Almost impossible by direct methods. For example: When he was in Atlanta last Spring, there was evidence dinned into his ears on every possible occasion that the colored people were receiving all the education, and the white people very little, and of course, the fact that there are four or five colleges for colored people in Atlanta made it quite plain to him. The result was, that he left Atlanta with the idea that more was being done for the Negro than for the White man in the state of Georgia. I happened to know that several strong men, including Mr. Ogden and others, made it possible during the trip North to change his opinion. They tried to point out to him how little the state of Georgia was doing for higher education, in fact, as you know, doing almost nothing, and in what poor condition the country public schools are in, and what little is being spent by the city of Atlanta for the education of the Negro in that city, compared with what is going for the education of the white children. Mr. Ogden has been discussing the matter from time to time, ever since, and believes he will be brought around to see his mistake. He will have to be changed gradually, and not in any direct manner.

My greatest concern just now regarding the race, is the condition of our people in the public country schools. I have just sent notice to twenty colored papers a strong appeal for them to put forth every effort in their power to improve the country schools, even though they have to pay for the improvement themselves. In this county, for example: Our people have built nine school houses, and we have ten others in process of erection; beside that, the school terms have been extended from five to seven months in nearly every country school in our county. We expect to do even better than that this year.

I wish very much that some equitable method could be found by which Mr. Carnegie could give the colored people of Atlanta a Library building. I think he is anxious to do so, and if it can be properly worked out by the local people, I am sure there will be no trouble in getting the Library. Very truly yours,

Booker T. Washington

TLpS Con. 323 BTW Papers DLC.

To William Dorsey Jelks

Tuskegee Institute, Alabama. December 14, 1906

Personal

Dear Sir: I am glad to know that you were pleased with the article describing the work of the Jesup Wagon.

In that same connection I want to tell you about other work that is being done in this county. I did not mention it in my former letter because I never like to speak of anything until we have gone far enough to demonstrate that it can be made successful.

In the way of taking improved methods of agriculture right home to the farmers doors in line with your own suggestion, several months ago we arranged through the Agricultural Department to carry on in this county in connection with the work of the Jesup Wagon 150 cooperative farms, that is, we are now selecting 150 farms in Macon County on the plan that the owners agree to set aside a few acres to be cultivated absolutely under the direction of one of our representatives. The Agricultural Department supplies the seeds, etc. In this way the farmer does not have to go to a school to get improved lessons, nor does he have to depend upon what he reads about or what he hears is being done on some other man's farm, but he gets the lesson of how to improve agriculture right on his own farm. Our man[1] is now at work every day and has already secured the consent of 30 farmers for this cooperative work, and I think by Christmas he will have secured 150.

I shall hope sometime next spring to report to you the results of this effort. Yours truly,

Booker T. Washington

TLS William Dorsey Jelks Papers A-Ar.

[1] Thomas Monroe Campbell.

To Ernest W. Thompson[1]

[Tuskegee, Ala.] Dec. 15, 1906

Dear Sir: I have noted the enclosed interview in the Montgomery Advertiser of December 13.[2]

In this connection I am writing to ask if you will give us the opportunity to put before you the facts concerning the land owned by this institution and how it is used. Personally, I have always taken the ground that any educational institution of this kind should not hold large acreages of land or other property which is not used for the purposes of the institution, and if it does hold land or other property not used for the purposes of the institution, it ought to pay taxes the same as a private person. This is my personal view, and as far as I have been able to do so, whenever any exceptions to this rule have been brought to my attention, I have tried to bring about a remedy.

Second, I find that a good many people have a wrong impression of the amount of land owned by this institution, for the reason that a number of our officers and teachers own land as individuals upon which they pay taxes; also a wrong impression is conveyed very often by people getting the idea that this institution owns the large tract of land operated by the Southern Improvement Association. The fact is, we do not own a single dollar's worth of interest in that property; it is a different organization and taxes, I understand, are regularly paid upon the property. I hope you will keep in mind that when this institution began, the great criticism brought against the Negro race was that it was being educated in everything except farming. In order to bring about a change, it was necessary for us to secure a large amount of land. Nearly all this land is being cultivated, and that which is not being cultivated is being used for pasturage and for the purpose of securing fuel. We have further pursued the policy of trying to produce, as far as possible, our own beef cattle right here on our own farm, realizing that every dollar we kept in the county, instead of spending it on the outside, would help enrich all of our citizens.

Third, if you will give me, or some one connected with the institution, the opportunity of putting the facts before you, I am quite sure that you will find that we are more than anxious to comply not only with the spirit of the law, but with the wishes of the officials and other leading people in Macon County. We are anxious to do our part toward supporting the county, and if those in authority will let us know in what way we ought to do more or ought to change our policy, I am sure our trustees will be very glad to comply with their wishes as far as possible. I have valued the good will and advice of people in Macon County more than in any other section of the world, and I believe that any changes can be brought about or any differences settled right here among our people at home.

I shall be very glad to have any suggestions in this regard that you may be kind enough to make. Yours truly,

Booker T. Washington

TLpS Con. 336 BTW Papers DLC.

[1] Ernest W. Thompson (b. 1881), son of Charles Winston Thompson and nephew of Joseph Oswalt Thompson, was an Alabama state representative from Macon County. From 1903 to 1904 he was editor of the Tuskegee *News*.

[2] The newspaper reported that Ernest W. Thompson planned to introduce a bill that would limit the tax-exempt status of Tuskegee Institute. Thompson denied that he was opposed to Negro education. He feared, however, BTW's power to acquire land, and thought Tuskegee Institute might ultimately own the major portion of Macon County. (Montgomery *Advertiser*, Dec. 13, 1906, 13.)

An Article in *Outlook*

15 December 1906

The Golden Rule in Atlanta

Three distinct movements looking to the improvement of the relations between the races have been started in Atlanta, Georgia, as a consequence of the September riots. The first of these, headed by ex-Governor Northen, aims to bring about the co-operation of the races along religious lines. The second has for its object the more practical education of the masses. The third is directed toward securing law and order through the practical co-operation of the better elements of both races. As a whole, I think I am safe in saying, the measures thus far taken and others proposed represent the most radical, far-reaching, and hopeful solution of the race problem that has ever been undertaken by Southern white people.

When a man's house is on fire, the fact easily publishes itself to the whole community. When he sets himself to rebuild it, the fact does not so easily attract attention. And yet if, warned by past experience, he builds in a way to avoid the danger of a second catastrophe, that may be the most significant fact about the whole matter. The illustration may fairly be applied to the city of Atlanta at the present time. There is hardly a man or woman in the United States who has not read of the September riots which resulted in the death of some fifteen or sixteen innocent negroes and some three or four equally innocent white people, one a woman and the other an officer of the law. On the other hand, the story of what Atlanta is doing in the direction of reconstructing the relations of mutual helpfulness between the races is probably only imperfectly known even in the city of Atlanta itself. This fact is my excuse for writing at this time of what I may call the work of "reconstruction" in Atlanta.

Immediately after the bloody and terrible events of September 22, 23, and 24, when the whole city was still in a state of terror, a public meeting of all citizens, white and black, was called to discuss the situation. As a result of that meeting a Committee of Ten was formed, as a "committee of safety," to recommend measures that should be taken to restore order and protect the lives of the inhabitants. Upon their recommendation all the saloons of the city, some one hundred and fifty in number, were closed, and remained closed for something like ten days; strict measures against loiterers and against all forms of disorder were taken. These were the measures taken to restore order and secure the public safety.

Meanwhile a committee of five prominent colored men had been appointed to confer with the Committee of Safety to aid and support them in the work they had undertaken. At the same time a meeting was held in which ten of the prominent white ministers and a similar number of the colored ministers took part. A member of the Committee of Ten appeared at this meeting for the purpose of assuring the colored people that the white people were their friends and intended to protect them as long as they obeyed the law. He asked the ministers to take this assurance to the members of their congregations and to use their efforts to induce the colored people of the city to return to their work. For by this time the industries of the city were fairly prostrated.

It was out of these two bodies and of the conferences which followed with the leaders of the colored people that the later organizations and the larger experiments in the co-operation of the races have sprung. The first thought of those who were principally concerned was in some way or other to make permanent the organizations that had grown up to meet an emergency, and to secure in this way the continued co-operation of the better elements of both races, looking to a permanent solution of the whole problem.

The first step taken in the direction of making permanent the co-operation of the races which the crisis had brought about was taken by ex-Governor W. J. Northen, President of the Atlanta Business Men's Gospel League. He proposed the formation of the Christian League. I can best indicate the character of this organization by quoting from the official statement of its purposes and the means by which it proposes to carry them into effect:

> The executive committee and general officers of the Business Men's Gospel Union, in consultation and co-operation with the ministers of the city, have undertaken the readjustment of the relations of the races at the South, through the formation of a Christian League, to which shall be eligible approved members of both races who will agree to promote, under the direction of the Gospel Union, the highest type of citizenship, maintain all existing laws, and promote peace and good will.

> The Christian League as such shall not be an organization, but its members shall consist of those who will agree to hold themselves subject to the call of the Business Men's Gospel Union, and who will agree to co-operate with the Union in its work, as outlined in its constitution.
>
> With the Christian League effected, its members, both white and colored, will constitute themselves a sort of Southern legion of honor, hoping to be more powerful in preserving patriotism and high morality than all laws or law officers elected to enforce them.

One of the first things undertaken under this arrangement was the designation of the second Sunday in December as a day when every minister in the city, white and colored, should preach a sermon upon law and order. Preparatory to this, and to other plans which the organization has in view, weekly prayer-meetings, at which members of both races are represented, have been held at the rooms of the colored Young Men's Christian Association.

It is the purpose of ex-Governor Northen, I understand, to extend the organization to every community in the South. I believe a similar organization has already been established at Nashville, Tennessee.

On November 18 there was published in the Atlanta Constitution a letter addressed to the people of Georgia by the Interdenominational Union of Colored Ministers. This letter recites the fact that of every one hundred persons in the State of Georgia over forty are colored, and that by the last Legislature something over $300,000 was appropriated for the establishment in every Congressional district in the State of an agricultural high school. With this preamble the letter proposes that a great central industrial school for negroes be established, and that schools of domestic science be established in the cities. The letter suggests "that such an arrangement would be positively helpful to the relations between the races, since it would tend to turn the minds of both away from their antagonisms and furnish a point of harmonious co-operation between them."

The purpose is to give the negro population what the white people are soon to have—thorough training in every department of labor in which they are now engaged. It recognizes the fact that the race question is and will probably continue to be for a long time to a large extent a question of labor. I understand that this project is favored by the white people, and that a sum amounting to something like $30,000 has already been subscribed toward carrying the plan into effect.

The third and perhaps the most important and far-reaching effort to bring about co-operation among the forces of law and order in both races has been due to Charles T. Hopkins, a young lawyer who has been prominent in politics in the city—a graduate, I am told, of Williams College and attorney for Atlanta University. Mr. Hopkins was one of the more influential members of the original Committee of Safety, and has taken a leading part in all the efforts to suppress violence since that time. The organization which he is now engaged in forming is to be known as the Civic League, and aims to make permanent the condition of peace that now reigns. This movement was started on Thanksgiving Day at a meeting of the Unity Club in Atlanta. The following is a copy of the notice which has been or will eventually be sent out to some five thousand prominent and public-spirited citizens:

> One of the results of the recent riot has been a rapidly growing sentiment that some intelligent action should be taken in order to prevent a repetition. Further loss of prestige, injury to business, anxiety, and bloodshed should be avoided if possible.
>
> Inspired with the belief that such measures should be adopted as will in the future prevent similar trouble, and in harmony with the growing sentiment, we, the undersigned, have consented to take the initiative towards an organization having but this one end in view.
>
> This is done after conference with a sufficient member of citizens to justify us in the statement that the great, overwhelming majority of law-abiding people in this country are opposed not only to riots and lynchings, but to any other form of injustice or violation of law.

The letter goes on to state that the objects of the organization are not political, and no one with a political ambition is desired as a member. The purpose of the organization will be to take such steps as will tend to promote peace between the races, secure an impartial administration of justice, and secure permanent protection to white and black alike. A similar association is in process of organization among the colored people. It is believed that no less than 1,500 members of the negro race in Atlanta will be eventually enrolled in this organization, the purpose of which is to co-operate with the organization of the other race in its efforts to secure peace and order in the community.

Already much has been accomplished by the co-operation of the races in this direction. Nineteen of the forty-two negroes originally indicted have been released. Twenty others remain to be tried. The cases against the members of the mob who attacked the negroes have been pressed, and if some who have been guilty have escaped, it has been due, perhaps, to the fact that it is impossible to change in so brief a time the state of feeling which made such an outbreak possible.

Meanwhile an earnest effort has been made through the medium of the newspapers to change public sentiment and enforce a new reverence for law and order. A remarkable series of letters from prominent ministers of the city has been published in the Atlanta Constitution. I can perhaps best give a notion of the tenor of these letters by quoting a few words from the letter of Bishop Seth Ward,[1] of the Methodist Church, to the Constitution, dated October 31. He says:

> The race problem in the South can only be solved by raising the moral tone of both races. . . . Dives and all sorts of evil resorts that breed crime in blacks and whites alike must be suppressed. The safety of our Southland demands it. But while the work of suppression and correction is going on, we must give ourselves earnestly to the work of making moral character among all our people. It can be done. The church, the pulpit, the industrial school, must undertake the task. We dare not shrink from the work because it is slow and beset with difficulties. We of the white race, boasting ourselves the "superior race," must show our superiority by treating with exact justice and Christian consideration the weaker race—the unfortunate race—that dwells in our common territory.

The discussions in the papers in emphasizing different sides of the question have widened the point of view from which the public at large has been disposed to look at the race problem and suggested many new methods for effecting improvement. One of the matters which have been discussed by the committees that are now engaged in forming the Civic League among the white and the colored peoples is the plan of establishing in Atlanta what already exists in Macon, Georgia, namely, a force of colored policemen to preside in the parts of the city occupied almost entirely by colored people. These policemen would be appointed on the recommendation of the members of the Colored Civic League, and, being in a sense their policemen, it is believed that they would have the moral support of the colored population.

Another measure that has been proposed by the League is to employ an attorney to attend the court and, where necessary, assist in the defense of negroes who, through ignorance and a sort of indifference of despair that seems sometimes to overtake them when they are brought before the judge, have need of a friend in court to look after their case. The necessity for this is emphasized by the experience which Charles T. Hopkins, and two other attorneys who recently defended a man who was charged with having committed an assault upon a woman, had. Joe Glenn, the man arrested, was a prosperous farmer and property-owner. He was arrested upon suspicion November 13, and taken to the house of the woman, who positively identified him. It was with difficulty that the officers succeeded in getting him to the city and safely lodged in the city prison. After this had been accomplished Mr. Hopkins went at once to Trial Justice Roan[2] and suggested to him that it was to the interest of the city at large that the man have a speedy but a fair trial. The Judge agreed, and appointed Mr. Hopkins to try the case, which he did with the assistance of two other well-known attorneys. Upon an examination of the evidence the attorneys became convinced that Glenn was an innocent man, and saw themselves compelled to secure the man's acquittal. They had taken up the case with no other expectation or desire than that the man should be quickly and decently hanged. They secured some of the best citizens in Atlanta to serve upon the jury. Glenn was regularly tried. Twenty-five of his white neighbors swore to his good character. The evidence was so strong that even though he was positively identified by the woman in question, who lost control of herself and denounced him on the witness stand, he was acquitted. The jury was out but four minutes. A circumstance that contributed to his acquittal was the arrest, upon another charge, of the man who has since turned out to be the real criminal.

In an editorial entitled "A Lesson to Rashness" the Atlanta Constitution says:

> Never was a stronger plea made for the saner course than in the dramatic ending of this remarkable trial. It is the province of laws to deal impartial justice -punishment to the guilty, vindication to the innocent. Here, without the intervention of the law, an innocent life would have been sacrificed.

This is the first important task accomplished in the spirit, if not in the name, of the new Atlanta Civic League. It is undoubtedly the first time that a negro accused of this crime, who had been positively identified by his supposed victim, ever escaped death. Glenn's attorneys brought him a suit of clothes and gave him a ticket to reach a farm in Alabama, where he might go and live safely until excitement in the neighborhood of his own home should pass away.

The foregoing, then, is my warrant for the statement that the efforts now being made represent the most radical, far-reaching, and hopeful solution of the race problem that has ever been undertaken by Southern white people.

Outlook, 84 (Dec. 15, 1906), 913–16. Dated at Tuskegee, Ala., Dec. 8, 1906. The editors wrote a headnote: "We believe that this striking article by Mr. Washington calls for no further comment than the mere expression of our opinion that the story of the trial told at the close of the article recounts an incident which, from the point of view of both races, is one of the most significant and promising in the whole history of the real Reconstruction Era."

1 Seth Ward (1858–1909) was assistant missionary secretary of the Methodist Episcopal Church, South, before being elevated to bishop in May 1906.

2 Leonard S. Roan (b. 1849), an Atlanta lawyer, was appointed judge of the circuit court in 1902.

From William Dorsey Jelks

Montgomery, December 18th, 1906

Dear Sir: I am in receipt of your letter of the 14th. I get up very little interest comparatively, in institutions whose business it is to turn out doctors, lawyers and even school teachers. One man who has, with a fairly trained mind, a love of the growing plant is worth a whole class of doctors and lawyers and other professional people.

Our general wealth is in our soil: the brick and mortar of the cities depend upon its productiveness: the doctor's patient and the lawyer's client go at last to the earth for a fee. Brick masons are good things to have. We cannot do well without them. Blacksmiths we need next to the farmer, and above them all and before them all, we need to educate men who are to be lovers of the soil. In my opinion we are stepping backward in Alabama, taking Alabama as a whole, and not forward. This much to premise, that I am gratified that you are running the "Jesup" wagon and the model school farm or "patch." The Japanese have an experiment station every few miles, and with less than the best the soil could give, would have been even at a greater disadvantage in the recent hard struggle against Russia. I think you are doing a great work for your people in taking improved methods of agriculture home to the farmers.

I am, my dear Sir, Faithfully,

Wm. D. Jelks

TLS Con. 324 BTW Papers DLC. A press copy is in the William Dorsey Jelks Papers, A-Ar.

An Article in *World's Work*

December 1906

A FARMERS' COLLEGE ON WHEELS

THE JESUP AGRICULTURAL WAGON OF TUSKEGEE WHICH EDUCATES THE FATHER IN THE FIELD WHILE THE INSTITUTE IS TEACHING HIS CHILDREN—A KINDERGARTEN METHOD OF MAKING THRIFTY LAND-OWNERS OUT OF HAND-TO-MOUTH NEGRO TENANTS.

The Jesup Agricultural Wagon stopped in front of a little cabin where an old Negro was unhitching a bony mule from a ramshackle wagon. He had evidently just returned from town.

"What is that in your wagon, uncle?"

"Hay."

"How much did it cost?"

"A dollar and a quarter a bale."

"What is that man doing out yonder in your cotton patch?"

"Chopping out the crab-grass."

"How much do you pay him?"

"A dollar a day—but my crop's behind and I have to have him."

"Don't you know, uncle, that if you had a field growing nothing but crab-grass, it would be worth more than the cotton field you are hiring a man to chop the grass out from?"

The old man had not thought of that before, so our horses are let rest while we try to show him the foolish waste that comes from buying hay in town and hiring a man to kill hay at home.

The Tuskegee Institute, whose object has always been the uplifting of the masses of the Negroes, has been confronted with the problem of reaching just such shiftless farmers as the man with the hay. It is not enough to get the sons and daughters into the Institute and teach them useful trades and give them object lessons in good farming: something must be done for the fathers and mothers who cannot come to school.

This problem is being solved, in a large measure, by the Jesup Agricultural Wagon, made possible through the generosity of Mr. and Mrs. Morris K. Jesup, of New York, friends of the Institute. The wagon itself and the harness were made by our own students, and two large mules were purchased. The outfit includes different kinds of plows and planters, a cultivator, a cotton chopper, a variety of seeds, samples of fertilizers, a revolving churn, a butter mould, a cream separator, a milk tester, and other appliances useful in making practical demonstrations. The expenses of operating the wagon are paid by the John F. Slater Fund.

FARM-TO-FARM DEMONSTRATIONS

Much previous work had of course been done through monthly farmers' institutes, and the results were far-reaching. But the wagon method has the immense advantage of going direct to the man in the field, where improved methods can be adapted to his particular conditions. We carry our implements out into his field. After he has plowed a few furrows, we hitch up one of our improved plows. "That may be a good plow for some," he says, "but for me, give me that old 'scutter.'" We use our plow for a few minutes and then ask him to compare the amount of work done and the kind of furrow. After that, we can hardly get away from him. They often try to borrow our implements and one man insisted that we remain at his house until he could plow over his cotton. When we come upon a man slowly plowing out his cornfield, we take out the cultivator and show him that he can make seven furrows where he is making one, and with the same animal. So convincing have these demonstrations been that many have at once bought improved implements. It generally means that boys between the plow handles may stay in school longer.

We often find the farmer's wife and children out in the field scattering fertilizer. A distributor taken from our wagon shows him that there is a quicker and a better way, and his family may at the same time be free to do something else. Great stress is laid upon the importance of the farmer's making his own fertilizers. Many of them are renting land at $2.50 an acre and paying out $1.50 an acre for fertilizer. The wagon carries samples of the different kinds and the farmer is taught the amount needed by his land for a certain kind of crop, and just how to mix it. As a rule, the few that have already learned this lesson are those who have previously come in contact with the Institute either as students or in some other way.

SOLVING FOOD-SUPPLY PROBLEMS

The operator in charge of the Jesup Wagon pays as much attention to the kitchen as to the field, for experience has shown us that the wife must be taught as well as the husband, if real advancement is to be made.

Very few of these people have gardens. The wagon carries with it the finest vegetables that are grown in the county and many run out to buy when they might just as well be growing them. We show them how every family can raise on a quarter of an acre vegetables enough to keep from buying $100 worth of meat. We tell them what vegetables can be grown each month in the year and explain just how and when to plant and cultivate. Garden plows and other implements are brought out and their use shown by actual demonstration. The women folks are shown the superiority of the revolving churn over the old "dasher" churn, and how the use of butter moulds would make the butter more salable.

When we ask a family if they raise chickens, they are often surprised. Strange to say, many do not have a chicken on the place, so we find it necessary first to teach the simple lesson of the economy of poultry-raising, and then to explain the best way. The same is true as to hogs. We urge every man to have at least two hogs for each member of his family. Some families with ten or twelve children have but one hog. The Wagon has charts showing the relative merits of different breeds and the operator shows how they may be raised on pastures and on the waste. It is proved to them that a 300-pound hog is worth more than a bale of cotton, and costs comparatively nothing. Over and over again is taught the importance of every man's raising his own food supply, so that his cotton crop may be a cash surplus.

Naturally, the feeding and care of farm animals comes in for consideration. The possibility for every farmer to raise his own mules is brought up also. Mules cost from $50 to $200 and numbers of men are always in debt for them. By the time they get a team paid for, one or both animals are dead. With a brood mare and proper management, a crop could be made and a colt raised, as well. Only a few have ever stopped to think of this.

OPEN-AIR MEETINGS FOR FARMERS

After the Jesup Wagon has in this way made the rounds of the large and small farms of a community, a mass-meeting is held in the open air at some central point. These are largely attended, and the women and children come also. There are always a few successful farmers in every community and these are induced to bring samples of their products and to speak at the gathering. The wagon, in the meantime, secures samples of poor crops, without explaining the purpose, and these are also on hand.

Two stalks of cotton are held up to view and the bolls are counted. Close attention is given while a comparison is made of the yield per acre. Two stalks of corn are produced—one green, with one or two well-developed ears, the other "fired" and dying without an ear of corn.

"What makes the difference?" we ask.

"One hasn't been worked," somebody answers.

Then the man who raised the good stalk is called out and asked to tell the others how he succeeds.

"I fertilize my ground," he says, in substance.

"I plow deep. I do not wait until the grass gets a start before I begin to cultivate. I spend my Saturdays in the field instead of going to town."

When the speaker sits down, we hold up a large bunch of grass, and show how the mass of roots runs down under the corn and cotton, absorbing the fertilizer and the moisture needed for the young plants. Demonstrations of this kind make lasting impressions.

Then other problems, say the question of acreage, are discussed in open meeting, in Sunday School fashion.

"How many acres did you plant in cotton last year," one man is asked.

"Forty."

"How many bales did you raise?"

"Twenty."

"And how many acres did you plant?" is asked of another.

"Twenty."

"And how many bales did you market?"

"Sixteen."

In this way, the farmers are put through the catechism as to crops of different kinds and on the replies is based the argument for a smaller acreage and a better distribution of the various crops. At the last meeting of this kind, it was agreed that they would not attempt more than twenty acres for each mule, and that the best arrangement would be ten acres in cotton, eight in corn, and two acres in potatoes, peas, sorghum cane, and peanuts.

THE NEGRO AS A LANDOWNER

These mass-meetings afford an excellent opportunity for emphasizing the gospel of Tuskegee, that every Negro should own his own home or farm. A typical case is taken of a tenant who moves from place to place every year, who plants no fruit trees nor beautifies his home, who cuts down the trees, allows the rain to make gullies in his field, and lets the farm "run down" generally.

"Why is this?" we ask.

"We don't want to work hard to cut off our own noses," somebody answers. "If we improve the place, somebody else will rent it over our heads."

"I have built up two farms and had to move," says another. "Now I let the place run any old way — and I can keep it."

"When I lived with Mr. Jones," says a third, "I set out a nice orchard, built a pasture fence, and cleared off a 'new-ground.' Then I was told that I couldn't stay the next year unless I paid more rent."

These replies give us a chance to bring home the fundamental duty of buying small tracts of land. The great question is — How? We urge them first to become the owners of a mule and the necessary tools; next, to buy a few acres of ground; then, when this is paid for — and not before — to build a good house on it. This means economy and self-denial, of course, but it can be done. We tell them of specific cases where Negroes have paid off debts of $1,000 and more with a single crop. Many of the landlords have large plantations and are paying taxes on land they never use. If a thrifty tenant remains on one place for a number of years, he ought to make an arrangement by which he will by that time become the owner of at least a few acres.

"But the landlords don't want to sell small tracts," somebody protests.

Then we explain how it was managed at Fort Davis by Rev. Moses Ellington. One of the Tuskegee Institute's teachers urged the Negroes of that vicinity to buy land. A small company was organized, a tract of 2,000 acres was bought, and it was then sold to colored farmers in lots of from ten to eighty acres. That was only five years ago, but most of these men now have nice homes and are good citizens. These farmers now have something to work for. When they set out an orchard, they know they can harvest the fruit. They reap the benefit of every gully they fill up, of every ditch they cut. They can say to their children: "This is your home; help to improve it." Within a few years, the colored people of one county in Alabama have bought more than 10,000 acres of land, and many of them have built nice houses.

Co-operation of the Whites

Since May 24th of the present year, this school on wheels has been moving throughout the farms of Macon and adjoining counties with instruction and appeals like these. It has brought these lessons home to an average of 2,000 people a month, and its circle of usefulness is steadily widening. Invitations are coming in from all parts of the county and from places many miles from Tuskegee.

The white people are taking great interest in the movement and many of them attend the meetings, listening as eagerly as their colored brethren. White men owning large plantations invite the Jesup Wagon to visit their tenants and they are active in working up the meeting.

They are, of course, quick to see that a movement of this kind not only has a direct bearing on the welfare of the community at large, but affects also their own individual prosperity. It requires no long-sighted wisdom to see that a tenant thoroughly aroused to the advantages of improved methods in farming is a more desirable tenant than one content to jog along in the ruts worn deep by generations of shiftless farmers.

The prevailing conditions and methods suggested by the incidents in this sketch are not exaggerated. They will be recognized as true to life in many parts of the South, particularly throughout "the black belt." The Jesup Wagon with its object lessons will do much to break through the hard crust of custom and prepare for a new agricultural era in the section over which its influence extends.

World's Work, 13 (Dec. 1906), 8352–54.

From Charles William Anderson

New York, N.Y., January 4, 1907

(Personal)
My dear Doctor: According to latest advices, Milholland has not dropped the soldier matter, but has merely retreated behind the ramparts. I am this day in receipt of a letter from Sol Johnson,[1] who is a very reliable person, and who keeps me informed of all that is said and done by Stewart. Johnson's letter reads thus:

"Roy Stokes, about whom you asked me this morning, has gone out West on a mission for Milholland. He is supposed to take in Brownsville, Texas, and several other points. I have not been able to learn the particular errand, but it is in connection with the soldier matter."

Thus you see Richmond is still in the field, but he is taking pains to conceal his hands.

The indignation meeting at Cooper Union last night was addressed by General Tremaine. Milholland contributed toward its expenses, but I have not yet learned whether he was among the speakers. Wetmore has just returned from Washington, where he went to put some so-called information in the hands of Senator Foraker. While there, he was a companion and co-worker of Mrs. Terrell.

Gilchrist Stewart is in town, and is informing his friends that Foraker's fight will kill the President's aspirations for another term, and thereby knock out "The Booker T. Washington Cabinet." This statement about "the cabinet" has reached me from several different sources. So you see there is some difference between that young gentleman's talk to you and his talk about you, and you also see that Stokes is playing the game that I predicted he would play, even if restored to the Age. Yours truly,

Charles W. Anderson

TLS Con. 35 BTW Papers DLC.

[1] Solomon C. Johnson, editor of the Savannah *Tribune* and a prominent black Mason.

From Andrew Carnegie

New York, January 5th, 1907

My dear Friend, I have been honored by being requested to deliver the annual lecture before the Philosophical Society of Edinburgh next October. You would be surprised to read the list of my predecessors, from Hume and Adam Smith, Carlyle, Gladstone, to Choate of recent date.

I was so deeply imprest by my visit to Tuskegee that I felt I could give Britain a startling surprise by a cold recital of what the negro was when a slave and what he is rapidly becoming as a free man. You are the foremost authority on this subject, but I do not wish to add to your labors. It occurs to me that it might be possible for you to employ a suitable man (a Tuskegee graduate), who could give me the outlines necessary for my subject, beginning with the first importation of slaves, noting the outstanding facts and the increase up to the time of emancipation, and of course the latest Census returns, giving their numbers, homes owned, land cultivated, property, churches, professions, occupations, etc. — everything showing that the race is advancing as I know it to be in all the elements of citizenship.

I noticed some figures from you the other day stating that so far you had not known a Tuskegee graduate committed for crime, and giving particulars and various occupations.

If your clever Secretary did not have enough to do, he would be the very man perhaps to give me the data in shape. I insist, however, that the one who does it must be liberally paid.

I think that I can surprise Britain, and of course the address would be printed here and might surprise most of our own people. I want facts.

Happy New Year, Always very truly yours,

Andrew Carnegie

Happy New Year from Mrs Carnegie & myself to you & Madam.

A. C.

TLS Con. 343 BTW Papers DLC. Postscript in Carnegie's hand.

A Sunday Evening Talk

[Tuskegee, Ala.] January 13, 1907

LOOKING AT THE BRIGHT SIDE OF LIFE

I think it is unfortunate for an individual to fall into the habit of always looking on the dark side of life. It is very easy for anyone to acquire the habit of always seeing the disappointing, the gloomy, and the unkindly side of life, to the extent that it shuts out from view all that is encouraging. You meet with so many individuals who from a physical point of view are never just right. They are always sick, always have a head-ache, the rheumatism, the tooth-ache, or something else. There is an ache somewhere all the time. They never know what it is to speak about health; they always talk about sickness; they are always groaning, or moaning, or gloomy. It reaches a point where people do not like to come into contact with individuals of that kind. They may not say so but when a person is always speaking about his sickness, his ailments, or anything else he can think of that is depressing, you will find people trying to keep from meeting that person, unless absolutely necessary. Very often such a one speaks as he does merely by force of habit. You very seldom meet a man of that sort when he is absolutely well; he is always "just tolerable" or something of that kind.

There is a class of men and women whose mind is always dealing upon the dark, distressing side of life merely by force of habit.

What is true of an individual is just as true of a group of people or of a race of people. I am more and more convinced that one of the mistakes that our race is now likely to fall into is that of behaving, to a certain extent, like the individuals to whom I have referred. Unfortunately, this attitude of mind is very largely encouraged by the type of colored newspapers, newspapers which, in a very large degree, make public sentiment. If you follow up the average paper, you will find that two-thirds of its columns are filled with expressions of disappointments, comments on the dark and gloomy outlook of life; every trial through which the race has passed, is passing, is given great prominence, while very little attention is paid to the inspiring side of racial life.

Now there is danger that the race, like individuals, may yield to the temptation of always calling attention to the failures, instead of to its success. There are times when races like individuals should speak out plainly and emphatically against wrongs, injustice, against anything that is not right. But no race should depend on its success in life merely upon the publication of its wrongs. If it does it is going to fail, because the world grows sick of a weak race, of a sick race, just as individuals grow sick of weak individuals, and of sick individuals. There is no pleasure, no encouragement in coming into contact with failure. The world likes to come in contact with success. The world does not honor failure. That is true with regard to a race, just as it is true with regard to an individual. I speak to you as I do because I want you to go out from here prepared to help the race learn to overlook the wrongs and injuries, to hold up its head, and go bravely on. Tell the world that your race is going to succeed, then the world will hold out its hand and help and encourage it.

There are times when it is wise for us to hold these indignation meetings to protest against injustice that is practiced upon our race. But it does not help to call indignation meetings merely to call attention to the weak side of the race. Whenever a race makes up its mind that it is sick all the time, you will never hear of that race organizing banks, department stores, great commercial enterprises, building railroads, or drug stores. My experience convinces me more and more that we do not gain anything in this way; but we do gain in proportion as we make up our minds to go forward bravely and make the most of our failures and our disadvantages. There is no reason why we should grow discouraged, no reason why we should become hopeless; no reason why we should assume the attitude of a sick people. I do not believe there is any race in history, in the same relative stage of civilization, that has made such a progress as is true of ten millions of the Negro race who dwell in the United States. I do not believe you will find ten millions of people of any race in possession of so many essentials of life, who have themselves paid such a small price for these essentials as the colored people of the United States.

One of the first essentials of life is being able to own a piece of property and a house. With few exceptions, a black man can own property anywhere in this country. You go into Russia, or South Africa, and you will find that many people can't own property; they haven't that privilege. A few days ago the Congress of South Africa, adopted a new form of constitution, a Federal Constitution, for the entire colony of South Africa, in which the Negro is formally debarred from citizenship to the extent that he is not permitted to vote. In some parts of South Africa he is not permitted to own land. In some places the native black men are denied the privilege of walking on the sidewalks in the cities, and in other places, the white man who would condescend to shake hands with a colored man would be ostracized. There are places in Russia where the people are not permitted to own land, and everywhere the common people are oppressed and denied many privileges that are granted to Negroes in this country. We call attention too often to the speeches of our enemies rather than to those of our friends. I never hear of a colored man getting up to speak who does not mention Senator Tillman. Because Mr. Tillman is not a friend to the colored people, they all have to make mention of him in their speeches. We know that he is an enemy to the race, but he is always being spoken of, because he emphasizes the wrong side of the race. The Negro of America occupies a peculiar position. He is permitted to work at any occupation that he happens to view. In most any part of America any man who has the ability, talent and money, can establish any line of business and succeed. With few exceptions, almost without money, when he has the ability, he can begin in a profession and make a success in that direction. There was never a time in the history of our race when there was such an encouragement for any young colored woman who has a talent in literature to succeed. There never was such a demand for literature, never a time when there was a field that is so large and encouraging for the literary work as now.

There is an opportunity for a colored man to get all kinds of education. We have opportunities, for the most part, to attend good public schools, to attend industrial schools, universities, colleges, professional education, and almost every kind that any other race is getting, we have an opportunity to get also. All over America we have religious freedom—we have the opportunity to belong to any religious sect we choose and worship in any kind of a church that we can build. Very little is denied us that is afforded other American citizens, and a race that does not make the most of what is in its hands, is not the race to get much that is not in its possession.

You will find that from every point of view our condition materially, educationally, morally and religiously is far more permanent than that of any similar number of people of our race anywhere in the world. You cannot pick out ten millions of colored people in the world, anywhere, whose educational and religious growth is so satisfactory as that of the ten millions of colored people in the United States. I repeat, under such circumstances we should not go about advertising our weakness to the public.

We want to learn a lesson from the Greeks who are coming into this country; they are going to Mobile, Montgomery, Atlanta and throughout the South, and they are quietly establishing themselves in business. They are holding no public meetings, but quietly and steadily they are getting a hold in the commercial world. They are educating their children, and building churches. In the city of Atlanta, one of the most interesting sights is that of a big resturant and soda fountains where all the colored people congregate every Sunday evening. They have to go there and get food and drink. These Greeks who can hardly speak the English language, have come here where the colored people have lived all their lives, they have gone into this business and are making money running a resturant for our people, who have not had the foresight to go into that business for themselves.

But let me repeat, we are going forward. There never was a time in the history of the race in America when it owned so much property; never a time when we had so many homes; never a time when we were engaged in so many business enterprises, owned and operated so many drug stores, grocery stores, and banks; never a time when there were so many public school buildings, and universities for the benefit of our race; never a time when we had so many ministers, doctors, lawyers, and churches, and when we had in our possession so much wealth of all kinds. There is no reason why we should become disappointed and grow into the habit of always complaining. There is every reason why we should hold up our heads and go bravely and courageously forward.

Tuskegee Student, 19 (Jan. 19, 1907), 1. Stenographically reported.

To Edgar James Penney

[Tuskegee, Ala.] Jan. 16, 1907

Mr. Penney In your statement before the committee Sunday, you said that part of the statements made by Flavia were true and a part were not true. Will you be kind enough to let me have this afternoon, if possible, in writing the portion of the statements made by her which are not true.

Booker T. Washington

TLpSr Con. 578 BTW Papers DLC.

From Edgar James Penney

Tuskegee Institute, Ala., Jan. 16 1907

Mr. B. T. Washington: The items in Flavia's statement, of January 13th, that are not true are these:

1. In general, I never kissed, nor attempted to kiss her; nor did such an idea enter my mind.

2. I remember saying to her, at my table, in company with my family, they joining me in the sentiment, that we wanted her to consider herself a part of our family, while with us, that is, a third daughter, &c.

3. She never slapped me in the face, nor attempted such a thing, there being no occasion for such action.

4. I never said, I was surprised at her; I never called her "a naughty girl."

5. She mentions two occasions, on which I had letters for her and took them upstairs, and called her upstairs, each time, to get them. Only once did I have a letter for her which I took upstairs; and, as nearly as I can recall, it was the second instance that she mentions. This was the only time. At that time, I was busy correcting papers, in my bedroom, which is my custom, afternoons and evenings, when I have time, putting in every spare moment, in this way. I had fifteen or twenty minutes before supper, on the evening in question, and was at my work, with my back to the door, across the room, with my face toward the window looking over to Mr. Gibson's. My coat was hanging on its usual nail by the dresser. As I heard Flavia's voice down stairs and my daughter talking with her, and not wishing to leave my work to go to supper, I called to her from the head of the stairs, saying I had a letter for her, and would not be down for sometime and that she might come up and get it if she wished it very much. I usually place each one's letters at their places, at table, when I first come home; but often forget to do so, sometimes keeping them till next day, unless asked whether I have mail. Hers I took upstairs, on this occasion, because my mind was on correcting my papers for next day. Before she reached the top of the stairs, I had placed her letter on the dresser which is by the door, returned to my seat and did not turn round to look at her, but simply said, "I hope its good news," and went on with my work. I ate supper when Mrs. Penney[1] came. This is the only time, I took a letter of hers upstairs and this is all that happened at that time.

6. The "gymnastic" incident was not upstairs, as she states; but in the dining room. My wife and Van, whom she mentions, being present. Flavia did *not* object to the gymnastic exercise, but my wife did, on the ground that it would be too violent both for her and "Van," as both were not strong. My children used to practice it with me. There was no "drawing her up to me," no "hugging," & no "kissing"; nor no thought of it.

7. There is no truth in the statement the "buggy in front of the

Whittaker's gate," when she claims I "started to pull" her into my room; but Mrs. Penney's coming prevented it.

8. I never "grabbed" and "kissed" her in my life, nor "laughed" when she spoke to me about it.

9. All those statements, about my pushing her on to the bed, either in her room or any where else, are absolutely without foundation.

There was not the slightest suggestion, in my conduct toward her, at any time, for such a statement from her.

10. The lighting the lamp statement is partly true and partly untrue.

When I have time, I clean the lamps, in order to help and because it is economical for me to do so. That day, I over ran some of the lamps with oil, which, by night, had filled the trough near top of one or two of the lamps. I also keep track of the matches, so as to avoid carelessness in their handling. When I heard her *asking* for matches, I was just coming in the back, down stairs door and ran upstairs, saying, "I will get you some." I went into Van's room, where I keep the safety matches and got two boxes, giving her one and lighting the lamp with one from my box, and observing the oil on the lamp, I told her to wait, and took a soiled handkerchief from my back pocket and wiped it off, Mrs. Penney standing by, at the time, and saw what was done. I have often used my soiled handkerchiefs in this way; and I often light the lamps, at night, when the people are busy. This was no new occurrence.

11. I never said, or hinted, by word or conscious look, that "I wanted her as bad as she wanted me," never! never!!

12. That statement about her menstrual period, &c. is all absolutely untrue. It makes me blush with shame, to have to write the word, in this connection.

13. The Chapel statement is true, excepting:

1) I did not "grab" her arm, but took her as I thought I ought to do, it being night and she being the weaker of the two, my daughter, Emma,[2] being her companion.

2) I bought the candy and *not* Emma, as Flavia states. I got five cents' worth for them which they ate before reaching home; and five cents' worth for Mrs. Penney.

3) I have no recollection of a conscious intention of "pulling"

at her dress or "pushing" her, on our way home. I may have jostled her, as we walked along the half lighted street, but I was not, nor am I now, aware of doing so.

I have tried to answer every item, mentioned in the statement, handed me, on last Sunday, at your house, as you request.

I have not, intentionally, omitted any point. Respectfully,

E. J. Penney

ALS Con. 578 BTW Papers DLC.

[1] Estelle C. Penney, born in Georgia in 1858.

[2] Emma Caroline Penney, born in 1882, E. J. Penney's daughter, was a Tuskegee graduate of the class of 1898 and later a student at Atlanta University.

To Francis Ellington Leupp

[Tuskegee, Ala.] January 18, 1907

Personal

My dear Mr. Leupp: I have both read and considered very carefully your letter of January 10. The questions raised in it I confess are puzzling and complicated. On one point, however, I am convinced, and that is I very much hope, if you can possibly avoid it without doing violence to the Indian Service, that you will not attempt to make any radical change at present, I mean not until after the feeling on the part of the colored people over the Brownsville affair has somewhat disappeared. If any move were made just now, it would be used by an element of white and colored people against the President. Of course I am not excusing or defending the attitude of the race toward the President, but I am simply putting a fact before you. Personally I have the most implicit faith in everything that the President does.

When the time comes to act, I should advise your trying the experiment of grouping the colored people at one school or agency. I believe that if the experiment could be made in connection with Indians who have been trained at Hampton and who I think would not share any prejudice against colored people, I believe it would be likely to succeed. I do not know how it is now, but when I was a student at Hampton, the Indian boys rather considered it an honor to be permitted to room with a Negro student. I can remember on social occasions the Indian boys would prefer to go with the Negro girls rather than with Indian girls. When I was in charge of the Indian boys at Hampton, I do not believe that they had the least feeling against me on account of my race or color, at least I never saw anything that indicated that such a feeling existed, and I think that one or two strong Indians trained at Hampton might be of great service in the experiment when you come to put it in operation.

I shall keep your letter before me, and if I can think of any other suggestion, I shall be glad to communicate with you, or perhaps I can see you for a few minutes sometime when I am passing through Washington. Yours very truly,

Booker T. Washington

TLpS Con. 352 BTW Papers DLC.

From Emmett Jay Scott

New York. January 18, 1907

Dear Mr. Washington: I have just wired you tonight. I think I have never been sent away to look after anything which has required more of tact and patience as this proposition. These men have a grossly exaggerated idea as to the value of their paper. When they came to conference yesterday they put their own interests at $30,000.00 and did not wish to discuss anything at all except on a basis of one-third interest which would require at once a cash outlay on our part of $10,000. Without revealing my own hand, I simply told them that it was an unfair capitalization and Fortune immediately dropped to $21,000. and wanted us to show $7,000. to begin with. We discussed and discussed every possible proposition until at last today we broke up at five o'clock with the agreement as wired you. This agreement means that they will capitalize at $50,000, and their holding in it will be $25,500 — a majority of $500 of the stock. Our interest will be the sum brought and in addition all that you have put into the business for the last two or three years. This will make our part in the capitalization a rather considerable sum. Fortune proposed and I agreed with him that it would seem reasonable to secure from persons outside of this group a sum to supplement this, to allow for larger equipment. The sum brought would not at all cover the items needed as they were unwilling to start except with three presses which would aggregate $3,000, two linotype machines to cost $3,000 each – making $6,000 and other appurtenances bringing the total up to $11,425. They have given me free hand to block out the campaign for carrying out our ideas and I have started on this work at once.

I am writing this immediately following the conference and am sorry not to have been able to report earlier, but as I said we have had to handle the proposition very carefully. As I have told you, as soon as any interest is manifested in the proposition, it immediately jumps up in value well beyond any serious consideration. Faithfully and sincerely,

Emmett J. Scott

I agree with you regarding non-publication of anything regarding Cleveland letter. I had not taken it up as I think to do so w'd only add to confusion &c &c.

E J S

TLS Con. 45 BTW Papers DLC. Postscript in Scott's hand.

To Braxton Bragg Comer[1]

[Tuskegee, Ala.] January 19, 1907

Dear Sir: I have not been to see you regarding the bill which has passed the Legislature calling for a special accountant to be appointed to examine into the finances of this institution for the reason that I did not care to disturb you or do anything that was not absolutely necessary. I have implicit faith in your sense of absolute justice towards the Negro race, and I do not believe that anyone would be appointed to come here by you who is prejudiced to the Negro and especially prejudiced against his education.

I presume, of course, that you are acquainted with the law originating this institution. We receive $4,500 from the State of Alabama; $3,000 to assist in paying normal teachers, and $1,500 toward the expenses of an Experiment Station. The total amount of money, however, handled by us for current expenses was last year something over $300,000, this latter, except the $4,500, coming wholly from donations of organizations and individuals. This money, for the most part, comes from the outside into Alabama each year, and would not come except for the work of this institution, and of course the bulk of it is spent within the borders of our state.

I take for granted that you will instruct the accountant just what you desire him to accomplish, that is, what the scope and character of the examination is to be, whether it is to be confined only to the money given by the State of Alabama, or whether you wish him to go into the use of money that comes from other sources. Of course I do not know how far you will desire the accountant to go into the examination of money that is not received from the State of Alabama.

If it is your wish or that of the State to have the examiner go into our other accounts aside from the money given by the State, I should like to have time in which to communicate with and get an opinion from the majority of our Trustees. I have no idea that they would oppose anything you or the State would desire, but I think it is such an important matter that it would be better for me to have an official expression from the majority of the Trustees.

During the twenty-five years that this institution has been in existence, we have built up a rather large establishment, large in the number of students and teachers and in the number of departments, and I hope the gentleman who is to make the examination will be prepared to go thoroughly into the work of each one of our numerous departments.

It may not be known to you that our Trustees employ a regular professional accountant who comes to the institution and audits our accounts and criticises our methods of bookkeeping two or three times each year. I have nothing to do with the appointing of this man, but, as I have said, he gets his authority wholly from the Trustees.

Enclosed I send you sample reports, my Annual Report, and the Report of our Treasurer, together with various balance sheets. These are the kind of reports that we have gotten out and given to the public during the last twenty years. I have sent my reports to all the State officers, members of the Legislature and to every daily newspaper in the state and, further, I have said to the public that if anyone desired to get copies of our financial report, we should be very glad to furnish them on application.

I also enclose a statement showing how our Endowment Fund is invested. Since this report was printed, a larger proportion of our Endowment Fund has been invested in Alabama State bonds as referred to in Governor Jelks' message to the Legislature.

Any number of white people from the town of Tuskegee and Macon County have been to me to suggest that they would be glad to go to Montgomery and see you in our behalf to let you know the standing of this institution in this community, but, except in two or three cases, I have suggested to these gentlemen that I did not think it necessary, that I thought you would do the right thing.

During all these years I have done my utmost to carry out the policy outlined in your message and inaugural address.

I am doing everything within my power to maintain peace and friendship between the races, and I believe that it is to the interest of all of us to avoid anything that will stir up strife and create suspicion, and for this reason I very much fear that the present effort on the part of the Legislature will be misunderstood. Yours truly,

[Booker T. Washington]

TLp Con. 6 BTW Papers DLC.

[1] Braxton Bragg Comer (1848–1927), a textile manufacturer of Birmingham, was governor of Alabama from 1907 to 1911 as spokesman of the New South, "business progressivism," and the northern section of the state. His constituency in the "White Counties" had often inveighed against the Black Belt planter-Negro alliance and occasionally threatened to deprive the black schools of even more of their proportionate share of school funds. Comer, however, was neither a racial demagogue nor a racial progressive, and made little change in the racial policies of his predecessors. His chief efforts at reform were railroad regulation and prohibition.

To Edgar James Penney

[Tuskegee, Ala.] Jan. 19, 1907

Mr. E. J. Penney: After giving the whole subject careful and serious attention, and I mean by this not only getting what information I could myself and considering views of other people, but getting the views of the most substantial friends and officers of the institution, I am compelled to reach the opinion that there is nothing left for me to do but to suggest that it will be better for all concerned for you to present your resignation. The plain fact that I must face is that this last occurrence, together with the other one, brings us to the point where it is practically impossible for you to render any further service to the institution that will be of any value. This latter view represents not only the attitude of teachers but students.

In writing as I do, I do not in any degree attempt to pass judgment upon your guilt or innocence, upon your discretion or lack of discretion, I am simply facing the hard, stubborn fact that you cannot in the present state of mind of all connected with the institution, render service of value. Since such a condition exists, I think it would be just as unpleasant and unbearable for you to remain longer as it would be for the school.

In reaching this decision, I hope you will bear in mind that I am not overlooking the long and valuable service which you have rendered this institution and which we have appreciated in the very highest degree. I am quite sure, however, that in the long run you will be happier and more useful elsewhere.

I shall ask you to turn over your work for the present to Mr. Whittaker who will take temporary charge of it.

If I can be of service to you or your family in any manner whatever, please do not fail to command me.

Booker T. Washington

TLpS Con. 578 BTW Papers DLC.

To Estelle C. Penney

[Tuskegee, Ala.] Jan. 19, 1907

My dear Mrs. Penney: In writing your husband as I have been compelled to do, I cannot refrain from making an exception to the general rule which I follow in such cases and express to you how very deeply every student and teacher, officer and friend of the institution sympathizes with you and your family in your present sorrow and trouble. I think it has perhaps seldom, if ever, been true where an individual has so ingratiated herself into the hearts of all the people connected with this institution as has been true of yourself. It has seldom been true, if ever, where there has been a woman connected with the institution who has had such unquestioned confidence of the whole school community as is true of yourself. All this, however, makes the duty which I have been compelled to perform all the more painful and difficult. If I can be of any service in the future to you or to those in your family, please be kind enough to command me.

We very much hope that Emma will decide to remain with the institution. Yours very truly,

Booker T. Washington

TLpS Con. 578 BTW Papers DLC.

To Edgar James Penney

[Tuskegee, Ala.] January 21, 1907

Dear Mr. Penney: I have read your communication of January 21 carefully, and I cannot see any justification or reason why there should be any change in my former decision.[1] I have given practically a whole week of time rather valuable to the school to the consideration of this case. I gave practically a similar amount of time to the consideration of the Lizzie Ranes case, and I am quite sure that it will be a waste of time to consider the matter any further. You will recall that you have had a week in which to state all that you had to say in connection with the case. I regret exceedingly the circumstances that force me to act in the way that I did.

Booker T. Washington

TLpS Con. 578 BTW Papers DLC.

1 Penney asked BTW to defer for a few days his request for resignation to give him time for an interview with BTW, "as I have some things on my mind that you ought to know that concern us both." (Con. 578, BTW Papers, DLC.)

From Charles William Anderson

New York, N.Y., January 21, 1907

(Personal)

My dear Doctor: Stewart called on me the other day, and informed me that Stokes had played false with both him and the Constitution League. He said that he had advised Milholland to send Stokes to Brownsville, for the reason that his color would allow him to get the desired information, without exposing him to the suspicion of acting in behalf of the soldiers. He also stated that Milholland advanced Stokes $375.00 as expense money, and as a precaution to protect him from harm, in case his real mission was suspected, he had him given a letter from one of the assistant editors of the "World," qualifying him as a reporter for that paper, and instructed him to send anything to the paper that he found, which would be of interest. Stewart now claims that Stokes has gone over to the other side. The article in last Monday's "World" (January 14th) was from Stokes's pen. Humphrey and Milholland are violent over Stokes's conduct. It all proves three things. First, that the soldiers actually did the shooting — which of course, nobody doubted, notwithstanding Stewart's lies. Second, that Milholland has not really quit the game, as Roscoe[1] informed you, but has merely withdrawn to cover, and is still furnishing supplies to the men on the firing line. Third, that Stokes cannot play square with any one. He seems to have a mania for double-dealing. As soon as he is given service under any man, he at once begins to look for a chance to betray him, or sell him out. I told you that Simmons was wrong, when he said that Milholland had retired from the game. I have a letter in my possession, which Emmett has read, from Stewart to Milholland, in which Stewart speaks of his negotiations with Simmons, and assures Milholland that Simmons is ready to turn his paper over to the League. Of course, Milholland cannot be so big a fool as to buy this "hand-bill," for it is not worth a drawing of tea, but it shows that Roscoe would play both ends against the middle.

I know of nothing else of interest at this time. Yours truly,

Charles W. Anderson

TLS Con. 35 BTW Papers DLC.

[1] Roscoe Conkling Simmons.

From Francis Ellington Leupp

Washington January 21, 1907

Personal

My dear Dr. Washington: Your letter of January 18 was exactly the sort of thing that I had reason to expect I would get from you—full of good common-sense and constructive suggestion besides. I had no idea of acting immediately in any course that I might decide upon. It was because I wanted to take deliberate counsel, and consider all sides, and consult all authorities whose opinion I respected, that I wrote to you as I did. I believe as heartily as you do in the doctrine of "the psychological moment." The biggest mistakes made in administration unquestionably are the result of taking a wrong time to do a right thing.

I want you also to acquit me, if you have not already done so, of any sympathy with the feeling that prevails among the Indians. The intent in my letter was to convey to you the underlying idea that this was a case of "condition, not theory." I should have taken no notice of any race feeling but for the desire not to let the issue come up in any such way that that feeling might be aggravated.

I am very much obliged to you indeed for your suggestion about Hampton graduates. You struck a fine lead there. You will understand, of course, that my great desire is to get Indians to teaching and governing Indians wherever that can be done under conditions which will assure me that the Indians employed are sympathetic with their own race. I have no use for the professional Indian any more than for the professional negro or the professional anything else — by which I mean the man who makes a livelihood out of an accident of birth, either by vaunting his superiority or inflating his humility. Your suggestion has added one more point to the general programme I have had in mind. A faculty for a school, in which the Hampton-trained Indians and the very best of our negro employees could be brought together, would offer a very interesting field of experiment in the humanities. I shall keep it in mind, and trust you will let me hear from you whenever any additional suggestions occur to you. Sincerely yours,

F. E. Leupp

P.S. Certainly, come to see me whenever you are in Washington and can spare the time. I need not assure you of the cordiality of your welcome.

TLS Con. 352 BTW Papers DLC.

From Emmett Jay Scott

New York, N.Y. Jan. 22, 1907

My dear Mr. Washington: Yesterday (Monday) Fortune, Peterson and I were together with Attorney Smith, to finally settle matters in connection with our affair here. At the last minute, the first named tried to reopen the whole thing and make my visit amount to naught. In spite of my disgust I was compelled to preserve an equable attitude until we could finally decide something.

Although they have no capital now, practically, Mr. Fortune wanted to make the capital stock $100,000. To this I demurred and finally won my point. Then, he wanted the incorporated name to be Fortune and Peterson Co., but I tried to show them that THE AGE PUBLISHING COMPANY would be better, and this name was finally decided upon after considerable discussion.

When we came to the matter of naming directors, he attempted to "fly the coop" by contending that he had stood out in the open for you all these years and that if you were not willing to stand out in the open with him we might just as well call the deal off. He also stated that the idea of incorporating was to get new blood and money into the scheme and he could not understand why you would not be willing to stand out in the same way he has. If you do not come on the directory, he wants me to come on, but I had him consent to hold off the matter of directors until I could talk with you or you with him.

The Conference wound up with an agreement upon all essential matters, and Mr. Smith left the meeting to draw up such agreements as may be necessary, together with articles of incorporation.

In the mean time, Mr. Attwell and I have been plugging away with our plans, and I think we have everything in what might be considered good shape.

I send you herein certain copies which explain themselves. Among others, a subscription offer, a letter which goes to each of the regular agents, a letter to be sent to various individuals whose names are on attached copy soliciting their good offices in connection with our plans. You will notice that the whole correspondence is written in their name and we appear nowhere. In addition, I have drafted a letter to go to all of the names we can get in any part of the country and I have had them agree upon a special offer to these proposed new subscribers at $1.00 each, per year, to begin with. Five thousand of these letters will be sent out.

In addition, I am having a stereotyped advertisement with reference to the subscribers offer and that is to be placed with the important colored newspapers of the country.

In addition also, we are making a bid for advertising with some of the firms and we hope to get them started in this direction.

There are insurmountable difficulties in the way of getting a plant at once for the simple and only reason that Fortune and Peterson absolutely refuse to assume any obligations whatever, either personally or as a firm, unless the money is in sight, and so we will have to get the plant from what money we raise outside. I have got them absolutely to agree, however, that every cent of money raised from capitalization or sale of stock is to be used exclusively in the development of the paper.

I have stuck to this job every moment since I have been here and while a great deal has been done, I could have done considerably more with co-operation from them.

I shall not give up, but shall try to make this thing a go, in spite of them.

Unless I hear from you to the contrary, I shall plan to leave here Thursday or Friday night. Yours truly,

Emmett J. Scott

TLS Con. 45 BTW Papers DLC.

From Braxton Bragg Comer

Montgomery, January 23, 1907

Dear Sir: Yours of the 23rd received and carefully noted.

I do not think the State intends any persecution of your school, and as stated before, you can communicate with me very freely any time you desire. Yours very truly,

B. B. Comer

TLS Con. 6 BTW Papers DLC.

A Sunday Evening Talk

[Tuskegee, Ala.] January 27, 1907

I am going to speak tonight for a few minutes concerning a subject that is not new to you.

People, as a rule, take two views of the object of work. One is the old view; the other is the new view. The old view considers work as something placed in the world as a curse, as a punishment for people; and then in connection with that same idea, people formerly regarded work as being something placed here for the purpose of enabling one to earn a living.

Both of these views are short-sighted. There is scarcely a pig in Alabama that is not able to earn its living. A human being who is only able to do this, is not very much beyond the pig. The new view changes this view of labor. Persons have learned by experience to look upon work as a privilege, as something that is placed here for the highest benefit of human beings, and I want tonight, if possible, for a few minutes, to help you to accept that as the new view of labor. It doesn't apply to any special race, to any special nation, or to any special period of time. You will find that when races or nations get to the point of looking upon labor as a privilege, they are making real progress.

If you will call to mind the successful nations or races, all that have really made a place in life, you will find always without exception, that they are the races or nations that have learned how to work, to labor; they have learned that it is a privilege to work. They have learned that labor constitutes a part of the highest service of any race or nation. And you will learn further in studying history that not only the races and nations that have learned to work are the most successful, but they are also the most happy.

Now there are two classes of people who do not work: the rich who do not work because of an over-abundance of riches — now, none of you have yet reached the point where you are in danger of being considered in the first class: and a second class of people who do not work because of their poverty and ignorance. No matter which class, whether he does not work because of an over-abundance of riches, or because of poverty and ignorance, and natural slothfulness, I wish you would get it thoroughly fixed in your minds that in either case the individual who does not work is the most unhappy, whether a black, or a white individual. Such an individual, whether ignorant, in poverty, or in wealth, is an unhappy individual. One cannot find happiness for any length of time in idleness. It is only in hard work with the hand or head, or both that people find genuine happiness. The persons who are the strongest in body, and healthy are the people who work most with their hands and head. It is impossible for you to enjoy real life unless you have learned to work, and to work hard. Persons who do not work are persons who do not enjoy life. You cannot enjoy your food unless you have a good appetite induced by real, earnest work. It is impossible for persons to live high, moral and spiritual lives unless they have a right view of work.

I want the students of Tuskegee Institute to get it fixed in their minds that there is genuine happiness in work. Never grumble about your work. You never will get all there is out of life until you get away from the old idea that labor is put here to curse individuals; you will never get all out of life until you begin to long for the time to come when you can begin your work. Never be satisfied until you get some kind of employment that will make you happy.

The persons who learn to get real happiness out of employment are the persons who do not commit crime. Think of that.

From now on, I hope that all of you will seek to change your whole point of view with regard to labor; no matter what your work in this institution may be, whether it be sweeping the floor, working on the farm, in the shops, in the class room, in the sewing room, the laundry — no matter where, remember you want to get to the point, as soon as possible, where you will long for the hour to come for the beginning of your labor. If it is the use of the hands in the Industrial Department, or the use of the head in the Academic Department, or in some other department, try to get yourselves to the point where you will get genuine happiness out of everything you do.

If you learn to take this higher view of labor, you will find that you will be laying the foundation for a success that will help you in reaching the topmost rounds of life regardless of opposition. The person who learns to labor for its own sake is the individual, who, when employed, can be found at his duty, ten, fifteen or twenty minutes before the other fellows get there, and will find himself remaining five, ten or twenty minutes after the other fellows have gone. He has learned to accept the new view of labor, and finds that it helps him. It is only in this way that we can make people honor us for what we are in ourselves.

Tuskegee Student, 19 (Feb. 2, 1907), 1.

From Edgar James Penney

[Tuskegee, Ala.] Jan. 28, 1907

Dear Sir: Your last note to me, declining an interview, has been by me for several days.

While I will not trouble you with the things on my mind, since you do not desire to listen, I feel, however, that I must bring to your attention two matters that are vital to me, at this time:

1. Since you have taken my regular work from me, which leaves me idle, I would like to know what arrangement you have made for my salary for the remainder of the year?

2. I would also like to know definitely what is the charge you base your action upon in demanding my resignation? I can not comply till I have a good reason for so doing.

Since you no longer want me at Tuskegee, I do not desire to remain; but wish to be relieved in a proper and honorable manner.

I am still unsettled and am tired of idleness. Respectfully,

E. J. Penney

ALS Con. 578 BTW Papers DLC.

From Pixley ka Isaka Seme[1]

Jesus College, Oxford, England 1, 29, 1907

Dear Sir: I have a cousin in New York City who desired to learn some trade. I have suggested to him the printing trade. I visited Tuskegee last summer with the League, and was carried away with your plant. We need your spirit in South Africa.

My cousin wishes to learn printing and with this can be of untold good at home where we are anxious to establish a sound and intelligent native public opinion. The verdict of my observation comes to this that printing or the press is the greatest emancipator.

Sir, you can do a great deal for our country if you can open the way for this ambitious young man to study under you and particularly printing. Of course the funds to pay his way are ready. If you have an opening for him at once, we should be very glad to have him come. The name of the young man is Bea Mabelubelu Dube.[2] The full particulars about him you may obtain from Mr. Louis Stoiber,[3] 722 Broadway, acting guardian.

I am the Zulu who graduated from Columbia last spring. I am studying law here. Oxford is full of inspiration. Your older son ought to be here. Please give him my address he will remember me. I will be pleased to correspond with him.

Again let me ask that you communicate with Mr. Stoiber about my cousin. Yours very truly

P. ka Isaka Seme

TLSr Copy Con. 359 BTW Papers DLC. Original sent by BTW to BTW Jr.

1 Pixley ka Isaka Seme (1880–1928), a South African black nationalist, graduated from Columbia University and then studied in England before returning to Johannes-

burg, South Africa, in 1910. He then launched a career as a pioneer Bantu lawyer, politician, and journalist. In 1912 he founded and became first president of the African National Congress. He also edited *Abantu Batho*, and in 1913 organized the South African Native Farmers' Association.

2 Not listed in Tuskegee Institute catalogs.

3 Louis Stoiber was for many years chairman of the American committee aiding the Zulu Christian Industrial School at Ohlange, Natal.

To Emmett Jay Scott

Tuskegee Institute, Alabama. Jan. 31, 1907

Mr. Scott: Answering your note regarding your willingness to prepare the data for Mr. Carnegie's speech, I would say that I shall be very glad to have you undertake it. Mr. Carnegie wants to have it thoroughly understood that whoever does this work is to be paid for it.

I would suggest that there are certain parts of it that Mr. Bruce, since he is in Washington where he can get the statistics, might prepare.

I have talked with Mr. Carnegie about it, and I suggest that it be begun so as to have plenty of time to get it up before the time to send it to him. You need not be afraid to put the matter in just the form that he would be likely to deliver it. He wants definite facts showing the material, commercial, educational, moral and religious progress of the race since its freedom. He also wants facts showing how the race is increasing. Under the head of commercial progress he would want, for example, to know the number of drugstores, the number of banks, the number of acres of land. He wants you to show how you reach the conclusion that the Negro is worth, for example, $400,000,000 worth of property. You will remember that we reached that conclusion in correspondence with Mr. Willcox by taking the state of Georgia where it is definitely known how much property the Negro owns by reason of the fact that the tax list for the races is kept separate, and making an estimate based upon that statement. He wants to bring out the fact that the conclusion is reached in this manner.

He wishes to know the number of towns, for example, that have been established and are governed by Negroes. He would like to know the number of industrial schools and colleges, the number of public schools, the number of churches and ministers of various denominations. He is also anxious to have you name a number of individuals who have exceptionally successful careers in one of these three departments. For example, Wm. J. Edwards, of Snow Hill, or some minister who has achieved great success. Also under the head of education he would want all the facts about the Tuskegee Institute, especially those showing how the school has reproduced itself in the growth of the other institutions like Denmark and Snow Hill.

Together with Mr. Carnegie's letter I send you the Willcox correspondence.

Booker T. Washington

TLS Con. 343 BTW Papers DLC.

To Timothy Thomas Fortune

[Tuskegee, Ala.] Jan. 31, 1907

Dear Mr. Fortune: I send the enclosed over the name of "American Spectator" so as to absolve you from responsibility therefor. I shall hope from time to time to contribute other articles over this same nom de plume. Yours truly

Booker T. Washington

[*Enclosure*]

Age If one wants to be made to feel real sick and disconsolate he needs but to share the experience of sitting in an Afro-American meeting and hear two or three Negro speakers speak for two or three hours describing the ills of the Negro race. The chances are, nine out of ten, that during the entire three hours that he may listen to these speeches, not one of the speakers will relate a single fact in connection with the race that everyone in the audience was not previously acquainted with; not only that, the chances are that most of those in the audience will have experienced the very injustice and wrongs which the speakers are describing. Most of the audience could describe better the evils under which the race lives than the speakers themselves. If any one thing in life is certain, it seems to the "American Spectator" it is the sheerest waste of time for so many of our people to spend so much of their valuable hours in listening to these descriptions. No one goes away from such a meeting inspired, no one goes away knowing a single thing that he did not know before. If these speakers would point out some practical method of remedying conditions, it would be quite a different thing, but they confine themselves in most cases to an attempt, and they are usually successful, to work on the emotions of the audience which is wrought up to a high pitch of fervor and enthusiasm through a description of wrong, but as soon as the meeting is over, everyone grows conscious of the fact that not a single new thing has been heard by the audience, that the speaker has taught no lesson, that the people who have heard him are not any more prepared to fight life's battles than they were before, in fact, not as well prepared because in many cases they go away completely discouraged. The time has come in the opinion of the "American Spectator," when much of this policy should be changed. The race should not fail to recognize the wrongs under which it suffers, but it should devote more of its time and energy to finding ways to make progress in the commercial, educational, moral and religious world just as other races are doing, despite the wrongs under which they live. An old colored man down in Mississippi a few days ago paid an admission fee of twenty-five cents to hear a lecture delivered by a very prominent individual of our race. After he had listened for an hour and a half to a description of the wrongs under which the Afro-Americans in Mississippi and elsewhere were living, the old man expressed himself in this way, that if he had known the speaker had come there for the purpose of telling about the wrongs of the race, he could have delivered a much better lecture on that subject than was true of the learned gentleman on the platform, and so it is throughout the country. Our people are fast getting to the point where they are tired and sick of the eternal calling of the attention of the country to their sickness and wrongs. There are not a few members of our race who try to make their living by going about through the country reminding the race of the wrongs under which it suffers. In some places the race makes no effort to go forward in the direction that other races are making progress because it has gotten into the habit of crying and can do nothing else.

American Spectator

New York City

TLpS and TLpSr Enclosure Con. 37 BTW Papers DLC.

To Ray Stannard Baker

[Tuskegee, Ala.] February 1, 1907

Dear Mr. Baker: I beg to return herewith proofs of your article which is to appear in the April American.

Let me tell you how much pleased I am with the careful and impartial way in which you have chronicled events leading up to and succeeding the Atlanta riot. I do feel, however, that I ought to express my disappointment because you use the small N (n) for "Negro" through it. I believe Negro should be capitalized as much as Indian, Filipino, or any other of the race varieties. The New York Tribune, and the Doubleday Page publications carry the capital N for Negro, and I believe you could well do the same thing. Self-respecting Negroes who are not ashamed of the term Negro, are always very much disappointed when they find themselves treated as a common noun, instead of as a race variety carrying capital letters in publications, just as others of our citizenship.

I am sure that great good will follow as a result of the publication of your articles. I have read this one with real interest. Yours truly,

Booker T. Washington

TLpSr Con. 261 BTW Papers DLC. Signed by E. J. Scott.

To Andrew Carnegie

[Tuskegee, Ala.] February 2, 1907

My dear Mr. Carnegie: I hope that you and Mrs. Carnegie are well, and that your daughter is being greatly improved by the Florida climate.

We are gradually getting the memoranda together to be used in connection with your Edinboro speech.

We have just had an expert organ man here in order to decide the question as to which will be the best kind of an organ for our Chapel. I have told him and all others that we must be guided by your suggestion, and it is mine also, that we are to put no organ in the Chapel which will overshadow the voices of the students. This we have kept in mind. I find that the very smallest and cheapest organ that will in any degree answer the purpose will cost $7,500. I have told the dealers that I would not move in the matter until I heard from you. Yours truly,

Booker T. Washington

TLpS Con. 343 BTW Papers DLC.

To Robert Curtis Ogden

[Tuskegee, Ala.] February 4, 1907

My dear Mr. Ogden: I have your good letter of February 1st, and you do not know how very grateful I am to you for it.

I often note that a problem seems more discouraging and disheartening when you are far from it than when you are right in the midst of it. I think if I were to live in the North I would become thoroughly discouraged and disheartened concerning Southern conditions, but being right on the ground one is likely to get many glimpses of light and encouragement which one would not get at a distance; I am not meaning to say, however, that there are not enough happenings to discourage the average man.

I am more and more convinced that you are on the right track in lending encouragement and help to the right-thinking, right-acting white people in the South, that is, in re-enforcing them. The South is full of white people who see all these questions from a right point of view, but they are timid and not willing to speak and act out their convictions as yet.

I spoke in the opera house in Columbia, South Carolina, a few days ago, to an audience composed of blacks and whites. I suppose there were a thousand white people in the audience, and I was told a thousand more were turned away. I have never spoken to a more sympathetic audience. I was told on every hand that the number of people who have no sympathy with Tillman and his utterances is growing.

Of course I may be mistaken, but I think our new Governor[1] is far above the average. So far he has shown interest in the work of this institution, and I hope we may not be disappointed in him in the future.

You do not know how much it pained and disappointed me to be compelled to remain away from the Hampton meetings in New York, and vicinity and also not to be able to deliver the Founder's Day address at Hampton, but as a matter of courtesy to the Governor, as well as a matter of duty, all felt that I ought to be on hand when the commissioner came here. Yours very truly,

Booker T. Washington

TLpS Con. 37 BTW Papers DLC.

1 Braxton Bragg Comer.

To Timothy Thomas Fortune

[Tuskegee, Ala.] February 5, 1907

Dear Mr. Fortune: Enclosed I am sending you some matter of great importance, in which I am deeply interested, relating to the clearing off of the debt on the Frederick Douglass homestead. I am most anxious that you give this matter a prominent place in your paper during the week of February 14th. Other prominent papers are to use it during the same week, and I am very anxious that you do the same thing.

May I further ask that you be kind enough to accompany this with a strong editorial, urging our people to give something to this worthy cause? If each will give just a little, the debt will be cleared off. I shall see that two cuts to illustrate this matter are promptly sent you, and I will be willing, if necessary, to pay any reasonable cost for it, if you will send me bill to cover same.

My whole object in undertaking this matter is to save the homestead of Frederick Douglass, our greatest hero, and I very much hope that we shall have the co-operation of not only the prominent editors, but of the entire race.[1] Yours truly,

Booker T. Washington

TLd Con. 355 BTW Papers DLC.

[1] BTW also wrote to James A. Cobb, urging him to work with the Pen and Pencil Club of Washington in the campaign to raise money for the Cedar Hill mortgage. (Feb. 5, 1907, Con. 344, BTW Papers, DLC.) The Pen and Pencil Club had sent to BTW three weeks earlier a list of forty-two subscribers to the mortgage fund. BTW was the largest contributor on the list at $150. (William L. Pollard to BTW, Jan. 16, 1907, Con. 347, BTW Papers, DLC.)

To Braxton Bragg Comer

[Tuskegee, Ala.] February 5, 1907

Personal and Confidential

Dear Sir: Taking advantage of your kind suggestion to communicate with you freely concerning any matter that we are interested in, I take the liberty of enclosing to you a legal publication which explains itself. This will complete the fourth consecutive week of this publication, and the bill can be introduced any time, as I understand it, after next Thursday.

I think I need not call to your attention the injustice of such a measure, to say nothing of the possibility of its being unconstitutional. I do not think that any such tax is imposed on any institution, white or colored, anywhere in the state of Alabama. This institution is not asking for any additional money from the state, at the same time it does not want to be hindered or oppressed in its work. I know thoroughly the substantial and conservative element of white people in this county, and I know that they have no sympathy with such efforts.

While writing, let me thank you for the kind of a gentleman whom you have appointed to examine our accounts.[1] While I have not been here, from all I can hear of him he is just the kind of man that we wanted you to appoint. Yours truly,

Booker T. Washington

TLpS Con. 6 BTW Papers DLC.

[1] William Wallace Haralson (1861–1938) was a prominent Alabama attorney and judge. A graduate of Cumberland University and of the law school of the University of Alabama, he served in the state senate (1888–89) and house (1900–1901).

To Edgar James Penney

[Tuskegee, Ala.] February 6, 1907

Mr. Penney: Replying to your letter of February 4 I would state that my letter to you of January 30 it seems to me was perfectly clear and self-explanatory in every sentence, and I cannot see the necessity of writing you further on the subject. I meant exactly what I said.

I must call your attention, however, to another matter. In my first communication to you dated January 19, I gave you as you will recall, the opportunity of resigning. I have not received such resignation and unless I do by Friday of the present week I shall have to take a different course to bring about the desired result.

Booker T. Washington

TLpS Con. 578 BTW Papers DLC.

From Edgar James Penney

Tuskegee Institute, Ala. Feb. 6/07

Dear Mr. Washington: Your note was received this afternoon, in reply to mine of Feb. 4, asking for the meaning of yours of Jan. 30, offering me one half of my usual salary, till further notice and the use of my house till further notice.

When I first read the proposition, it seemed like a good offer, and I was about to accept it; but the more I read it, the more indefinite it seemed. That is why I ask for an explanation.

I am very anxious to have this matter settled, in some way, honorable to all concerned. I suppose you are also. I would very much dislike to resign, under pressure, with my salary and good name involved. Both are in your hands.

Allow me to suggest this proposition as a final settlement of this unfortunate affair:

1. That I be paid one half my usual salary till June 1. For, as I stated to you in a former note, I have obligations that are depending upon my salary. It would be a great hardship to be deprived of it, in the middle of the year, without warning.

2. That I be allowed the use of my house, at least, thirty days longer, so as to dispose of my household goods and get away.

Allow me to add further, that I fear you misunderstand my attitude toward you in this sad affair. I am simply trying to find out what is my duty at such a time.

You can afford to be both just and generous to me in this matter. The school, as well as I have been unfortunate in this trouble and should be willing to bear its part.

If you can see your way to accede to the above suggestions (which are really yours made more definite than in your note), I will hand in my resignation by or before Friday, as you requested in your note.

Awaiting your reply I am respectfully,

E. J. Penney

ALS Con. 578 BTW Papers DLC.

From Andrew Carnegie

Fernandina, Florida, Feby 7 1907

My Dear Sir No organ of that kind shall ever be got from me to spoil the finest vocal choir I have listened to since I was in Russia where no instrument is used. Vocal music in our Country is being pushed aside rapidly. You make a great mistake in my opinion in falling into the practice.

You dont know what a perfect choir you have—dont spoil it. Yours always

Andrew Carnegie

ALS Con. 343 BTW Papers DLC.

An Article in the Birmingham *Ledger*

Tuskegee, Ala., Feb. 7 [1907]

WHY CHAPLAIN WAS DISMISSED

From Washington's Institute at Tuskegee

YOUNG GIRL THE CAUSE

Dr. Washington Says Reports of Imprudence Necessitated This Action

On account of the persistent gossip over the resignation of Rev. E. J. Penney, the chaplain of the Tuskegee Institute, the staff correspondent of The Ledger came to this town from Montgomery to investigate.

It seems that three or four days ago there was considerable talk and rumors alleging that Rev. Penney had had improper relations with a ward, who had been placed in his charge by the principal of the Tuskegee Institute. These reports soon became public property, and were being freely discussed in Tuskegee, as well as elsewhere in the state. Following hard upon the rumors was the announcement that Principal Washington had demanded Penney's resignation and that the same had been turned in.

As soon as The Ledger correspondent reached Tuskegee he took a hack for the institute. Principal Washington was called on and informed of the nature of the correspondent's visit. Prof. Washington frankly stated that Penney's resignation had been asked for on grounds that the reports and gossip which were going the rounds concerning him had in the opinion of the trustees brought his usefulness as a member of the Tuskegee Institute faculty, to an end.

Prof. Washington then sent for his secretary and brought in the correspondence between Penney and himself. He also produced a letter which Penney's wife had written, appealing to Dr. Washington to retain Penney. Several letters passed between Washington and Penney in which the former chaplain sought earnestly to have the charges against him dismissed, and begging to be allowed to retain his place in the faculty.

To each one of these appeals Dr. Washington answered that the trustees had considered the case carefully and in view of the rumors they thought it would best subserve the institute for Penny to sever his connections therefrom.

In asking for the resignation Washington made it plain that he was not passing upon Penney's guilt or innocence.

In discussing the case with the Ledger correspondent Dr. Washington said:

"Rev. Penney has been with the Tuskegee Institute for fifteen years. He has made a splendid record. He is naturally of a nervous temperament, but has rendered some very efficient service to the school. Several months ago there was a student sent to the institute from Louisiana. She was very delicate and by request was assigned to board in Rev. Penney's family. Several days ago the gossip became current that Penney had acted very imprudently and that he had over stepped the bounds of propriety in that he had kissed his ward and boarder.

"Without passing upon the veracity of these reports I, with the advice and consent of some of the trustees asked for Penney's resignation, which request has been complied with.

"The records in the case as well as the reports on which I based my action are open to the inspection of the public. It has been stated by one or two persons connected with the institute that if there was any grounds on which to bring proceedings against Penney or if the institute could find any grounds on which to bring proceedings that the same would be done."

The incident has created considerable interest around Tuskegee and many rumors have gotten out concerning the case, but the above facts can be substantiated.

Birmingham *Ledger*, Feb. 8, 1907. Clipping Con. 578 BTW Papers DLC.

From Robert Curtis Ogden

New York February 11th, 1907

Dear Mr. Washington: I am extremely grateful for your two recent interesting letters. I am greatly encouraged by the fact that you believe in my feeling toward the best South as I understand it, whose voice is not heard in any aggregate and consolidated way — here and there a man speaking with human sympathy and conscience, but alone like the voice of one crying in the wilderness. I have felt that there is a slowly developing consciousness that will eventually make itself heard, but I chafe under the delay and am impatient over the things that must be endured in the meantime. My best thinking can reveal no other potent source of progress and reform in our race relations.

There is a fine touch of humor in your experience with the State Commissioner. I am encouraged to think, but without any specific authority, that Mr. Low has accepted the situation concerning Tuskegee and will become the President of your Board of Trustees so soon as the official opportunity may appear. Yours very sincerely,

Robert C Ogden

TLS Con. 37 BTW Papers DLC.

From Adrienne McNeil Herndon[1]

Atlanta Feb. 12th, 1907

My dear Mr. Washington: Last year we broke up our home, took our little son to Philadelphia, put him in school there and since my return we have been occupying rooms in the Univ. dormitory.

The house we occupied for ten years was Dr. Bumstead's home so that I feel we have never had a real home.

The riot and the unsettled conditions here make us feel that we can never hope to have one in this ungodly section. Some times I doubt if there is any spot in this country where one with Negro blood can plant a home free from prejudice scorn & molestation.

The sanctity of the Negro home is to the majority (the vast majority) of the white race a thing unrecognized.

I thank you for the honor you confer upon me by selecting me among the women for your magazine article.

I appreciate it most highly, but I have come to feel that I should like to hide from the eyes of the white man, or any rate the Southern white man the things, I, as a Negro woman hold most sacred for fear they pause & look to jeer and ridicule.

You'll say I am growing pessimistic. Perhaps so, I was born and reared in Ga you know and I live in Atlanta.

My kind regards to Mrs. Washington and my best wishes for the success of your great work there. Gratefully yours,

Adrienne McNeil Herndon

ALS Con. 358 BTW Papers DLC.

[1] Adrienne McNeil Herndon (1869–1910) graduated from Atlanta University in 1891 and became a prominent elocution and drama instructor at her alma mater. She was well known for her dramatic readings and her portrayals of characters from Shakespeare. She married the black businessman Alonzo F. Herndon.

From Timothy Thomas Fortune

New York Feb. 12, 1907

Dear Mr. Washington: The nervous collapse which has been coming for some time, as the result of too much work, reached last Wednesday, and have been doing all I could under disadvantages to keep things in shape. Mr. Malone was to have come two weeks ago, but has not showed up as yet.

I have deemed it necessary to take Peterson back into the office as he is expert in handling copy and as a bookkeeper, and under the incorporation, subject to the laws, I want the responsible secretary and treasurer to handle all of the accounts and keep them straight and to be directly responsible in his position for all of the moneys received and disbursed. He will come into the office as soon as Mr. Anderson can find a man to fill his place. And in the meantime I have transferred to him responsibility for all of the accounts.

It will be my aim to keep the expenditures as closely within the receipts as possible with the proper pushing of the extension of the paper.

In reply to your letter of the 5th instant, I will use the Douglass matter this week, and will try to make the editorial, which I have not been able as yet to do.

I have been grieved by your letter of the 7th, and by letters from Mr. Scott of same date, in which it appears that I have made myself misunderstood by both of you as to the matter you should send and the advice you should give me. I want all of the advice and all of the matter for publication both of you care to send, as I am always receptive of both from all sources, and peculiarly so from you and Mr. Scott, in whom I have implicit faith, both of you furthermore being parts of the business now and as much interested in its well-doing as I am. I may have written out of the ordinary to both of you about this matter because of overwork and nervousness, and if so I regret it, as I want the utmost freedom on the part of both of you to send me matter for publication and advice.

But we should have an understanding of the policies upon which we agree and disagree for editorial treatment. You send me two editorial notes this week which put me in reversal of policy if I should use them — advising the race to remain out of the North and endorsing the President as against Foraker. To adopt either and hammer it would smash the paper with its readers. I have nothing to say over your signature or nom de guerre, say what you will and I will use it. I have lost faith in Roosevelt, lost it before we reached the Gauley, and his action in the soldier business and appointment by threat to worry his enemy in Ohio is bad policy, not based in sincerity. He had done you dirt in the soldier business and the Ohio business, as he should not have dragged you into it. But I have nothing to do with all this except that I will not subscribe to it editorially because I donot believe in it and because it would ruin the paper. And I am not stuck on Foraker. But I only wish you to see that we must have an understanding as to policies and men to be treated editorially, and we can well reach a conclusion.

As to matters of business I am writing to Mr. Scott by this mail. I thought it best to fetch the letters of both of you to Red Bank and answer them to-day, rather than dictate them.

With my kind regards, and hoping all goes well, Yours sincerely,

T. Thos. Fortune

TLS Con. 35 BTW Papers DLC.

From George Bruce Cortelyou

Washington February 16, 1907

Personal.

My dear Mr. Washington: I have your letter of the 7th instant,[1] and beg to state that the gentleman[2] you mention is not an employee of this Department. At one time he was president of one of the pneumatic tube companies which had a contract with the Department, but recent correspondence has elicited the fact that he is not actively connected with any of those companies at the present time. Very sincerely yours,

Geo. B. Cortelyou

TLS Con. 7 BTW Papers DLC.

[1] Not found in the BTW Papers or the Theodore Roosevelt Papers.

[2] John E. Milholland.

From Anna Thomas Jeanes

Friends Home Germantown [Pa.] 2/16–1907

You read an Item in my Will, I wish to carry it out in my life time — but do not rush an old lady in her Eighty-fifth year, my disabled hand interferes with my copying the Item, and I do not want it done by another.

The friend who was to help me wants his own way and I do not approve, he talks of one Trust Company in the North with a Trustee, I would rather you and Hollis Burke Frissell would think it out and let me know what is best.[1] Respectfully

Anna T. Jeanes

ALS Con. 796 BTW Papers DLC.

[1] Frissell replied to Jeanes, after discussion with BTW, that it would be better not to have on the board of trustees the officers of the trust companies, who might be good businessmen but not necessarily interested in black rural education. (Feb. 22, 1907, Con. 348, BTW Papers, DLC.)

From Anna Thomas Jeanes

Friends Home Germantown [Pa.] 2/17–1907

I did not approve of only *One* Trust Company to hold the Fund, but the securities divided equally between three of our best Philadelphia Companies is satisfactory to me. The deed of Trust says

"*In Trust* to keep the said fund invested in good and safe securities and after the payment of all necessary expenses, to pay over the net income thereof, from time to time, to Booker T. Washington and H. B. Frissell, or to such association or corporation as they, in conjunction with the Trustees above mentioned may hereafter form, having for its sole purpose the maintenance and assistance of rudimentary rural and community schools for Colored people."

Do you, and H. B. Frissell, approve? Respectfully

Anna T. Jeanes

ALS Con. 796 BTW Papers DLC.

From Edgar James Penney

Tuskegee Institute, Feb. 18, 1907

Dear Sir: I have considered, from every point of view, your letter of February 9th, offering me half salary and the use of my house "until the close of the present school term" "unless there is some special reason for the revocation of this promise." This seems much more definite than simply "till further notice," of your former note, and even here the words, "special reason" put me entirely at your discretion. But, as it seems the wisest course to pursue, under the circumstances, I accept the conditions, and shall endeavor to keep my side of the arrangement, whether "the school term" means till June 1st, or August 31st.

Please, remember, however, I do this, 1st admitting no guilt in this affair, but under pressure, as I told you in another note. Being innocent and not responsible for this state of things, I can not plead guilty. I am poor, helpless and *alone*, therefore I, to this extent, yield. 2nd, I accept this arrangement, not admitting you have any right to deprive me of any of my salary for the year Sept. 1st 1906 to Aug. 31, 1907. Nine ($950) hundred and fifty dollars.

The salary is mine, with "one month or six weeks vacation." The rest of the time is the school's, and well have I, till now, used it, in the school's interests, as well as the most of my vacation time.

But you have treated me in this case, as though I had had a fair trial and had been found guilty and dismissed, in disgrace. That is the news that has gone out to the country. I have heard of it from several states already, and it has hardly begun to travel. You could not have planned better to do me and my family the greatest human injury, and all, because you would not listen to but one side and acted prematurely and hastily in not granting me the asked for interview; and in demanding my resignation & in taking my work from me, before knowing all the facts.

I feel it my duty, as a man and a father to say these last words to you.

Might may not always make right. I am still trusting God. I can not, yet, see why He has allowed you to treat me thus. I can wait His time.

Permit me one more thought. I am seeking new work. It is natural that I should have a suitable line or two from you after such a long service at Tuskegee.

Will you give me a recommendation, so that I may, in part, the easier, overcome this false rumor (that has already divided itself into several versions), and "in the long run be happier and more useful elsewhere"? (See your letter, Jan. 19, 1907).

I do not know, now, how you could be of better service to me and my family than in some such way (see same letter). I await your answer. Meantime, I am preparing to leave Tuskegee, whenever I secure other work. I shall always love Tuskegee Institute. It is our school; we helped to make it. I would not, willingly, lift a finger to harm it. I wish I might also continue to be your friend. Respectfully,

E. J. Penney

ALS Con. 578 BTW Papers DLC.

From William Estabrook Chancellor

Washington, D.C. February 22, 1907

Dear Dr. Washington: I have not answered your letter with regard to my impressions of white teachers at Hampton as compared with colored teachers at Tuskegee until now, as I had not fully made up my mind. For your purposes at Tuskegee I believe the introduction of a considerable number of white men would be very unfortunate. For the purpose of the elevation of the colored race, I believe that at present for the good of the South, the more positions of honor and responsibility that can be created and maintained for colored men and women, the better. I don't believe from what I saw at Hampton that the difference in the quality of the work is due so much to the quality of the white teachers as such as it is to the proportionate cost per capita of the instruction there. I believe, if you had enough colored teachers in Tuskegee on equally good salaries as those of the white teachers at Hampton, that you could get as good results. There was an enthusiasm in the relation of the colored youth to the colored teachers at Tuskegee that I missed between the white teachers and colored youth negro and Indian at Hampton. I believe that this enthusiasm is priceless in the elevation of a race. Permit me to renew strongly the expressions that I used when I was at Tuskegee, regarding the magnitude and value of your work. Anything whatever that I can do to encourage men in the North to support that work I shall be only too glad to do. Very sincerely yours,

Wm E Chancellor

TLS Con. 364 BTW Papers DLC.

To Andrew Carnegie

[Tuskegee, Ala.] February 23, 1907

My dear Mr. Carnegie: I meant to have written you earlier about the organ matter. The fact is, you know more about organs than all the rest of us. I shall follow your advice and let the matter drop.

Our choir is improving all the time, and I hope you will hear it again. Yours truly,

Booker T. Washington

TLpS Con. 343 BTW Papers DLC.

To Henry Huddleston Rogers

[Tuskegee, Ala.] February 25, 1907

My dear Mr. Rogers: I thought you might like to see the enclosed copy of a letter written by Mr. Seth Low.

I think it is very probable that a friend will make a considerable donation soon for the same kind of primary school work that you are so generously helping. That will enable us to extend the work over a wider territory. Yours truly,

Booker T. Washington

TLSr Copy Con. 37 BTW Papers DLC.

Charles William Anderson to Emmett Jay Scott

New York, N.Y., February 25, 1907

(Personal)

Private.

My dear Mr. Scott: Replying to your favor of the 22nd instant, permit me to say that from a source which I do not care to mention on paper, of which the Doctor will advise you, I learned that Du Bois, Wetmore and Owen Waller met in Wetmore's room at the Hotel Marshall, during Du Bois's recent visit to this city. At this conference, or interview, Du Bois took occasion to criticise the Doctor and myself as frauds, and to say that you were a very mean and rascally person. He paid you the very high compliment of being the man who inspired all the mischief that is hatched out at Tuskegee. As for myself, he found no colors black enough in which to paint my picture. The same was true with reference to his estimate of the Doctor. The Doctor will tell you that I have a way of finding out what goes on in the office or the apartment of Brother Wetmore.

I learned from the same source, that during Wetmore's visit to Washington, Judge Terrell accused both the Doctor and myself of working against Gilchrist Stewart. This accusation was made to Wetmore in strictest confidence. Terrell volunteered the statement that I was working in New York to have Stewart unseated, as a member of the Republican County Committee, and that I ought not to do it, because of Stewart's great services to the race in the Brownsville matter. He said much more along this line that is not worth repeating. As you know, Stewart is a member of the Contesting Delegation from the 13th Assembly District, to the Republican County Committee of this County. This Delegation was unseated in all of the preliminary conventions, and its contest is now before the Committee on contested seats of the County Committee. I have never opened my mouth to Congressman Parsons,[1] who is Chairman of the County Committee, against Stewart or any of his colleagues on the Delegation. Stewart, however, has written the Congressman, that to unseat his crowd, would leave the impression that it was done because of his interest in the Brownsville matter. Thus you will see, that while he is using the soldier incident to have his contest decided in his favor, he is accusing others of using the same incident to have it decided against him. I wrote these facts to Congressman Parsons, and am enclosing copies of his answers to me. I need not assure you, that whatever I have done toward building up Solomon Johnson, who lives in Stewart's district, was to gain strength for myself, rather than to weaken Stewart. I don't want to make enemies for any man in politics; I only want to make friends for myself. I think Judge Terrell had better take a stitch in his tongue. The trouble with him is, that his term of office covers the term of the President, and he, therefore, feels that the Doctor can be of no more service to him. Hence, he is "a

Washington man" when the Doctor is around, and yet he manages to give his approval and support to all of his enemies.

Please pardon me for wasting so much paper on such cattle. Please let the Doctor read this letter. Yours truly,

Charles W. Anderson

TLS Con. 35 BTW Papers DLC.

[1] Herbert Parsons (1869–1925), a New York lawyer, was a member of the board of aldermen in New York City from 1900 to 1904 and served in the U.S. House of Representatives from 1905 to 1911. He was a delegate to the Republican national conventions of 1908, 1912, 1916, and 1920.

To Hollis Burke Frissell

N. Y. [City] Mar 1 [190]7

Important that you meet me here Monday or Tuesday. As matters now stand should Miss J.[1] die we would get nothing. She is not well.

Booker T. Washington

AWcSr Con. 796 BTW Papers DLC. Addressed to Frissell at Penn School, Frogmore, S.C.

[1] Anna Thomas Jeanes.

From Horace Bumstead

Boston, Mass. March 1, 1907

My dear Dr. Washington: The recent action taken at Tuskegee in regard to Rev. Edgar J. Penney has raised some questions which it seems desirable to bring to your attention. As Mr. Penney is not only a graduate but also a trustee of Atlanta University, his reputation and future usefulness cannot fail to be matters of deep concern to our Board as well as to all friends of our Institution.

We realize that all the facts in the case may not be before us, and if we have been misinformed we shall be grateful for any correction.

As we understand it, Mr. Penney has been dismissed from Tuskegee, or his resignation required, because of certain charges of immoral conduct which he positively denies and the truth or falsehood of which has not been determined by any impartial tribunal. If Mr. Penney is morally unfit to be a teacher at Tuskegee he is also unfit to be a trustee of Atlanta University. But how are we to know whether he is or not if you do not know?

If this question is left to our Board to determine, there are certain points on which it is important that we have accurate information. So far as we have been informed, the charges referred to are based solely on the testimony of a young girl student whose own character and testimony have been impeached by letters found in her trunk, the discovery of which has resulted in her own dismissal from Tuskegee. If there has been any corroborative evidence of her testimony, it would seem important for us to have it.

We understand also that in all the many years that Mr. Penney has worked at Tuskegee his moral character has never been assailed but in one previous instance, in which case, after careful investigation, he was completely vindicated; and yet that this former case has been coupled with the present one as a basis of the action just taken against him. If we have been misinformed as to this, we desire to know the truth.

I trust that you will realize that in making these enquiries I have in view not only the preservation, if possible, of the good name of a man who for more than thirty years has been rendering faithful and valuable Christian service, but also the good name of the two institutions with which he has been so closely identified. Yours very sincerely,

Horace Bumstead

TLS Con. 364 BTW Papers DLC.

Emmett Jay Scott to Theodore Roosevelt

Tuskegee, Alabama, March 8, 1907

My dear Mr. President: I have the honor to ask you to issue an order that six of the batteries of Field Artillery and not less than eighteen of the companies of the Coast Artillery added by act of congress, approved January 25, 1907, be recruited with colored men.

I ask the above favor for my race for some of the reasons which follow:

1. Their bravery in the Civil War, in the Indian Campaigns, in the War with Spain. In this latter war they fearlessly used four Hotchkiss mountain guns with good effect. (See "The Colored Regulars in the U.S. Army," a book by T. G. Steward, Chaplain 25th Infantry, U.S.A.)

2. Some of the best shots in the army of the U.S. are colored men belonging to the colored cavalry and infantry regiments. A man that can learn to shoot one gun can learn to shoot another.

3. They possess sufficient intelligence. Many of the men at present in the army are especially intelligent, alert and ambitious fellows. They do the most, or all, of the clerical work of their regiments.

4. There are not many desertions from the colored regiments. Cognizance has been taken of the fact that there is increased desertion by white soldiers from the army and navy, and the credit on this score is altogether with the colored soldiers.

5. Last but not least, our population and the progress we have made since slavery was abolished entitle us, we believe, to the recognition above sought. There has never been in the regular army a company of colored artillery, and as only men of superior intelligence are enlisted for that branch of the service, our most intelligent men deserve a chance to prove their ability and serve their country in the artillery branch of the service the same as white soldiers of similar qualifications do.

I have been informed that the War Department in the past has been of the opinion that colored men with sufficient intelligence to make good artillerymen cannot be found. This was doubtless true in the '60s and in the period immediately following, but does not hold good now as a trial, I am sure, will show. Whenever given an opportunity, as at Las Guasimas in 1898, they have acquitted themselves creditably.

Since the four lone regiments by which we are represented in the army give a ratio not at all equal to that of the white regiments to the white population, it has occurred to me that as a matter of simple justice you might care to consider the above suggestion.

During the many changes or reorganizations which have been made in the army since the first reorganization after the Civil War, the Negro people since the first six regiments were authorized, have received no favors at the hands of congress or the War Department. In 1866 two full regiments of cavalry and four of infantry were authorized by an act of congress. In 1869 the four colored regiments of artillery were [merged] into two.

In 1898 the five regiments of artillery were increased to seven.

In 1901 five regiments of infantry were added to the army, also five regiments of cavalry, and the artillery was reorganized and changed from regimental to the corps formation.

The 14 or 15 batteries of light or field artillery were increased to 30, and the 70 or 80 batteries of heavy artillery increased to 120 and designated as Coast Artillery.

In all of these reorganizations, as you will note, nothing has been done for the colored regiments aside from reducing them from six to four regiments. Not one addition of any kind has been made.

In conclusion, I am pleased to say, and with pride, and as testified to by yourself on a number of occasions and by the honored Secretary of War, Hon. William H. Taft, in his address at Tuskegee in April, 1906, the Negro people have made great progress along intellectual and financial lines commensurate with the opportunities which have been offered them. The colored soldiery I feel have done likewise, and if given this opportunity will be encouraged and helped.

Thanking you in advance for any consideration you may be able to give this matter, I am, Yours very truly,

Emmett J Scott

TLSr Copy Con. 7 BTW Papers DLC.

An Item in the *Tuskegee Student*

Cambridge, Mass., March 12, 1907

PRINCIPAL WASHINGTON AT HARVARD UNIVERSITY

Dr. Booker T. Washington of the Tuskegee Institute, spoke to Harvard students in the Harvard Union Building last night. The room was crowded and even the windows and gallery were filled. The speaker was introduced by President Eliot who emphasized the importance of young men getting a clear conception of Dr. Washington's life and work. The address was full of enthusiasm and candor and wisdom; it was oratorical and witty and forceful from beginning to end, and time and time again the speaker was cheered to the echo.

The applause went wild when the speaker, raising himself to his full height, and taking on a most serious and earnest look, remarked with a slightly nervous tremor of the hand and lips:

"If I could be born again and the Great Spirit should say to me: 'In what skin do you wish to be clothed,' I should answer, 'make me an American Negro!' "

These words lent inspiration to every Negro present, and won for the speaker and the race immeasurable respect from the whites.

After the address, Messrs. Edwin French Tyson[1] and Walter S. Buchanan,[2] both of the class of 1907 at Harvard University, escorted Dr. Washington to their room, 22 Hastings Hall, where he met and addressed informally all of the young colored men in the University. Mr. Buchanan graduated from Tuskegee Institute with the class 1899.

Booker T. Washington, Jr. and Mr. Charles Alexander, Editor of Alexander's Magazine, were in the party.

Tuskegee Student, 19 (Mar. 16, 1907), 1.

1 Edwin French Tyson received an M.D. degree from Howard University Medical School in 1911.

2 Walter Solomon Buchanan (b. 1882) later became a president of Alabama State A & M College for Negroes in Normal, and a director of the Standard Life Insurance Co.

From Harry C. Smith

Cleveland, O. March 13, 1907

Dear Mr. Washington: Your letter of the 9th received. For more than a year I have noticed at frequent intervals that you have been quoted in exchanges as using the expression "that the southern whites were the best friends of the race" and I have an indistinct remembrance of having read words to that effect quoted as coming from your speech or speeches. If the papers quoting you as making this expression and my remembrance are wrong, I am glad to know it I assure you, and with your permission will take pleasure in trying to correct the wrong impression which I am satisfied many others hold beside myself.[1] I believe you are satisfied that The Gazette tries to be fair, just and right and will not wrong you or any other person or thing intentionally or knowingly.

I noticed in the New York World a statement relative to the probable finding of the committee of the Alabama legislature which has been investigating Tuskegee's financial conduct and the probable outcome of the effort to tax the grounds of the institution, with a great deal of satisfaction. If the information given out by that paper is correct, please accept my sincerest congratulations. There have been Ohio "Solons" who have been silly and foolish enough to introduce measures directed toward our people as contemptible as those you call attention to, of the Alabama assembly.

Trusting you will find time to call when in the city en route to Oberlin and have a talk, as indicated, and with sincerest best wishes, I am, Yours for the race,

H. C. Smith

TLS Con. 382 BTW Papers DLC.

1 BTW replied: "In regard to the statement, what I have said is that we have some white people in the South who are as good friends as can be found anywhere else." (Mar. 19, 1907, Con. 382, BTW Papers, DLC.)

To Samuel Laing Williams

[New York City] March 21, 1907

My dear Mr. Williams: In connection with my visit to Chicago, April 5th, 6th and 7th I wish you would if possible arrange for me to meet the colored students of the University of Chicago. When I spoke at Harvard a few days ago I had the pleasure of meeting all the colored students in a separate meeting and if it is possible I should like to meet the colored students of the University in the same manner. Very truly yours,

[Booker T. Washington]

TLc Con. 37 BTW Papers DLC.

From John Perry Powell

Zeidab-Soudan, Egypt, Mar. 23, 1907

Dear Mr. Washington, I have been wanting to write you for some time and let you know how I was getting on with my work in the Soudan but as I was so long settling on some particular work, I thought that I had but a very little to say.

When I arived here in January 1905, I was put in charge of the garden whitch covered about two acres of land. I remained at this work for about two Mounths and after this I was transfured to take charge of the company's farm whitch was about five miles away and contained about one hundred acres of land. My principal work here was to harvest the crop and I employed on an average of thirty men and boys daily. As there was no one here for me to converse with in English, I soon learned to speak Arabic well enough so as to transact any business with the natives whitch fitted me for the following work that I am about to mention.

After the harvesting of this crop, this farm was closed out & was transfured to the head quarters so as to open up a new and larger farm. This farm now covers more than three thousand acres of land most of whitch I cleared.

After making a very good start in opening up our new farm, our assistant manager of this company who was also superintenden[t] of canalization died. The manager sent for me and told me that he wanted me to take charge of canalization and one after noon I went with him over the work whitch he explained and turned over to me. At that time this work covered about five hundred acres and I extended it over three thousand acres of land with out any complaint against my work and during this time I worked more than seven hundred men at a time and my average number daily was about five hundred men all of whos[e] work I had to direct and whos[e] account I had to keep.

Near the completion of this work, the season opened up for planting crops so I thought that I could make more by taking up a farm of my own and then gave up this work and took up a farm. I think I have made a very fair crop & will make some money. It was judged that my crop was the best grown at the Syndicate and I was rewarded the *first* agricultural prize being twenty five dollars ($25.00). On [owing] to the fact that our water supply was late, we have not grown very much cotton but with what little we have grown here I would say that this is a very good country for cotton growing & most general agricultural products. Our principal crops have been wheat, barley, clover & native corn.

All of the other boys have been in very good health with an exception of a little fever, nothing serious or unusual.

Each of them Messrs C. W. Triplett; J. B. Twitty[;] Ocie R. Burns & Poindexter Smith have done good service for themselves the Syndicate especially and for the school. Mr. Triplett has done excelant work at his trade & also teaching the native boys to speak English. He has taught many of them to read & write a little. The school he operated it in his own time and expence with the cooperation of the other boys mentioned above. Mr. Twitty has done some excelant work in construction of a short railroad line. I am very sorry that I have no illu[s]tration to send you of the work that Mr. Smith has done in puting up an eighty feet smoke-stack for a boiler on the banks of the Nile river. He does all the blacksmithing and machine shop work for a Thirty H Power engine & a sixty H Power engine. Mr. Smith now gets a salary of $100.00, one hundred dollars per mounth.

My best wishes for yours and the success of the school. I am,
Yours most sincerely

John P. Powell
Class, '03

ALS Con. 357 BTW Papers DLC.

To Carroll Davidson Wright

[Tuskegee, Ala.] March 26, 1907

My dear Mr. Wright: I want to write you regarding a matter which for the present I wish you would consider as confidential, and which I feel deeply concerned about.

I see in the newspapers and also in one of the publications of the Department of Economics and Sociology of the Carnegie Institution that Mr. Alfred H. Stone is to make an investigation covering the life of the Negro in slavery and freedom so far as the economic elements are concerned. I think I have read with some care almost everything that Mr. Stone has printed on this subject, and I think I am safe in saying that without exception there has been but one conclusion to his investigations, and that is in plain words, to damn the Negro. There are very few white men who have been reared in the South who would be capable of not putting prejudice into such an investigation, and I repeat that I feel quite sure, judging by Mr. Stone's previous utterances, that he is not the man to make such an investigation, I mean that will demand respect and confidence. He and I have had considerable correspondence on the subject of the progress of the Negro and I know him pretty well. I have tried over and over again to get him to come to Tuskegee or go to Hampton or some other institution and see something of the effects of rational education on the life of the Negro, but I have never succeeded in getting him to go where he could see for himself what is being accomplished. I think the man, in the second place, has been soured by failure in cotton raising in Mississippi.

I should raise practically the same argument against a Negro making this investigation, he would be too much biased in the other direction. Of course I suppose such an investigation will cover the effect of industrial education on the life of the Negro. You can see for this reason alone, if for no other, that a man ought to be appointed to this work who is of the highest scientific ability and who would not let his feelings or previous association enter in any way into it. Already quite a number of colored people have spoken to me about this matter and they feel the same way that I do. You have perhaps noticed that only a short time ago Mr. Stone made a comparison between Italian labor and Negro labor in Arkansas with the usual result of his investigation, that is, to prove the Negro a failure as compared with the Italian. Yours truly,

B. T. W.

TLI Copy Oswald Garrison Villard Papers MH.

To Horace Bumstead

[Tuskegee, Ala.] March 27, 1907

Dear Dr. Bumstead: Replying to your letter of recent date, bearing upon the case of Mr. Penney, I would state that, I do not see how I can serve you better than to send you a copy of the letter which I wrote Mr. Penney. Your letter raises the question as to several details or incidents in connection with this case. It seems to me I had better not enter into a discussion of details, for if I do so in one case I should have to do so in others and that would result in a very long correspondence.

I would state further that our Trustees and other officials considered carefully and fully the seriousness of the case both as regards Mr. Penney and his family and other connections as well as the interest of the institution. We took plenty of time in which to weigh all points and could reach no other conclusion than the one indicated in my letter.

As pointed out in my communication to Mr. Penney, some years ago a similar charge was brought against him; and after careful consideration of the matter we decided to give him the benefit of every doubt and he was retained, but in that case several members of the committee who sat upon the case, as well as other prominent officials, felt that we made a mistake in retaining him in the service of the school, and for a number of years his influence at the school was seriously crippled and hampered by reason of the charge brought against him. The memory of the first case was beginning to completely disappear when the second case came to light. You can easily understand that under the circumstances Mr. Penney's influence at this institution was at an end, and we felt that it would be the most kindly thing for him, and certainly the best thing for the institution, to be frank and firm and say as much to him. We have always taken the position that a school is not a court of law, that it is the duty of the court to prove a person guilty; in the case of a school we take the position that whenever a student or teacher gets into a position where his influence is hurtful that the school has a right to part with such an individual.

Enclosed I send you a copy of a letter which I wrote Mrs. Penney which I think embraces the universal opinion of all upon our grounds.

You do not know how seriously we regret this unfortunate occurrence, but there was but one course to pursue in the matter. Yours truly,

Booker T. Washington

I think you will find that you have a record at Atlanta University to the effect that he was charged with a similar offense while a student at Atlanta. This is the information I have received from a graduate of Atlanta University who knows about it.

TLpS Con. 364 BTW Papers DLC.

An Address to the Theological Department of Vanderbilt University

Nashville, Tennessee, March 29, 1907

Dean Tillett and Gentlemen: I am very glad to be here; I have never been in the city of Nashville without hearing from the leading colored people and from the officers and instructors in the large colleges and universities for my race located in this city about the interest that Vanderbilt University is constantly manifesting in the education of the colored people right here in this city. In fact, it has been less than two hours since I met a company of men who were speaking to me about the special acts of kindness shown by members of the faculty of the Theological Department of Vanderbilt University.

I was born a slave. I was born here in the South and I am proud that I have always lived in the South. By the grace of God, I intend always to live here and teach my children to live here, and right here in the heart of the South I hope to be buried.

In considering the claims of my race upon your sympathy and upon your thoughtful and unselfish helpfulness, I think it should always be borne in mind that, unlike any other portion of the American people, we did not come here of our own accord. Whatever problems, whatever difficulties have grown out of our presence here, please always remember that they are not of our especial making; so far as our desire to come to America is concerned, we were forced into this country against our will and against our most earnest protest. That fact alone, it seems to me, gives us a claim upon the generous and helpful consideration of the Christian men of America that cannot be true in the same degree of any other race.

Now, if in my talk this afternoon, I seem to omit the duty which the Negro race owes to himself and owes to you in the working out of the problems to which reference has been made, I hope you will bear in mind that when I am speaking to my own people, I speak frankly and plainly and pointedly concerning their duty to you. There is quite a difference, however, between speaking to a people and about a people. I was in New York City a few days ago and in an address which I was to deliver there, a gentleman urged me to speak something about the white people of the South. Well, I said to him, when I am in the South I will say to the Southern white people what I have to say to them.

I shall try to follow the instruction given me by your Dean, to speak to you for a minute concerning the manner in which I think the Christian men of the South can be of service to my race, and therefore, of service to our entire Southland.

In my opinion, we are here to stay. So far as I can discern the activities and the ambitions of the masses of my race, I do not believe that the time will come in this or any other near generation, when any large proportion of them will leave the South for any other portion of the United States, or for any foreign territory. So, it seems to me, that we had just as well make up our minds that both of us are here to stay, as I discern no signs of your going away. (Laughter.)

I suppose you have heard the story of the old colored man in Virginia who had lived on a plantation up there for about seventy years, in slavery and in freedom. One of the young men who used to be a part owner of this old fellow went to New York to live and afterwards went back to his Old Virginia home for a little visit. He found this old colored man around there and he got a little impatient with the old fellow because of his slothfulness and because of the way in which he performed some of his duties. He said to him one morning, "Jim, I think we will have to part; I can't put up with your slothfulness and carelessness any longer; Jim, I think we shall have to part." The old fellow replied, "Boss, I's sorry for it, but I don' know whar you is a-goin." (Laughter.)

We don't want to part from you and you don't want to part from us. If you want to see a real lonesome Southern white man, meet him in Europe or somewhere in a portion of the world where he can't see any colored people; he is the most lonesome creature you ever saw. Both of us, in my opinion, are here to stay. When two races are living in the same country, are living side by side, it seems to me that the only logical, the only sensible course for those races to pursue is to find methods by which they can live together in peace, in harmony and in complete friendship.

It is so often true of races as of individuals, each race becomes so wrapped up in the prosperity or happiness of its own race that in too many cases it forgets the duty that it owes to the other race, especially to the weaker race that is right by its side, forgetting the fact that it and its interests are not the only interests to be considered.

I believe that the educated young men of the South can be of service in the present condition of our progress in a larger degree than has been true in the past if in every large — perhaps I should modify that and say — if in many of the large colleges and universities there were sociological departments in which young men of education, of proper balance, of command of mind and body, could pursue, in a larger degree than has been true, original investigation as to the condition existing among our people right here in the South. And I wish very much that, more in the future than in the past, educational institutions might pursue lines of original, first-hand investigation as to the physical, the industrial, the educational, the moral and religious condition of the colored man who is right in their community. It is too often a fact, my friends, that the white man who lives nearest to the Negro is ignorant in regard to the Negro's real progress. Too often ignorant of what is taking place right in the community where he lives. Something is said by A regarding the condition of the colored people, that is repeated to B, then he repeats it to C, and then to D, and very soon that remark goes all through the county, and then all through the state, not one person stopping to make an original, first-hand investigation for himself. For example, I was with a gentleman of considerable prominence not very long ago who was discussing the Atlanta riot which took place last September, and this gentleman was above the average in intelligence and in general information, and he remarked in my presence once or twice during the conversation, that hundreds of Negro students in the Atlanta colleges were the leaders in that riot, that they were the leaders in hiding the colored criminals. Well, now, as a matter of fact, not a single Negro college in Atlanta was in session during the period of that riot, not one had opened its doors for the admission of students for the fall session. But that gentleman had simply heard that remark and had not stopped to find out the untruthfulness of it, and so the statement went the rounds.

In material, industrial and economic directions, I fully realize all the shortcomings of my race; I never attempt to hide them, never attempt to minimize them; but I believe you can help us, again, in this regard: You can help us in economic and industrial directions and to make ourselves of greater service to the communities in which we live, of greater service to the white people where we reside, by exerting an influence wherever you can, from the pulpit, from the public platform, through the medium of the public press — an influence that will call attention to the Negro or Negroes in that community who perform service well. Now, so often you see this statement in many of our newspapers: The Negro is a failure as a laborer; the Negro as a race is worthless. I suppose within the past year I have read, in effect, that statement more than a dozen times in some of our best newspapers. Now those writers did not mean exactly that. They meant to say that some Negroes are shiftless and lazy; some Negroes cannot be depended upon. Every one of those individual writers could have called the names of dozens and perhaps scores of colored people right in their community who, in the matter of industry and in the matter of promptness, who in the matter of conscientious service or reliability, were equal to almost any members of any other race in the same relative stage of civilization. Now, you do not know, my friends, how much it will help the best among our people to grow better; you don't know how much it will encourage them if, through your various public utterances, you try to call attention to the helpful Negro, to the successful Negro. It is not very encouraging when all of them are put in a "bunch" and all damned together. If you would single out these individuals, single out these groups and hold them up to the masses of the white people and the masses of my people as examples and place the emphasis upon the positive instead of the negative side of life, I believe that in that respect you would prove of great service to us as a race.

And I believe, too, that the South should call attention more often than it does to the general progress that our people are making. And you have a right to be proud of this progress. I shall never forget the impression that a Southern white man, in the little town of Tuskegee, where I live, made upon me some weeks ago when he passed a grocery store, and with one exception I think it is the largest and most successful grocery store in that town, owned by a colored man, and pointed to that Negro merchant and pointed to his store and said, "I am proud of that man. I owned the father of that man and I am proud of his success." We get so much in the habit of dwelling upon our difficulties that I am afraid too often we fail to emphasize the progress that both races are making in the working out of this tremendous problem. But when we consider, my friends, the complications of this problem, when we consider the seriousness of it, when we consider your part and my part, when we consider where we started forty years ago, I believe that we have every reason to congratulate ourselves that we have done as well as we have and have had as few difficulties as we have had. We have every reason to feel proud of the success that has been made in the solution of this problem. (Applause.)

Why, a few days ago, a gentleman in another part of the country was referring to the woes existing down here, and I said to him: Do you know that the Negro race in the South, since it became free, in the state of Virginia, for example, has gotten to the point where it pays taxes upon one twenty-sixth of the land in that state; that in the counties east of the Blue Ridge Mountains in Virginia it owns one-sixteenth of the soil. I said to him, do you know that in the state of Georgia, the Negro owns and pays taxes upon $18,526,000 worth of property? And that statement, my friends, leaves out of consideration what the Negro owns in the state in the form of town and city lots, and perhaps it also leaves out of consideration the further fact that the Negro might have learned the lesson from his white neighbor, not to give in his property for taxation purposes at its full taxable value either. Why, my friends, the statistics show that the Negro in the South owns an acreage of land that is equal to the combined acreage of the kingdoms of Holland and Belgium. Now, unless we were getting on reasonably well, unless we were making some progress in working out this problem, the Negro could not have acquired all of this property; he could not have done it; he would have been afraid to have done it. I believe in calling attention to this side of the progress that we are making here in the South. If, in every community, the black man had been oppressed and discouraged, as some people would emphasize, it would have been impossible for him to have made any such material progress as I have indicated.

Now, I know that there is criticism, and true, a just criticism, in regard to the Negro as a laborer, in regard to his unreliability, whether it is on the farm or in the shop or in the kitchen or in the dining room or in the laundry or elsewhere. But, we must remember that, in a state of freedom — other conditions perhaps will control in slavery — but in a state of freedom, along with the elements of industry there has got to go one other element, and that is the element of intelligence, the element of education. For a number of years, beginning in a little shanty, at Tuskegee, I have been trying to combine the elements of industry — we teach the Negro, first of all, the dignity of labor — with the element of intelligence.

Some would argue that it is a mistake to give the Negro education if you want him to be reliable as a laborer. I was in a coal mining community not very long ago and I found that the proprietor of that mine was in great difficulty because, as he stated to me, notwithstanding he paid a very high wage to the miners, they would not work with system or regularity. He said that they would work from three to four days during the week and then they would stop working and no influence could induce them to work any longer, and he was not always sure when he paid them off on Saturday night that any large proportion of them would report for service on Monday morning. Well, now, at his request, I went through this community pretty generally, and I found that for the most part they were ignorant, so far as education was concerned. In that community, in my opinion, here was the trouble: Those people had been trained to use their hands, but their wants had not been increased, their ambitions had not been aroused, they were ignorant to the extent that they knew only a few simple and crude things; and they could satisfy the few wants that they knew anything about by working three or four days out of the six, and then when they had satisfied all the wants they knew anything about, they naturally argued: "What is the use of working any longer?" There is a good deal of human nature in that.

Not very long ago I talked with a gentleman who has large industrial interests in South Africa, and there, he told me, with few exceptions, he could not get the native Africans to work longer than two or three days out of each week. Now, what is the difference? In South Africa, for the most part, those people have never been touched by Christian civilization, they have not come into contact with white men, they have not received education, in church, or in Sunday school, or in day school; they have few wants, these are very crude and they can satisfy these wants by working two or three days out of each week and no influence can get them to work longer.

In the South where, as I said a minute ago, the Negro is not satisfactory as a laborer, he is far in advance of his South African brother, because through contact with the white man, through education in the church, in the Sunday school, in the day school, in a large degree, taking the race as a whole, its wants have been increased, its ambitions have been aroused; the Negro wants a little piece of land; after a while, as he gets more education, he wants to put a house on that land with three or four rooms in it, he will want furniture of a good character, he will want some newspapers, he will want some books, he will want to educate his children, he will want to build a new church house, he will want to support his minister; after a while he will want a bank account, and as he goes on making that kind of progress, hand education going with head and heart education, his wants will be multiplied, will be so increased, that he will be compelled to work five and six days out of each week.

And then, I believe from a mere material point of view, from a mere selfish point of view, if I may so describe it, that it will pay every white man in the South who operates a large plantation to see to it that on that plantation or near it there is a good church with a good minister, that there is a school that is comfortable so far as the house is concerned, that the school session lasts from six to seven or eight months, from a mere selfish point of view, if from no higher element; I believe it will pay every planter to see to it that good, comfortable houses are provided for the colored laborer. In proportion as that is done, what will be the result? Instead of the owner having to seek labor, labor will seek him, because it will soon become noised abroad in the community that there is an owner, there is a planter who is taking care of his laborers, who has an interest in their physical, in their mental, their moral and Christian welfare. There are those in this room who remember that during the days of slavery, it was the master who was most kind to his slaves, who looked after their bodily comfort, who provided them with comfortable houses, who saw to it that they were protected, that they led moral and decent lives, the master who was most kind and considerate, was in most cases the individual who, from a money point of view, made his plantation pay; while the master who was careless in those respects, in many cases, ended his industrial or business career in bankruptcy.

Now, in the matter of education, I believe that the Christian men of the South can be of service to us. First, I believe that all of us had just as well make up our minds that the Negro race is going to be educated by somebody, at some time, at some place. Since this is true, I believe that it is vastly better for all concerned for the Negro to be educated by the South, for the most part, for him to be educated by the South so that he will keep in touch with the conditions and opportunities that prevail in the South, so that he shall always feel a sense of gratitude for the education of his children to the Southern white man who is right at his door. I believe that the South should, in the main, win credit for the education of the Negro. Now, in this remark, bear in mind that I am not overlooking what has already been done, but I believe that there is a greater work yet to be done.

In my opinion, the most difficult problem that you have got to face, that I have got to face, is in some manner to so articulate the education of the colored youth into the life of the community in which that youth lives so that the Southern white people will feel and see, day by day, the benefit of Negro education. Now, right there, in my opinion, is the crucial point. In that respect, you must be patient with us. You must remember that it was very natural for a race just coming out of slavery into freedom, to yield to the temptation of jumping from one extreme to the other. For a number of years at Tuskegee, in the earlier days of that institution, I met that problem and had the difficulty of getting the Negro to feel and see that education was a rational, was a sensible thing; that it meant nothing to anybody except as that education could be used right in the community where that individual lived in a way to make every one feel that because of that individual's having education, he was more useful to the community. I often say to the members of my race, that the greatest protection which the Negro can have in the South, or anywhere else, is the usefulness of each individual member of my race. I urge upon them to make themselves so useful to the community where they live that that community will feel that it cannot dispense with the service or with the presence of that race or with those individuals.

Now, there has been a great deal of jumping about in matters of education. It is going to take, perhaps, another generation for my people to learn what education is really meant to accomplish, perhaps another generation for any large proportion of them to get right down to bed rock, to learn that they must begin the using of their education right in the communities where they live, that their service, whether in the field or in the shop or in the kitchen or in the laundry or anywhere else, must be of higher value than the service of the individual who has not had education; to get them to feel and see that all kinds of labor is honorable and all kinds of idleness is a disgrace. In my opinion, we are making a tremendous advance in that direction. We have not reached perfection yet, we have not gotten to the point where many white families, for example in the Southern States, can experience the value of this education; but, remember first, the great problem that we had to overcome was to get our people to see the dignity of labor; to overcome the old idea that when a person got education it was a disgrace for him to use his hands in service for colored people or in service for white people. That difficulty in a very large degree we are overcoming. I remember how for years at Tuskegee parents used to object to our teaching farming, object to our teaching carpentry, object to our teaching sewing, cooking, laundering, and all that. My friends, it has been ten years since I have heard a single objection at Tuskegee from a single parent or from a single student about teaching the industries; and I do not overstate it, when I say to you today, that our students at Tuskegee are just as happy when it comes their turn to take their places upon the farm or in the kitchen or in the sewing room, in the carpenter shop, or in the blacksmith shop, as when it comes their turn to recite their lessons in the history class, in the algebra class, or in any other class of the Academic Department. We feel that in this respect we have made advancement, and gradually you will find that our entire race will make something of the same kind of progress.

I believe that there should be in every large center of population, such as Nashville and Atlanta, a local training school for the training of colored people in the service that is needed to be performed in the community.

Now, in a large institution such as we have at Tuskegee, it would be useless and folly for us to undertake to turn out from there, cooks for individual families; we could not do that. But what is a sensible and logical thing is for these larger institutions to train the leaders in these directions, who could come into a community like Nashville or New Orleans or Montgomery — and we have such a school right in the little town of Tuskegee — leaders who will give training to the colored people in these domestic service lines. And I believe that those institutions, those training schools, should be supported in a large measure by the white people in those various localities. It is mighty important, in my opinion, that you exert your influence and interest in the elevation, in the education of the Negro race.

If you go into a store in the city of Nashville to buy a pair of shoes, I doubt not that in nine cases out of ten the person who fits the shoes upon your feet will be a person of education, will be a person of cleanliness, will be a person of considerable refinement; that happens in reference to the putting of a piece of leather on the outside of your feet. In most cases, taking the average white families of the South, the woman who prepares the food that goes, not on the outside of the foot, but goes on the inside of the stomach to make blood and bone and heart-beat, that woman in most cases is ignorant, in many cases is filthy, untrained. My friends, I claim that it is just as important that the person who prepares the food to go on the inside of the stomach, shall have some training, as it is for the man who puts a piece of leather on the outside of the foot.

In the average white family of the South, you will find that the white child spends a large proportion of his life in the arms or in the company of a Negro woman or of a Negro girl. During the years when that child is most impressionable, when he is at a point where impressions are perhaps most lasting, that child is in the company of this black woman or this black girl. My friends, it is mighty important, in my opinion, for the civilization, for the happiness, for the health of the Southern white people that that colored nurse shall be intelligent, that she shall be clean, that she shall be morally fit to come in contact with that pure and innocent child. (Applause.)

Now these things some of us at least have in mind in the education of my people. I confess that when I began my work at Tuskegee I began it with a selfish ambition, the desire to lift up the Negro alone; but my friends, I thank God that I have long since outgrown that selfishness. (Applause.) I have long since outgrown that narrowness, and I am just as happy today when I can perform any service, however little, for the man or the woman of your race, as when I am working for the elevation and happiness of my own race. We can neither of us, my friends, be utterly free until we are free from racial prejudice. (Applause.)

Now, in these respects, I believe that if this question is brought home — and I have friends on every hand in my community, in my county, in my state, among the best Southern white people, and I find that whenever I want to make an impression upon them, all I have got to do is go to them, look them in the face, and talk to them plainly and frankly. Now, they do not like to be talked about, but you can talk mighty plainly to a man when you can't talk about him; and in proportion as the cultured young white citizen of the South, in my opinion, brings these facts before the masses of white people in the South, showing to them how vital it is to their interest, to their happiness, that the Negro shall be elevated, will he, in my opinion, help mightily in the solution of what is termed this racial problem. And in that regard, my friends, you should take pride, a just degree of pride in the enlightenment that the Negro race has achieved right here in the South.

If you will go into Italy I think you will find that thirty per cent. of those people cannot read or write, and this, after years of freedom and opportunity. In Spain I think it is true that sixty-two per cent. of the people can neither read nor write. In Russia, over seventy per cent. of the people can neither read nor write. In the average South American country perhaps eighty-five per cent. can neither read nor write. In the United States, taking the Negro as a whole, we have already reached the point where more than fifty-six per cent. can read and write. And we should be proud of that, not only my race but your race, as well.

Now, I grant that the mere fact of an individual learning to read and write does not mean always all that the average man thinks that it stands for, but it means something in making progress. Now just in the degree that we can take hold of this book knowledge and weave it into our civilization, into practical measures, in the same degree will both races be helped and both made more happy and more prosperous.

In regard to what you can do to help us in moral and religious directions: In the first place, I believe that you can be of great service to us in helping to get rid of the idea wherever it prevails that in proportion as the Negro gets education — and that is one of these fallacies that gets abroad in the land; one person repeats it and it keeps going all over the community without a person stopping for a moment to make first-hand, clean-cut, scientific investigation as to the facts — he becomes morally weak, or that education does not help him in his moral and religious life. In answering that argument I use the same process that the modern school teacher does; that is, I argue from the known to the unknown. I speak to you about the institution that I happen to know most about. At Tuskegee we have a man who devotes his entire time to keeping in touch with our graduates. He visits them in their homes, in their places of labor, he gets the testimony concerning their character and concerning their work from colored people and from their white neighbors. And, being in possession of that information as I am, I am prepared to say to you today, my friends, that you cannot find in a single penitentiary of this country a man or woman who holds a diploma from the Tuskegee Institute. (Applause.) And I doubt not, if you will go and make an investigation for yourselves, go to Fisk, to Roger Williams, to Walden University, and these other institutions of learning here in Nashville, you will be surprised to find the very small proportion of the men and women who have been thoroughly educated at those institutions who have ever been charged with any kind of crime or who have ever gone to prison. And what is true of these institutions is true in a larger or less degree of the institutions for my people throughout the South where they have received rational education.

So it is not true that the Negro who gets education goes straight to the penitentiary or becomes an idler. Investigation would show, in the case of the men and women who have gone out of Tuskegee, that you could scarcely find in any season of the year as many as ten per cent. who are in idleness. They are in work of some kind, employed in some way, because they have learned the disgrace of idleness and the dignity of labor.

Wherever you find a low state of morals existing among my people, my friends, you will find that in some degree that condition extends to the members of your race. And in my opinion — Dr. Tillett told me to speak plainly and frankly — in my opinion, the degradation of the Negro woman will in many cases, prove the damnation of many of your best Southern white men, unless that Negro woman is gotten hold of and lifted up and given a higher ideal of a moral and virtuous life. I believe that the time has come when many of the ripest and best Christian white men of the South are feeling and seeing that it is just as much a part of their duty to elevate and to Christianize — and when I say Christianize, I mean to Christianize in a practical way, because a large proportion of the members of my race belong to the church already, a larger proportion it is true perhaps, than in any other race; but belonging to the church does not, as you know, always mean what it may seem to mean — I believe the time has come when some of the best Christian men and women of the South are beginning to feel and see that it is just as much a part of their Christian duty to help elevate and Christianize the black persons who are at their door, as it is a part of their Christian duty to extend a helping hand to the people in China, in Corea or the central part of Africa. (Applause.)

But let me try to be more practical. How can you, as Christian men and women, assist in this regard? In the first place, I want to see us get back to the old days where the white minister will be invited, and if he does not receive the invitation, will ask for the invitation, to preach in Negro pulpits, as was true many years ago. I want to see us get to the point where at least once a month every white minister will feel it a part of his duty, a part of his mission to appear in some of the Negro churches in that community. My friends, our people will welcome you in their pulpits, and you don't know how far your presence and your words and your example in this respect will go toward helping to encourage our people. And further, I believe that everyone of these large centers of population should plan that once a month or once a quarter or several times a year at least, the white ministers and colored ministers should meet together and talk out these problems plainly one to the other. This can be done, my friends, it has been done in many of our Southern States. It is being done in Birmingham, it is being done, I am glad to say, in the city of Atlanta. The Atlanta riot, as unfortunate as it was, has cleared the atmosphere in this respect and has made the Christian ministers in that city feel and see their duty in regard to the colored people, in my opinion, in a way that no other occurrence has done perhaps since my race received its freedom. And almost every week since this riot the colored ministers and the white ministers have been meeting together for seasons of conference and for seasons of prayer. And they are getting a better understanding, an understanding that they did not have concerning their problems and their mutual interests, that has never existed before.

And I believe further that you can help us not only by visiting our churches, but by going into the Negro schools and seeing for yourselves what is being taught in these Negro schools; seeing for yourselves what progress the colored people are making. Not by taking somebody else's word for it, but by finding out for yourselves what effect Negro education is having upon the masses of my people.

During the past year at Tuskegee I have had a series of lectures and I have asked such men as Dr. Rice,[1] formerly of Montgomery, of your own church, to come to Tuskegee to speak to our people frankly; I have had the leading ministers from Montgomery, from Mobile, from Atlanta and throughout that section; they have been there this year. Others will be there during the coming year. I want them to see for themselves what we are doing and I want our students to hear at first-hand from the lips of these representative Southern white people what their attitude is toward the race and what they expect from our people.

I believe further, my friends, that it is the duty of my race to help get rid of the idle and vicious class, and I believe that you can help us in the lifting up of our race and especially of our women by generating in your social and educational circles a public sentiment which shall ostracize a white man who has immoral relations with a colored woman. (Applause.) It is not always easy for us to draw the line, it is not always easy for us to make such a woman feel the weight of our condemnation when in too many cases she is supported in ease, sometimes in luxury, by members of your race. And in all these respects it is the duty of the Negro to help, to co-operate with the white officials in this regard.

Only day before yesterday the Sheriff of my county spent an hour in my office and we talked over frankly the problems relating to the moral uplift of our people in that county. And that Sheriff said to me — and he is an honest, intelligent, conscientious official — "We have got to the point in this county where there are only eighteen cases of immoral relations existing between white men and colored women, and by the grace of God, we will get rid of those eighteen." I said to him, we will help you. And, speaking of this question of co-operation between the races: We have twenty-four hundred colored people living in our little community where our school is located, and I cannot recall a single instance where an official of that county has come into that community to arrest one of our people. I do not mean to say that one has not been arrested, but I do mean to say that those officials, from the Sheriff down, have such confidence in us that whenever a crime is charged or suspected, the Sheriff telephones to my office or comes to my office and says to me that a certain individual in that community has been charged with that crime and he wants that individual, and that man is always found and is turned over to the proper county official. They have faith in us and we have faith in them. And I wish, in this regard, that more responsibility, wherever it can be done, might be placed upon our people in regard to finding criminals, but Negroes, in most cases do not feel such a responsibility. We feel in our community this responsibility because the officers trust us, because we know if we deceive them once they, themselves, will come into that community and will ferret out these persons charged with crime. If, in every community, there could be such co-operation between the officers of the law and the leading colored people, I believe that many of the criminals, who now hide and perhaps in some cases are harbored by members of my race, would be brought to the light and turned over to the proper officers.

This brings me to the discussion, briefly, of another subject which is of vital concern to both of us. The one subject which perhaps is more discussed in the newspapers in the South and throughout the South and throughout Europe for that matter, as bearing upon the South, is the subject of lynching.

In the first place, I think you will agree with me that lynching has its beginning in punishing individuals of my race for assaults upon women. It was thought in the early years that that kind of punishment would get rid of that kind of crime. I believe that, for the most part, we are agreed that that punishment, that kind of punishment, has not, in most cases, rid our country of that kind of crime. In the first place, I believe that there is only one safety for all of us, one safety for your race, for my race, and that is in the absolute enforcement of the law. When we go outside of the law we are treading upon dangerous ground. The Governor of Alabama said in a public speech not long ago that during his administration he knew of at least five colored men who had been lynched when they were wholly innocent of any crime. To quote his exact words, he said, "They were as innocent as the Governor of Alabama is of any such crime."

When I was a small boy, during the days of the Civil War, I used to hear a great deal about deserters from the Southern army and from the Northern army, and I was always told that if a deserter met a small colored boy in the road, the first thing he would do was to cut off his ears. Well now, nobody could have convinced me that that was not true and I made up my mind that if ever I saw anybody coming in my direction in a public road that looked like a deserter, I was going to run and scream with all of my might. Well, I very much fear that the unusual punishment inflicted through lynchings and sometimes through burnings, the constant discussion of that subject in the public press, the large, flaring and scary headlines which are often given in the public press give many timid white women the impression that if they meet a Negro, especially a strange Negro, in the road he will be guilty of some attempted assault — the same as I was afraid that a deserter would cut off my ears if ever I met him or he ever met me in the road. In some cases, my friends, I know that persons, by reason of the constant discussion of this subject, by reason of the advertisement which it gets growing out of this unusual and unlawful punishment, have gotten the idea that innocent colored men, whom they have met in the road have meant harm; they have become frightened and run, the noise has gone through the community that some colored man has attempted criminal assault, everybody becomes excited, no one stops to inquire into the facts, the man is rushed upon and put to death. Innocent people in many cases, I fear, have been put to death under such circumstances. I know, my friends, of one case, a friend of mine, a colored man of some education, or some standing in this community, who almost had that experience. And it was by the merest chance that the life of that individual was saved. Everybody took for granted that he was guilty and nobody had perhaps the self-poise or had the influence to check the onslaught of the mob except one individual to whose house this friend of mine had fled and who shut him in his house and held the mob off until the facts were found out. You see how easy it is to grow in the wrong direction when we first break the law. As a matter of fact, you will find that at the present time, or it was true last year, that two thirds of the lynchings in the United

States of colored people, were not for crimes that had any relation to assaults upon women. If you will make the examination for yourselves, you will find that that statement is true. Breaking the state law is like breaking a moral law; when you begin you don't know where the individual is to end. And these lynchings, this unusual method of punishment gives to the South a reputation of lawlessness which it does not deserve. You will find if you will make the examination that in the city of Chicago alone two years ago there were more attempts made by white men at rape than there were throughout the whole of the Southern States, so far as the colored people are concerned. I repeat, for sake of emphasis; if you will go into Chicago and make an examination through the proper officials, you will find that two years ago, in one year, there were more attempts at rape or more actual committings of this crime than there were by colored people in all the Southern States put together.

In nine-tenths of our Southern communities there is peace and harmony, good will and friendship; but when one goes outside of the Southern States, when one goes into the North, into Europe, as I have done, and reads the dispatches that come from the South, it is always one thing — lynchings. And you never hear of any other news from the South except of lynchings. Those people naturally get the idea, other people get the idea, through this unusual punishment, that we are living in a state of turmoil, at daggers-points, throughout the South, whereas, as a matter of fact, as you go through the average Southern community, you will find a feeling of mutual confidence, a feeling of friendship existing between the races — each race interested in the progress of the other. And for that reason alone, my friends, if for no other higher consideration, I believe we owe it to ourselves to bring about such a public sentiment as will get rid of this unusual and barbarous method of punishing criminals. And in the case of my race, I believe you will find that many of our criminals — and you will find that this crime is usually committed by wandering colored people — have no homes, no trades, no bank accounts, no permanent abiding place; in many cases, they are half-witted. And this condition has been emphasized by the use of bad whiskey — those people read the newspapers, they hear in public discussion about these crimes and many of them, by reason of the mere publicity of this unusual punishment, are led to attempt these assaults, when if the individuals were punished in an orderly, sober, quiet method, they would never hear of them. And I believe, for these reasons, and for many more, that we of both races should insist that we are gaining nothing in any community by ever condoning what is termed mob or lynch law.

Now, before I conclude, I believe that you can help us further by being the leaders and makers of public sentiment. It takes a strong man to make and mould and lead public sentiment. The average man, the weak man usually falls in with public sentiment just as he finds it in his community, and he rarely takes a step outside of that circle. Now, to be still more frank: In my opinion, one of the reasons why many of the best and brightest Southern men have not taken hold and helped in the directions that I have tried to emphasize as they would like to have done, has been the scare, the bug-bear of what is called "social equality."

Now, my observation is, that the man who really has high social standing is not very much afraid of his standing being affected by contact with a weak race. It is the fellow, in most cases, whose social standing is shaky — (Laughter and Applause) who makes the most noise on that point. I need not say to persons such as I am addressing today that it is true that Robert E. Lee and his family, Stonewall Jackson and his family, and men of that stamp, in the old state of Virginia, used to go into the Negro Sunday school every Sunday and teach Negro classes. They were not afraid of their standing being affected by helping to lift up and Christianize the lowly who were right about them. (Applause.) There is not a white man in the city of Nashville today, my friends, however high he may stand in social or business circles, who is afraid that my friend — and he represents the highest type of education and Christian citizenship among the Negroes of the city of Nashville — Mr. J. C. Napier, will ever intrude himself into your social circles where he is not asked or where he is not wanted. What is true of him, my friends, is true of the average educated, sensible colored man. In reality, in actual practice, there is little in it. And you agree with me. But still that is used to frighten off, to hinder, and very often to check some of the best efforts that our Southern white friends want to put forth in the direction of helping us.

And another bug-bear that is used is "Negro domination." Negro domination! Now, my friends, there is nothing in either of those things. I think I know the ambitions and the activities of the colored people throughout this country pretty well. And I am safe in saying to you that it is not the ambition or the desire of the Negro in this country to intermingle socially with the white people. Neither is it his ambition or his desire to domineer the white man in matters of politics. You can help us by making that fact known. You can help us, again, by using your influence to check the work in many cases of the sensational daily newspapers that use these incidents in connection with the Negro to give them circulation, to give them popularity among a certain class of people.

And you can help us again by using your influence by bringing to bear your Christian ideas of citizenship upon the public mind of the South so that in the future they will not, as they have in so large a degree in the past, ride into office or attempt to ride into office on the Negro. My friends, there are some men in office who never would have seen an office, except for the Negro. And on every possible occasion, when they want to go to the Legislature, when they want to go to Congress, when they want to be Governor, or to be United States Senator, these men who have no ideas of constructive, progressive statesmanship, they fall back on the old idea of "Negro domination," and they just go through the country harping on the Negro all the time, all the time. I believe we have gotten to the point where not very much can be accomplished in the working out of this problem by the passing of laws — by the passing of laws that forbid, or the passing of laws that are of a positive character.

I think in one of his letters to the Galatians, St. Paul says something like this:

"And the fruit of the spirit is love and joy and peace and long-suffering and temperance and self-control."

And then St. Paul ends that great passage with these pregnant words: "Against such there is no law."

My friends, the best and most far-reaching and most fundamental influence in this life for your race, for my race, in my opinion, is far above the reach, is far above the control of any law that men can pass.

I believe that it will help us both in proportion as we get up, way up into St. Paul's atmosphere in the working out of this great problem. The greatest injury that can come to either your race or my race is for individuals to grow embittered. An embittered man loses power for usefulness, whether he is black or whether he is white. As I speak to the educated men and women of my race, I always say to them, I pray God that they may never grow bitter toward any man or toward any race; that they shall always keep a beautiful, sweet and Christian spirit.

My friends, the feeling of mutual confidence, the feeling of friendship and of sympathy that was planted in the hearts of the young white man and the young colored man, of the old colored man and the old white man of this Southland fifty years ago, must remain there, and you and I, who have honored them and are honoring their traditions, should not dare to uproot what they have planted. Let us, as we go out into the world, cultivate that feeling of friendship and trust; and let us not dig up the rose bush of friendship which was planted during the days of slavery.

If you want to know how to solve the race problem, place your hands upon your hearts and then with a prayer to God, ask Him how you today, were you placed in the position that the black man occupies, how you would desire the white man to treat you, and whenever you have answered that question in the sight of God and man, this problem in a large degree will have been solved. (Long continued applause.)

PD Con. 956 BTW Papers DLC. Stenographically reported. Occasional asterisks, indicating omitted passages, have been deleted. Reprinted in E. Davidson Washington, ed., *Selected Speeches of Booker T. Washington* (Garden City, N.Y.: Doubleday, Doran and Co., 1932), 160–89.

[1] John Andrew Rice (1862–1930), a Methodist Episcopal clergyman, was president of the Columbia, S.C., College for Women from 1894 to 1900, and later served pastorates in Montgomery, New Orleans, Fort Worth, St. Louis, and other cities. From 1902 to 1907 he was pastor in Montgomery, Ala. BTW considered Rice among the few liberal southern clergymen on the race question.

To Charles Waddell Chesnutt

[Tuskegee, Ala.] April 3, 1907

Dear Mr. Chesnutt: This letter is my receipt and acknowledgment of the twenty-five dollars sent by you as a contribution toward the

Douglass Memorial Home Fund. We are deeply grateful for the interest manifested and for the substantial contribution made. It will serve to help us preserve Mr. Douglass' late home as a memorial in honor of himself as well as a memorial to the Negro people. It will become in time, we hope, what Mount Vernon is to white Americans.

Anything you may do in the direction of bringing this matter to the attention of others will be greatly appreciated.

I shall hope to read Mr. Merriam's book, "The Nation and the Negro"[1] very soon. Yours very truly,

Booker T. Washington

TLpS Con. 794 BTW Papers DLC.

[1] George S. Merriam, *The Negro and the Nation: A History of American Slavery and Enfranchisement* (New York, 1907).

To William Loeb, Jr.

[Chicago, Ill.] April 6, 1907

Personal.

My dear Mr. Loeb: I have just learned that Mr. J. W. Johnson has been transferred from the Consulship of Puerto Cabello, Venezuela to a small African port at the *same* salary.[1] I should be very happy if it can be arranged whereby if Mr. Johnson cannot be promoted at this time the President, can see his way clear, acting through Secretary Root, for Johnson to be left at Puerto Cabello unless he can secure a substantial promotion.[2]

I am not writing at all at Johnson's suggestion, as I am not even sure he knows of the intended change, but Mr. Johnson, who was the President of the Colored Republican Club of New York, along with Mr. Anderson, have done such effective work in that state that I would like to see him promoted rather than transferred without promotion. Very truly yours,

Booker T. Washington

TLdS Con. 249 BTW Papers DLC. Written on stationery of Tuskegee Institute.

[1] Charles W. Anderson wrote an even stronger letter of complaint. On hearing

of Johnson's transfer to a consulate at Goree-Dakar, French West Africa, he wrote Loeb that the news "has pained and disappointed me inexpressibly." He pointed out that Johnson measured up to every demand of the consular service and was a loyal party man. "We haven't got many men who can 'stand upon their feet and play the game,' " he observed, "and when we find one, he certainly deserves good treatment at the hands of those he is serving." (Anderson to Loeb, Apr. 5, 1907, Con. 7, BTW Papers, DLC.)

2 After receiving copies of BTW's and Anderson's letters, Assistant Secretary of State Robert Bacon wrote Loeb: "Under all the circumstances, Mr. Johnson will be left at Puerto Cabello for the present." He pointed out that Johnson could hardly expect promotion after only one year. (Apr. 9, 1907, Con. 7, BTW Papers, DLC.)

From Horace Bumstead

Brookline, Mass. Apr. 10, 1907

My dear Dr. Washington: Replying to your letter of Mar. 28, in answer to mine of Mar. 1, I would say:

The purpose of my former letter was to get at the essential facts in the case of Mr. Penney in such a way as to enable our Board of Trustees, of which he is a member, to know what action it ought to take in regard to him. For this reason I regret that you have not answered my questions more definitely. The points raised, which you speak of as "details or incidents in connection with the case," and which you prefer not to enter into, seem to me of vital importance to a just decision of the question as it comes before us, if not as it came before you.

However, I will not press you for further reply if you feel that it would involve too long a correspondence and is not worth the time and effort involved. But it seems only fair to you that I should state how the matter now lies in our minds, with such evidence as is now before us, in order that you may still have an opportunity to correct us on any matters of fact or inference before we take action which might seem to reflect in any way on the action taken at Tuskegee.

The case against Mr. Penney, as we understand it, is based upon the testimony of two girl students who, ten or a dozen years apart, have charged him with immoral conduct. In neither case was there any corroborative evidence aside from the word of the girl. In both cases the word of the girl has been impeached in such a way as to show her testimony to be worthless.

In the first case, after careful investigation Mr. Penney was exonerated and retained and the girl sent away. You intimate that the case was not wholly clear when you say that you decided to give Mr. Penney the benefit of every doubt and that some of you felt it was a mistake to retain him. But you do not allude to the subsequent confession of the girl herself who, as we are informed, acknowledged that she had nothing against Mr. Penney and only brought the charges that she might force her parents to take her home when they had been unwilling to do so. This, if true, would seem to settle the case so that it should never be brought up again.

In the recent case the girl's testimony is invalidated by the character of the letters found in her trunk. These letters are from her physician, a married man, apparently white, who mingles medical advice with love-making. Some of his expressions give strong intimation of improper relations between them in the past. He was anxious to take her north with him last summer, to have her sent north to him after he had gone, and to get her into his home in New Orleans after she had gone to Tuskegee. More than this, he had been practicing hypnotism with her and had taught her how to hypnotize herself. This fact would be enough in itself to throw grave doubt on any statements she might make, however sincerely made at the time, but in connection with the other facts revealed in the letters would seem to render her testimony worthless. In addition to this, she is said to have told at Tuskegee how she had been chased by men at her home and that her brother had given her a stiletto to protect herself against them; yet in the face of this and of the revelations of the letters found in her trunk she declared, as shown in the typewritten charges against Mr. Penney, that she had never, anywhere, in her life before, had any such experiences as she said she had had with Mr. Penney.

It is pertinent to add here that the girl's father and aunt (the mother being dead) disbelieve the charges she has made and have written letters of regret and sympathy to the Penneys. You yourself have discredited her in sending her from Tuskegee.

Against the testimony of these two discredited girls, one of them a confessed liar, stands the positive denial of the accused, backed up by the record of more than thirty years of faithful service and an unblemished life otherwise unstained by calumny. More than half of this time has been spent at Tuskegee where Mr. Penney's service has won from you the highest praise even when asking him to resign.

You say you take the position that a school is not a court of law and so not bound to prove the guilt of a teacher. But is it not bound to be governed, in dealing with him, by the ordinary laws of evidence which prevail among men even outside the courts?

You say when a teacher gets into a position where his influence is hurtful the school has a right to part with him. But has it a right to do so in a way to besmirch his character? And is it not bound to consider whether he "gets" into such a position or is *put* into it by no fault of his own? Does a school owe nothing to a teacher in the way of protection from the calumnies of irresponsible students?

You say Mr. Penney's usefulness at Tuskegee was at an end. We are compelled to enquire why this should be so. Is the voice of wicked slander so powerful there that the record of a long, useful, unblemished life counts for nothing against it? Is it possible that even you, with your great influence, are unable to overcome it? We do not like to think of Tuskegee as an unsafe place for a teacher who values his reputation and future influence and usefulness.

I hesitate to refer to another matter in this connection lest you misinterpret my motive for doing so, but it is so vital to the question you raise about Mr. Penney's usefulness at Tuskegee that you must pardon my frankness. I refer to the effect upon the question of his usefulness produced by your own personal attitude toward him. From the information before us, you seem to have treated him from the outset as a guilty man. You denied his request before the committee to be confronted with the girl who made the charges — a claim which even a guilty man should hardly be denied. You refused his subsequent request for a personal interview with you. You forced his resignation and the quitting of his work within a week of his first arraignment. You refused to recognize any further financial obligation to him, granting him only as a matter of favor half salary till June with the use of his house, revocable at any time. What must have been the effect upon the minds of teachers and students at Tuskegee produced by this summary treatment if it was not that you believed him guilty? And would not this impression have been increased rather than allayed by your statement to Mr. Penney, which was also furnished to the public press, that you did not pass upon the question of his guilt or innocence? Whatever may have been the situation on Mr. Penney's first arraignment before the committee, it would seem that the discovery of the letters in the girl's trunk several days later would have given you ample opportunity for announcing to the school that newly discovered evidence had satisfied you of the worthlessness of her charges and convinced you of Mr. Penney's innocence. Would the school have disbelieved you if you had?

We realize that, in spite of all, you may still believe him guilty or probably so. With the evidence before us we do not see how you can. But if you do, we think our Board is entitled to know the reasons why.

You say in your letter to me that you think I will find a record at Atlanta University to the effect that he was charged with a similar offense while a student at Atlanta, and that you have received this information from a graduate of Atlanta University who knows about it. This charge I never heard of, though I was Mr. Penney's teacher for the year preceding his graduation, nor does Prof. Chase know about it, though a teacher during the whole of Mr. Penney's career there. Diligent search has just been made at Atlanta and no such record found. If there had ever been any such charge, it was evidently dismissed as untrue, for otherwise Pres. Ware[1] would never have consented to his graduation.

The only incident I know of that might be tortured into being a "similar offense" is the one which Mr. Penney himself voluntarily told you and your committee at the time of his recent arraignment — the mischievous tale of a girl about his alleged kissing of another girl. As Mr. Penney told you this of his own accord, and in self-defence, that he might illustrate how easily false charges are set afloat, it would seem incredible that you should turn the incident against him as supporting the charges at Tuskegee, and give it to me as coming from "a graduate of Atlanta University who knows about it." Who then was the graduate who informed you? It seems due to us that we should have his name and learn what he knows.

The circumstances have made it necessary that I should write you very frankly and at greater length than I could have wished.

It seems only right that you should know how we view the matter, with our present knowledge, and that you should take the pains to correct us if we are in error. We feel that you have done Mr. Penney a grievous wrong, besmirching his character and injuring him financially, while bringing great grief and sorrow to his innocent wife and children, and all upon utterly insufficient grounds. In doing this you have also put an undeserved stigma upon Atlanta University and its Board of Trustees, which you should not blame us for wishing to wipe off so far as we can. If Mr. Penney is unworthy, we are ready to put him off our Board.

The fact that you and your associates have already spent much time on this case should not, it seems to me, deter you from spending more in some effort to reach a more harmonious understanding of it than now exists between us. I need not tell you how deeply I regret that any difference of this sort should have arisen between our two institutions and my earnest desire that it may be adjusted.

Now that Mr. Penney has gone from Tuskegee, no one would think of his returning. But is there really any good reason why you might not, on a reconsideration of the evidence, clear his character from the smirch that has been put upon it and make up to him the financial loss he has incurred, all, as we believe, through no fault of his own? Some such action as this would go a long way toward healing deep wounds and promoting a good understanding. It is never too late to rectify a mistake like this, if one has been committed, and I earnestly hope that Tuskegee will be courageous enough and magnanimous enough to consider further action. Yours very sincerely,

Horace Bumstead

TLS Con. 364 BTW Papers DLC.

[1] Edmund Asa Ware.

To D. Robert Wilkins

[Tuskegee, Ala.] April 17, 1907

Personal and Confidential.

My dear Mr. Wilkins: I am agreeably surprised as well as gratified to read the generous expressions from yourself in the last issue of your paper. I was sorry not to see you while in Chicago.

As a matter of fact, there is no difference between your position and mine, the only difference being that you are working to secure certain ends by traveling in a certain route, and I am working to secure the same end by traveling perhaps a different route. Since we are all aiming at the same thing, there is no earthly reason why there should be bickerings, jealousies and cursings, especially when there is so much hard, earnest work to be done in order to lift the race up and secure for it all the rights which are guaranteed by the Constitution of the United States. No man in recent years, in my opinion, has undergone more suffering for the sake of the race than I have, and I have done so without murmuring and complaining, and often in the face of danger which I could not describe to you. The fellows, nine cases out of ten, who are in favor of keeping up quarreling and strife between members of the race and between newspapers are those who in reality care little for the race except to use it to advertise themselves. In most cases they belong to what they call the "upper ten," who very seldom mingle with the masses, who in fact think themselves and their families too good to even touch the hem of the garment of the ordinary man and woman, but through the public press and on public occasions they lose no opportunity to take advantage of their connection with the race to boost themselves into prominence. That is the element that is in favor of continual strife. I am sure that if you and I could have a good heart to heart talk, we would find that there is no difference between us.

I wish at some time you could find your way clear to visit Tuskegee. I wish you could see for yourself what we are doing right here in the heart of the Black Belt of the South to lift up the masses of our people.

I shall be very glad to hear from you at any time. Yours truly,

Booker T. Washington

TLpS Con. 385 BTW Papers DLC.

To Horace Bumstead

Tuskegee Institute, Alabama. April 18, 1907

My dear Dr. Bumstead: Replying to yours of April 10 I would state that, I sympathize with you and with Mr. Penney and his family most deeply concerning the matter of their leaving Tuskegee. There have been very few occurrences in the history of the institution that have pained me more deeply. While this is true, I cannot consent, without our Trustees requesting or ordering me to do so, to go into any detailed discussion or defense with you in regard to Mr. Penney's leaving this institution. Such a course would be a most unusual one in the case of one institution dealing with another. In the first place, the matter is between Mr. Penney and this institution, and my taking it up at all with a third party was simply through courtesy, and I ought not to be expected to continue explanations, defenses and discussions with another party. So far as I know, the custom of institutions dealing with each other is to take for granted that each institution acts in good faith without attempting to go back of its actions, and this policy I think I must pursue in the present case.

My reference in the latter part of my letter to some charge brought against Mr. Penney at Atlanta University was merely incidental and had nothing whatever to do with his leaving here, in fact the decision had been reached before I came into possession of that information from the Atlanta graduate to whom I referred, and of course we would not have acted upon a mere hearsay. Yours truly,

[Booker T. Washington]

TL Copy Con. 364 BTW Papers DLC.

To Alfred Holt Stone

[Tuskegee, Ala.] April 19, 1907

Dear Mr. Stone: I have received your letter of April 10 and am writing to say that, I shall be very glad to cooperate in any manner

I can with you or others in covering the subject that you have been requested to deal with by the Carnegie Institute.[1]

I must say in this connection, however, in order to be perfectly frank with you, that I have had fears in the past which I think I have not withheld from you, that some things you have spoken and written have been rather unfair to the Negro, growing out of the fact that you had not come into contact with the results of rational education. In most I have read from your pen, the conclusion seems to have been reached by you that the Negro was a failure in the labor world. I may be wrong, but this is the impression I have formed. I think you have reached this conclusion very largely owing to the fact that your contact has been with a certain element of colored people in Mississippi. I believe that a broader contact with the whole problem will give you a different view.[2]

For example, I send you a copy of a letter which I have just received from a large firm in Birmingham. This firm has been using our graduates and former students for the past six or eight years. We can hardly keep the students in our departments long enough for them to get trained in any measure because there is such a demand on the part of white as well as colored people for their services.

I hope before you are through with your investigation that you will visit Hampton and Tuskegee and similar institutions. I hope you will also go into some of the small communities where the graduates of these institutions have been exerting their influences.

What I am most interested in is facts as to our real progress. I do not want to cover anything over. No one would suffer more than the Negro by a false view being taken simply for the purpose of pleasing the race.

I repeat, if I can serve you, please be kind enough to let me know. Yours truly,

Booker T. Washington

TLpS Con. 360 BTW Papers DLC.

[1] Stone's letter to BTW mentioned that he had secured the cooperation of W. E. B. Du Bois and R. R. Wright, Jr., for his volume on "The Negro in Slavery and Freedom" in a Carnegie Institution series on the industrial history of the United States. He briefly outlined his book, expressed his favorable opinion of the influence of Hampton and Tuskegee, and said he hoped to visit Tuskegee. (Apr. 10, 1907, Con. 360, BTW Papers, DLC.)

[2] Stone denied that anything he had written was anti-Negro, and said the mis-

understanding might have arisen "through my failure to make it clear that I was dealing with a specific class of Negro labor—that living under the plantation system." He thought that "the proper study of the Negro was a study of local conditions." BTW replied that "I do not want any thing over or under stated regarding the Negro, simply the facts. . . ." (Stone to BTW, Apr. 23, and BTW to Stone, May 1, 1907. Con. 360, BTW Papers, DLC.)

From Emmett Jay Scott

Tuskegee Institute, Alabama April 23, 1907

Dear Mr. Washington: There is something rather interesting in considering Wilkins' letter, which I send you today, and the following sentence from Du Bois' part of the April number of the "Horizon." In speaking of some man he says: "He knows not even the Conservator, of his own Chicago, the doughtiest champion, next the Guardian, of the rights of the Negroes and edited by an unpurchasable man."

When he reads Wilkins' editorial of last week, I am sure he will have fits! Yours truly,

Emmett J. Scott

TLS Con. 574 BTW Papers DLC.

An Item in the *Tuskegee Student*

Tuskegee Institute, Alabama May 4, 1907

MONEY FOR NEGRO SCHOOLS

DR. WASHINGTON AND DR. FRISSELL OF HAMPTON TO HANDLE BIG FUND

To her already numerous and liberal contributions to educational and philanthropic purposes, Miss Anna T. Jeanes, of this city, yesterday added a splendid gift of $1,000,000 to be used in giving rudimentary education to the Negro children in the rural districts of the South. Desiring to see the work in which she is so deeply interested started during her lifetime, Miss Jeanes, who is 85 years of age, on Monday executed a deed transferring this large amount of money to Booker T. Washington and Hollis Burke Frissell, who are vested with full power to use the income in such manner as in their judgment may seem best.

Miss Jeanes, who now spends most of her time at the Home for Aged Hicksite Friends, which she built and liberally endowed, has for more than a year had this gift under consideration. Having made up her mind she last week summoned to this city Dr. Washington, the famous Negro who is at the head of the Tuskegee Institute, Alabama, and Dr. Frissell, who is president of the equally famous institution at Hampton, Virginia. They reached Philadelphia on Monday and were amazed and delighted at learning for what purpose they had been asked to meet the venerable philanthropist. Having perfected the details of her great undertaking, Miss Jeanes handed to her visitors copies of the deed of trust and bade them go to work as soon as possbile and to save her from publicity as far as the nature of the action would permit.

Absolute Control of Fund

The two men are named as trustees of what is to be known as "The Fund for Rudimentary Schools for Southern Negroes," and are given practically absolute control of the income from the big fund. This money is to supplement cash that is being appropriated by the Southern States toward the education of the Negro and none of it is to be used for higher institutions of learning. The fund must be invested in bonds of specified states and cities, and the accruing interest, which will aggregate about $40,000 a year, is to be expended by the two trustees in such manner as they may determine.

Only one other bequest of a like amount of money has been made to the colored race. That was given over twenty years ago by John F. Slater of Norwich, Conn. Unlike Miss Jeanes' gift, this fund was used for the establishment and maintenance of higher institutions of learning for the Negro. As fiscal agent of this fund Miss Jeanes named the Pennsylvania Company for Insurances on Lives and Granting Annuities, of this city. The power to appoint a Board of Trustees is given to Mr. Washington and Mr. Frissell, but none of these has been named as yet.

GIVER SHUNS PUBLICITY

Miss Jeanes could not be seen last night at the Germantown Home for Friends, which is located at Washington Lane and Greene Street. She refused to see reporters or to discuss her latest gift. It was Miss Jeanes' wish, Dr. Washington said, that the affair be given no more publicity than necessary.

Miss Jeanes has endowed a number of institutions, and most of her benefactions have been in the names of her dead brothers and sisters, whose shares of the family fortune she inherited. She is a daughter of Isaac Jeanes. She had four brothers and one sister. One brother, Dr. Jacob Jeanes, with Dr. Constantine Hering and Dr. Walter Williamson, founded the Hahnemann Medical College in 1848. The other three brothers — Samuel, Joshua and Joseph — built up a large fortune in the dry goods business in this city a number of years ago. She has at all times sought to avoid publicity in her gifts, and until a few years ago, lived alone with her servants at No. 1023 Arch Street. Her fortune now amounts to nearly $5,000,000.

TEXT OF DEED OF TRUST

The deed of trust which she on Monday signed to make her gift to Negro education imperative reads as follows:

Know all men by these presents: That I, Anna T. Jeanes, of the city of Philadelphia, trusting and believing in the practicable and far-reaching good that may result from the moral and elevating influence of rural schools for Negroes in the Southern States, taught by reputable teachers, do hereby make, constitute and appoint Booker T. Washington, Tuskegee, Ala., and Hollis Burke Frissell, Hampton, Va., and their successors in the trust appointed or created as hereinafter directed, the trustees of an endowment fund in perpetuity of one million dollars, which is hereby created, to be known as "The Fund for Rudimentary Schools for Southern Negroes," the income whereof shall be devoted to the sole purpose of assisting in the Southern United States, community, country and rural schools for the great class of Negroes to whom the small rural and community schools are alone available; and I further nominate, constitute and appoint the Pennsylvania Company for Insurances on Lives and Granting Annuities as and for the "fiscal agent" of the said trustees and their successors in the trust, with full power to safely hold said fund, to collect all income thereon and from time to time, as directed by said trustees, to pay over said income unto them.

If at any time in the future the Board of Trustees of the said endowment fund hereby created shall determine upon some other fiscal agent for any part or all of said fund, in the administration of said fund, I confer upon it ample power and authority to change the fiscal agent.

In consideration of the permission therefore, I hereby, give, grant, transfer, set over and assign unto the said Booker T. Washington and the said Hollis Burke Frissell, trustees, and their successors in the trust, absolutely all and every, the securities and cash to the amount of one million dollars ($1,000,000) set forth specifically in the list hereunto annexed and made a part hereof, marked "Exhibit A."

THE INVESTMENTS SPECIFIED

In trust, nevertheless, for the following uses and purposes: In trust to keep the said fund invested in United States Government bonds or bonds of the States of Pennsylvania, New York, Massachusetts, Alabama, Virginia, Maryland and Missouri, and of any city or cities in said states having a population of 500,000 or more inhabitants and after the payment of all necessary expenses to apply the net income toward the maintenance and assistance of community, country and rural schools for colored people in the Southern United States.

And I further request, empower and direct the said Booker T. Washington and the said Hollis Burke Frissell to nominate and appoint a Board of Trustees, of such number as they may think desirable, of the aforesaid endowment fund, and to secure a succession of the members of the Board thereof, and to take any and all steps that they may deem necessary and expedient to connection therewith. And further, I request that both the said Booker T. Washington and the said Hollis Burke Frissell shall be members of the said Board of Trustees.

Should, however, the said Booker T. Washington or the said Hollis Burke Frissell die or decline to serve before they shall have established the Board of Trustees of said endowment fund, or if for any reason the same shall not be constituted by them within a period of six months from this date, then and in that event I request and empower the Trustees of the Hampton Normal and Agricultural Institute and the Trustees of the Tuskegee Normal and Industrial Institute to select and create from members of their own Board of Trustees of such numbers as they may deem best, to act as Trustees of the said endowment fund in perpetuity hereby created; and I direct that such Board apply the income upon said fund in like manner solely toward the maintenance and assistance of rural, community and country schools for the Southern Negroes and not for the use or benefit of large institutions, but for the purpose of rudimentary education as herein above referred to and to encourage moral influence and social refinement which shall promote peace in the land and good will among men.

The Trustees have given out the following statement:

It is impossible to express in proper terms the gratitude of the Negro people, as well as the whole country, to Miss Anna T. Jeanes, for her great generosity in giving one million dollars to assist in the education of the Negro children in the South in the small rural schools. This fund will greatly aid local communities and Southern States in carrying the burdens of rudimentary education.

This money will, of course, help to educate only a small proportion of the Negro children in the South; it will, however, help much, and we hope it will result in inducing other people to give money for the same purpose.

Through the wise use of this fund, we believe an object lesson in the way of the best kind of rural schools can be placed in many counties in the South. The interest from this fund can only aid a few schools in each state, but these being made object lessons can influence the character of education throughout a single county.

While we cannot speak definitely, we feel quite sure that it will be the aim of the Trustees of this fund to work in hearty sympathy and close co-operation with the county and state officers in assisting schools, and that it will be the policy of the Trustees to use the interest of this fund in a way to stimulate self-help and not replace local schools, but supplement the money being appropriated by Southern States toward the education of the Negro. The states, we feel sure, will be encouraged to do more for the Negro children because of this gift.

We think it cannot be too emphatically stated that not one cent of this money will go to help the Hampton Normal and Agricultural Institute nor to the Tuskegee Normal and Industrial Institute, and in no way relieve the pressing needs of these institutions, but every cent will go toward helping the rural schools, according to Miss Jeanes' wish and directions.

Booker T. Washington
Hollis Burke Frissell

Tuskegee Student, 19 (May 4, 1907), 1. Reprinted from the Philadelphia *Record.*

Helen Van Wyck Lockman[1] to Julius Robert Cox

[New York City] May Seventh [1907]

Dear Sir The Huntington place adv. on Sunday is charmingly located by the Harbor side with no road or nuisance of any kind between.

It is a double old fashioned house with parlor, large living room, large dining room with three windows on the water and eight bedrooms. An extra could be provided for a man in one of the outbuildings. There is a private lane leading down a hillside to the house. Perhaps three acres of land are enclosed with it. I own six hundred feet of the water front. There are four stalls in the barn. I have an other barn on my land should extra stalls be required. The modern improvements are being put in now. Possession June 1st. Rent for four months or longer $1000.00.[2] Should you wish to see it please notify me.

(Mrs) M. A. Lockman

ALS Con. 7 BTW Papers DLC.

1 Helen Van Wyck (Mrs. Myron A.) Lockman (1863–1944) taught for many years at the Bovee School in New York.

2 Four days later Lockman acknowledged receipt of $100 from Cox, representing BTW, toward a total of $750 according to agreement in the lease. (Lockman to Cox, May 11, 1907, Con. 7, BTW Papers, DLC.)

To Charles Woodroph Hare

New York, May 15, 1907

Dear Sir: I am very glad indeed to see, in The Tuskegee News, an account of the movement to get rid of the dispensary. If this can be brought about it will result in Macon County being one of the cleanest and most orderly counties in the South. It is my opinion that the colored people will see that "blind tigers" are not supported if the dispensary is out of the way.

It is bad for an individual to be engaged in the sale of liquor, and it is much worse for an entire community to be engaged in the traffic of liquor, through the agency of a dispensary. The money derived from the source may accomplish some good, but the presence of this evil in a community, and the harmful influence it exerts over the growing lives of young men, will more than offset the good accomplished.

I hope to be home in a few days and confer with you about several matters. Very truly yours,

[Booker T. Washington]

TLc Con. 36 BTW Papers DLC.

To William Howard Taft

Tuskegee Institute, Alabama. May 21, 1907

My dear Secretary Taft: This note will be handed you by Mr. Charles W. Anderson, Internal Revenue Collector for the Second District of New York. Mr. Anderson is one of the wisest and strongest members of our race. He is an ardent admirer of yours and has often expressed an earnest desire to meet you, so it is for this reason that I am taking the liberty of giving him this note of introduction to you.

You can talk with Mr. Anderson freely and fully regarding any matters. Mr. Anderson is a member of the New York State Republican Committee and it was through his lead that an action, which might have been hurtful to the President and yourself, was prevented a few days ago. Very truly yours,

Booker T. Washington

TLS William Howard Taft Papers DLC.

To Ray Stannard Baker

[Tuskegee, Ala.] May 23, 1907

My dear Mr. Baker: I read the manuscript for the August number[1] with interest. I make only one suggestion. You state in the first paragraph: "It is this element which has driven the Negroes out of many communities in the South and it commonly forms the lynching mobs."

I know of very few communities in the South where the Negroes have been driven out. There are, however, a great many communities and counties where practically no colored people live, and in most such cases you will find that the whites have gotten in there first and the colored people stayed away. It would be almost as correct to state that the colored people had driven the white people out of many strictly white communities. There is one county in Alabama where I think there is only one or two colored people: I do not think it would be safe to say that the colored people have been driven out of this county; the fact is, as I have said, the whites got in there first, and they were a poor class of white people who were not able to employ colored people or who did not wish to do so or who wished to do their own work, and hence the colored people remained away.

I think the article on the whole is very good. Yours truly,

Booker T. Washington

TLpS Con. 35 BTW Papers DLC.

[1] Ray Stannard Baker, "White Man and Negro in the Black Belt," *American Magazine,* 64 (Aug. 1907), 381–95. Baker saw the secret of success for southern blacks in hard work, thrift, sobriety, and high moral standards. Only with these virtues could blacks become landowners. Landownership, Baker maintained, would lead to the desire for education and responsible citizenship. Baker also declared industrial education an important factor in racial advancement.

To William Hayes Ward

Tuskegee Institute, Alabama May 24, 1907

My dear Dr. Ward: I wonder if you could use this letter which I am sorry to say I have been compelled to dictate, during the next few days in The Independent? If you can use this, I want to follow it up in a day or two with an article regarding a meeting of the Alabama Negro doctors. I can send you a fine photograph to be used in this connection. When I came to Alabama twenty-five years ago there was not a single physician of the race in the state. When the State Negro Medical Association met in Birmingham a few days ago there were over seventy present. Yours very truly,

Booker T. Washington

TLS Francis Jackson Garrison Papers NN-Sc.

To Booker Taliaferro Washington, Jr.

[Tuskegee, Ala.] May 27, 1907

My dear Booker: During the next few weeks I am going to have large expenses in many directions, that is, I will have a great deal of money to pay out, and I hope you will be just as economical as you possibly can in the use of every cent I send you. Do not spend any money for anything unless you are absolutely compelled to do so.

Before leaving New York, I went down to look at the house we are to occupy during the summer. It is a beautiful house right on the salt water and the surroundings are very fine. I am quite sure that both you and Gomez will enjoy it.

My present plan is to have Mr. Owens[1] spend two or three days in Exeter in order to find out the methods which they use in teaching, also to find out just the ground which you and Gomez should cover during the summer. He will be ready to begin teaching soon after your school closes.

As soon as you receive this letter, please let me know the exact date when Dummer closes.

Also let me know the date when the prize contest occurs. I hope that you will be successful in winning the first prize.

I think it well for neither you nor Gomez to say anything to the people there about whether you are going to return next year or not. I advise that you pack your things carefully away in your room, that is those that you are not going to bring away with you, so that they can be removed if necessary at any time.

Be careful and do not make the mistake of spending too much time on your motorcycle.

I want your mark to be higher this month even than it was last month.

As you know, we are now getting ready for the closing of the school. Yesterday was Commencement Sunday, and the Commencement exercises occur next Thursday.

You have not acknowledged the receipt of that check which I sent you. You ought to make it a rule to acknowledge promptly the receipt of all money which you get from any one. Your papa,

B. T. W.

TLpI Con. 363 BTW Papers DLC.

[1] T. Edward Owens taught mathematics at Tuskegee from 1903 until after BTW's death.

From Charles William Anderson

New York, N.Y., May 27, 1907

(Personal) *Private & Confidential*

My dear Doctor: Following up my telegram of last Saturday, I beg to say, that I told "our friend"[1] that, in my judgment, it was time we took some action against the people who are inspiring these newspaper attacks, and informed him that the man[2] in the Interior Department was the leading spirit among them. I said that I felt that he would come to his senses if a reduction in rank should happen to take place, or if that was impossible, a transfer to some very hard and disagreeable service. I then asked him to give me a letter to Secretary Garfield,[3] whereupon he sat down and penned the following note with his own hand:

"Dear Garfield:

Mr. Anderson is one of our very best friends. You can talk absolutely, freely to him, as he is a safe man to follow.

Signed."

I took the note over to Mr. Garfield, who received me most cordially and agreed with me, that the course I suggested ought to be pursued. He sent for his Secretary and had him look up the exact position occupied by the man in question and made a note of it. He asked me very particularly if I was *absolutely certain* that this man was engaged in writing editorials and stories of the nature I had described, and I replied, that there was no sort of doubt about it. I told him that I had investigated it personally and knew him to be the leader in this work. He promised to find some way to do exactly what I requested. If reduction could not be accomplished, then a transfer to something hard and disagreeable is the plan. I think the thing will be clinched if you will write him at once, assuring him that *there is no doubt that this particular man is the head devil.* Of course I said nothing about the man's attitude toward you, but contented myself with showing up his attitude toward the present administration. It is now distinctly up to you to reinforce my work by convincing Garfield that there is no doubt about the guilt of this man. I may add that the Secretary treated me with much consideration.

"Our friend" asked me to see Secretary Taft and talk over the artillery matter. I called at the War Department and sent in your letter and was immediately shown into the Secretary's private office. He gave me one of his big, hearty hand-shakes, and put me at ease at once. He seemed to know all about me and my little activity in the Republican State Committee. He asked me several questions about the different members of the Committee, and during my description of some of them, I thought he would split his sides with laughter. We got on famously together, and established a perfect "entente cordiale." We went over the army matter fully, and I quite agreed with your and his position. He ended the discussion on this subject by requesting me to write him a letter about it, after I had thought it over fully. By this, I presume he means to commit me along with all the others. I then told him that I had noticed an advertisement of a mass meeting to be held Monday evening (May 27th), at which Rev. Corrothers, Archie Grimke, George White,

Chase and Judge Gibbs of Arkansas were to speak and Rev. Waldron[4] was to preside. The meeting was to protest against the consideration of Taft's name for the Presidency. The Secretary at once set up and began to take notice. Seeing that he was concerned about the protestants, I then told him that this thing would go on as long as men in the government service secretly aided and inspired this opposition. I told him all about the man in the Interior Department, and then reminded him that he had one such in his own Department — by the name of Murray.[5] I told him what I thought his friends ought to do with people of this sort, and how quickly this thing would end, if once the kickers were convinced that it was unsafe to be engaged in this sort of work. I would not be surprised to learn in the near future that Murray was having a hard row to hoe. From this you will see that I had rather a successful day of it. I think I left a distinctly favorable impression on Secretary Taft, and I know he made a great hit with me. It didn't take me five minutes to learn that he was my kind of a man. I am really delighted with him.

I forgot to say that "our friend" told me that he had fixed up Lewis of Boston in the manner that you desired. I was glad to learn this. In introducing me to Senator Hemenway,[6] "our friend" said "Senator, I want you to know Collector Anderson of New York. He is just about straight goods, and you will hear of him in national politics before you are much older. I want you to know him for he is a good man to tie to." This was said out loud before fifteen or twenty people in the Cabinet room, and immediately after this speech, I requested him to write the note to Secretary Garfield.

I was greatly surprised to find the name of Judge Gibbs of Arkansas among the speakers at the Taft protest meeting. Gibbs was formerly Consul at Tamatave, Madagasgar, but resigned and had his son-in-law[7] named as his successor. A few months ago the administration promoted Hunt to the Consulate at St. Etienne, France. When I attempted to have Johnson sent to France, Mr. Bacon replied that as Hunt had already been promoted there, and Jackson[8] was at La Rochelle, it would be impossible to send another colored man to France. Thus you see Hunt's recent promotion prevented Johnson from realizing his ambitions, and now his backer and father-in-law (for Hunt has no strength of his own) is out making speeches against the administration's policy. It is a shame that our own friends have to suffer, while the friends of the other crowd receive exceptional rewards. I wish you would write "Our friend" at once, and lay this matter before him, and tell him that Gibbs would probably recover his senses if his son-in-law were transferred and another colored man (Johnson) given St. Etienne. This is the only remedy for these evils, and it ought to be applied all along the line. I am writing such a letter myself to-day. Please advise me on this point. Yours truly,

Charles W. Anderson

TLS Con. 35 BTW Papers DLC.

1 Theodore Roosevelt.

2 Lafayette M. Hershaw.

3 James Rudolph Garfield (1865–1950), the son of President James A. Garfield, was U.S. Secretary of the Interior from 1907 to 1919.

4 John Milton Waldron (b. 1863), a Washington, D.C., clergyman, socialist, and anti-Bookerite, was educated at Lincoln University (A.B. 1886) and Newton Theological Institute in Massachusetts. Waldron lectured widely on the race problem at churches and YMCAs and held several editorships in Washington, D.C., and Florida. In 1901 Waldron organized the Afro-American Industrial Insurance Society in Jacksonville, Fla. Originally a church-oriented society, it became a full-fledged insurance company. Waldron was a member of the Niagara Movement, and was among those Niagarites who endorsed the Democrats in 1908 and organized the National Negro American Political League, later the National Independent Political League. Beginning in 1906 Waldron was pastor of Shiloh Baptist Church in Washington, D.C. He was a founder of the NAACP and served on the Committee of Forty in 1909 and the NAACP's first executive committee in 1910. In 1913 Waldron broke with Woodrow Wilson over the issue of segregation in federal offices. He was also active in the temperance movement and in housing reform in Washington. (Sherman, *Republican Party and Black America*, 79–80, 109–10; Fox, *Guardian of Boston*, 162–79; Link, "The Negro as a Factor in 1912," 81–99.)

5 Freeman Henry Morris Murray (1859–1950), born in Cleveland, Ohio, was a clerk in the War Department and also worked with his family business in Washington, D.C., Murray Brothers Printing Co. With W. E. B. Du Bois and Lafayette M. Hershaw, Murray was a publisher of *Horizon* from 1907 to 1910. In 1915 he received a law degree from Howard University. For more than two years Charles W. Anderson sought to get Murray fired from his government job. (See Anderson to BTW, July 12, 1909, Con. 43, BTW Papers, DLC.)

6 James Alexander Hemenway (1860–1923), Republican U.S. senator from Indiana (1905–9).

7 William H. Hunt, of New York, was appointed U.S. consul at St. Etienne, France, in 1906.

8 George H. Jackson, born in Massachusetts, was a resident of Connecticut when appointed to the consular post at La Rochelle, France.

To James Rudolph Garfield

[Tuskegee, Ala.] May 27, 1907

Personal and Confidential

My dear Mr. Garfield: I write to second most heartily what Mr. Charles W. Anderson, of New York, said to you lately regarding the bad influence of a colored man by the name of Hershaw. I perhaps understand how difficult it is to deal with such cases and how much you dislike to even notice such people, but it is a fact which I could easily make you understand if I should have opportunity to talk with you, that this man, and others in Washington, is doing much to injure not only the colored people but to the administration by constantly misrepresenting the President and his officials and by keeping the colored people stirred up, especially in such matters as the Brownsville affair. He is so sly and deceitful in his methods that it is very difficult for a man who has not known him for years not to be deceived by him. If he cannot be removed, if some change were made in his work or his salary lowered or something done to indicate that the administration had its eye upon him it would have a far-reaching effect. He, together with Du Bois and one other man in the War Department, publishes a monthly paper called The Horizon, and it is full each month of matter abusing the President and at the same time putting wrong and false ideas into the heads of the colored people. Yours truly,

Booker T. Washington

TLpS Con. 6 BTW Papers DLC.

Emmett Jay Scott to John A. Hertel

[Tuskegee, Ala.] May 27, 1907

Personal

My dear Mr. Hertel: At your request and suggestion I am writing you. Of course, since what you told me is wholly confidential and has been treated as such, I must ask you to treat what I am going to say as completely confidential.

Could that property[1] be secured by paying the printer's bill, which I understand is not more than $600?

Would the paying of this bill secure the good will and subscriptions and all other property belonging to the magazine?

Could you see that the transfer of all this is put in legal form so there would be no question as to my getting the good will and all the property connected with the magazine?

Would it help matters for Mr. B.[2] to be given employment as editor or one of the editors by those who bought the magazine? It would not be the policy to throw Mr. B. overboard but to let him remain as one of the editors, giving him an opportunity to make a career for himself, but it would be the policy to gradually change the policy of the magazine in constructive directions and cease the policy of merely calling attention to the faults of white people and condemning people right and left. It would be the policy to see that more can be accomplished in race building by actually doing something than by merely whining and complaining.

It seems to me the question is, is it better to transfer the magazine in an honorable way to another concern ready to live, or let it remain as it is and die. The concern to which I am referring has ample facilities to get out the magazine promptly and to keep it up to the high plane which it has heretofore sustained.

Please telegraph answer to this letter as far as you can, and then write me fully later covering each of the points raised in this communication. Yours truly,

Emmett J. Scott

TLpS Con. 36 BTW Papers DLC.

1 *The Voice of the Negro.*

2 Jesse Max Barber.

To William Howard Taft

Tuskegee Institute, Alabama. May 28, 1907

Personal and Confidential

My dear Mr. Secretary: I am now replying to the question which you asked me and which was raised by my secretary, Mr. Emmett J. Scott, to give my opinion in regard to the advisability and wisdom of organizing a colored regiment of field artillery. I have thought carefully over this matter in all of its bearings since I saw you, and have taken the liberty of consulting with several persons in whose judgment I have confidence. Most of the persons with whom I have consulted are thoroughly in sympathy with you and the President and believe thoroughly in the policy of President Roosevelt. I have considered the subject not only as to the actual usefulness of the regiment but also the matter of public criticism that might be aroused by reason of the organization of such a regiment. Everything considered, I am prepared to recommend strongly that the regiment be organized, and I have no question in stating that, in my opinion, it will do much good in many directions.

Aside from the reasons which I have mentioned to you, you will note that in most of the states the colored state militia has been abandoned. This has served in many cases to discourage the colored people. The organization of this regiment will stop much of the senseless and useless criticism that is now in the air and will let the country see and feel that the President and the administration are in favor of doing the right thing by all races regardless of praise or blame.

The enclosed letter from Mr. Villard, of the Evening Post, I thought you might like to see. Of course I know what is his general attitude toward the President, but he has made a careful study of military matters, and, besides all this, I thought it would help matters to have him committed to such a policy. Please return his letter after you have read it.

Enclosed I also send an article, "The Negro in the Regular Army," written by Mr. Villard some years ago.[1]

If you desire to discuss this matter further, I can do so when I see you on the 6th.[2]

If the regiment is to be organized, I hope for certain reasons it can be done during the month of June, or the fact made public during this month. Yours truly,

Booker T. Washington

TLS William Howard Taft Papers DLC. A press copy, badly faded, is in Con. 537, BTW Papers, DLC.

[1] Oswald Garrison Villard, "The Negro in the Regular Army," *Atlantic Monthly*, 91 (June 1903), 721–29.

[2] Taft replied that he would discuss the matter when he met with BTW on June 6. (June 3, 1907, William Howard Taft Papers, DLC.)

To William Howard Taft

Tuskegee Institute, Alabama. May 29, 1907

My dear Secretary Taft: You have no doubt received notice from Dr. Frissell that the Trustees of the Jeanes Fund will meet in New York June 6th. Then it is the plan to adjourn to Philadelphia, mainly as a compliment to Miss Jeanes, and for the purpose of seeing her.

When in Philadelphia a few days ago, I mentioned to her that you had accepted a place on the Board and she seemed exceedingly pleased. She is an old lady over eighty-five years of age, and I am sure that nothing would better please her than for you to call, with the rest of the members of the Board, if you, in your busy life can possibly spare the time to do so. And I very much hope that your plans will enable you to do this. Very truly yours,

Booker T. Washington

TLS William Howard Taft Papers DLC.

To Emmett Jay Scott

Tuskegee Institute, Alabama May 29, 1907

Mr. Scott: Please instruct everybody connected with the office that it is against the rule of the office to have gum chewing in the office.

B. T. W.

TLI Con. 574 BTW Papers DLC. Docketed in Scott's hand: "Pls acknowledge this notice with initials."

From Seth Low

New York May 29th, 1907

Confidential.

Dear Mr. Washington; Since I saw you I have given much thought to the question of the chairmanship of your Board,[1] with the result that I feel it very essential to take some step that will protect me from embarrassment on the financial side, and that will also protect the Institute from suffering because its friends may think that I have made myself responsible for its financial success. I have therefore written the enclosed letter to the Board of Trustees, with the idea that it might be read to the Board before they act, and subsequently be given to the public. I am sending it to you for your criticism and suggestions, and I shall consult with some of the Trustees whom I can reach here. I daresay the letter can be improved in form by more careful consideration; but on the substance of it I must stand, that, while I am Chairman of the Board of Trustees, I will make no contribution in money to the Institute.

It is due to you to say what impressions I have formed by my general reflection upon the situation; for I should not wish to accept the chairmanship of the Board unless I felt that you would move willingly along the general lines that good judgment seems to me now to indicate. As you know, the great value of Tuskegee has always seemed to me to be that it is altogether the creation and the work of negroes, and I have not the slightest desire to impose upon you a policy which you yourself may think unwise; for there would be little gain and much loss in such a course. Several things, however, seem to me to be so clearly called for by the situation that I should not wish to accept a position of even indirect responsibility for the Institute unless I know that you feel as to these things as I do.

1. Tuskegee has come into being in response to your personal efforts. Without these it could not have been made, and without these it could not be maintained. If, however, it is to be permanent, that is to say, if it is to remain of value to the country after your death, I think the time has come when the management of it must lose, as far as practicable, the personal note and take on the impersonal. This is the whole trend of the new By-Laws; and, as you have approved of these in their general scope, I assume that you are in sympathy with this idea. One of the very first steps to be taken, in my judgment, is for the Trustees to appoint, upon your recommendation, a Vice-Principal, who can have full charge in your absence, and who can be in the way of being trained to step into your place in case of emergency.

2. While I appreciate the force of the argument which has led Tuskegee to accept a great many students even if they can stay at

Tuskegee for only a few weeks, I think the time has now come when it is in the interest of the Institute to insist upon better quality of work, even at the expense of smaller numbers. At Harvard and at Columbia, and I have no doubt elsewhere, it is quite customary to begin a new enterprise on a lower basis than is represented by the ultimate ideal; and I think that Tuskegee, not only for its own sake but for the sake of negro education at large, ought to move along the same path; for Tuskegee is no longer one of a great number of negro schools. It is the typical institution conducted by negroes for the education of negroes, and the standards which it sets up will profoundly affect the work done in negro institutions throughout the land. I am fully in sympathy with your idea of placing the emphasis of Tuskegee's work on the industrial side; though, naturally, I should like to see the academic side made at the same time as strong as possible. But it is evidently quite as important that the students of Tuskegee should have a good reputation industrially as academically; and it is impossible for this result to be obtained unless the students stay at Tuskegee long enough to be moulded by Tuskegee. I know the almost irresistible strength of the appeal to give a little to those who need everything; but I cannot help thinking that the typical position of Tuskegee in relation to the negro race makes it important for it to do what other institutions cannot afford to do; namely, show how thorough an education negroes can give to negroes, both in industrial and in academic lines.

3. I speak of the farm with much reserve, because my own experience in that line is limited. I cannot help thinking, however, that the loss under that head is too large to be permanently tolerated. I know that the processes of farming are slow, and that it takes several years to bring up soil that has been neglected. I feel, nevertheless, that this branch of the activities of Tuskegee will call for the most careful consideration. It may be better to work in that field on a smaller scale until experience has shown how to bring about better results; for the present situation not only throws heavy financial burdens upon the Institute, but it is also a showing calculated to discourage, rather than to encourage, resort to agriculture as an occupation.

The only other point which occurred to me in examining the Budget is one as to which I may easily be mistaken; for I made no attempt to go into the matter in details. It seemed to me that perhaps the administrative expenses of the School bear rather a large percentage to the academic expenses. I observed, also, that between 1904–05 and the present year the salary of almost every stenographer, for example, had been increased; but I did not notice a corresponding increase either in the salaries of teachers or in the number of teachers employed. I dare say that my impression was a mistaken one; but, if you have not looked into this matter recently, perhaps it would be worth while for you to do so.

I shall be glad to know whether your judgment moves with mine along these lines.

Replying to your letter of the 20th May, I have to say that Monday, June 24th, in New York, would be perfectly convenient to me as the time and place for the annual meeting of the Institute. Yours, very truly,

Seth Low

TLS Con. 991 BTW Papers DLC.

[1] Robert C. Ogden resigned as chairman of the Tuskegee Institute Board of Trustees on account of ill health. (Ogden to BTW, May 28, 1907, Con. 37, BTW Papers, DLC.)

From James Hardy Dillard[1]

New Orleans May 30, 1907

My dear Mr Washington: I have written to Dr. Frissell expressing my regret that I must be late for the first meeting in New York. I cannot possibly leave until Tuesday night, on the train due in New York at one on Thursday. I have been thinking about the great work before us, and the more I think of the practical side of it, the more clearly it seems to me that we should as far as possible try to act through the State superintendents. They ought to be, and certainly in most cases they are, most familiar with the local needs and the best points of attack. I had a talk with our superintendent, Aswell,[2] last Saturday. I mentioned to him that I had already received two letters from different points in the state. He said at once, "one of these men is all right, both negroes and whites in his community believe in him; the other one ought not to be helped, he is a sham, and is looking out only for himself." He then told me of five communities in the state where help from this fund would be of immense benefit at the present moment. After talking with him, I was all the more convinced that we should make every effort to work in conjunction with, and as far as possible, through the State Superintendents.[3] Yours sincerely,

James H. Dillard

ALS Con. 796 BTW Papers DLC.

[1] James Hardy Dillard, born in Nansemond County, Va., in 1856, was president of the Jeanes Foundation from 1907 to 1931. A graduate of Washington and Lee, he taught in many southern schools and was professor of Latin (1891–1907) and dean of academic colleges (1904–7) at Tulane University. Besides his direction of the Jeanes Foundation, he was also director of the John F. Slater Fund from 1910 to 1917, and its president after 1917, member of the Southern Education Board from 1908 to 1913, and member of the General Education Board after 1917. In 1928 the Harmon Foundation gave him its annual award for promotion of better race relations in the South. Dillard was remarkably free of racial bias and condescension.

[2] James Benjamin Aswell (1869–1931), former president of Louisiana Polytechnic Institute (1900–1904), was Louisiana state superintendent of education from 1904 to 1908 and an ally of the Ogden Movement. During his term as superintendent he reorganized the public school system. From 1908 to 1911 he was president of Louisiana State Normal College at Natchitoches. From 1913 to 1931 he was a Democratic member of the U.S. House of Representatives from Louisiana.

[3] Two days later, apparently in reply to a letter from BTW, Dillard wrote: "I may have appeared somewhat 'brash,' and I may have been thinking too exclusively of our own excellent man in Louisiana. I can well believe that some of the Southern superintendents would not be good for our purpose. My main feeling was that we should, as far as possible, work through the organized school authorities." (June 1, 1907, Con. 70, BTW Papers, DLC.)

To William Howard Taft

Tuskegee Institute, Alabama. May 31, 1907

Dear Mr. Secretary: Please consider the enclosed suggestions as confidential. I should like to know by the time we meet what you think of these suggestions. Yours truly,

Booker T. Washington

[*Enclosure*]

Memoranda regarding Jeanes Fund

1. The selection of the General Agent or Executive Secretary, who can devote his whole time to the administration of this fund with

such assistance as he may need, preferably a Southern white man of high standing and strong executive ability, who is thoroughly in sympathy with the education of the Negro child.

2. Consider the wisdom of having headquarters either at Atlanta, Ga., or Montgomery, Ala.

3. Would it be wise to decide, before expending any money for direct educational work, to find out the exact condition of the schools in the rural districts as to school houses and equipment, length of school terms, amount spent on each pupil per capita, amount spent for teachers salaries, and the attitude of the state and county officials toward Negro schools. With definite facts as to present conditions in hand, it seems that we might be in position for more effective work.

4. Would it be wise to pursue the policy for several years of spending money exclusively in the direction of providing comfortable school houses, to give money for school building on condition that for each dollar given by the trustees that the people must secure a dollar. This, in my opinion, would enable us to secure the erection of at least from 75 to 80 school houses a year. My experience and observation convince me that whenever the people secure a good school house that this within itself settles many other problems. In the first place, the parents take more interest in the school, they are willing to tax themselves to extend the school term, and a good school house means a good teacher, and, besides, the school house serves as a sort of social center for the entire neighborhood. The people are much more willing to give money for the building of a school house than for the extension of the school term because the building of a school house presents something that is tangible and visible.

In this connection, I might add that for a number of years I have been expending a sum of money given by Miss Jeanes previously for the improvement of rural schools, and have devoted it almost wholly to the building of school houses with the result that I have named. Or, would it be better to pursue the policy of securing a good teacher first and put the burden of details in providing the school house upon the teacher rather than have these details to be assumed by the Trustees of the Jeanes Fund.

5. In administering this fund, would it not be wise to pursue the policy of dealing wholly with the state superintendent, county

superintendent, township officials, making the public schools the basis of our work rather than independent schools, rather than to have the General Agent or Secretary have any direct dealings with the individual school teacher? Unless this fund is administered very judiciously, there is great danger that harm may result in causing the school officials to get the idea that this fund is going to educate the Negro children and therefore they may feel free to withdraw state and county aid. Clinging to the policy of dealing with the officials and using this money only on condition that an equal amount is raised in the county or given locality will obviate difficulty.

6. Would it not be wise to first select a few county superintendents in each state who are already thoroughly interested in Negro education and believe in it and begin working with and through them with the idea that the neighboring superintendents who may not be so friendly may see just what is being done through the friendly county superintendent and be induced to take more interest in the education of the Negro child.

7. The General Agent or Executive Secretary should keep in his office information regarding the condition and needs of rural schools throughout the South.

TLS and Enclosure William Howard Taft Papers DLC.

To the New York *American*

[Tuskegee, Ala.] May 31, 1907

Only foundation I know for such report[1] is that I am going to live on a farm during part of summer at Huntington, Long Island. Have bought no property in that vicinity. Do not know that place is anywhere near Sagamore Hill.

Booker T. Washington

TWpSr Con. 355 BTW Papers DLC.

[1] On the same day, the owner of the house wrote: "Reporters got news from telephone Co. All on hand last night. No information given." (Helen Van Wyck Lockman to Julius R. Cox, May 31, 1907, Con. 7, BTW Papers, DLC.) "Do not let any one know that I made a reduction for you," she urged. (Lockman to Cox, June 1, 1907, Con. 7, BTW Papers, DLC.)

Emmett Jay Scott to Oswald Garrison Villard

[Tuskegee, Ala.] May 31, 1907

(Personal and Confidential)

Dear Mr. Villard: I am very glad that you have so heartily endorsed the artillery matter. Dr. Washington has shown me your letter. I think you know that it was through my efforts that Secretary Taft was led to pave the way for the appointment of colored men as bandmasters in the Negro regiments, a few weeks ago.

For your personal information, I beg to hand you herewith a letter to the President bearing date March 8th, with which I sought to get representation in the artillery branch of the service. A personal letter to the President accompanied this communication, and if I can find copy in the next day or two, I will send you a copy of it. Yours truly,

Emmett J. Scott

TLpS Con. 37 BTW Papers DLC.

Julius Robert Cox to Emmett Jay Scott

[Tuskegee, Ala.] May 31, 1907

Mr. Scott: I have noted the attached note.[1] Some 15 or 16 years ago, acting upon the advice of a physician, I commenced chewing gum as an aid to indigestion. Since that time I have been chewing it, not as a habit or for the sake of the gum, but for a purpose as I have found it beneficial.

I do not consider chewing gum a pernicious habit, a vicious practice or an immoral act, but rather one within the rights of personal privilege, which injures, or interferes with, no one else. Very truly yours,

Julius R. Cox

TLpS Con. 574 BTW Papers DLC.

[1] See BTW to Emmett Jay Scott, May 29, 1907, above.

MAY · 1907

An Article in the *Ladies Home Journal* by Emmett Jay Scott

May 1907

MRS. BOOKER T. WASHINGTON'S PART IN HER HUSBAND'S WORK

Of Booker T. Washington and of the great Tuskegee School for Negroes[1] he has builded the public has heard much. It knows but little, however, of the woman who is to him both helpmeet and companion. Nevertheless, not the least factor in the success of Mr. Washington and his school has been the support and cooperation of the woman who divides with him the responsibilities and the labors of a leader of his people.

Even before the War closed there came to the South on the heels of the army of emancipation an army of school-teachers. They came to perfect with the spelling-book and the reader the work that the soldiers had begun with the sword. It was during this period, in the little straggling village of Macon, Mississippi, that a little girl, called then Margaret Murray, but who is known now as Mrs. Booker T. Washington, was born. When she grew old enough to count she found herself one of a family of ten, and, like nearly all children of Negro parentage at that time, very poor.

In the grand army of teachers who went South in 1864 and 1865 were many Quakers. Prevented by the tenets of their religion from entering the army as soldiers these people were the more eager to do the not less difficult and often dangerous work of teachers among the freedmen after the War was over.

One of the first memories of Mrs. Washington's childhood is of her father's death. It was when she was seven years old. The next day she went to the Quaker school-teachers, a brother and sister, Sanders by name, and never went back home to live.

And so it was that Margaret Murray became at seven a permanent part of the Quaker household, and became to all intents and purposes, so far as her habits of thought and religious attitude are concerned, herself a Quaker.

The books she found in this Quaker household were, as may be imagined, of the sober sort. The passionate interest with which this little girl consumed them merely reflects the interest that seized the whole race of enfranchised people at that time. The great mystery of letters had so impressed the imagination of the Negro people during the period of slavery and after emancipation that they were possessed with a fanatical desire for knowledge.

She Taught School When Fourteen Years Old

Never in the history of the world have people made such sacrifices to get knowledge as the masses of the Negro people have since the War. And after they had learned, their next greatest desire is to teach others who have not yet had an opportunity to learn.

When Margaret Murray was fourteen years old the good Quaker teacher said one day, "Margaret, would thee like to teach?" That very day the little girl borrowed a long skirt and went downtown to the office of Judge Ames, and took her examination. It was not a severe examination. Judge Ames had known Margaret all her life and he had known her father, and in those days white people were more lenient with Negro teachers than they are now. They did not expect so much of them. And so, the next day Margaret Murray stepped into the schoolroom where she had been the day before a pupil and became a teacher.

Then Margaret heard of the school at Nashville, Fisk University, and she went there. She had a little money when she started to school, and with that and what she was able to earn at the school and by teaching during vacations she managed to work as, what was termed rather contemptuously in those days, a "half-rater." It was not the fashion at that time, in spite of the poverty of the colored people, for students to work their way through school.

In those days very little had been heard at Fisk of Tuskegee, of Hampton, or of Booker T. Washington. Students who expected to be teachers were looking forward to going to Texas. Texas has always been more favorable to Negro education than other Southern States, and has always got the best of Negro public-school teachers.

But upon graduation day, June, 1889, Booker T. Washington was at Fisk, and he sat opposite Margaret Murray at table. About that time it was arranged that she should go to Texas, but, without knowing just how it came about, she decided to go to Tuskegee and become what was then called the Lady Principal of the school. She has been at Tuskegee ever since.

Is a Sort of "Mother Confessor" at Tuskegee

Mrs. Washington's duties as the wife of the Principal of the Tuskegee Institute are many and various. She has charge of all the industries for girls. She gives much time to the extension work of the school, which includes the "Mothers' Meetings" in the town of Tuskegee and the "plantation settlement" near by. Her most characteristic trait, however, is a boundless sympathy which has made her a sort of Mother Confessor to students and teachers of the Institute.

The Mothers' Meetings grew out of the first Tuskegee Negro Conference held at Tuskegee in February, 1892. Mrs. Washington, as she sat in this first meeting of Negro farmers and heard what they had to say, was impressed with the fact that history was repeating itself. Here again, as in the early days of the Woman's Suffrage Movement, women had no place worth mentioning in the important concerns of life outside the household. While there were many women present at this first conference they did not seem to realize that they had any interest in the practical affairs that were being discussed by their sons and husbands. While her husband was trying to give these farmers new ideas, new hopes, new aspirations, the thought came to Mrs. Washington that the Tuskegee village was the place for her to begin a work which should eventually include all of the women of the county and of the neighboring counties. Accordingly, the first Mothers' Meeting was organized in the upper story of an old store, which then stood on the main street of the village. Mrs. Washington says: "That first meeting I can never forget. The women came, and each one, as she entered, looked at me and seemed to say, 'Where is it?' We talked it all over, the needs of our women of the country, the best way of helping each other, and there and then began the first Mothers' Meeting, which now has in its membership two hundred and twenty-nine women."

The meetings are now held in a large, roomy hall on the main street in a brick building owned by a colored merchant, a graduate of the Tuskegee Institute. Women now come long distances on foot to attend the meetings. They bring the little girls whom they cannot afford to leave at home. The presence of these children raised another question: "What should be done with the children?" A plan has been carried out which is doing for the children somewhat the same service that the Mothers' Meeting is doing for their mothers. The children now number fifty. They are taught simple lessons, and at the same time receive practical talks on behavior at home and in the streets and elsewhere. A small library-room is also provided for them, with picture-books and simple games on the tables.

There is marked improvement among the women in the matter of dress and care of the hair, the old plantation habit of "wrapping" it being almost entirely done away with. The women no longer go barefooted, nor do they sit around the streets in listless fashion indulging in a kind of reckless familiarity with the men. Thousands of papers and picture-cards sent by friends of the school have been distributed, so that the cracks of the cabin homes may be closed against the wind, and in order that the children may become accustomed to seeing something besides the cheerless logs that usually face them inside their homes.

Very few of the women can tell how old they are. Mrs. Washington has them recall some incident in their lives as near as possible the time they were born, and in this way their ages are discovered.

THE PLANTATION SETTLEMENT SHE STARTED TEN YEARS AGO

About eight miles from Tuskegee there is a large plantation where some thirty families are living. Many other families live in the vicinity. It was here that some ten years ago Mrs. Washington started what she called a "Plantation Settlement."

She asked some of the teachers at Tuskegee to begin to help these people. At first they went to the plantation on Sundays only. Mrs. Washington selected what seemed to be the most promising cabin, and asked the woman who lived there if she could come to that house the next Sunday and hold a meeting. When the party went down early the next Sunday morning a stout new broom was taken along. Making the woman a present of the broom, it was suggested that all take a hand in cleaning the house a little before the people should begin to come. The woman took the broom and swept half of the room, when Mrs. Washington volunteered to finish the job.

She had not gone far along on her half before the woman said: "Oh, Mis' Washington, lemme take de broom an' do mah half ovah." Mrs. Washington says: "I have always thought that that one unconscious lesson in thoroughness was the foundation of our work on that plantation."

The people came out quite largely to the meeting, and after a few Sundays they gladly accepted the offer to have a day-school opened. The owner of the plantation gave the use of an old cabin for the teacher and the school, and a teacher, an earnest young woman who had been a student at the Tuskegee Institute, was secured. With a few simple household belongings this young woman moved into the cabin which was to be at once her home and the schoolhouse.

The Children Are All Taught to Do Something

The expense of this school at first was borne largely by contributions from the teachers of the Tuskegee Institute — from their none too large salaries — and from some money given Mrs. Washington for this work by generous Northern friends, but after a little the people of the community began to realize its value to them and to give what they could to its support. Provisions and supplies for the teacher were brought by those who could not pay money. After a time, too, the school began to help support itself.

Few of the children could even read when the work began, but school for them meant much besides the alphabet. The girls were taught — and are now — to take care of the house, to wash dishes, scrub and make beds. The boys split wood, kept the yard clean, and planted and cared for the garden about the cabin, and learned to raise poultry. From the first the influence for good of the teacher, Miss Annie Davis, began to be evident in the community. The one-room cabin homes were kept neater, the moral life of the place was better. A Sunday-school was established, and a rough little board church built.

After three years in the old cabin the school was such a success that it was decided to provide for it larger accommodations. Ten acres of land were bought adjoining the plantation, and a neat, comfortable, frame house of three rooms was built. One of the rooms is the schoolroom, and the other two are the teacher's home and the practice-rooms for the girls' housekeeping. Around the house is a large garden in which the boys and girls raise good crops of many kinds of vegetables.

The rest of the land has been broken up and planted in various crops. In the summer months the teacher closes school at two o'clock and goes out with the children into the fields to work. During the last two years good crops have been grown on the place, and have been used for the teacher's food, or toward the support of the school. With money given by visitors at Tuskegee Institute who occasionally drive down to see this plantation, the teacher has been able to buy a cow, and now the boys learn to care for the cow, the girls learn how to make butter, and the teacher's table is just so much better supplied.

SHE IS "COMPLETELY ONE" WITH HER HUSBAND IN THEIR WORK

Not the least of the duties which fall to Mrs. Washington is that of caring for the distinguished people who visit the Tuskegee Institute. The Tuskegee rule that everything must be in readiness for the inspection of visitors, as much so in the kitchen as in any other department of the school, prevails in her home also.

An interesting part of this home life is the Sunday morning breakfast. The teachers have slept later than usual, and, when Mr. Washington is at home, they are invited in groups of three and four to share their morning meal. In this way he keeps in personal touch with each of his teachers; he knows what they are doing; he hears their complaints, if they have any; he counsels with them; they "get together."

Mrs. Washington's labors for the good of her people are not confined to the school. She is President of the Southern Federation of Colored Women's Clubs, and editor of the official organ of the National Federation of Colored Women's Clubs, of which she is also an officer.

Mr. Washington's estimate of his wife's helpfulness to him may be gathered from his tribute in his autobiography, "Up from Slavery": "She is completely one with me in the work directly connected with the school, relieving me of many burdens and perplexities."

Ladies Home Journal, 24 (May 1907), 42.

1 Scott corrected the galley proof to capitalize the word *Negro*. (Proof in Con. 17, BTW Papers, DLC.)

To Arthur E. Whatham

[Tuskegee, Ala.] June 1, 1907

Personal

Rev. Arthur E. Whatham, I come into contact in one form or another with the discussion of the subject which your letter raises almost constantly, and especially during the last two or three years.[1]

I can remember some years ago when the subject was first brought up of having a Negro Bishop in the Episcopal Church, quite an element of colored people in that organization were opposed to it. I have noted the change in recent years, so much so that I know of no members of the Clergy who would not favor a Negro Bishop. Some have gone so far as to state that the membership of the Episcopal Church, as far as the Negro is concerned, has grown about as large as it can be without a Negro Bishop. I am quite sure if I were asked to give my opinion on the subject it would be in the direction of electing a Bishop of our race.

If I can be of further service, please let me know. Yours truly,

Booker T. Washington

TLpS Con. 363 BTW Papers DLC.

[1] Whatham, of St. Peter's Church in Louisville, asked BTW's opinion on the question of Negro bishops "for our colored work." He deplored the increase of racial discrimination in the South and in the Episcopal Church, but as though frightened by his own words he underscored at the top of his letter, "Both present letter and reply, private." (May 25, 1907, Con. 363, BTW Papers, DLC.)

John A. Hertel to Emmett Jay Scott

Chicago 6/1/07

Dear Mr. Scott: I am wiring you as you suggest that $600. won't buy it. There are other people that would snap at it at this price, whether or not they would have the ability to make it a success is the question.

To make a long story short, Mr. Scott, I am heartily in sympathy with Dr. Washington's educational policy, I believe he is on the right track and on the other hand I believe that Barber is on the wrong track. I have studied Barber's methods and his policy for about three years, and I am convinced that the young man, though sincere and enthusiastic and determined is nevertheless in error in his method of solving or contributing towards the solution of this race problem.

I like your idea of retaining Barber, we can get together on this proposition. He has considerable ability, and I for one would be heartily in favor of giving him a place on the staff and carrying out the ideas that you suggest.

On Tuesday we had a business meeting, and I find that the receipts for two months were over $1500., over $800. worth of stock was sold by Barber, and I might say to you confidentially that I can, by investing another $300. or $400. have the control interest in this enterprise, and can turn it over to you free and un-incumbered for between $1200. and $1800. and for my equity I would arrange with you for advertising space because if a new company takes hold of this enterprise I want to advertise "The Negro in Business" in this magazine to beat the band this Fall.

My object would be to work in harmony with Prof. Washington's educational policy. I want to contribute my little mite towards the solution of the negro problem in which I have been intensely interested and I think the fact that I have invested over $10,000. in this enterprise already ought to be sufficient evidence to you that I was really in earnest.

I write you strictly confidential, you have got to be mighty careful who you take into your confidence so that this matter will not come to the ear of Mr. Barber, otherwise the transfer might not be made in a pleasant, amicable and equitable manner.

The matter can go on in its present form another month if you see fit, but you better write me fully in reply to this letter and give me your scheme. You can be frank with me regarding this business proposition and depend upon it absolutely that I will divulge nothing. I have been in business too long to swap information on important matters of this kind with any man. Yours truly,

John A. Hertel

TLS Con. 36 BTW Papers DLC.

To Emmett Jay Scott

Huntington, L.I., June 9, 1907

Dear Mr. Scott: You will be interested to know that I had a very satisfactory conference with the President Saturday night.

In all the years I have known him, I have never seen him looking better or in such fine spirits. He says that notwithstanding all the criticism heaped upon him from a certain element of the Negro race he is not soured or discouraged in the least. He said that he intends going right on doing what he believes to be for their interest, as he has done in the past.

He further said that the Negro race had not acted near so badly over the Brownsville matter as the laboring element had acted over the Haywood affair.[1] He spoke freely of other matters which I will tell you about when I see you. Very truly yours,

Booker T. Washington

TLS Con. 359 BTW Papers DLC.

1 The arrest and trial of labor leader William Dudley "Big Bill" Haywood, accused of ordering the murder of former Idaho governor Frank Steunenberg in 1906. Haywood and two other labor leaders were arrested in Denver and moved to an Idaho prison, where they were held for a year and a half before coming to trial in May 1907, with Clarence Darrow as attorney for the defense. Haywood was eventually found not guilty.

To Seth Low

Huntington, L.I., June 18, 1907

Dear Mr. Low: Replying to yours of May 29th, I would say that the statement which you propose to issue to the public, with possibly some changes in detail, is very satisfactory and I think will be wise. It would be hurtful to the institution if it should be thought that you, or any individual, was in a large degree, responsible for the financial support of the institution.

I realize fully that the time has come when the Tuskegee Institute must be placed upon such a footing as will secure its future and not make its existence and policy so thoroughly dependent upon the life of one man, as has been true of it in the past. In your efforts to bring about this result, you will have my hearty cooperation and approval. The main thing to be guarded, is to make any changes, decided upon, gradual[ly] rather than abruptly. I agree with you as to the importance of the Trustees selecting a Vice-Principal. In this connection I wonder if it would not be wise to appoint a small committee to consider this subject so far as the person to be selected or recommended is concerned.

Any policy that looks toward the securing of more regularity in the attendance at Tuskegee and in the rounding out of the student body and securing more thorough work will meet with my approval. In this connection there are several points which I cannot cover in a brief letter. We have gradually secured, from year to year, a more regular attendance, but are far from our ideal in this respect. It seems almost impossible to prevent the crop conditions from affecting, seriously, the attendance. Perhaps 75% of our students are dependent, directly or indirectly, upon the cotton crops for their support. This means that a large number cannot enter our school until a portion of the cotton crop is gathered, and that they must leave in the early Spring to plant.

Within the last ten years, however, I think I am safe in saying that we have improved 50% in the matter of regular attendance. Another element which enters into the situation is that we have refused to follow the custom of many schools in the South, of securing personal help for our students. If this were done many students who go out to earn money for present expenses could remain throughout the nine months, but in real education and character building we have thought it wiser to place the responsibility of paying his personal expenses upon the student, to be paid either in labor, if not in cash. I am guided a good deal in my judgement, as to the result of our work, by my personal inspection of the work and standing of the men and women whom we have turned out, and in most cases they have more than met our expectations.

In regard to the farm. Your criticism, if I may describe it as such, is perfectly justified. In this matter, however, I want to make a request that the Trustees permit me to continue a policy, for the next three years at least, which I have carefully mapped and thought out, of improving the farm thereby increasing its income and decreasing its losses. I am giving the farm more of my personal attention, at present, than any other part of the institution and I believe that if I am permitted to carry out my plans, for the next three years, which will mean the selling of a portion of our land and buying tracts nearer the school, thus putting the farm in a more compact body, also making improvement in the land, buildings and other changes, that I can show gratifying results. In holding and operating so large an acreage, as we now have, I am keeping in mind that as our building operations will soon cease or greatly decrease, that a larger number of our students will turn to the farm, than is now true, and also the further fact that the colored people are engaged most largely in agriculture, and they are at their best in it, therefore this should be the largest industry at Tuskegee.

As to the cost of the administration expenses, it is perfectly natural that this item should call for comment. If the Tuskegee Institute was conducted as an ordinary institution with the same number of students and teachers, with no other responsibilities and relations, I would say that the expenses of administration could be cut in half. I am now going to make a statement, which I have made to no one else, excepting my Secretary, Mr. Scott.

I think I am safe in saying that at least one-half of the mail which comes into my office is concerned with matters not strictly bearing upon school work. The letters frequently reach more than a hundred a day. They come from all classes, in and out of this country, including the President of the United States and Cabinet members. I have done my best to rid myself of everything not strictly bearing upon our work at Tuskegee, but the fact remains that hundreds of matters bearing upon the interests of the ten millions of Negroes in this country center at Tuskegee, and these matters help to pile up the expenses of the administration. Not only this, but a large proportion of my time and strength is taken up in racial matters which I seem unable to throw off. Visitors are continually coming to Tuskegee to consult with me regarding racial and other educational matters. A large proportion of my time is given to attending public meetings in the North and South that do not strictly bear upon our work. To what extent all this extra effort is justified I leave to the Trustees to decide.

In this connection I ought to add that when President Roosevelt went into office, he asked me to assist him in certain matters pertaining to our race. I placed the suggestion fully and frankly before Mr. Ogden, Mr. Peabody and Dr. Frissell, and they said that they thought I ought to accede to the President's wishes.

The organizations of the Negro Conference and the Negro Business League were both started at Tuskegee and now have become national in character. I started these for the purpose of directing the attention of the race from its ills to its opportunities and from politics to a larger and more encouraging field of material development, considering this kind of work, in a large sense, educational. But I repeat that I wish the Board of Trustees would consider the whole question, broadly, and decide. Very truly yours,

Booker T. Washington

TLS Seth Low Papers NNC. A draft of this letter is in Con. 348, BTW Papers, DLC.

From Wilbur Patterson Thirkield

Center Marshfield, Mass. 7/2/07

My dear Dr. Washington: Your telegram was forwarded to this place & delayed. I promptly wired you.

I also would like to have an interview with you on one or two matters of importance. If you will not be over this way soon I might arrange to come to N. York. Let me hear from you.

You may observe that your election to our Board has stirred up the extremists. This does not disturb us & we know that you are used to it. My mail shows that it will gain to your support an element that will make your hold on the race stronger. The replies I have rec'd from influential men who have, for some reason been out of touch with you, are most gratifying. I am sure we can work together for the best interests of the race & of the Nation. Yours faithfully

W. P. Thirkield

R R Station — "Marshfield Center" — N.Y. N H & H. Ry. 30 mi. from Boston 12 mi. No. of Plymouth. Lv. Fall River 7:07 A. — Ar.

Plymouth 8:50 A – Ar. Marsh. Center 9:30 a m. If practicable, come & *see us.*

ALS Con. 362 BTW Papers DLC.

To Arthur Isaiah Vorys[1]

Tuskegee Institute, Alabama July 8, 1907

(Personal and Confidential)

My dear Mr. Vorys: I have your favor of July 1st. I happened to be in New York a few days ago and Mr. Anderson very kindly spoke to me of your letter to him bearing upon a Washington man. What Mr. Anderson says of that man voices my own opinion thoroughly. He is the very last man to be touched.

I strongly advise that for the present you will not excite any of the colored people by giving any special attention to individual men or individual newspapers except in a very cautious way. The minute one hears that you are paying attention in certain directions, you will have the whole body of the colored politicians down upon you for something and there will be probably a rough and tumble scramble.

You can consult freely and safely at all times with men like Mr. Chas. W. Anderson and a few others who have no selfish aim to gratify.

I shall be returning to Huntington, N.Y. again soon and if you are likely to be in that vicinity I shall be glad to see you.

I agree with you thoroughly concerning the danger that there is to the Negro race in this Brownsville agitation and am doing some quiet and effective work with colored newspapers in changing that tendency. I will from time to time let you know of the results of this work. Very truly,

Booker T. Washington

TLS Con. 362 BTW Papers DLC.

[1] Arthur Isaiah Vorys (1856–1933), an Ohio lawyer and insurance executive, was a member of the Republican National Committee from 1908 to 1912 and managed Taft's presidential campaign in Ohio.

From Samuel Edward Courtney

Boston July 12th 1907

My dear Mr. Washington: Duckery promised to let me see those letters last Sunday but failed to keep his agreement. I have hired our friend Wootton[1] to get them by *any* means. It will take a little time but feels quite certain he can get them long enough to make a copy. Very truly yours,

S. E. Courtney

ALS Con. 345 BTW Papers DLC.

1 Paul L. Wootton, a pressman residing in Cambridge according to the 1910 city directory. A supporter of BTW in the Boston area, where the Tuskegean had many critics, Wootton occasionally did favors for BTW. (See Fox, *Guardian of Boston*, 97.)

To William Wallace Haralson

Huntington, L.I., July 22, 1907

My dear Sir: While I have not as yet had an opportunity of seeing your official report I have seen enough of it to convince me that you have made a fair, thorough and just report and I want to let you know how very much I feel obligated to you in the matter.[1] In saying this I know full well had you found anything wrong you would have been just as quick to say so as you were to say that everything was all right, as you meant to do your full duty in the matter regardless of who was pleased or displeased.

I shall hope to write you about the other matter very soon. Very truly yours,

[Booker T. Washington]

TLc Con. 350 BTW Papers DLC.

1 Haralson's report, done for Governor Comer of Alabama, was reprinted in the *Tuskegee Student*, Aug. 3, 1907, 1. It was a glowing account of the school's financial operation. "The business organization of the Tuskegee Normal and Industrial Institute, looking at its purely business side, is a model of perfection," Haralson wrote. The school's physical appearance, the student body, and the curriculum also received praise.

To Oswald Garrison Villard

Huntington, L.I., July 23, 1907

Personal

My dear Mr. Villard: The enclosed statement regarding the taxes for educational purposes is perfectly trustworthy, as it was prepared by an intelligent and conscientious man. So much is often said about the South dividing the school fund equally and the white man paying for the Negro's education that I think the fallacy of the statement should be shown.

Please return the statement to me when you are through with it. Very truly yours,

Booker T. Washington

TLS Oswald Garrison Villard Papers MH.

To Ray Stannard Baker

Huntington, L.I., July 23, 1907

My dear Mr Baker: There are three subjects which come to my mind in connection with the South, that I hope you will treat before you finally get through, and they are the Convict System, the Public School System and Voting.

I think the public should know all the facts regarding these matters. Some very interesting things could be brought to light regarding all these subjects. Very truly yours,

Booker T. Washington

TLS Ray Stannard Baker Papers DLC.

From Emmett Jay Scott

Tuskegee Institute, Alabama July 23, 1907

Dear Mr. Washington: You can be very sure that nobody from Montgomery wrote the report which appears on the front page of the Guardian of this week, which I have marked and sent to you.

I wonder also if anybody has called your attention to the effort being made by certain of the newspapers to take the statement emanating from the White House, to the effect that you had counseled the President that only Negro politicians were stirred up over the Brownsville affair, as a means of proving, as they say, race treason. The more I think of it, the more I think that report was uncalled for, especially in the references made to you. Our friend does not protect you, & has given Trotter, Harry Smith & the whole brood a new weapon to defeat their own purposes. Yours truly,

E J Scott

TLS Con. 574 BTW Papers DLC.

From Seth Low

Bedford Station, N.Y., July 28. 1907

Confidential

Dear Mr. Washington: I am, as you know, a member of the Episcopal Church; and perhaps you also know that there is going on in that body a warm discussion as to the wisdom of appointing Colored Bishops with missionary jurisdiction over the Colored people in adjoining dioceses. These bishops would have seats in the House of Bishops of our general convention, which meets every three years, and the negro missionary jurisdictions would be represented by a clerical and lay delegation on the same basis as other missionary jurisdictions.

I do not wish to quote you, but I would like very much to know, for my own guidance, how this proposition strikes you.

As a matter of theory, I confess that a racial separation seems to me out of place in a religion that claims that in Christ there is "neither barbarian, Scythian, bond, nor free." I confess, also, that I do not pretend to know how two races are to continue to live together on terms of industrial and political amity who will not mingle socially even in their churches.

On the other hand, dealing with the question as a condition and not a theory, is not this proposal in line with the general educational policy which seems to so many of us not only inevitable at the present time, but on the whole advantageous for the negro as well as for the whites. In other words, how is the negro to develop leadership without opportunity? And how is he to get opportunity if not among his own people?

Personally, I am not at all interested in the ecclesiastical aspect of the question. But I am very greatly concerned that our Church shall not take a step that will make all other problems harder, if that would be the effect; nor decline, on the other hand, to adopt a policy that promises to be helpful now, even if no one can see the outcome of it in the long future.

I shall be more than glad to have your views on this subject. Yours, very truly,

Seth Low

I have your letter giving me the result of the vote on the proposal to tax the Tuskegee property, in the Alabama legislature. I congratulate you on the decisive defeat of the proposal.

S. L.

ALS Con. 36 BTW Papers DLC. A typed copy is in the Seth Low Papers, NNC.

From Winfield Forrest Cozart[1]

Manitou, Colorado. 7-29 1907

Dear Sir: Several copies of the Boston Guardian has been sent me in which you have been severely criticised, especially in refer[e]nce to the discharged Colored Soldiers.

I am sure that the Guardian has placed you in a false light, the same as it has always tried to do, and I assure you that I do not believe what has been said.

I also wish to assure you that I am still with you in your great industrial movement, which I believe is beneficial to the masses, of both races.

In refer[e]nce to the discharge of the Colored Soldiers I wish to state that the race stands almost a unit, in condemnation of their discharge without trial and nothing short of restoration will settle the matter, especially, if the Senate Committee do not find evidence enough to convict.

We believe that the President me[a]nt well and we are still devoted to him, and do not question his honesty, and sincerity of a "Square deal," because we have faith enough in him to believe that when he is thoroughly convinced of his mistake he will rectify same.

It is indeed unfortunate that this regretable incident happened.

I like thousand of others has kept silent and watched with great interest the result of the investigation and final result. As much as I appreciate the effort of Senator Foraker, to secure a trial like millions of others I have remained silent.

But the time is near at hand, important moves on the political chess board will soon be made and if the administration and the party wish to retain the support of the Colored Vote in the next National election, the time of action has come. As you know I am in a business where I come in direct contact with voters.

I have spent some time in the various big cities between here and Atlantic City, and I have only met one Colored man who says that the dismisal of the troups was right.

You know I have been in the employ of the National Republican committee during the last two National campaigns, and that I am usually conservative. I will tell you how I felt about the dismisal of the troups, I had an application on file in the State Department for appointment in the Consular Service. As soon as the Soldiers was dismissed, I wrote Sec. Root, Saying owing to recent happenings I have decided to withdraw my application for appointment in the Consular Service. Accordingly my papers & endorsment was returned. The above explains how I felt, and there were million others.

I write you thus freely, with the best intent, that you may know how I and many others stand on the Soldier question.

I hope that you will pardon me for assuming the liberty to write you on this subject but do so through friendship.

I wish to congratulate you upon your election to the Trustee Board of Howard, and I feel that in Dr. Thurkiel we have an able and competent president.

Thanking you in advance for receiving this letter in the spirit in which it is sent, and hoping for your continued success I remain, Yours Very Sincerely,

W. Forrest Cozart
Author "The Waiters Manual"
"The Chosen People"
Headwaiter Cliff House

ALS Con. 345 BTW Papers DLC.

[1] Winfield Forrest Cozart (b. 1867), waiter, author, and Republican politico, wrote several books on proper dining-room techniques as well as a book on mixed marriage. In 1916 he was a delegate from New Jersey to the Republican national convention.

An Article in *World's Work*

July 1907

A TOWN OWNED BY NEGROES

Mound Bayou, Miss., An Example of Thrift and Self-Government

Bolivar County is noted among the counties of Mississippi for two reasons: it contains the richest soil in the famous Yazoo Delta, and it possesses the only regularly constituted Negro town in the Southern States. This town, called Mound Bayou, gets its name from a large mound, a relic of the prehistoric inhabitants of the country, which marks the junction of two of the numerous bayous that make so important a part of the natural drainage system of this low and level land.

Situated in the heart of the wide alluvial plain between the Mississippi and the Yazoo Rivers, Mound Bayou is the centre of a Negro population more dense than can found anywhere else outside of Africa. The Negroes outnumber the whites seven to one throughout the Delta. There are whole sections of these rich bottom-lands where no white man lives. Mound Bayou and the territory for several miles around it on every side is one such section — a Negro colony, occupying 30,000 acres, all of which is owned by Negroes, most of them small farmers who till 40 and 80-acre tracts. The town itself has, at present, a population of about 500. Of these, eighty-three are registered voters.

Mound Bayou is a self-governing community. That is one of the interesting things about it. It has had, since it was incorporated in 1898, a mayor, three aldermen, a constable, and a town marshal, all of them Negroes. This was necessarily so, because no white man has ever lived in this community since it was established, except the man who introduced the telephone system, and he remained only long enough to teach some of the townspeople how to manage the exchange.

The colony, of which Mound Bayou is, so to speak, the capital, grew out of a correspondence and an interview between Maj. George W. McGinnis, land commissioner of what was known at that time as the Louisville, New Orleans, and Texas Railway, and Isaiah T. Montgomery, the man who founded the colony. The railroad, now known as the Yazoo and Mississippi Valley, wanted to settle the vacant lands along its right-of-way. It was Montgomery's idea to establish on these wild lands a Negro colony, and his plan was heartily seconded by the officers of the railroad. In the spring of 1887, accompanied by a civil engineer, he made a personal inspection of these lands and finally located a site for the present town on the line of the railroad 104 miles south of Memphis and 116 miles north of Vicksburg.

Twenty years ago, this whole region was wild and inaccessible. The country was covered with a heavy hardwood forest, which united with a dense undergrowth of briars and cane to make a dense jungle, through which it was only possible to thread one's way by the use of a magnetic needle, cutting the path as one proceeded. Through this semi-tropical jungle, the railroad had blazed a wide furrow for a distance of 200 miles from Memphis to Vicksburg, along which were scattered a few straggling villages, with here and there a larger town.

One morning in the fall of 1887, a northbound train stopped in the midst of this wilderness, a party of Negroes stepped off, and the train went its way. The leader of the group, a small, slender man, with strongly marked features and a deliberate and thoughtful manner, held in his hand a plot, which he looked at from time to time. This was Isaiah T. Montgomery and the men with him were the first contingent of prospective settlers.

It was not easy, as I have often heard Mr. Montgomery say, to find settlers in that early day. The task of taming this wild country seemed hopeless to men with so few resources and so little experience. On this particular morning, Mr. Montgomery thought it best to make a little speech before proceeding with the work that had brought them thither.

"You see," he said, waving his hand in the direction of the forest, "this is a pretty wild place." He paused, and the men looked hesitatingly in the direction he had indicated, but said nothing.

"But this whole country," he continued, "was like this once. You have seen it change. You and your fathers have, for the most part, performed the work that has made it what it is. You and your fathers did this for some one else. Can't you do as much now for yourselves?"

The men picked up their axes and attacked the wilderness. The idea of the thing got hold of the minds of some of them, so they went back home and prepared to return and take up the work of pioneers. It was not until February, 1888, however, that the first permanent settlers moved in. A month later the ground was cleared sufficiently to set up a small store. Two dwellings were also erected. A few of these early buildings may still be seen in remote corners of the community. They were constructed of the materials at hand, walls of rough-hewn logs, roofed with a sort of shingle split with an axe from hardwood blocks.

There was, of course, no land to be cultivated when the first settlers arrived on the scene and no crop-lien system to provide in advance for provisions until something could be earned from the land. But the railroads needed cross-ties for their constantly extending lines. Timber agents came along in search of stave-bolts and spoke-material. This gave the settlers a chance to earn something while they were clearing the land. In this way the colonists solved the problem of living off the wilderness while they were engaged in subduing it. At the end of three years they had located and purchased 4,078 acres of land and had cleared and made ready for cultivation some 1,250 acres. They had earned during this time $8,780 from their timber operations and had raised 379 bales of cotton and 3,045 bushels of corn on the 655 acres of land which they had cleared.

The wilderness had become the frontier. The colonists came in faster now. The ragged outline of the forest steadily receded in all directions and large areas were opened for cultivation in the surrounding territory.

The Growth of the Colony

It was not the ordinary Negro farmer who was attracted to Mound Bayou colony. It was rather an earnest and ambitious class prepared to face the hardships of this sort of pioneer work. The scheme was widely advertised among the Negro farmers throughout the state and drew immigrants from all parts of Mississippi, and a certain number from other states. Some of the most valuable settlers in the community came from the "white-capping" counties in the southern part of the state. No doubt, the fact that the men who settled Mound Bayou are a select class has been an important factor in its success.

After twenty years of existence, Mound Bayou colony numbers about 800 families, making a total population of some 4,000 persons. Of the 30,000 acres of land owned by members of the community, about 6,000 acres are already under cultivation. This land produces annually about 3,000 bales of cotton and from one-half to two-thirds of the corn and fodder consumed by the community. The original site of the town has been extended until, including the thirty acres in the original plot and the several additions that have been made since, it embraces a tract of ninety-six acres.

With the influx of population, the value of land in the town and the surrounding country has greatly increased in value. Property inside the town that formerly cost from $7 to $9 an acre sells at present, in the form of building lots, at prices ranging from one to three cents per square foot. This land, which was assessed at one time at two dollars an acre, has now an assessed valuation of $23,073.55.

The business of the town has grown with the growing population. There are thirteen stores and a number of small shops in the town which do an annual business of something like $600,000. The express business at Mound Bayou amounts to $250 per month. The railroad station is the tenth in importance between Memphis and Vicksburg, according to a writer in the *Planter's Journal,* and the railroad traffic amounts to $40,000 a year.

There are six churches and three schools in the town. One of these, the Mound Bayou Normal and Industrial Institute, conducted by B. F. Owsley, has a building which, with the seven acres of land belonging to and adjoining the school, is valued at $3,500.

This school was started by the American Missionary Association before the town was incorporated. The expenses of maintaining it, about $1,500 a year, are met in part by the society that founded it, but in part by a tuition fee of $1 a month from its pupils. A second school, established and maintained by what are known familiarly as the "Sister Workers of the Colored Baptist Church of Bolivar County," has a large two-story building for recitations, and plans are now being made for the building of a dormitory to provide accommodations for pupils who come in from the surrounding farms to get the advantages of better schools than the county can provide.

The town is gradually increasing its facilities for doing business and is acquiring all the machinery of a highly organized community. Mound Bayou has a bank, three cotton gins, a telephone exchange, a weekly newspaper, and is preparing to issue bonds for the construction of waterworks and the erection of a system of electric lighting. It is an indication of the progress of the town that a well-kept cemetery — an institution too often neglected by Negroes — has been established on one side of the town, and a public park of five acres has been laid out on the other. Mound Bayou, though an exclusively Negro town, keeps up its connection with and interest in the outside world. The post-office business amounts to between $400 and $500 a quarter. Fifty Memphis papers are sold every day in the town and there are a number of subscribers to the magazines of general information.

The business interests of Mound Bayou town and community centre in the Bank of Mound Bayou, organized March 8, 1904, with a capital stock of $10,000. The earnings of the bank during the first eight months of its existence amounted to 17 per cent. In 1906, it paid a dividend of 16 per cent. and set aside a considerable sum as a surplus. The following statement indicates the condition of the bank on Feb. 12, 1907:

LIABILITIES

Capital paid in	$ 8,300.00
Deposits for capital account	2,500.00
Total	$10,800.00
Undivided profits	645.41
Deposits subject to check	29,545.33
Total	$40,990.74

ASSETS

Loans and discounts	$26,394.36
Building	4,000.00
Fixtures	2,004.02
Overdrafts secured	1,054.65
Cash and sight exchange	7,537.71
Total	$40,990.74

As practically all of the business of the colony centres in the bank, it is natural that nearly all the prominent business men of the town should be represented on the board of directors. Charles Banks,[1] the founder and cashier of the bank, was a successful business man at Clarksdale before he came, in 1903, to Mound Bayou. He became interested at that time in the success of the enterprise, sold out his business interests at Clarksdale, and cast in his fortunes with the colony. He is the youngest and most aggressive business man in the town. John Francis, the president of the bank, came to the settlement in an early day from New Orleans and worked for a time as a clerk. The Bradstreet and Dun mercantile agencies assess the value of his property at $20,000 to $25,000. His neighbors say that he and his wife are worth $50,000. W. T. Montgomery[2] – who is the postmaster, the brother of the founder, and vice-president of the bank – is a man of independent means. He owned and conducted for twelve years a farm of 640 acres near Fargo, N.D., which he sold at the time of the rise in Dakota lands at an advance of from $20 to $25 per acre over what he paid for it and invested in other lands in the neighborhood of Winnipeg, Canada.

Among the directors of the bank are R. M. McCarthy, who owns 450 acres of land in the colony and runs a cotton gin. T. C. Jordan has a bakery and meat market. He started in the colony as a farmer. He is now said to be worth something like $8,000 or $9,000. J. Barker is the town marshal. C. R. Stringer is treasurer of the town. H. A. Godbold, who came into the settlement as a farmer about 1895, runs a general store. The bank and its directors, because they represent and are so completely identified with the interests of the town, have come to have the position of a sort of chamber of commerce, guarding the credit of the various enterprises and directing and inspiring the economic and business development of the colony.

There are some special difficulties in the financial direction and development of a town and colony like Mound Bayou. For instance, it has been the constant aim of the men who founded the colony to preserve it as a distinctively Negro enterprise. Separated from, yet intimately bound up with the commercial and political interest of the other communities about it, the problem of preserving this isolation has often been a perplexing one. A difficulty arose a few years ago when the Louisville, New Orleans, and Texas Railway was sold to the Yazoo and Mississippi. Practically all the lands purchased from the railroad company had been subject to a lien for deferred payments. With the change of ownership in the railroad, a wholesale foreclosure of these mortgages seemed imminent. Charles Banks and his associates in the bank managed, however, to have the loans renewed and upon terms by which the mortgages were to bear 6 per cent. interest instead of 8 per cent.

In time, all of the original purchase money for these lands was paid, but many of the colonists had borrowed money for improvements. There was, therefore, a constant danger that farmers who were not able to discharge the mortgages when they came due would lose their holdings. To provide against this, the Mound Bayou Loan and Investment Company was formed, with a capital stock of $50,000. W. T. Montgomery was made president of this company and Charles Banks secretary and treasurer. The plan of this company was to sell stock to the farmers in the community. The price of shares was fixed at $50, payable in monthly instalments of one dollar. By this means, a capital was secured to take over the mortgages of those members of the community who were not able to pay the loans as they fell due, and at the same time provide a way by which the owners of the land might accumulate a sum sufficient to pay off the indebtedness for which the mortgage was issued. It is expected that the capital accumulated in this way will eventually be used to assist settlers coming into the colony to acquire and pay for lands, and in this way extend thc holdings and the influence of the colony.

The Town's Local Government

Mound Bayou has been from the first, at least in the minds of the men who founded it, more than a business enterprise. As a matter of fact, its most conspicious success has been its local government.

The records of the mayor's court shows that, as Delta towns go, Mound Bayou is a remarkably quiet and sober place. There have been but two homicides in twenty years. Both of these were committed by strangers — men who drifted into the community in the early days before the local self-government and the traditions of the town had been established. One of the men killed was Benjamin T. Green, who was the partner of Isaiah T. Montgomery in the early days of the town. The man who committed this crime was afterwards identified as a fugitive from justice, who was wanted for some desperate crime committed in the vicinity of Mobile. The murder was the result of a trivial altercation in regard to a box of tacks.

During the whole twenty years of the town's existence, only three persons have been sent to the circuit court for trial. Two of these were men convicted of theft. Since the town obtained its charter in 1898, there have been, up to February, 1907, but 163 criminal cases tried in the town. Of these, fifty were committed by strangers or by men who had come into town from the surrounding community. Twenty-eight cases were either never tried or were of so trivial a nature that no fine was imposed. Sixty-four were cases of disturbing the peace.

It is interesting to read the records of the mayor's court. They are an index to the life of the village and reflect the changing current of public opinion in regard to the moral discipline and order of the town.

In July, 1902, the records show that fourteen persons were arrested and fined for failure to pay the street tax. Every citizen of the town is required to do $3 worth of work on the streets every year. Some had neglected to pay this labor tax and allowed the streets to fall into a condition of neglect. As a result of a discussion of the matter in the town council, a number of the delinquents were arrested and compelled to pay fines amounting to $3.30 and costs amounting to $1.40 each.

Again, in 1904, a man was arrested for gambling. He had established what is known in sporting parlance as a "crap" game, and on Saturday nights a number of the young men of the village were accustomed to gather at his place to gamble. He was repeatedly warned and finally the town marshal and some of the more substantial citizens made a raid upon the place and arrested fifteen persons. The cases were dismissed after each man had paid a fine of $2. A year later, another man was arrested for running a "blind tiger," selling liquor without a license. He formerly owned a store in the town but began selling liquor, then commenced to drink, and was rapidly "going to the dogs." After his place had been closed, he went out into the country and took up farming again. It is reported that he is doing well there.

During the year 1905, there were several disturbances in the town which were traced directly to the illicit liquor sellers. Men would come into town on Saturdays to do their marketing, fall to drinking, and end in a fight. Things became so bad at last that a public meeting was held in regard to the matter. As a result of this meeting, the town marshal, the mayor, and the treasurer were appointed to get evidence and secure the conviction of those who were guilty. Six persons were convicted and fined at that time. One of these, a woman, left town. Another is still under suspicion and the rest, now on their farms, have become respectable citizens. To my mind, the interesting fact in regard to these prosecutions is that they served not merely to correct a public abuse but to reform the men who were prosecuted. In most cases, these men went back to the farms and became useful members of the community.

It seems to be pretty well agreed that the moral conditions of the Mound Bayou colony are better than those in other Negro settlements in the Delta. Some years ago, when the question was an "issue" in the community, a committee was appointed from each of the churches to make a house to house canvass of the colony, in order to determine to what extent loose family relations existed. The report of this committee showed that there were forty families in the colony where men and women were living together without the formality of a marriage ceremony. As a result of this report, the people of the town gave notice that these forty couples would have to marry within a certain length of time or they would be prosecuted. Nearly all of them acted upon this suggestion; the others moved away.

"Since then," said Mr. Montgomery, in speaking about the matter, "we have had no trouble of this kind. Upon occasions, the women who are conspicuous in towns and cities and who travel in the Delta, making the various camps on pay-days and who more or less infest the larger plantations, have tried to get a footing here, but have never succeeded. They can get no place to stay and have to leave on the next train. This is now generally known and we have no trouble on that score."

When I asked Mr. Montgomery how he explained the fact that they had been able to obtain such good results in the way of order and morality among the people of the colony, he said: "I attribute it to the force of public opinion. The regulations that we enforce have public sentiment behind them. The people recognize that the laws, when they are enforced, represent the sentiment of the community and are imposed for their own good. It is not so easy for them to realize that where the government is entirely in the hands of white men."

One thing that has helped to maintain order in the colony is the fact that Bolivar County prohibits the sale of liquor. More than once the liquor men have attempted to pass a law that would license the selling of liquor in the county. Some years ago a determined effort was made to repeal the prohibition law. In order to secure the vote of Mound Bayou, which seems to have the balance of power in the county on this question, a "still hunt" was made among the voters in the community. A plan was arranged by which a saloon was to be established in the town and one of the citizens made proprietor.

"This scheme came very near going through," said Mr. Montgomery. "The plan was all arranged before we heard of it. Then we called a meeting and I simply said to the people that experience in our own town had taught us that a saloon was a bad thing to have in the community. I said that if the law was passed, a colored man might run the saloon here, but in the rest of the county they would be in the hands of white men. We would pay for maintaining them, however, and we would be the ones to suffer. We voted the law down and there has been no serious attempt to open the county to the liquor traffic since."

In a certain sense, it may be said that the Mound Bayou town and colony have been a school in self-government for its colonists. They have had an opportunity there, such as Negro people have rarely had elsewhere, to learn the real meaning of political institutions and to prepare themselves for the duties and responsibilities of citizenship.

It is interesting to note, in this connection, that this is one of the few instances in which Negroes have ever organized and maintained in any Southern state a government which has gained the entire respect of the Southern people. A writer in a recent number of the *Planter's Journal,* published in Memphis, says:

> "Will the Negro as a race work out his own salvation along Mound Bayou lines? *Quien sabe?* These have worked out for themselves a better local government than any superior people have ever done for them in freedom. But it is a generally accepted principle in political economy that any homogeneous people will in time do this. These people have their local government, but it is in consonance with the county, state, and national governments and international conventions, all in the hands of another race. Could they conduct as successfully a county government in addition to their local government and still under the state and national governments of another race? Enough Negroes of the Mound Bayou type, and guided as they were in the beginning, will be able to do so."

The story of Mound Bayou would not be completed without some account of the man who founded the colony and to whose patience and wisdom it owes the greater part of its success. Isaiah T. Montgomery was born on the plantation of Joseph E. Davis, a brother of Jefferson Davis, the President of the Confederate States. The plantation where he was born, in 1847, was known as "The Hurricane" and was situated in Warren County, Miss. His father, Benjamin Thornton Montgomery, came originally from Virginia. He was purchased in Vicksburg by Mr. Davis, while he was still a boy. He had picked up a little education from his young master in Virginia before he was sold South. After he came into the possession of Mr. Davis, he managed to acquire, in some way that Isaiah could never account for, a very good practical education, so that he was able to make surveys and draw plans for buildings, and for years he was in practical control of the plantation upon which he was employed. There were four children, all of whom received the rudiments of an education from their father.

When he was nine years of age, Isaiah was set to work sorting and filing letters and papers in Mr. Davis's office, and from that time he lived in his master's home. He had a great deal of copying to do for Mr. Davis and it was in this way that he gained a practical knowledge of written English that has stood him in good stead ever since. As he grew older he became the special attendant of Mr. Davis, having charge of all his public and private papers, and he worked steadily in his office until the breaking out of the Civil War. In 1863, Mr. Davis retired, upon the approach of the Federal armies, to the interior of the state, taking with him his slaves. Young Montgomery was left behind with his father, however, to assist in taking care of the plantation.

After the destruction of the Federal gunboat *Indianola*, at Hurricane, and the passage of the Federal gunboats under the batteries of Vicksburg, Isaiah entered the service of the United States as a cabin-boy for Rear-Admiral Porter. He was present, in his capacity as cabin-boy, at the battle of Grand Gulf, accompanied the first expedition up Red River, and was a witness of the operations at the siege and capitulation of Vicksburg. In the winter of 1863, he lost his health and was discharged from the navy at Mound City. From there he went to Cincinnati, where, through the kindness of Admiral Porter, his parents had been able to precede him.

Immediately after the war, Isaiah's father returned to the plantation and in 1866 put himself in communication with Mr. Davis. Very soon they had perfected plans with him for the purchase of the Hurricane and Brierfield plantations, containing something like 4,000 acres of land, upon which the elder Montgomery and his sons, under the name of Montgomery & Sons, conducted the third largest plantation in the state.

It was the desire of Joseph Davis, after the war, to keep together as far as possible the slaves who had grown up on his plantations. His notion was, no doubt, that the interests of all concerned demanded that there should be just as little break in the old relations as possible and that the transition from slavery to freedom should be made gradually, with the idea that the freedmen should, however, eventually become the owners of the land upon which they had previously been slaves. The plantations were conducted with this end in view until 1880, when it became apparent to the Montgomerys that unless there was a modification of the terms upon which the project had been left to them after Joseph Davis's death, it would be impossible to succeed. The heirs could not agree to an alteration in terms, and so the scheme was finally abandoned.

It was with the same notion of carrying out, under new conditions, the plan which his father and his former master had formed years before, that, in 1887, Mr. Montgomery — as he says in a brief autobiography — "sought to begin anew, at the age of forty, the dream of life's young manhood," the dream of doing something to build up the fortunes of his race. It thus appears that the history of Mound Bayou is deeply rooted in the past, and is, in a certain sense, a carrying out of the scheme formulated by the elder Montgomery and his former master for the welfare of that master's former slaves. Others than were intended have become heirs to the plans of these men, but their good will and their forethought have made the success of Mound Bayou possible.

As the colony grows older and the life of the community becomes more complicated, new problems present themselves to the men who are still planning and directing its future.

The success of the present community has suggested the formation of others similar to this one. Already there are the beginnings of such communities at other points above and below Mound Bayou. Mr. Montgomery believes that the success of these new communities, as well as the future of the Mound Bayou colony, depends largely upon the ability of the new generation, now growing up, to profit by the experience of the older. It is with this idea that he and his associates are even now studying out a scheme by which the work of the schools can be brought into closer touch with the actual work of the colony.

"What we need," said Mr. Montgomery, "is an agricultural school, something that will teach the young men to be better farmers than their fathers have been. But, more than that, we need here a system of education that will teach our young men and women the underlying meaning of the work that is being done here. In some way they must be taught the importance of carrying forward this experiment in the spirit in which it was begun. The problem of education is at present the most important which the town and the colony of Mound Bayou have to solve."

Some time ago, Mr. Montgomery was asked by a newspaper writer what he thought of the future of the colony. What he wrote in reply shows his confidence in the outcome:

> "What Mound Bayou is now, and what it has already accomplished is largely prophetic of its future. Situated in the great alluvial Delta district, lands whose productive qualities are not surpassed by any in civilization, timbered by hardwood that finds ready sale at almost fabulous prices, no part of this great section has yet reached its full development. The thriving, hustling towns dotted here and there throughout the Delta, with their factories, waterworks, electric lights and other modern improvements, have become what they are with the Delta only partially developed. What may we expect when practically all the lands have been cleared, properly drained, with a full supply of contented and efficient labor to do the necessary work? In proportion as the whole Delta approaches these conditions, Mound Bayou will progress also.

"There is another distinction that is more than likely to come to Mound Bayou as the years go by, and our schools and churches improve in power and capacity; as our streets are drained and paved, our oil lamps replaced by electric lights, and the old, antiquated, characteristic Delta pump is replaced by clear streams of artesian water. Negroes will begin to make this their resident home, even though they are engaged in business or make their livelihood elsewhere. There will be an atmosphere in which to raise their children, and they will find here social conditions for their wives and daughters very much to their liking. There are those who ask, 'are you not afraid that some day the whites will be moved to wipe out Mound Bayou by violence?' Knowing the controlling force among the whites in this section, as I do, gathered by a stay of thirty-three years among them, I say, 'No, we are not afraid.' The Negroes who have shaped and controlled the destiny of Mound Bayou understand conditions too well to allow any radical or indiscreet policy to prevail here. On the one hand, there are too many white men around us or in easy reach who are our friends and willing to see that no impediment is thrown in our way, or undue advantage is taken of us by irresponsible parties. This has been demonstrated on several occasions."

Isaiah Montgomery is hopeful and confident of the future. He is now sixty years old, but takes an active part in every movement that relates to the upbuilding of the colony which he founded. He believes that his work at Mound Bayou is only just begun and his townsmen share that belief.

World's Work, 14 (July 1907), 9125–34.

1 Charles Banks in the early twentieth century took over from Isaiah T. Montgomery the leadership of the all-black town of Mound Bayou, Miss. Born in nearby Clarksdale in 1873, Banks was educated at Rust College. From 1891 to 1903 he was the senior partner of Banks & Bro., a general store in Clarksdale. In 1903 he founded the Bank of Mound Bayou, serving as its cashier until 1914. In an effort to strengthen the economic base of the town as well as to advance his fortunes, he founded the Mound Bayou Oil Mill and Manufacturing Company, which processed cotton-seed oil. He was also active in an insurance company and a loan and investment company. A leader of black Masons, Banks used his fraternal connections throughout the state in search of capital for his enterprises. A Republican, he was a delegate to the national conventions of 1904, 1908, and 1912. BTW befriended Banks's business enterprises as part of his encouragement of the town of Mound Bayou and of Banks as a symbol of black economic success. At a meeting with Banks at Tuskegee the philanthropist Julius Rosenwald agreed to lend money to the Mound Bayou cotton-oil mill in 1913, and Banks also raised funds from BTW's New York banker friends for the Bank of Mound Bayou in 1914. (See Meier, "BTW and the Town of Mound Bayou," 396–401.)

2 William Thornton Montgomery, brother of Isaiah T. Montgomery, was vice-president of the Mound Bayou Bank and president of the Mound Bayou Business League. He also was a land agent for the Y. & M. B. Railroad, a merchant, and a lumber dealer in Mound Bayou.

Extracts from an Address at the Jamestown Tercentennial Exposition

[Jamestown, Va.] August 3, 1907

I wish to express the gratitude of my race to the management of this Exposition for the opportunity here presented to exhibit our progress as a people. I also wish to congratulate Mr. Thomas J. Calloway and his Board of Assistants, as well as Mr. Jackson,[1] for their successful efforts in making the Negro Department a matter of pride to our race. Everyone who has contributed, in a slight degree, to the success of this Exposition deserves the thanks of our entire people.

Since coming upon these grounds I am free to say that I have been pleased and surprised at the neat and attractive appearance of the Negro Building. From an architectural point of view it does high credit to Mr. Pittman and all connected with its construction. I have been equally surprised and pleased at the large exhibit which has been installed in such an attractive and instructive manner. I am equally free to say that I wish that every member of my race could come here and witness these evidences of progress in agricultural, mechanical, house-keeping, educational, moral and religious development. In all these matters, those in charge of the Negro department deserve the highest praise.

I have been equally interested and gratified on the account of the deportment of the thousands gathered upon these grounds today. They present a clean, orderly, sober, industrious appearance. This deportment on a public occasion, such as this, is within itself the highest evidence of our progress.

Whenever an opportunity to see the slightest evidence of the progress of our race, presents itself, there, our people should not fail to put in appearance in large numbers.

I believe that our people should take advantage of every opportunity, no matter wherever presented, North or South, to show to the world the progress that we, as a race, are making. No battle was ever won by an army standing still or sulking in tents. Racial battles are to be won by marching forward, not by halting.

There are some special reasons why we should have a part in the

Jamestown Exposition. It was near this spot, nearly three hundred years ago, that the first representatives of our race were brought into America. It is especially fitting, therefore, that since here we entered slavery that on the same spot we should show results of improvement both in slavery and in freedom. When our first representatives landed we were only 20 in number, now there are nearly ten millions; when our first representatives landed here we had no uniform language, now we speak the English tongue. For the most part, we were pagan, now, we profess Christianity.

More and more as a race I believe that we should emphasize our opportunities, as is being done at this Exposition, rather than our disadvantages. In the fundamental things of life we have great opportunities before us as a race, in this country. No one who would be honest should deny or overlook the fact that we have disadvantages with which to contend and that acts of injustice are often perpetrated on us, as a race, but in spite of all this, in the fundamental consideration of securing a home, of earning and saving money, of finding employment, either in skilled or common labor, in entering into business or professional life, no one can deny the fact that in America, and especially in the South, that we have a rare opportunity. These are the things in hand, and we should get all out of them, possible.

In the matter of securing and using education we have, in this country as a whole, an opportunity which we should highly value. While in many sections there are discouragements, acts of unfairness, yet taking the country as a whole, the public school system is wide open to our race; further, without hindrance, we are at liberty to establish private schools, industrial schools, colleges, and professional institutions. One of the peculiar advantages presented by the South consists in the fact that we are at liberty to use whatever education we receive in promoting our own welfare, as well as the welfare of others.

No one event during the past year, has been so important as the magnificent gift of $1,000,000, by Miss Anna T. Jeanes, of Philadelphia, the interest of which is to be used in promoting rural schools. So long as the race finds such friends we need not despair.

Again, we not only have an opportunity to make progress in material and educational lines, but we are in a position where no man can take from us the privilege of living a high moral life. No one can take from us the privilege of having a beautiful well kept home with high moral standards. Throughout this country we have freedom of religious worship and the progress that we have made in the number of Ministers and Church organizations clearly proves that we are taking advantage of that opportunity.

. . . .

We of both races, here in the South, have the opportunity of teaching the world how two races, dissimilar in many respects, can live together, side by side in peace and harmony, each promoting the welfare and happiness of the other.

. . . .

I believe, too, that the South should call attention more often than it does to the general progress that our people are making. And you have a right to be proud of this progress. I shall never forget the impression that a Southern white man, in the little town of Tuskegee, where I live, made upon me some time ago when he passed a grocery store, and with one exception I think it is the largest and most successful grocery store in that town, owned by a colored man, and pointed to the Negro merchant and to his store, and said, "I am proud of that man. I owned his father and I am proud of his success." We get so much in the habit of dwelling upon our difficulties that I am afraid too often we fail to emphasize the progress that both races are making in the working out of this tremendous problem. But when we consider, my friends, the complications of this problem, when we consider the seriousness of it, when we consider your part and my part, when we consider where we started forty years ago, I believe that we have every reason to congratulate ourselves that we have done as well as we have and have had as few difficulties as we have had. We have every reason to feel proud of the success that has been made in the solution of this problem.

. . . .

Each race is in [a] degree dependent upon the other. For ex[am]pl[e] in the average white family of the South, you will find that the white child spends a large proportion of his life in the arms or in the company of a Negro woman or of a Negro girl. During the years when that child is most impressionable, when he is at a point where impressions are perhaps most lasting, that child is in the company of this black woman or this black girl. My friends it is mighty important, in my opinion, for the civilization, for the happiness, for the health of the Southern white people that that colored nurse shall be intelligent, that she shall be clean, that she shall be morally fit to come in contact with that pure and innocent child.

. . . .

In nine-tenths of our Southern communities there is peace and harmony, good will and friendship; but when one goes outside of the Southern states, when one goes into the North, into Europe as I have done, and reads the dispatches that come from the South, it is always one thing — lynchings. And you never hear of any other news from the South except lynchings. Those people naturally get the idea, other people get the idea, through this unusual punishment, that we are living in a state of turmoil, at daggers points throughout the South, whereas, as a matter of fact, as you go through the average Southern Community you will find a feeling of mutual confidence, a feeling of friendship existing between the races — each race interested in the progress of the other. And for that reason alone, if for no other, higher consideration, I believe we owe it to ourselves to bring about such a public sentiment as will get rid of this unusual and barbarous method of punishing criminals. And in the case of my race I believe you will find that many of our criminals — and you will find that this crime is usually committed by wandering colored people who have no homes, no bank accounts, no trades, no permanent abiding place; in many cases, they are half-witted, and this condition has been emphasized by the use of bad whiskey — those people read the newspapers, they hear in public discussion about these crimes and many of them, by reason of the mere publicity of this unusual punishment, are led to atttempt these assaults, when if the individuals were punished in an orderly sober quiet method, they would never hear of them. And I believe for these reasons, and for many more, that we of both races should insist that we are gaining nothing in any community by ever condoning what is termed mob or lynch law.

. . . .

In my opinion, one of the reasons why many of the best and brightest Southern men have not taken hold and helped in the directions that I have tried to emphasize, as they would like to have done, has been the scare, the bug-bear of what is called "social equality."

It is used to frighten off, to hinder, and very often to check some of the best efforts that our Southern white friends want to put forth in the direction of helping us.

Another bug-bear that is used is "Negro domination." Negro domination? Now there is nothing in either of these things. I think I know the ambitions and activities of the colored people throughout this country pretty well, and I am safe in saying to you that it is not the ambition or the desire of the Negro in this country to intermingle socially with the white people. Neither is it his ambition or his desire to domineer the white man in the matter of politics. You can help us, again, by using your influence to check the work in many cases of the sensational newspapers that use these incidents in connection with the Negro to give them circulation, to give them popularity among a certain class of people.

. . . .

You can help us again by using your influence by bringing to bear your Christian ideas of citizenship upon the public mind of the South so that in the future they will not, as they have in so large a degree in the past, ride into office or attempt to ride into office on the Negro. My friends there are some men in office who never would have seen an office, except for the Negro. And on every possible occasion, when they want to go to the Legislature, when they want to go to Congress, when they want to be Governor, or to be United States Senator, these men who have no idea of constructive, progressive statesmanship, they fall back on the old idea of "Negro domination" and they just go through the country harping on the Negro all the time.

. . . .

If you want to know how to solve the race problem, place your hands upon your hearts and then with a prayer to God, ask Him how you, today, were you placed in the position that the black man occupies, how you would desire the white man to treat you, and whenever you have answered that question in the sight of God, and man, this problem in a large degree will have been solved.

The two races are not going [to] be enemies but friends. The white man in America cannot afford to be unjust to the Negro. Every act of injustice will remain to weaken further generations. Every law so administered to mean one thing for a black man and another thing when applied to a white man means the moral degradation to the individual who enforces such law.

. . . .

Finally above all things we should not be discouraged, as a race. No man, discouraged, ever wins a victory. There is more in our favor than there is against us. We have a magnificent opportunity to teach the world how, by patience, courage, and work we can overcome difficulties and secure and maintain our rightful place as useful citizens in our common country.

TM Con. 956 BTW Papers DLC. Minor changes and editing in BTW's hand. The second, third, and fourth paragraphs were at the end of the manuscript labeled "Insert A." BTW marked a large "X" at the end of the first paragraph, which seems to be the proper place for the insertion. Many of the passages are verbatim repetitions of his address at Vanderbilt University. (See An Address to the Theological Department of Vanderbilt University, Mar. 29, 1907, above.)

1 Giles Beecher Jackson.

An Address at Hampton Institute

[Hampton, Va., Aug. 4, 1907]

THE HIGHER AND THE LOWER LIFE

There are two kinds of lives presented to every young man and every young woman, to every individual — the higher life and the lower life. The question which presents itself to you every day is: Will you lead the higher life, or will you lead the lower life? One leads to success and happiness; the other leads to misery and failure every time. If one yields to the temptation of getting hold of money, of getting hold of material possessions, in order that he may ride over his fellows, in order that he may set himself upon a pinnacle higher than others and thereby minister to his own selfish ambition, his own desires, however great his success in business, in the material life, that individual is leading the lower life. On the other hand, the world is full of men who get hold of large wealth, of beautiful homes, of large farms, of fine business establishments, not as ends but that they may have these possessions as means through which to serve their fellows. So long as persons learn to use material wealth, material success, not as an end but as a means to reach the highest life for themselves and to help their fellows to reach and live the higher life, it seems to me that they are worthy of the highest praise.

In the matter of labor and study you are having the opportunity presented to make the choice every time you go into the shops on these grounds, every time you go out on the farm, every time you go into any domestic department. You are called upon day by day to make the choice between the lower life and the higher life. The average individual asks this question when he begins his day's work: How little can I put into this hour's work and get my wage? How little can I do? He does not ask how much but how little he can afford to give. Each student will find himself making that mistake if he is not careful. As you go to the farm, the shops, the classroom, you will find yourselves yielding to the temptation and asking the question: How little service can I perform to-day and get my proper wage and proper credit? That individual fails while he is in school and after he goes out into life. On the other hand, the student who asks these questions: How much can I put into this service? How many hours of work can I put in? How can I improve upon the kind of labor that I performed yesterday? gets ahead of the other fellow every time, my friends. If the time to begin work is seven o'clock in the morning, you be there ten minutes before seven. If the time to quit work is five o'clock, you remain fifteen minutes after five o'clock. After the other fellows are gone you stay a little longer, and ask: Is there not some service I can perform; is there not something else you want done? The fellow who is always considering his own selfish interests is not the man who succeeds. The man who is trying to live the higher life in all lines — is the individual who will not only succeed here, but also will succeed after he leaves school. In the classroom and elsewhere that individual who sees all that he can do finally succeeds.

No man's life is really complete until he owns a Bible that is part of himself. One of the most valuable lessons I ever learned at this institution was the value of the Bible. For the first time in my life I had put into my hands a copy of that book which I could call my own. And ever since I have possessed that Bible. No matter how busy I may be and no matter how many responsibilities crowd upon me, I never have let a day pass without taking my Bible and reading a chapter or at least a few verses. It is valuable from an historical and a literary point of view; it is more valuable from a spiritual point of view. This morning I read from the tenth chapter of Luke the story of the Good Samaritan. You remember how the other fellows acted when they saw this unfortunate individual across the street, wounded and helpless. The Good Samaritan went to him and took care of his wounds. That did not impress me a great deal. Any individual with a heart in him would have done that. Anybody with human feeling seeing a human brother in misery would have gone there and done what he could to relieve his pains and heal his wounds. The Good Samaritan did two other things which were not his duty. He performed more than his duty. A man does not deserve credit for doing his mere duty. The Samaritan did two other things before he left the helpless man. He took out two pence and gave them to the innkeeper and said, "Take care of him; and whatsoever thou spendest more, when I come again, I will repay you." Add the extra two pence of labor in the classroom or wherever you can and you will find that you will succeed. The world will be looking for you, instead of your looking to the world for service.

You can ask yourselves this question in the schoolroom, in the dining room, and in dealing with your teachers. The question is constantly presented to you: Shall I lead the higher life, or shall I lead the lower life? When the new student comes to this school next fall will you try to satisfy your own selfish ambition, your own selfish desires? Go out of your way; take hold of that new student and ask if there is not something you can do for him. Give up your seat in the dining room in order that he may have a better seat. Give up your own bed if that is necessary in order that he may have a better bed. The fellow who is thinking of himself all the time lives in the mire. Many people in our communities yield to the temptation of spending much of their time and energy in dealing with little mean gossip. Time and strength are thus wasted which ought to be spent in reading, in higher endeavor, in doing things which lift one into the Christ atmosphere.

The higher life, is serving others and not ourselves: the lower life, is serving ourselves and not others. I believe that one of the most serious difficulties of the Negro race, one of the most deplorable conditions, and one for which we are not altogether to blame, consists in the fact that we are almost forced to spend all our time when we come together in public gatherings, in thinking about ourselves, in talking about ourselves, in preaching about ourselves, and in writing about ourselves. I do wish the time would come when the subjective element in connection with our race will not be so largely emphasized as it is to-day. I wish to see our race get to the point where we can discuss some other fellow; where hundreds and thousands of representative men and women of our race can come together in a great convention, where the ills of the Negro race will not be mentioned, but where, for two or three days, we can consider the needs of some other fellow who is down in the world. It is unfortunate for the Negroes to be always forced to think, read, and study about themselves.

I have spoken of the unselfish life. You have before you as an example every day in the year (and sometimes we do not rightly appreciate the riches right about us until it is too late) passing in and out among you a man who, in my opinion, represents most completely the life which I am trying to describe. I refer to Dr. H. B. Frissell. I have seen Dr. Frissell under all kinds of circumstances. I have studied him in the North and in the South, in private and in public, and I know I have met few men in all my experience who are able in such large degree to forget themselves so completely, crush themselves, in order that they may serve others. I am glad to make this statement in his absence rather than in his presence. My friends, study and follow his example, for thus only can you in any measure compensate him and those who stand and hold up his hands.

In leading this life, place yourselves on the constructive side of life. The man who gets real happiness out of life is the fellow who is doing something. That is the element at Hampton which makes it a pleasure to come here. You are building a little heaven around here. I do not know as the theologian will agree with me, but I believe it is possible to have a little heaven right here on earth. You are approaching that condition here at Hampton, and you are approaching that condition because you are all doing something. Do not spend any time with the fellow who is simply on the negative side of life. Get on the positive side of life every time. I was in Atlanta. An old colored minister, without very much education but interested in his race, had built a fine and useful building there, which he had dedicated as an orphan asylum. A younger minister came to visit the new building. This young fellow said, "That is a pretty good building but it has certain faults." The old minister said, "You stop right there. You have the advantage of me. I can't discuss the orphan asylum *you* built." The old fellow was on the constructive side of life. Do not get discouraged because we have a hard row to hoe. I like a real, hard, tough proposition. It is interesting to work on the hard problem. Any fellow can solve an easy one. You honor the fellow who can work out the tough, perplexing problems. I like to belong to a race that has hard, knotty, problems to solve. I would not care to live in an age when there was no weak portion of the human race to be lifted up and helped and encouraged. It is only as we meet these great problems and opportunities that we gain strength.

Southern Workman, 36 (Sept. 1907), 478–80. Address delivered in Cleveland Hall Chapel.

To Gordon David Houston

Huntington, L.I., August 5, 1907

Dear Sir: When in Baltimore last winter, when Dr. Waring[1] told me that you had applied to him for a position in the city schools of Baltimore, I recommended you to him for a position and was glad to do so, in the same way I recommended you to Dr. Chancellor of the Washington public schools. It is my purpose now to withdraw my recommendation, in both cases, unless a satisfactory explanation is forthcoming from you in regard to the following matters, or a straightforward statement made acknowledging your mistake and wrong act.

In writing you this note I need not recall the circumstances in detail that led to your coming to Tuskegee, neither do I need to remind you how I have exhibited my interest in you from year to year in seeing that you were promoted and in having your salary increased. I refer to these matters simply to make plain the fact that in what I am now going to say I have no personal feelings against you.

Letters have been placed in my hands which make it clear, first, that during a portion of the time while you were at Tuskegee you were disloyal to the Institution, which you were paid to serve; second, that you were making efforts to get away from the institution at any time in any manner without regard to your promise or contract to remain through the year; third, the statements made in these letters are false to the extent of being almost ridiculous.[2]

I am taking this action first because I feel that I owe it to the teaching profession, and to the friend in Cambridge who recommended you. There ought to exist among teachers, the same as among other professional men, a certain degree of honor that one should hesitate to trifle with. Second, I am taking this position because I owe it to the Tuskegee Institute, and thirdly, because I want to serve you. I have, as I stated, no personal feeling against you because of these acts and falsehoods, but I feel that I would be doing you a gross injustice to permit you to go further in life on a false foundation, that of insincerity and lack of truth. Now, I must ask you to do one of two things, either to prove the statements which you have made or to make a complete unequivocal and frank statement to the effect that you have told an untruth and regret your action. This is the only course that you can pursue in order to reinstate yourself in my confidence and the only course that you can pursue in order to begin, as I have said, on a solid foundation instead of a false one. I have no desire to punish or embarrass you, I am simply trying to help you and at the same time defend the interests of our institution and the teaching profession. Very truly yours,

[Booker T. Washington]

TLc Con. 36 BTW Papers DLC.

[1] James Henry Nelson Waring, a graduate of Howard University Medical School in 1888, was principal of the Colored High and Training School in the Baltimore school system for a number of years beginning in 1903. In 1927 he was president of Downington Industrial and Agricultural College, Downington, Pa.

[2] An agent of BTW purloined Houston's letters from the desk of his former pastor in Cambridge, Mass. (See Samuel Edward Courtney to BTW, July 12, 1907, above; Harlan, "Secret Life of BTW," 409.)

From Samuel Edward Courtney

Boston Mass Aug–6 1907

Ducker[y] will come when you want him wire.

S. E. Courtney

HWSr Con. 345 BTW Papers DLC.

From Gordon David Houston

Cambridge Mass., Aug. 6, 1907

Dear Sir: In reply to your letter of Aug. 5, I beg leave to admit the guilt of the charges that you bring against me, and to state that I regret very much my action. I thank you heartily for the assurance of your renewed confidence in me. Very truly yours,

G. David Houston

TLS Con. 574 BTW Papers DLC.

From Ernest Lyon[1]

Monrovia, Liberia. August 10, 1907

My dear Dr. Washington: As I took you into *confidence* in my letter of the 12th ultimo I am under further and more pressing necessity by recent developments to bind you to a stricter confidence in what I shall herein impart.

Intelligence has just come to Liberia from England that the Delimitation question on the France-Liberia frontier has reached an acute state as to demand the presence of the President[2] of Liberia at a conference in London. Liberia is located between two formidable powers, each of which is determined that neither shall secure any territorial advantage over the other.

England on the northwest declares that she has no desire for Liberia's territory, but if French encroachments in the southeast are not checked she will be obliged for national defence to imitate France on the northwest.

Liberia is unable to check France and unless the United States interferes the impairment of the independence of Liberia is inevitable.

This same mail carries an appeal from Liberia for diplomatic interference. The appeal is a confidential expression of the situation and therefore cannot be given out.

We must come to the rescue of our people over here. The grasping policy of these nations must be checked if it can. They now have everything on the west coast, yet Ahab like, they covet Naboth's little vineyard.

What can you do? Our Government I am confident will act if the proper influence is brought to bear on it. *I simply ask that the source of information be withheld for diplomatic reasons.* God give you wisdom to act in this crisis.

In conferring with Bishop Scott, he says that if you find it absolutely necessary to give up the source of information why you can use my name. Sincerely,

Ernest Lyon

TLS Con. 7 BTW Papers DLC.

[1] Ernest Lyon (1860–1938), born in Honduras, migrated to the United States in the early 1870s. He attended Straight University and Gilbert Seminary before receiving an A.B. from New Orleans University. Lyon was a Methodist Episcopal minister in Baltimore. In 1901 he became professor of church history at Morgan College, and was a founder of the Maryland Industrial and Agricultural Institute for the education of black youths located near Laurel, Md. A friend of BTW and an active Republican, on BTW's recommendation he became U.S. minister and consul general to Liberia, serving from 1903 to 1911. He then returned to Baltimore and was minister of the Ames Methodist Episcopal Church until his death. In 1927 Lyon took part in the negotiations that resulted in the payment of Liberia's war debt to the United States.

[2] Arthur Barclay.

To Ray Stannard Baker

Huntington, L.I. Aug. 21, 1907

My dear Mr. Baker: Your kind letter of recent date has been received. One point which you seem to have overlooked, and that is the Convict System of the South.[1] It would be of considerable interest and very instructive to show to just what extent that Negro convict labor goes to pay the expenses of states. The amount cleared by the states on convict labor is something enormous. Very truly yours,

Booker T. Washington

TLS Ray Stannard Baker Papers DLC.

[1] In *Following the Color Line,* Baker devoted a page to the large profits made by the state of Georgia from the convict lease system.

From James A. Cobb

Boston, Aug. 26 1907

Dear Dr. Washington: I am here in the City where the Niagara Movement is expected to hold forth, and expect to attend sessions, if I can find out where it will meet. There seems to be no Esprit de Corps — everybody is up in the air — in fact there is no definite program as yet. The leaders seem to be disgruntled among themselves. However, I shall remain and see the outcome. Very truly yours,

James A. Cobb

ALS Con. 344 BTW Papers DLC.

James A. Cobb to Emmett Jay Scott

Washington, D.C. Sept. 5, 1907

Dear Bro. Scott: I have just returned home after a three weeks visit out East. Found your two several communications waiting me upon desk on my arrival. Thank you very much for badge and receipt and glad to know that you had such a good meeting of the Business League; sorry that I can't say as much for the N. M., which met in Boston, and of which I was in attendance, it seemed to have been beset with misgivings and discord. Only one public meeting and no well arranged program at that, the others were committee meetings where Trotter and Morgan[1] wrangled.

I think the Movement has about met its "watermellon-lou" as would be said by Bob Cole in the Shoo-fly Regiment, when something is about to be smashed up. I shall hand your letter to Mr. Waller[2] upon his return to the city, he is now in New York. Sincerely,

James A. Cobb

TLS Con. 344 BTW Papers DLC.

1 Clement G. Morgan.

2 Possibly the George Waller listed in the 1905 Washington, D.C., city directory as a cook.

Timothy Thomas Fortune to Emmett Jay Scott

Red Bank, N.J., Sept. 7, 1907

Dear Scott: Recognizing the shattered condition of my health and the imperative urgency of taking a long rest, on the 4th instant I transferred my interest in the New York Age Publishing Company to Fred R. Moore. A meeting of the stockholders was called for yesterday afternoon to elect new officers and define a new policy.

Of course Mr. Moore could only pay for my stock in notes, for the most part.

How am I to live? There is little enough in sight, but God will provide. He never fails those who repent of their sins and accept His promise to the Believer. As soon as I have completed the transfer of interest I plan to go to Tuskegee to remain indefinitely, where I am very sure the ravens will feed me. With love for you and the dear house, Yours in Christ,

Timothy Thomas Fortune

ALS Con. 45 BTW Papers DLC.

From Emmett Jay Scott

Tuskegee Institute, Alabama September 10, 1907

My dear Mr. Washington: The enclosed letter from Dr. Ernest Lyon explains itself. It is quite probable that you will not be reaching Washington far ahead of the hour you are to speak, but this matter is so important that I have decided to burden you with it. A few minutes private conference with some of the officials of the State department would accomplish great good, I am sure, and, at the same time, your influence at the critical moment would be thrown on the side of preserving the autonomy of the Negro Republic of Liberia.

You will, I am sure, as Dr. Lyon suggests keep in mind his suggestion that his communication *is confidential* and that nothing

whatever can be said connecting him as the source of information.
Yours truly,

Emmett J. Scott

TLS BTW Papers ATT.

An Announcement of the Engagement of Portia Marshall Washington and William Sidney Pittman

Tuskegee Institute, Ala., Sept. 14 [1907]

PITTMAN — WASHINGTON

Mr. & Mrs. Booker T. Washington announce the engagement of their daughter, Portia Marshall, to Mr. W. Sidney Pittman, of Washington, D.C.

The marriage ceremony is to be solemnized at Tuskegee Institute during the latter part of the month of October.

TD Con. 355 BTW Papers DLC. The item appeared in the *Tuskegee Student*, 19 (Sept. 21, 1907), 1.

To Ernest Lyon

[Tuskegee, Ala.] September 18, 1907

My dear Mr. Lyon: All of your communications have been received. There has been a delay in answering them owing to the fact that I have just returned to the school from my summer home.

I am writing to say that I shall decide within the next few hours what will be the best manner of taking up the case of Liberia. The more I think of it, the more I am convinced that the wisest thing will be to make a perfectly frank statement of the case directly to the President. I feel reasonably sure that he will do something to relieve the situation if it is possible for any American to do so.

Please say to Bishop Scott that I am very grateful to him for his letters and will write him soon regarding all the matters raised in his communications.

I shall hope to write you more fully within a few days. Yours truly,

Booker T. Washington

TLpS Con. 7 BTW Papers DLC.

To Theodore Roosevelt

[Tuskegee, Ala.] Sept. 19, 1907

My dear Mr. President: I had the privilege of speaking last week to the National Negro Baptist Convention in Washington, which is the largest and most representative body of Negroes in America, there being present about 3,000 delegates and I was very glad to note, that with the exception of a few extreme radicals, that the feeling toward you and your administration was kindly. The day after my address, an effort was made to get through a resolution in condemnation of your course bearing upon Brownsville, but the effort failed, the President, Dr. E. C. Morris, taking a firm stand against it and his hands were held up by the strong men in the Convention. The feeling indicated at this Convention, I think is representative of the change that is taking place gradually among our people in most parts of the country.

Mr. Scott is going to see you within a few days especially regarding the following matters. You know, I think, the history of Liberia, Africa, how it was established by Americans during President Monroe's administration and how its interests have been safeguarded in many ways by Americans ever since its foundation. I have information from reliable sources that both France and England are seeking to take large parts of the Liberian territory. I am sure that you will prevent this, if it can be done.

The other matter is this: one of the white Justices of the Peace in the District of Columbia has recently died. I think it would be a good thing from many points of view just now, if you could put on the Bench in his stead, Mr. James A. Cobb, a fine colored man, or some other man an equal of Mr. Cobb. He is very popular among the white lawyers and stands high among all classes.

I thought you might like to see the enclosed clipping regarding the success of Judge Terrell and his conduct of his office.

As soon as you return from your western trip, I am planning to see you myself concerning several matters. Yours sincerely,

Booker T. Washington

TLpS Con. 7 BTW Papers DLC.

From John Langalibalele Dubé

Phoenix, Natal, So. Africa. Sept. 21st, 1907

My dear Dr. Washington / I am in receipt of your letter and I was glad to hear from you for your devoted life in the interest of the Negro race has made me love you dearly. I am sending you per even mail a copy of the "Native Affairs Commission Report["] which was appointed by the Natal Government after the rebellion. This Commission has just completed its inquiries in native matters and its comments on the position of native administration will tell you briefly how we have been ruled in the past. The Commission says of the policies of past Governments that "It was weighed and found wanting." You may regard me as a political agitator from reading my speech to the Zulu people, but I am sure if you knew me, you would know that I am not in the habit of speaking as I did upon that occasion. Things had gone so bad, that I as one of the leaders of the people felt it my duty to speak the whole truth. You will be interested to know that I am better respected by the authorities for that reason; for they had come to a point in their rule of the natives when they wanted to know how the natives felt. The translation is very poor, but I have no time to translate it and am sending you a clipping from the "Natal Advertiser" of my speech to the Zulu people and you may find something to give you an insight to our life in South Africa. I am also sending you a copy of my Zulu newspaper "Ilanga." There is a portion of it in English and an article in reference to the Native Commission will interest you probably. My work (educational) is very much like yours. I believe in Industrial Education. Some of my scholars work hard during their vacation to earn money for their school fee. A great number of civilized natives are anxious to push forward in spite of the prejudice of our white people. The condition is much like that in the Southern States in America. They want our ignorant people to stay in their heathen condition so that they can only use them as beasts of burden. Those who aspire to something higher are not wanted.

I am pressed with work and shall be glad if you will write to Mrs Byron Horton of 421 *a* Hancock St. Brooklyn N.Y. Secy. to our American Committee to give you full information [as] to our School.

The Government is taking interest now in my efforts. The Minister for Native Affairs has just sent word to the Prime Minister of Cape Colony to ask if they have a skilled Agricultural teacher to teach agriculture in our school and be paid out of Government funds. Before this my scholars were not allowed even to take Government examinations and we had no financial help from the Government, but my efforts are beginning to bring good results. I wanted some one either from your School, or Hampton to teach farming, but the authorities objected to that. They fear that American Negroes would teach our people racial ill-feeling.

I trust you may be in a position to assist me. You can see by these documents that I cannot expect a great deal of financial assistance locally. Yours respectfully,

John L. Dube

P.S. If you care I can send you from time to time any documents especially official "Blue Books" dealing with native affairs.

I regret that the translation of my Zulu address to our people is so poor, but you will get the idea from it.

Our people are anxious to do something for their welfare but they have no organization strong enough to bring them together. If it were possible to unite them in all their efforts they would be irresistable both financially and politically.

I am hoping to come to America in the course of a year (D. V.) & will be glad to go So. & learn something of your Farmers Conference & other organization.

J. L. D.

TLS Con. 346 BTW Papers DLC. Postscript in Dubé's hand.

From Joseph Fels[1]

London 25th September 1907

Dear Sir As some introduction to my writing you, I may say that I am the senior member of Fels & Co (Fels-Naptha soap) Philadelphia, and divide my time between the two countries, we having a flourishing selling branch of our business on this side.

I am greatly interested in the land question on both sides of the Atlantic.

About two years ago I spent a few hours looking over your enterprise there; but, much to my regret, neither you nor Mrs Washington were at home. I received all possible courtesies, however, from your representatives.

I have just received a letter from W. Ryan, 56 Pine Street, New York, who, like myself, is greatly interested in land and social reform. In it he quotes from an address delivered early in the month in Delaware by Mr J H Amies, and which I repeat at foot hereof.[2]

I was born in Virginia, and raised in North Carolina. I think I understand the Negro question, and certainly appreciate its difficulties. Perhaps you are cognisant of the work being carried on near Jackson City, and will know if it is successful and otherwise.

The Fairhope experiment, referred to in Mr. Ryan's letter is at Fairhope, Ala., 15 miles across Mobile Bay, from Mobile. I have for many years been interested in helping to develop Fairhope, which Colony now owns about 4,000 acres of land; and, while it is not growing as a 'boom' town, it is exercising an influence on the land question, and calling people's attention to that question as *the* economic one.

I am expecting to come across there again in December; and, intending to visit Mexico in January on business connected with Colonization matters, may be able to visit you on my way.

Meanwhile will you please give the matter such consideration as its importance would seem to deserve, and let me hear from you at this address. Believe me Yours very truly

Joseph Fels

TLS Con. 350 BTW Papers DLC.

[1] Joseph Fels (1859–1914), soap manufacturer and philanthropist, was an advocate of Henry George's single-tax philosophy. In 1899 he became the major benefactor of

the Fairhope, Ala., single-tax colony and supported it for ten years. The colony grew from an original population of twenty-five persons in 1894 to more than 4,000 in the 1950s, when it was still run on the single-tax principle.

2 Appended to the letter was an argument for black land ownership on single-tax principles as the solution of the race problem.

To Ernest Lyon

[Tuskegee Ala.] Sept. 28, 1907

My dear Mr. Lyon: According to my last letter, Mr. Emmett J. Scott, my secretary, went to Washington for the purpose of having an interview with the President concerning the interests of Liberia. I have just received a telegram from him, a portion of which I quote — "Liberian matter amicably settled. President says he will go to limit of all power and moral force to protect Liberia."

I shall send you a fuller report when Mr. Scott returns. Please communicate this information to Bishop Scott. Very truly yours,

Booker T. Washington

TLpS Con. 7 BTW Papers DLC.

An Article in the *Congregationalist and Christian World*

28 September 1907

THE NEGRO IN THE NORTH

ARE HIS ADVANTAGES AS GREAT AS IN THE SOUTH

My attention has been repeatedly called in recent years to the rapid increase of the Negro population in Northern cities, particularly in the larger cities of the North Atlantic States, that is, New England, New York, New Jersey, and Pennsylvania. These states have already considerably more than one-third of all the Northern Negroes and statistics show that from 1880 to 1900 this portion of the population increased one-third more rapidly than the white.

The Negroes in Philadelphia increased in the ten years, between 1890 and 1900, from thirty to sixty-two thousand. The colored population in New York was 23,606 in 1890, but in 1900 it had risen to 60,666. Boston's colored population grew more slowly, but it has grown steadily. In 1880 the Negroes of Cambridge and Boston were 7,377, but in 1900 this number had increased to 15,497.

Under normal conditions I doubt whether the existence of 900,000 Negroes scattered over the whole Northern and Western country, and permanently settled on farms and in small towns, as they are to a very large degree in the South, would have attracted particular attention. But the fact is that the Negroes in the Northern States are, to a large extent, part of the floating population. While eighty-two per cent. of the Southern Negroes are on farms and plantations in country districts, more than seventy per cent. of the Northern Negroes are in cities.

This Negro element in the floating population of the Northern cities has grown so rapidly in recent years and has to such an extent complicated the problem of city life, already difficult enough, that some persons have come to regard it as a distinct menace.

City Life Unfavorable to Health and Morals

I have more than once said that the masses of the colored people are not yet fitted to survive and prosper in the great cities North and South to which so many of them are crowding. The temptations are too great and the competition with the foreign population with which they come in contact is too severe. Many of these young colored men and women, who leave the country for the city, go almost directly from the farms and plantations of the South, where they have been living on the same soil on which their fathers and mothers worked as slaves and under conditions not far removed from those that existed before emancipation. It is not difficult, under these circumstances, to understand that the colored immigrants from the South are not able at once to adjust themselves to the crowded, strenuous and complicated life of these great modern cities. The vital statistics, which are perhaps the best indicators we have in this matter, show that, of all the races now pouring into the larger American cities from various parts of the world, the Negro is the least prepared to meet the conditions of city life.

It should always be borne in mind that there is this difference between the Negro in the North and the average colored man living on plantations of the country districts in the South, that while he is ignorant he has not been degraded, as a rule, except in rare cases, by vicious habits. In the large cities of the North, it is true of a large element of the Negroes, as it is true of the same class of other races, that they have injured body and soul by degrading habits. There is a vast difference between pure ignorance and degradation.

My own conviction is that this problem, like others which the presence of the Negro race in this land has created, must find its solution ultimately on the farms and plantations of the Southern States. So far as I can understand the disposition of the masses of my own people they have determined to remain for all time upon the soil of the Southern States, where their future, in my opinion, is inextricably bound up with the prosperity of the soil. I do not believe that any large proportion of the Negro people intend to live permanently outside of the South, and I doubt very much if any laborer will be found to supplant permanently the Negro in the Southern cotton field. The problem of the Northern Negro will, to a very large extent, find its solution in the efforts now being made by the United States Department of Agriculture to improve the character and quality of the Negro farmers; in the efforts now being made to increase the number and efficiency of country schools; in the growing disposition among the better class of the white people to secure justice for the Negro and protect him against hectoring and abuse to which he is so often subjected, and finally in the encouragement the Negro is receiving in certain parts of the South to buy land, to build houses and permanently settle on the soil.

The security of the South against danger of race riots and the evils that cause them demands that every man, white and black, should, as far as possible, own a home; a hearth stone around which the interest of the family can find a center; and a permanent place of abode on which the wholesome influences of family life can find a prop.

I believe that those who are seeking a solution of the problem of the Northern Negro will find that they can co-operate in this direction with the more thoughtful class of the Southern people who find that the South is being slowly drained of the labor it needs in the fields and in the trades by emigration Northward.

I have spoken thus far of that part of the population which has but lately arrived in the North. It represents the element of unrest among the Negroes of the South. While a large number of these people have left the South upon a definite promise of higher wages or better treatment, a greater number are mere social drift, drawn into the cities with the tide that sets to the large centers of population from all over the United States.

While I do not deny that there are some advantages for the Negro in the North which he does not have in the South, there are also disadvantages. There are the advantages of better schools and better teachers. The Negro has, for example, the opportunity of using the public library, of entering the colleges and universities. The Northern cities are farther advanced, on the whole, in their methods of dealing with the problem of city life. The Northern people are not haunted by the fear of social equality, and are therefore able to take hold in a more practical way of the problem of uplifting backward races. The Northern cities are richer and more able to provide special education to meet the special needs of special classes of the population.

Difficulties in Finding Labor

But on the whole I am convinced that the condition of the great mass of Negroes in the Northern cities is not only worse than that of the Negroes on the farms in the South but worse than that of any other portion of the city population. The statistics show that the death rate is much larger among Negroes in the North than it is among the whites, and this greater death rate is, no doubt, the result, not of one, but a number of influences which, in the Northern cities, work to the detriment of the race. The Negro has greater difficulty there in finding satisfactory employment. Large numbers of Negro laborers are induced to leave the South to meet the emergencies of Northern industry. They were brought to Chicago to help dig the Chicago Drainage canal. They were imported to New York to work on the building of the subway. The labor unions, to whose interest it is to limit the supply of labor, have never been favorable to the employment of Negroes. The fact that Negroes are frequently brought North as "strike breakers" helps to intensify the prejudice against them. The tendency of all this is to force the Negro down to the lowest rung of the industrial ladder and to make him, in short, a sort of industrial pariah.

But in spite of these difficulties the facts show that a considerable number of exceptional colored men, spurred on by contact and competition with the swift and thrifty race about them, have made their way and been successful. The number of successful Negro business and professional men is probably larger in proportion to the Negro population in the North than it is in the South. Many of these have become men of influence in the communities in which they live and have worked quietly and steadily in their professions and in other directions for the benefit and building up of the Negro people.

GREATER OPPORTUNITIES IN THE SOUTH

But the Northern Negro who makes a success in business or in a profession must, in most instances, live beside and work for a people who have no special need of his talents. At best he can but perform for them a service that can be performed as well, if not better, by some one else. In the South, on the contrary, a Negro professional or business man has an opportunity to work for his own people who need his services and will respect and honor him for his work. Land is still cheap in the South. Negroes are better able there than in the North to buy and own their homes, to build their own communities, where they can have their own churches, schools, banks and other places of business, and where the masses of the people are not placed in such direct competition with a race centuries ahead of them in habits, instincts and education. In these communities the masses of the people are enabled to grow slowly and normally, and the educated Negro, the preacher, physician, teacher and business man has an opportunity in directing and controlling the development of his own people, to assist in building up his race and his country, and to gain for himself the honor and gratitude with which the world everywhere rewards real service.

But there is another disadvantage under which the Northern Negro labors which, while it is not so obvious, is none the less real. He is, in relation to the lives and interests of the masses of the Negro race, in a certain sense, an exile, condemned to witness from a distance their struggles to rise, but not able to give them any effectual aid. Very often it happens that the Northern Negro knows little or nothing, except what he can learn from the newspapers, of the actual condition under which the majority of the Negro population live. He hears much of the crime and violence and sees nothing of the deeper constructive forces which are working quietly in the minds and hearts of Southern people, black and white. His protests against what he regards as the wrongs committed against the members of his race in the South are often inspired by impatience and contempt for the Southern Negroes themselves who, as far as he can see, are willing patiently to suffer wrong.

The result has been that while Northern and Southern white people have been steadily coming closer together upon the race question, the Northern and Southern Negro seem to be steadily growing farther apart.

There is a radical group among the Northern Negroes, just as there is a radical section among Southern whites, who insist on making the racial question a political and sectional issue. They are seeking to solve the problem of the races by keeping the North and the South apart and preventing the co-operation of both sections and both races in the task of reconstruction.

My own opinion is that this policy is not only hopeless but mistaken. What the ultimate effect of any systematic effort to intensify the sectional and racial antagonisms that already exist might be I dare not say. Some persons have suggested that it would result in making the Negroes the permanent wards of the several states or of the United States. I do not believe that either the white people or the black people of the South are yet prepared to accept this solution. On the contrary I believe that the races that have lived and worked together for 250 years in slavery will be able, in spite of difficulties, to solve the problem of living together in freedom.

The Negro has too long been a battledore and shuttlecock of political parties. What the South at the present time needs most is racial and sectional peace. What the Negro wants is justice, protection and encouragement to put forth his best efforts in fruitful and productive labor for his own welfare and that of the country as a whole. This is not a sectional, but a national issue.

Congregationalist and Christian World, 92 (Sept. 28, 1907), 403–4. The article also appeared in *The Interior*, 38 (Sept. 26, 1907), 1259–60.

To Charles William Anderson

[Tuskegee Ala.] Sept. 30, 1907

Humphreys to have meeting tonight his headquarters. Think important you have friend on inside.

B. T. W.

TWpIr Con. 35 BTW Papers DLC.

To James Hardy Dillard

[Tuskegee, Ala.] Sept. 30, 1907

My dear Prof. Dillard: Please forgive the delay in answering your letter of Sept. 21. I was away from home when it came and am just now getting to my mail.

Permit me to say, first, that it is a matter of great gratification to me, and I am sure it will be to the others, to know that you are considering favorably the proposition which our Board made to you. Without at present going into details, I want to say that, in my opinion, you are the one man for the place. I repeat my opinion to the effect that you are the one man for the place. Of course, I should have to consult with the other members of the Board as to several questions which you raise in your letter, but I do not think there will be serious disagreement regarding them.

By this mail, I am sending you a copy of the book containing the history of the Peabody fund. It is written by Dr. Currier.[1] If you have not seen it, every line of it is worth reading. It contains an immense amount of information that will be valuable to us in administering the Jeanes Fund.

The mere matter of distributing through the South $35,000 or $40,000.00 each year, in my opinion, is a very small part of the work needed to be done by the general agent. The main thing to consider, it seems to me, is that this fund provides a basis for moving and guiding Southern thought and activities in reference to the whole subject of Negro education. The opportunity that it furnishes to make and lead public sentiment is of more value than the distribution of the money. I am sure that you realize that there never was a time when there was greater need for a strong sane influence to be put on foot that will combat the present tendency to decry, discourage and hamper Negro education. In many parts of the South, the Negro is not only being injured by disinterest and unfairness in reference to the handling of school funds, but worst of all, the white people are degrading and weakening themselves by yielding to dishonest habits in reference to the distribution of Negro school funds. The injury done to the white man is worse than that perpetrated upon the black man. So you see that there is a great opportunity for service to both races in this matter.

In the matter of the detailed organization of the Board, to which you refer, I am free to say that I do not care anything about the detailed method of organization, except to have the greatest good accomplished. I am willing to hold any office that the Board thinks it well for me to hold or I shall be just as happy to hold no office. If you and other members of the Board think that it will be well for the general agent to be the President of the organization, that will suit me. I am only anxious to get into a position where we can accomplish the greatest amount of good and the detailed organization and the machinery is a matter of minor importance to me.

I was in Boston a few days ago and had a talk with Wm. Lloyd Garrison and his brother and I was very much pleased to know that they knew you through correspondence.

Just as soon as I can get into touch with other members of the Board, I will write you further. Yours very truly,

Booker T. Washington

TLpS Con. 796 BTW Papers DLC.

[1] J. L. M. Curry, *A Brief Sketch of George Peabody, and a History of the Peabody Education Fund through Thirty Years* (1898).

An Article in *World's Work*

September 1907

A NEGRO COLLEGE TOWN
THE UPLIFTING INFLUENCE OF FIFTY YEARS' GROWTH OF WILBERFORCE, O.

A few miles west of Xenia, O., there is a quiet little community of which one occasionally sees the name in the newspapers, but in regard to which very little is known by the outside world, even among its immediate neighbors. This is the Negro town of Wilberforce, which is, however, not a town in the ordinary sense of the word, but rather a suburb of Xenia, from which it is distant an hour's walk and with which it is connected only by a stage.

The road which takes you from the city runs through a pleasant, rolling country, between wide stretches of rich farm land, dotted with little patches of woodland and large, prosperous, and well-stocked farms. Green County, in the centre of which the community is located, is one of the most prosperous counties in the whole rich farming region of southern Ohio, and is noted as a centre of the stock-raising industry of the state.

Approaching from the city, there is nothing, at a little distance, except the college buildings to distinguish Wilberforce from any of the other country villages which one meets in this part of the country. It is merely a little cluster of houses against a background of pleasant woods, a little centre of country residences with lawns and gardens, and a few farmhouses on the outskirts.

But turning from the country road into the wide avenue along which the town is arranged, you find yourself in the midst of a quaint and beautiful little college town, which has some of the rustic charm of a country village, with something, also, of that flavor of refinement and grace which inevitably comes, with time, to every college town, where men are permanently bound together for a high purpose. On one side of the long avenue, along which the town has arranged itself, are the college buildings, and on the other are the homes of the teachers and officers of the school. The road terminates in a little wood, and rambles off into the meadows beyond the town.

A Contrast to Mound Bayou

Different in almost every way from the sprawling frontier village of Mound Bayou, which I have described in a previous article, Wilberforce is quite as distinctively a Negro community. Mound Bayou, situated in the wilderness of the Yazoo Delta of Mississippi, is a pioneer town. It exhibits in a picturesque and unique way the struggle of the masses of the Negro people in the South to get possession of the land and make it their own. Wilberforce is older, slower, less enterprising, and more beautiful.

Mound Bayou has sprung up as the centre of an industrial enterprise. Wilberforce has grown up about a school and reflects in its homes the slow, refining influence of half a century of Negro education.

It is only during the last twenty or twenty-five years that the masses of the Negro people have begun to seek a solution of their problem in industrial progress. The first great passion of the Negro race after the war was for education. If the church stands for the first great interest in which the Negro, as a race, has sought salvation, it may be said that the schoolhouse represents the second. The College of Wilberforce, which is, so far as I know, the first permanent institution of learning founded by Negroes in this country, gave at an early period a definite expression to that aspiration. It came into existence in the midst of the commotion of the great Civil War, at a time when the masses of the people were still in slavery: at a time when everything that concerned the Negro people, their fitness for freedom and their capacity for education, was looked upon with much more doubt than it is to-day. In the half century since that time the scattered Negro community in which the College began its work, while it has not to any great degree increased in size, has grown to represent in a very concrete way, in its homes and the habits of the people, the spirit and influence of the College.

There are a certain number of persons who are in the habit of saying that Negro education has been a failure, for the reason that it has tended rather to increase than to diminish the number of Negro criminals. It is my experience that whenever a permanent school for Negroes has been established, there has almost always grown up around it a permanent, decent, and orderly Negro community. I do not know where one can better study the actual effects of education upon the Negro than in these communities, where one can see the concrete results of its permanent and lasting influence.

If Mound Bayou represents what Negroes have accomplished in the direction of industrial progress and political self-control, then Wilberforce may be said to represent the slower and subtler influence which the patient struggle to gain an education has had upon the life and character of the race.

Wilberforce is both a college and a town. But many persons who know something of the College and its history know nothing of the community that has grown up around it, though the community is older than the College. Its history reaches back into the days before the war, when the Northwest Territory, made free by the ordinance of 1787, was a refuge for Negroes who sought permanent freedom.

How the Community Started

In its origin, Wilberforce is at once a representative and a survivor of a number of somewhat similar Negro communities which were established in different parts of Ohio in the period before the war. Most of these communities have disappeared and been forgotten, but traces of them may still be found under obscure names in forgotten corners of Ohio, and in other portions of the original Northwest Territory. More than one of the families now living in Wilberforce can trace its history back to some one of the Negro pioneers who crossed the mountains from Virginia in the early days in order to find a home in the free territory of the Northwest.

The conditions under which this and the other Negro communities of which it is a type were established in Ohio will be better understood, perhaps, if I recall the circumstances under which the state was settled.

A century ago one might have discovered in Ohio a situation not unlike that which may be seen to-day in the new state of Oklahoma. Two currents of immigration, one from the North, the other from the South, pouring into the state and mingling on the same soil, brought into touch with one another two widely different traditions, particularly with regard to the Negro and the treatment that he deserved at the hands of his white neighbors. The effect of this was to produce a number of abrupt changes in the situation of the free Negroes, according as, in the course of history, the anti-slavery or the pro-slavery element had control of popular opinion. For instance, by the terms of the Constitution, as it was first adopted by the constitutional convention in 1802, Negroes were given the right to vote. A motion subsequently made to strike out the provision was carried only by the vote of the presiding officer. This was followed, however, a few years later, by the enactment by the Legislature of a so-called "black code," so vigorous in its terms that, if it had been enforced, it would have made the position of the free Negroes of Ohio quite as difficult as it ever was in any of the slave states. Laws were passed which were intended not merely to prevent the further settling of Negroes in the state, but which aimed to drive out those already there.

One thing about the character of the people who settled the southern part of Ohio was peculiar. Though most of the settlers in the two or three tiers of counties were from Virginia or Kentucky, a large number were people who had moved from the South for the purpose of freeing their slaves. Mount Pleasant, Smithfield, and several other neighboring towns in Jefferson County were settled by Quakers who had liberated their slaves in North Carolina and after the adoption of the ordinance in 1787 settled in the free territory. It was at Mount Pleasant that Benjamin Lundy, the founder of the Abolition movement, started the first Abolition paper, in 1821.

But not merely Quakers and those of severe and earnest religious views migrated to the new country to secure freedom for their slaves. Some of the men who were most prominent in the early history of the state were drawn to this new country for the same reason.

Thus, from earliest times, it had become a custom for masters who did not believe in the institution of slavery, or who, for any reason whatever, wished to free their slaves, either to emigrate to the free territory or send their slaves there to enjoy the fruits of freedom. This practice of settling emancipated slaves on the free soil of the Northwest Territory was continued until the Civil War put an end to slavery.

The little Negro community at Tawawa Springs — now known as Wilberforce — was Southern in its origin, and the school out of which the present College eventually grew was an attempt to redress some of the wrongs that sprang from slavery.

THE FOUNDING OF THE COLLEGE

In 1856, when the anti-slavery agitation was at its height in Ohio, the Methodist Conference in Cincinnati, in conjunction with the Conference of the African Methodist Episcopal Church, established at Tawawa Springs a school for the Negro immigrants and refugees who had settled there. Salmon P. Chase, the first anti-slavery Governor of Ohio, was one of the board of trustees. Governor Chase's interest in the school continued throughout his life, and when he died, as Chief-Justice of the United States, he left $10,000 to assist in providing an endowment for the institution.

At the time of the breaking out of the war, this school had nearly one hundred pupils. Many of these came from the families settled in the neighborhood. Others were the natural sons and daughters of Southern planters who had sent them North to be educated. But with the breaking out of the war the school, deprived of its principal patrons, fell into decay, and in June, 1863, it was sold for a debt of $10,000 to the African Methodist Episcopal Church. This was the origin of Wilberforce College.

The community which has grown up about it is composed of a few farmers, who have been attracted to the place by the College; a few former students, who, after succeeding elsewhere, have gone back there to make their homes; the officers of the school, some sixty families in all, and about 400 students. Of the little colony of Negro refugees who settled in this neighborhood before the war, there still remain a few families. On a little height on the edge of the town there still stands a modest cottage in which lives the only one of the early pioneers who still remains. The memories of others are preserved in the names of some of their descendants who occupy farms in the neighborhood.

THE TOWN'S UPLIFTING INFLUENCE

I have referred at some length to the early history of Wilberforce, in order to emphasize the permanence (I am almost tempted to write, the antiquity) of the community, and to suggest something of the interest and attraction that the place has come to have for those who have grown up there. Permanence and stability are always important factors in the development of a people. They are, perhaps, more important to the Negro race at the present time than they are to any other element of the population. The individual who grows up without feeling himself a part of some permanent community, which exercises at once a controlling and an inspiring influence upon his life, is placed at a great disadvantage. In the Negro communities like Wilberforce, we may see, I believe, the growth of a moral control within the Negro race, which is taking the place of the control that was formerly imposed upon it from without.

The influence of Wilberforce is reflected in the character of its homes and of the people it has gradually, in the course of years, drawn about it. I doubt whether there is any Negro community in the United States in which there is so large a number of beautiful and well-kept homes.

One of the most characteristic of these is that of Professor William S. Scarborough, Professor of Ancient Languages. Professor Scarborough has been at Wilberforce for about thirty years. He has made himself an authority in his studies. He is member of a number of learned societies, and is the author of a text-book on the Greek language. He has traveled widely in Europe, and his home is filled with the fruits of his journeys. He has an extensive library, and he and his wife, who is the head of the Normal Training Department of the school, have devoted much time to local history, particularly to the history of Negro schools in Ohio. His home has the refined, studious atmosphere of a scholar.

A Wealthy Negro College Professor

President Joshua H. Jones, whose home directly adjoins that of Professor Scarborough, is a different type of man — the modern type of college president, an administrator and a business man. He is an enthusiast in agriculture and, in addition to his work as teacher and head of the college, is an extensive landowner. President Jones is, to a greater degree than any other member of the community, a self-made man. He was born on a plantation in South Carolina, and, until he entered Claflin University at nineteen, he had a very imperfect education. He was for ten years a student, first at Claflin University, in South Carolina, later at Howard, and finally at Wilberforce; during all this time he supported himself mainly by teaching in the summer months. His school training fitted him to be a minister. He got the training which made him a business man outside of the school, and the story of how he obtained it is interesting.

"While I was in Lynn, Mass.," he said, "I saved a few hundred dollars and put it in the savings bank. Somehow or other some promoters who had come East for money for their speculations learned of it. They wrote to me. I replied courteously, asking for further information. Then they called on me, and outlined their plans and projects. I listened to all they had to say, attentively, and with great interest, for they were introducing me into a new world. But I did not give them my money. I continued to receive circulars, to which I always replied. Evidently the promoters did not understand me. Perhaps they thought just because I always listened and inquired, that I had more money to invest than I had. Anyway, this thing went on for years. After some years I began to get reports from some of the investments that had been offered me, and I was able to see the other side of the transaction. All this time I was observing and studying. I never put any money into any one of the schemes that were offered me, but I learned the methods of business investment. After I came to Columbus, I made up my mind to put into practice what I had learned, and I was successful."

President Jones made a fortune, I am told, of something like $30,000 before he came to Wilberforce as president of the College.

PROMINENT CITIZENS OF WILBERFORCE

I was impressed with the fact, during my visits to Wilberforce, that one thing which has given character to the community is the number of distinguished men who have lived and worked here.

The house which President Jones occupies at present was formerly occupied by Bishop James A. Shorter, one of the founders of the College. Bishop Daniel A. Payne, who was more than any one else responsible for the existence of the College, lived near by for many years, until he died, in 1892. Bishop B. W. Arnett, who, until he died in the fall of 1906, was one of the most influential men in the African Methodist Episcopal Church and one of the trustees of the College, lived for thirty-five years in Wilberforce. Bishop Arnett was born in a Quaker settlement at Brownsville, Pa., in the same year as James G. Blaine, whose parents lived directly across the street.

Though these men are little known to the world at large, they did good service for the uplifting of the Negro race and are remembered with reverence and gratitude by the people they served, both outside and inside of the church whose influence they have helped to extend all over the United States and even to Africa. Every year brings a considerable number of students who come from Africa to prepare themselves for the ministry at the theological seminary connected with the College here.

One of the most interesting little homes in the community is that of Miss Hallie Q. Brown, who has been for years a public figure. She is an elocutionist, and in the course of a long professional career has traveled all over the world. She was at one time what used to be known as "Lady Principal" at Tuskegee. Although by the nature of her profession she is constantly moving about, she has maintained her home in Wilberforce ever since her graduation from the College in 1873. The house is occupied at present by her mother and sister. Mrs. Brown, her mother, is an interesting old lady whose memories go back to the days before the war, in Virginia. In 1860, she, with her husband and a number of other colored people, went from Pittsburg to Canada, and lived for a time in what was known as "Kings Settlement," one of several refugee settlements founded near Chatham, Canada. Her son, Jere Brown, is immigrant inspector at Detroit, Mich. He is one of a considerable number of successful young men, in different parts of the country, who have gone out from Wilberforce and still claim it, in a way, as their home.

Another former student, who after some years in the West has returned to Wilberforce to make his home, is W. A. Anderson, who conducts a grocery business. He lives in a comfortable and well ordered little home which, like nearly all the homes in this community, displays a thrifty sense of order and a discipline in the household virtues, which is, after all, perhaps the most important product of Christian civilization.

THE PROSPERITY OF WILBERFORCE NEGROES

Of the sixty families that make up the Wilberforce community, forty-seven own their own homes. Four farmers of the community own land in a surrounding country which is valued at about $100 an acre. The College has 350 acres. President Jones has 280 acres, a part of which he hopes to add to what the school now possesses, should the agricultural school eventually be established. In all, there is owned by the school and members of the community about 1,700 acres.

During the last few years, several handsome new homes have been erected, fitted with all the comforts and conveniences of modern city houses. The home of Bishop Lee, valued at $6,000, is one of these. Bishop Lee graduated from Wilberforce in 1872, and was president of the College from 1876 until 1884, when he resigned to accept the editorship of the *Christian Record*, one of the publications of the African Methodist Episcopal Church. He makes his home in Wilberforce, though his duties take him away a large part of the time.

Joseph P. Shorter, superintendent of the Normal and Industrial Department, which was established by the Ohio legislature in 1887, owns a farm of eighty acres in the community, the work of which he superintends, in addition to his work in the College. Caleb Nooks, a former student who is a cattle-buyer for the Xenia markets, has a farm of 100 acres in the neighborhood. James E. Smith, of the class of 1891, a carpenter by trade, has a farm of 100 acres near the school.

Among other homes are those of James P. Maxwell, treasurer of the College, who has lived here for twenty-five years; Horace Talbert, who has been for ten years secretary of the College; Mrs. S. T. Mitchell, wife of a former president of the College; James Masterson, whose house is now occupied by Lieutenant Davis, teacher of military tactics, and Edward H. Clark, professor of physics and astronomy. He is a descendant of a family that came out to Cincinnati from Virginia at an early day, members of which have been connected with the University almost since its foundation.

Among the other members of the community who have been attracted to Wilberforce by the advantages that it offers as a place of residence and the opportunities for education of their children, is Thomas Perkins, a retired farmer from Mississippi. Mr. Perkins is the owner of a plantation of 1,200 acres near Belzoni, on the Yazoo and Mississippi Valley Railroad. He was employed for a number of years as a laborer on the farm he now owns. At the death of the owner the heirs first rented it, and finally sold it to Perkins. He managed the property with such thrift that he was able to pay $20,000 for it within a period of about six years. After he had acquired the property he was induced to come North on account of malaria, and decided to settle in Wilberforce, where he could conveniently give his children the benefit of an education. Mr. Perkins is now a man of independent means. He has a fine house, surrounded by wide lawns, and has been living for some years past on the earnings of his Mississippi plantation, which has greatly increased in value in recent years.

One of the most successful farmers in the neighborhood is J. Fowler, who owns 150 acres a few miles from the College. Fowler and his wife walked over the mountains from Virginia in 1860. He worked as a farm-hand in the neighborhood of the College in the early days, and has, as he says, "dug his fortune out of the earth." He lives in a fine old country place, built of stone and bearing the date 1821 carved over the entrance.

Another farmer, who came to Wilberforce community some years ago to educate his children, is J. J. Turner, who, with his sons Arthur and Cyrus, conducts a dairy farm of some 200 acres not far from the school. They have a dairy herd of 250 cows and dispose of their milk and butter in Springfield. Cyrus Turner went to the State University at Columbus, after his graduation at Wilberforce, and devoted himself for several years to the study of agriculture. They have a fine home, which, like most of the other farms in this vicinity, is connected with Xenia by telephone, and are rapidly increasing a fortune that is already considerable even for an Ohio farmer. They sell about 500 pounds of butter fat a month in Springfield, and secure two cents a pound premium on each pound of their product. Cyrus Turner received the highest mark at college in the butter-making contest, and his scientific knowledge, added to the practical experience of his father, has contributed to the business success of the dairy farm.

Linked as it is by its history with the past and possessing for colored people a certain historic interest as the first college established in this country by Negroes, and for many years almost the only college exclusively for Negroes north of Mason and Dixon's line, Wilberforce occupies a position of importance in the rapidly increasing population of the southern section of Ohio.

In the county adjoining it is Springfield, the scene of the race riots of 1905. To the west is Dayton, the city in which the late Paul Laurence Dunbar, the Negro poet, was born and raised. The constant, steady influx of Negro immigration from the southern shore of the Ohio River has brought to this whole region of southern Ohio, under somewhat changed conditions and with different motives, the same struggle for the adjustment of the races that one meets elsewhere. If in other parts of the country Negroes have been made to feel that they were alien and intruders, here, where they are firmly planted in the soil, they have been able to feel at home.

One of the subtle charms of Wilberforce is that in this place a people that for almost 250 years has been almost without a tradition of its own is beginning to make a history. This is, no doubt, why so large a number of the students who have gone out from here into the world have returned to make their homes. It is one of the things that make the Negro communities that are growing up elsewhere in the South and in the West interesting and important.

World's Work, 14 (Sept. 1907), 9361–67.

From Roscoe Conkling Simmons

New York Oct. 2, 1907

Personal

Dear Uncle Booker: I have not before written you on the "Conference" because I wanted to get my editorial matter out of the way for the current week & I am not to write you voluminously; yet I want to write intelligently.

The "Conference" was interesting. Besides Mr. Milholland, who presided, there were present: A. B. Humphries; Miss M. W. Ovington; a Major Gardner[1] (?) (white) O. M. Waller; G. F. Miller; R. C. Ransom; Wilford H. Smith; Gilchrist Stewart; J. L. Curtis; B. F. Thomas, several white men who were not introduced; Granville Martin (Guardian) and myself. Dr. Sinclair[2] could not remain over. The Rev. Messrs; W H Brooks, M. W. Gilbert and C. S. Morris sent letters, subscribing to any action the "Conference" might take. My presence was anything but pleasant to several of the brethren, who talked at me until I arose to reply. As to what I said, or how I said it, perhaps some time Mr. Smith might tell you. I served notice on the Constitution League that it could never hope to win anything, not even the respect of men, unless it ceased to conspire against the reputation of the leader of Negroes; that I was not a black-guard, and intended never to be one; nor to give quarter to those who sanctioned any such methods; that it was simply chiseling its own headstone by standing with or for those men amongst us, who, like the woman crusader of olden times, stood in the roadway, a porringer of fire in one hand; a pail of water in the other – with the fire she would burn up heaven; with the water she would put out hell; nor offered anything for the loss of either. Mr. Milholland responded by offering me the Editorship of all matter emanating from the League, much to the evident chagrin of some of the elders.

Now, the Conference specifically considered the advisability of holding a "huge" demonstration in Cooper Union; and definitely decided to "pack the house" on the evening of Nov. 14th; aiming to attract the attention of the country towards the Senate investigation of the Brownsville riot, which, you will remember, resumes its hearings on Nov. 18th. This meeting is to immediately follow a Conference to be held in Philadelphia for several days during the same week. This Conference is to be, from all reports, quite an affair, as no few of the reformers of first one thing and then the other, are to participate in the deliberations, and sign the address to the country. The event however that is to shake the foundations of many mountains and set the earth a trembling, is the Cooper Union "protest." The speakers for that occasion are (we were implored to hide them under our tongues) Congressman McCall[3] of Mass.; Mrs. M. C. Terrell; Alexander Irvine[4] (who investigated peonage); Manning and Middleton[5] of Alabama; Rev. Mr. Ransom and Miss Ovington. Miss Ovington is to work up interest in the meeting among the leading whites of New York; that class which most likely would pack Carnegie for Tuskegee or to honour Schurz. There is some talk of Senator Foraker coming over; but I can head this off, I am positive, if I could get to Cincinnati. You will instruct me here.

The bone for the mouth of the growlers on this occasion is to be the abuse of Mr. Roosevelt and the scorn of Mr. Taft. Mr. Hughes[6] is to be extolled for "his many virtues." Both Mr. Smith and myself refused places on the program. I also declined the Editorship or Censorship of the periodical publications of the League and as the spokesman, so far as the public press is concerned of this particular event. Likewise I would not take up the work of a "Press Bureau" on pay, graciously tendered me in open Conference.

I have given you substantially the plans and purposes of the "Conference." Behind it all is the political note; that note tunes and hums against the Administration of course. This New York meeting is to be the official protest of the Negro and his "friends" against the "infamy" of the man on "horst bac'" to quote Col Giles Jackson.

Whatever is done be careful of my part. The whites do not, but the blacks do fear me, saying I am too independent to be so conspicuously put forth. You can write me fully with perfect freedom and confidence. Whatever you instruct will be carried out. By the way, it is possible that Du Bois will speak at the Cooper Union meeting. I tried to get a place for Ben Davis, and had his name recorded, when this Martin of the Guardian, sprung this editorial of Ben's on Roosevelt and the Soldiers, which appeared a week or so ago. I knew if Ben could have been placed he would have rung true, and most likely attacked the spirit of the meeting. This, I believe, is a full and faithful report of the word and spirit of the "Conference."

With genuine affection for all at home, I am Your devoted nephew

Roscoe

Don't forget to have me meet you Phila; when you start towards Pittsburgh. If you want me to prevent Senator F.'s coming to this meeting, let me know.

R

Very soon, perhaps next week, a "Conference" is to be held to begin work for delegates to the National Convention.

ALS Con. 37 BTW Papers DLC.

1 Probably Augustus Peabody Gardner (1865–1918), a Republican congressman from Massachusetts from 1903 to 1917.

2 William Albert Sinclair (1858–1926), a Philadelphia physician, became field secretary of the Constitution League. He wrote *The Aftermath of Slavery: A Study of the Conditions and Environment of the American Negro* (1905), which contained a defense of black reconstruction.

3 Samuel Walker McCall (1851–1923), editor of the Boston *Advertiser*, served in Congress from 1893 to 1913 and as governor of Massachusetts from 1916 to 1918.

4 Alexander Fitzgerald Irvine (1863–1941), born in Ireland and educated at Oxford and Yale, was an ordained Congregational minister in Connecticut and then New

York. He was a Christian Socialist who worked with the poor on the lower East Side of New York City and once disguised himself as a common laborer in the South to gather information about peonage, especially among immigrants.

5 J. Osmond Middleton (b. 1882), an Alabama lawyer and politician, was an Alabama state representative from 1906 to 1922.

6 Charles Evans Hughes (1862–1948), governor of New York (1907–10), associate justice (1910–16) and chief justice (1930–41) of the U.S. Supreme Court, and Republican presidential candidate in 1916.

To George M. Warner[1]

[Tuskegee, Ala.] Oct. 3, 1907

My dear Sir: It is very difficult to reply to your inquiries in a brief letter. The subject is a very large one and requires much in the way of explanation.

I might say in brief that peonage in the South is on the decrease, though there is no doubt that a great deal of it still exists. If you will look up the back numbers of The Cosmopolitan Magazine, I think you will find in the January, February or March numbers an interesting article that describes the existence of peonage in the state of Florida. Enclosed I send you a pamphlet on the subject written by a colored woman in Atlanta, in whose word I have a good deal of confidence. I would state that if a small sum of money, say, $500.00 or $600.00 could be secured, that it could be used in a way that would go a long distance in breaking up this practice. What is needed is for a case to be properly brought before a court, and if this is done, an example could be made that would result in great good. I cannot explain in a letter all the details of what I mean, but if there was any probability of getting such a sum, I could explain just how it could be used. In a few words, the plan would be to test constitutionally having prisoners work out fines as punishment for crime committed. The practice of having prisoners work out fines lays the foundation of peonage in many cases. Many eminent lawyers claim that this practice is unconstitutional. Very truly yours,

Booker T. Washington

TLpS Con. 363 BTW Papers DLC.

1 George M. Warner was a Philadelphia grain and feed dealer.

To Frederick Randolph Moore

[Tuskegee, Ala.] October 5, 1907

Personal and Confidential

My dear Mr. Moore: You have now in your hands the greatest opportunity, in my opinion, that any individual has had in many years to influence and make public sentiment and therefore bring about sane and helpful efforts on the part of our people that any individual has had, as I have stated, within recent years. It is a tremendous opportunity as well as a serious responsibility. Because of this significant honor and because of the great chance afforded you, I want you to forgive and excuse me for being very frank with you regarding one or two matters. It is because of my high regard for you and friendship for you that I am going to speak as I do.

In the first place, I think you owe it to yourself and your business to be more considerate of your health. Not only that, but the actions of a man so far as his habits are concerned have a good deal to do with the confidence which people share in his business. I think you make a great mistake by not getting more regular and systematic sleep than you do. People who are thoughtless may joke with you for a while about sitting up until two and three o'clock in the morning and then rise again at seven, but deep down in their hearts such people know that that is poor business. You may keep your bodily and mental health for a while at this rate, but not long. You would be in a vastly better shape for first class business the next day if you were to get from eight to ten hours good sleep every night. Every man owes it to himself as well as to his business and those associated with him in business. If one is seen out late at night continually, it reflects upon his business capacity.

Secondly. There are a good many of your best friends who criticize you for being too prodigal of your time, that is in spending too long a time in talking to inconsequential individuals on the streets and elsewhere, that is, in a word, they criticize you because you do not at all times show the business spirit which comes right down to hard[pan][1] business and gets through with a subject or an individual and takes up something else or another man. Simply as a business proposition, it pays an individual to seem to be busy even though he may not be busy, but if one gets the reputation of always having plenty of time for talking it becomes hurtful to himself and to those associated with him in business.

The third suggestion or criticism is contained in the following quotation which comes to me from a friend where you have traveled in the interest of the Business League:

"A man who smokes continually on the streets in the presence of women and children as well as men, and also smokes continuously in the homes wherever he is, does not set a good example as a man of affairs and business. In this community there are a good many prominent business men who smoke, but most of them do so after meals or confine it to their office or home. Very few of them are seen puffing cigars on the street."

All three of these points are in a way trivial, but they mean a great deal in the direction of helping you to succeed.

I think I know you well enough to know that you will take all I have said in the very best spirit and will not misunderstand me. Yours truly,

Booker T. Washington

TLpS Con. 949 BTW Papers DLC.

[1] Word partly obliterated.

To Robert Russa Moton

[Tuskegee, Ala.] October 5, 1907

Personal and Confidential

My dear Major Moton: I thank you very much for the intimate information which you have given me. I shall treat it, of course, as wholly confidential. This information interests me, not as much from the view point of Miss Ovington and her group of friends, as it does in showing the attitude and character of those with whom she associates. No person could be in such relations with Miss Ovington without sympathizing with her. So far as the other phase of it is concerned, it only represents the howlings of a group of second or third rate white people who are trying to meddle into colored people's affairs and become their perpetual advisors or leaders. I understand perfectly the little group with whom Miss Ovington is in contact. The individual referred to as giving her this information bearing upon conditions in Alabama is either John E. Milholland, A. B. Humphrey, or a discontented politician in Alabama by the name of Manning. These are the three persons with whom Miss Ovington has in some way become enraptured. Neither one has a bit of standing among white people of any standing either in the political or business world.

I have been accused of a good many crimes, but rarely have I been accused of wasting away time and effort. Any one who is at all acquainted with public affairs in Alabama knows that so far as the political situation is concerned that the President has the state wholly in his grasp and that the leaders are willing to go in any direction that he wishes, and hence it would be folly for me, even if I were inclined to do so, to seek to get something for the President which he already has and aside from this it is absolutely folly that I have given time to an effort to try to get delegates for the President.

It is possible that persons who are able to accomplish good in directions that Miss Ovington is able to do, should yield to the temptation of giving time and strength to mean, little, greedy gossip to directions that will do good for no one. As I stated in my address at Hampton,[1] [every] one should seek to get up to the highest atmosphere and not descend to the lowest.

Thanking you again for the information, I am Yours truly,

Booker T. Washington

TLpS Con. 949 BTW Papers DLC.

[1] See An Address at Hampton Institute, Aug. 4, 1907, above.

From Ralph Waldo Tyler

Washington, D.C. Oct 5/07

Dear Doctor: I have Mr. Vory's (Tafts manager) permission to go ahead an[d] inaugurate a Colored Press Bureau here, at their expense.

My idea is to place it in the hands of Thompson, let him get up a newsy letter each week and send to colored newspapers. In this letter he will incorporate, judiciously, pro-Roosevelt and pro-Taft matter, and in such a manner as to not aro[u]se suspicion. He will notify the Colored press that because of the desirability of having a regular Washington letter each week, he has decided to begin the service of a weekly syndicate letter covering news, comment at the Capitol, and in order to give each paper an opportunity to fully test the advantage of using such a letter, he will mail it each week for a period of 6–8 or 10 weeks gratis. Quite all will take it, and once they begin it, the letter can be continued on indefinitely gratis, and without even so much as reminding them of the expiration of the gratis period.

I would sort of supervise the service, and if it was found expedient to disarm any possible suspicion, at the end of the gratis period, a nominal charge of say 50 cents a letter might be made, Thompson receiving it for himself — if any of them remit.

What do you think of the plan? I await your opinion before taking the work up. Sincerely

Ralph W Tyler

ALS Con. 8 BTW Papers DLC.

A Sunday Evening Talk

[Tuskegee, Ala.] October 6, 1907

One object of a school is to help people to break up old lines of action, to throw off old habits that are not of the most helpful character, and to take on in their place new and more helpful ones. It is surprising to note to what an extent people get into the habit of thinking or talking or acting in a certain direction without any special reason for it, to what extent in that way they make themselves slaves of a certain line of thought, talk or action.

There are some people, and I am very much afraid they constitute a very large proportion of the human family, who do very little thinking for themselves, and usually repeat day by day in one form or another that which they have heard from the lips of others. The people who are strong enough and brave enough to think for themselves are very few. You can go through certain communities, and be perfectly sure how every individual in those communities will express himself regarding certain subjects, be perfectly sure of almost the very words these people will use to express themselves. I had this emphasized some years ago when I was on the Pacific coast. I was very anxious to know the opinions, or what was called the opinions, of the people there concerning the Chinese, and practically every individual that I met had the same opinion and expressed it in almost the same words.

Now, it is impossible to make me believe that many of those people had been thinking for themselves; that they had really, by proper research, by hard endeavor, found out anything upon which to base their thoughts. The facts were, that they had gotten into the habit of hearing certain opinions expressed day by day concerning the Chinese, and without original investigation, without any attempt on their part at original thinking, they had gone on, parrot-like repeating the same things that they had been hearing for years.

One of the first things that education should do for an individual should be to make him strong, courageous; should be to give him that kind of courage and that kind of faith which will make him find out for himself what is true and what is untrue; should be to make him by original research separate the false from the true, and then after he has found the truth, make him brave enough to express his opinions, no matter whether it makes him popular or unpopular — for the time being. The same weakness not only extends to our habits of thought, our habits of expression, but it goes still further. You will find, I think, the habit of thinking in certain directions perhaps without being able to get out of a groove, has a stronger hold upon people who live in a warm climate, upon people who live in tropical climates, than upon those who live in colder climates. For example, you will find, with very few exceptions, people who live in a warm country grow into the habit of thinking they must put off things today for tomorrow. They are always going to do a thing tomorrow, and the hotter the section in which they live, the more they talk about tomorrow; you will find that they grow into the same habit of saying that they are going to begin to do work on Monday. I find about here that there are very few people who, if you ask them to do a certain piece of work after Wednesday, will not say they will do it on Monday. You cannot get a person to begin building a house on Friday — always Monday! They have got into the habit of thinking and acting in that way.

The same habit will apply to other things, and I want to impress upon you this line of suggestion, that education here, education everywhere, is meant to help people break up old lines of thought and habit and seek that which is best.

Now, I suspect that many of you know families, have known them for a good while, who have been eating the same thing for breakfast and for dinner and for supper for twenty years, without any variation. You can go to certain houses and can be almost absolutely sure what those people are intending to have for breakfast. They have it every day in the year. It usually is grits, meat and corn bread, is it not? They have the same thing in the spring that they have in the winter, the same thing in the fall that they have in summer — always the same thing over and over!

Education is meant to help people to search out that which is best in relation to eating, and to use that which is best — to throw off the old habit and not grow into the slavery of using a certain thing on the table because it has been used in that way generation after generation. Why, I have actually seen people living right in the midst of a peach orchard and when there were berries of the most delicious character all around, bananas and oranges not very far away, when those delicious things could be placed upon their breakfast table at a price that was almost half what they paid for the corn bread, meat and grits, but still they would not touch the berries and the tempting fruits of various kinds. They would rather stick to the old things, simply because it is a habit. Now, education, I repeat, is meant to help you to find out what is best — to throw off the old things and put on the new things, no matter how much you have been a slave to the old thing. It is meant to help you girls and you boys find the best thing to use here at school, the best thing to use after you go away from here.

You will find the same habit, the same weakness, entering into one's life very largely in regard to dress. You have seen individuals in your community, individuals sometimes with considerable book education who get into certain slovenly, uncouth habits of dress. You have seen such individuals who never have all of the buttons in the proper place on their coats; you have seen such individuals whose dress, whose coat, is always filled with grease spots — always untidy, never clean, never pressed.

You have seen individuals who were school teachers and sometimes preachers, who have worn the same old necktie, it has seemed to me, in some cases, for ten years. No matter where you meet them, they always have on that slovenly, greasy, old coat and the same old slovenly, dirty, greasy necktie. Now, education is meant to help such persons to see these weaknesses and to throw them off.

You will see the same thing exemplified again in home life. You know houses that have had the window-glass out — been out for many years. Some of you can see the picture of that glass now. You know where it is and you have seen the old piece of cloth, an old pillow, stuck into that window, which has been there — right there — for many years, and some of you could go right now and put your hand on that window-glass and on that old pillow which was there when you left home; it will be there I fear when you get back home.

Education is meant to help you take hold of that kind of thing and change it. Why, it does not matter a snap about your studying mathematics and history and all those kind of things, if you can not use this increased knowledge and this increased strength of mind in a way to make you change such things.

You know people, some of them people of considerable wealth, of considerable education, who have lived in houses for years that have never had a single ounce of paint on them, or a drop of whitewash, and still simply by force of habit, they have lived there in that old house in the same old way.

The question that I want to put to each one is, are we going to be able to give you enough strength, enough of new vigor, enough of education at Tuskegee, that will enable you to go home and in spite of criticism, in spite of the slavery of old habits, get the paint brush and whitewash brush, and even if you have to do it with your own hands, notwithstanding you are girls, see to it that a change is brought about?

I referred briefly, last Sunday, I think, to some of the evil habits of farming. Let me illustrate one of them: I remember that I had in my office not long ago a farmer with whom I was talking about the kind of crops it was best to grow. I found that he had got into the old habit of raising nothing but cotton on his farm. The old fellow had been raising cotton for thirty years. I began to ask him a few questions. He acknowledged that he never got more than $12.50 worth of cotton off of each acre of land. I made the old fellow do some figuring with me — tried to make him do some thinking. I finally showed him that he could plant the same amount of land in sweet potatoes and make that land realize a cash amount of $25.00 an acre over against $12.50 an acre. I went over the subject with him two or three times, and each time he agreed with me that if he would plant sweet potatoes he would get $25.00 to the acre, whereas if he planted in cotton he would get only $12.50 per acre. He acknowledged that I was right, and then I asked him what he was going to plant next year, and he scratched his head and said he guessed he would have to stick to cotton. He just could not get out of the habit of making $12.50 on an acre of land or exchanging $12.50 for $25.00, because he had been in the habit of making $12.50 so long.

This is one of the weaknesses that we expect you to grow out of. I was talking a few days ago to the ministers that meet in this county in Phelps Hall about the same weak habits, the slave habits of the average man or woman connected with the church, for which the ministers in a large degree are responsible. I pointed out to them, as best I could, pictures of some of the churches that they were using, old houses with no window-glass in them — old houses with the door hanging on one hinge — old houses that were so old and broken down that whenever it rained, as much rain came into the house through the roof as was kept out — church houses that have never been painted, that have never seen any whitewash, and those people had been praying there in those old houses for twenty-five years for the Lord to help them. The Lord is not going to help a man preaching in such a house as that. What those people want to do is to help themselves — to get some paint, plaster and hinges and beautify the church of God. Then the Lord will help them.

You will find some school teachers that are so slovenly and untidy they teach in the same kind of old schoolhouses year after year simply through the slave habit, without attempting in any way to improve the school building, without attempting in any way to beautify the yard or surroundings.

And then there are some people that grow into the habit of standing perfectly still each year in relation to their reading. They get hold of the daily newspaper and that is all they read. The same old thing day after day. They read it and are satisfied with it. There is no possible growth in such a habit as that. You want to be very sure that in your reading, you are in contact with the very richest and best in this and all other countries, and you can only be sure of that as you form the habit of searching after that which is newest and best in literature, whether it is in the form of a daily paper, the weekly paper or the magazine.

Now, this school and all schools are meant to help you find the best, are meant to help you become proficient in finding the best — the best in thinking, in talking, the best in all kinds of activity, and above all, let me repeat, all kinds of education is meant to help you find the best, to help you find the truth, and then after you have found it, to see to it that you utter the truth, that you act the truth at all times and under all circumstances.

Tuskegee Student, 19 (Oct. 12, 1907), 1. Stenographically reported.

To Joseph Fels

Tuskegee Institute, Alabama October 12, 1907

My dear Sir: I recall being informed of your visit at Tuskegee along with your brother several months ago. If you happen to be coming this way again, I very much hope I may have the privilege of meeting you at the school.

I make note of what you say, and also of the extract from the letter written by Mr. Ryan, of 56 Pine St., New York. You may be interested to know that there are a number of Negro towns which are developing in a most helpful and satisfactory way. Of one of these, Mound Bayou, Miss., I wrote an article for the World's Work which was published in the July number. The experiment as it is being carried out there seems to promise very gratifying results. Another Negro town, Boley, I. Ter., seems to be started on a very substantial foundation.

Thanking you for your kind letter which I have read with great interest, I am, Yours truly,

Booker T. Washington

TLpSr Con. 350 BTW Papers DLC. A copy is in the Fairhope Colony Archives, Fairhope, Ala.

A Speech at Hampton Institute

[Hampton, Va.] October 13, 1907

THE PRIVILEGE OF SERVICE

I had planned to speak to the Tuskegee students tonight, but some matters of business made it seem wise for me to come here to see Dr. Frissell, so I am speaking to you instead. It is always a pleasure and, I might add, a sacred privilege, for me to be permitted to come here and stand upon this platform, to look into your faces, and to take by the hand those whom I have known for so many years. All of this is a privilege which I cannot describe to you in words. As I pass through these grounds, as I look into your faces and hear these beautiful songs, you do not know how many memories of days gone by come into my mind. I sometimes wish that I might come back to Hampton and be a student over again.

I remember that when I came to Hampton [Dr. Washington entered in 1872] there were just three industries for young men. One was farming; the others were carpentry and shoemaking. Aside from my entrance examination, to which I often refer and which consisted in dusting a room, my first industrial lesson was in shucking corn. One of the boys had a shoemaker's bench in the hall in Academic, and that was the shoemaking department; and the carpentry, I think, was in the charge of one person. When I came here there was just one brick building, the old Academic Hall. What changes have taken place since that time in order to make the institution more instructive and more useful! I remember that when I was here all the boys, with few exceptions, slept in Academic Hall; we had our classes there and our chapel; nearly everything was in that one building. I suppose that now there are three or four boys — no more — in a room. Then there were often as many as ten and we had a pretty good time. I remember one winter we got so crowded that General Armstrong put up some tents. When the General got hard up for a building he would go out and dig a hole, then when people came to the school he would show it to them and say that he had got that far and could not go further without money. One winter he had done this but had not received money enough for a building, so he put up a number of tents and called for volunteers to sleep in them. I had the privilege of being one of the boys who volunteered to sleep in one of them. I remember one cold night the wind got under that tent and lifted it completely off. We used to have some interesting times in those days. Great changes have taken place in your comforts, in your rooms, in your opportunities. I remember when I first came the dining room was in the barracks and there were no tablecloths. We had no cups and saucers and no spoons — no small spoons. Our tea and coffee — nobody ever knew what that was. We sometimes called it tea; sometimes coffee. It didn't make any difference. It was served in yellow bowls. I suppose now you have "light" or white bread every day. In those days we had it twice a week, and those were great days. We used to look forward most anxiously to Wednesdays and Sundays, for those were the days when we were sure to get light bread and molasses with it. The boys always prepared for those days and ate very sparingly the day before.

To me one of the most interesting lessons in connection with our efforts as a race is to know what wonderful and tremendous ramifications this institution has in the life of our people. You can scarcely go anywhere — North, South, East or West — where you do not meet from one to a dozen men or women who have had their lives shaped through the training received here. It seems to me more and more that if there is one thing for which we as a race, you as students, ought to feel thankful to God, it is for the privilege of work, the privilege of living in an age when you can be identified with a cause and with a race where you can find service at all times. No man or woman of our race with education needs to wait for an opportunity for service. Every part of the country has need for those who can perform all kinds of work. Tuskegee and Hampton men and women are a privileged class in this respect. We have the privilege of serving our own race and have an opportunity to lift it up, as it were, from the very bottom. The more I observe conditions in the South, the more I am convinced that in an increasing degree we should make an effort not only to perform this service to our own race, but to perform also the service to the white people about us of letting them know the work that is being done for our own people in their midst. It is pathetic that so many of the Southern white people, those who should know most about it, know, in many cases, least of what is going on among our people as a race. Perhaps any other people with their environment, with their past, would be just as hard to reach, would know just as little about what is taking place about them; but I feel that it is one of the duties of institutions like this, and of the graduates who go out from such institutions, to get hold of the white people and bring them in contact with what our people are doing. Very often we take too much for granted. My experience teaches me that when people are brought in contact with what is being done they become friends and supporters of the work. I know you hear much that is of a disappointing nature. No individual need hide the fact that there is much that is hard, much that is unjust, much that tends to discourage and dishearten us, but we must keep our hopefulness.

Now and then come things to encourage us. Last Tuesday it was my privilege to be present at the dedication of the Negro Y.M.C.A. building in Columbus, Ga. This building, and I believe it is one of the finest and most expensive colored Y.M.C.A. buildings in the country and perhaps in the world, is there chiefly through the generosity of our friend, Mr. George Foster Peabody. It cost twenty thousand dollars and is now complete and in use. Though Mr. Peabody gave the greater part of the money for the erection of this building, at least five thousand dollars were given by the white people of Columbus, Ga., and two or three thousand dollars were given by the colored people. I spent the day in Columbus and it has never before been my privilege to go into a community where such a feeling of friendliness exists between the two races as in that city of Columbus. White men have not only given generously of their money, but I noticed that when the building was opened for inspection it was crowded not only with colored people, but with white people who seemed proud that the colored people had this building. I had the privilege of speaking to them in the evening. Four or five hundred of the audience of twelve hundred were white people. It is not alone in this way that they show their interest in the welfare of the colored people; if you could go through the city schools of Columbus you would see how, under the direction of a brave and capable city superintendent, the same opportunities are provided for the colored children as for the white. They have the same course of study. There is a slight difference in the construction of the buildings, but in the length of term and in the equipment there is no difference. The superintendent explained, with a great deal of pride, the plans for the new building which is to be erected for a colored school. It is to be a model one, to make sure that there shall be at least one city in the South where colored children shall receive the best possible educational training. Besides the usual public school studies, industrial training is given in connection with the Columbus school system. No one can spend a day in contact with these people without having more and more hope. This is not the only green spot in this country, and they will increase as we go on doing our privileged work.

I sometimes fear that we advertise our enemies too much to the world. We do this rather than advertise those who are friendly to us. There are some people perhaps who do not wish us well, and these are people who make a great deal of noise. I am going to illustrate my point by telling a story. Down in Alabama there was once an old colored man who lived near a frog pond. There was one very large old bullfrog who made a great deal of noise every night, so that the man could not sleep. He found out that a summer hotel not far away would purchase frogs' legs, so he went there with a great deal of interest, found the proprietor of the hotel, and said that he had heard they would buy frogs' legs. The proprietor said he would buy as many as he could get, and the old man said he could bring a cart load. The old fellow went home much encouraged. He went down to the pond and searched a long time, but he would find nothing but the bullfrog. After a few days the old man went down town and saw the proprietor, who asked why he had not brought the frogs' legs, and the man had to tell him that there was only the one bullfrog in the pond. Our enemies are not so many in number but they make a great deal of noise; we must not be deceived by these bullfrogs. Very many people in the South are interested in the development of our race.

There is another phase of development in the South, a most significant one. I do not believe there is anything in history equal to the present temperance wave that is sweeping through the South, so far as the Gulf States are concerned. There is something in it that is hard to understand. Not long ago the state of Georgia passed a law that made it impossible to sell whiskey legally within the borders of the state. I saw an article in the Outlook a few days ago which said this law was passed mainly because they wished to take the whiskey from the Negroes. It is something more than that. All through the South the people are talking about it and praying about it. I believe that within ten years from now there will not be a single place in the state of Alabama that will sell whiskey legally. In Tennessee there are now only four cities that sell it; in Kentucky nine-tenths of the counties have decided to stop its sale. And this is not a momentary impulse but a public sentiment that, in my opinion, is not only going to pass the law but see that it is enforced after it is passed.

Here and there throughout the South are things that bring the greatest amount of hope and encouragement. It seems to me that one of the greatest evils that could befall our people at the present time would be to have any large proportion of them suffer themselves to grow embittered, to learn to hate the people of any other race, to cherish hatred in their hearts because of what people do to them. To be useful in the world, to exert the most lasting and deepest influence one must always be calm, cheerful and self-controlled in action. Such people exert the greatest influence in life and will help most in the solution of the problems in which we are most interested.

Some time ago one of our young men invited me to make a visit in a back country of Alabama where he had been teaching school. We had lost sight of the young man and were not sure what kind of work he was doing. I went out there and one day he had a Farmers' Institute, which he called an experience meeting. An old farmer was asked to go up on the platform. He had a handful of cotton stalks. He picked up one stalk and began his address: "I never had no chance to study no science, but I has been trying to make some science for myse'f." "This stalk of cotton," he said, "growed only one boll to the stalk." He picked up another stalk of cotton and told how he had fertilized his land until he got three bolls to the stalk. Then he picked up another, and another until he showed one which had six, and "las' year" he concluded, "I got to the p'int where one stalk growed fourteen bolls." After he had taken his seat somebody said, "Uncle, what is your name?" Then he got up and made another little speech. "In de ole days when I didn' have no learnin,' an' lived in an ole log cabin, in them days dey uster call me 'Ole Jim Hill.' Now I owns houses, I is educatin' my chilluns, I has no mortgage on my buildin's, an' I has some money in the bank. Now dey calls me 'Mr. James Hill.' " Without any arguing and without abusing anybody the old man had solved his problem. Patiently and persistently we must go on and solve our individual problems and the racial problem. There is something in human nature which whether the individual be black or white, compels one to respect success.

Tuskegee Student, 19 (Dec. 14, 1907), 2–4. Reprinted from the *Southern Workman.* Brackets in original.

To Lyman Abbott

Tuskegee Institute, Alabama October 17, 1907

My dear Dr. Abbott: I thank you very much for your kind letter of October 10, and am writing to say that I shall keep your suggestion in mind regarding a visit to Cornwall.

The wave of temperance reform which is now sweeping through the South is most miraculous. There is scarcely a week now that some county in Alabama or some Southern state is not voting out whiskey. Wherever the question is put before the voters with few exceptions it carries by a very large majority. Two of the largest towns in Alabama have just voted this last week in favor of no license. Yours truly,

Booker T. Washington

TLS Lyman Abbott Papers MeB. A press copy is in Con. 811, BTW Papers, DLC.

To Samucl Sidney McClure

[Tuskegee, Ala.] Oct. 19, 1907

Personal.

My dear Mr. McClure: Some time ago, when we happened to meet in the streets of New York and you gave me a forecast of the ground which you expected to have your magazine cover during the next two or three years and put among other features, the Temperance Movement and said that within a few months, that would be the great question of America, I doubted your wisdom. Since then, I have come to realize, especially in the South, that you were right. The wave of temperance which is now sweeping through every section of the South is something akin to the miraculous. At the present rate of progress, I predict that within the next five years that no liquor will be sold in any of the Southern states legally, except perhaps Louisiana and Texas. There is scarcely a week that whiskey is not swept out by vote of some county in Alabama and the same is true of other Southern states. It is hard to understand the origin and meaning of the movement. People talk about it in the cars and on the street, discuss it in churches and in commercial organizations. In interest, it takes precedence of all else just now, but I do not need to give you any pointers in that direction. Yours very truly,

[Booker T. Washington]

TLc Con. 353 BTW Papers DLC.

From Frederick Randolph Moore

New York, 10/19 1907

Personal Private

My dear Mr Washington Fortune was up today. Gave me an article to publish signed answer to editorial "The Brownsville Ghouls."[1] No objection to publishing except that he uses following as part of article "Just before he went to Panama President Roosevelt wrote a letter to Dr Booker T Washington in which he assumed sole responsibility for the order. The letter was not marked personal. I believe I saw it. The letter has not been published I believe. Then in the language of the Scriptures the President raised the color question when he issued the order.["]

Telegraph me if you object to this portion. Do it immediately on receipt of this at Age office.

Fortune is bitter. Dont you send him any more money or, any more invitations. He goes to Chicago Friday or, Saturday. Full of religion and bitterness. I would like Scott to transfer all stock standing in his name to me and I will sign in blank new stock to him that he can hold – and will protect interests. He can say he has sold out to me (to Peterson) and the books will show at anytime here-after that Tuskegee is not interested. I will then be able to keep books away from office — for then absolute right will be mine. I think you will agree (both of you) to the wisdom of this request.

Kindly send order for $100 I borrowed this until Monday. You know you gave me $600 note was $700. Will send Business League matter within the next 12 days. I am sure you will recognize that I havent had any time to give to same in the last five weeks. Sincerely yours,

Fred. R. Moore

Balance in bank today $320 all bills paid.

Telegraphed Rev [Moore?] Cleveland immediately on receipt of your telegram. Am advised that Council adjourned when telegram was received so same is undelivered. Where can I reach him in *D.C.*?

ALS Con. 378 BTW Papers DLC.

1 Written by Ralph W. Tyler. See Tyler to E. J. Scott, Oct. 9, 1907, Con. 8, BTW Papers, DLC.

A Sunday Evening Talk

[Tuskegee, Ala.] October 20, 1907

Some days ago I received a letter from a missionary friend in Liberia in which he referred to the fact that several years ago some friends had very kindly presented him with a small boat to enable him to cover his mission fields more quickly and with less difficulty than he had been accustomed to do. He said that at the time he wrote this letter, he was in great trouble, because in some way his boat, which was a small steam affair, had gotten out of order and he could find no one in that part of the Republic who knew anything about repairing steam engines or steamboats. That incident impressed upon me a lesson which I want to try to impress upon you tonight — the lesson that every country and every people at a certain stage of its career is bound to give attention to certain fundamental things of life, otherwise there is going to be trouble, and this is true, I repeat, with a nation as with an individual.

Now in every new country, and with every new race, there are certain things in the way of laying the foundation that must receive attention in their proper order and at the proper time, and unless these fundamentals are emphasized and do receive attention at the proper time, there is going to be trouble.

Let us take, for example, the Republic of Liberia. Many of the lessons I shall suggest as coming from it will apply to our own people, especially here in the South, which, in a very large degree, is a new country, inhabited by a new race of people. Here in the South, I may say, so far as freedom is concerned, we are not so old as are the people in Liberia. Now, there are certain temptations that every new country and every new race are bound to avoid, if they would get upon their feet and stand firmly there. There is a temptation to seek to get into an artificial atmosphere; a temptation to ape nations that are thousands of years old, to ape the manners of individuals that have made a success and have laid the foundation for that success in those things to which I shall call your attention.

Now, what are the things that people most want? Suppose, for example, that you were going into a new country such as Liberia was fifty years ago (and I fear it is very much the same today). Some of the first things you would want would be shelter and perhaps before shelter or along with shelter, food. Among the first things to which any new race, any new country has got to give its attention is the cultivation of the soil, the getting all out of the soil that it will produce in order that there may be life, in order that there may be stability and in order that there may be progress. People who have been to Liberia, for example, have told me that they have seen school teachers eating canned tomatoes from Germany and England. Just think of it! People teaching school buying their vegetables in a market thousands of miles away.

This is a thing for our schools to consider. The thing to do in our schools — in private schools, high schools, in every school, no matter what its character — is first of all to bend education in the direction of helping the people to get their living out of the soil.

In the old days, education used to mean something that would help the person get away from the soil, away from the farm, away from the kitchen, and away from the country. Education in the new day, or the newer education means that which will help a person get the most out of the soil, the most out of the kitchen, the most out of the laundry, and enable him to put the most energy, the most skill in all of these activities.

Now they have education in Liberia — and I am only using this as an example; it is not the only country that has made the same mistake for years — they have education, as I have said in Liberia. They study the classics and they study the sciences, but they do not marry education to the soil, do not bring it into touch with the forests and the fields, do not train the hands of their men and women along with the mind, so that they can go to the soil, go into the forest and go into the mines and into the rivers and into the air and get the riches that are there, take them out and throw them upon the markets of the world.

The new education, in the newer day, is meant to accomplish all of these purposes. Why, it is perfectly ridiculous, perfectly absurd in a new country, where people are learning mathematics, where people are learning history and literature and all that kind of thing, as they are doing and have been doing for fifty years in Liberia, to be told you can not find a single decent public road in the entire Republic. What is education for, if it can not produce a public road? What is mathematics for? What is the use of studying arithmetic? What is the use of studying geometry, unless in some way people can make mathematics teach how to make public highways. You can scarcely find a wheelbarrow, scarcely find a cart in the entire Republic, and still we speak of people getting education while they omit these fundamental things of life. Education should produce railroads, should bring about the use of telephones, should bring about the construction and the use of all kinds of the latest and most approved kinds of vehicles, so that there can be communication from one part of the country to the other. Education should help every country produce more in that country than it consumes, should help the people of that country to send out of it more than they produce, and wherever you find a country that is buying more than it is selling, that country gets into debt. It gets into debt and very soon it gets into difficulty.

Education should be so directed, should be so harnessed to practical things as to enable any new people, no matter what their race, no matter what their color, to go into the soil, into the forest, into the mines, into the rivers — go everywhere — and get out of the natural resources of that country the riches of that country and throw them upon the markets of the world. There will be no poverty in that kind of country, no lack of progress there. What is true of Liberia, I am sorry to say, is true of other new countries: is equally true of Hayti, of San Domingo and many of these West Indian countries. These countries have attempted to build without first laying a foundation.

This newer kind of education to which I am referring, which brings people into touch with first and fundamental things, has not only come into use in a measure in the industrial schools for our people in the South, but in a larger degree, you will find, this kind of education is being used in all parts of Europe. It is being used in the West. Go into the Western States — Wisconsin, Iowa, Montana, California, as well as in the North — you will find that education is responding to this newer and more insistent demand in a way that has never been equalled in the history of the world.

I wish very much that some time during this present year, each one of you might find an opportunity to read the report of the Commission of Industrial and Technical Education — a report made by a committee appointed by the Massachusetts legislature some two or three years ago for the purpose of examining into the education of the state of Massachusetts. You can get this report at my office or at the Library. At any rate, if you will come to the office, we will show you how to get it. It is a document worth reading. I wish very much that you might carefully examine this report and see how in the great and intelligent and wealthy state of Massachusetts this committee recommends that there be introduced into the public schools, into the high schools, and, in a large degree, into the colleges and universities of the state of Massachusetts, the study of agriculture, the study of mechanics, the study of all kinds of domestic arts. They go still further. They recommend that in a certain grade of schools, pupils should study the books half a day and work at these industries half a day. You would think they were making a report on Tuskegee. They go still further and recommend that in many of the high schools they have the night school system and the day school system, the same as we have here at Tuskegee. Education in all parts of the world is moving in this direction. Every country and every race that wants to keep up with the best that is being done in the world, must study these newer educational systems.

Now, I have called your attention to the need of Liberia mainly for the purpose of emphasizing that our people in the South, so far as the country is concerned, so far as our race is concerned, are, in a degree, in the same condition as they are in Liberia and the other places I have mentioned. We have before us many of the same fundamental needs that they have and we must more and more devote ourselves to these fundamental needs. When a people, a race or a nation, become interested, as a gentleman suggested out here at the Fair yesterday, in these industrial affairs of life, it not only affects their industrial, their economic prosperity, but it has a lot to do with their moral standing, their moral status as a race or as a people. When people become interested in business, in production along these lines, they do not spend all their time in discussing politics, they do not spend all their time in abstract speculation, they do not have time to get into trouble with their neighbors. All this has a fundamental bearing upon the moral welfare of individuals and the community.

Nothing that I have suggested would indicate, or should indicate that a people who pursue this course are not to get everything they possibly can in all walks of life. Go as high as possible in literature, in mathematics, in science — in all directions. There should be no limitation; but the laying of this foundation is the main thing. The more carefully it is laid, the more firmly it is laid, the higher can nations and races mount in the scale of human progress, and without such foundation, it is impossible for them to travel very high, or stay up very long when they do get up. They must stick to these fundamentals. You will find that the races of earth and the nations of earth, those that are making the greatest progress today — Germany, Sweden, Norway and Holland — these nations that have their education in the closest touch with all of these material and industrial affairs of life, are the same races and nations that are succeeding most in giving and securing what the world calls the highest education — the highest things of life. They are succeeding in the higher because they have laid the foundation first in what the world calls the lower or more fundamental things of life.

Tuskegee Student, 19 (Oct. 26, 1907), 1. Stenographically reported.

To Emmett Jay Scott

Tuskegee Institute, Alabama. Oct. 21, 1907

Mr. Scott: I have read with interest Mr. Baker's letter. I confess, however, that I have little hope of your doing much with him. I think the other crowd have gotten pretty thoroughly hold of him and then the thing which they din into his ear is the kind of thing that a writer, such as he is, rather likes, I fear. Then, we have this disadvantage – the other crowd have nothing to do but talk, while we are busy in trying to construct and operate something. The crowd that can talk most, I am sure, is the one that gets his attention.

B. T. W.

TLI BTW Papers ATT.

From Charles William Anderson

New York, N.Y., October 21, 1907

(Personal)
My dear Doctor: Moore came in this morning with an article from the pen of the "Sage of Red Bank," in reply to the leading editorial of the Age of Last week. He (Fortune) took exception to the use of the terms "ghouls," "parasites," etc. and imputes the authorship of the editorial in question to you. In his reply he states that he happened to know that the President had made a color issue of the soldier incident and that he saw the letter from the President to you, to that effect. He also says that you inspired his attack on A. H. Grimke and a lot of other stuff of that character. Moore told me that he had promised him to print the reply, with the reference to the letter from the President to you, cut out. I advised Moore emphatically not to print any of it, but to send it to you by special delivery. I told him that it would only serve to show that the man at Red Bank was fighting mad, and the Boston crowd would certainly get hold of him, and after filling him with soda water, would wring from him a lot of drunken balderdash which could be made to appear damaging. So much for this heading.

The Guardian printed a New York letter last week, which I feel confident came from Bruce Grit, to the effect that Fortune had made you famous, and had been repaid by being kicked out of the property which he had spent a lifetime in building up. It also stated that here in New York there was another man who had been written into prominence by a Boswell, whom he had now forgotten. This last reference was undoubtedly meant for me. The reason advanced for kicking Fortune out was that he would not support Roosevelt and Taft. Now the writer of this article is himself an employe of the administration, serving under General Clarkson, and yet he is contributing articles to a paper that is assailing the administration in the most scurrilous manner. This ought to be called to the attention of "our friend" at Washington, and he ought to be asked to take immediate action with the Surveyor of the Port here. I fear it cannot be done through the medium of a letter, as it would be only forwarded to Clarkson. A year or so ago Mr. Scott sent an editorial to Washington, written by this man Bruce, in which he assailed President Roosevelt, which was sent to Clarkson and by him turned over to Bruce. Hence this editorial only had the effect of intensifying Bruce's hatred of you, and did not in any way effect his standing as an employe of the government, or make him mend his manners. Thus you see, the next move along this line must be made in a personal interview. This should be had at once with "our friend" himself, as soon as he returns to Washington. I do not think much good will come of conferring with Loeb, for some reason or other, he seems to have confidence in Clarkson.

I have hurriedly dictated a little editorial for this week's paper under the heading, "Accelerating" Race Hatred. It is not much in itself, but I think it is pointed in the right direction.

I sent you a wire this morning asking you to send John B. Nail, #450–6th Ave. an invitation, if you had not already done so. I would not have him overlooked, for despite his faults, he is a loyal, zealous and untiring supporter of yours. He never fails to preach on you, in his place of business, whenever an opportunity presents itself.

Moore tells me that you mentioned Simmons as a suitable man for editor, in case he could be kept in check. Great heavens! Has not your experience with Red Bank been sufficient to warn you against surrounding yourself with men who play double, and who are in your counsels and in the counsels of the enemy at the same time? If not, you are certainly a most unpromising pupil. Men of this type can never be trusted. You never know the minute when they will desert and go over to the enemy with all of your plans, past and future. I do not like friends whom my enemies will trust, or confer with. A friend, if he is made out of the right material, will display that spirit which convinces the enemy that they ought not to talk with him or trust him. If his zeal is less than this, he is no friend. I hope you will cut out these last two or three sentences and put them in your scrapbook. By and by you will find them weightier and truer than they now appear. But always remember that absolute loyalty is more to be desired in a lieutenant than brains, experience, or power, as valuable as these latter qualifications are. The best title that a subordinate officer can show in time of war, is loyalty to his colors. Without this, all others are worse than useless. So if you have Simmons in your mind, perish the thought. I am not a philosopher nor the son of one, but Marcus Aurelius never penned any wiser counsel than this. Yours truly,

Charles W. Anderson

TLS Con. 35 BTW Papers DLC.

To Charles Satchell Morris

[Tuskegee, Ala.] October 26, 1907

Personal.

My dear Dr. Morris: I was in New York for a few hours last week and called to see you, but unfortunately it was so late in the evening that you had retired and I asked that you not be disturbed. I shall be in New York again in the near future when I shall hope to have a long talk with you on several important matters.

The more I think of it, the more I admire the stand you have taken to throw the force of your energy and influence in the direction of racial unity. I have mentioned this to a good many people lately. There are many matters in which we can be of mutual assistance through a clear understanding and by cooperating with each other. Yours truly,

Booker T. Washington

TLpS Con. 344 BTW Papers DLC.

From Charles Satchell Morris

New York City, Oct 28th 1907

My dear Dr Washington, Your letter duly received. I regret that I did not know you were at the door, I should of course have been glad to have seen you.

In speaking about the necessity for a larger toleration of opinions that differ from our own, I express a conviction that grows deeper as the days go bye. Nothing perhaps could happen to us from the outside quite so unfortunate as our ceaseless suspicion and aspersion of the motives of men whose every act proves that they are as loyal as honest as true as any of the rest of us, and sometimes a great deal more serviceable. I shall be glad to see you when you are in New York again. Wishing you abundant success in your great and inspiring work fit for a titan I am yours sincerely

Charles S. Morris

ALS Con. 354 BTW Papers DLC. Docketed by Fred R. Moore: "*OK.* but bears watching — careful correspondence FRM."

To Wallace Buttrick

[Tuskegee, Ala.] Nov. 1, 1907

Personal:

My dear Dr. Buttrick: I am just writing you a letter in a way of "thinking out loud" as Mr. Baldwin used to say.

What do you think of the idea of our spending a large proportion or perhaps nearly all of the Jeanes Fund for a few years in a campaign in the direction of inducing the Colored people to better their own schools through extra contributions or taxation. The same campaign might include a movement to interest and get hold of the state and county officials. This suggestion might have this advantage. It would prevent the direct expenditure of any money in counties for the present. Of course the money would go very largely to the employment of a large corps of a considerable number of assistants perhaps, who would go directly into the counties and carry on a campaign of education for a given number of months, something in the same way that Dr. Knapp is in the direction of improving the soil. I think the county officials would be rather more inclined to increase the proportion for Colored schools, if they knew that no money was coming through the outside, but all was coming through the direct self-help efforts of the people. The Colored people have within themselves tremendous power for self-help. In the first place, their interest is weak and besides being weak, is not properly guided. It is surprising to know how much they can raise in the direction of school house building and school extension, where they have the proper leadership and guidance.

These suggestions of course on practical value may amount to very little, but I should like to have your opinion upon them. You will note that these are modelled very largely after Dr. Knapp's work. Very truly yours,

Booker T. Washington

TLpS Con. 70 BTW Papers DLC. Original in General Education Board Collection, Rockefeller Archive Center, North Tarrytown, N.Y.

To Alphonsus Orenzo Stafford[1]

[Tuskegee, Ala.] November 1, 1907

My dear Mr. Stafford: The last chapters have been received and are first rate. I want to get an outline as soon as possible of all the chapters that you have in mind.

One other suggestion. I think we ought to have a chapter showing what Negroes themselves did to bring about freedom. We could use in this chapter such persons as Douglass, Harriet Tubman, Judge Gibbs and other strong characters that are little known about. Of course, you have already treated this same subject under another head, but I think you could make a real romantic chapter under this head. Yours truly,

Booker T. Washington

TLpS Con. 360 BTW Papers DLC.

[1] Alphonsus Orenzo Stafford (1871–1941), of Cheyney, Pa., was a ghostwriter for much of BTW's *The Story of the Negro* (1909).

To Charles William Anderson

[Tuskegee, Ala.] Nov. 1, 1907

Understand Fortune is in Chicago forming alliance for trouble with Max Barber publisher of Voice. If you think wise you might control situation quietly through Motts.[1]

B. T. W.

TWpIr Con. 340 BTW Papers DLC.

[1] Robert T. Motts (1861–1911) moved to Chicago from his birthplace in Washington, Iowa, in 1881 and worked as a coachman before opening the Pekin Theater on Chicago's South Side. He succeeded John "Mushmouth" Johnson as the city's most powerful black gambling lord. Motts had wide influence with police and city officials, and controlled many black jobs. He was instrumental in securing the seat of the black Illinois state legislator Edward Green.

Emmett Jay Scott to Timothy Thomas Fortune

[Tuskegee, Ala.] November 1, 1907

Dear Mr. Fortune: The Doctor leaves here November 6 for the North, and will be in New York and Boston until nearly the Christmas season.

I hope that your health is picking up in a satisfactory way. Your handwriting does not seem very natural to me and has caused me some uneasiness.

I make note of your suggestion that you have bought an interest in The Voice. Do I understand that you have bought a half, a third or an entire interest in the concern?

All my family keeps well. With kindest regards from all of us, I am, Yours very truly,

Emmett J. Scott

Moore has made an overture for ~~our~~ the holdings in the Age: & soon as it can be arranged — next few days — will turn it over to him. He seems to have a white. . . .[1]

TLpS Con. 363 BTW Papers DLC. Postscript in Scott's hand.

[1] The letter ends here. Scott may have failed to complete his thought, or a second page is missing.

From Samuel Laing Williams

Chicago Nov. 1—1907

My Dear Dr Washington Your telegram received.[1] Fortune came to the city and was here several days before I saw him. He came to the house last Saturday Oct. 26 and found no one home. He left a card stating that he would come back for breakfast Sunday a.m. He came about 9-30 and had breakfast, and din[n]er and then went with me to the Men's Forum where he spoke very intelligently. He left me and went with W. H. H Moore. I have not seen him since. He ha[d] a definite engagement with me for Monday but he did not come. I saw a memorandum on my desk yesterday stating that he had been in to see me. I have learned on good authority that Fortune Barber and Moore are about to start a paper here. I think this is what they are figuring on. I have not been consulted on the matter and know nothing about it.

Fortune was in good shape while he was with us on Sunday. He talked rationally and was in good spirits. He was some what indefinite as to what he intended to do. At one time he spoke of going to Tuskegee to stay for some time, at another, buying him a little place in the suburb, and settle down to literary work. He always spoke kindly of you. There were some other things about his domestic relations which he revealed to me but which I do not need to speak of now.

I am going to make an effort to see him. I cannot understand why he has absented himself so completely since Saturday.

Since writing the above I have been to the Palmer House. Mr Fortune must have received telegram etc as there is no mail or message in his Box. He still has a room here — 62. Yours Etc.

S L W

ALI Con. 37 BTW Papers DLC.

1 BTW had wired Williams to tell Fortune there was an important telegram for him at the Palmer House. "Don't use my name in connection with information," he wired. (Nov. 1, 1907, Con. 37, BTW Papers, DLC.)

From Samuel Laing Williams

Chicago Nov 2—07

Dear Dr Washington I wrote to you yesterday replying to your telegram. I was on the car with Barber this morning on my way down and he talked with me quite freely about F. He tells me that F has bought the entire interest of Jenkins and Hertel in the Voice, and that he and F. are planning to publish a weekly here in Chicago under the name of the Voice.

I cannot understand why he has not taken me into his confidence in this particular matter, as he had already revealed to me certain things that are peculiarly confidential. Even in the preparation of the legal papers needed in the transfer of the interests sold, my associate Mr Wilson was called in. This howev[er] is of no consequence. I am afraid he is getting himself involved in a way that will embarrass him. The Voice Company is in debt yet from which I can understand he invested without looking into the matter of the Corporate indebtedness.

Barber assured me that in these transactions F. was fully in his right mind and alert. He admitted however that their one embarrassment was a lack of money.

The Fortune policy in the proposed paper is to support Hughes for president.

Barber also intimated, or directly stated that F. had been forced out of the Age because he would not support the president and Taft.

All this of course is confidential, and written on the presumption that you are interested in what is going on.

Is there any truth in the report that Dancys place is to be open? If so the president has a good chance to redeem his promise as to the "next place." If you can learn anything about the matter please let me know, what I can rely upon. Yours Etc.

S L W

ALI Con. 37 BTW Papers DLC.

An Account of the Wedding of Portia Marshall Washington and William Sidney Pittman

Tuskegee Institute, Alabama, November 2, 1907

THE PITTMAN-WASHINGTON WEDDING

The chief social event of the year at Tuskegee Institute was the marriage Thursday evening, October 31st, at "The Oaks," Principal and Mrs. Washington's residence, of Miss Portia Marshall Washington and Mr. William Sidney Pittman of Washington, D.C. The whole affair was simple and impressive in its dignity. The Electrical Division of the school transformed the entire grounds of "The Oaks" into a blaze of light by utilizing colored lights in the trees, among the rose bushes, hedges, and in the various nooks and corners. Similarly, on the inside of the house, decorations of grasses, ferns, wild Southern smilax, white roses, with multi-colored lights, made the interior most beautiful. A great canopy in the main reception room had been erected, and it was under this that the ceremony was performed by Chaplain J. W. Whittaker.

Just before the wedding procession formed, Mrs. Washington and her son, Davidson, took their places to the right of the canopy. Miss Gertrude Washington[1] played the solemn Mendelssohn Wedding March, and the ushers, Messrs. Nathan Hunt, John Washington, Jr., George Austin and G. W. A. Johnston led the procession. Then followed the groom-elect and his best man, Mr. W. R. Griffin,[2] of Washington, D.C., and, in order, the bridesmaid, Miss Gertrude Watkins of Montgomery, Ala., and last the bride-elect, Miss Washington, leaning on the arms of her father, Dr. Booker T. Washington. After the ceremony, congratulations of the assembled guests were earnestly and sincerely bestowed.

The refreshments were particularly dainty, chicken salad, rolls, cheese, olives being served, followed by ice cream in the form of red apples, lillies, white and green colored, pears, busts of famous characters, roses and many others of similar kind. The cutting of the bride's cake, a particularly formidable looking affair, was accompanied with a great deal of merriment as slices were distributed to all of the guests.

Many presents were received by the bride and groom, coming from all parts of the country, from distinguished men and women who are friends of Principal Washington, as well as from many of their own friends. Those presented by members of our own community were also beautiful and in many instances very valuable.

Miss Washington is a graduate of the Tuskegee Institute, receiving the school's diploma and also a certificate from the Dressmaking Division. She also took a short course in the Millinery Division. Afterward she studied and graduated from Bradford Academy, Massachusetts, one of the oldest schools in the country for young women, being one of the only two young ladies of the graduating class to appear on the program. The next year she went to Europe for two years of study under Professor Krause, of Berlin.

Miss Gertrude Watkins, the bridesmaid, is a relative of Mr. Pittman's, and has been Miss Washington's life-long friend.

Mr. Pittman, as is well known, is a graduate of the Tuskegee Institute, and of Drexel Institute, Philadelphia. He was Tuskegee's instructor in architectural drawing for a number of years, severing his relations voluntarily two years ago to establish an independent office in Washington. He has already won a high place as an architect.

The couple, followed by the congratulations of many friends who came here from other parts of the country, as well as of the whole Tuskegee Institute community, departed for their future home, Fairmount Heights, Washington, D.C., Friday morning, November 1st.

Tuskegee Student, 19 (Nov. 2, 1907), 1.

[1] Gertrude L. Washington (b. 1889) was the daughter of John H. Washington.

[2] W. R. Griffin (b. 1870) was an organizer for the United Order of True Reformers from 1894 to 1903. In 1903 he became head of the Washington, D.C., division of the order, and also was president of the Colored Grocerymen's Union and an executive of the YMCA.

To Roscoe Conkling Simmons

[Tuskegee, Ala.] November 4, 1907

My dear Mr. Simmons: Mr. W. H. Ferris, of Boston, whom I think you know, has some very interesting stuff that I happen to know he is trying to get published. If you could drop him a line indicating you would like to see the matter and would perhaps publish it, without letting him know how you got the information, I think it might result in your getting the matter. It exposes the inside work of the entire Niagara movement. It is a pretty long letter and you might publish it in sections from week to week. I think it would create great interest and result in the increased circulation of your paper. Yours truly,

Booker T. Washington

TLpS Con. 37 BTW Papers DLC.

To Ralph Waldo Tyler

[Tuskegee, Ala.] Nov. 4, 1907

Personal and Confidential.

Dear Mr. Tyler: I have read yours of Oct. 30, together with the enclosure. I really suspect that the matter to which you refer ought to be decided altogether by Moore as to whether the suggestion is altogether a wise one or not. I do not know just how he will look upon the suggestion and of course any final word as to whether he would want this scheme carried out would have to come from him. I have written Mr. Moore, however, my frank opinion, that as I now notice it, the editorial on "Brownsville Ghouls" has proved a boomerang, as it has too quickly, after his taking charge of the paper, following his purchase of Fortune's interest, suddenly changed its attitude.

I return the editorial herewith. Very truly yours,

Booker T. Washington

TLpS Con. 8 BTW Papers DLC.

From Daniel Hale Williams

Chicago. Nov 4th 07

Personal

My Dear Sir, Your letters received. Please accept thanks for your generous reply, so full so frank. Mrs Williams[1] and I have always marked you as the exceptional man, of all modern men. We never give our full confidence to but a very limited few. You are the exceptional one. We believe in you and your work and take great pleasure in assisting in our humble way. Situated as you are among a pack of wolves, vicious wolves. You need brave trusted true friends where they can best serve you. We have been watching the game here, since this poor demented friend came on to the scene, some two weeks ago. Poor fellow we pity him. The once brilliant mind is being gradually obliterated. Cerebral changes are taking place slowly. Gradual softening of the Brain is going on. We went to hear him preach a "Lay Sermon" last night. We sat through it with but one thought, Pity, and Sympathy, as to facts, the wolves have already gathered him in, he talked rather freely to me. He is at the Palmer House. Has bought the majority of the stock of the Voice and that he intended making it an up to date publication. That a stock company had been organized with the following names as directors, Barbour, Morris, Bentley, and one other I could not catch.

There is a woman in it. Who I have had occasion to suggest

her treachery before. They have long been friends — (?) He spoke of having called a meeting last night and of the absence of M & B. He tried to get the Conservator but failed. From this you can see the play, they have fleeced the poor fellow and are making him believe that they will back him. The object is plain. We feel and ardent pleasure in not being know[n] in your interest. Mrs W. will be active in anything of interest to you. We have some plans to work out in this matter. Mr F. will dine with us during the week, advise me if anything or anyway we can serve you. Sincerely

Dan'l H Williams

ALS Con. 363 BTW Papers DLC.

[1] Alice Johnson Williams (1879–1926) was the daughter of the white sculptor Moses Jacob Ezekiel and a mulatto maid. Alice Johnson never used her father's name but maintained a close relationship with him. She grew up in Washington, D.C., graduated from Howard University, and married Daniel Hale Williams in 1898. In Chicago she headed the kindergarten at Reverdy C. Ransom's Institutional Church Social Settlement. She crossed the color line frequently, entertaining members of the black elite and also joining a white literary club. Apparently some of Dr. Williams's friends found her pretentious and overly class-conscious. She influenced her husband to move into a white neighborhood in Chicago. (Buckler, *Doctor Dan*, 147–58, 226–27.)

To Timothy Thomas Fortune

[Tuskegee, Ala.] Nov. 5, 1907

Personal and Confidential

My dear Mr. Fortune: Both of your very kind letters have been received.

I would be very glad to help some at once, but for the fact that the money situation here is more serious than it is there; in fact, every bank is holding on to all that it has and it is almost impossible to do any business. I could not see my way clear to take up the note however, but I think I might help you personally in some other way that would relieve the situation. I hope you will consider very seriously each step that you take. Would it not be wiser to get your magazine thoroughly upon its feet before starting a weekly newspaper? Both of these factors will call, you will find, for a good deal of cash outlay and we should go slowly, but surely into them. There is a field for a first-class magazine, such as I am sure you can edit. I do not believe, however, that there is much money or much glory in jumping on somebody. I have tried and have found it does not pay in any direction, and I am sure you will agree with me in the end, if you do not already.

The first news I received about the possible change of ownership in The Age came from you. Later, I heard rumors which were confirmed by a visit made by Mr. Scott to New York to the effect that Moore had received backing. I want to say to you, however, for your personal information that Mr. Moore now owns and controls the entire property. I question very much whether President Roosevelt knows whether there has been any change in the editorship and ownership of The Age. This is a subject that I never discussed with him or ever heard him mention. You will find that no one can get any real satisfaction out of his work or out of his life, except [as] it is thrown along constructive lines.

I am absolutely sure that no one connected with this Institution wrote the "Brownsville Ghouls." I agree with you, however, that as a business matter alone, it was a mistake to have printed something that would indicate a sudden change of policy in the paper. If Moore is wise, for a long time at least, he will continue substantially your own policy in the conduct of the paper.

When are you coming East? I want to have a long talk with you, when I can go over matters more fully than I can in writing. I start for New York on the 9th and plan to be in New York and in Boston for at least two weeks. I am not sure that I shall be passing through Chicago, until after the holidays have passed. I shall, however, be in Tuskegee again before I go to Chicago. In that case, if I do not see you in New York, how would it do for you to come here and stay several days? I imagine that you are going to find the winds from the lakes very disagreeable and trying in Chicago during the winter and a few days at Tuskegee, I take it, would be quite a relief.

I have noted the insinuations that some of the Colored papers have made, but you of course know better than anybody else, that there is no foundation for these.

I note what you say concerning my sticking by the President. In some way, I have a feeling that I do not like to break friendship with one with whom I have associated and had confidence in for a number of years, even though it may some time prove disagreeable to one. I think it best in the long run for one to be loyal to his friends. Of course, if it is true that he does some things that his friends disagree with him in, if the majority of things he does are right, we will have to try and forgive him for some of the errors. I think there is no Colored man in America who will not agree that in many things, he has been our friend.

Aside from the one editorial, to which you refer, I have not kept up closely enough with the policy of The Age to determine to what extent it seems to be supporting the President or anybody else.

Please remember me to the Williams' and all our good friends there. Very truly yours,

Booker T. Washington

TLpS Con. 814 BTW Papers DLC.

From Samuel Laing Williams

Chicago Nov. 6/'07

Dear Friend Your favors of recent date with enclosures concerning F. and in reference to Federal matter are both received.

For some reason F does not come to see me. On Sunday night he attempted to deliver a sort of lay sermon at the Institutional Church. It was wretchedly incoherent and meaningless. I went over to the Palmer House Monday morning and found him apparently well and mentally normal. He assured me of his success in purchasing the Hertel interest in the "Voice." He had in his possession the Subscription list of 16000 names. The new paper is to be named "Justice," and opposition to Taft is to be the slogan. Things are at a stand still however until he gets his money from the Age, or the nex[t] installment. I delivered to him your letter addressed to him in my care. He eagerly read it without comment.

He promised to go home with me in the evening for dinner, and afterwards to a meeting at All Souls Church, but he did not show up and sent no explanation. I have not seen or heard from him since. He seems to have no sense of obligation in keeping appointments with me at least. I cannot understand why he evades me, for when I see him he is cordial and disposed to be confidential.

In reference to the Federal matter, the chances for the U.S. District Office are altogether uncertain. A recommendation has been made to the Dept. of Justice for an increase of 7 men.

The letters from Mayor Busse[1] and Hopkins[2] Etc last sent to the president ought to be satisfactory for the president to act in my behalf on the very "next opening." If there is to be a vacancy in the Recorder's Office at Washington and the president wants to redeem his promises to you there ought to be no hesitancy. Truly yours

S. Laing Williams

ALS Con. 37 BTW Papers DLC.

1 Fred A. Busse (b. 1866) was Republican mayor of Chicago from 1907 to 1911.
2 Albert Jarvis Hopkins.

To Joseph Oswalt Thompson

[Tuskegee, Ala.] November 8, 1907

Dear Mr. Thompson: The enclosed memorandum is the gist of what I said to you last night concerning the distribution of the school fund. Yours truly,

Booker T. Washington

[*Enclosure*]

The amount per capita for the education of all the children in Alabama this year is $2.07. On this basis, money is sent into each county in Alabama. For example, the amount sent into Lowndes county is based upon the total number of white and black children in that county. The amount sent into Marshall county, for example, is sent on the same basis as that sent into Lowndes county. The difference in the distribution of the money is this: In Lowndes county where 4/5 of the children are black, and in Marshall county where practically all the children are white, each white child in Marshall receives only $2.07 while the few white children in Lowndes county on account of the unequal distribution of the fund between the races receive, it is safe to say, from $6 to $7 per capita. That is to say, the white child in the Black Belt counties of Alabama instead of getting only $2.07, receives from $6 to $7 for his education, while the white child in Marshall county receives only $2.07. This will constitute an interesting subject for the people living in the white counties of Alabama.

TLpS Con. 362 BTW Papers DLC. The enclosure appears on the same press sheet as the letter.

From R. R. Varner

Tuskegee Institute 11-8-07

I hereby give B. T. Washington permission to hunt on all lands owned or Controlled by me in Macon County for one year.

R R Varner Agt.

ADS Con. 362 BTW Papers DLC. On stationery of the business agent's office. Varner apparently borrowed the stationery while at Tuskegee Institute, and wrote as agent of the lands in his control, not as Tuskegee Institute's business agent.

To Daniel Hale Williams

[Tuskegee, Ala.] November 9, 1907

Personal

My dear Dr. Williams: It is very good of you to write me so fully and frankly as to the situation there. It is amusing and pathetic. I have letters almost daily from our friend F. He is hard up for cash and wants me to advance him some money with which to carry out the plan of getting out a weekly newspaper or of getting out the edition of The Voice. Of course I am furnishing no money, but answer his letters.

The pathetic part of the situation is this: Within a few months he will have spent all he gets from the sale of The Age and then he will have nothing upon which to live the remaining portion of his life. When I see him I plan to talk to him frankly in that direction.

I am planning to write you more fully soon.

I shall be in Washington within a few days, and am going to suggest to Mr. Garfield that he invite you to see him and have a talk with you. I am also going to ask him to give Dr. West[1] an interview in order that his case may be put squarely before him. Yours truly,

Booker T. Washington

TLpS Con. 363 BTW Papers DLC.

[1] Charles Ignatius West (b. 1869), a graduate of Howard University Medical School in 1895, was first assistant surgeon at Freedmen's Hospital from 1902 to 1905 and then became professor of anatomy at Howard University Medical School. Daniel Hale Williams considered him one of the most brilliant black surgeons and sought to have him appointed surgeon-in-chief at Freedmen's Hospital. William A. Warfield, a rival for the position, fabricated stories about West which led to his dismissal. In an attempt to get West a position in a new division in the hospital, Williams sought BTW's aid, but BTW supported George Cleveland Hall for the position.

To Emmett Jay Scott

Boston. November 16, 1907

My dear Mr. Scott: I had a very interesting and lengthy interview with the President and Mr. Loeb as I came through Washington. I think I have gotten at the bottom of things. The President was most free and confidential in all that he said.

I question whether, under the circumstances, you can carry through the plan in reference to the Age and Mr. Vorys, though you may be able to succeed. I will tell you all about it when I see you.

I suppose you have seen the speech which the President delivered at Howard University. It was composed almost altogether of facts which I gave him and information which he gleaned from the article in The Independent on the Negro doctor in the South which I wrote sometime ago. Yours truly,

Booker T. Washington

TLS BTW Papers ATT.

From Emmett Jay Scott

Tuskegee Institute, Alabama November 18, 1907

My dear Mr. Washington: I regret to have to advise you that it has become necessary for Mr. Pollard[1] to retire from the Institution. He has undeniably been guilty of some of the same kind of offences as those charged against him last year by a student. In the present case, the direct charge is, that he made an effort to embrace and kiss one of the girl students. Major Ramsey and I, at Mrs. Washington's request, talked with the girl and confronted her with Mr. Pollard, on Saturday evening, and substantially he confessed his guilt.

Yesterday, Sunday morning, he sent to my house a letter of resignation addressed to you. I simply send this word to you, that you may be advised. The whole thing has been handled in such a way as not to create on the school grounds a great scandal, such as would have ensued, if a formal investigation with a great many witnesses, etc. had been called in. Very truly yours,

E J Scott

TLS BTW Papers ATT.

[1] N. E. Pollard was a steward in the boarding department of Tuskegee Institute from 1902 to 1907.

Wilford H. Smith to Emmett Jay Scott

New York, November 18th, 1907

Dear Mr. Scott: In compliance with your letter of the 12th instant, I turned over the six shares of stock in the New York Age Publishing Company, held by me, to Mr. Fred R. Moore, and took his receipt for the same.

I found it necessary to strike out the name of our friend in the transfer made by you on the back, and to insert the name of Mr. Moore. I suppose that this will meet with your approval, since we did not wish at this time for our friend's name to appear on the books of the Company.

With kindest regards, I remain, Very truly yours,

Wilford H Smith

TLS Con. 382 BTW Papers DLC.

From Charles William Anderson

New York, N.Y., November 19, 1907

(Personal)

My dear Doctor: I have yours of the 16th instant, with enclosure, which was interesting as a study in aimlessness. That gentleman does not appear to know what to do, or how to do it.

I see that Fortune has written Trotter a letter of congratulation, and advised him to keep up the fight. The letter is printed in the Guardian of last week. I also notice that he has written Smith of the Cleveland Gazette, a similar letter. Hence, you see he has gone over, horse, foot and dragoon to the enemy. Smith's paper also published a letter from Judge Gibbs, congratulating him on the defeat of Burton,[1] and expressing the hope that Roosevelt will share the same fate, in case he runs for President again. This is the sort of talk that the father-in-law of the present Consul to St. Etienne is indulging in. What a fish, a frog is! And Johnson is still at Puerto Cabello, Venezuela, while Gibbs' son-in-law is in the good berth in France. Yours truly,

Charles W. Anderson

TLS Con. 35 BTW Papers DLC. Addressed to BTW in Boston. The last sentence is in Anderson's hand.

1 Theodore Elijah Burton (1851–1929) was a congressman (1889–91, 1895–1909) and U.S. senator (1909–15) from Ohio.

From Emmett Jay Scott

Tuskegee Institute, Alabama November 20, 1907

My dear Mr. Washington: Dr. Williams came down from Nashville to Atlanta and on to Tuskegee, without any charge whatever, to perform two very difficult operations for Dr. Kenney, one upon a charity patient from the town of Tuskegee, and the other upon the Japanese student[1] here. Both of them have proved successful.

I had opportunity to talk quite at length with him with reference to our friend, who has recently gone to Chicago. In him, Dr. W. you have a real jewel of a friend. He is into the situation and knows what is transpiring all the time. It has been rather industriously circulated in Chicago that Fortune is out of The Age by reason of your action, despite the evidence to the contrary, which Fortune has placed in our hands, namely, his letter notifying me of transferring his interest to Moore. He thinks that Mr. F. is almost irresponsible and that he is undoubtedly suffering even now from softening of the brain. He has pretended to the Chicago people that he has a great deal more money than is anywhere in sight. The woman, whom Dr. Williams has written you about, has also given a good deal of currency to this statement. He certainly does refer to her in biting terms and she must be unusually treacherous and mean, considering all that has been done for her and hers.

While in Atlanta, he took an hour off and went up to call on Du Bois. He tells me that Du Bois confessed to him that he, too, has an interest with Fortune and the rest of them in the publication to be launched in Chicago. He says that Du Bois insists that what they really need is the Conservator and that he, Du Bois, is urging them to that effect. Dr. W. will watch the case, however, and thinks he can altogether thwart their efforts to secure it. I told him the beginning and the ending of F's negotiations with Moore for his interest, showed him a copy of letter that F wrote me and told him just how much money he was receiving from Moore and how often. Dr. W. thinks that he is now altogether or practically out of money and hopes that you will not be too swift to send any money from yourself, as it would only go into the hands of the wolves.

He spoke to me, also, respecting the Freedman's Hospital matter and I told him that you were working on that; also, he is anxious

to have you interest yourself in securing a building for Meharry Medical College. They have ten thousand dollars, but want to secure ten thousand dollars additional from Mr. Carnegie. All of his motives in these matters are entirely disinterested and I find him, in every way, as you already know, one of the rarest of men. He has asked Dr. Hubbard[2] to write you in the Meharry matter.
Yours very truly,

E J Scott

TLS BTW Papers ATT.

[1] Iwane Kawahara of Saga, Japan, the only Japanese student, was in the A middle class in 1906–7 and the senior class in 1907–8.

[2] George Whipple Hubbard, a white physician on the faculty of Meharry Medical School. In 1916 he became president of Meharry.

Emmett Jay Scott to Henry Connard Binford[1]

[Tuskegee, Ala.] November 22, 1907

My dear Mr. Binford: Perhaps you are not acquainted with the fact that I have "approached the East" and am now a full fledged member of your fraternity. The special point of this letter, however, is to bring to your attention the following:

Friends of mine, who live in Boston, have just written me that, while Dr. Washington is there prosecuting his regular campaign in the interest of the school, they would like to make him a Master Mason "by sight." This does not mean that he would join the Boston Lodge, because his membership would be in the lodge here in Tuskegee. Prince Hall Grand Lodge of Massachusetts, as you know, is the oldest in the country and their idea is to ask him to take a certain part in connection with the One Hundredth Anniversary of Prince Hall Grand Lodge, next September. You most likely will be written a letter by Grand Master Lloyd Marshall[2] of Massachusetts at an early date.

I very much hope that you will feel willing to consent to this arrangement and that you will so advise Grand Master Marshall, when he writes you.

Hoping to hear from you at your convenience and with sincere regards and profound respect always, I am: Yours in A. F. and A. M.

Emmett J. Scott

TLpS Con. 341 BTW Papers DLC.

[1] Henry Connard Binford (b. 1874) was a graduate of Howard University (1897). He taught school in Huntsville and Baltimore before returning to Huntsville in 1908 to become principal of a black high school there. Binford was a prominent member of the black Masons beginning in the 1890s.

[2] William Lloyd Marshall was active in the Prince Hall Grand Lodge beginning in 1898, when he was a junior deacon. From 1907 to 1908 he was grand master of the lodge.

An Article in the *Tuskegee Student*

Tuskegee Institute, Alabama, November 23, 1907

WHAT IS IT THAT THE NEGRO NEEDS MOST?

PRINCIPAL WASHINGTON, IN THE COLUMBUS (OHIO) STANDARD WORLD

The colored people of this country need a great many things.

What is it that we need most?

If I were to answer this question quite frankly, seeking to put my meaning in its most comprehensive form, I should say that the thing that the colored people of this country need most at this time is: SOLIDARITY! We need as a race to learn to pull together.

We have made as individuals enormous progress in this country. Despite much talk to the contrary, the Negroes are going steadily forward. The race owns today an acreage of land in the United States that is equal to the combined acreage of two entire states of Europe, Holland and Belgium. Negroes own more houses, more stores, more banks this year than they did last, and they will own more next year than they do this year.

There used to be a question as to whether or not the Negro could be educated — that is, in the ordinary sense in which we understand education. There is no longer such a question in the minds of any people whose opinion is worth considering. During the last forty years the American Negro has convinced the world that he could be educated in literature, science, mathematics, agriculture, mechanics and the household arts, and in the professions. We have won this victory not by depending upon empty talk, not by depending upon abstract argument, not by abuse of some one, but by actually doing the thing, by filling every public school, every college, every industrial and professional school that has ever been opened for us. We have won this victory by having living, tangible object lessons in every part of the United States that within themselves were indisputable evidences of our ability to receive education. When proof is asked of our ability to receive education, we can point to the little bareheaded and barefooted boy in the Mississippi log cabin school, or we can point to the Negro youth in the cap and gown in Oxford University, England. So much is settled.

To a large extent this progress has been made, as I have said, by individuals. But there are ten million Negroes in this country. We are a nation within a nation. There is within this ten million individuals a vast latent power, a power which can be awakened only by united action — united action along business, along educational and along religious lines.

Now to accomplish results such as this, we must be united in a business way. By this I do not mean that we should trade at a Negro store simply because it is a Negro store and not a white store; I do not mean that we should place our money in a Negro bank simply because it is a Negro bank. But I mean that we should take a pride in the business conducted by our people; that we should take particular care to see that they are conducted just as neatly and as orderly as the store of a white man; that we should take particular care that they do not suffer from the fact that they are dealing with Negro people, for the reason, as is sometimes said, that Negro people do not pay their bills as promptly as other people. On the other hand, the Negro business man, on his side, should feel a pride in dealing as justly, as fairly and giving as much and as good quality for the money as any other store, or as if he were dealing with any other people. In these respects, the Negro business men and the Negro people can do much for each other at this time. And this is the sort of unity that I believe should prevail among us, a unity that I may characterize as a solidarity of purpose and of interest.

The same thing is true as to education. We do not accomplish as much in our schools at the present time as we could if we were more united — more united inside of our schools and more united out of them.

I might say the same thing about our religion. Here, too, we waste too much time in discussing and emphasizing sectarian matters, in emphasizing those things which divide us instead of those things in regard to which we are united.

Civilization in any people is to a large extent the ability of the individuals of that people to combine their efforts for the good of the whole; it is the ability, while holding fast to individual differences of opinion and sentiment on minor matters, to be able to put these differences in the background whenever it is necessary to unite for the benefit of the whole community or the whole state.

In this direction — in the direction of this solidarity of which I spoke — we are making progress. This is evident by the large number of organizations of all kinds which have grown up among us in recent years. It is evident, also, by the number of Negro banks now in existence. These banks and these large business organizations indicate there is a growing confidence among our people in their own business men and in their own business institutions. We need to encourage this confidence. We want to see it grow and extend. All the more important is it that the greatest possible care should be exercised in the control and in the administration of these organizations. If through neglect or the dishonesty or incapacity of any of their officers this growing confidence and this growing business solidarity should be destroyed, the loss to our people would be immense.

But finally we need unity in another direction; we need a clearer, more definite and more harmonious conception of our duty and our policy as a people and as part of these great United States.

In reference to our interest and our duties as a people we have too frequently mistaken the shadow for the real substance. Too frequently we have wasted our strength and our efforts on trivial and unimportant issues and have divided among ourselves in regard to the important things.

For one thing, we should make our platform broad enough, so

that all good men, black and white, North and South, can stand upon it with us. It would be fatal to our future in this country to proceed in a way to discourage and alienate our friends, to unite the whole or even the majority of the white race of this country against us. And it is not necessary. Our interests as a people are one with the deepest interests of the country and of humanity. Let us steer our course by the stars and not be led away by false lights. The main thing is that, in our relations with the world, we ourselves should be right. It is not so necessary that we should convince the world that our opponents are wrong. Eventually the world will find that out for itself.

In the meantime, should I interpret and analyze the feelings and ambition of the black man in America it is this: He is not seeking to dominate over others in matters of government, nor is he seeking to intermingle with others in strictly social matters where he is not wanted or asked, but he is asking that in every community and state where he resides that equal justice shall be meted out to him in the courts and elsewhere, and that at all times his family and property shall be protected by those who administer the laws. This, I believe, in the end, the great American people will grant to ten millions of their citizens.

Tuskegee Student, 19 (Nov. 23, 1907), 1.

To Thomas Washington Talley[1]

Boston. November 24, 1907

My dear Professor Talley: I am writing concerning a matter that I am deeply interested in. It is this. I am very anxious that Booker have considerable training in the direction of strengthening his memory. He is weak in that point.

I am also anxious at the same time that he be given training in the matter of public speaking. If he is not doing it, could it not be arranged in some way that he might be required to commit to memory good specimens of literature, either poetry or prose, and also have an opportunity to speak before his class or some other body once a month, or something like that. Without using my name, if this is not being done, perhaps you might find a way to have it done.

I am constantly grateful to you for your help and interest. Yours truly,

[Booker T. Washington]

TLc Con. 362 BTW Papers DLC.

[1] Thomas Washington Talley, a graduate of Fisk University (A.B. 1890, M.A. 1892), taught chemistry and biology at Fisk beginning in 1903. He served on the faculty at Tuskegee during the 1902-3 school year.

From William Henry Ferris

Cambridge, Mass. Nov. 26th, 1907

My Dear Sir, Enclosed you will please find a letter of mine which recently appeared in the Boston Herald.

While I do not always agree with everything you say, I believe that the greatness of your work & grandeur of your achievement, & your grasp of the industrial conditions in the South entitles you to rank with the great constructive geniuses of the century. I remain Very truly yours

W. H. Ferris

P.S. Our friend Trotter like the cat in the story seems to have nine editorial lives. But I believe that he is almost at the end of his tether. The fight in the Niagara Movement means that the conservative wing has cut loose from Trotter.

W. H. F.

ALS Con. 348 BTW Papers DLC.

To James Griswold Merrill

Parker House, Boston, Mass. Dec. 2, 1907

My dear President Merrill: Your kind letter regarding the library has just been received. I do not remember the exact sum that Mr.

Carnegie promised to give for the erection of the library, but I have an idea that it was $25,000. Am I right in this.

In case Mr. Carnegie were to remove the condition, that is that you raise $25,000 in addition to his gift, would you be able to keep the library going from year to year in good shape? Would the American Missionary Association or any other responsible body guarantee to see that the library is kept going and not permitted to degenerate?

The plan which I have in mind is this: Mr. Carnegie is very fond of Mrs. Washington, and I am quite sure if she were to make a personal appeal to him on the grounds that she is a Fisk graduate, to leave off the condition and to give you $25,000 straight for the erection of the library that he would accede to her request. I might say to you privately that he has done several such things for me when I have made a personal request of him. Mrs. Washington I think has never asked anything personally of him. It is probable that Mrs. Washington will be going to New York sometime in the near future, and if this suggestion meets with your approval I think it will be well for you to write her directly. You need not tell her I have made this suggestion because I have not mentioned it to her, but, of course, if she goes to New York we will talk the whole thing over so as to have everything well understood before she sees Mr. Carnegie. I was with him for a while a few days ago, and in discussing the subject of higher education I had the privilege of telling both him and his secretary that in my opinion Fisk was doing the very best work of any of our Southern institutions. He is having his Edinburg speech recast for the purpose of wide circulation, and he has inserted a paragraph concerning the work of Fisk. Yours truly,

[Booker T. Washington]

In case Mr. Carnegie makes an exception in your case, it is important that the matter not get into the newspapers, I mean the fact that he has made an exception.

TLc Con. 344 BTW Papers DLC.

To Timothy Thomas Fortune

Boston, Mass. December 2, 1907

My dear Mr. Fortune: Yours of November 29th has been received. I am surprised that you did not receive the telegram. It was sent to 415 Dearborn St. The following is a copy of it:

"Absolutely out of money myself. Can see Moore in New York Wednesday morning. Will make effort to get party who is backing him advance something on note. Will try get him telegraph it to you Wednesday. Will that be satisfactory. Answer here."

It is barely possible that Moore will be able to carry out this suggestion; at any rate I will urge him to do so if you think it wise. Yours very truly,

[Booker T. Washington]

TLc Con. 814 BTW Papers DLC.

To Charles William Anderson

Parker House, Boston, Mass. Dec. 5, 1907

My dear Mr. Anderson: What became of you Tuesday, you seemed to have completely disappeared. I waited at the Manhattan for two hours. You said you would be there at four. I had some very important matters to discuss with you. One relates to Johnson. I shall be in New York next Sunday. Can you take breakfast with me at the Manhattan Hotel Sunday morning at eight o'clock; or, if not, can you call there to see me at nine o'clock in the morning?

In regard to my speaking at Brooks' church. I perhaps do not look at the matter as you do. I understand, of course, thoroughly the untrustworthy and changeable character of such would-be leaders. They never deceive me, when I once find them changing from one position to the other I never thoroughly trust them any more. That I understand is the program which you follow. But in this case he has come to me and I have not gone to him. He professes all kinds of allegiance. Of course I know how much dependence to put upon that, but this is my main point, to keep in touch with the masses of our people. We must not let these would-be leaders frighten us away from the masses of the people whom you and I depend upon to support us and carry out our wishes and policies. The masses are all right, as you know. I find, however, that unless once in a while an individual actually appears among these people and lets them know what his views and wishes are, they are rather inclined to grow discouraged and get their views second-hand. In the meantime it gives an unscrupulous fellow an opportunity to lead them astray. In a word, what I have in mind is to take advantage of every decent opportunity to meet the masses directly, disregarding the false leaders. If we are to keep the masses on the right track, they will take care of the leaders. It has been my experience in the past that in several cases where I have not let the masses hear from me directly as to my views and wishes that they have been led astray by unscrupulous individuals. The ranks and file are all right, but they do like to have those whom they trust and are trying to follow get near to them as often as possible. I believe you will agree with me that this is the proper policy, although in getting near them we may have to do disagreeable things.

Ransom was here Tuesday night and spoke in Faneuil Hall. One paper gave him an inch of space, the others scarcely mentioned his name. Yours very truly,

[Booker T. Washington]

TLc Con. 35 BTW Papers DLC.

To Droop and Company[1]

Parker House, Boston, Mass. December 6, 1907

My dear Sirs: My daughter, Mrs. Portia Washington Pittman, and also my wife, I think, have had some conversation with you regarding a piano.

Will you be kind enough to let me know by return mail what is the very lowest price you will take for the piano that my daughter wishes. We have many obligations at this season of the year, and cash, as you know, is very hard to secure, and it is for this reason, among others, that a decision has been delayed.

I am writing you in behalf of Mrs. Washington. Yours truly,

[Booker T. Washington]

TLc Con. 6 BTW Papers DLC.

[1] A firm in Washington, D.C.

To Charles Waddell Chesnutt

Parker House, Boston, Mass. Dec. 6, 1907

My dear Mr. Chesnutt: I have just read your letter to Mr. Browne regarding the interpretation which you put upon Mr. Carnegie's remarks based upon my position bearing upon the franchise, and also what you say regarding my own position. I confess that after reading your letter I have almost reached the conclusion that it is impossible for me to ever get my thoughts regarding the franchise through the brains of any human being; whether the trouble is with my thoughts or with the brains of the other fellow I am not prepared just now to state, but there is trouble in either one or the other direction.

In your letter you say: "On one point, however, I do not at all agree with Mr. Carnegie or with Dr. Washington, whom he quotes, in holding it 'the wiser course' to practically throw up the ballot, or the demand for it."

In the first place, Mr. Carnegie has said no such thing. I have never said no such thing. If you can put your finger or eye on a single sentence in all my writing that will bear out this statement, I will agree to send you a first class Alabama possum for your Christmas dinner. Suppose you re-read what Mr. Carnegie has said. I feel quite sure that when you wrote Mr. Browne that there was something in the lake breeze which was troubling your brain. I have said, and do so now, that to any people living under a republican form of government the ballot is a consideration of the very highest importance, and there is no disagreement between you and me as to the importance of the ballot; however, perhaps, we do not agree as to the methods of attaining to the permanent and practical use of the ballot. Some of our people maintain that the ballot is a matter of first consideration in our present condition. This I do not agree with. Practically you do not agree with their contention. Practically, the matter of earning your daily bread and banking your money is a matter of the first consideration. You vote perhaps once in two years. The average brother in the North does not vote even that often, but you earn your daily bread once every day in the year, excepting Sundays. The matter of the next consideration to you is the education of your children, something that you put into practice every week in the year. The next is the matter of attending church, or "should be" with you, something that you practice every week in the year. If the ballot were a matter of first consideration, one would vote every day in the year instead of spending his time in the laying of an economic foundation every day in the year. Take the people of the Republic of Liberia, they might vote every hour and every day in every year. At the end of the period they would not have improved their economic condition nor moral status before the world one iota. There is something deeper in human progress than the mere act of voting, it is the economic foundation which every race has got to have. But I shall not burden you further. We will try to finish this out when we meet again.

I think after Mr. Browne and Mr. Carnegie have gotten through trying to weave your ideas into the address that you will be satisfied with the changes. Yours truly,

[Booker T. Washington]

TLc Con. 35 BTW Papers DLC.

From Daniel Hale Williams

Chicago, Dec 7th 07

My Dear Mr Washington. I want to apologize if I am guilty of an omission. Your telegram was received twenty four hours late and I waited for some definate information from Tuskegee, as soon as it came I wrote you. I have also written you that I will be on my way in a few hours. I have but one thought now i.e. to see Mr

Scott safe. I shall wire you on my arrival and when operation is completed. I shall keep you fully advised.

Have not seen F. for a week. Your plain to let him learn his lesson is good. *I do not think Mr Scotts condition is serious,* but is to him, and you well know a man worrying [about] anything personal soon makes him a sick man.

He has an affected appendix without doubt and the safest thing for him or any man that is conscious of a diseased condition is to relieve him of it. I want to relieve your anxiety about Mr Scott and will soon. Very truly yours

Dan'l H Williams

ALS Con. 363 BTW Papers DLC.

Timothy Thomas Fortune to the Editor of the Indianapolis *Freeman*

Chicago, Dec. 7 [1907]

To the Editor of The Freeman — In The Freeman today I find an editorial paragraph, the sentiments of which are misleading and which, like the editorial in The Age referred to, are likely to work me mischief. The Age states a possible fact when it declares that Dr. Washington does not own a dollar's worth of stock of the New York Age Publishing Company. You say "Mr. Washington insists that the charge (that he owns stock) is a falsehood, which has been circulated by those who know what such a charge means."

Who circulated the "charge?" What does such "a charge" mean? That it is or was dishonorable for Mr. Washington, or anybody else, to own stock in The Age when I was president of it? What is "the tempest in the teapot" about? Is somebody after me? It looks that way. Is somebody after Mr. Washington? It looks that way. Is somebody after President Fred R. Moore of The Age corporation? It looks that way. Now, if somebody is after somebody, who is it and what is the object of the chase? Now, if the chaser is after me here am I. I have no dirty linen to wash in private or public. My dirty linen is entirely a personal matter, between God and me.

Now, while The Age was about it why did not President Fred R.

Moore tell the whole truth? While Mr. Washington was "insisting," why did not he "insist" as to the whole business? What is there to conceal? Nothing but the facts. Will they hurt Mr. Washington or Mr. Moore? They appear to think so. Will they hurt me? Not if I know it.

When I sold my 1,250 shares of stock to Mr. Moore last September and took his paper in payment for most of it, Jerome B. Peterson owned 1,250 and Booker T. Washington owned 950 shares, Emmett J. Scott being stockholder of record, the shares being of the par value of $10. A few shares of the total capitalization were held by other parties, mostly friends of Mr. Washington. If Mr. Washington has disposed of his stock I don't know it and I don't care about it. How did Mr. Washington secure his stock? That is his business. Why does he "insist" that holding such stock, or having held such stock, would "work him mischief?" That is his business. Why did I sell my stock? Guess. Why do I not state the facts? Because somebody wants to make dirt out of an ant heap, and seek by evasion and iteration to confuse the facts and tend to make me appear crooked. Am I? Not if I know it.

When President Roosevelt and his people are endorsed by me I will be a dead man. Am I dead? Here am I.

T. Thomas Fortune

Indianapolis *Freeman*, Dec. 14, 1907, 4.

Extracts from an Address in Brooklyn

St. Ann's on the Heights, Brooklyn, N.Y., Dec. 8, 1907

To give you an idea of the advancement of the colored race in the direction of self-help, I wish to state that the students in attendance at the Tuskegee Institute last year paid $41,000 toward their expenses in cash. In Macon County, Alabama, where the Tuskegee Institute is located, the colored people, mainly in the country districts, raised $2,700 toward the improvement of their school houses and the extension of their school terms last year.

While there are serious and perplexing elements connected with our Southern situation, still at the same time, no one can live right in the heart of the South from year to year, without noting many evidences of most satisfactory progress as a result of the education of both races. During the past year, the most encouraging and striking evidence of progress is to be noted in the almost miraculous sweep of temperance sentiment through the South. I question, whether in all history, there has been any movement in favor of temperance that equals that which has now taken hold of the people of the South. In my opinion, the getting rid of whiskey in the way that is now being done, means a long forward step in the working out of our racial problem. A large proportion of the difficulties that have occurred in the past, have grown out of the fact that bad whiskey has got into ignorant and bad people. When you mix ignorance and bad whiskey, you will be sure to have a difficulty, whether the individuals are black or white. Most of the lynchings in the South, which have disgraced our civilization, have been the result of whiskey and ignorance. Almost without exception the educated black men and women are cooperating with the best class of Southern white people in this effort to get rid of whiskey. Many of the Tuskegee Institute graduates are leaders in the temperance movement. I think I do not exaggerate when I predict that within two years, with the exception of two of our states, I do not believe that whiskey will be sold legally anywhere in the South. In Florida all the counties now have prohibition except 13. Georgia will be completely under prohibition after January 1st. Mississippi has only 7 counties in which liquor is sold. In Tennessee there are only 6 towns and cities where liquor is permitted. There are two or three counties in Alabama which are voting out whiskey now every week. The majority in favor of prohibition averages almost six to one. Not a single county, which has voted in Alabama within the past few months, has gone in favor of whiskey. Nine-tenths of the counties in Alabama will have prohibition after Christmas, and within a few months the whole state will be under the prohibition law. The rank and file of the people are back of this movement. It is not a sentimental movement. It is not a movement placed upon mere sentiment or hysterics, but the people have thoroughly thought it out, have planned for it and are determined that the law shall be enforced. There is something in the whole movement that is hard to understand. It has come about, seemingly, with no special planning, without any special leadership, or the expenditure of any large sum of money, but it has taken thoroughly hold of the people. Individuals discuss it on the streets, in the cars and in all kinds of gatherings. It is the uppermost subject of conversation, and I repeat, in my opinion, the law will be enforced where prohibition laws are enacted.

To us, who are engaged in the uplift of the Negro race through education, the progress in favor of prohibition brings to us an encouragement for the future that is hard for you to realize. Not only has whiskey been the influence more than any other that has brought about friction between the races, but it has been the influence which has degraded our people morally and, perhaps worst of all, has caused them to spend their hard earned money to waste their money, instead of investing it in their homes and putting it in the banks.

There is another element in the Southern situation that is satisfactory. During the past few years, there has been much agitation in the direction of getting foreigners into the South to take the place of the Negroes as laborers. This experiment has been tried in several of the states, but almost without exception where it has been tried, people have come to the conclusion that the effort to replace the Negro by white foreigners is a failure. Especially is this true in the Carolinas and in Georgia, where considerable money has been spent in getting white foreigners as common laborers. They have not proved satisfactory. It has been demonstrated that they cannot take the place of the Negro, and public men and newspapers that years ago were loudest in their demands for foreign labor, now state unhesitatingly that the Negro is the best laborer that the South has ever had, or is likely to have.

The result of this is, that the leaders of Southern thought and activity are more and more inclined to settle down with the idea that the Negro is to remain in the South, that he has to be the main dependence of the people for labor, and for this reason, are advising that he be educated and trained into the very highest usefulness. Only a few days ago, the president[1] of the Georgia Federation of white women's clubs made the following remark on this subject:

"In distress, our people have turned to immigration as a proper solution. The experiment has been tried and proved a failure. Rather than flood our country with a foreign population, unable to stand our climate and unfitted to conditions of life around them, rather let us use the labor which has served us for so many years, and has grown up under our present civilization. True, their relations have been changed to us, but we must readjust these relations. The state has it in her power to do this by a compulsory law of education."

I have referred to two classes of Negroes in the South. I would not be just and frank unless I added that there are also two classes of white people. Most persons get the idea that all white people in the South are opposed to our progress or to our having our rights as citizens. I grant there are a class who make a great deal of noise, who talk about pressing and keep the Negroes down, but there is another class that does not make so much noise, but are as interested as any class to be found here in the North or anywhere. In proportion as this class of white people respects us, we are going to have different conditions existing in the South.

The work of spreading and deepening education in the South must be continued through such institutions as Tuskegee, Hampton and many others. You ask how can you help us? Our needs are as follows. The most pressing ones are:

1. $50 a year for Annual Scholarships for the training of one student a year.

2. $1,000 for permanent scholarships.

3. Money for current expenses in any amounts, however small.

4. The increase of the Endowment Fund to at least $3,000,000.

I am more and more confident that our work will prosper and continue to grow in usefulness just in proportion as we continue to pursue the policy of keeping it close to the masses of the Negro people by closely studying and seeing that our educational efforts respond to their needs and condition.

. . . .

If possible, I want to give you an idea of the progress of the Negro race in a single county in one of the Southern states. For this purpose I select Gloucester County, Virginia. I take this one for the reason that I had the privilege of visiting it a number of years ago, just about the time when interest in the education of the colored people was beginning to be aroused, and for the further reason that this is one of the counties in Virginia and the South that has been longest under the influence of graduates of the Hampton Institute, as well as men and women trained in other centers of education.

Gloucester County is in the tide-water section of eastern Virginia. According to the census of 1890, Gloucester County contained a total population of 12,832, a little over one-half being colored, and both sets of schools are in session from 5½ to 6 months, and the pay of the two sets of teachers is about the same. The majority of the colored teachers in this county were trained at Hampton, and have been teaching in this county for a number of years. For the most part, the teachers of Gloucester County are not mentally superior, but what they lack in methods of teaching and mental alertness is more than made up for by the moral earnestness and the example they set. Most of the teachers are natives of the county, and, what is more important, most of them own property in the county.

Now, what is the economic or material result in one county where the Negro has been given a reasonable chance to make progress? I say "reasonable," because it must be kept in mind that the great body of white people in America, with whom the Negro is constantly compared, have schools that are in session from eight to nine months in the year. According to the public records, the total assessed value of the land in Gloucester County is $666,132.33. Of the total value of the land, the colored people own $87,935.55. The buildings in the county have an assessed valuation of $466,127.05. The colored people pay taxes upon $79,387 of this amount. To state it differently: the Negroes of Gloucester County, beginning about forty years ago in poverty, have reached the point where they now own and pay taxes upon one-sixth of the real estate in this county. This property is very largely in the shape of small farms, varying in size from 10 to 100 acres. A large proportion of the farms contain about 10 acres. It is interesting to note the influence of this material growth upon the home life of the people. It is stated upon good authority that about twenty-five years ago at least three-fourths of the colored people lived in one-room cabins. Let a single illustration tell the story of the growth. In a school where there were thirty pupils, ten testified that they lived in houses containing six rooms, and only one said that he lived in a house containing but a single room.

I repeat, I have always believed that in proportion as the industrial, not omitting the intellectual, condition of my race was improved, in the same degree would their moral and religious life improve. Some years ago, before the home life and economic condition of the people had improved, bastardy was common in Gloucester County. In 1903 there were only eight cases of bastardy reported in the whole county, and two of those were among the white population. During the year 1904 there was only one case of bastardy within a radius of ten miles of the court house. Another gratifying evidence of progress is shown by the fact that there is very little evidence of immoral relations existing between the races. In the whole county, during the year 1903, about twenty-five years after the work of education had gotten under way, there were only thirty arrests for misdemeanors; of these 16 were white, 14 colored. In 1904 there were 15 such arests — 14 white and one colored. In 1904 there were but seven arrests for felonies; of these two were white and five were colored. In one point at least the colored people in Gloucester County have set an example for the rest of the religious world that ought to receive attention. It is in this regard: there is only one religious denomination in all of this county, and that is the Baptist. No over-multiplying, no overlapping, no denominational wrangling and wasting of money and energy.

TMf BTW Papers ATT.

[1] Mrs. M. A. Lipscomb, president of the Georgia Federation of Women's Clubs from 1906 to 1908.

To Theodore Roosevelt

[Boston, Mass.] Dec. 16, 1907

Personal and Confidential

My dear Mr. President: I happen to have been in Boston during the greater part of the canvass covering the election of Mayor, and I have watched with a good deal of interest to see what the influence on the Negro voters of the Brownsville episode would be. Here, as you know, has been the center of the agitation against you and Secretary Taft on account of the dismissal of the soldiers. During the recent campaign that matter was worked for all it was worth. I am glad to state to you, and I believe that any keen observer will agree with me in this, that the Brownsville matter had practically no influence in alienating the Negro vote from the Republican party.

A gentleman who is pretty close to Boston politics told me that he felt rather sure that not more than a hundred colored men voted the Democratic ticket. I do not believe that the Brownsville matter will hurt seriously Secretary Taft in his canvass for the nomination nor for election in case he is nominated. Yours very truly,

[Booker T. Washington]

TLc Con. 7 BTW Papers DLC.

From William Henry Ferris

Cambridge, Mass. Dec. 16th, 1907

Dear Dr. Washington, I read your note of the 12th inst. with interest. I believe that your position regarding a gentleman & a blackguard is the true one.

I listened to you with a great deal of interest yesterday. On the whole, it was the most inspiring & most optimistic address that I have ever heard you deliver. There is no doubt but that you possess the masterful personality, which makes you a born leader of men. With a keen gray eye, a quick brain, an iron will, & a magnificent physique, you have the faculty of sweeping men up into your own personality & charging them with your own energy & enthusiasm. There can be no question as to the fact that you are endowed by Nature with the qualities of leadership.

As to the content of your address, I have this to say, I met some of the most prominent members of the Niagara Movement to day. They think that you have sympathy for the higher aspirations of the Negro; but think the vulnerable part of your address is that a man must have a bank account or own a brick house before he can be regarded as a full fledged, full orbed man. For myself, I haven't reached final & definite conclusions upon the debated points of your address.

I hope though to see you before you leave.

Thanking you for your cheery greeting of yesterday I remain Faithfully yours

W. H. Ferris

ALS Con. 348 BTW Papers DLC.

From Booker Taliaferro Washington, Jr.

Fisk University Nashville, Tenn. Dec. 18, '07

Dear Father, Please telegraph me $5 to get some Xmas presents for my friends here. There are some people here who have been *very, very* kind to me since I have been here, and for this reason I want to get something for them before I go home. Please father telegraph me the money right away, as I want to purchase the presents this coming Saturday. *Father please dont dissapoint* me.

We leave here Tuesday morning for Tuskegee. Hope that you are well

Booker, Jr.

ACS Con. 363 BTW Papers DLC.

To Arthur Isaiah Vorys

[Tuskegee, Ala.] December 25, 1907

Personal and Confidential.

My dear Mr. Vorys: On my return home a few days ago, I find the Colored people considerably stirred up in this state over the fear that something is going to be done by Secretary Taft's friends and representatives to put the political machinery in this state in the hands of the "lily whites" again and the feeling seems to have gotten abroad in some way among them that Secretary Taft and his friends favor the lily white movement. Of course you and I know how absurd this feeling is, but it is something that we have got to face. I want to urge that you do nothing or permit anything to be done in your name that will give color to such a feeling among the people. Of course, the injury in Alabama and other Southern states for Secretary Taft's name to be connected with the "lily white" movement would not be insurmountable, but the fact that his name was identified with the lily white movement in the South would injure him greatly among the Colored people in Ohio and elsewhere, not only during the canvass for the nomination, but in the canvass for the election after his nomination.

Secondly, I want to urge that you do not permit yourself to be made to feel that it is necessary to spend any money in this state. I believe that if matters are properly managed, that Secretary Taft can secure the vote of every man that goes to the Convention in Alabama without an expenditure of fifty cents.

Third. As I understand it, what you and the Secretary want is delegates secured in an honorable way from this state, who will vote for the Secretary. Do not permit yourself to be used by any faction, or by any individual in order to punish enemies, or to promote personal interests. Unless these matters are handled very carefully here, there will be a split that will cause you trouble. You have enough to do in other states.

I shall hope to see you soon and will tell you more plainly just what I have in mind. Practically everybody in this state is in favor of the Secretary, but there are individuals who differ in their methods of bringing about the same result. It is not necessary for you, or the Secretary to become entangled in these local and personal difficulties.

I am writing you all the more plainly and frankly on these subjects, for the reason that no one knows better than yourself that we *have a hard battle* for ourselves to win over the Colored people of the North and doubtful states to the Secretary and I am very anxious that nothing be done in this or any other Southern state that will make the effort to overcome the Brownsville influence more difficult than it is.

I think you understand that the Constitutional League is on the alert, is spending money to keep the Colored people stirred up and alienate them from the Secretary.

I am watching every one of their movements and will continue to do so. Yours truly,

Booker T. Washington

I sum up in a sentence the main thing that I want to suggest and that is, there is no use of going to the trouble and expense of building up a new organization in the state to support Mr. Taft, when the old organization can be used just as well without any work and without any expense on your part.

B. T. W.

TLpS Con. 362 BTW Papers DLC.

To William Howard Taft

Tuskegee Institute, Alabama December 28, 1907

My dear Secretary Taft: You will see announced, perhaps, in the public press in a day or two that Governor Hughes of New York is to be one of the speakers at a meeting sometime in January in the interest of this institution. Before inviting Governor Hughes to be one of the speakers, I consulted with the President through Mr. Loeb as to the effect of having him speak at such a meeting, and the President felt that it would not have any hurtful effect on your interests, and therefore I went ahead with the arrangements. The Governor and his friends know that I am unreservedly committed to you and your candidacy with all my power. The meeting, of course, has absolutely no political significance. I thought it well to inform you about it, however, in advance, so that no one could get the impression that I am playing a double game.[1] Yours very truly,

Booker T. Washington

TLS William Howard Taft Papers DLC.

[1] Taft replied that he was glad BTW had secured Hughes as a speaker, "and I should not have misconstrued the action in any way." (Jan. 1, 1908, William Howard Taft Papers, DLC.)

From Frederick Randolph Moore

New York, 12/30/07

My dear Mr Washington: Telegram received. Fortune came to town today. Called here and tryed to raise a row. I slapped his hand down and told him I would put him out. He had been drinking and was nasty. Afterwards calmed down and cried like a child and apologized. At the same time was nasty and abusive of you to the extent of villification until I told him I would not permit him to talk further. I cant put it all down. The gist of his talk is that I am too strong to go with you and support you and an effort to persuade me to take Barber and himself into the Age. He was equally abusive of

Scott. I dont want you to write him a line or, see him until you have seen me and then when you do I want you to see in the presence of a 3rd party. As a matter of fact you should ignore him entirely. See me as soon as you come to town. He threatens to remain here. There is nothing to fear — but he is nasty and crazy. His religion is a farce. Threatens if I dont go with him to start another paper.

I hope you are very well and that you may have with Mrs Washington a most pleasant new year.

I think the Taft people should be seen at once and matters started. The other people are working. Tyler has written me that a news article on record of Foraker can be had and 2000 copies taken. I have written him that as a matter of news I would take it — but no declaration as to our choice — for Prest.

The Taft people should see the wisdom of using both the Age and Magazine — and the time is now ripe when others are beginning to line up. These two publications are the strongest and most helpful.

We would too be positioned to get a good strong *Editor*. Kindly see what can be done. Advise me. Sincerely yours

Fred. R. Moore

Dont worry about Fortune he aint worth it.

F.

ALS Con. 36 BTW Papers DLC.

To James Griswold Merrill

[Tuskegee, Ala.] December 31, 1907

My dear President Merrill: My son tells me that he owes you five dollars. Enclosed you will find my check to cover same.

I am rather anxious that every influence possible be used to have him feel that money is not the main thing, to make him just as careful and economical in handling money as possible, and to make him use just as little money as possible. Most boys, as you know, of his age, do not consider how hard money is to get nor how hard it is to keep.

He and Mr. Brady[1] and Alice S[im]mons[2] have been spending the Holidays with us, and we have been enjoying their presence with us very much. Mr. George W. Moore[3] is also here, and he is helping us in many ways.

In case Mrs. Washington succeeds in getting the library building without condition for Fisk, both of us very much hope that no public mention of either of our names will be used in connection with the gift. Yours very truly,

Booker T. Washington

TLpS Con. 344 BTW Papers DLC.

1 St. Elmo Brady graduated from Fisk in 1908 and later did graduate work at the University of Illinois (Ph.D. 1916). He was professor of chemistry at Howard University in the 1920s.

2 Alice Carter Simmons graduated from Fisk in 1908 and then attended the Oberlin Conservatory of Music. She headed Tuskegee's division of instrumental music beginning in 1916.

3 George Washington Moore (1854–1920) was a black Congregational minister in Nashville. Born of slave parents in Nashville, he graduated from Fisk University in 1881 and from Oberlin Seminary in 1883. After a post as professor of biblical history and literature at Howard University (1887–92), he became an American Missionary Association field secretary in 1892, rising to the superintendency of the A.M.A. southern church work with headquarters in Nashville. He was a Fisk trustee for more than thirty years beginning in 1885.

From Charles Waddell Chesnutt

Cleveland, O. Jan. 1, 1907 [1908]

My dear Dr. Washington: I received your long and interesting letter. I shall be glad the [to] thresh the ballot proposition over with you sometime. As to the ballot, the importance of a thing is not to be measured by the number of times you do it. Some of the most important & vital things of life are done only once. A man is born only once, but on that act depends his whole life; he dies only once, which ends all his hopes & fears & usefulness. He marries only a few times.

The importance of the ballot is to me a paramount element of citizenship. A man can earn his daily bread easier and bank more money with it than without it. You argue the question as though the Negro must choose between voting & eating. He ought to do both, and he can do both better together than he can do either alone. It is not the *act* of voting I speak of — it is the right of every citizen to have some part in the choice of those who rule him, and the only way he can express that choice is at the polls. It is just as effective if he votes once in five years as once a day. Would you maintain for a moment that the economic conditions in the South, which crush the Negro & drive away white immigration, would continue to exist if the Negroes could vote, and their votes were directed by intelligent leadership? If they could vote, and you with your power of leadership, would direct their votes in the right channel, do you believe their conditions would not be materially improved? I do, and you do. It is not all of life to eat or to put money in the banks, but, as I say, a free man can do both of those things better than a mere praedial serf, yoked to the mule, with no concern in life but his belly & his back. If the colored people ever expect to cut any figure in this Republic they must not pitch their ideals too low; tho their feet must of course rest upon the earth, it should not be forbidden to them to lift their eyes to the Hills.

Wishing you a Happy & prosperous New Year, Cordially yours,

Chas. W. Chesnutt

ALS Con. 886 BTW Papers DLC.

From Edwin Doak Mead

Boston Jan. 2, 1908

Personal

Dear Mr. Washington: I wish you would tell me in a word what the facts are in this matter of the "N.Y. Age" ventilated by Mr. Trotter in the last no. of his "Guardian." Mr. Garrison and I have determined to put a stop, if possible, to this chronic row in the "Guardian," which is making our colored people here as a body almost inefficient for any good purpose. Garrison, whose name was used in the "Guardian" in opposition to you, has sent them a very stiff letter for publication. They are trying to avoid its publication; but they will have to publish it — probably this week — or its publication immediately elsewhere will be the worse for them. And now comes this blast about the "Age" – concerning which we should like the simple facts, to use or not, as the exigencies of a probably hot controversy following the publication of Garrison's letter may demand.

I wish you a happy new year. The colored people in the South have rare good fortune in securing young Ware[1] for the presidency of Atlanta University. Mrs. Mead and I have known him and his family intimately for many years; and I do not know a finer fellow in the world. Yours truly,

Edwin D. Mead

ALS Con. 376 BTW Papers DLC.

1 Edward Twichell Ware.

An Article in *Outlook*

Jan. 4, 1908

BOLEY, A NEGRO TOWN IN THE WEST

Boley, Indian Territory, is the youngest, the most enterprising, and in many ways the most interesting of the negro towns in the United States. A rude, bustling, Western town, it is a characteristic product of the negro immigration from the South and Middle West into the new lands of what is now the State of Oklahoma.

The large proportions of the northward and westward movement of the negro population recall the Kansas Exodus of thirty years ago, when within a few months more than forty thousand helpless and destitute negroes from the country districts of Arkansas and Mississippi poured into eastern Kansas in search of "better homes, larger opportunities, and kindlier treatment."

It is a striking evidence of the progress made in thirty years that the present northward and westward movement of the negro people has brought into these new lands, not a helpless and ignorant horde of black people, but land-seekers and home-builders, men who have come prepared to build up the country. In the thirty years since the Kansas Exodus the Southern negroes have learned to build schools, to establish banks and conduct newspapers. They have recovered something of the knack for trade that their foreparents in Africa were famous for. They have learned through their churches and their secret orders the art of corporate and united action. This experience has enabled them to set up and maintain in a raw Western community, numbering 2,500, an orderly and self-respecting government.

In the fall of 1905 I spent a week in the Territories of Oklahoma and Indian Territory. During the course of my visit I had an opportunity for the first time to see the three races — the Negro, the Indian, and the white man — living side by side, each in sufficient numbers to make their influence felt in the communities of which they were a part, and in the Territory as a whole. It was not my first acquaintance with the Indian. During the last years of my stay at Hampton Institute I had charge of the Indian students there, and had come to have a high respect both for their character and intelligence, so that I was particularly interested to see them in their own country, where they still preserve to some extent their native institutions. I was all the more impressed, on that account, with the fact that in the cities that I visited I rarely caught sight of a genuine native Indian. When I inquired, as I frequently did, for the "natives," it almost invariably happened that I was introduced, not to an Indian, but to a Negro. During my visit to the city of Muskogee I stopped at the home of one of the prominent "natives" of the Creek Nation, the Hon. C. W. Sango, Superintendent of the Tullahassee Mission. But he is a negro. The negroes who are known in that locality as "natives" are the descendants of slaves that the Indians brought with them from Alabama and Mississippi, when they migrated to this Territory, about the middle of the last century. I was introduced later to one or two other "natives" who were not negroes, but neither were they, as far as my observation went, Indians. They were, on the contrary, white men. "But where," I asked at length, "are the Indians?"

"Oh! the Indians," was the reply, "they have gone," with a wave of the hand in the direction of the horizon, "they have gone back!"

I repeated this question in a number of different places, and invariably received the same reply, "Oh, they have gone back!" I remembered the expression because it seemed to me that it condensed into a phrase a great deal of local history.

One cannot escape the impression, in traveling through Indian Territory, that the Indians, who own practically all the lands, and until recently had the local government largely in their own hands, are to a very large extent regarded by the white settlers, who are rapidly filling up the country, as almost a negligible quantity. To such an extent is this true that the Constitution of Oklahoma, as I understand it, takes no account of the Indians in drawing its distinctions among the races. For the Constitution there exist only the negro and the white man. The reason seems to be that the Indians have either receded — "gone back," as the saying in that region is — on the advance of the white race, or they have intermarried with and become absorbed with it.[1] Indeed, so rapidly has this intermarriage of the two races gone on, and so great has been the demand for Indian wives, that in some of the Nations, I was informed, the price of marriage licenses has gone as high as $1,000.

The negroes, immigrants to Indian Territory, have not, however, "gone back." One sees them everywhere, working side by side with white men. They have their banks, business enterprises, schools, and churches. There are still, I am told, among the "natives" some negroes who cannot speak the English language, and who have been so thoroughly bred in the customs of the Indians that they have remained among the hills with the tribes by whom they were adopted. But, as a rule, the negro natives do not shun the white man and his civilization, but, on the contrary, rather seek it, and enter, with the negro immigrants, into competition with the white man for its benefits.

This fact was illustrated by another familiar local expression. In reply to my inquiries in regard to the little towns through which we passed, I often had occasion to notice the expression, "Yes, so and so? Well, that is a 'white town.' " Or, again, "So and so, that's colored."

I learned upon inquiry that there were a considerable number of communities throughout the Territory where an effort had been made to exclude negro settlers. To this the negroes had replied by starting other communities in which no white man was allowed to live. For instance, the thriving little city of Wilitka, I was informed, was a white man's town until it got the oil mills. Then they needed laborers, and brought in the negroes. There are a number of other little communities — Clairview, Wildcat, Grayson, and Taft

—which were sometimes referred to as "colored towns," but I learned that in their cases the expression meant merely that these towns had started as negro communities or that there were large numbers of negroes there, and that negro immigrants were wanted. But among these various communities there was one of which I heard more than the others. This was the town of Boley, where, it is said, no white man has ever let the sun go down upon him.

In 1905, when I visited Indian Territory, Boley was little more than a name. It was started in 1903. At the present time it is a thriving town of two thousand five hundred inhabitants, with two banks, two cotton-gins, a newspaper, a hotel, and a "college," the Creek-Seminole College and Agricultural Institute.

There is a story told in regard to the way in which the town of Boley was started, which, even if it is not wholly true as to the details, is at least characteristic, and illustrates the temper of the people in that region.

One spring day, four years ago, a number of gentlemen were discussing, at Wilitka, the race question. The point at issue was the capability of the negro for self-government. One of the gentlemen, who happened to be connected with the Fort Smith Railway, maintained that if the negroes were given a fair chance they would prove themselves as capable of self-government as any other people of the same degree of culture and education. He asserted that they had never had a fair chance. The other gentlemen naturally asserted the contrary. The result of the argument was Boley. Just at that time a number of other town sites were being laid out along the railway which connects Guthrie, Oklahoma, with Fort Smith, Arkansas. It was, it is said, to put the capability of the negro for self-government to the test that in August, 1903, seventy-two miles east of Guthrie, the site of the new negro town was established. It was called Boley, after the man who built that section of the railway. A negro town-site agent, T. M. Haynes, who is at present connected with the Farmers' and Merchants' Bank, was made Town-site Agent, and the purpose to establish a town which should be exclusively controlled by negroes was widely advertised all over the Southwest.

Boley, although built on the railway, is still on the edge of civilization. You can still hear on summer nights, I am told, the wild notes of the Indian drums and the shrill cries of the Indian dancers among the hills beyond the settlement. The outlaws that formerly infested the country have not wholly disappeared. Dick Shafer, the first Town Marshal of Boley, was killed in a duel with a horse thief, whom he in turn shot and killed, after falling, mortally wounded, from his horse. The horse thief was a white man.

There is no liquor sold in Boley, or any part of the Territory, but the "natives" go down to Prague, across the Oklahoma border, ten miles away, and then come back and occasionally "shoot up" the town. That was a favorite pastime, a few years ago, among the "natives" around Boley. The first case that came up before the Mayor for trial was that of a young "native" charged with "shooting up" a meeting in a church. But, on the whole, order in the community has been maintained. It is said that during the past two years not a single arrest has been made among the citizens. The reason is that the majority of these negro settlers have come there with the definite intention of getting a home and building up a community where they can, as they say, be "free." What this expression means is pretty well shown by the case of C. W. Perry, who came from Marshall, Texas. Perry had learned the trade of a machinist and had worked in the railway machine shops until the white machinists struck and made it so uncomfortable that the negro machinists went out. Then he went on the railway as brakeman, where he worked for fifteen years. He owned his own home and was well respected, so much so that when it became known that he intended to leave, several of the County Commissioners called on him. "Why are you going away?" they asked; "you have your home here among us. We know you and you know us. We are behind you and will protect you."

"Well," he replied, "I have always had an ambition to do something for myself. I don't want always to be led. I want to do a little leading."

Other immigrants, like Mr. T. R. Ringe, the Mayor, who was born a slave in Kentucky, and Mr. E. L. Lugrande, one of the principal stockholders in the new bank, came out in the new country, like so many of the white settlers, merely to get land. Mr. Lugrande came from Denton County, Texas, where he had 418 acres of land. He had purchased this land some years ago for four and five dollars the acre. He sold it for fifty dollars an acre, and, coming to Boley, he purchased a tract of land just outside the town and began selling town lots. Now a large part of his acreage is in the center of the town.

Mr. D. J. Turner, who owns a drugstore and has an interest in the Farmers' and Merchants' Bank, came to Indian Territory as a boy, and has grown up among the Indians, to whom he is in a certain way related, since his brother married an Indian girl and in that way got a section of land. Mr. Turner remembers the days when every one in this section of the Territory lived a half-savage life; cultivating a little corn, and killing a wild hog or a beef when they wanted meat. And he has seen the rapid change, not only in the country, but in the people, since the tide of immigration turned this way. The negro immigration from the South, he says, has been a particularly helpful influence upon the "native" negroes, who are beginning now to cultivate their lands in a way which they never thought of doing a few years ago.

A large proportion of the settlers of Boley are farmers from Texas, Arkansas, and Mississippi. But the desire for Western lands has drawn into the community not only farmers, but doctors, lawyers, and craftsmen of all kinds. The fame of the town has also brought, no doubt, a certain proportion of the drifting population. But behind all other attractions of the new colony is the belief that here negroes would find greater opportunities and more freedom of action than they have been able to find in the older communities North or South.

Boley, like the other negro towns that have sprung up in other parts of the country, represents a dawning race consciousness, a wholesome desire to do something to make the race respected; something which shall demonstrate the right of the negro, not merely as an individual, but as a race, to have a worthy and permanent place in the civilization that the American people are creating.

In short, Boley is another chapter in the long struggle of the negro for moral, industrial, and political freedom.

Outlook, 88 (Jan. 4, 1908), 28–31.

[1] E. M. Shute of Boston, who had recently spent six or seven months in the Indian Service in Oklahoma, wrote to the *Outlook* that it was untrue that Indians had degenerated. Many of the leading businessmen of the Indian Territory, he wrote, were Indians. (Jan. 5, 1908, Con. 42, BTW Papers, DLC.)

To James Bertram

Hotel Manhattan, New York   January 9, 1908

My dear Mr. Bertram: Mr. Carnegie told Mrs. Washington this afternoon that he would take up with you tomorrow or sometime soon the case of Fisk University which she presented to him. I am simply calling the matter to your attention to restate briefly what she said.

In the first place, I appreciate fully the importance of your having a rule in regard to libraries and sticking to it. I believe that Fisk University, however, presents a case where much good would be accomplished by perhaps breaking the rule. It is an old institution, the very best institution in the South for college education. It has a large library so far as books are concerned, and these books in their present cramped condition are well taken care of, but they have needed for a long while a library building. The application on file in your office from President Merrill asks for $20,000 for a building. President Merrill has had a hard time in getting the money for current expenses during the last two or three years and has not, therefore, been able to get anything toward meeting the condition named by Mr. Carnegie. President Merrill represents one of those cases where a college president is able to do excellent work on the grounds, but has little ability in getting money on the outside. There would be no risk whatever, in my opinion, so far as the up-keep of the library building and books is concerned, for the reason that they have a system the same as we have at Tuskegee by which the library is carefully and systematically cared for by teachers and students. Mrs. Washington is a graduate of Fisk and knows its condition thoroughly, and both of us feel quite sure that the money for the library building with the condition left off would accomplish a great deal of good. Yours truly,

[Booker T. Washington]

TLc   Con. 41   BTW Papers   DLC.

From William Henry Ferris

New Haven, Conn. Jan. 9th, 1908

My Dear Dr. Washington I thank you for writing to Dr. Frissell in my behalf. I trust that something may result from it. I am now putting the finishing touches upon My History of the Negro Race. I will entitle it "The Negro in American Civilization." The book now numbers nearly one thousand typewritten pages & I expect to finish it next week.

I have been thinking over the Southern situation. The white man of the South never will be dominated by the Negro. The Negro follows the white man step by step & he wants everything the white man has. So the problem will be "What will be the outcome when the Negro gets wealth & education & outnumbers the white man in the Southern communities? Will that millennium come when the Lamb & the Lion shall lie down together & a little child shall lead them?"

It doesn't look as if any process can be discovered whereby the Negro can bleach his complexion, straighten his hair, pinch in his nostrils & thin his lips. As long as there is the physical difference between the races, there will be more or less race antagonism.

I am inclined to believe & I put it forth as a tentative hypothesis & not as a theorem that can be demonstrated, that if some means could be found whereby the South could be relieved of its congested condition, where the blacks outnumber the South that the friction between the races would decrease. It might be well for some of the Southern Negroes to go to the forest lands of the West.

The Greeks & the French are the most brilliant & versatile races that have appeared upon the stage of History. But the Romans & the Anglo Saxons are the races that preeminently have a genius for war & government. They are the masterful & dominating races.

One white man wrote me yesterday "I have lost hope for your people. I do not see how their condition can be bettered — indeed I am convinced that their condition will grow worse & worse instead of better — for reason inhereing in themselves as well as those outside of them. All the powerful forces of our civilization are coming more & more to be exerted against them — they are doomed."

I think this is a rather gloomy picture. I believe that if the Negro will absorb & assimilate & appropriate the Anglo Saxon's civilization, he will ultimately come to his own in this country. The race problem will solve itself or rather time the alleviator of all wrongs, the righter of all grievances will solve the delicate & complicated problem caused by two races differing in hair, feature & complexion dwelling side by side in the same country. Meanwhile we need leaders like yourself, who will tell the Negro to get money & land & become an industrial & financial factor in this country. And we also need leaders like Du Bois who will tell the white people, "The Black Man is not only a Physical Organism of the *Genus Homo*; but a *Moral Personality of the Genus Vir.*

This is the conclusion that I finally arrive at in my prospective book.

I trust that my long letters have not wearied you. But these thoughts that I have been expressing to you are what I am putting into the preface to my book. I believe that if a man will solve his own problem that he can best serve his day & generation. I haven't attempted to solve the race problem in my History; but I have endeavoured to present a picture of the Negro, surrounded by his peculiar environment. Very truly yours

W. H. Ferris

ALS Con. 887 BTW Papers DLC.

William Lloyd Garrison, Jr., to the Editor of the Boston *Transcript*

Lexington, [Mass.] Jan. 11 [1908]

To the Editor of the Transcript: There exists in Boston a group of colored men possessing a weekly organ conspicuous for its hostility to Booker T. Washington. Viewing him as a self-seeker influenced by unworthy motives, they lose no opportunity to criticise his acts and asperse his character. Agreeing with them, concerning the value of agitation to rectify wrongs, and uncompromisingly demanding for the Negro equal civil and political rights, I, nevertheless, protest against the unfair spirit of their attacks upon Mr.

Washington. To my mind it betrays a personal animosity and a distorted vision.

This condition of things, beginning with a lawless attempt to interfere with free speech in a public meeting, which culminated in the arrest of the ringleader, has reached the proportion of a scandal, grieving many steadfast friends of the race. Affecting to see in Mr. Washington's recent address at the Whittier celebration in Amesbury indications of veering in the direction favored by the paper in question, the editor thus insultingly declares: "In all of his speeches we have noticed the results of the flogging which it has been our painful duty to inflict, 'many a time and oft.' "

In the number of the paper containing these words, I was made inferentially to appear in harmony with such an attitude, detached quotations from Mr. Washington and myself being printed in contrast, and with the prominent headlines: "William Lloyd Garrison vs. Booker T. Washington." Disclaiming the antagonism, and expressing my plain opinion of the proceeding, I wrote a dissenting letter to the editor. As its publication was refused, I am constrained to give it publicity through other channels. Excepting the introductory paragraph, the following is substantially the rejected communication:

"The assumption that such critics are actuated by a superior fidelity to principle is unwarranted. Had Mr. Washington ever betrayed a purpose to sacrifice principles for the prosperity of his institution, these frequent attacks upon him by members of his race would be intelligible. But upon the two distinct points of censure — those limiting the Negro to industrial pursuits and an indifference to the suffrage — he speaks with no uncertain sound. He sets no metes or bounds to the Negro's aspiration for learning, nor does he acquiesce in the annulment of the Fifteenth Amendment. While naturally giving emphasis to the particular field which Tuskegee covers, he is careful to demand for the race every right conceded to white fellow-citizens.

"There is cruelty in these aspersions. Mr. Washington is working in the most inflammable portion of the South. He not only carries the burden of a great university, but upon his shoulders has fallen the mission to disarm sectional hostility, to draw support from Southern whites with inherited prejudices that must be allayed, ever to keep a hopeful front under circumstances which must at times chill his heart, to discern events in their proper proportion, never to allow discouragement to blind him to the real signs of promise, and to preserve a serenity and poise that are a marvel to his friends and a confusion to his enemies. What unusual qualities meet and blend in one capable of such achievement!

"How easy for colored men with academic advantages, secure in the stronghold of anti-slavery sentiment, to affect disdain and indulge in bitter speech! It costs nothing and is no evidence of courage. Where an occasional office is tossed to a colored man by way of reward for political service, how quickly, as is the case with the white officeholder, do circumspection and subservience overtake him. He may be eloquent in denouncing the rendition of fugitive slaves when the law demanded it, and yet evince no scruple in helping to deport poor Chinamen for the crime of seeking larger opportunity and freedom in Boston. And a salaried position under the City Government insures his support of a corrupt administration. Yet Booker Washington is held to an ideal standard which not one of his critics would dream of realizing in the same situation.

"To twist my statement of expressed conviction into an intended reproach on this leader of his race is to convey a false impression. I appreciate the difficulties which encompass him. I wonder at his patience, wisdom, courage and sagacity. For myself, with no restraint of speech, save those of fealty to truth and the requirements of justice, I am able to wield a free lance. He, on the contrary, lives in a region where a whisper at times precipitates the avalanche. That he is permitted to declare himself with the frankness that he does, is only explicable on the ground that his sincere purpose and upright character compel public respect and confidence.

"But, however the colored people may differ with each other regarding methods and policies, there is room enough for all to help in the regenerating work without the unseemly strife that divides and weakens their efforts. Personally, I beg to be spared further employment of my words to discredit one who, in the consideration of the thinking civilized world, is the most remarkable living American, black or white, and to whom both races owe an immeasurable debt."

William Lloyd Garrison

Boston *Transcript*, Jan. 13, 1908, 9.

From Daniel Hale Williams

Chicago, Jan 12th 07 [1908][1]

My dear Dr. Washington, I am writing you of a condition that is existing here, one that I think your attention should be called to. The Conservator is in sore straits, caused by a persistent attempt to divert or control its policy. A Preacher has it under obligations to him, he being the dominant force has a decided influence over the Merchant[2] who has the largest interest in it. Urged on by the continued force of enemy has almost squeezed the life from the paper. If the present managers of the Paper will concede or capitulate things will run smoothly. They have been ejected from their office during the past week with a fiendish glee that is well understood. I have been helping them right along in every way that I could, so have others, but now their condition is so serious that I thought I should at least call your attention to it as much as I dislike to do so. This is on purely personal grounds, as I am sure that you have quite enough always on hand to be shielded from annoyance in these matter[s] that may seem trivial to you, yet I feel that in this quarter, at this time, it is important, decidedly important. Nothing could be made by F. in the other venture hence they have turned their attention to the matter I refer to. Very Sincerely

Dan'l H. Williams

P.S. Enclosed find letter from Editor. A very worthy and reliable man. Kindly return it.

ALS Con. 385 BTW Papers DLC.

1 Williams wrote "07" but the year was 1908, as his letter of Jan. 16, 1908, below, and other subsequent correspondence about the Chicago *Conservator* make clear.

2 Sandy W. Trice, born in Tennessee in 1866, was for many years a Pullman porter. He operated a clothing store in Chicago from 1900 to 1909. He was active in the NNBL and worked to secure favorable press coverage for BTW in Chicago. In 1908 he bought an interest in the Chicago *Conservator* and helped oust J. Max Barber as editor. By 1909, however, the *Conservator* was again hostile to BTW, and the Tuskegean refused to help Trice make another attempt to find a friendly editor, preferring to let the newspaper die. (Spear, *Black Chicago*, 74.)

To William Lloyd Garrison, Jr.

Hotel Manhattan, New York City January 15, 1908

My dear Mr. Garrison: I want to thank you most earnestly and sincerely for your fine and generous letter recently published in the Transcript. I am sure that it will accomplish a great deal of good, and I hope that it will teach Mr. Trotter a lesson which will do him good. There is too much serious work on hand at the present time to be done for any one who is really interested in bettering conditions to spend his time in personal blackguarding and bickerings. If Mr. Trotter could just learn the lesson that what the terms "courage" and "manhood" do not consist in [is] low personal abuse, he would be helped immensely.

I have just been reading this week a little book called "Garrison, the Non-Resistant," by Ernest Crosby,[1] and the words of your father point out more clearly than I have realized before what true courage means. You will be interested to know that this little book was bought and presented to me by a white man from Louisiana.

With feelings of high esteem and great gratitude, I am, Yours very truly,

[Booker T. Washington]

TLc Con. 371 BTW Papers DLC.

[1] Ernest Howard Crosby (1856–1907), a former judge of the International Court in Egypt, became an advocate of the single-tax ideas of Henry George and began a life of social reform, championing anti-militarism, vegetarianism, and settlement work. He was a founder and president of the Social Reform Club and the author of several books on reformers such as William Lloyd Garrison and Leo Tolstoi.

From Daniel Hale Williams

Chicago, Jan. 16th, 08

My Dear Dr Washington. I write to advise you of some important changes going on. The Conservator has changed management. Mr Max Barbour has been installed as Editor. L. B. Anderson[1] and Mr. Trice and a Mr Washington[2] are holding the managerial end of the Company. I do not know what their policy will be but will advise you if anything of interest comes up. Yours truly

Dan'l H. Williams

ALS Con. 385 BTW Papers DLC.

[1] Louis B. Anderson, born in 1870 and admitted to the Chicago bar in 1897, was assistant Cook County attorney from 1898 to 1915. He was an alderman from Chicago's second ward from 1917 to 1933 and a longtime Republican regular. He was closely allied with the black businessmen of Chicago and, less directly, with the Tuskegee Machine. In 1913 Anderson was a partner in the Anderson-Watkins Film Co. in Chicago, which produced and distributed a three-reel motion picture *A Day at Tuskegee.*

[2] A. W. Washington worked for the *Conservator* beginning about 1905. Sandy W. Trice reported that A. W. Washington was trustworthy, presumably meaning he was pro-BTW. (See Trice to BTW, Mar. 12, 1908, below.)

To James Bertram

Hotel Manhattan, New York City January 17, 1908

My dear Mr. Bertram: I have received yours of January 15th concerning the Fisk University library building. Mrs. Washington and I are most grateful to Mr. Carnegie for granting this request, and I am sure that Fisk University and the trustees will thoroughly appreciate what Mr. Carnegie has done.

I shall see to it personally that no mention is made publicly concerning the waiver of the endowment. Yours truly,

[Booker T. Washington]

TLc Con. 886 BTW Papers DLC.

To Abram L. Grant

[Tuskegee, Ala.] January 23, 1908

Personal and Confidential.

My dear Bishop Grant: I spoke to the President as I passed through Washington concerning the meeting of the three Boards of Bishops. He suggests that, instead of his coming to the church — something that he very rarely does — that he receive the Bishops in a body in the east room, that is the large parlor in the White House, say, at 2:30 on February 14. Does this meet with your approval?

He states that, if you desire it, he can arrange to have no newspaper reporters present, and in that case, he can speak as freely and frankly as he desires. He has left the matter largely in my hands. I told him, however, that I would co-operate with you and that you are the one that I should depend upon and that seemed to satisfy him. Now if this plan is carried out, there must be no mistake.

In the first place, if the President makes an address, which he is likely to do, someone — I should prefer yourself — should be selected to reply to the address. If either Bishop Turner or Bishop Walters are permitted to speak in reply, I think it better for the Bishops not to go to the White House. Bishop Turner, in the first place, would say some foolish thing because of his age and child-like condition. Bishop Walters would say something in order to play to the gallery. He would say some foolish thing, or brave thing, in order to have it published in Negro newspapers. As I suggested, the proper thing would be for the President to make his address, then for you, or some level-headed Bishop to reply briefly and then for the President to meet each one personally for a chat.

This, I am sure, would be a dignified proceeding and would accomplish a great deal of good.

I shall not write to Mr. Loeb about final arrangements until I have heard from you. Please write at once. Yours truly,

Booker T. Washington

TLpS Con. 41 BTW Papers DLC.

From Charles William Anderson

New York, N.Y., January 23, 1908

(Personal)

My dear Doctor: I wired you on yesterday, but am writing you more at length. During the recent financial stringency I accepted checks in payment of internal revenue tax, and I believe, was the only Collector in the country to do so. This materially assisted in relieving the situation here, and helped the merchants greatly in the conduct of their business. Some of the merchants hearing of the proposed dinner to me, concluded that they would take occasion to make me some sort of a present, in recognition of the services rendered to them, as above stated. To that end a representative called on me, and I told him that I could not accept any gifts from the merchants doing business with this office, as it would be highly improper. It was then suggested that a sum of money be raised to be given to Tuskegee in my name, and to this proposition I heartily consented, if it was not thought improper at Washington. I at once wrote the President, and am now awaiting his reply. These merchants assured me that every wholesale dealer in the district is ready to subscribe a sum, which the Committee have fixed upon, not to exceed $10 each, and the whole to be turned over to Tuskegee. I assured them that this would please me immensely, if the authorities at Washington would permit it. Please take this up at your end of the line.

The compliment intended, certainly is a very satisfactory one, for as you may know, many of these merchants are Southern men, from Kentucky and Maryland. That they should unanimously agree to give me some testimonial, rather looks as though I had not altogether failed in handling this office in a satisfactory way. Yours truly,

Charles W. Anderson

P.S. They say that [they] will be able to raise about one thousand dollars, the sum to be presented at the dinner on the 30th. The whole proposition was voluntary. I had no knowledge of [it] until yesterday.

C. A.

TLS Con. 38 BTW Papers DLC.

From William Henry Ferris

New Haven, Conn. Jan. 24th, 1908

My Dear Dr. Washington, When I criticized you ten & five years ago, I didn't understand you quite as fully as I do now. I analyzed your statements then; but not your personality.

But when I began to write my History of the Negro race two years ago, I soon discovered that you were an unusual Negro. I saw that while our race had produced many scholars, theologians, philosophers, artists, painters, poets, writers, orators & politicians, it had produced few men of constructive & creative genius. Then I saw that you were a masterful strategist, a resourceful tactician & an astute diplomat. I saw that you possessed remarkable executive ability & that you had shown considerable constructive ability in organizing & marshalling your forces at Tuskegee. In a word you were a born general of the Oyama[1] & Count von Molkte[2] types.

III. I believe that it is recognized at present that the masses of the Negro race need Industrial Education, while the Talented Tenth need the Higher Education.

IV. The difference of opinion between you & my Niagara Movement friends comes in with regard to the delicate situation caused by the Negro desiring the manhood rights guaranteed by the Constitution of the U.S. I have no solution of the race problem to offer; but here are five axiomatic truths, five facts of human nature.

First. The world never puts a higher estimate upon a race or individual than that race or individual puts upon himself or itself. *Secondly.* The world as a rule does not give a race or individual more than he or it asks & claims for. *Thirdly.* Men *tolerate* but do *not respect* the race or individual, who will be kicked & cuffed without an audible protest. *Fourthly.* The world only respects the individual, who regards himself as a man. *Fifthly.* A completely disfranchised & segregaded race will lose the respect of mankind.

But on the other hand, the *South* says "Go back to the farm & leave the government in the hands of white men." There is the dilemma. I believe that ultimately an adjustment will be reached in the South satisfactory to both races. Faithfully yours

W. H. Ferris

P.S. Some of my friends say that if I adopt the Kelly Miller role of taking a middle ground between you & Trotter, I cannot logically & consistently ask any favors of you or any aid from you.

The Niagara Movement fight last summer convinced me that with Trotter, you must go the whole distance or not go at all. That is what caused the split? We were willing to go half the way with Trotter but not all the distance. Trotter has written to his friends that I have sold out to you.

W. H. F.

P.S. This is a summary of the last chapter of my History. W.F.

ALS Con. 887 BTW Papers DLC.

1 Iwao Oyama (1842–1916), the Japanese general and hero of the Sino-Japanese and Russo-Japanese wars.

2 Helmuth von Moltke (1800–1891), the Prussian field marshal.

To Daniel Hale Williams

[Tuskegee, Ala.] January 25, 1908

My dear Dr. Williams: Both of your kind letters have been received.

I appreciate more than I can express your deep interest. It is always very difficult to reach any decision concerning such a case as your letter covers.

In the first place, even if one had the funds, it is difficult to tell how to help, how far to go and where to stop. In many cases, one has to shoulder all the responsibility or assume none of it. The main difference seems to be that our people have such little business ability, that it is almost impossible for them to carry any business enterprise to success, however much they are helped. Then in the case of the newspapers, the owners and editors seem to depend almost wholly upon graft rather than upon strictly business principles for success. Since your letter, however, was written, I find that the problem has in a measure solved itself, judging by a clipping which someone has sent me.

It is difficult to conjecture, I presume, in what way the new editor will shoot, except one can be perfectly sure that he will go in the most foolish direction. When in New York, I saw some letters which the new editor wrote to Mr. Fortune. They would amuse you. The question discussed was — "In What Way Was He to Sneak out of Chicago?" "Would it be wise to notify the one he was going to leave with his debts unpaid?" Another question was — "Whether or not he could be arrested, if he had left."

Fortune was in New York during the time that I was there, but I did not see him. I am sorry to say that I heard that he was under the influence of liquor during the greater part of the time and I fear is destined to remain in that condition for a while.

I shall be passing through Chicago during the first or second week in February and shall hope to have a word with you. I have just received a letter from Dr. Carey's church inviting me to deliver an address, but I am not sure that I can find time to do so.

Enclosed, I return Mr. French's letter. . . .

[Booker T. Washington]

TLpf Con. 385 BTW Papers DLC.

To William Howard Taft

Tuskegee Institute, Alabama January 27, 1908

My dear Secretary Taft: Some days ago some one informed me that according to a published report from the War Department, six regiments of light artillery had already been filled and that consequently there seemed to be no chance for a colored regiment to be organized in the way we discussed some months ago.

I very much hope that there is still an opening left for the organization of a colored regiment at the proper time. Colored men as a rule are anxious to enlist in the service, while I understand white men are difficult to get. This, it seems to me, offers an adequate reason why you would be justified in disregarding other considerations in organizing the regiment at the proper time.

Of course, you will understand that what I am writing is only suggestive. Yours truly,

Booker T. Washington

TLS William Howard Taft Papers DLC. Docketed: "Talk with President."

From Robert Ezra Park

[Wollaston, Mass.?] Jan. 28. 1907 [1908]

My dear Mr Washington: I send you enclosed my notion of the sort of replies I think it would be well to make to the enclosed letters. I am sorry that I allowed the people of Boley to deceive me in regard to the number of inhabitants of the town. My impression is that they told me that a census had been taken sometime before I was there and that the town had greatly increased since then.

With regard to the second letter, that is, in my opinion, mere pettyfogging. Your article puts the finger on the most striking and most palpable fact in regard to the relations of the races in Indian Territory. Perhaps it could have been expressed more precisely but it never could be expressed in a way that would be palatable to the person who believes there is something essentially noble in the red man and something essentially ignoble in the Negro.

One fact you should emphasize in the Story of the Negro and that is this: The Negro had risen in the scale of civilization to the point where he kept slaves. So far as I know the Negro is the only savage people who has done so. A system of government based on slavery is essentially higher than one based on the mere tribal or family relations. The Southerner will appreciate that. I am very truly

Robert E. Park

P.S. Would it not be a good plan to send copies of these replies to the Outlook, *not* for publication.

TLS Con. 42 BTW Papers DLC.

To William Loeb, Jr.

Hotel Manhattan, New York February 3, 1908

Personal

My dear Mr. Loeb: I received your telegram regarding the division of the state between the two referees[1] just as I was leaving Tuskegee. Of course I will do my best in the future, as I have always tried to do in the past, to try to carry out any policy or any wish that you and the President may desire. I telegraphed you as I did because I felt strongly that the dividing up of the state would tend to emphasize, and perhaps keep alive longer, the differences between Mr. Thompson and Mr. Scott. Before leaving I fulfiled my promise to make another effort to get Mr. Thompson and Mr. Scott together. I succeeded in getting Mr. Thompson to modify his demands in certain directions; one was, Mr. Scott had the idea that Mr. Thompson wished to secure his place as National Committeeman; Mr. Thompson said he would not make any such claim before the state convention and would not agitate that question. That was the point that seemed to be agitating Mr. Scott most. I got hold of Mr. Nathan Alexander, the colored Receiver of Public Money in Montgomery, whom both of these men very highly respect. He will put this phase of the case before Mr. Scott and make an effort to get him to work in harmony. Of course, no one can tell what the final outcome will be, but I have felt that the dividing up of the state would mean a permanent breach. As soon as I return to Alabama, which will be within a few days, I am going to continue to work in the direction of getting them to harmonize, no matter what is done in the meantime. They are both strong men, and it is too bad to have them apart as they are.

I attended the Anderson banquet here on Thursday night. It was a magnificent success. There were more than five hundred men present from different parts of the country. It was a deserved tribute to Anderson. The point I want to mention, however, in this connection, for the information of the President is that whenever the President's name was mentioned by any speaker, or even directly referred to, it was cheered most heartily, and I was pleased to note with that group of colored men present, the Brownsville matter seemed to have had very little permanent influence. Yours truly,

[Booker T. Washington]

TLc Con. 7 BTW Papers DLC.

[1] Joseph Oswalt Thompson and Charles Herrington Scott.

From William Howard Taft

Washington, February 5, 1908

Personal

My dear Doctor: I am in receipt of your letter of the 27th ultimo, and have seen the President about the matter. He seems favorably inclined toward the creation of a colored regiment of artillery, but before definitely deciding prefers to see the character of the report on the Brownsville affair, which the Senate Investigating Committee is expected to make some time in the near future.

As for myself, I have always been in favor of having one of the artillery regiments consist of colored men, and had this matter thoroly investigated and reported upon by my subordinates. I had just about decided to give the order to organize one of the new artillery regiments with colored men when the Brownsville affair suddenly took a political turn. Realizing that no matter what I might do at that time would be liable to be attributed to political motives rather than to my own personal convictions, I decided to postpone action in that connection awaiting further definite developments in the Brownsville investigation.

Just as soon as I find it possible to take any action favorable to your desires, without subjecting myself to the suspicion of being influenced by political motives, I will take pleasure in considering this matter again. Very sincerely yours,

Wm H Taft

TLS Con. 7 BTW Papers DLC.

To Sandy W. Trice

[New York City] February 10, 1908

Personal

My dear Mr. Trice: I thank you for your kind letter of recent date. It is a great satisfaction for me to know that the arrangements for the meeting on Friday night are all right and in accordance with your wishes. I am very anxious that there be present a large representation of the ordinary, hard-working people, men and women.

I thank you very much for what you say regarding the policy to be pursued by your paper. I appreciate this thoroughly. Nothing whatever is to be gained by any effort on the part of a newspaper or on the part of individuals to tear down organizations and individuals of our race. The newspapers should devote the main proportion of their efforts to progressive, constructive work rather than mere criticism and fault-finding. You never could have built up your own business in the way you have if you had merely depended upon finding fault with the other fellow. I shall hope to have a talk with you when I see you. Yours very truly,

[Booker T. Washington]

TLc Con. 383 BTW Papers DLC.

Charles William Anderson to Emmett Jay Scott

New York, N.Y., February 15, 1908

(Personal)

My dear Emmett: I want to thank you for your letter of the 12th instant, and to take proper shame on myself for not having before sent you a word of thanks for the splendid service rendered me in the dinner matter. The write-up pleased me immensely, and is all due to you. I feel certain that it would not have pleased me, had it been left to the present presiding "genius" of the Age. I have not seen Mr. Moore since the night of the dinner, although I am in receipt of a bill from him for $18.75, for making the cuts. The dinner is still the talk of the town here, and everybody seems to feel that it was a great success. Naturally, I am highly gratified.

Confidential In strictest confidence, I want to suggest that the Doctor reduce his points of contact with men who are under pay from the Constitution League. I fell in with Napoleon Marshall last week, and spent some hours with him, during which time I learned that their forces were familiar with every move the Doctor has made, and is making along political lines. He was frank enough to confess that the information came from two gentlemen who live in New York, and are drawing salary from the League. I hope the Doctor will understand that it is always dangerous business to deal with men who are playing two ways. If he does not suffer injury from it, he will be the only man that the world ever produced who did not. My experience is, that if you want to win a battle, you had better confer only with your officers, and keep your plans unknown to the enemy. This can only be done by dealing with men who are faithful and single-hearted. I think I have said enough on this score.

With kind regards to Mrs. Scott and wishing you all sorts of good luck and success, and with many thanks for the splendid service rendered me in the dinner, as in other matters, I remain, Yours truly,

Charles W. Anderson

TLS Con. 38 BTW Papers DLC.

To Samuel Laing Williams

[Tuskegee, Ala.] February 18, 1908

Confidential.

My dear Mr. Williams: Enclosed, I send you copy of a letter which I wish you would treat as confidential.

I am simply sending it to you as a sample of what I am doing constantly to help young Colored men through college. This, of course, is in the face of the charge that I try to hinder rather than to help that kind of education.

This young fellow is in the Law School of Harvard University. Yours truly,

Booker T. Washington

TLpS Con. 42 BTW Papers DLC.

To Robert J. Reyburn

[Tuskegee, Ala.] February 22, 1908

Personal.

My dear Dr. Reyburn: I am writing you about a matter, which I hope will not be displeasing to you.

As a public man, and as one deeply interested in the education and elevation of my race, I am most anxious that you stand by the President of the United States. I have known Mr. Roosevelt. I knew him before he went into his present office. I have been in close touch with him ever since and I, also, know that, taking him on the whole, there is no man who has been in the Presidency since Lincoln, who has been so deeply interested in the permanent and sensible elevation of our race. Time will show that there has been no man who has done more to help us than is true of Mr. Roosevelt. The time has come, you will agree with me, when the true friends of the race must not be led away by temporary spasms or by any attempt to secure momentary glorification or popularity, but must be guided by those who are permanent and have nothing but the highest good of the race in mind.

As a Negro, living right in the heart of the South, where the bulk of our race dwells, I am in a position to know what the President has done in the way of standing by us here, often in the face of the severest and most unreasonable criticism and condemnation. I, also, know what he has done in the way of encouraging and helping the race in the North and West, and if I did not feel that he has our best interests at heart and is doing that which will permanently help us, I should not stand by him or his policies for a minute.

It is impossible for any public man to hold such an office as he holds without now and then performing specific acts, with which we do not agree, but it is unfair to condemn unreasonably any public servant simply because he does one thing with which we do not agree and does nine things with which we do agree.

I feel all the more at liberty to write you, because my personal friend and your friend, Mr. Whitefield McKinlay, has spoken to me often concerning your high character and strong interest in our race.

There is a movement going on in most parts of the South to get up spurious delegations to attend the Chicago Convention, with the hope of defeating the policies of the President, or embarrassing him. You will be surprised to learn that some of our pretended friends in the North are now working hand in hand with the "lily white" element in the South, ready to do anything to embarrass the President. I do not believe for a minute that you will have anything to do with such company. Yours truly,

Booker T. Washington

TLpS Con. 380 BTW Papers DLC.

To Whitefield McKinlay

[Tuskegee, Ala.] February 22, 1908

Personal

My dear Mr. McKinlay: I have received your telegram regarding the Bishops. I can hardly understand how the matter got out that I had spoken to the President concerning the Bishops. I did not tell anybody in Washington except yourself. Of course I only mentioned the matter to the President because I had been requested to do so by a member of the Board of Bishops.

I have received a letter from Mr. Loeb in which he expresses some apprehension about the position of Dr. Reyburn. I hope you will keep in close touch with Dr. Reyburn and see that he stands by the President and is not led off to favor the spurious delegates which will go from the Southern states. He ought to stand by the regular organization.

It will interest you to know that many of the Lily Whites are now being taken up by the friends of Foraker.

It is absolutely necessary that all that passes between us be kept in the strictest confidence, otherwise there will be trouble and embarrassment. Yours truly,

Booker T. Washington

TLpS Con. 41 BTW Papers DLC.

To William Loeb, Jr.

[Tuskegee, Ala.] February 22, 1908

Personal and Confidential.
My dear Mr. Loeb: I telegraphed you yesterday, as follows: "Am writing today strongly as I can to Dr. Reyburn. Matters going pretty well in Alabama. Ninth district voted for the secretary this week making two districts in all."

I have written Dr. Reyburn as strongly as I could. I, also, have written Mr. Whitefield McKinlay to see him and keep in close touch with him. McKinlay has quite an influence with him.

You will be interested to know that the Constitutional League Convention and some other of Mr. Foraker's friends, are now trying to get the support of the "lily white" element in the South. They are ready to do anything to embarrass the President. They will not succeed in Alabama. Yours truly,

Booker T. Washington

TLpS Con. 7 BTW Papers DLC.

From Alphonsus Orenzo Stafford

Cheyney, Pa. Feb. 25, 1908

My dear Dr. Washington: Your favor of February 22d is at hand.

I only trust that when all the chapters are read in their entirety, in their regular order that the completed structure will be as satisfactory as the single chapters have been.

From the beginning I have been deeply sensible of the rare opportunity you have offered me and the wish to measure up to the opportunity has been my main desire in my efforts in this matter.

No authority known to me for information on the history of the Negro has been neglected. I confess that I wish the work were a hundred per cent better.

Prices for work of this kind are unknown to me and I have no standard of valuation as a guide. However, I shall make an attempt — so please don't smile or frown — when my terms are read.

Ten dollars a chapter I ask — all expenses incurred to be paid by me. At this rate you have already settled for seven chapters.

The World's Work material will be gathered and put into shape at once into one chapter. In that I shall include your "Boley, A Negro Town in the West" article from The Outlook of January 4th 1908, if you wish.

My thanks are due to you, Doctor Washington, and which I now sincerely give for your kindness and the unusual privilege this matter has offered to me to do a kind of work that appeals strongly to me and for one who could put it to the very best and most effective use. Very truly,

A. O. Stafford

ALS Con. 382 BTW Papers DLC.

From Oswald Garrison Villard

New York February 25, 1908

Dear Mr. Washington: I enclose, as you request, Mr. Taft's letter — mournfully, for it is extremely discreditable reading and confirms my own unfavorable impression of the man as a candidate. You will observe that he says that he had decided to organize a colored regiment, that is, the best interests of the military service demanded it, but then purely personal considerations kept him from doing his duty. Pray, when did the Brownsville affair take a fresh political turn? Was it not political from the start? And since when have we in our political officers an inability to do what is right and just and fair to the negro race lest they be accused of political considerations?

As a matter of fact, Mr. Taft does not meet the point that the regiments are already organized in full, and that he cannot create a negro artillery regiment without *mustering out* one of whites. On the whole I am sorry that I have seen this letter. Yours sincerely,

Oswald Garrison Villard

TLS Con. 42 BTW Papers DLC.

To Frank Harris Hitchcock[1]

Hotel Manhattan, New York City, March 1, 1908

Personal

My dear Mr. Hitchcock: Since talking to you over the telephone last night, I have decided to recommend to you the following persons for the work that we discussed:

Gov. P. B. S. Pinchback will call to see you tomorrow. The Governor is one of the few old time politicians who still retain the entire respect and confidence of the Southern colored people and who has great influence on them. The mere fact that it is known that he favors Secretary Taft will count for much. His presence in a community will always carry large weight, and I advise that he be permitted to circulate quietly through the South in the way I suggested. He has about as much influence in one state as another. He is a good "mixer," and I strongly advise that he be permitted to spend as much money as you can afford in entertaining friends where he goes.

2. Mr. S. Laing Williams, 184 Dearborn St., Chicago. Mr. Williams is a lawyer in Chicago but is well acquainted with the South, having taught school in Alabama and traveled in other sections. He is a thoroughly honest man and an admirer of Secretary Taft. He can be depended upon to do effective work. In his case it may be that you will have to pay him $125 or $150 a month as I hardly think he could afford to leave his office for less than that.

The third man is Mr. Ad Wimbs, of Greensboro, Ala. Mr. Thompson can tell you about him. He is wide-awake and an experienced man in such matters as you want attended to and is well acquainted throughout the South.

While Mr. Williams lives in Vorys' territory, I understand that you want the work done in the South and I do not suppose that would be an objection.

Since telephoning you last evening I have also reached the conclusion that Thomas J. Calloway, 1732 V St. N.W., Washington, D.C., will be a good man for the work that you have in mind, I mean the newspaper work.

I also believe that Col. Lewis will do good work in the direction you mention. While he is not as outspoken as some other parties would be, still at the same time his non-combative nature will give him certain advantages in doing just the work that you wish done. Charles Banks, of Mound Bayou, Miss., is a good man also, but none of these I have named are stronger than Pinchback or Williams. Yours truly,

[Booker T. Washington]

TLc Con. 381 BTW Papers DLC.

[1] Frank Harris Hitchcock (1869–1935), manager of William Howard Taft's campaign for the presidential nomination in 1908, was chairman of the Republican National Committee from 1908 to 1909. From 1909 to 1913 he was postmaster general, establishing postal savings banks, parcel post, and airmail service. In 1916 he managed the campaign of Charles Evans Hughes for the presidential nomination.

To Emmett Jay Scott

Hotel Manhattan, New York March 2, 1908

Dear Mr. Scott: Mr. Baker was kind enough to let me see the proof of the article[1] which he has written concerning Du Bois and myself. I have read it very carefully. It is a fine article, clear and clean-cut, and I am satisfied with his treatment of the subject. He certainly has a way of getting at the truth. When Du Bois, Trotter and his crowd read what Baker has written I think they will squirm.

I wish you would let Dr. Park read this. Yours truly,

[Booker T. Washington]

The gist of the matter is to the effect that all the Negroes in the South are with me, that the masses are with me in the North and only the "intellectuals" in the North are against me.

TL Con. 582 BTW Papers DLC. Postscript in BTW's hand.

[1] Ray Stannard Baker, "An Ostracized Race in Ferment: Story of the Conflict of Negro Parties and Negro Leaders over Methods of Dealing with Their Own Problems," *American Magazine*, 66 (May 1908), 60–70. Baker described BTW as the undisputed leader of the black masses both in the North and in the South and one of the greatest men in the country. Du Bois, on the other hand, was not a leader of men, according to Baker. He characterized Du Bois as a promulgator of ideas, a lonely critic upholding lofty goals. Where BTW sought to cultivate friendship between the races, Du Bois remained aloof from whites, Baker wrote.

To Sandy W. Trice

New York March 2, 1908

Personal and Confidential

My dear Mr. Trice: I thank you so very much for your kind letter of February 24th. I appreciate it all, I assure you.

As I said to you when I saw you, the party[1] that you write about is wholly dependent upon the position which he now holds. I happen to have inside information to the effect that he was to the point of nearly starving when you gave him something to do.

I feel quite sure that the individual[2] whom I wrote you about will either send for you soon or have some important person see you. Just now he is much occupied in Ohio, but will have time to attend to matters after this week.

I shall hope to keep in close touch with you. Yours truly,

[Booker T. Washington]

TLc Con. 383 BTW Papers DLC.

1 Jesse Max Barber.

2 Either S. Laing Williams or Ralph Waldo Tyler, both of whom saw Trice during March.

From Emmett Jay Scott

Tuskegee [Ala.]: March 6/08

Dear Mr. Washington: The chief complaints against Secretary Taft as expressed in the Negro newspapers are:

1. That he Endorses the Disfranchisment Laws of the South & refer to his Tuskegee and Greensboro and Kansas City speeches in proof thereof: also that he is opposed to colored republicans having any part in party politics:

2. That he first held up the President's order as to the Dismissal of the Colored Soldiers and then put the order in to effect, & followed it up with an arraignment of the soldiers more bitter even than the President's arraignment of them:

Of course the Secretary will not discuss this second complaint (in re Brownsville) in any way but I am sure he can make very clear the fact that he favors (as he does) the highest citizenship of the Negro, & is not in favor of his disfranchisement *as a Negro*: in fact he calls for the equal treatment of the illiterate & property-less classes, but he can put in clearer language just what he does stand for: I wish the Secretary might emphasize as he did in his letter to the Cleveland Journal the faith he has in the capacity of the race: and also the position which his father & his family have taken in the past with regard to the freedom & elevation of the Negro. If he would also call attention to the high class of Negroes who have had recognition from the President — Anderson, Lewis, Cohen, Rucker & others — I am sure it w'd not be a bad thing to do: Yours very truly

Emmett J. Scott

ALS Con. 261 BTW Papers DLC.

Emmett Jay Scott to Joseph Oswalt Thompson

[Tuskegee, Ala.] March 7, 1908

Dear Mr. Thompson: I hand you herewith code to be used in telegraphing the Doctor at any time. If any of these names are to be referred to, you will use the code name instead of the person's proper name and, if you sign the code name to the telegram, we will at all times understand who the telegram is from. In the same way, if we wire you referring to any of these persons and using the code name, you will know to whom reference is made, and also you will know from whom the telegram is. It seems desirable to have such a code, so as to save having to expose in telegrams just exactly whom you may be referring to. The Doctor will have a copy of this code, I will have a copy, and you will have a copy, and in that way, it will always be easy for us to communicate. Yours truly,

E J Scott

[*Enclosure*]

Telegraphic and writing Code:

Proper Name:		Code Name:
J. O. Thompson	—	Freeman
F. H. Hitchcock	—	Remorse

William Loeb	–	Saturday
The President	–	Claudius
A. I. Vorys	–	Brutus
Charles W. Anderson	–	March
Emmett J. Scott	–	Harris
Booker T. Washington	–	F. B.

TLpS Con. 382 BTW Papers DLC.

To Alphonsus Orenzo Stafford

New York March 9, 1908

My dear Mr. Stafford: Enclosed please find $120 which, according to your suggestion, settles the bill for your work. I wish to assure you that your charge is entirely satisfactory and reasonable. I wish it were within my power to be even more generous with you for your satisfactory work.

I have made this settlement on the basis of 19 chapters. Am I right in this regard? If not, please let me know and I will settle the difference. Yours truly,

[Booker T. Washington]

TLc Con. 382 BTW Papers DLC.

To Theodore Roosevelt

Hotel Manhattan, New York March 9, 1908

My dear Mr. President: It is very important, in my opinion, that every influence possible be used by you to see that the leaders of the Republican party in North Carolina and Virginia especially, have a fair proportion of colored men in the state and district conventions & delegates to Chicago. I understand on pretty good authority there was not a single colored man present at the last state convention in North Carolina. You can easily see that if this occurs again it will be used with tremendous effect against Secretary Taft in

Chicago; and not only there, but will hurt very much in the effort to elect Secretary Taft after he is nominated. Already those opposing Secretary Taft are using the fact with effect among the colored people that the Republican party is composed wholly of white people in North Carolina and Virginia and that the Negro is ignored.

I am planning to be in Washington on the 19th and shall hope to see you. Yours truly,

[Booker T. Washington]

TLc Con. 7 BTW Papers DLC.

To Robert Ezra Park

Hotel Manhattan, New York March 9, 1908

My dear Dr. Park: I am working from time to time on The Story of the Negro. The publishers are becoming impatient. We shall have to begin definite work at once. I see nothing to do but for me to send you the matter just as I write it. You can take it and enlarge upon it wherever you see fit or change it in any manner that you deem wise, and also placing it in the form of chapters. The first batch of material I shall send you will be, I am sure, rather trying for you to put in shape, but as soon as I get started out, as it were, it will come to you in better shape. I hope you will make your plans so as to give as much time to it as possible. Yours truly,

[Booker T. Washington]

TLc Con. 249 BTW Papers DLC.

To William Howard Taft

Hotel Manhattan, New York March 9, 1908

My dear Secretary Taft: I told you I would write you regarding the address which you are to deliver at the Hampton Institute meeting in Brooklyn on the evening of March 16th.

Of course, in an address at an educational meeting such as this is to be, you will perhaps not consider it advisable to touch upon several points that at another kind of meeting you might touch upon. My general idea is that more will be gained by your taking a strong affirmative position on matters relating to the education and general progress of the race rather than by attempting to combat directly the charges which the enemy bring against you. I believe much in the scriptural injunction, "Overcome evil with good."

In the first place, I think that you would do well to enlarge mainly upon the points brought out in your letter to the Cleveland colored paper, that is, touching upon the interest of yourself and family in the Negro.

Second. I think it well to make clear that you take the position, as you did at Tuskegee, that wherever any restriction is put upon the use of the ballot that such restriction ought to apply with equal certainty to the whites as well as to the Negro voter and that it is unfair and unjust to place a burden upon one race that is not shared by the other race. The Negro does not oppose an educational and property test for voting, but he does ask that in the making of the law and in its administration that no loophole be left by which he is treated unjustly.

Third. I think you could well call attention to the immense material, educational, moral and religious progress made by the race since it has been free.

Fourth. If you deem it advisable at such a meeting, it might help to call attention to the high class of colored men that the present administration has put into office.

Fifth. I think also it will be well for you to call attention to your interest in and work for the dark races in the Philippine Islands and elsewhere.

By this mail I am sending you some publications from the Hampton Institute that will give some definite facts regarding the work of that school. I am also sending you a book recently published by me called "The Negro in Business." You will find some facts in it that I thought you might like to refer to. I have noted the places in the latter part of the book.

If you are going to prepare this address in advance, I wish very much I might see a copy of it, if convenient, before it goes out to the press.

This will be my address until the 16th. Yours truly,

[Booker T. Washington]

TLc Con. 6 BTW Papers DLC.

From Samuel Laing Williams

Chicago 3/10/08

Dear Mr. Washington: I have received several notes from you, but have not answered any of them knowing that you were busy in the extreme in your strenuous efforts, at this time, in behalf of the school.

Your letter to Dr. Hall was very apt in every way. I have seen them both several times, but they have not mentioned the matter further.[1]

Barber is no longer editor of the Chicago Conservator. Trice asked for his resignation. He threatens to take the public into his confidence and tell why he was "forced out" – intimating that it was due to pressure from the outside. He has sued the Conservator for $500. alleging "breach of contract." I saw Trice this morning and he says he has a good defense.

Referring to the Amanda Smith matter,[2] an architect friendly to the old lady is working on some plans and specifications for a new Dormitory. In her letter to Mrs. Smith, Mrs. Emery expressed a desire to see the plans. I want to ask you, if we shall send them together with a letter of explanation, to Mrs. Emery, or would you prefer to look them over and send them yourself to her. Please let me hear from you in this matter as soon as you can conveniently.

Referring to the possibility of my going South to do some work [for] Taft, I hope to be able to go, if I can be of any service. Very truly yours,

S Laing Williams

P.S. I was talking to Barber to-day and drew out of him how he felt concerning his upset with the Conservator. I did this because it has been intimated that he blames you for his summary dismissal. I learn that he does blame you for his present predicament. The fact that the Conservator did not print the report of the Tuskegee Conference is, in his opinion, the cause for his being let out. I don't know [how] far Trice is to blame for giving Barber a chance to feel sore and to blame you. Trice probably, was not so tactful as he ought to have been.

I protested to Barber that he was going a long way about to connect you with the matter of his separation from the paper, but he insists that "you have been pursuing him for several years trying to make it impossible for him to succeed in any thing, etc."

I am not sure that it is the right thing to write you all this stuff, but I thought perhaps you ought to know just what is being said. Again, I am Very sincerely yours.

S L W

TLS Con. 42 BTW Papers DLC.

[1] George C. Hall was miffed that D. H. Williams rather than he was chosen to perform E. J. Scott's appendix operation. Hall also complained that John A. Kenney, the school physician, extravagantly praised his rival, Williams, in a signed article in the *Tuskegee Student* (19 [July 20, 1907], 1), after a three-week visit with Williams in Chicago. (Scott to BTW, Mar. 10, 1908, Con. 582, BTW Papers, DLC.) The bitter rivalry continued for years. Hall eventually became BTW's personal physician.

[2] The Amanda Smith School for Negro Girls in Harvey, Ill., about twenty miles south of Chicago.

From Sandy W. Trice

Chicago, Ill., March 12, 1908

Personal and Confidential.

Dear Sir: This will inform you that I have made a change in the editors of the Conservator and in doing so I have been made a defendant in a suit for $1000.00 five hundred against the company and five hundred against me personally and in order to defend myself and the company I have had to employ a high class lawyer in the person of Patrick H. O'Donnell. This is a move I am sure on the part of the Niagara Movement people to get the paper which they have been after for some time, and now to make a long story short I want to tell you that in order to maintain the stand that I have taken I must have some immediate financial assistance as I have a hard fight on my hands.

The gentleman that you spoke with me about called on me and we have things arranged satisfactory but that does not relieve my immediate needs, so I appeal to you to help me out of this difficulty, if you can possibly do so, so that nothing will hinder the progress of the paper during the period of litigation. The paper has been in bad circumstances for some time, Wilkins left it in very bad circumstances. Now, I ask you this providing you can consistently do so, I hope you can see your way clear in the matter.

The Local Business League meets this evening and we are going to discuss and formulate plans for a Negro Bank in this city. The subjects that you sent us will be used.

Mr. A. W. Washington, a man that has been with the Conservator for more than two years, and a man that I can trust will have charge of the paper for the time being.

Wishing an immediate reply, I remain Yours very truly,

Sandy W. Trice

TLS Con. 383 BTW Papers DLC.

From Emmett Jay Scott

Tuskegee Ala Mch 12 190[8]

See Code. Alexander[1] reached home last night, says mission entirely satisfactory. Saw Remorse[2] Claudius[3] and Saturday[4].

Also taft. Each expressed himself as being entirely satisfied. They say they will not need party opposing freeman[5] at all. Alexander will write.

E J Scott

HWSr Con. 582 BTW Papers DLC.

1 Nathan H. Alexander.
2 F. H. Hitchcock.
3 Theodore Roosevelt.
4 William Loeb.
5 J. O. Thompson.

An Article in *Outlook*

Tuskegee Institute, Alabama [Mar. 14, 1908]

Prohibition and the Negro

What are the results of two months of prohibition in two large Southern cities, Atlanta, Georgia, and Birmingham, Alabama? The answer to this question contains some very interesting facts. It will be recalled that on the first of January of this year all the bar-rooms in Atlanta, Georgia, and throughout the state for that matter, and all the bar-rooms in the city of Birmingham, Alabama, were closed. Of course two months is too short a time in which to draw definite and permanent conclusions, but nevertheless this period emphasizes some valuable lessons.

I have read much in the Northern papers about the prohibition movement in the South being based wholly upon a determination or desire to keep liquor away from the negroes and at the same time provide a way for the white people to get it. I have watched the prohibition movement carefully from its inception to the present time, and I have seen nothing in the agitation in favor of the movement, nothing in the law itself, and nothing in the execution of the law that warrants any such conclusion. The prohibition movement is based upon a deep-seated desire to get ride of whisky in the interest of both races because of its hurtful economic and moral results. The prohibition sentiment is as strong in counties where there are practically no colored people as in the Black Belt counties.

If I mention these facts here, by way of introduction to what I have to say in regard to the results of prohibition where I have been able to observe them, namely, two typical Southern cities, Birmingham and Atlanta, it is because I want to emphasize the fact that the contrary is true: prohibition in the South is essentially a moral movement, the first effect of which has been a remarkable reduction in crime. Putting it roundly, according to the reports of the police magistrates, prohibition has reduced the amount of crime in Birmingham one-third and in Atlanta one-half, since January 1, when the law went into force.

The significance of these facts will be appreciated when you consider the extraordinary number of people who are arrested and sent to the mines and penitentiaries every year by the criminal courts of these two cities. During the year 1907 the police of Atlanta, according to a report in the Atlanta Constitution of January 1, made 24,332 arrests. This means that during the year, on an average, one person out of every six in the city of Atlanta was arrested. And this number has been increasing. There were 2,630 more persons arrested in 1907 than in 1906. This is an increase of considerably more than twelve per cent in one year.

Of course this does not mean that one person in every six in Atlanta is a criminal, because a good many persons represented in these statistics were arrested several times during the year, and a good many others were arrested but not convicted. Putting the best construction upon the facts, however, they indicate an abnormal drain upon the ranks of the peaceful and law-abiding people of the city into the classes that fill the penitentiaries and supply recruits to the chain-gangs, which are already doing too large a portion of the work of the State. It should be taken into account also that, under present conditions, Southern prisons are conducted too largely for the purpose of punishing men rather than reforming them, and they are therefore constantly discharging back into the ranks of the industrious and law-abiding populations a stream of hardened and embittered men and women, which in turn pollutes the masses of the people with which it mingles.

Prohibition has attacked this evil at its source, and the results which the enforcement of this law brought about serve to indicate to what extent evils that the South has accepted as human and inevitable can be modified and cured, if proper measures are taken and these measures are backed by the will of the people.

In his report to the Mayor at the end of the first month of prohibition, Judge N. B. Feagin,[1] of Birmingham, makes the following statement:

"The decrease in arrests average about as follows, in comparing January, 1908, under prohibition with January, 1907, with saloons: Aggregate arrests, decrease 33⅓ per cent; for assault with intent to murder, 22 per cent; gambling, 17 per cent; drunkenness, 80 per cent; disorderly conduct, 35 per cent; burglary and grand larceny, 33 per cent; vagrancy, 40 per cent; wife beating, 70 per cent."

There were 33 arrests for drunkenness in January, 1908, as

against 174 for the same month of 1907. There were 56 arrests for disorderly conduct in January, 1908, as against 90 for the same month of 1907.

Several times during the past eight weeks there has not been a single prisoner before the Recorder's Court at Atlanta charged with drunkenness. The first instance of this kind was January 4, when there were but 17 cases on the docket; nine of these were cases of children. On the same day a year before 63 cases were tried in that court, of which 32 were for drunkenness and 28 for disorderly conduct. Wednesday, January 29, at the session of what was called by the local papers "the smallest police court ever held," there was only one prisoner at the morning session. It was about this time that the newspapers recorded another extraordinary event in the history of the city. For the first time in many years, the jail was for several days empty.

The records of arrests for the month of January show a more extraordinary decrease in Atlanta than in Birmingham. For the month of January, 1907, 1,653 cases were put on the docket of the Recorder's Court in Atlanta. During the month of January, 1908, on the other hand, there were but 768 cases on the docket, a decrease of considerably more than 50 per cent. During January, 1907, there were 341 cases of drunkenness tried, but in 1908 only 64, a decrease of more than 80 per cent.

The Justices of the Peace, before whom warrants in minor criminal cases are issued, report a similar falling off. Three classes of warrants ordinarily taken out by negroes and the poorer classes of whites show, according to reports in the newspapers, a falling off equal to that of the Recorder's Court. These are the warrants charging abandonment of minor children, dispossessory warrants — taken against people unable to pay their rents — and warrants charging various kinds of larceny. A good many of these cases grow out of family quarrels, and serve as a sort of barometer of the condition among the poorer classes in the city. These evidences indicate that the closing of the saloons and the breeding-places of crimes and disorders has brought a remarkable change into the homes of the poor, where, finally, the effects of crime and disorder are always most keenly felt.

Commenting on the situation as it is in Atlanta and Birmingham, the Birmingham News says: "For ten years Birmingham has not enjoyed so orderly a period as it has since the 1st of January. The moral improvement in the city has been marked since prohibition went into effect. The newspapers are no longer giving space to reports of murders, shooting and cutting scrapes, personal altercations and other disorders, as they formerly did, for the reason that the regard for law and order in this community is very much more in evidence since the removal of the whisky traffic."

In Birmingham the demand for reform has not stopped with the closing of the saloons. Since January 1, seventeen gambling-houses, many of which had been running for years in a more or less public way, have been closed. A Law and Order League has been formed, and vigorous measures are being taken throughout Jefferson County to do away with the "blind tigers" and to suppress the vices that have centered about and in these moral cesspools.

The interesting thing about the prohibition movement in the South is that it goes out from and is supported by the churches. The campaign in Jefferson County, Alabama, which changed Birmingham from wet to dry began, as I have been informed, in a ministers' meeting. The superintendent of the Anti-Saloon League in Alabama, Mr. Brooks Lawrence, is a minister and a Northerner. One of the charges brought against him during the campaign was that he was a carpetbagger, and that the prohibition movement was an attempt "to dump Northern ideas" upon the South, where they did not fit conditions.

It was predicted that prohibition would demoralize business. In Birmingham alone one hundred and twenty-eight saloons, fourteen wholesale liquor stores, and two breweries were closed as a result of the law. But the predictions do not seem to have been fulfilled. It has recently been announced that a fourteen-story building was to be erected on the site of one of the oldest saloons in Birmingham; and Atlanta is preparing to pave and improve the notorious Decatur Street on which the larger part of the dives of the city were located. It is promised that it will soon become one of the best streets in the city.

Prohibition has been the popular issue, and it has the South behind it. Many of those, I am informed, who voted for prohibition were men who themselves belonged to the class that has supported the saloon. On the other hand, many of those who opposed prohibition were men who rarely, if ever, entered a bar-room.

Directly and indirectly, the members of my own race have suffered, perhaps more than any other portion of the population, from the effects of the liquor traffic. But the educated men and the leaders of the race have been quick to see the advantages that would come from the total suppression of the saloon. Everywhere in the South this class have given their votes to the support of prohibition even where it brought them in opposition to the men whom they have been disposed to regard as their friends, in the support of those whom they have been accustomed to regard as their enemies. In Birmingham the negroes formed an organization, and cast nearly all of the registered colored vote for prohibition.

Prohibition in the South is to a certain extent a women's movement. In the campaign in Alabama it was the women, the mothers and the wives and the children of the men who supported the saloon with their earnings, who marched in the processions, and stood all day at the polls to see that their husbands, sons, and fathers voted "right."

No one who is at all acquainted with the conditions in the South can doubt the depth and the genuineness of the feelings that are behind prohibition in the South, which is in no way a political maneuver, but an inspired movement of the masses of the people. Its great importance, it seems to me, consists in the fact that it is bringing the ordinary conservative elements in the community, the women, the ministers, and the people in the churches, into close and intimate contact with actual conditions and with the real problems of the South. It is at the same time, if I may say so, an intellectual awakening and a moral revolution.

Outlook, 88 (Mar. 14, 1908), 587–89. Reprinted in the *Tuskegee Student*, 20 (Mar. 21, 1908), 1–3.

[1] Noah Baxter Feagin (b. 1843), a Birmingham criminal court judge from 1895 to 1910. Feagin introduced juvenile courts and other court reforms during his tenure on the bench.

To James Hardy Dillard

Hotel Manhattan, New York, March 16, 1908

My dear Dr. Dillard: I am writing to make a mere suggestion which may or may not have any value in it. You can think it over.

Would it not be a wise plan to try the experiment of spending some money in a few counties in paying the salary of a county superintendent with the understanding that he [is] to actually visit and try to help the Negro schools in his county. Two results might follow; one, that he might prove of some actual service, the other, that he might become so interested that he would use his influence in seeing that the Negro schools were treated justly.

I go to Tuskegee this week. Yours truly,

[Booker T. Washington]

TLc Con. 40 BTW Papers DLC.

From Pinckney Benton Stewart Pinchback

Orangeburg S.C. Mch 17, 08

My Dear Doctor: Have been to Columbia to attend Com'ee Meeting. Quite harmonious. Capers assured me he was glad I came; that my presence helped. I am sure of it. Well, from all I can learn the situation is improved.

Taft will have 3 delegates from state at large. Viz: Capers Blaylock[1] and Grant, and about 9 or 10 from the Districts.

Quite sure I have done much good here. Full report to Mr. H. by the same mail as this.

Am quite under the weather with cold and hoarseness. May have to remain here a couple of days to recuperate. Will go direct from here to Atlanta. I will be in and about Atlanta several days. Would like to have a line from you if convenient.

Have requested Mr. H. to write me there. Yours very truly

Pinchback

ALS Con. 379 BTW Papers DLC.

1 Loomis Blalock.

To Frederick Randolph Moore

[Tuskegee, Ala.] March 21, 1908

My dear Mr. Moore: Last week's paper on the whole was very good, but I wish to submit herewith certain criticisms for your guidance in the future. All these matters, it seems to me, deserve attention.

For instance, on the front page you say in the second line that Secretary Taft got a rousing reception "last night," when you really mean to say Monday night of this week. My opinion is that his address should have been briefed to about one-third the space taken up, and I am further of the opinion that instead of the few lines of introduction that the whole address should have been treated from the point of its significance, that is, much should have been made of the event itself, of the persons who were present, of how the address was received by the public and of much else of that kind of feature work which, while calling for a little energy on somebody's part, would have made the whole thing more interesting.

While all of the address in the main is very good, at the same time it occurs to me that there are parts of it which have already been widely published and which take up space which should not have been taken up. I am also of the opinion that this address should have been carried only two or three columns on the front page and whatever additional over on the inside pages.

In the editorial which you carry, you say in one place "they met with these recalcitrant preachers constantly while they were HERE." Now, as a matter of fact, the Age is published in New York and the meeting was held in Washington, and so any clear minded man can easily see that the editorial was written in Washington instead of in New York. These kind[s] of things reflect on the discrimination of those in charge of the paper, and I am sure that you can easily see that you play into the hands of the enemy.

Mr. Henderson's article bears no date nor post office address, and it is hard to tell from where he is writing you. It seems to me that his address should be at the top or bottom of his article.

I cannot help but feel that a whole page devoted to theatricals is too much for a costly paper like the Age. I am sure that three columns, or four at the most, would be a plenty. If you should cast up accounts I am sure you will find that the results from this source are not going to be great. I think it is a good feature of the paper, but I am sure it is now being over-played.

In connection with the notes which come to you from various cities, I want to suggest that the Cleveland Journal handles these items in a rather admirable way in that they run two or three stars between each item. If you will see the paper of March 14th you will get some idea as to what I have in mind.

Further, with reference to this week's paper, I advised you that I thought it hardly necessary to run my address, but I notice that you did so. I do not think that the readers of the paper should be made to feel that matter will be simply dumped in to fill space. Everything that goes into the paper should have a straight significance, and this significance should be easily seen by every reader of the paper. The present jumble, to my mind, does not make the paper look as satisfactory as I think it should look.

I make note of the fact that you are having our friend to write editorials for you. Now the point which I have had in mind to suggest is that the paper does not need so much to have one write for it as it does need to have some one go critically through the matter each week and wield it into a somewhat satisfactory shape. The very things which I call attention to this week come under the head of what an editor should really do. I have asked Mr. Scott to mark some of the things to which I have called attention and I send the paper along with this letter. Of course, I know that you are working to make the paper in every way a decent publication, but these things deserve attention. Yours truly,

Booker T. Washington

TLpS Con. 261 BTW Papers DLC.

To Ralph Waldo Tyler

[Tuskegee, Ala.] March 21, 1908

Personal

Better get in close and immediate touch with Trice. Plans may be thwarted and enemy get charge of paper unless you keep in close touch. May have to render little extra help.

B. T. W.

TWIr Con. 8 BTW Papers DLC.

To Theodore Roosevelt

[Tuskegee, Ala.] March 21, 1908

My dear Mr. President: There are two matters in which I think you can do a great deal, within the near future, to change the attitude of many Colored people and to put a few of the loud talking enemies into an awkward position and, at the same time, accomplish a great deal of good.

I refer, first, to the matter of the Liberian Commission, which is coming to this country on an official visit soon, as I understand. The second is the matter of the separate coach law. I shall write you regarding this latter subject on Monday.

As I understand it, the Liberian Commission is coming here to see you in reference to the encroachments of foreign governments upon Liberian soil. I do not know, of course, what the custom of the State Department is regarding such matters, but I am wondering if in some way some special attention cannot be shown to this Commission. This is the first time that any such Commission, composed of Negroes, has visited this country and I am most anxious that they be treated with just as much courtesy as the customs of the United States will allow; even if an exception has to be made, I think it will be a fine thing.

I understand, of course, the delicacy of handling the situation. I am already planning, in connection with others, to pay this Commission a good deal of attention. I am hoping, among other things, to have them visit Tuskegee and shall be willing to bear a good part of the expense of their entertainment, personally, if necessary.

If I can serve you in any manner in carrying out the wishes of yourself or the State Department, please be good enough to command me.

Whatever is done, or is not done, will attract a good deal of attention and result in wide comment among the Colored people. Yours truly,

Booker T. Washington

TLpS Con. 7 BTW Papers DLC.

To Ulysses Grant Mason[1]

[Tuskegee, Ala.] March 23, 1908

Personal and Confidential.
Dear Dr. Mason: I am writing you about a very confidential matter but at the same time, one in which I think you will agree with me, that both of us are deeply concerned. In doing whatever you deem fitting in regard to it, I hope you will not use my name. I need not tell you who the "lily white" party in Alabama is and what they stand for. You know their disgraceful actions toward our people a few years ago in Birmingham. This party is now seeking to secure power and recognition again in Alabama. If it does, it will throw the Negro over-board the same as it did when it got temporary control a few years ago.

My special point now, is to urge you to see all the individuals of our race over whom you have any influence, in any conventions, either county, congressional or state. A good personal talk with the individuals will help. Yours truly,

Booker T. Washington

P. S. I send you herewith a list of names of individuals who have been suggested to me as persons who perhaps are on the other side, among whom you may be able to do a little "missionary" work.

TLpS Con. 7 BTW Papers DLC.

[1] Ulysses Grant Mason (b. 1872), a prominent black surgeon in Birmingham, was vice-president of the Alabama Penny Savings Bank from 1897 to 1908, organized the Prudential Savings Bank in 1910, and served as a trustee of Central Alabama College. Mason was a delegate-at-large to the Republican national conventions of 1908 and 1912.

To Theodore Roosevelt

[Tuskegee, Ala.] March 23, 1908

Personal
My dear Mr. President: I am very anxious that if anything is done regarding the improving of the railroad accommodations for colored people in the South, that the first public utterance bearing

upon it initiate with you rather than with the Inter-State Commerce Commission. Perhaps a letter from you to the Inter-State Commerce Commission might accomplish the purpose that I have in mind.

In case you write such a letter, I think it well for you to keep in mind the following points:

First, the colored people as a whole are opposed to the principle of separation, and it would be unfortunate for you to say anything that would seem to endorse the principle of separation. Since separation has been provided for in all of the Southern states, you could insist that the accommodations be equal in convenience and in comfort for the same money.

Enclosed I send you an exact extract covering the Alabama Law. It is practically the same in all of the Southern states.

As I stated, I think the safest course for you to pursue would be to emphasize the fact that where separation is made that the colored people receive the same treatment for the same money that the white people do. The principal grounds of complaint at present among the colored people are as follows:

The cars are often filthy. The compartments for colored people are not only filthy, but are in many cases too small, lacking in proper ventilation. The news boy takes up a large portion of the space with his goods. In many cases all the colored people, including women and children, are required to pass through the white men's smoking compartment in order to get into the part of the coach reserved for colored people. In many cases no smoking room whatever is provided for colored men. In most cases the waiting rooms provided for colored people are filthy and not given anything the same kind of attention that is given those provided for white people. Yours very truly,

Booker T. Washington

In case you prepare anything on the subject, I wish very much I might have the privilege of looking it over before giving it out if it is at all practicable.

B. T. W.

TLpS Con. 7 BTW Papers DLC.

To Josiah Thomas Settle

[Tuskegee, Ala.] March 23, 1908

My dear Mr. Settle: As you perhaps know the Southern Education Conference meets in Memphis the month of April. This is an important gathering bringing together not only Southern educators but Northern educators.

I want to suggest as strongly as I can that a committee be appointed from among the colored people whose duty it will be to get hold of especially the Northern people and take them around to the business enterprises as well as the schools and colleges for our people in that city. In many cases when Northern white people go to Southern cities they are shown only the worst side of Negro life and the best side of white life. This comes about largely by the fact that our people do not get hold of these visitors and take them to places where they can see the most encouraging features of our life. I urge that you take this matter up at once. Yours very truly,

Booker T. Washington

TLpS Con. 381 BTW Papers DLC.

To Sandy W. Trice

[Tuskegee, Ala.] March 24, 1908

Personal.

My dear Mr. Trice: On my return to Tuskegee Institute I find your kind letter of March 12. I hope that you will be able to get matters in very satisfactory shape. I have already wired to party[1] who saw you last, and asked him to see what he could do for you. I very much hope that something very satisfactory will come out of it. I do not think that you need have any fears at all with reference to the suit about which you write me. Yours truly,

Booker T. Washington

TLpS Con. 383 BTW Papers DLC.

[1] Ralph Waldo Tyler.

From William Vivian Chambliss

Tuskegee, Ala., Mar. 26th 1908

Dear Sir: I am sending you a list of the persons whom I think all are registered voters, and there may be others out there. On the 1st Saturday in April (4th day) as Chairman of the Republican Ex. Committee I have call[ed] a mass meeting to be held in Tuskegee, to elect Chairman, Committeeman, delegates to the District and State Conventions, and transact such other business as may come before the meeting. We can not hold a meeting unless we have persons who are registered voters. To make a creditable show as a party I insist on these persons attending and participating in the meeting. I'd thank you very much, in any way, to notify and impress upon those persons who are quallified voters to attend this meeting. I'm sending out printed notices to the different beats of the County. Yours truly,

W. V. Chambliss

[*Enclosure*]

Registered Voters:

Prof. Logan
Mr J B Washington
" M D. Garner
" Wm. Gregory
" J C Green
" Chas H. Gibson
" Chas Evans
" E. J. Scott
" E. H. Gamlin
" Thos. A. Harris
" J. N. Calloway
" C. J. Calloway
Capt Seals
Mr. C. W. Greene
Prof Geo. W. Carver
Mr. L. G. Wheeler
Mr. E. A. Atwell[1]
" C. R. Bridgeforth[2]
Rev. J. W. Whittaker
Mr. Lafayette Moore
" B. C. Stevens[3]
" H. E. Thomas
" J. A. Bynes[4]
" T. J. Murr[a]y[5]
" J. M. Flournoy
Mr. Diggs
Maj. J. B. Ramsey
Capt Austin
Prof R. R. Taylor
Capt Richardson
Mr. M. B. Lacy
" W. J. Carter[6]

" J. H. Washington
" Cum[m]ings[7]
Dr. J. A. Kinney[8]
Mr Chas Kelley
" Thos Campbell

ALS Con. 367 BTW Papers DLC.

[1] Ernest Ten Eyck Attwell.
[2] George Ruffin Bridgeforth.
[3] M. B. Stevens.
[4] John A. Bynes taught founding at Tuskegee Institute beginning in 1906.
[5] Thomas J. Murray, nephew of Margaret M. Washington, was cashier of the Tuskegee Institute savings bank.
[6] William H. Carter.
[7] Edward W. Cummings taught blacksmithing at Tuskegee Institute.
[8] John A. Kenney.

To Theodore Roosevelt

[Tuskegee, Ala.] March 28, 1908

Personal

My dear Mr. President: I thank you very much for letting me see the draft of your letter to the Interstate Commerce Commission.[1] Enclosed I am returning the draft to you just as you sent it, also another copy with some suggestions which I have underscored in red ink. If in some way you could bring out the fact that you want to be just as careful in seeing that justice is done in regard to human beings as in the matter of freight, it would be a strong point, I think. I attach herewith two paragraphs which may convey the sense of what I am trying to say.[2] I am not sure that I express the thought very clearly, but I think it might be well if the suggested paragraph could be used in some way. Several of the roads in the South really strive to do justice to the colored people, and I note that you give them credit for doing so, but this sentence appears at the bottom of your letter and there is opportunity for the newspapers to leave this sentence off if they desire. Could it not be woven in in some way into the body of the letter so that it could not be left out? Yours truly,

Booker T. Washington

I think your letter to the Interstate Commerce Commission is an admirable one from every point of view.

B. T. W.

TLpS Con. 7 BTW Papers DLC.

[1] On the issue of segregated railroad accommodations Roosevelt wrote to the Interstate Commerce Commission: "I entirely agree with the action of your Commission in insisting that the accommodations be equal in convenience and comfort, for the same money, wherever separation is made." He urged the ICC to investigate unfair practices, lack of equal accommodations, and filthy conditions in black cars and waitings rooms. (Mar. 25, 1908, Copy, Con. 7, BTW Papers, DLC.)

[2] BTW wrote: "We have been seeking to see that there is no discrimination in the transportation of freight from one state to another; we should be even more careful to see that there is no discrimination in the matter of conveying human beings from one state to another.

"We should be just as careful to see that there is no discrimination in transportation of human beings from one state to another as we are in seeing that there is no discrimination in freight rates." (Con. 7, BTW Papers, DLC.)

A Sunday Evening Talk

[Tuskegee, Ala.] March 29, 1908

ON NOT BEING EASILY SATISFIED

No one can pass along through the Southern part of our country, whether on the railroad trains or on the public roads, without getting the idea pretty firmly fixed in his mind that the average person, who lives in this part of the country, is pretty well satisfied with his lot — is easily satisfied; that it does not take much to satisfy all of his wants.

Education should tend to make people industrious, to make them love labor — to make them love it so much that they will be willing to and anxious to work five and six days out of each week. The only way to get persons to work more than two or three days in each week is to increase their wants. Go into any country among people without education and you will find, that as a rule, they work only two or three days, at most, out of each week. This is true in many parts of Africa, in many parts of Mexico, and all through the South American countries. The fundamental difference is, that these people have never had their minds awakened: their ambitions have not been quickened. They have few wants, and those few can be satisfied by working two or three days out of six days; and when they have satisfied all of the few wants they know anything about, they wonder, what is the use of working any more, and that is not very unnatural.

Tuskegee and other educational institutions should seek among other things, to increase the wants of the people. This institution will have accomplished a great deal of good for the uplift of this part of our country, especially, if through the influence of the hundreds of men and women who go out from here each year, we can multiply the wants of the population where their influence touches. If you can multiply these wants, so that our people will have the reputation of being everywhere an industrious people, a people who are ready, anxious and willing to work five or six days out of seven days, we shall be fulfilling our mission.

Let me be more specific in my suggestions: One way to increase the wants of the people is to teach them not to be satisfied with so little. At present, they are too easily satisfied. You pass by on the railroads and you can see any number of houses with no paint anywhere on the outside, or on the inside; no paint or whitewash on the fence or on the palings — nothing indicating that there is any such thing in existence as whitewash or paint. This picture is not new to you. The question I wish to put to you is, is your education here going to make you dissatisfied with such a condition of things, so that you will go back to your homes and see to it that, among the first influences you exercise, in your community, is to see that there is some whitewash and paint put upon the fence about you? See to it that there is a new condition of things and that you use your influence to make our people dissatisfied with their present condition.

We want to make our people dissatisfied with the size of the houses in which most of them live. You know it is common for our people to live in one and two rooms, where there should be at least three or four, or in some cases five rooms. Our people are too easily satisfied in the matter of their dwellings. We want to wake them up in all these respects — get them dissatisfied, increase their wants; we want you to go out from here carrying an influence that will mean the civilization and redemption of our people in the highest sense.

Our people are too easily satisfied in the matter of the amount of land they own. They will get a little piece of land, a little patch, and they will work it year after year in a certain old way, planting a little cotton on it, and coming out in debt at the end of the year; beginning again in September, in January or February, planting again the same amount of cotton, working in the same old way, and coming out in debt again in the fall, satisfied with the same old condition of affairs from year to year.

Education means that we should wake our people up and get them dissatisfied with the old condition of things. Help to get them to get to the point where they will want more land — better land — where they will be continually seeking through conversation, through hearing lectures, through reading newspapers, through reading magazines and books, continually striving to find better methods of cultivating the land, continually striving to find something different to grow upon the soil. We want to get them to the point where they will be dissatisfied in all respects, where they will crave newer, more inspiring and encouraging conditions.

We want not only to have these outside appearances changed, but also the inside of the houses. We want to see to it that our people get to the point where they will want something that is beautiful, something in the way of convenience, in the way of comfort in their houses where they will want more books, more newspapers and a piece of carpet upon the floor and some pictures upon the walls. In all these respects, we want to get our people to the point where they will be dissatisfied with the old life. I beg of you not to yield to the temptation of falling into the old way when you go back to your communities, because it takes a person a very little time, unless he has very great strength of character, to get used to the old conditions. It will take you but little time to get used to the old broken window pane; it will take you but a short time to get used to seeing the old knob left off the door. Before you get used to it, see that there is a new knob put there; see that a new pane of glass is put in the window instead of an old pillow. See to it that you cultivate that strength of character that will make you dissatisfied with such physical surroundings. See to it that you infuse new life in all these respects, and what I am suggesting not only applies to the house, to the farm but it applies to any kind of business in which you may engage.

Our people are too easily satisfied. Their ambitions are too easily satisfied. You go into many communities where our people are trying to run a little grocery business, or a little barber shop, or a restaurant, and in too many cases, they have a little room around the corner, and carry on their business in the most primitive manner. All people have to begin in that way, but there is no reason why it should be said from year to year, that they have made no progress. See to it that under all circumstances, you make progress; that you are dissatisfied next year with what you have had this year. See to it that the year following you are even more dissatisfied, and so on and on. You cannot make this progress in farm life, in the home, in carrying on a mercantile or any business, unless you, yourselves, are thoroughly awake, unless you get yourselves in touch with the best that is going on in the world, unless you get in your minds the spirit of progress. That is what we are trying to do here for you. If you enter into the business of building up a school, do not be satisfied with a little school. Don't be satisfied unless your school is better next year than it is this year. I do not mean necessarily that you should enlarge it, so far as the physical equipment is concerned, but see to it that the schoolhouse is more convenient, that it is made more attractive every year. See that the teaching is better each year, that everything is on the move, that you never get to the point where you are satisfied. When your eye rests upon the old thing year after year, you begin to feel that there is nothing new that you can learn, that there is no improvement you can make. Never get to the point in farming, in housekeeping, in business or in school teaching, where you feel that you have reached the end of all you can accomplish.

And in higher matters, in reading, in studying, see to it that you are never satisfied. If you are reading a newspaper, week after week, see if there is not a better one you can find. If you are reading a magazine, seek continually to find out if there is not a better one. Seek continually to find out if there is not some idea that you can get hold of in some book, some magazine, in some newspaper, that will make you more progressive, that will make you more dissatisfied with your personal surroundings, that will better fit you for your life's work.

In a word, all that I am trying to suggest to you tonight is, that you keep yourselves informed of the best things taking place in the world, whether in farm life, in business life, in school teaching and in every respect, see to it that you never become completely satisfied; keep alive an ambition to improve every year – improve your physical surroundings, improve your mental strength, improve your spiritual life.

Tuskegee Student, 20 (Apr. 11, 1908), 1, 4. Stenographically reported.

To Robert Robinson Taylor

[Tuskegee, Ala.] March 30, 1908

Mr. Taylor: I understand there is a great deal of vulgar writing on the walls of the girls toilet rooms. Please see that they are whitewashed as soon as possible.

B. T. W.

TLpI Con. 584 BTW Papers DLC.

To Sandy W. Trice

[Tuskegee, Ala.] March 30, 1908

Personal:

My dear Mr. Trice: I am especially pleased to learn from your letter of some days ago that my friend Dr. Majors[1] has been put in charge of the editorial policy of the "Conservator." He is a strong man and I am sure will help you to build a magnificent newspaper.

I just received a letter today from a Washington friend whom I saw sometime ago and he writes me as follows: "Mr. Trice of Chicago has my assurance that he will be treated right and he is now satisfied." You can see that I have not been asleep in the matter. Yours truly,

Booker T. Washington

TLpSr Con. 383 BTW Papers DLC. Signed in E. J. Scott's hand.

[1] Monroe Alpheus Majors (b. 1864), a graduate of Meharry Medical College (1886), was a black physician, lecturer, writer, and poet. He was editor of the *Texas Search-*

light from 1893 to 1895, and served in editorial capacities with the Indianapolis *Freeman* and the Chicago *Broad Ax* before assuming the editorship of the Chicago *Conservator* in 1908.

From Charles William Anderson

New York, N.Y., April 1, 1908

(Personal)

My dear Doctor: The Primaries in this City were held yesterday, and Parsons[1] defeated Odell[2] all along the line. The Fifteenth Congressional District, in which San Juan Hill is located, where Gilchrist Stewart was encouraged to make his fight for a delegate to the National Convention, was carried by the Parsons forces, although Stewart's own district, the Thirteenth Assembly District was lost by a few votes. This district has always been Anti-Parsons, and always gave an overwhelming vote against him. This time, under the leadership of Sol. Johnson, it was nearly carried. Of course, the Odell forces never intended to send Stewart. They supported him in that district to hold the big colored vote there, but had they won, their plan was to send Senator Saxe[3] and Abe Gruber.[4] Now that they have lost, they will probably pay the empty compliment of casting their 66 votes for him, to show that they were really in earnest in their desire to have a colored man go to Chicago, and to put Parsons in a hole. The Convention will be composed of 180 delegates, 114 of whom are Parsons men and 66 Odell men. Hence, the 66 will probably be instructed to vote for Stewart. As I also live in that district, it would be a fine play for Parsons to have me elected. He can do it easily. Please wire or write our "friend" to have Parsons send me from this (the Fifteenth) District. I am writing Loeb in this connection today. I do not think there will be any trouble about it, if the President makes the request, as Mr. Parsons agrees that I did as much hard work to win the fight in the district as he did, or any other man. He was very fearful of losing it, and didn't even hope to carry it by such a splendid plurality. Do this at once, as the Congressional Conventions are to be held very soon. Make your letter as strong as possible.

As you may have heard, the meeting held in Stewart's interest last week, at which Bishop Walters, A. H. Grimke, Max Barber, J. Douglas Wetmore and Jim Hayes spoke, both you and I were as savagely denounced as the President and Secretary Taft. In fact, the meeting, while ostensibly in Stewart's behalf, seemed to be really in opposition to you and myself. Walters, Grimke, Wetmore and Barber were especially bitter in their references to us. The net result of their work and the expenditure of large sums of money along San Juan Hill by Milholland and Odell, was that they came nearly losing the district, which they had carried by a vote of almost three to one at the last Primaries. In other words, a district which was carried by Odell at the last Primaries before the Brownsville episode, by a tremendous vote, was only carried by less than a hundred votes, with Brownsville as the battle cry. The republican vote in this district, as you know, is almost exclusively a black vote. Thus you see, Brownsville didn't cut much of a figure. Yours truly,

Charles W. Anderson

TLS Con. 38 BTW Papers DLC.

[1] Herbert Parsons.

[2] Benjamin Barker Odell, Jr.

[3] Martin Saxe (1874–1967), a New York lawyer, was president of the New York Tax Commission and served as a state senator from 1905 to 1909.

[4] Abraham Gruber (1861–1915) was a prominent criminal lawyer and Republican politico, often called "Little Napoleon." A foe of Theodore Roosevelt, Gruber supported the campaign of Benjamin Odell to defeat Herbert Parsons in the 1908 primary election in New York City.

From Daniel Hale Williams

Chicago Apr. 2nd 08

My Dear Dr. Washington, Have just returned from Washington to day. Saw and had a very pleasant and satisfactory conference with the Secretary.[1] It is necessary that I see you on very important matters while you are here. I have a verbal message from the Secretary to you. Any arrangement other than my office hours would suit me. At your Quarters, my office, or our home. If you will give me a little time for this interview much can be accomplished. With profound Respect I am, Very truly yours

Dan'l H. Williams

ALS Con. 386 BTW Papers DLC.

[1] James R. Garfield.

To William Loeb, Jr.

Chicago, April 3d, 1908

Personal

My dear Mr. Loeb: Mr. Anderson tells me that he has already written you concerning his being elected as a delegate to the National Convention from the Fifteenth District in which he lives. If this could be brought about it would be a fine play and do much good, especially in view of the fact that the opposition has tried to elect Gilchrist Stewart. Anderson has done a great deal of hard work recently in defeating the opposition. Perhaps if you would consult Mr. Parsons about it, letting him know what ought to be done, he would find a way to do it. Yours truly,

[Booker T. Washington]

TLc Con. 7 BTW Papers DLC.

William Burke to Tuskegee Institute

Birmingham, Ala. Apr. 4th 08

To Member of said Institute I wish today before you the Horible treatment you have heard before now about the Turpintine farms of the south, in regard to making Peons and Slaves of the colored people and how bad they are treated is unable to show in writting.

I have spent 4 months time in the chain Gangs of Georgia and must say it is time for you to seek and help those of your color as they need assistance at once as the parties that runs those Turpintine farms are working and whiping those helpless people to death.

I am a white man by name Wm Burke. I was convicted at Quitman Ga for 10 months on the chain Gang in 2 cases. 1 case for vagrancy 4 months and 1 case of Pitel [pistol] carring 6 months. I served 2 months at Capt. Balls Turpintine farm begining Dec. 11 '07 and remained there untill I and 4 colored men was sold to Capt. Davis of Eldorando Ga. 11 miles north of Bainbridge, Ga. About the latter part of Feb. is the time of said transfer.

During the time I was at Ball place, I ought to by right term Balls Place, as Balls Hell for it Equal can not be found in the savages of Africa or the heatherns of India or the cannibals of West Australia and such is the real condition on this christian soil of a supposed sivilized People.

I plead with you for God sake and Humanity form an investigation committee and go to Bainbridge, Ga.

For the want of space I will make a long story short.

I made my Escape from the man Capt Davis the party that bought me from Capt Ball of Reynoldsville, Ga.

Several Insidinst that occured that I may state here. A Boy 13 year old col. was whipe like a man would be. A Col. woman ther is whiped in a brutish manner I can say is beyond a human principal. A strap applied to her bare skin with to col. men to hold her face down.

I had a 12 lick sampl of the strap and it to me 3 months to loose all its efects.

Tuskegee Intu. Arthorities I wish to inform me that what I have wrote is not hear say, but it is the real thing and should this letter not receive its weight in Gold in exposing one of backest deeds perpatiated by white men to get Gloriously rich of off the labor of others when it is a violiaton of our national laws to sell men or women as slavery was abolished by the war of 1863.

I hope this letter will be placed in the proper hand by said Instu if it is out of place there.

I want Mr Booker Washington to see it and have him to investigate the Chain Gang Laws of Georgia and see if they are carried out in the Turpintine belt of South Ga.

I write this to you as a respect for you people and as I have had 4 months experience my writting surely must have some weight. I must close for this time as it is a week last thursday morn when I got my Freedom by my night operations. Ever yours

Wm Burke

ALS Con. 365 BTW Papers DLC.

Charles Wesley Archbold[1] to Henry Huddleston Rogers

Parkersburg, W.Va., April 4, 1908

My Dear Mr. Rogers: On returning North from a sojourn at Thomasville, Ga., my wife and I made a visit of three days at Tuskegee Institute, in response to a cordial invitation from Principal Washington. We had expected to be very deeply interested in what we might see there but the results achieved exceeded our most sanguine expectations. We visited several times the handsome and commodious administration building which you gave the Institute. We were fortunate in finding Dr. Washington at home during most of our stay and we had favorable opportunities for conversation with him and Mrs. Washington regarding their work at Tuskegee. We were pleased to receive an invitation to dine with them in their beautiful home. During the dinner Dr. Washington sent for your picture which you had kindly sent him, which was passed around the table and all agreed it was the picture of a handsome man. Dr. Washington is evidently very proud of it as he has a right to be. He explained to me that it was your desire not to have your name published in connection with what you have done for the Institute, but in view of my long acquaintanceship with you he felt satisfied as I did there could be no objection to our talking together freely about you. I explained to him that I had known for many years of your sincere desire to help those who were worthy and who needed your help. Dr. Washington showed me a statement of what had been accomplished in the past year in the way of raising the standard of the rural schools, chiefly in Macon County, Alabama, through the use of funds contributed by you, supplemented by subscriptions from colored people in the various school districts selected for this work. At the suggestion of Principal

Washington my wife and I accompanied by Mr. Calloway, who is his chief assistant in this work, rode out perhaps five miles from Tuskegee to the school house at Solomon's Chapel, where Mr. Calloway explained to us the kind of work that is being done. The school house in question had been recently painted and was abundantly supplied with blackboards, and with a little flower garden in front of the school house. The teacher of this school came out from Tuskegee to teach it. It was explained that this work was not to supplant but rather to supplement the work the State of Alabama is doing in the way of educating the colored children, and to furnish an object lesson which will be useful not only to the State of Alabama but to the South generally. Allow me to say our judgment is that the money contributed by you for this work is very wisely applied. Principal Washington spoke to me many times of his very warm regard for you and I was happy to say to him that I heartily concurred with him in the expression of such sentiments.

I sincerely trust your health is now much better and with very kind regards, I am Yours sincerely,

C. W. Archbold

TLS Seth Low Papers NNC. BTW forwarded the letter to Seth Low on Apr. 12, 1908.

[1] Charles Wesley Archbold (b. 1843), an oil company executive, was the brother of John Dustin Archbold (1848–1916), vice-president of Standard Oil Co. from 1875 to 1911, and president from 1911 to 1916.

Daniel Hale Williams to Emmett Jay Scott

Chicago, Apr. 5th 08

Personal

My Dear Friend Mr. Scott, Your cordial letter received. Sorry that you would not be in position to be with us. We will nevertheless stand guard over you and see that no one steals you while here. When you may have an hour we will care for you. I've just returned from Washington, had a most satisfactory and pleasant two hours with Sec'y Garfield, he is a fine manly man and spoke cordially and complimentary of you. Things about F. H.[1] are in bad condition, he understands fully the situation and the needs, and will deal with them. His type of mind is very much like that of Mr. Washington. Society Doctors, lazy Drs. and Drs looking for an easy place or position, and radiation, will find no place with him. Is it not discouraging to be made to feel that in over 3000 Colored men with Diplomas, he cannot satisfy himself that the one man of proper attainment, class, and real scientific turn, can be found to fill this exceptional opportunity. He knows them all. Political pull, counts for nothing. He selects his subordinates as Dr Washington does. The best in the market. He said he "must have results." Nothing else will be considered. I shall be in close touch with him at his request. *I trust that he understands that I want nothing,* that I am perfectly unselfish in my interest. I recognize this one grand opportunity of our time for progress along this important line. If it is lost or carelessly handled, it will put our Doctors and nurses back 25 years. I so much, want your interest and help in this important matter. You can do so much to finally develope an exceptional institution. Dr Washington is fully advised of the situation. I had an hours visit with him yesterday.

I want to suggest that you be out of doors as much as possible. Play Tennis. Ride Horseback. Walk and Play. Do not eat but little meat or sweets. Drink lots of good water and use a coarse towel after Bathing. Windows open while asleep. Mrs Williams kindest regards to you and Wife. Sincerely yours

Dan'l H. Williams

Write me soon.

ALS Con. 386 BTW Papers DLC.

[1] Freedmen's Hospital.

To Daniel Hale Williams

New York, April 9, 1908

My dear Dr. Williams: I called to see the Secretary as I came through Washington and had quite a talk with him. Nothing definite was decided upon except that he wants me to put in writing recommendations as to reorganization. This I shall do as soon as

I can get time. I would like, however, to go over the whole matter with you before submitting it to him.

Can you send me by return mail the names of six or eight colored doctors who, in your opinion, represent the very highest and best in the medical profession, men, as far as possible, who have specialized in various directions. Dr. Roman,[1] in Nashville, I should think would be a type of man I want to get hold of. Of course I do not know what you think of him, but I mention his name as an example. The Secretary's present idea, among other things, is to have a staff of visiting lecturers in the medical school and nurse training school whose expenses will be paid and who will receive an honorarium for their lectures. Of course, we want to include your own name.

There are other and more important matters I want to take up with you. Yours very truly,

[Booker T. Washington]

TLc Con. 386 BTW Papers DLC.

[1] Charles Victor Roman, born in Pennsylvania in 1864 and reared in Canada, was a graduate of Meharry Medical College and the first black specialist of the eye, ear, nose, and throat in the South. A professor at Meharry, he also edited the *Journal of the National Medical Association* and was a director of the One Cent Savings Bank in Nashville. In 1911 Roman published *A Knowledge of History Is Conducive to Racial Solidarity*, in which he postulated that black children should learn of their own heroes before learning of national heroes in order to promote race pride and solidarity and ultimately end racial strife. Five years later he wrote *American Civilization and the Negro*, which advocated a biracial society and parallel civilizations. (Meier, *Negro Thought*, 262).

From James Weldon Johnson

[Puerto Cabello] 4/9/08

My dear Dr. Washington: It is needless for me to tell you what sort of effect your letter had upon me; I might say, a kind of Emancipation Proclamation effect. I feel quite confident that it is now only a matter of weeks before I shall be sent to another and better post. To say another is almost equivalent to saying a better; for at the Department it is recognized that there are few more undesirable posts in the Service than this.

It is also useless for me to try to express to you my appreciation for your efforts in my behalf; I'm sure you know how I feel. We are at this moment on the thin ice of diplomacy; I hope however that nothing will happen to make it necessary for me to remain at this post just as promotion is coming my way.

As to our relations with Venezuela, I don't know whether our government understands that much of the antagonism here to the United States really finds origin in our race question at home. You know from an Anglo-Saxon point of view, none of the South American countries, with the possible exceptions of Argentina and Chili, can be called a "white man's country"; and I feel sure that here in Venezuela they are constantly fighting against any possible chance of a Saxon standard being set which would place them in any grade below that of equals. This feeling is partly shown in the way the local press culls the American press and copies all accounts of violence to Negroes in the States. Hardly a day passes in which there is not recorded in the papers here news of that character. Often these happenings occur in towns in the States so obscure that I never heard of them; this, and the omission of other more important news make it plain that the papers of this country make it a business of hunting out and republishing news of that sort. The object undoubtedly is to warn Venezuelans, without saying it in so many words, against any increase of Saxon influence in the country, on the ground of racial discrimination. As I said, perhaps, this most delicate phase of questions affecting the relations between the United States and the South American Republics has not been considered by our government, nevertheless, it is of importance.

Some months ago I wrote giving you some of my observations concerning internal racial conditions here in Venezuela; I have since then been using my eyes and ears, and I should like to talk with you further on the subject if I am so fortunate as to see you this summer.

I hope that you and Mrs. Washington are both well. Please give her my kindest regards. Yours very truly,

James W. Johnson

ALS Con. 374 BTW Papers DLC.

Emmett Jay Scott to Daniel Hale Williams

[Tuskegee, Ala.] April 9, 1908

My dear Dr. Williams: I have your very interesting communication of April 5 and thank you for your courtesy in writing me at such length.

As soon as I saw by the Washington papers that you were there, I became interested to learn as to how your interview with the Secretary terminated. I am pleased to find that, on the whole, it was so satisfactory and that you found him the kind of man you would like to have him be.

I am sorry from the race point of view that matters at F. H. should be in such a condition as you mention. It is most desirable that the very best man possible be secured for the headship and I know of no one better circumstanced than yourself to help select the proper man. To be perfectly frank with you, however, I do not know in just what particular I can be of any direct personal service, but in any way I can advance the general cause, I hold myself in readiness to do it. I hope that he was well dispositioned toward the party whom you have had in mind. I take it for granted, of course, that you assured the Secretary you personally want nothing at his hands. For my part, I believe that you, the most competent and best known of our physicians and surgeons, should be at the head of this hospital, but the sacrifices would be too great, as I have already said to you and as you, yourself, have indicated. I feel a direct interest in the matter, however, and hope that the race is not to lose this splendid opportunity of controlling the magnificent plant which Congress has just given us.

Thank you heartily for your kindly suggestions with reference to my personal welfare. I seem somehow to keep so tired these days and have not felt strong enough to take up playing tennis again, or even to go horseback riding, but now that I have your suggestion, I am going to go after both again. I have cut out meats altogether, but it was pretty hard to give up sweets. I read your letter in its entirety to Mrs. Scott and she is especially glad of the recommendations, which you send with reference to my keeping well and plans, she says, to see that I observe all of your regulations.

Do not fail to remember both of us most heartily to Mrs. Williams.

I still have no word with reference to going to Chicago. I wish I knew just what was going to be expected of me. Yours truly,

Emmett J. Scott

TLpS Con. 386 BTW Papers DLC.

From Ralph Waldo Tyler

Washington April 11/08

Dear Doctor: Yesterday I called on Mr. Hitchcock, with reference to keeping Governor Pinchback in the field. I had already taken the matter up with Mr. Vorys, who talked with Mr. Hitchcock over the long distance phone. Mr. Hitchcock received me kindly, *after a wait of one hour and a half,* by the watch, and I spent perhaps twenty minutes with him. I said to him that I did not believe he appreciated fully what it meant to have a man like the governor on our side. Mr. Hitchcock gave me no satisfaction, and if it were left to me to be the judge, I would say that he negatived all that I advanced. I tried to make it plain that the action of the Virginia convention had a tendency to neutralize the good effect of the President's letter to the Department of Justice, and that offered another reason why a man, like Governor Pinchback should be kept in the field, and particularly so in view of the fact that he asked, nor would he accept any remuneration.

Confidentially, I don't believe Mr. Hitchcock appreciates either the gravity of the situation or places a just estimate on colored men of character and standing. He may be just a cold, shrewd manager who prejudges all men, and prejudges them all alike.

A rather embarrassing thing took place, or rather developed during the conversation, and that was that Mr. Vernon had been given money, by Mr. Hitchcock, to defray the expenses of Chase to Philadelphia, but at the same time had led me to believe that he was defraying half of it personally, on the agreement that I would pay the other half. The discovery was a blow to me. I did not think a man of his standing would practice deception to such an extent, nor did I believe a man in his position would stoop to such petty larceny. I made it plain to Mr. Hitchcock my understanding of the agreement, and fortunately for me, Moore happened to be present at the time, and heard the entire conversation.

After leaving him, I was so worried over it, that I felt I must, in justice to myself, place the matter in black and white, and over my own signature, and so wrote, and mailed to him a letter, the enclosed being an exact duplicate.[1]

You can read this letter and form your own opinion.

Mr. Vernon's action has a depressing effect upon me, not so much because of it involving me, but because of the fear that Mr. Hitchcock may entertain the belief that all Negroes are grafters. And I don't believe, honestly, that Mr. Hitchcock has any especial desire to recognize or accept advice from a Negro. I may be doing him an injustice, but that's how I have sized him up. I don't think he intends to use the Governor further, and I believe that his opinion and conclusion controls the action of Mr. Vorys. At least in this particular matter. Sincerely yours,

Ralph W Tyler

P.S. Kindly return me the copy enclosed.

TLS Con. 8 BTW Papers DLC.

[1] Tyler to Hitchcock, Apr. 10, 1908, Con. 8, BTW Papers, DLC. Tyler reported that he had given Vernon $12.50 to give to W. C. Chase toward his expenses at a Philadelphia black meeting with the understanding that Vernon would match the amount, with another $12.50 each to be paid to Chase if he secured results favorable to Taft's candidacy. He said that Vernon and he had a clear understanding that the Taft managers would not be appealed to.

To Theodore Roosevelt

Hotel Manhattan, New York April 12, 1908

My dear Mr. President: The Liberian Commission is composed of the following persons, and they will reach this country about the 12th or 15th of May:

Mr. G. W. Gibson,[1] ex-President of the Republic, also an old and sensible man; Mr. J. J. Dossen,[2] a former Vice President of the Republic; Mr. C. D. H. Dunbar,[3] a lawyer.

I spoke to McKinlay and Tyler about the matter, and they will handle this party in a way to comply with your wishes.

Bishop I. B. Scott, formerly of New Orleans, whom you at one time thought of appointing Naval Officer for New Orleans, has been spending the last four years in Liberia and knows the Republic thoroughly. He has just come to this country. I am wondering if you would not like to have a talk with Bishop Scott sometime previous to your seeing the Commission. He could give you important facts. Bishop Scott can be thoroughly relied upon. At the time you were considering him for Naval Officer at New Orleans he was not a bishop but has been elected to that office since. He says he will be glad to see you, say the second week in May if that will suit you and if you desire it. Yours very truly,

[Booker T. Washington]

TLc Con. 7 BTW Papers DLC.

1 Garretson W. Gibson (1832–1910), former president of the College of Liberia, was president of Liberia from 1900 to 1904.

2 James Jenkins Dossen, former vice-president of Liberia, was elected president of the College of Liberia in 1913. He later was chief justice of the Liberian supreme court.

3 Probably Charles Benedict Dunbar (d. 1918), a lawyer, senator, and officer of the College of Liberia.

From Theodore Roosevelt

The White House Washington April 14, 1908

My dear Mr. Washington: I suggest that Bishop Scott bring those three gentlemen to see me when they come. Unfortunately, I am afraid the Liberian Republic is in a pretty bad way, and I do not think it advisable that any official prominence that can be avoided should be given their visit. Sincerely yours,

Theodore Roosevelt

TLS Con. 16 BTW Papers DLC.

To James Rudolph Garfield

Hotel Manhattan, New York, April 15, 1908

Personal

My dear Secretary Garfield: I shall be sending you within a few days the list of doctors that we discussed. I find that there is no trouble in getting hold of first class talent.

As a beginning for the re-organization and general betterment of the medical department and hospital, would it not be a good idea to make Dr. Daniel H. Williams, of Chicago, a member of the Board? I believe it is called the Board of Visitors. I think he would have constantly wise and good suggestions. I am recommending him because I do not think he wants anything for himself. Of course his traveling expenses to and from Washington when he is attending the board or lecturing would have to be paid.

Anything sent to this address will reach me. Yours truly,

[Booker T. Washington]

TLc Con. 371 BTW Papers DLC.

From Pixley ka Isaka Seme

Oxford–Jesus College. April 15th 1908

Dear Sir, I take great pleasure in bringing to your notice the fact that I am trying to urge the African students here in England to form a club or society for the interchange of ideas.

In preaching this movement I realize the fact that here are to be found the future leaders of African nations temporarily thrown together and yet coming from widely different sections of that great and unhappy continent and that these men will, in due season, return each to a community that eagerly awaits him and perhaps influence its public opinion. Sir I beg to leave the possibility of this text to your well-known imagination – but permit me to add that this movement is not fastened to any daring or even lofty star – violence in word or deed has no place in our programme – We meet as brethren, sons of a common fatherland for the interchange of general ideas and for self-educations in the problems of the unhappy fatherland receiving her story from the lips of her own sons.

The call of my circular-letter was most enthusiastically greeted and supported throughout and I am happy to say that the idea of *union* was carried and that there and then I was commanded to reconvene the meeting as soon as I shall be ready with details. This I propose to do very early in May. I hope I shall be able, then, to present the infant society inter alia with your correspondence.

In closing I beg to say that publicity and all species of notoriety are not connected with our movement – our programme is very simple but I believe that in God's time this movement will prove very eventful toward bringing about the "regeneration of Africa."

With my highest respects I remain Yours truly,

P ka Isaka Seme

ALS Con. 381 BTW Papers DLC.

From Daniel Hale Williams

Chicago Apr. 17th 08

Personal

My Dear Dr Washington Your letter of the 15th inst. received. When I wrote you I thought it well to leave my designation to you, but as you have suggested, "Clinical Surgery." I have taught surgery by lecture, or Didactic, for many years. One cannot impress practical things by talking. I firmly believe in showing, and then repeat again, and again, in that way it sticks. From the list I sent you, I inadvertintly omitted the name of Dr John E Hunter[1] of Lexington Ky. one of the most progressive men of his time, he has the respect of all classes in his home city and is a man of fine ability. I would like much to see him honored by adding his name, as surgical gynecology. With reference to the party you mentioned in your letter.[2] In selecting the names sent you I drew upon my knowledge of what each individual had actually done to merit recognition, and not upon newspaper notoriety. I believe the names seldom appear in the Negro Press, though they are powerful factors in race progress. They are doing something. You know that I am a great admirer of the doctrine you advocate. "The man who is doing something," quietly adding something to the sum total, that is the man who can get my endorsement. I cannot say that I consider the party you named in this class. There is so much that you do not know and have no way of knowing. All of the gentlemen I named are not friends of mine some of them I never saw, but I do know of their ability and honor, and assure you that they are men of such standing that I would be perfectly willing to serve with them – and again I want to impress most sincerely Mr. Washington that I am in this for the love of the work and the advancement of my people, to make conditions better for them, to prepare them for serious life work and am too much of a friend of yours to embarress you in any way. I am serious in everything I undertake. If I go into this it is not for social prestige or outside show, it means to me long days of patient hard work from home. I shall be deeply obligated if you would keep me posted on what is done and the names of those appointed or to be appointed.

I am not so sanguine as to the success of this departure, but as the Secretary thinks well of it and he is such a grand man with a humane heart, a noble spirit I would be willing to work hard to support his idea. The Secretary advanced the idea of making the Hospital assist in supporting itself by arranging for pay patients. This is quite feasible and can be worked up into a fine Revenue & support. Enclosed find statement, which may interest you. Kind regards Very truly Yours

Dan'l H. Williams

[*Enclosure*]

Pay patients

15—at $15.00 per wk.	private room	$225.
20 " 10.00 " "	Two in room,	$200.
	Per week total	$425.

This can be done at very little increase in expense. It would raise the tone of the hospital and attract a good class of people to it.

D H W

ALS Con. 386 BTW Papers DLC.

[1] John Edward Hunter (b. 1864) received his M.D. degree from Western Reserve University in 1889, and opened a private surgical practice in Lexington, Ky., the same year.

2 George Cleveland Hall. BTW suggested to Williams in a letter of Apr. 15, 1908, that he include Hall's name, on the ground that "It pays to overcome littleness with bigness and to do our whole duty regardless of how people may feel toward us." (Con. 386, BTW Papers, DLC.)

From Daniel Hale Williams

Chicago April 18th, 08

My Dear Dr. Washington, I have re-read your letter and incline to the view that I have not been frank enough to you in my statement regarding the make up of the proposed staff and the party you suggested as being added to "some Department." Under no circumstances would I embarress you. I am loyal to you and want nothing. I am sure to add the party would dismember the working and harmony of the board in short order. I have tried it. I have subserved many times for peace and harmony, but it never came. I cannot see my way clear to serve in association with him or on a staff which I am again sure, would eventuate into cliques and factions and accomplish nothing. That is what would happen by the inclusion. I think I know you well enough to say, that I believe you want me to be frank.

I go to Kansas City Kan. April 24th 25th & 26th to be present — make an address, and operate the three days opening of a hospital, owned and controlled by A. M. E. Church. Bishop A. Grant in charge. I want to get them started right. It is a fine addition to the number now in existence. Very Sincerely Yours

Dan'l H. Williams

ALS Con. 386 BTW Papers DLC.

To Oswald Garrison Villard

Hotel Manhattan, New York April 20, 1908

Personal

My dear Mr. Villard: I call your attention to the enclosed statement clipped from the Montgomery Advertiser bearing upon the earnings of the convicts in Alabama. You will note that the state cleared $437,000 from convict labor during a period of ten months. What is being done in Alabama in this regard is typical of what is being done in other Southern states.

First, you will note that it seems to be the object of the Southern states to make money out of their convicts without [with] little or no regard to reforming.

Second, of course three-fourths of the persons serving as convicts are colored people, but no credit is given them for the large amount of money that they are turning into the state treasury toward the expenses of the state. Yours very truly,

Booker T. Washington

I think an investigation would show that the the colored convicts alone turn much more into the state treasury than the state spends every year for the education of the whole Negro population in Alabama.

TLS Oswald Garrison Villard Papers MH. A carbon is in Con. 42, BTW Papers, DLC.

From Ralph Waldo Tyler

Washington April 20/08

Dear Doctor: Yours of the 11th. at hand. As yet Mr. Hitchcock has not replied to my letter, copy of which I sent you. The letter, however, was not one that really called for an answer, unless just the courtesy of an acknowledgement.

One more thing I heard today, in connection with the matter, and that is this. I left the making of the arrangements with Chase in the Register's hands. He gave Chase the amount agreed upon between us, but asked Chase to give him a personal receipt, and to sign that receipt in blank. Now the question [that] naturally arises in my mind is — for what reason did he request a receipt in blank unless it was to give him an opportunity to fill in amount greater than what he had actually given Chase. For instance; make the amount to cover what I had given also, and thereby bring the total up to such amount as Mr. Hitchcock had given him to give Chase.

Fortunately for me I gave Chase my personal check, or rather I drew it payable to Chase and gave it to the Register to hand to Chase. I am protected to that extent. But, on the other hand, a man who will play deceit to the point that he did, might also give Mr. Hitchcock the impression that he had reimbursed me for the expense I went to personally.

The whole thing leaves a bad taste in one's mouth.

I sent Trice a check, as I said to you I would, but as yet he has not acknowledged it. I presume he got it however.

I am satisfied that Foraker intends to keep up his fight to divide the Negro vote, and is willing to lose his seat in the senate to accomplish it.

This Vernon transaction clearly illustrates the necessity of a thorough understanding among the Taft Negro supporters, and also should be accepted as evidence that some Negro, or a committee of them be recognized in matters pertaining to the race, so as to prevent the crossing of trollies. The Foraker, or rather the Negroes at work for the "allies" are organized, and there is some head and tail about their work, while we are sort of every fellow following his own line of work.

I don't think Mr. Hitchcock has any too high an opinion of our men, and does not feel to ask or accept their judgement in affairs, and this Vernon transaction simply strengthens him in his apparent decision. I think, when you have an opportunity, it would be well for you to take the matter of Negro recognition, and system, in his campaign up with the Secretary. With high regards, I am, Sincerely yours,

[Ralph Waldo Tyler]

P.S. Presume you have seen the Governor.[1] He returned to New Rochelle last week, Hitchcock being through with him.

The enclosed letter from Vorys I think you enclosed under the impression you were enclosing copy of my letter to Hitchcock.

TL Con. 8 BTW Papers DLC. Written on stationery of the Office of Auditor for the Navy Department, U.S. Treasury. The last paragraph is in Tyler's hand.

[1] P. B. S. Pinchback.

To James Rudolph Garfield

Hotel Manhattan, New York City, April 21, 1908

My dear Secretary Garfield: Enclosed I send you a list of the leading colored doctors in the country with their specialties indicated after their names. All these are not only men of fine standing in their immediate profession, but of high character.

I take for granted that you received my letter regarding Dr. Williams. Yours truly,

[Booker T. Washington]

[*Enclosure*]

The following is a list of names of men who have been trained or have done special work along lines indicated:

Clinical Surgery . . . . Dr. Daniel H. Williams, Chicago
Surgical Gynecology . . . . Dr. John E. Hunter, Lexington, Ky.
Pathology, Physicial
Diagnois . . . . Dr. F. A. Stewart,[1] Nashville, Tenn.
Physiology &
Electro Therap[e]utics . . . Dr. Wheatland,[2] Newport, R.I.
Eye, Ear, Nose & Throat . . . . Dr. Roman, Nashville, Tenn.
Anatomy and Surgery . . . . . . Dr. C. I. West, Washington, D.C.
General Medicine . . . . Dr. Henry M. Minton,[3] Philadelphia.
Materia Medica
& Therap[e]utics . . . . Dr. Henry McCord, Baltimore.
Obstetrics . . . . Dr. John Francis, Washington.
Minor Surgery & Anesthetics . Dr. Jno. Kenney, Tuskegee.
Practical Laboratory Worker in
Pathology, Bacteriology, Blood,
Urinalysis, Historian and
Photographer, for recording progress
and advancement of the work, ... Dr. Antoine, Chicago.

In addition may be added — Head Surgical Nurse to have charge and train nurses in operating room technique.

Dietitian and Diet Kitchen nurse, to prepare food for the sick.

TLc and Enclosure Con. 371 BTW Papers DLC.

1 Ferdinand Augustus Stewart (b. 1862), a graduate of Fisk (1885) and Howard University Medical School (1888). Stewart was professor of pathology at Meharry Medical School from 1889 to 1908 and professor of surgery from 1889 to 1931.

2 Marcus Fitzherbert Wheatland (b. 1868), a graduate of Howard University Medical School, was examining physician for the Rhode Island State Sanitarium.

3 Harry McKee Minton (b. 1871), a Philadelphia pharmacist, received an M.D. from Jefferson Medical College in 1906 and practiced medicine in Philadelphia.

To Frank Harris Hitchcock

Hotel Manhattan, New York April 22, 1908

Personal

My dear Mr. Hitchcock: The following point you may be already guarding, but I thought it might not be out of place to remind you of its importance.

Mr. Scott[1] of course is going to have an advantage over Mr. Thompson from the fact that Mr. Scott will be on the inside of the National Committee, and I have the feeling pretty strongly that when Mr. Scott finds how strongly the tide is going for Secretary Taft when he goes to Chicago that he will flop over to the support of Secretary Taft and attempt to impress the Committee with the idea that he has favored him all along with the object of preventing Mr. Thompson's being recognized with his followers in Alabama and get on the inside himself with his followers which are the Lily White faction. I have not corresponded with Mr. Vorys on the subject and do not know whether he is aware of Mr. Scott's treachery in Alabama; if he does not know of it, I hope you will inform him.

I stopped at the White House some minutes as I came through Washington, and I am glad to find there that they are thoroughly disgusted with Mr. Scott and understand fully now that he has been treacherous from the beginning.

I hope that matters are going well with you.

This will be my address for several days. Yours truly,

[Booker T. Washington]

TLc Con. 6 BTW Papers DLC.

1 Charles Herrington Scott.

To James Hardy Dillard

Hotel Manhattan, New York, Apr. 23, 1908

My dear Dr. Dillard: One other thought comes to me which may or may not be of value. It is this: Would it not be within our rights and wise for us to consider the matter of spending a certain sum of money in employing one or more strong influential white men to go through the South during a few months each year talking to the people, I mean the whites, in regard to the education of the people, bringing out emphatically the value that it will prove to the whole South to educate the Negro. I find that in many cases while individual school officers want to do the right thing regarding the Negro, they are timid and backward because they are not supported by public opinion. The value of this suggestion, if it has any, would be in rallying the masses to the support of liberal school officials. A man like Dr. Rice, if his services could be secured for a few weeks in each year I think would accomplish a great deal of good. Yours very truly,

[Booker T. Washington]

TLc Con. 40 BTW Papers DLC.

From W. B. Watkins[1]

Richmond, Virginia, April 24, 1908

Dear Sir — I enclose herein a clipping from the News Leader of April 15th.[2] Speaking for myself and all of my friends, and in fact every Virginian, with whom I have talked, I can say that the white people of this state, and I believe of every Southern state, do not want Italians under any circumstances. The state of Virginia spent more money in education last year than ever before, for both races, appropriated a handsome sum for a negro deaf and dumb institution, and is doing all within reason to uplift both the negroes and the poorer whites. To introduce a foreign race, and a very low form, perhaps one of the lowest, of the white races into the South, will mean a serious complication. To educate the negro, and then have a foreigner work for half of what he can live on, means offsetting the good effect of proper education and training. Further than that it may mean driving the negro into pauperism. Of course, this applies with equal force to the poorer whites. To cite a few cases: ten years ago all the barbers in Richmond were negroes, and they were good ones too. Now nine tenths of them are Italians. The Richmond Locomotive Works is supplanting its negro laborers with Italians. In Richmond as yet there are too few of them to have done much harm, but there is a danger which looms ahead. Governor Swanson[3] is opposed to indiscriminate immigration. The Commissioner of Agriculture is only bringing in English and Scotch immigrants to work on farms, and he is getting only a few picked men, so that does not enter into the labor question. The Legislature of Virginia at its recent session passed a resolution *unanimously* requesting its representatives in Congress to vote for stringent restriction of immigration, and to do all they could to keep Italians out of Virginia. In spite of this, Powderly[4] seems to be endeavoring to neutralize the effect of this resolution by advertizing Italians in every manner possible. Last Fall I had some correspondence with him in regard to a similar utterance, and he claimed he was misquoted. This could hardly happen twice in succession, and from friends in the North, I am led to believe that he is unduly influenced by the foreign steamship lines. At a so-called Immigration Convention in Washington in 1905, one Bonaventure F. Broderick,[5] a Roman Catholic Bishop delivered an address strongly advocating Italians for the South. The fact that Powderly is a Catholic is another reason why he is trying to force Italians on the South. In Virginia there are comparatively few Italians, and our people don't like the few we have. The division over which Powderly is chief, only has authority to send immigrants to any section on request, and has absolutely no authority whatever, to criticise any section because it may not want a certain class of immigrants, and this article, which he does not deny having authorized to be published, (as I wrote him some time since asking him if he had not exceeded his powers, and have heard nothing from him, and if it were untrue he would have denied it) clearly lays him open to severe censure from the proper authorities in Washington.

The best thing for the South is to have Powderly removed from office. I have written my representatives in Congress but as they are

Democrats and have little political influence, I thought if you could get some of your influential friends in the North to try to have Powderly removed, or failing in that to have him properly disciplined, as his stubborn insistence in ignoring the wishes of the Southern people is fraught with great danger to this section.

Hoping you will take this matter up promptly while Congress is in session, Very respectfully,

W B Watkins

TLS Con. 386 BTW Papers DLC.

1 W. B. Watkins, listed in the Richmond city directories as a salesman.

2 The item quoted Terence V. Powderly's statement that Italian immigrants were in demand for work in southern agriculture. "What the South needs is immigration," Powderly said. (Richmond *News Leader*, Apr. 15, 1908, Clipping, Con. 386, BTW Papers, DLC.)

3 Claude Augustus Swanson (1862–1939), a Democratic congressman (1893–1906) and governor of Virginia from 1906 to 1910. He then served in the U.S. Senate from 1910 to 1933, until he was appointed Secretary of the Navy by Franklin D. Roosevelt, a position Swanson held until his death in 1939.

4 Terence Vincent Powderly (1849–1924), the American labor leader, was mayor of Scranton, Pa. (1878–84), U.S. commissioner general of immigration (1897–1902), and chief of the division of information in the Bureau of Immigration (1907–21).

5 Bonaventure Finnbar Broderick (1868–1943), ordained a Roman Catholic priest in 1896, served several offices in Hartford, Conn., Cuba, and the Philippine Islands. He was elevated to bishop in 1903. For many years after 1910 he engaged in literary and editorial work.

To Ralph Waldo Tyler

New York April 26, 1908

Personal

My dear Mr. Tyler: Please attend to this matter at once, it is very important. Keep it wholly confidential:

Mr. John C. Laughlin, the staff correspondent of the Washington Post, has recently made it known that he is preparing an article for the New York Times showing to what extent the Negro vote is disaffected and opposed to Secretary Taft. This, I take it, is to be rather an important article.

Put yourself into touch with Mr. Laughlin at once. Show him the Negro papers from all over the country that are favorable to Secretary Taft. Also impress upon him the fact that the same colored people are traveling around from one city to the other getting up these so-called indignation meetings. They are under pay for the most part of John E. Milholland, who hides himself behind the name of the Constitutional League. The Constitutional League means practically nothing except John Milholland and A. B. Humphrey who are trying to work the old carpet bag game of going to a National Convention and saying to the candidates that they have charge of the Negro vote and will trade the vote for a cabinet office or some high official position. After you have impressed him with this view of the case, I wish you would see further that you judiciously have Judge Terrell, McKinlay and other sensible people get into touch with him. Of course you will have to keep from him the fact that you have heard of his preparing this article, unless he brings it out himself. The names of the people in the pay of Milholland are, as you know, such men as "Dr." Sinclair, R. C. Ransom, J. Max Barber, Bishop Walters, Wm. M. Trotter and a few others of that stripe. Impress him with the idea that while these people make a good deal of noise, they are not representing the masses of our people.

Do not hint anything to the effect that you have heard from me on this subject.

You might show him the signed letter sent out from Boston a few days ago by the colored people there in favor of Secretary Taft. Yours truly,

[Booker T. Washington]

TLc Con. 8 BTW Papers DLC.

From Emmett Jay Scott

Tuskegee Institute, Alabama April 27, 1908

My dear Mr. Washington: I have your kind letter of April 24th advising as to Mr. Carnegie's provision with reference to the Committee of Twelve. I am slightly disappointed, however, as I have been laboring under the impression that there was a possibility of a permanent fund for the distribution of facts bearing upon Negro progress. To my mind, $2,700 to $3,000 is a rather small amount for the purpose I suppose you have in mind and would hardly warrant the employment of a man expressly for that work. It would be no use to print either facts or documents without they were in such form as to insure they would be not merely read, but quoted in the press and so make an impression on public opinion. That means, in the end, that you would have to have a man of considerable ability and I fear that he would have to be directed and coached from this office. Besides there is the matter of postage, printing, clerk hire and the additionals which count up.

I know your delicacy about centering matters at Tuskegee, but nevertheless, I am going to submit a suggestion just the same. Since you, in the main, will have to be responsible for the distribution of this money and for the efficiency of the work, would it be out of place to suggest that the work be done here at Tuskegee under your general supervision? In the collection of the facts and in their publication, we could use the knowledge and the methods we already have our hands on and when we had shown what could be done, it is possible that Mr. Carnegie would be willing to permanently endow the work.

When a permanent endowment was secured, we might consider making a position for some one. In the meantime, we could, if necessary, employ different individuals to make special investigations and they could be made under your direction with the assistance of Dr. Park and myself and SENT OUT BY THE COMMITTEE OF TWELVE AS BEFORE. I have talked with Dr. Park and he agrees with me that the plan you have in view is of the highest importance, but personally I think you need more money and in order to get it, we ought to make a showing with what we now have. It will be difficult to do that if we load ourselves up with a permanent salaried man, who will, after all, have to be taught to do the work you want done.

I fear I may already have written too much. Yours sincerely,

E J Scott

TLS Con. 582 BTW Papers DLC.

From Samuel William Bacote[1]

Kansas City, Mo., April 28, 1908

My Dear Friend: I desire a little information concerning the discharge of the Negro soldiers by the President. And if you are in a position to give that information, it will be considered *strictly private*. You probably are aware of the fact that I am Gen'l Statistical Secretary of the National Baptist Convention and am always in touch with the brethren. For some months past I have been called upon from time to time to "DECLARE" myself. This I have never done, not wishing to involve myself in a controversy, the outcome of which is so problematic and upon which there is such a diversified opinion.

1. Kindly give me the benefit of your investigation of the affair.
2. Do you think Pres. Roosevelt would have treated white soldiers in the same manner as he did the Negroes under similar conditions? In view of what the President has done for the Negro race, it is difficult for me to believe he intended to do injury to the race by the discharge of the troops.

Thanking you in advance for an early reply, I remain, Yours truly,

Sam'l W. Bacote
Ed. Bapt. Year Book

TLS Con. 365 BTW Papers DLC.

[1] Samuel William Bacote (1866–1946) was born in Society Hill, S.C., of slave parents. He graduated from the normal department of Benedict College in Columbia, S.C., in 1886 and then completed the "higher English course" in 1888. He served as principal of Johnston Academy in Edgefield, S.C., for a year and then attended Shaw University in Raleigh. Bacote graduated from Richmond Theological Seminary in 1892, and was ordained a Baptist minister that year. Later he received degrees from Kansas City University in Kansas City, Kans. In 1895 he became pastor of the Second Baptist Church in Kansas City, Mo., a position he held for fifty-one years. In 1901 he was appointed statistician of the National Baptist Convention, and also edited the *National Baptist Yearbook* for many years.

From Emmett Jay Scott

Tuskegee Institute, Alabama April 28, 1908

Dear Mr. Washington: I have exactly the same chagrin and disgust as Mr. Tyler expresses in the attached letter,[1] which I *am going to ask you to read carefully at your convenience.* He sets forth clearly Vernon's larceny and this, I think is what you will want to be advised about. I really think that you owe it to yourself to know something of the type of man whom you are from time to time compelled to deal with. I cannot help feeling that Vernon is considerable of a scamp and to think of the Registrar of the Treasury being caught red-handed in stealing $75. is simply awful. Yours truly,

E J Scott

TLS Con. 582 BTW Papers DLC.

[1] Ralph W. Tyler reported to Scott that he had caught William T. Vernon, register of the treasury, in an act of petty larceny. "*I caught Mr. Vernon red-handed,*" he wrote Scott. According to Tyler, Vernon had pocketed some Republican travel money earmarked for W. Calvin Chase. This revelation occurred in the office of Frank H. Hitchcock, manager of William H. Taft's 1908 campaign for president. Vernon received money from two sources and instead of returning the funds pocketed $75. "I would have rather lost $500," Tyler wrote, "than to have had Hitchcock know that a colored man holding so high a position would stoop to petty larceny." (Apr. 25, 1908, Con. 8, BTW Papers, DLC.)

An Account of the Cosmopolitan Club Dinner[1] in the New York *American*

New York, April 28, 1908

WHITE GIRLS AT AN "EQUALITY FEAST" WITH NEGROES

Banquet of the Cosmopolitan Society Proves Too Much for Rev. Dr. Peters[2]

BOOKED TO SPEAK; FLEES

Orators Openly Advocate the Intermarriage of Whites and Blacks

Social equality and intermarriage between the races were advocated last night at a banquet of the Cosmopolitan Society of Greater New York, where twenty white girls and women dined side by side at table with negro men and women.

Whether by accident or design, all of the white women save three found, when they reached the tables in Peck's restaurant, at No. 140 Fulton street, that the seats beside them were to be occupied by negro men.

The Rev. Madison C. Peters, who had intended to speak to the society, remained only long enough to view this startling seating arrangement. As the first course of the dinner was served he called Andre Tridon,[3] the treasurer of the society, aside, and, pleading as an excuse another speech which must be delivered uptown, hurried from the room. In spite of promises that he would return and speak, Dr. Peters failed to come back and the speech was not delivered.

White Girl among Negroes

Miss Mary White Ovington, a Brooklyn society girl, who has been prominent in settlement work, and whose father is proprietor of the Hotel St. George, was the only white woman who occupied a seat at the speakers' table. Negroes were clustered all about her. On her right hand sat William H. Ferris, colored graduate of Harvard, who told later of his effort to implant his "Boston education" in the South. At this table also sat Hamilton Holt,[7] introduced as "editor-in-chief of The Independent," and whose subsequent utterances on intermarriage stirred his auditors to enthusiastic applause.

At the left of Miss Ovington was Editor Harold G. Villard,[5] of the New York Evening Post, and his plea for "equality and abolition of caste spirit" a few minutes later drew forth another wild outburst.

But the one table in particular which attracted attention was that [at] which half a dozen white women were seated, and where the dashing young negro, Captain H. A. Thompson, sat between two prominent white girls from Greenpoint.

MISS EATON AND MISS DOOLITTLE

These young ladies were Miss Isabel Eaton and Miss Marion Doolittle. They laughed and chatted with their negro entertainer during the meal, while he retold his exploits at San Juan Hill, where he served as adjutant of the Eighth Illinois Colored Infantry. One of his apparent interesting recitals was dramatically interrupted by a violent attack of nose bleed, which caused his unceremonious and hasty departure from the table, but he was received with evident pleasure when he returned, five minutes later, and renewed his attentions to the young ladies.

At this table were also seated Mrs. J. W. Gates and her sixteen-year-old daughter, Bessie. The latter was a very attractive blonde girl, gowned in a blue creation, slightly decollete. She wore a light straw hat trimmed with brilliant poppies. Treasurer Tridon announced that Mrs. Gates and daughter were prominent in society in Seattle and were in New York "studying art." Directly across the table from the little debutante sat Edward C. Walker, President of the Sunrise Club, which organization was among the first to rush to the defense of "Affinity" Earle and which later attracted attention by preaching of polygamy.

Blackest Man at the Feast

Mrs. A. Stirling,[6] a white woman, occupied a seat at the same table at the left hand of Dr. John A. Morgan, a West Indian, who was the blackest man in the assemblage. Mrs. Morgan sat near Professor Walker and importuned him with questions during the dinner.

Mrs. L. Landis, said to be a prominent Brooklyn woman, sat at an opposite table at which were ten negroes, men and women. Her husband also occupied a seat at this table. Miss M. Lyons, one of the colored women speakers, sat directly opposite Mr. Landis. The Landis party, however, left the room before the speaking concluded when the place became quite warm.

All of the attention was not that paid by the colored men to the white women. One large negress attracted much attention. She wore a large hat with white plumes and brilliant diamond ear pendants. The manager of the banquet announced that she was Mrs. Anna Allen, a "wealthy colored lady of Brooklyn, who owns many houses, not tenements either." Mrs. Allen was surrounded during the evening with plenty of attention.

Dominated by Military Man

Miss Marie Perrin,[7] who did not give her address, was a young white girl who sat at the side table which was dominated over by the gallant negro army captain. She sat close to Miss Martha Thompson, a colored girl and a relative of the military negro.

The "social equality" of the affair acted like new wine upon the diners, two-thirds of whom were negroes. The free license of the speeches was received with loud outbursts. Groans greeted the names of Roosevelt, Taft and Bryan, and wild applause followed every mention of Socialism. But the greatest demonstration was drawn out by direct or indirect allusions to intermarriage, whether through the gentle discussion of "social equality," as spoken by Miss Ovington, or the broad, bald advocacy of the direct intermarriage.

Hamilton Holt, editor of the Independent, struck the keynote of the feelings of the negroes when he said: "Intermarriage, if continued long enough, would solve the race problem. I do not believe that the white man would be so anxious to marry the negro woman, as would the negro man to wed the white girl; but this would continue, the negro man marrying the white woman, until the dark race would gradually bleach."

Mr. Holt had spoken of the race problem as one of the four great questions of the present day, enumerating the international peace question, the woman question and the industrial questions as the other public matters. Then he said:

"Conditions are going to get worse in the South before they get better. When the colored people get educated the whites in the South will have to recognize them as their equals." A great outburst of applause and hand clapping greeted this statement. The speaker continued:

"What must the remedy be? To let things remain as they are is unsatisfactory: deportation is impossible; then it must be amalgamation and education. Intermarriage, if continued long enough, would solve this race problem." The applause that this received was not stopped for several minutes.

"I am surprised," continued the speaker, "that we have no great white man, who has championed the colored race."

Cries of "Foraker, Foraker," interrupted him.

"No, no," shouted the speaker, "I don't mean that; I mean a man who will consecrate his life. Nothing ought to appeal more to a white man than this great field for a philanthropist."

At this point Mr. Villard, of the Evening Post, was called to speak, but a diversion for a time threatened to stop the dinner. A newspaper photographer had mounted his camera upon a stepladder to obtain a flashlight picture. The white women began to fidget and cast appealing looks about for aid as they saw the camera trained upon them and their negro dinner partners. A bustle followed at the speakers' table, and Manager Tridon, who was busy arranging for the photograph, received a penciled note, warning him that no picture must be allowed. The women refused to pay any attention to the speakers until the camera was taken from the room.

Miss Ovington did not touch upon race equality as bluntly as Mr. Holt had done. Still she grew enthusiastic when she got to speaking, and said:

"Move your chairs nearer together and get up closer." That invitation was greedily accepted by the colored dinner partners of the white girls, and a great noise of chair crowding continued for some minutes.

She Calls the Work "Human"

"I am very glad I have been asked to welcome you in behalf of the Cosmopolitan Club," said Miss Ovington. "We hope to have many of such clubs as this soon and we shall know by next season if our movement is going to be a success. Caste spirit is not simply a race question. I am in this work because it is human. The danger of this caste spirit is not a racial matter, but relates to we men and women of this republic. It means moral and physical ruin, especially in the South.

"I like to think that we are going to eat with and stand up for our colored brothers and sisters whenever and wherever we meet them or wherever we can. I believe it would be a terrible state of affairs when the negro gives up any of his rights as a man.

"He should never be satisfied until his equality is recognized. The power of love overruns caste and brings people of all castes together. I should like to think that our society stood for the Hunger of Brotherhood among all human beings."

The efforts of the young lady evidently pleased her hearers. They cheered and clapped when she sat down.

Then came Editor Villard. He said: "This spirit of caste is the most dangerous spirit that can threaten any land, particularly a democratic form of government. We stand in this country for equality — equality of rights, liberties, and to do as we see fit. It is a question of whether one believes in Christ or not."

About this time Dr. Ferris, the colored collegian, was called upon. He was delighted to speak, and said:

"Is it too soon to admit the negro into the brotherhood of equality in the human family? This meeting means more to the negro of the Black Belt of the South than to the negro of the North. It marks an epoch for the down south negro. It is a question of recognizing them as a man and as an equal. There is only one way to succeed — demand your equality.

"We have two leaders. Booker Washington advocating peaceful resistance, and then there is Du Bois saying, 'Exercise your rights.' Now, which shall it be?"

"Exercise our rights!" shouted a voice followed by great applause, which was joined in by white and black alike.

PASTOR SEES LIFE IN SOCIALISM

Rev. George Frazer Miller, a negro, declared the great bugbear to abolition of caste was the "social equality." He said the natural remedy was in the ballot. He declared he could see no reason for giving the negro vote to Roosevelt, Taft or Bryan, and that he owed the Republican party nothing. "Our rising sun is Socialism, which promises true equality without reference to race or society," he shouted.

Vice-President Humphries, of the Colored Republican Club, felt called upon to say "Race prejudice is not going to be settled with peaceful means. The man with the hoe should not hesitate to use it at both ends — to belabor with the handle. You must have equality."

John Spargo,[8] a white settlement worker, was applauded when he shouted: "You negroes must assert your powers — you, my friends, whose skins are tanned darker than mine. The equality of opportunity must be placed before every child born into this world."

Max Barber, a Chicago negro editor, spoke of Candidate Taft as the "heir apparent to the throne," and declared he would not give the negroes "untrammelled use of the ballot." He said the opportunity was at hand to wipe out caste by use of the ballot.

Dr. O. M. Waller, a negro, who is secretary of the Cosmopolitan Society, presided.

New York *American*, Apr. 28, 1908, 1, 4.

1 The Cosmopolitan Society of America, often called the Cosmopolitan Club, was founded in 1906 by Mary White Ovington for the purpose of promoting interracial understanding through a series of meetings and dinners held first in Ovington's Brooklyn Heights home. In 1908 the club met in a New York restaurant, attracting about a hundred persons. BTW's role in the adverse publicity the dinner received is not clear, but he did secretly undermine the same group at a 1911 dinner. (See An Account of the Cosmopolitan Club Dinner in the New York *Press*, Jan. 25, 1911, below, vol. 10.) Before the 1911 dinner BTW wired Charles W. Anderson: "Regarding black and white dinner be sure get hold of same reporter who reported for *American* year or two ago." (Jan. 21, 1911, Con. 52, BTW Papers, DLC.) BTW was at a New York hotel during the 1908 Cosmopolitan Club dinner and made an extra effort to avoid the press on the night of the affair. (See Kellogg, *NAACP*, 71–72; Harlan, "Secret Life of BTW," 413–15.)

[2] Madison Clinton Peters (1859–1918), a white Presbyterian clergyman, lecturer, and author. He wrote several books promoting justice for Jews and blacks in America.

[3] André Tridon (1877–1922), a French newspaperman and socialist, came to the United States in 1903 and wrote for the New York *Tribune* and the New York *Sun.* After 1914 he was noted for his translations of Freud and Adler and wrote several works on psychoanalysis.

[4] Hamilton Holt (1872–1951) was managing editor of *The Independent* from 1897 to 1913, and its editor and owner from 1913 to 1921. Under his editorship *The Independent* championed the major progressive causes of the era, and was outspoken in favor of civil rights for blacks. Holt believed that education was the key to solving race problems, but he also believed in protest, and denounced lynching and Jim Crow practices. He was a founder of the Cosmopolitan Club in 1906, and a signer of "The Call" in 1909 which led to the creation of the NAACP. Later Holt was active in the promotion of international peace, and served as president of Rollins College from 1925 to 1949.

[5] Oswald Garrison Villard.

[6] Ada Sterling, later secretary of the American Polish Relief Committee.

[7] Marie R. Perrin (1870–1957), one of the first teachers at the Ethical Culture School in New York City, was head of its household arts department from 1891 to 1931. During World War I, she returned to her native country, France, and was active in war-relief work.

[8] John Spargo (1876–1966), an Englishman who became a socialist at the age of eighteen, came to the United States in 1901 and lectured and wrote on socialism. He was one of the founders of Prospect House Social Settlement in Yonkers, N.Y., served on the national executive committee of the Socialist Party, and was a director of the Rand School of Social Science in New York. He wrote several books on socialist principles and *The Bitter Cry of the Children* (1906), a tract opposing cruelty toward and exploitation of children.

An Excerpt from an Article in the Norwalk (Conn.) *Evening Hour*

New York, April 28 [1908]

. . . .

Booker T. Washington, head of Tuskegee Institute, who is at the Manhattan Hotel, was greatly agitated when he read the story of the Cosmopolitan club banquet, and especially over the frank statements made by Hamilton Holt.

He sent word to the desk of the hotel that he was "not to be disturbed," and notified his two secretaries that he was "not at home" to reporters.

An effort to see him was met by the sending back of the card with the message that "Dr. Washington is engaged." Persistence met with a visit from one of the secretaries. He had been well coached.

"You want to talk with the doctor regarding certain speeches made at a so-called dinner last night; well, the doctor will not talk about what any one else might have said."

A call of Washington's on the telephone resulted in the interrogation of the inquirer who was asked what he wanted to talk about. When he explained the answer came back: "Doctor Washington has nothing to say."

Norwalk (Conn.) *Evening Hour*, Apr. 28, 1908 Clipping Con. 1050 BTW Papers DLC. This clipping was a fragment of a longer article.

To Pixley ka Isaka Seme

[Tuskegee, Ala.] April 29, 1908

Dear Sir: I read with interest your communication of April 15, 1908, and dated from Jesus College, Oxford, and am glad to learn that the educated young men of our race in England are coming together to seriously discuss the problems and conditions of their people in Africa. It is a great task that you have before you; but great tasks have their rewards.

I am sure that English statesmen, the men whose counsels will finally prevail, believe as you and I do, that in the long run Africa can prosper only on condition that, not only the riches of the soil and the mines but the latent powers of the native people are developed in a rational manner. What that implies is a practical problem that can only be solved by study and experiment. You can and should help in the solution of that problem and there are ways that you can be helpful, as no one else can, both to your own people and to the government. More and more I am learning that you face in South Africa, in a somewhat different and more difficult form, the same task we have in this country.

I wish you Godspeed in your work and hope that you will keep me informed of your success. Yours truly,

Booker T. Washington

TLpSr Con. 381 BTW Papers DLC. Signature in E. J. Scott's hand.

From Alfred M. Colby[1]

Dayton O May 1st 1908

Dear Sir. I have long been an admirer in your work and a believer in your efforts to show your race wherein lies its real salvation.

After the unfortunate exhibition which took place in New York a few days ago I feel very much in the mood of telling you that your work is admired and appreciated by the great mass of American citizens both black and white. You have heard that before and from men whose judgment is worth much more than mine but as a representative of the *average* man I feel like saying to you that we believe in you.

A colored man has been a servant in our family for twenty years. He had no early educational advantages but has taught himself to read. He is an intelligent upright man and he may be fairly considered as typical of the average better class negro of the North. Here is what he has to say about the Cosmopolitan Club affair:

"Now, that's all foolishness, those people whoopin' and hollerin' about race equality and intermarriage. If those negroes go on about their business and quit making fools of themselves the negro race would be helped lots more that they will by all that fuss.

["]What the negro wants is to quit botherin' about the negro problem and go on about his business. Let the white folks worry about the negro problem. Every negro ought to have his own problem: how to be a good citizen, how to be decent and how to help somebody else get a start."

So you see he has the common sense view of it. He lacks the learning of some of the Cosmopolitan Club folks but he has what they need somewhat, common sense. With best wishes, Sincerely,

Alfred M. Colby

ALS Con. 368 BTW Papers DLC.

[1] Possibly the Alfred M. Colby listed in the 1910 Dayton city directory as a travel agent.

From Hamilton Holt

New York, May 1st, 1908

My Dear Dr. Washington: I am planning to leave for Tuskegee probably next Tuesday afternoon or evening — I have not decided which, but I will notify your Secretary, Mr. Scott as soon as I look up the trains and definitely decide.

In view of the malicious misrepresentation of the Cosmopolitan Club Dinner last Monday night printed in The American,[1] and which I have learned, has been copied all over the South, you may think that if I should go to Tuskegee my presence there would be an injury to the School. Of course, I do not care for myself, but you have to exercise care and prudence. I leave the matter entirely in your hands. Very truly yours,

Hamilton Holt

P.S. I enclose a clipping from The Times[2] which corrects the misstatements made about me, but as you know "truth never catches up with error, if error gets the start."

TLS Con. 372 BTW Papers DLC.

1 See An Account of the Cosmopolitan Club Dinner in the New York *American*, Apr. 28, 1908, above.

2 The New York *Times* reported on Apr. 28 that what was first described as a socialist affair was actually a majority of white men sitting with a majority of black women for the purpose of decrying the caste system in America and promoting a closer relationship between the races. No mention was made of Holt or his speech in this item. (New York *Times*, Apr. 28, 1908, 1.) The next day, however, the *Times* contained a report that only one person at the dinner advocated interracial marriage. The item contained a denial by Holt that he advocated intermarriage and reiterated his solution to the race problem, which was education. Mary White Ovington also denied believing in intermarriage, the *Times* reported, but said she saw nothing wrong with educated blacks and whites sitting together. (New York *Times*, Apr. 29, 1908, 2.)

To Oswald Garrison Villard

Hotel Manhattan, New York May 2, 1908

My dear Mr. Villard: Please forgive me for disturbing you with a little matter that disturbs me frequently, and I have also heard other people express the same feeling.

We do not understand why you spell the word "Negro" in your paper with a small "n" and "Indian," for example, with a capital "I." Many of us have been trying for years to get this custom changed in the newspapers, and we very much hope that the Evening Post sympathizes with us in this respect. Yours very truly,

[Booker T. Washington]

TLS Oswald Garrison Villard Papers MH. A carbon is in Con. 42, BTW Papers, DLC.

From Carrie C. Smiley Fortune[1]

Red Bank N.J. Sunday night [ca. May 3, 1908]

My dear Mr. Washington: I saw our Dr. down here, and he told me that Mr. Fortune was not himself he has mental prostration and that if he doesn't have some thing done for his condition, he is liable to go crazy any time, he came in and had a long talk with him, and after that he said that by all means I ought to do some thing for him I ought to have a specialist to talk with him, he could go to see him with some friend and be introduced as some person of note and then he could draw him out, and cross examine him and he would not know it. Now Mr. Washington, I am very much grieved, the condition of things is almost killing me. Mr. Fortune is financially crippled, he is bound by the law to give me so much a week, but, he does not do it. I am strained here and am in an awful fix. I have not been able to pay for living here in four months, and the creditors are all restless he has only promises to give them and I don't know what to do. I appeal to you to ask your advice. I've been to Mr Moore and he tells me to keep at him, although he knows that Mr. F. has no money. I wonder if you could help me in some way make him give me one of the notes due him from the "Age" I have just got to have some money from some where soon. Of course Mr. F. is all tangled up with this white woman, and since she came back to N.Y. he has become quite insolent. I threaten him that I will arrest her, and he doesn't want me to do any thing like that, that he had trouble enough that he had no money, and when he got some, I will get some and not before. I am to be in New York Friday the 8th instant and if you will be there till then, I will call and you can talk to me and perhaps help me a little. Mr. Washington the matter is very important, and I desire very much for some one to advise with me a little, so will you please let me hear from you soon so as I can know what to do, for some thing must be done soon. He is not safe, and I am afraid of him, he is always talking about "tired of living[") and he wants me to die with him etc, etc, I am getting a little uneasy now.

Hoping to hear from you soon, or I don't know what I will do. ever very truly

(Mrs) C. C. Fortune

P.S. He has not given me but $15. since the 1st Jan. I hate to take Fred from school to go to work. I am sewing and doing all I can, but I must have more money.

C. C. F.

ALS Con. 370 BTW Papers DLC.

[1] Little is known of Carrie C. Smiley Fortune, wife of T. Thomas Fortune. She was from Florida and about sixteen years of age when she married. In New York she was active in the Brooklyn Literary Institute and several musical clubs. She was also a member of the Afro-American Women's Club. In October 1906 she separated from her husband, probably because of his severe depression and continued problem with alcohol. In 1912 T. Thomas Fortune sought a reconciliation with his wife, but she refused. (See Thornbrough, *T. Thomas Fortune*.)

From Oswald Garrison Villard

New York May 4, 1908

Dear Mr. Washington: In reply to your note I beg to state that we have always declined to capitalize "negro" because we have not wished to emphasize in that way the doings of any particular negro. On the same theory we do not capitalize "white man" or "white." When this matter was brought to my attention a couple of years ago, I consulted with my uncles about it and they approved of our position. I admit that there is an inconsistency in our capitalizing "Indian," but you must remember that we still consider the Indian as a member of a tribe with a tribal, if not a national, entity. Yours very truly,

Oswald Garrison Villard

TLS Con. 42 BTW Papers DLC.

To Samuel William Bacote

[Tuskegee, Ala.] May 5, 1908

Personal and Confidential.

My dear Dr. Bacote: Replying very briefly to your kind letter, I believe that the President would have acted just as he has acted, if the troops had been white. I think in such a case, even granting that some may believe that the President has made a mistake in this one particular, where a man has been a friend to us in nine cases out ten, I think we ought to remember the nine cases of friendship, rather than the one case of enmity. The Colored people of this country cannot afford to place themselves in continued opposition to the President of the United States, no matter who he is.

Again, it must be borne in mind that there is a difference between civil government and military government. What is done in relation to charges brought against an individual in civil life is not followed in military life in any country in the world.

In a word, I believe that we shall gain more by acting in a conservative, sensible manner under such conditions as we are now facing than by being radical and abusive.

What I have written is, of course, confidential.

I shall be glad to hear from you at any time. Yours very truly,

Booker T. Washington

TLpS Con. 365 BTW Papers DLC.

To Joseph Oswalt Thompson

[Tuskegee, Ala.] May 6, 1908

Personal and Confidential

My dear Mr. Thompson: I hope you are preparing to have some of the strongest talent in the state represent your interest before the Committee in Chicago. You will have to keep in mind that Mr. Scott[1] is going to have a tremendous advantage in being a member of the Committee himself.

One of the strongest points you can possibly use, it seems to me, is the fact that *yours is the organization which elected Mr. Scott to membership on the National Committee.* If you do not *represent the legal organization in Alabama, then Mr. Scott is not a member of the National Committee himself.* Yours very truly,

Booker T. Washington

TLpS Con. 8 BTW Papers DLC.

[1] Charles Herrington Scott.

To Frederick Randolph Moore

[Tuskegee, Ala.] May 6, 1908

Dear Mr. Moore: I wish very much that you would use the enclosed as your leader, and lead it heavily. Yours truly,

Booker T. Washington

[*Enclosure*]

Editorial

In our news columns we re-publish extracts from interviews and addresses of the leaders of the "lily white" movement in Louisiana. These extracts indicate already how the "lily white" party in that state regards the Negro.

A few days ago the "lily white" party of Alabama headed by Davidson[1] and aided by J. C. Manning held their meeting in Birmingham, Alabama. Both of these organizations have put themselves on record, as against the organization for their rights of Negroes in county, state, or national convention. They boast of what they have done and say that these are white men's organizations. Four years ago, when the "lily whites" under Davidson and others held their meeting in Birmingham, they refused to allow Negroes to even sit in the galleries.

These are the organizations that are going to Chicago, to ask to be recognized as representing the republican party in the South. There is but one republican organization in Alabama and that is the regular organization headed by Mr. J. O. Thompson and backed by the best white and colored republicans in the state.

The recognition of the Davidson faction, which is the "lily white" faction, or of the "lily whites" in Louisiana will prove an insult to every Afro-American in the western and northern states, and we might as well put ourselves on record now as being opposed to the recognition of the "lily white" element in the southern states.

The "lily whites" are the worst enemies of the political rights of the Negro in the South. The democratic party sought to disfranchise mainly the ignorant Negro; the "lily whites" go a step further and seek to take away the political rights of the intelligent Negroes, as well.

In every part of the South we should make it known that we are opposed to anything, in the way of "lily whiteism." The "lily white" party has not helped the South or any southern state where it was in control; on the other hand, the republican party has less votes, where the "lily whites" have dominated.

At Chicago the regular republican party, headed by J. O. Thompson in Alabama, should be recognized, and the "lily whites," headed by F. B. Williams in Louisiana should be turned out.

Of course, it is likely that both the "lily white" party, an element in Alabama and in Louisiana will try to secure a few weak colored people to go to Chicago on their delegations, merely to make the proper appearance. We hope, however, that no Negro in Alabama, or in Louisiana will be so lacking in racial loyalty and in honor as to suffer himself to be used as a cat's paw.

We hear that an effort is being made in Alabama to get Dr. Pettiford, President of the Alabama Penny Savings Bank, to go with the "lily whites," but we cannot believe that Dr. Pettiford would suffer himself to be used in this manner. Dr. Pettiford's bank is supported by the Negroes of Alabama, while the "lily whites," we presume do not have one cent deposited in his bank.

In the case of Louisiana, not a single Negro is on the "lily white" State Executive Committee of 96 members. This is the strongest kind of proof, as to how the "lily white" party regards the Negro in that state.

TLpS and Enclosure Con. 41 BTW Papers DLC. A note on the letter in E. J. Scott's hand reads: "send 50 copies here."

[1] J. W. Davidson.

To Carrie C. Smiley Fortune

[Tuskegee, Ala.] May 7, 1908

Dear Mrs. Fortune: Your letter which went to the hotel has followed me here. I am very sorry I had no opportunity while there to go over the matter mentioned by you as requested. I am especially sorry to make note of all that you call my attention to. I hope, however, to have a chance to speak to you sometime when I am in New York again. Yours truly,

Booker T. Washington

TLpS Con. 370 BTW Papers DLC.

To Frank Harris Hitchcock

Tuskegee Institute, Alabama May 7, 1908

Personal and Confidential.

My dear Mr. Hitchcock: In your own way and at your own time, I very much hope that you can do something to bring about an improvement in the condition of affairs in Louisiana. I am sure you do not know to what lengths the "lily white" party in that state is going in order to show their hatred of the Negro. No Negro with a drop of decent blood in his veins, or with any racial loyalty, can support a party that is acting as the "lily whites" are in that state. The only object, of course, of the Colored people, like all other races in aligning themselves with any political party, is to better their condition. They have nothing to hope for from such people as the "lily whites" in Louisiana. They are more hurtful, more bitter in their opposition to the Negro than the Democrats are. If they are permitted to keep the upper hand in Louisiana and spread their present movement, the time will soon come in the South when no Negro will have any rights left.

I know it is a delicate situation and I appreciate the perplexity that surrounds you in this as in other cases, but I am sure in the long run, when we consider the tremendous amount of work to be done among the Negroes in the North, that nothing will be gained by letting the "lily whites" go further in Louisiana unchecked. I presume you know that they do not have a single Negro on their state committee.

Mr. Thompson is to come here this week and we are going to form some plans, which we are going to put before you. I do not want to make any movement without your knowledge and approval. Yours truly,

[Booker T. Washington]

TL Con. 372 BTW Papers DLC. The original letter is unsigned and was not mailed.

From Charles Knowles Bolton[1]

Boston 7 May 1908

My dear Dr Washington: I wonder if you will pardon me who is not a politician writing to you on a political subject? I see frequent reference to a national *race* movement among negroes to defeat Mr Taft. This seems to me to be a false move on the part of the negro. Many thousands of Northern men want Mr Taft to be president and if they are thwarted in their desire by negroes *as a* race on a race issue will that not weaken the North's wish to have the negro in politics? There is a discernible trend in the North to let the South handle the negro problem — even more, I believe: to treat the negro in the North socially & politically as the South treats him.

If the negro is to fight a popular northern man like Taft by making a *race* issue he plays with fire. The Jew & the Chinaman unite their opposition. Will not this Taft question unite those at the South who want the negro barred from politics to those at the North who sympathize with the South or are wavering?

I have no particular interest in Mr Taft nor in Brownsville. I think the negro perfectly justified in voting against him if he has been in the wrong, but I do not believe a race issue ever helps the race which sets itself apart in politics & acts as a race unit. Do you? I write to you because I believe your work for the race is based on sound principles. Very truly yours

C. K. Bolton

ALS Con. 365 BTW Papers DLC.

[1] Charles Knowles Bolton (1867–1950), a graduate of Harvard (1890), was librarian at the Boston Athenaeum Library beginning in 1898. He wrote several books on historical subjects and articles on library administration.

An Article in the *Tuskegee Student*

Tuskegee Institute, Alabama, May 9, 1908

THE NEGRO IN BUSINESS

I have in the past advised the progressive business men of the Negro race to go South. In spite of the disturbances that have recently taken place there, I believe I am justified at this time in repeating this advice. In saying this I am not moved by any sentimental attachment to the South, though I do not deny that, like others of my race, I have a peculiar feeling of attachment to the Southland. I advise the business men of my race to come South because there are, I believe, business opportunities here that do not exist elsewhere.

As an evidence of this I might mention that there are now no less than thirty-three Negro banks in the Southern States owned, controlled and capitalized by Negro business men.

In considering this question one should bear in mind, first of all, that the masses of the Negro people are now and are likely for all time to remain in the South. They were born there, bred there, and I believe they are better fitted to live there than elsewhere on this continent or in Africa.

I saw a statement recently that until the beginning of the nineteenth century no city has ever increased in size by the natural growth of its native population. Where great cities sprang up they grew and maintained their population by constant accessions from the country districts. The same causes which operate to destroy the population of the cities a hundred years ago are still operating today, though to a less degree, no doubt, in the crowded city districts which most of the colored people usually live in in the North.

I do not believe the masses of colored people are yet fitted to survive and prosper in the great Northern cities to which so many of them are crowding. The temptations are too great and the competition with the foreign population is too fierce.

But on the farms and in the small towns of the South, where great masses of the Negro population are, there are the best opportunities for Negro business men. Experience has shown, I believe, even in the North that the largest opportunities for the Negro in business are in providing for those needs of other members of his own race which the white business man, either through neglect or lack of knowledge, has failed or been unable to provide. The Negro knows the members of his own race. He knows the Negro people of his neighborhood in their church and in their family life and is able to discriminate in his dealings with them.

This superiority in the matter of credits is in itself a business advantage of which competition cannot easily deprive the Negro.

Tuskegee Student, 20 (May 9, 1908), 3, 4.

From Jane E. Thompson[1]

Washington, D.C. May 11, 1908

Personal.

Dear Dr. Washington: Thanking you for your kind letter of May 9, 1908,[2] I write to say I think you better not try to see me as I asked you to, owing to the very strong race feeling here just now — some reporter might get hold of the fact that you called to see me, and misrepresent you, and make it to your [dis]advantage. As much as I desire to discuss certain things with you just now, I know I better not.

You don't know how I hate to say this — I honor you and your great work so much. But it is the unhappy result of Mr. Villard's ill-advised Cosmopolitan dinner. The amount and bitterness of remark would suprise you. Your Atlanta speech in 1894 did so much for the amity of the races, but temporarily this N.Y. episode has set things back greatly. I hope you will make another speech soon and reassure the public. Faithfully, your friend,

Jane E. Thompson

ALS Con. 383 BTW Papers DLC.

[1] Jane E. Thompson, of Thoroughfare Gap, Va., a white woman whose family had owned slaves, was a founder, with Jennie Dean, of the Manassas Industrial School for Colored Youth, where she served on the board of directors, taught, and helped with fund-raising. She later resided in Washington, D.C.

[2] BTW wrote in reply to Thompson's letter on an undisclosed matter, probably related to the Manassas school, saying he would try to see her about it when he was next in Washington. (Con. 383, BTW Papers, DLC.)

To Charles Knowles Bolton

Tuskegee Institute, Alabama May 12, 1908

My dear Mr. Bolton: Replying to your kind favor of May 7, I would state that I thank you very much for your kind letter and for the sentiments which you express regarding the Colored people's opposition to Mr. Taft. Your sentiments really are my own. I want to urge, however, that you do not suffer yourself to be misled concerning the attitude of the Colored people by a few noisy ones, especially around Boston. The great body of the Colored people are all right. When the proper time comes, they will cast their votes and their influence in a sensible direction. No one need try to hide the fact that there has been and is considerable feeling among the Colored people against the President and against Mr. Taft on account of the dismissal of the soldiers at Brownsville, but the sensible Colored people, and they are in the majority, take the view that even though a mistake has been made in this one case, they ought to overlook it in view of the many fine things that have been done for the race on the part of the President and the Republican party.

If you will read the newspapers closely, you will find that while a good many meetings are held by Colored people to express opposition to Mr. Taft, the same people appear on the program at all these meetings in every part of the country. The fact is, that for a number of months, they have been paid to get up these meetings for the purpose of injuring Mr. Taft. They have, however, now about reached the end of their rope. Since it is practically certain that Mr. Taft is to be nominated, these people who have been furnishing the money to get up indignation meetings, are ceasing to do so.

Your letter is so finely and sensibly expressed that I am going to take the liberty of having it used in an important Colored newspaper without, of course, using your name or printing anything to indicate from whom it is, unless you will give me the liberty to use your name.[1] Yours truly,

Booker T. Washington

TLS Bolton Collection MWA.

[1] Bolton replied that he was pleased with BTW's reaction to the letter and had no objection to the use of the letter or his name. (May 14, 1908, Con. 365, BTW Papers, DLC.) BTW probably sent a copy of Bolton's letter of May 7 to the New York *Age,* for in the original copy BTW's name is deleted and "To the New York Age" added as a salutation. (Con. 365, BTW Papers, DLC.)

To Ernest Lyon

[Tuskegee, Ala.] May 12, 1908

Personal and Confidential.

My dear Dr. Lyon: I have your letter of April 15th.

I have arranged in New York for accommodations of the Liberian party at a hotel. Later, friends will arrange for their accommodation in Washington. When Bishop Scott sees you, he will give you important information in detail.

I am writing now, however, to say very confidentially that arrangements have been made by which the President will receive these envoys unofficially. This, of course, gives them a certain great advantage, as under ordinary circumstances, the President himself would not, I think, receive persons of such a mission, but would let them have their entire business connection with the State Department.

Further, I am planning to bring these parties to Tuskegee arranging for special railroad accommodations. I am hoping to have them remain here several days, also, to see something of the best life of our people in other parts of the South and in America. I shall propose to bring them to Tuskegee at my own expense.

Let me know whenever I can serve you. Yours truly,

Booker T. Washington

TLpS Con. 375 BTW Papers DLC.

From Charles William Anderson

New York, N.Y., May 12, 1908

My dear Doctor: I am this day in receipt of a letter from John W. Conner,[1] inviting you to be present at a game of Base Ball between the Royal Giants, and the Cuban Giants on May 30th, at the Polo grounds. These are the two champion colored base ball teams of the country, and Conner who manages one of them, is very anxious to have you present, and to have you throw the ball to the "umpire." This is the usual bit of stage craft incident to the opening of a series of base ball games, and is usually performed by the Mayor of this city for the New York League Team. Hence, Conners wants you to act for these colored teams. It is a rather peculiar invitation to extend to you, but I promised to pass it along — so here it is. If you have any sporting blood in your veins you may desire to accept it, if not, please advise me at an early date.

I see that Cohen has allowed the Lilly Whites to out-general him in Louisiana. Their star play in instructing for Taft yesterday, and electing a colored delegate-at-large, will probably result in their being seated in the Convention. I am afraid he has mismanaged his fight. His timidity, with reference to Taft, gave the other side their opportunity, and they have promptly made the most of it. I am now at a loss to see how any sane man can prevail upon Taft's friends in the National Committee to seat Cohen. I, for one, shall keep my hands out of it. When a man ceases to be brave enough to stand by his friends, I soon lose all interest in him. Every report that I have had from Louisiana, either states or intimates that Cohen is for Foraker. If so, let him take his reward from the friends of Foraker.

The newspapers throughout the country are beginning to talk about two great negro factions, one of which is led by you. The only way to put the quietus on all of this, is to close up the ranks, stand by those who are loyal to you, and drop those who flirt with your opponents. If Cohen is in this latter class, let him drop too. Yours truly,

Charles W. Anderson

TLS Con. 38 BTW Papers DLC.

[1] John W. Connor, born in Virginia about 1874, was owner of the successful Royal Cafe in Brooklyn and the Royal Giants baseball team. Conner served in the U.S. Navy during the Spanish-American War, retiring after the war to open his restaurant in Brooklyn. He was active in several black lodges, the Spanish-American War Veterans, and the H. H. Garnet Republican Club. (New York *Age*, Aug. 23, 1906, 7.)

From Samuel William Bacote

Kansas City, Mo., May 16, 1908

My Very Dear Friend: Your kind missive came just as I was about to take train for Little Rock, Ark. I have just returned.

I heartily agree with your position, and believe as you, that the President would have acted just the same, if the discharged regiments had been white. In view of what Mr. Roosevelt has done for the race, it is difficult for me to believe him its enemy.

Sometime ago, I listened to an address by Sec'y Taft, in this city and was convinced that he is not only the true friend of the Negro, but should he be nominated for the Presidency, the Negro would receive considerably more recognition than from any other man the Republicans could nominate and elect. The time has come for the best element of the Negro ministry to take a hand in directing the professional politician to a back seat in the leadership of the race. After the Chicago nomination, I shall have something to say in a quiet, yet positive manner, upon the position the Negro should assume in the campaign.

Thanking you for your letter and assuring you that I shall hold it strictly confidential, I remain Yours

Sam'l W. Bacote

TLS Con. 365 BTW Papers DLC. A copy was sent to William Howard Taft.

To Ernest Hamlin Abbott

[Tuskegee, Ala.] May 20, 1908

Personal and Confidential

My dear Mr. Abbott: Replying to yours of May 12th regarding the National Negro Political League, I would state that this organization is about as near nothing as it is possible for any organization to be, that gets its name into the newspapers. It is purely an artificial creation that has taken place within the last few months. I know this part of the movement fully and understand their motives. No one need regard them seriously. With one or two exceptions, the persons identified with it are individuals who have a wide reputation among colored people for looking for notoriety or seeking money. All told, I am quite sure they could not influence two hundred votes.

I do not mean, however, to give you the impression that there is not considerable opposition to Secretary Taft among the Colored people, for there is, but the organization referred to has practically no influence one way or the other among the thinking people of our race. The opposition will gradually disappear, you would find, after the Secretary is nominated and people come to understand him better, in fact, it is already disappearing very fast.

I hope you understand that most of the loud talk against the

President and Secretary Taft has been carried on by a few colored people who have been paid by certain parties in New York to keep up this agitation, but since the money has ceased to appear, the agitation is disappearing. Yours truly,

Booker T. Washington

TLpS Con. 364 BTW Papers DLC.

From Samuel Edward Courtney

Boston May 23rd 1908

My dear Dr Washington: Your letter of the 20th rec'd. I hasten to write you so you can understand the situation to date. When I wrote you last, I thought everything was adjusted satisfactorily. The Grand Lodge was called last night, to which the Centennial Committee was invited. Gilbert Harris[1] & I would not attend, being already thoroughly disgusted with the cheap Negroes who are members of the Grand Lodge. They did what I expected, voted to ask you to resign as Orator of the occasion of the Centennial Celebration, and you are to be informed by the Secy. of the Grand Lodge, Bro. Monroe of New Bedford. Reed was elected by the Grand Lodge to be Orator. You know the Grand Lodge is greater than the Centennial Committee & therefore has the power to undo what the Committee has done. This entire thing has been the work of Reed, Teamoh[2] & The New Bedford set who are all members of the Grand Lodge. I at first thought I would have you withdraw your acceptance before the Lodge met, but after thinking it over, your friends thought it would be best to let the Lodge do what *they* thought best & wise. They did it, now we, your friends are in a position to show the entire thing up to the Country. Gilbert Harris has resigned from the Committee entirely. I shall stay on the Com. long enough to put them in a bad light before the country, then resign myself and take all of *our* friends from participation in the celebration. I am thoroughly disgusted with the letter Reed sent you.[3] It's false from start to finish, and if this is a sample of the letters he has sent out as Secy. of the Com. no wonder we are in such a muddle. With your permission I will read it to the Committee. He has been the "Nigger in the woodpile" althrough this affair.

I am pleased to inform you that Grand Master Marshall and Chairman the Com. Wentworth[4] stood by you to the end. When the whole affair was over the Grand Lodge was *worried* as to the out come of the affair, which simply means we are now to have a small Negro affair as there will be no attraction to outsiders. I feel sure the Masons of the Country will resent the insult, & show it by staying away from Massachusetts this fall. I shall certainly make an explanation through the city press of the whole affair when it gets to the public. Anything you may wish said, thro. me, I will see that the people get it. Shall write you again soon. Very truly yours,

S. E. Courtney

ALS Con. 369 BTW Papers DLC.

[1] Gilbert C. Harris owned a wig-manufacturing company in Boston that supplied theatrical groups. The Boston branch of the NNBL was founded in his office, and he became its first treasurer.

[2] Robert T. Teamoh, former editor of the Boston *Courant*, had served one term in the Massachusetts House of Representatives in the 1890s.

[3] William L. Reed, without mentioning that he was selected to be centennial orator, wrote BTW that he regretted the change in the program, and blamed the situation on the "lack of tact on the part of some of the members of our committee." (May 4, 1908, Con. 380, BTW Papers, DLC.)

[4] Nelson P. Wentworth, an employee of the U.S. Appraisers' Office in Boston, was a leader in the Prince Hall Grand Lodge for many years beginning in the 1890s.

Emmett Jay Scott to Walter L. Cohen

[Tuskegee, Ala.] May 25, 1908

Confidential.

My dear Walter: I have been absent from Tuskegee for a considerable period of time, as you most likely know, having gone on from Philadelphia to Norfolk and Hampton and afterward to New York and Washington. On my return I find all of your several communications. I confess, however, that I am slightly in the air, taking them as a whole, and I think at the same time that even our friend is in a measure embarrassed for some of the reasons which are herewith set forth.

In the first place, you will remember that he has suggested at various times that you go directly on to Washington and see Secretary Taft himself. This you did not see your way clear to do.

Then he suggested that you make a trip to Washington to see Secretary Garfield. This you did not see your way clear to do.

Then, you will remember, you made two applications for leave of absence, one through Pearl Wight,[1] and again direct, asking for leave of absence June first.

The embarrassment comes about, although you cannot go on to Washington to see Secretary Taft or Mr. Garfield, you were able to go to Chicago to confer with Mr. New, Senator Scott, Elmer Dover, etc. Now as you know positively, Senator Scott and Mr. Dover are not in favor of Secretary Taft's nomination. Mr. New of course is for Fairbanks. Under the circumstances, then, you see it seems a bit out of the way for you to be able to confer with three men who are opposed to Secretary Taft's nomination and are not able to confer with any of the men who are directly involved in bringing about his nomination. You can easily see that if Senator Scott and Mr. Dover and others begin making a fight for your presence at Chicago, you will only stir up the administration men to the fact that you are working along with their enemies. It is certainly hardly necessary for you to make a trip to Chicago to find out from Mr. New that *Secretary Taft is going to be nominated,* because this was known to you and all the rest of us weeks ago.

You cannot fail to appreciate, as we all do, that you are going up against a pretty strong combination at Chicago. In the first place, you have never declared for Taft while the other people have. In the next place, some of your strongest friends have received intimation that you are for Foraker and not for Taft. In the next place you have been in conference from time to time with men who are generally regarded as non-administration, and when Pharr walked out of the convention and two colored men were placed on the Lily White delegation, you can see that they have been placed in a somewhat strong position when they go on to Chicago.

Our friend is really in the air. He does not know what to do. You have so many influences working already through the various applications that he thinks he should wait the conclusion of them all before doing anything. You will keep us advised as to how your various communications are coming out, and it may be, toward the end, our friend can think of something effective. Just now, however, as above indicated, he does not feel that he should obtrude himself in the present situation. If you do not become antagonistic, as I have already indicated to you, he feels that the matter of your own retention in office is secure.

I am not writing this letter for any one but yourself, and I hope that you will not take it up with any of your political friends. I am simply placing before you the situation as I find it and as it seems to appear to our friend. Yours truly,

Emmett J. Scott

TLpS Con. 40 BTW Papers DLC.

[1] Pearl Wight (1844–1920), a prominent New Orleans white merchant and shipbuilder, was a member of the Republican National Committee beginning in 1905. In 1907 Theodore Roosevelt appointed him Commissioner of Internal Revenue, but Wight declined the position. From 1912 to 1916 he was a member of the Progressive party's national committee.

To William Howard Taft

Tuskegee, Ala., May 27, 1908

Liberian envoys spending two days here looking through our work. They are anxious to have interview with you while in this country and I strong[ly] urge you grant an informal interview to them and myself. I shall probably be in Washington to see President with them some time between June eighth and tenth and if agreeable could see you at your house preferable evening after they see President. Please answer my expense.[1]

Booker T. Washington

TWSr William Howard Taft Papers DLC.

[1] Fred W. Carpenter, Taft's secretary, replied: "Secretary Taft will be very glad to see Liberian envoys when you are in Washington between eighth and tenth June." (May 28, 1908, William Howard Taft Papers, DLC.)

From Frederic S. Monroe

New Bedford, Mass. May 27th, 1908

Dear Sir and Brother: At a Special Communication of the M. W. Prince Hall Grand Lodge F. & A. M. of Massachusetts, holden May 22d, 1908, one of the calls for which is herewith enclosed, it was voted:

"That Dr. Washington be officially notified by the Grand Secretary, in a courteous and fraternal letter, that his selection as Centennial Orator has created such serious discord in this and other jurisdictions, that the M. W. Prince Hall Grand Lodge finds it imperatively necessary in the interests of harmony to withdraw the invitation extended to him by the Executive Committee."

These dissensions are of such a nature as to permanently threaten the peace and harmony of the jurisdiction, but are not as yet in any way personal to you. On the contrary, they are the expressions of a deep-rooted, earnest and sincere conviction on the part of a very large majority of the brethren, that they should be represented on this occasion by a Massachusetts Mason; one identified by years of association with the Grand Lodge; one familiar with its history and traditions; one who has contributed to its growth and development. This protest would have been none the less urgent if some one else — other than yourself — not a Massachusetts Mason had been selected as orator. To the refusal of the Chairman of the Executive Committee to consider these feelings, to his inability properly to appreciate the conditions, is due in no small degree the present situation, compelling Grand Lodge action in the way herein before stated. Of course you can have no desire to be a source of contention, or to be the cause of lasting discord, for there is neither honor nor profit in that.

It is therefore respectfully suggested, as a courtesy to which you are entitled — and this in accordance with instructions given the writer by his Grand Lodge — that you forward through this office your withdrawal of any acceptance of invitations extended to you by the Executive Committee to be present as a speaker at the Centennial, placing it upon such grounds as may commend themselves to your judgment.

I should be remiss in my duty as the representative of this Grand Body, if I did not say that the vote of the Grand Lodge renders null and void all that the Executive Committee has done in this direction, and has taken it out of its hands altogether. As the Grand Lodge is the Supreme Governing Power its action is final. The question has been seriously and carefully considered, with due regard for the interests of all concerned, and we believe you will be willing to cooperate with us in the way suggested, as the wise and proper thing to do under present conditions.

It is necessary that this change in the programme be given to the public as promptly as possible, as the time is very short. It is the desire of the Grand Lodge to accord you the fullest possible consideration, but if this is not permitted, it will necessarily be obliged to publish the Grand Lodge action, and it is to be hoped that this will not be forced upon us. Trusting for an early and favorable reply, I am Fraternally yours

Frederic S. Monroe

TLS Con 376 BTW Papers DLC. On stationery of the Prince Hall Grand Lodge, of which Monroe was Grand Secretary.

From William Howard Taft

[Washington, D.C.] May 28, 1908

Personal.

My dear Doctor: I write to inquire what you would think of the wisdom of having Lewis, of Massachusetts, act as one of those who second my nomination in the Chicago Convention. I believe it would be better to have a colored man from the north do it, and I am sure he could not come from a better state than Massachusetts. Will you let me hear from you on this subject as soon as possible? I know you have talked with Vorys about this business, and I do not want to act in it until I get your judgment. Very sincerely yours,

Wm H Taft

TLpS William Howard Taft Papers DLC.

Walter L. Cohen to Emmett Jay Scott

New Orleans, La., May 31, 1908

My dear Emmett, I forgot yesterday was Decoration Day or I would not have promised you to write again as I did. I went down to Chalmette and took part in the services and hence did not get back in time to write.

I don't agree with you in that I am going up against a tough proposition at Chicago. Of course if the fight is a close one I don't expect to win out because I know the Taft forces will use their utmost to seat the other crowd. It is true I have never declared for Taft but to you and our friend I have been very outspoken. If you consider the fight I had I think you will agree that I have done very well in having a delegation elected that at least two thirds will be for Taft. If I had not taken hold of the opposition here the entire crowd would be anti-Taft. As it is there is no telling if barely the entire delegation will not cast their votes for him on the very first ballot. There is another side of the question and that is this. If you remember Mr. Hitchcock did not play square with the Taft people when the National Committee met in December. He was then acting in the interest of some other candidate. If he had acted on the square the convention would have been at Kansas City. If you will look over the votes for Chicago you will see the name of Pearl Wight. I say to you that Mr. Wight at that time told me that he thought Cortelyou was the strongest candidate. Of course he was simply voicing Hitchcock's sentiments.

As for the "Lily Whites" electing a negro on their delegation I will be prepared to meet the issue. If what you say about it being too late for me to declare for Taft it seems the same ought to hold good in their case of electing a negro after it was plainly told to them that unless they did there would be no chance of their getting a "peep in" at the Convention.

With the friends I have and with what you and our friend can do I feel satisfied that I will get the victory. The only man in our way is Hitchcock and from what our friend did for him it seems to me that he can pull him off. I some time[s] think that Hitchcock is playing a certain game so as to be able to hold certain delegation[s] so as to turn the tide if necessary. As for myself I have lost faith in him. While speaking of Hitchcock it might be well for me to recall to you that in keeping with your advice when I went to Washington in December I called on Hitchcock three times. At no time did I get any satisfaction out of him. His last advice was to go home and act along with Pearl Wight and I told him I did not see my way clear to do this when he told me well if you don't you will be shut out [of] the convention. He no doubt will try and keep his word.

As I wrote you I am expecting to leave here Tuesday night unless you write or wire me you will leave during the week. In that event I shall wait for you.

With best wishes I am, as ever, Yours faithfully,

Walter L. Cohen

TLS Con. 40 BTW Papers DLC.

To William Howard Taft

[Tuskegee, Ala.] June 3, 1908

Personal and Confidential

My dear Secretary Taft: I am writing on a very confidential subject and one on which I fear you will think I am meddling into matters in which I am not concerned.

But I must say that I consider it will be a great mistake if Mr. Luke Wright is made your successor. It will place a heavy additional burden upon your canvass after the nomination. Rightfully or wrongfully, the masses of the colored people have the feeling that Mr. Luke Wright is responsible for the interjection of much color prejudice in the Philippines. They have the feeling that he was not in favor of giving the Filipinos a square deal by reason of their color. Aside from all this, he is a Democrat, and our enemies are making a good deal over the fact, or trying to do so, that the President is a Southern Democrat. You know my own personal feeling in regard to these matters is in the direction of liberality and common sense, but just now I feel it would be a pretty dangerous experiment to place Mr. Luke Wright Secretary of War. If you feel that I ought to say this to the President I shall be very glad to do so.

There are already many apparent signs to the effect that our enemies are waiting to seize hold of this appointment and use it for all that it is worth against you and the President. Yours very truly,

Booker T. Washington

TLpS Con. 6 BTW Papers DLC.

To William Howard Taft

[Tuskegee, Ala.] June 3, 1908

Personal

My dear Secretary Taft: I have just sent you a telegram in answer to yours of May 28th reading as follows:

"After thinking matter over carefully think W. H. Lewis of Boston would be a safe and good person to second nomination. Of course I presume you realize that Lewis is not a delegate or alternate and will have to get a proxy."

After consider[ing] the matter fully I rather think that Lewis is the best man to second the nomination. There are several elements of weakness in his case, but there are also elements of strength. In the first place, he will be sure to make a capital speech and a good impression on the Convention. One of the elements of weakness is the fact that he is an office holder and is not a delegate but, as I have suggested, he can of course secure a proxy. It is much better to have a colored man from the North than from the South.

I hope to send you tomorrow a suggestion for a plank in the platform at Chicago referring to our race.

I shall hope to see you within a few days. Yours very truly,

Booker T. Washington

TLpS Con. 6 BTW Papers DLC.

To Ernest Lyon

[Tuskegee, Ala.] June 3, 1908

Confidential

My dear Mr. Lyon: I am simply writing to say that the Envoys spent two days here covering our Commencement period, and we are all more than delighted with them, and we all feel that they got a great deal that will be of value to them out of the visit. All of us are immensely pleased with the personnel of the party; their modesty, common sense and deep earnestness pleased every one. They were given a great deal of attention while here, and we would have given them more but we did not want to do anything to detract from their opportunity of seeing the school in its actual work.

I have made an engagement with President Roosevelt to go to the White House with them on the night of June 10th. I have taken the liberty to arrange the meeting at the White House in the evening because I have found that this is really the way to get a full, free and frank conference with the President. Whenever I want to accomplish anything of value I get him to permit me to come to the White House at night when he is free from other cares and duties, and in this way I am quite sure we can arrange to have an hour with the President, something that very few people get. In addition, I have made an engagement for them to call with me on Secretary Taft. I think in view of the fact that it is practically certain that Secretary Taft will be in the White House during the next four, or perhaps next eight, years it is important that they get acquainted with him, and get his influence and good wishes.

If you will permit me to say rather frankly, it is my opinion that Liberia has made a mistake in the last few years in not cultivating the good will of the people in America. The fact is, Americans have in a large degree forgotten Liberia. They are interested in Liberia, but their interest must be kept awake and alive in some way. I very much fear that Liberia has drifted too much toward other countries and not kept alive the original and historic attachment between America and Liberia that it should have been done. The visit of these Envoys is going a long ways toward re-awakening and reviving the old interest.

I have sought as far as possible to keep the Envoys from attending public functions which our own race is anxious to provide for them until they are through with their diplomatic work at the State Department and at the White House. You of course can easily understand that somebody might make some fool utterance that might damage their mission. Of course after they are through with their interviews with the Secretary of State and the President, matters will be different.

All this of course is wholly confidential. Yours very truly,

Booker T. Washington

If it is known in Washington that the three million Negro voters in the United States object to any foreign nation encroaching upon Liberian territory, a way will be found to carry out the wishes, in my opinion, of the American Negroes.

TLpS Con. 375 BTW Papers DLC.

To Charles William Anderson

[Tuskegee, Ala.] June 3, 1908

Our big friend asks for my advice regarding having Lewis of Boston second nomination. Think we had better agree to this. While he has several weak points if we dont get him we may get somebody worse.

B. T. W.

TWpIr Con. 38 BTW Papers DLC.

To Charles William Anderson

[Tuskegee, Ala.] June 3, 1908

Personal

My dear Mr. Anderson: I have just received the enclosed copy of a letter from our friend in Washington. I have advised him to have Lewis do this, although of course I realize as you do, that there are several weak elements in his doing it, and some stronger man might have been selected, but I feared that if we did not clinch the matter at once with Lewis the fellow from Kansas[1] might be selected which would have been disastrous, or if not him some other fellow who would have been untrustworthy or disloyal. Of course, you would doubtless have been considered or selected but for the fact that your delegation is committed to Mr. Hughes. Yours very truly,

Booker T. Washington

TLpS Con. 38 BTW Papers DLC.

[1] William T. Vernon.

To William Howard Taft

[Tuskegee, Ala.] June 4, 1908

Personal and Very Confidential

My dear Mr. Secretary: Enclosed I send you some suggestions for a plank in the Chicago platform. Of course, I presume the wording will be changed, but I have tried to make my meaning clear. I think I know the situation pretty well among the colored people and I do think the substance of what is stated in this suggestion ought to go in the platform in some form. I have put it in plain language as the situation demands plain language, something which cannot be misunderstood or misinterpreted.

My own view is that something like the enclosed would do more good than the meaningless platform about reducing Southern representation. That was in the last platform and made no impression because it did not mean anything, and if another plank goes into the platform about reducing Southern representation I do not believe it will make the least impression, but what I have suggested, in my opinion, if put in some form would help the situation tremendously.

The words "Lily Whitism" may seem inelegant, but the meaning will be clear to all. Yours very truly,

Booker T. Washington

[*Enclosures*]

Suggested Plank for Platform:

The Republican Party had its origin in an effort to secure equal justice to all men. Above the tariff, above the currency question, is the matter of justice between man and man and as between race and race. The Republican Party, as now constituted, cannot afford to deviate in any degree from the principles of its founders. If the party anywhere has drifted from its original moorings, it should as speedily as possible get back to the original starting point and demand justice for all men regardless of race and regardless of color.

In this connection we applaud and commend the efforts of President Roosevelt to secure equal accommodations on railroads and other public carriers for the white and black races.

The Republican Party demands that wherever any law relating to the civil or political conduct or rights of individuals is framed and promulgated, that that law shall apply with equal and exact justice to all races; especially is this true in regard to the exercise of the franchise. The weak need the protection which the ballot affords. No color line should be recognized in the American ballot. The provision known as the "grandfather clause" in some state constitutions is an insult to American manhood and we condemn and oppose it as unwarranted and un-American.

The National Republican Party unequivocally records itself as opposed to the recognition of any party organization which excludes or discourages men from joining county, state or national organizations because of their race or color; and especially does the party record itself as being opposed to the doctrine known in some parts of the country as "Lily Whiteism." This departure from Republican principles must find no place in the plans or policies of the Republican Party.

Rights of the Negro:

The Republican party has been for more than fifty years the consistent friend of the American Negro. It granted to him the freedom & the citizenship which he earned by his valor & service. It wrote into the organic law of the land the declarations that proclaim his civil and political rights, and it believes today that his noteworthy progress in intelligence, industry and good citizenship has earned the respect and encouragement of the Nation. We demand equal justice for all men, without regard to race or color; we approve the efforts of President Roosevelt and the vote of the Republican majority in Congress, over a solid Democratic opposition, to secure equal accommodations on railroads and other public carriers for all citizens, whether white or black; we declare once more, and without reservation, for the enforcement in spirit and letter of all those amendments to the Constitution which were designed for the protection and advancement of the Negro, and we condemn all devices like the so-called "grandfather clause" that have for their real aim his disfranchisement for reasons of color alone, as unfair, un-American and repugnant to the supreme law of the land.

TLpS and Enclosures Con. 7 BTW Papers DLC. Editorial changes in the enclosures are in E. J. Scott's hand.

To Hugh Mason Browne

Tuskegee Institute, Alabama June 5, 1908

My dear Mr. Browne: Perhaps I have missed some of your letters. In your last one, you referred to some work that Mr. Wright[1] is preparing to do. What is this? You, also, referred to what Mr. Forbes is preparing to do. What is that?

In setting the price for work, I think we might use somewhat as a model the price being paid Mr. D. W. Woodard, who is a first-class man. He is to spend three weeks in Jackson during the summer getting the data and is to prepare the pamphlet and the whole expense, including travelling and everything else, is not to go beyond $105.80.

I think you will have to be very careful in dealing with such a man as Forbes to see that we do not pay for a mere voice in the wilderness without any definite end in view. It is the easiest thing in the world to get up a lot of discouraging figures showing the bad side of the Convict Lease System. This we should not include in the pamphlet and my opinion is that the best thing to ask Mr. Forbes to drive at is to show in what way the Convict Lease System in the South is supporting the state and local governments. This would be a strong and interesting point, for example, I believe that a careful investigation will show that last year there was turned into the state treasury over Four Hundred Thousand Dollars net as a result of the Convict Lease System. Of course, nine-tenths of this money was earned by Colored convicts. It would be interesting to show what proportion of the state expenses is thus borne by colored people. This would be an off-set to the oft repeated cry that the Negro does not bear his proper share of the burden of taxation. On the whole, I agree with what you have said to Mr. Forbes in your letter. Yours truly,

Booker T. Washington

TLS BTW Papers ATT. A press copy is in Con. 39, BTW Papers, DLC.

[1] Richard Robert Wright, Jr., born in Cuthbert, Ga., in 1878, was one of the most highly educated black Americans of his time. He graduated from the school his father founded and presided over, Georgia State Industrial College. He then earned A.M. and B.D. degrees at the University of Chicago, studied in German universities, and took a Ph.D. in sociology at the University of Pennsylvania. Ordained an A.M.E. minister in 1900, he divided his efforts between church work and social work, being the founder of a social settlement for blacks in Philadelphia. After six years as president of Wilberforce University, in 1936 he was elected an A.M.E. bishop, and presided over districts in the United States, the West Indies, and South Africa.

To William Pancoast Clyde

[Tuskegee, Ala.] June 5, 1908

My dear Mr. Clyde: I have just returned from my South Carolina trip. After speaking in Beaufort on Saturday, a party of us, including about eight, spent the day on Hilton Head. We went over the island thoroughly and saw a good deal of conditions there. I am more encouraged than I have ever been.

To begin with, the land is much better than I thought it was, much more fertile and lays better. We shall have to, in my opinion, interject a little new blood into the island. The people are about as run down as the animals, but there is a foundation for a good work there.

We had an interesting and large meeting in the Baptist Church, where several of us spoke to them for nearly two hours. Tommie Wright and others did all they could to make our visit successful and pleasant.

A white family who keeps the store was extremely kind. Mrs. W. D. Brown served a very nice dinner to our party and in every way went out of her way to be attentive to us. In fact, the white people seemed just as much interested as the colored, and all seemed anxious for anything to be done that would help conditions on the island.

I think it well that several additional Tuskegee men be sent there to take up farms, in the same way that other people are taking farms.

It seems to me that we are going ahead in the right and proper way and that is slowly and carefully.

When I see you again, I shall hope to tell you and your son, more in detail about our visit. Yours truly,

Booker T. Washington

TLpS Con. 367 BTW Papers DLC.

To Charles G. Kelley[1]

Tuskegee Institute, Alabama June 5, 1908

Mr. Kelley: I find that there is considerable criticism, based upon the report that your house is used pretty freely by teachers of the opposite sex who wish to be in company with each other. I think it wise for you and Mrs. Kelley to guard against this. It is always hurtful for a family to get that kind of a reputation. It does no one any good for people to get the idea that they can go to visit a family, not because they are interested in the family, but simply because they want to use the convenience that the family has for their own selfish purpose.

Booker T. Washington

TLS Con. 6 BTW Papers DLC. On the bottom of the letter Kelley replied: "Mrs Kelley, & Myself will guard against any such criticism in the future; While I think that any information you may have has been grossly exaggerated I never the less feel that your calling my attention to it is right.

I would like to have a copy of this letter to show to all couples who may call."

[1] Charles G. Kelley served in the business office of Tuskegee as freight agent (1903–7), receiving clerk (1907–13), and assistant business agent from 1913 until after 1915.

To Frederic S. Monroe

[Tuskegee, Ala.] June 5, 1908

Dear Sir and Brother: Please forgive the delay in answering your letter of May 27th. When it reached my office I was away in South Carolina and did not receive your letter until my return home.

Please permit me to say that from a personal point of view I am heartily glad to be relieved of the duty and responsibility of preparing an oration for the Centennial. Especially is this true because of the numerous other engagements which I have at about the same season.

Really I cannot see that the situation demands any action on my part. In a word, as I see it, it is as follows: Your Executive Committee extended me an invitation to speak. I accepted. Later the Grand Lodge rescinded the work of its Executive Committee—that is, withdrew the invitation. That, it seems to me, ends the whole matter from an official point of view.

In your kind and courteous letter you were kind enough to use the following words:

"It is therefore respectfully suggested, as a courtesy to which you are entitled — and this in accordance with instructions given the writer by his Grand Lodge — that you forward through this office your withdrawal of any acceptance of invitations extended to you by the Executive Committee to be present as a speaker at the Centennial, placing it upon such grounds as may commend themselves to your judgment."

I am very sorry that I cannot bring myself to take this view of the case or to act in accordance with the suggestion. If I have learned anything of value from our grand order during the time that I have been connected with it, it is that one of the things that it stands for is truth, frankness, squareness between man and man. To write such a letter as is suggested would be to deceive, to make something appear which was not real; would be to give the impression that I was withdrawing from something when something had already been withdrawn from me. For a number of years I have been a teacher of youth, and have always taught that short cuts and pretenses never pay, but in the long run it pays better to be square, frank and open, even though by so doing one may seem to meet with momentary defeat and embarrassment.

Just one other consideration. I am so new and young in the order that I hardly dare suggest it, and that is in the future it might be wise when one considers the ancient, honorable and dignified character of an organization which we all hold in such high esteem to so safeguard the actions of the order itself as well as its agencies, that whatever is done will carry with it the element of deliberation, decisiveness and dignity, and will not be dependent upon the whim or reported untactfulness of some individual or individuals.

The awkward turn that affairs have taken I wish to assure you, however, does not in the slightest degree diminish my interest or faith in the organization which all of us hold so dear, nor does it diminish my interest in the success of the Centennial Celebration of one of the greatest organizations in the world, nor can it diminish the esteem in which I hold the memory and the deeds of Prince Hall, whose name the jurisdiction bears. Yours with fraternal regards,

Booker T. Washington

TLpS Con. 376 BTW Papers DLC.

To Emmett Jay Scott

Tuskegee Institute, Alabama June 5, 1908

Mr. Scott: I really want you to go to the Chicago Convention. The only question is the method of providing the expenses. I do not feel that it is a matter that I ought to ask the school to take care of and I have been drawn upon so heavily personally lately, that I feel I would be doing an injustice to myself and family to advance money for the purpose, but as I have said, I really want you to go and I think you better prepare to do so.

B. T. W.

TLI Con. 582 BTW Papers DLC.

To William Howard Taft

[Tuskegee, Ala.] June 5, 1908

Personal

My dear Secretary Taft: I have just received your telegram asking me to telegraph Mr. Hitchcock giving my views as to Mr. Thompson and Mr. Scott. I have sent Mr. Hitchcock a telegram which he could put before the members of the National Committee endorsing Mr. Thompson as strongly as I could.

Anticipating that the Alabama case was going to be a pivotal one, I began work several weeks ago to back up Mr. Thompson in Chicago. In the first place, I arranged for a half dozen of the strongest colored men in Chicago and vicinity to get hold of Mr. Lowden,[1] the Illinois Committeeman, and also to be present during the sessions of the Committee and impress the members of the Committee with the idea that Mr. Thompson had friends among the colored people in the North. I also arranged for Gov. Pinchback to go to Chicago with the same end in view, at my expense. I have also arranged that Mr. Tyler and other colored friends be present with the same end in view. In addition to all this, I have written individual letters to every member of the Committee whom I personally know.

I know that matters will turn out all right in the end. Yours very truly,

Booker T. Washington

TLpS Con. 7 BTW Papers DLC.

[1] Frank Orren Lowden (1861–1943), an Illinois member of the Republican National Committee from 1904 to 1912, served in the U.S. House of Representatives from 1906 to 1911 and later was governor of Illinois (1917–21).

From William Howard Taft

Washington June 5, 1908

My dear Doctor Washington: I have your letter of June 3rd. I sent you a telegram last night with reference to the Alabama delegation in order that if possible there might be no doubt that Thompson's delegation represents both races and that the Davidson crowd are the Lily Whites. I have consulted with Senator Lodge with respect to the Lewis matter and he objects to Lewis making the nomination on the ground that he is an office-holder. They will have to make some selection of a colored man in Chicago. I wish you could suggest some others to Hitchcock and write him at the Auditorium Annex in Chicago. Very sincerely yours,

Wm H Taft

TLS Con. 7 BTW Papers DLC.

To William Howard Taft

Tuskegee, Ala., June 6 [1908]

Personal very much hope you will stick to Lewis to make address seconding nomination I am to see you Wednesday next in case you think of changing to another person but Lewis I am sure will be best all things considered.

Booker T. Washington

TWSr William Howard Taft Papers DLC.

From Joseph Oswalt Thompson

Chicago. June 6–08

My Dear Doctor: We dont know how to thank you for the great aid you gave us throughout this fight. We saw evidence of it on every hand. The contest did good as it gave the Committee a chance to see the personel of our delegation both white & colored, in comparison with the other crowd.

We hope to be able to make a good showing at the polls in Ala. this fall.

Lily Whitism is forever stamped out in Alabama. Your Friend,

Jos. O. Thompson

Let me know through Mr. Scott just whom to provide tickets with.

We would so much like to see you here.

ALS Con. 363 BTW Papers DLC.

From Charles William Anderson

New York June 6 1908

Quite agree with you concerning Lewis Bishop Derrick is working for Vernon We ought to defeat Vernon at all hazards.

Chas W Anderson

HWSr Con. 38 BTW Papers DLC.

From William Howard Taft

Washington June 6, 1908

My dear Dr. Washington: I have received your kind telegram of June 5th, congratulating me on the seating of the Thompson delegation at Chicago.[1] I am very much gratified about this.

I have sent word to Mr. Hitchcock that I am very anxious that he should not take a position in favor of Lily White delegations like that one in Louisiana. I believe they have some colored men on the delegation, and I am quite sure that Cohen and his men ought to be given substantial recognition. There are places, however, where negro delegations are hunting for recognition that are merely frauds and ought to be thrown out without respect to the general question, upon which I have, as I have already expressed to you, a very deep feeling, to wit, that the negro vote in the south should not be ignored, but fully recognized. Sincerely yours,

Wm H Taft

TLS Con. 7 BTW Papers DLC.

[1] The telegram is in the William Howard Taft Papers, DLC.

To William Howard Taft

Tuskegee, Ala., June 7th 1908

Have just telegraphed Mr. Hitchcock as follows: "Hope you will be as generous and considerate as possible in case of Cohen of Louisiana. In my opinion it is quite different from others as Cohen has been fighting for a principle. He has made definite promises all along that no matter what happened his support would go to the Secretary. Faction he has been opposing in Louisiana has been badly tainted with Lilly Whiteism."

Don't know whether you feel like sending any word to Mr. Hitchcock. Colored people of North, especially are closely watching Louisiana case.

Booker T. Washington

TWSr William Howard Taft Papers DLC.

To William Howard Taft

[Tuskegee, Ala.] June 7, 1908

Personal

My dear Secretary Taft: I have just received your very kind letter regarding the objection made to Lewis by Senator Lodge. By the time I see you Wednesday I would suggest consideration on your part of the two following persons:

First: Charles Banks of Mound Bayou, Mississippi, who is the cashier and controlling influence in a Negro bank there and a delegate-at-large to the Convention. Banks is very black, has a pleasing appearance, is a good speaker and stands well with the strongest of both races in Mississippi.

Second: Bishop Abraham Grant of Kansas City, (not Missouri). He is not a delegate to the Convention but can easily, I am sure, secure a proxy.

I shall try to think of one or two others by the time I see you.

From several points of view, I think it would be better if this matter could be decided before the delegates go to Chicago. Yours truly,

Booker T. Washington

TLpS Con. 7 BTW Papers DLC.

To John Clarence Wright[1]

[Tuskegee, Ala.] June 7, 1908

Mr. Wright: There are some special reasons why I think this ought to be called to your attention.

B. T. W.

[*Enclosure*]

Experience has proven that it is best for the school to pursue the policy of asking its unmarried teachers, to refrain from making the mistake of too frequent association with the same individuals of opposite sex. Such constant association, experience has proven, weakens the influence of the individual teachers and damages the influence of the school, and sets a bad example before the students.

For reasons mentioned, it has been found necessary to call the attention of the teachers, whose cases come under the above statement, to this policy. In fact, the above is not meant to cut off or to unduly restrict such association, but when it becomes a subject of general gossip among the teachers and students, the influence of the Institution and the teachers is injured.

TLpI and Enclosure Con. 581 BTW Papers DLC.

1 John Clarence Wright was head of the English department at Tuskegee Institute from 1907 to 1910.

To Lila M. Taylor[1]

[Tuskegee, Ala.] June 7, 1908

Miss Taylor: There are special reasons why I think this ought to be called to your attention.

B. T. W.

[*Enclosure*]

Experience has shown to us that it is not wise for teachers to become intimately associated with individual students, and when ever teachers make the mistake of growing so intimate with one of the students, it becomes a subject of gossip among the students and teachers, and the influence of the teacher is injured and the standing of the student is injured, and besides a bad object lesson is presented to the other students. The only safeguard is for teachers not to make the mistake of growing too intimate with an individual student or seen too frequently in the company of one student.

TLpI and Enclosure Con. 581 BTW Papers DLC.

1 Lila M. Taylor taught geography at Tuskegee Institute from 1907 to 1909.

To Charles William Anderson

[Tuskegee, Ala.] June 8, 1908

Personal and Confidential.

My dear Mr. Anderson: A sentence in your telegram[1] reading as follows — "Our friends all have offices" is very suggestive. That is just what the other fellows have been saying, that we have no friends except those who hold offices. That will be a good sentence to give Trotter.

I am very much afraid if we should suggest Morris, our enemies would say that we had to get a crazy man as no sane man would second the nomination. I think we shall work out of the difficulties some way. It may be that we shall have to fall back upon your friend, Bishop Grant of Kansas. Yours very truly,

Booker T. Washington

TLpS Con. 38 BTW Papers DLC.

[1] Anderson had wired BTW on the same day: "Scarcely know whom to suggest. Our friends all have offices. How about Chas Morris he seems sane and favors Taft." (Con. 38, BTW Papers, DLC.)

To Harry T. Pratt[1]

[Tuskegee, Ala.] June 8, 1908

My dear Mr. Pratt: I am answering in part the very kind letter which you have addressed to Mr. Scott.

I am writing only to say, please do not secure the Richmond Market Hall for our meeting. It is entirely too large. We cannot hold a successful meeting in such a hall. That mistake has been made before, and we do not want to repeat it. In the first place, bear in mind that at most we have present only three to four hundred members. Add to this an equal number of visitors from a distance and then the local attendance, and you can see that this will make a ridiculously small number of people in such a hall. Aside from this, the main objection is in the fact that the men and women who speak at our meetings are not trained public speakers and it places them at a tremendous disadvantage to place them in a large hall where their voices cannot be heard. It is better from every point of view to have a hall that is too small than one that is too large. It creates a better impression and arouses more enthusiasm to have people standing up than to have vacant seats. Vacant seats in any kind of an audience room always bring a chill on a meeting. For the ordinary meetings a hall that will seat twelve hundred or two thousand people is all that is necessary, for the night meetings the place that you mention might be all right. On the night that I speak, however, I do not want any charge made at the door.

It will be a fine thing to have Secretary Taft present, but we shall have to wait until a later date to determine this.

Mr. Scott will be writing you on other matters. Yours very truly

Booker T. Washington

TLpS Con. 379 BTW Papers DLC.

[1] Harry T. Pratt was proprietor of a laundry in Baltimore, beginning about 1904, until his son took over the business in 1928. Pratt was also a principal in the black elementary schools of Baltimore for many years beginning about 1913, and was active in the black Baltimore Educational Association. During World War I he was treasurer of the Maryland Colored Public Health Association.

To John Massey

[Tuskegee, Ala.] June 8, 1908

Dear Sir: I hope you will excuse me for taking the liberty of writing for the purpose of letting you and Mrs. Massey know how deeply grateful and happy all of us connected with this Institution are because you have decided to continue as President of the College and to make your permanent home in the town of Tuskegee. The Kind Father, I think, had seldom given two individuals so great an opportunity to be a continued blessing to so many people as is true in your case. Personally, I feel constantly indebted to you for your help and influence, which has always been exerted in wise and conservative directions. During all the years, now more than twenty-five, that it has been my privilege to live in Tuskegee, I have never heard a single individual, white or colored, utter a single sentence that was not in your praise.

I trust that both of you may be spared many years to this community and the larger circle which God is permitting you to serve. Yours truly,

Booker T. Washington

TLpS Con. 377 BTW Papers DLC.

To Clara J. Johnston[1]

[Tuskegee, Ala.] June 8, 1908

Dear Clara: I meant to have written you several days ago in answer to yours of May 27th.

I am having the New York Age sent to your mother, and there will be no charge for it. I am very glad that Mr. Strawder and others read it.

Mrs. Washington and I are interested in your coming marriage, and hope that it will prove a happy and prosperous one.[2] We shall be writing you again before the date. We are very glad that you are going to continue to stay at home. Your uncle,

Booker T. Washington

TLpS Con. 6 BTW Papers DLC.

[1] Clara J. Johnston, BTW's niece from Malden, W.Va., enrolled at Tuskegee Institute in 1893 and attended somewhat irregularly for eight years, appearing last in the A middle class in 1901–2. She returned to Malden, where she frequently lived with her mother Amanda Ferguson Johnston.

[2] A wedding invitation is in Con. 374, BTW Papers, DLC. It announced the coming marriage of Clara J. Johnston and John L. Cheatham on June 30, 1908. The records of Kanawha County, W.Va., show that the marriage was recorded, but little is known of John Cheatham, listed on the marriage certificate as age twenty-one. All references to Clara after 1908 were to her maiden name. In 1914 BTW addressed a letter to "Miss Clara Johnston."

To Walter L. Cohen

[Tuskegee, Ala.] June 8, 1908

Personal and confidential.
Message from Secretary[1] states he recognizes difference between your case and others and that he is in favor doing all he can to help you. Do not show this telegram to anyone. Advise you get close Mr. Hitchcock and have frank talk with him. He means to do right.

Booker T. Washington

TWpSr Con. 40 BTW Papers DLC.

[1] William Howard Taft.

From William Howard Taft

Washington D C June 9–08

Have informed Hitchcock that what I desire is that in the Louisiana Contests as in all others before the National Committee, the regularly elected delegates should be seated, and if the Committee feels that the Cohen delegates are the regular delegates they should all be seated, that I am opposed to lily white-ism and that if anyone is excluded entitled to representation in the selection of any delegation that is a reason either for rejecting the entire delegation or only giving it part representation but that the whole matter should be submitted to the Committee as a question for its decision and discussion.

Wm H. Taft

HWSr Con. 7 BTW Papers DLC.

From Ralph Waldo Tyler

Chicago June 9/08

Dr. Booker T Washington I leave tomorrow night for Columbus, returning to Chicago next Monday, accompanied by my wife, Myers and wife of Cleveland, and Terrell and Cobb, whom I am to meet in Cleveland.

With the settlement of the Louisiana case, our work here is practically over, and with Alabama and Louis[i]ana settled our way, I think our work has been accomplished. Of course I am not unmindful of the fact that after all, you were the very potent influence that brought results. Governor[1] and I were simply small factors.

There is no mistaking the fact that the Louis[i]ana settlement was a popular one. When the result was announced a great applause went up from the colored men assembled in the lobby. Governor and I were practically ignored by Hitchcock. I did not bother him, and neither did the Governor. I may be wrong, but it is my candid opinion that he has about as much use for a Negro as I have for poison. Up to Monday noon Walter Cohen's case was a hopeless one. It was a fight against odds. The "allies" had about one hundred Negroes here, under pay, with ample funds to make a show. Governor and I were practically alone, and that too at no expense to Taft's managers, for not one penny have they offered towards defraying the Governor's expense, and that is all I ever asked of them.

Governor will remain here until after the convention stopping at 3254 Wabash Ave. On my return, I expect to smooth out the wrinkles.

I think we have done good work in spreading a good opinion of the Secretary.

Practically alone, we have stalled the advance of the "allies" one hundred Negroes. It has been a hard, fast and furious week, and I am now ready for a couple days rest. From the 16th up to and including the 19th I will be at the Palmer House. Sincerely,

R W Tyler

ALS Con. 8 BTW Papers DLC.

[1] P. B. S. Pinchback.

From William Howard Taft

[Washington, D.C.] June 10, 1908

My dear Dr. Washington: I have your letter about Luke Wright. It isn't true that Mr. Wright is responsible for the interjection of any color prejudice in the Philippines, and I am quite sure that that will appear when the nomination is made. The President has already decided on it and told General Wright that he would appoint him, so that I think we must regard the matter as closed. I am sorry that you think it will have a bad effect. Very sincerely yours,

Wm H Taft

TLpS William Howard Taft Papers DLC.

From Pinckney Benton Stewart Pinchback

Chicago, Ill. June 10—08

My dear Doctor: Both of your wires recvd. Mr Thompson told me he had wired you as to result in Alabama case etc:

Tyler and myself wired you relative to Louisiana case to urge full vote because we feared Hitchcock's influence would be used against giving Cohen even a half vote. I felt quite sure a half vote could be secured for Cohen but I desired to make it certain. Hence contended for full vote. See! In my opinion Cohen has won a signal victory in getting a half vote.

Well, as you see by the papers the draft is all one way — Taft. It is probable the opposition will move to make his nomination unanimous on the first ballot. That would be good politics.

I cant sufficiently thank you for your foresight and generous kindness in getting me to come here. It has been a great help to me in many ways. We will go over it when we meet.

Hastily and nervously Yours etc.,

Pinchback

ALS Con. 379 BTW Papers DLC.

From Samuel Laing Williams, Louis B. Anderson, and Oscar DePriest

Chicago Ills June 11—08

Lyons defeat certain for committeeman. Lincoln Johnson[1] of Atlanta only available man. Important that Colored men be chosen for moral effect. No other Colored man in South has chance. Hitchcock holds key of situation. Can you reach Hitchcock to help case or keep hands off. Matter excites much interest if committeeman lost to race Taft forces will be blamed.

S. Laing Williams
Louis B. Anderson
Oscar DePriest

HWSr Con. 42 BTW Papers DLC.

[1] Henry Lincoln Johnson (1870–1925), a black Georgia politician and officeholder, was educated in Atlanta University (A.B. 1888) and the University of Michigan (L.L.B. 1892). He practiced law in Georgia and was active in Republican politics, attending national conventions beginning in 1896. At the 1904 Republican national convention, Johnson led an abortive effort for a plank in the platform supporting federal legislation against peonage. Johnson, never really part of BTW's circle, succeeded in Republican politics nonetheless. In 1910 William Taft selected Johnson to succeed John C. Dancy as recorder of deeds in Washington, D.C., a position he held until 1913. His political fortune picked up again in 1920 when he was named Georgia national committeeman of the Republican party, a move which incensed many whites in the state. Warren G. Harding, in an attempt to attract black votes, used Johnson to help arrange speaking engagements before black groups. Harding rewarded him by appointment to his old post as recorder of deeds in Washington. Johnson's appointment, however, was blocked by Georgia senator Tom Watson.

From Walter L. Cohen

Chicago, Ill. June 11, 1908

My dear Dr. Washington, Words cannot express the feeling I have for you for the extraordinary good work you have done for the true and tried republicans of Louisiana. Without your aid the fight would have been lost. To you is due entirely our success, and, while I know you would not like to give publicity of your good work yet it will be impossible for me to refrain from letting my friends and other colored leaders throughout the country know of your good work.

I inclose you a copy of a letter I received from Mr. Taft also my reply. The possession of this letter will enable me to speak in a very positive tone as to his attitude toward "Lily Whiteism."

The "Lily Whites" threatens to take the contest before the Committee on Credentials and even to the Convention floor. I have no fear of this threat. I wish they would for it would give me an opportunity of refuting some of the most reprehensible misstatements made by them before the National Committee. They took advantage of the rules of the Committee. The rules compelled us to use up our entire time straight, in the presentation of our side. When this fact was made known to me I made the request to reserve five minutes of the time to be used in refuting any false statements made by them. This they ("Lily Whites") objected to. This gave them an opportunity of making some most outrageous false statements. Kennedy[1] surprised me in a very bitter attack on Vance[2] and myself. He became so abusive that it was necessary for me to say to him that I would hold him personally responsible for his remarks. Of course I did not want to act other than a gentleman, and, therefore during our stay here will not take the matter up except if the case is heard before the Credential Committee I shall take the opportunity of correcting the statements.

You will observe that under the compromise we are to have a thorough reorganization throughout the entire State under the auspices of a Committee of the National Committee to be composed of one member with the Chairman and Secretary. The member of the National Committee from the State is to be appointed by the Chairman of the new National Committee. This will give the power of forming an organization completely in sympathy with the incoming administration.

When Mr. Hitchcock called me to talk about a compromise he mentioned he was very much interested in Mr. Pearl Wight going back on the National Committee. I told him I felt very kindly toward Mr. Wight. That if our delegation had been seated I had been slated for membership of the National Committee, but in the interest of harmony I would yield whatever claims I might have, but thought that if the concession was made, in equity our side of the house ought to have the Chairmanship of the State Committee. I also told him that as I was the Chairman of our side but realizing that it would be to the interest of the Party to have a white man Chairman I would relinquish my title and have a white man selected. He expressed himself as perfectly in accord with this and we parted. I don't know that the "Lily Whites" will agree to letting us have the Chairmanship but if Mr. Wight is to be the member of the National Committee we shall insist.

If this agreement is not to be carried out I have a suggestion to make to you at the proper time.

Gov. Pinchback is here and working like a youngster in the interest of Mr. Taft. He always get into the groups and try and impress them that Mr. Taft is the only one to nominate and that there has not been a single member of the Taft family who has not been friendly to the colored people. His manner of putting things is very impressive and his arguments are so clear.

Again thanking you for your help, I am, Yours faithfully,

Walter L. Cohen

TLS Con. 40 BTW Papers DLC.

1 Alexander B. Kennedy.

2 J. Madison Vance, a graduate of Straight University in 1886, was a New Orleans lawyer who was active in the black Odd Fellows.

George A. McQueen[1] to Emmett Jay Scott

Birmingham, Ala., June 12th, 08

Dear Sir: I wish you would secure, if possible, a copy of Mr. Villard's paper, in which he used the data referred to in your letter, and mail the copy to Mr. Gilreath, and oblige.

I am sending you letter from the Associate Editor of the Wall Street Journal,[2] New York, confirming figures of $400,000,000.00 carried away from this country by the Italians during 1907. Mr. Gilreath had these figures confirmed in order to be sure there was no mistake as to the amount. As stated, we enclose Mr. Crowell's letter, and will ask you to please show the same to Mr. Hare, as he seemed interested in these figures, and put it before Dr. Washington also, in order that he may be sure of its correctness.

Mr. Gilreath has no objections to the Italians or any other nationality making money in this country and carrying it away. In fact, he is glad that we had the surplus to spare to help the poor of other countries. But he also thinks such figures show the importance of encouraging and developing our own people here to the highest extent, who are investing all of their earnings here among us, as your race and ours do.

We hope this data will be of some service. Very truly yours,

Geo. A. McQueen

TLS Con. 371 BTW Papers DLC.

1 George A. McQueen was secretary to Belton Gilreath, the Birmingham coal executive and trustee of Tuskegee Institute.

2 John Franklin Crowell (1857–1931), an economist and educator, was on the editorial staff of the *Wall Street Journal* from 1906 to 1915.

From C. R. Branch[1]

Washington, June 12th, 1908

Dear Doctor Washington: I have the honor, by direction of the Liberian Envoys to forward to you the enclosed copies of the documents received at the Department of State, Monrovia – three in number,[2] which they most respectfully ask you to treat privately outside of Government Officials.

The Envoys desire me to express to you their cordial thanks and appreciation for the very masterly and helpful service you have so kindly given them in their mission to this Great Government. They will not forget to carry your name, your great work at Tuskegee as well as your worth to the Negro race, to President Barclay when they shall return home.

With sentiments of distinguished consideration, I have the honor to be, Your obedient servant,

C. R. Branch

TLS Con. 366 BTW Papers DLC.

1 Secretary of the Liberian diplomatic delegation to the United States.

2 The enclosures are with the letter in Con. 366, BTW Papers, DLC. They express the friendly interest of the governments of Great Britain and the United States in Liberia's desire to remain independent from foreign encroachment.

To John Thompson Emlen[1]

Tuskegee Institute, Ala., June 13, 1908

Personal & Confidential

Dear Sir: Replying very briefly to yours of June 11th, I am sorry to say that your answer has been delayed, which, of course, is due to my absence.

I would say that the gentleman whose name you mention in your letter[2] is about as unfitted for such work as is needed to be done in Dr. Anderson's school, as any man that I can think of. I do not know a single qualification which he has for that kind of work. I have known him for a number of years. He has failed at everything that he has undertaken, besides he has a bad influence. He stirs up racial strife wherever he goes, teaching colored people to hate white people. Aside from this, he has been connected with a number of newspapers and magazines, and in one of them he has most heartily and inconsistently opposed industrial and manual training in every conceivable way. He is now only seeking a position in a manual training school because he cannot get anything else to do, and is forced to do that or starve. Aside from the matters which I have mentioned, he is a pessimist, and I do not believe that any pessimist can properly lead and inspire young people.

I am very glad, indeed, to learn that you have succeeded in getting manual training into the grammer grades of some of the public schools, and I hope that you will succeed still further.

Of course, I shall take for granted that you will not use my name in connection with this information, unless it is absolutely necessary.[3] Yours truly,

Booker T. Washington

TLSr Copy Con. 370 BTW Papers DLC. "Personal and Confidential" is written in Emmett J. Scott's hand.

[1] John Thompson Emlen (b. 1878), a Quaker former teacher at Hampton Institute, was active in social work in Philadelphia and served on many boards, including the Public Education Association, the Armstrong Association, and the Council of Social Agencies.

[2] Jesse Max Barber. See Emlen to BTW, June 11, 1908, Con. 370, BTW Papers, DLC, writing as a trustee of the Berean Manual Labor School for blacks in Philadelphia.

[3] Emlen promised not to allow BTW's letter to go beyond a few influential members of the board, who would keep it in confidence. (Emlen to BTW, June 19, 1908, Con. 370, BTW Papers, DLC.)

From Charles William Anderson

Chicago, June 13, 1908

Lyons openly working with Gilchrist Stewart. Hitchcock said to be against Lyons for committeeman. His defeat would have us unrepresented on committee. I suggest that convention elect colored member at large as suggested in my letter.

Chas. W. Anderson

TWSr Con. 38 BTW Papers DLC.

To Emmett Jay Scott

Tuskegee Institute, Alabama June 14, 1908

Dear Mr. Scott: I forgot to say to you that in his conversation with me, the President seemed evidently nettled on account of the opposition of Cohen to the other faction of the party in Louisiana. While Secretary Taft expressed himself as greatly admiring the course which Cohen had taken, and especially did he express himself as pleased at the manner in which Cohen agreed to the compromise, the President I think, hardly looks at the matter from the same point of view. For this reason I telegraphed you to be very sure to urge Cohen in your own way and in your own words, to keep close to Hitchcock so as not to alienate himself from the President. Yours truly,

Booker T. Washington

TLSr Con. 582 BTW Papers DLC. Addressed to Scott in Chicago.

To P. O. Gray[1]

[Tuskegee, Ala.] June 15, 1908

My dear Sir: I thought that you and your readers[2] would be interested in knowing something about the manner in which the Liberian Envoys have been received in America. It is very seldom that a visit of any foreign representatives creates more interest and attracts more attention, than is true of the Liberian Envoys.

They have been quartered at the best hotels in New York and in Washington and have received the very best attention.

After spending several days in New York they arrived in Washington and made a formal call on the Secretary of State, and were received formally by the President of the United States. From Washington they came to Tuskegee Institute, under the escort of Mr. T. J. Calloway, one of my assistants. They spent two days inspecting the work of this institution, and delivered addresses at our commencement exercises and at a special banquet given in their honor by the 20th Century Club.

The railroads went out of their way to provide extra accommodations for the trip of these Envoys from Washington to Tuskegee. The high officials of the railroads going so far as to telegraph their agents on the route, to give them special attention.

After finishing their visit at the Tuskegee Institute, where they made a special inspection of the operations of this institution, they returned to Washington, and had a second conference with Mr. Elihu Root, Secretary of State.

Arrangements had been made sometime ago by the writer for an extended visit to President Roosevelt. It will interest your readers to know that the President did something which he rarely does, and that is made arrangements to receive the Envoys and myself in the evening in the parlors of the White House, rather than in his office. There the Envoys spent an hour with the President, while they went over in a painstaking and careful manner every detail in connection with their visit. He assured them that the United States would assist and encourage Liberia in every way possible.

Immediately after concluding their interview with President Roosevelt, the Envoys were driven to the residence of Secretary Taft, where it had been previously arranged that the Secretary should receive the Envoys and myself for an interview. Notwithstanding the very busy season through which Secretary Taft is passing, owing to the near approach of the Chicago Convention, the Secretary received the Envoys in his parlors, introduced them to Mrs. Taft and spent an hour in discussing their problems. He too assured them that he had the most lively interest in all that concerns Liberia and its citizens.

The next day, notwithstanding that the Secretary of State, Mr. Root, had already made engagements covering every hour of the day, but when he found that the Liberian Envoys wished to have a concluding interview with him, he re-arranged the plan of work for the day and gave them a special audience, which lasted nearly two hours. The Secretary of State gave the Envoys every opportunity to present their views and assured them that the United States would do everything within its power to carry out their wishes.

On Friday night, the day after they visited the President, a reception was tended the Envoys by the colored citizens of Washington, in one of their large churches, at which prominent people spoke. This reception was held under the auspices of the Local

Negro Business League, of which Mr. W. Sidney Pittman is President. One of the noticeable features of this reception was the display of a large Liberian flag, together with several smaller flags, representing the same.

While they were in Washington, a reception was also tended them by Judge R. H. Terrell. I cannot take the time to enumerate the various functions that the Envoys have been invited to participate in, in which they have been accorded special honors.

The American Press, I am glad to say, both white and black was most friendly in discussing the mission of the Envoys to America. Wide and extensive publication of their mission has been made in the most influential news journals. This has helped the cause of the Envoys in a most satisfactory way I am sure.

This brief letter cannot be concluded without expressing the opinion, which has been expressed by everyone with whom the Envoys have come into contact; and that is in reference to the fine impression that they leave upon everyone who meets them. They impress us all as being a set of scholarly, dignified, courageous gentlemen, deeply interested in the welfare of their country; not the least characteristic of these Envoys is their modesty, at the same time earnestness and courage. Everywhere that they have gone, they have not failed to impress individuals, both private and public, that they represent a government and that they are maintaining the dignity of people, representing an independent State. Yours truly,

[Booker T. Washington]

TLc Con. 371 BTW Papers DLC. A copy is in Department of State Numerical File 1906–10, Vol. 794, Case 12083/50, RG59, DNA.

1 Editor of *African Agricultural World*, Monrovia, Liberia.

2 BTW's letter appeared in the *African League* (Buchanan, Liberia), 10 (Sept. 1908), 1–2, copy in Con. 1092, BTW Papers, DLC. A copy was also sent for publication to the editor of *Silver Trumpet*, Cuttington, Cape Palmas, Liberia. BTW sent the same information to Ernest Lyon, and also wrote him in confidence that the U.S. government had dispatched a general consular agent to Liberia to get firsthand information on the Liberian situation. (June 15, 1908, Con. 375, BTW Papers, DLC.)

From Emmett Jay Scott

Chicago. June 15/08

My Dear Mr. Washington: I got here & got right to work. I went with Mr Thompson at once to see Mr Hitchcock. Mr Thompson told him that *you* & you alone ought to name this colored man to second the nomination: he (H) said he was agreeable except *Banks*. He said Banks had been fighting him & could not accept him. I did not urge it as I have kept in mind your suggestion that we ought not to antagonize Mr H. Well, I went off to find Anderson & when I found him we got right down to business: and decided to recommend Alexander (as a clean man & a good orator &c) or to have them withdraw opposition to Lewis.

Then we went back & looked for H. We kept that up till 12 o'clock when I went to bed; then this morning I went back to look for him & Mr Anderson & I kept it up till 3 pm & we have not found him yet — we have telephoned his room; his secretary & yet he has refused to permit us to see him. Mr. Thompson is disgusted & so tonight I am going out to see the Tafts themselves so they wont run in some "fresh one" on us. I shall telegraph you.

Personally I dont mind for I shall keep on after Mr H — or anyone to accomplish a purpose — the purpose you have in mind — but both Mr. T. & Mr Anderson feel they have been treated discourteously because of the way he (H) has evaded us.

These Negroes here are in a frenzy. Their meetings here are wild. I send you two (2) clippings which show how they are going. Bishop Walters, Sinclair & that whole gang are here & they are doing their worst. I have not wired you today because I have not had anything to say. Moore is here but I have not seen him.

I think I am spreading in the best & most discreet way what you have done against Lily Whiteism & also your part about the plank. Yours Faithfully,

Emmett J. Scott

ALS Con. 381 BTW Papers DLC.

To Elihu Root

[Tuskegee, Ala.] June 16, 1908

Dear Mr. Root: I am writing you regarding a matter upon which I desire your personal opinion and advice, as far as you are willing to give it. If you think it wise, I should also like to have, through you, the opinion and advice of the President on the same subject, as I have not put it before him.

The Liberian Envoys, now in this country, have requested that I take the position of Charge D'Affaires for them in this country. I have told them that I would give them no answer until I had consulted you and the President.

I am really anxious to be of some service to Liberia, but the question arises, whether it would be proper or desirable for me to accept such a position; and the further question arises, whether I could not be of the same value to them, in acting in a private capacity or rather in a seemingly unofficial capacity. The official designation I care nothing about; my only object is to be of service, but they seem to be anxious that I should consent to take the position that they have indicated.

The only element that appeals to me, in favor of accepting the position, is perhaps in the fact that I might speak with some authority in helping the Republic carry out the advice and suggestions which you gave.

Liberia is practically the only portion of Africa, which is now left in control of the black man, and I am particularly anxious that the people of Liberia have a chance to see what they can do.

Fundamentally, I realize, as I think you do, that there is no hope for these people except as they are able to get right down to business and develop the natural resources of that country, in a way to give them wealth, and consequently strength and standing before the world.

The mere fact that they have the political control of this country means nothing, except as they can make themselves of service in the development of the natural resources of the country. In this direction I want to be of service to them, in sending them some strong men from Tuskegee and in getting some of their brightest men to come to Tuskegee to get hold of our ideas and methods of work, with a view of returning to Liberia and putting them into practice.

Before I close, permit me to thank you most heartily for the very frank talk which you gave these people, and for the sound advice which they thoroughly appreciated. After leaving the State Department, I went over your conversation fully with them again, and they realize now, as I think they did not before, that what you have suggested is the wisest course of action for them, and I think they will do their best to follow your advice. Yours truly,

[Booker T. Washington]

TLpS Con. 41 BTW Papers DLC. The original is in Department of State Numerical File, 1906–10, Vol. 794, Case 12083/30, RG59, DNA.

To Olivia Egleston Phelps Stokes

[Tuskegee, Ala.] June 16, 1908

My dear Miss Stokes: Replying to your kind favor of June 7th, I would state that I am always glad to give you any information that I have within my power.

In speaking of schools, I find that I can talk more frankly concerning them, if my name is not used in connection with the information that is given.

I have followed pretty carefully the Berea College matter[1] and I would state that not a few Colored people in Kentucky and elsewhere are strongly of the opinion that the change resulting in the separation at Berea could have been avoided and some go so far as to state that the present authorities have encouraged the separation, but however this may be, I have no hesitation in saying that matters have now gone so far that I do not believe it would be possible to have the two sets of students again together at Berea and the only way in which the Colored people can get any benefit from Berea is by having a separate institution, though I have not understood so fully as your letter seems to imply, that it was in any large degree an industrial school, but more in the nature of a college, but perhaps I am wrong in this. I do know, however, that they have said they were going to make industrial features rather prominent. I think if the institution is modelled, as they state, after Hampton and Tuskegee, that it can do a real needed work in the state of Kentucky. It would not have to be necessarily a large institution to meet the needs of the Colored people in that section. The total Negro population of the state of Kentucky is 284,706; the total white population is 1,862,309, while the total Negro population of Alabama is 827,307. To sum up the whole matter, I believe that help given to the new department of Berea College would be money well spent.

I am sorry to say that I have not changed my opinion in any appreciable degree regarding the work at Kowaliga under Mr. Benson.

Thank you for your suggestion regarding the opportunity to study the race problem in Brazil. I shall see if I cannot get hold of some direct reading matter on that subject. You will be glad to know that we have from time to time an increasing number of South American students and some are bright, but I think we have had none as yet from Brazil.

I am quite sure that you will, also, be interested to know that we have just had a visit from four men from the Republic of Liberia. One is the present Vice-President, Mr. J. J. Dossen, another a former President, Mr. G. W. Gibson and two others. They were fine men. They spent two days with us here looking through our work and I feel quite sure they got hold of many points which will be of value to them in Liberia. They are going to send some of their brightest young men here for training, in fact, we already have two. The Republic is getting into some entanglements with England and France and I spent two days with these envoys in Washington trying to secure the interest of Secretary Root and President Roosevelt in helping them out of their difficulties and I am glad to say we made considerable progress.

The work of re-modelling and enlarging Dorothy Hall is now underway.

Please remember my wife and myself kindly to your sister. Yours truly,

Booker T. Washington

TLpS Con. 47 BTW Papers DLC.

[1] Berea College was open to both blacks and whites for its first half-century, but a Kentucky legislative act in 1904 declared it unlawful to operate any college or

school for members of both races. The Berea trustees took the statute to a Kentucky court, which upheld it. Four years later, the U.S. Supreme Court upheld the Kentucky decision. While waiting for the final settlement of the case, the Berea trustees sent the school's black students to other colleges. After the decision, the trustees took $200,000 from the now all-white Berea College to found a black school, Lincoln Institute. (Peck, *Berea's First Century*, 50–55.)

From Emmett Jay Scott

Chicago June 16, '08

My Dear Mr. Washington: Last night (Monday) the Colored Taft League had its inning as against the Negroes who are here for the "allies." Things were quite stormy at once. When they went to light up Quinn Chapel the wires had been cut in the basement & they could not light up till nearly 9:30 o'clock. Anderson, Vernon & Governor were to be the speakers. Mr Anderson started off right from the shoulder; he did not mince matters at all, but they started in to interrupt him with *hisses*, groans & some remarks. He kept his fire up till they ceased. I think won many of them.[1] Vernon's talk was about everything under the sun; he called the names of all the great Negroes, alive & dead — that is all but *one*; then he never once called Secretary Taft's name. He contented himself mostly with urging them to stand by the nominee whoever he is. Gov. P. made a fine talk; then they had a banquet — & Nathan Alexander, Mr Napier & W H R [W. H. H.] Moore spoke. All were in good taste & everything went off all right. I enclose 2 clippings both from the Tribune. The editorial is strong & truthful. *All* of us are taking it as a text & showing up the folly of the present foolishness. I am urging *all* of our friends to keep references made to it in all their talks. I wired you about the man Alexander from *Md.* None of us know him but they say the Secretary has sent him here to do *it.* The Colored Taft League is doing good work all along the line. Faithfully,

Emmett J. Scott

ALS Con. 381 BTW Papers DLC.

[1] As reported in the black press, the anti-Taft men controlled the meeting and passed resolutions attacking the Roosevelt administration. (Fox, *Guardian of Boston*, 157.)

To Charles William Anderson

[Tuskegee, Ala.] June 19, 1908

My dear Mr. Anderson: I have just read your interview in the New York Sun, which was telegraphed from Chicago. It is *faultless* in its *strong breadth and accuracy of statement.* It ought to be published as *a campaign document and scattered widely among our* people, but I very much fear we should have *to beg for* the privilege *of having it so used.* I am going to try to get Moore to use it in The New York Age.

I see that the *Foraker forces* had no trouble in getting a Colored man to second his nomination, while the friends of Secretary Taft, of course, placed his Negro followers at the usual disadvantage in not providing such an opportunity. It would have been a tremendous advantage to the Secretary, if you, Lewis, Alexander, Banks or some other sensible Colored man had been asked a month ago to prepare a second address. In some way, we shall have to try to bring these people to their senses. Yours truly,

Booker T. Washington

TLpS Con. 38 BTW Papers DLC.

To Charles William Anderson

[Tuskegee, Ala.] June 19, 1908

My dear Mr. Anderson: Enclosed, I send you a sentence or two taken from a letter from a friend of mine in Chicago, who listened to one of your addresses.[1] You see it always pays to be brave and frank like you always are.

It is really a pity for a man, who has done as much and stands for as much as you do, to almost have to get down on his knees and beg certain officials, who are in power, for the *privilege of serving* a cause, especially when so much is being done against our friends, but in the long run, I think that matters will come out right. Yours truly,

Booker T. Washington

TLpS Con. 38 BTW Papers DLC.

[1] Three sentences from E. J. Scott to BTW, June 16, 1908, above, beginning: "Mr Anderson started off right from the shoulder. . . ."

To Wallace Buttrick

[Tuskegee, Ala.] June 19, 1908

My dear Dr. Buttrick, For your Lake George Conference, which I take for granted will be held next year, I will try to get hold of another set of figures showing the condition of the Negro schools in South Carolina. If you haven't got the reports in your office, I wish very much that you might have at that Conference the statements made by Mr. Sheats of Florida in his report ending June 30th, 1900, and the statements made by Superintendent of Schools in North Carolina in his report for 1905–1906. The Superintendent himself on page 34 of the North Carolina report makes some very strong statements and then follows on page 346 the report of Mr. Charles L. Coon,[1] with whose statements you are already acquainted. I believe if these matters were brought out pretty plainly before the Southern members at the Conference, that they would at least think a little, or try to do so. Yours truly,

Booker T. Washington

TLpS Con. 39 BTW Papers DLC.

[1] Charles Lee Coon (1868–1927), superintendent of schools of Wilson, N.C., after 1907 was one of the most effective proponents of educational reform and racial justice in the South. In 1903–4 he directed the educational information bureau at Knoxville, Tenn., established by the Southern Education Board. From 1904 to 1907 he was superintendent of black state normal schools. At the Twelfth Conference for Education in the South, at Atlanta in 1909, he delivered a paper on "Public Taxation and Negro Schools," one of the most forthright statements of the view that black schools, far from being recipients of white tax funds, did not even receive all that blacks directly or indirectly paid in taxes. The Committee of Twelve for the Advancement of the Negro Race reprinted it in pamphlet form. Coon's statement in the *Biennial Report of the Superintendent of Public Instruction of North Carolina, 1905–06* was an earlier version of his 1909 paper.

From Elihu Root

Washington. June 19, 1908

My dear Mr. Washington: I do not think it would to any degree increase your usefulness to the Liberians for you to be Chargé d'Affaires. Indeed, it would rather tend to detract from the weight of your independent expression of opinion and interest regarding their affairs. A chargé d'Affaires is a very low grade diplomatic representative, and your own personality would, I think, have greater weight without that small office than with it. It would not be a real relation but a mere false appearance. You can do them good as an American, which you are, not as a Liberian, which you are not.

I think very highly of your idea of sending some strong men from Tuskegee and bringing some of their brightest men to Tuskegee to get hold of your ideas of methods and work with a view to returning to Liberia and putting them into practice. This would require time, of course, and the first thing, it seems to me, is for you to send some of your men there. I hope you will be able to send them men who have not only the education acquired at Tuskegee, but who have strong characters and capacity for leadership and control.

I am much pleased that you liked the advice that I gave the Commissioners in our recent interview. I have already written to our Ambassador in London[1] to take the subject up with the British Government. Very sincerely yours,

Elihu Root

TLS Con. 41 BTW Papers DLC.

[1] Whitelaw Reid (1837–1912) was editor of the New York *Tribune* (1872–1905) and U.S. ambassador to Great Britain (1905–12).

To James Wesley Cooper[1]

[Tuskegee, Ala.] June 20, 1908

Personal and Confidential

My dear Dr. Cooper: I am writing you about a matter that is not of very great important, yet the suggestion may prove helpful.

I learn from several reliable sources that Mr. Pickens, of Talladega College, who is lecturing from time to time in the South bearing upon the interests of Talladega College, makes a statement involving a comparison of the work at Talladega and Tuskegee that is entirely uncalled for and unnecessary and gives people a wrong impression. I would not write you except that I have heard it verified from several sources that in his lectures he says something like this: "Tuskegee teaches girls to wash clothes; Talladega teaches them to think." There is entirely too much work in the South for Talladega, Tuskegee and all the other schools that we can plant and sustain to do for any of us who are in earnest to make these belittling comparisons, and I thought in some manner you might call the folly of this thing to Mr. Pickens' attention. I would write directly to Talladega but I do not know who is the actual head. Please do not let him know that I called this matter to your attention as it would serve no good purpose.

You will be glad to know, I am sure, that we have employed on our next year's force several of the recent graduates from Fisk.

When in Washington a few days ago, Secretary Taft read to me the address which he made at Fisk University. It is one of the best endorsements of college education from a public man I have seen. I have written to the Secretary for a copy of it with a view of asking Dr. Ward to publish it in full or in part in the Independent. Yours very truly,

Booker T. Washington

TLpS Con. 367 BTW Papers DLC.

1 James Wesley Cooper (1842–1916), a Congregational minister and trustee of Hampton Institute and Talladega College, was corresponding secretary of the American Missionary Association from 1903 to 1910 and vice-president from 1910 to 1914.

From Ernest Lyon

Monrovia, Liberia. June 23, 1908

My dear Dr. Washington: Upon my request the President of Liberia with the concurrence of his cabinet has made you a Knight of the National Order of "African Redemption." The insignia is very pretty and is worn and valued by Europeans. I am intrusted with the presentation and delivery of the same and it will be a source of pleasure to me to bring to you Liberia's highest recognition of your services for the race in particular and for humanity in general in the fall when I come home on furlough. Personally you deserve this and more. The Liberians as a general thing do not bestow their favors readily on American Col. men; but there was no hesitancy when I proposed it. I think you will like the collar and insignia which are worn on special occasions and look well over a full dress suit. Yours sincerely,

Ernest Lyon

TLS Con. 375 BTW Papers DLC. The last three sentences are in Lyon's hand.

To Clarence E. Woods[1]

[Tuskegee, Ala.] June 25, 1908

Dear Sir: I thank you for your kind letter of May 23d, 1908.[2]

I cannot but feel, as you undoubtedly do, that the younger generation of men in the South, both black and white, owe much to those faithful old servants, who have served to keep alive the good relations that so often existed in the old days between master and slave. I wish I might say or write something that would make the younger members of my race understand better than they now do the extent to which they are indebted to these old people for the kindness and the goodwill that each one of them has not failed to find somewhere and at some time among the white people of the South.

At the moment, nothing more happy suggests itself to me than this statement which I have often expressed before in one form or another, namely, "The world owes something to the man or woman no matter how humble, who has done a common thing in an uncommon way."[3] Yours truly,

Booker T. Washington

TLpSr Con. 385 BTW Papers DLC. Signed in Emmett J. Scott's hand.

[1] Clarence E. Woods was the Democratic mayor of Richmond, Ky.

[2] Woods had asked BTW for a suitable brief inscription "to place upon the monument of two faithful old colored servants who died here some time ago, and who were the incarnation of those lofty principles you have so nobly taught to your race —honesty, industry, frugality, fidelity, etc." It was on the death of their former owners—"fine people here"—that the monument was being erected. (Con. 385, BTW Papers, DLC.)

[3] Emmett J. Scott sent Woods's letter to Robert E. Park and asked Park to "write what you think sh'd be sent to Mr. Woods. . . ." The utterance was, however, typical of what BTW had said on many occasions. (Scott to Park, June 10, 1908, Con. 42, BTW Papers, DLC.)

From Joseph W. Henderson[1]

Providence, R.I., June 30 '08

Respected Sir: Over eight months ago, T. Thomas Fortune over his own signature told the reading public that in another man's name you owned $9500 worth of stock in the New York Age and that this owned sum together with the amount that you controlled owned by your friends made you the virtual owner or put you in actual control of the New York Age. During these long laps of months, no public denial of these statements have been forth coming from you and thus the public is justified in the belief that Mr. Fortune's published statements concerning your veiled ownership of the New York Age are true. What of that? What is it my business if you do own or control the New York Age? None until June 15, 1908 when a marked copy of the New York Age was handed me containing [a] false, slanderous and libelous article assassinatingly assailing my character.[2] Sir, character is all that I have, and I believe that you would not respect me if I did not go to the limit to defend it. I will. So contrary to your public teaching or utterances that it becomes a task for me to believe that you yourself would maliciously order or sign such a slanderous article as appeared in the Editorials of your paper against me. I could not believe that you would solicit and collect money from philanthropists of the country for the advertised purpose of educating the Negro, and yet spend [it] or any part of it to the ill purpose of destroying the Negro by murderous assaults upon the character of fellow members of your race and your country.

Again taking in consideration that you have publicly advised colored men to keep out of politics, it is hard for me to understand how you could consistently afford to stoop to political tricks so low and cheap as the above mentioned article would appear to show. Of course it would be nothing short of the most cowardly deceit for me to pretend that I am totally ignorant of the political interest that you took in helping to bring about Mr. Taft's nomination and that you are now working to bring about his election. I know what I did against his nomination, therefore was indignantly repugnant to your working desires. But I cannot see wherein such a slanderous article attacking anybody, much less a stalwart Republican who never supported or recommended a Democrat for any political position, how such a slanderous article could be expected to help Mr. Taft's canvass is beyond my ability to see. Even if such political trickery could incident[al]ly help the political canvass of your political friend, I cannot see why you should permit your paper, "The New York Age" to bring upon me this character damage that it has done through this stated article.

I have the right of defense. This you know. Following the high source of advice given me, I now ask you for a conference that this inflicted wrong may be righted. In the absence of such a conference being granted, I know that you cannot blame me justly for appealing to whatever other source of defense that may be left.

Awaiting your early reply, I am Respectfully yours,

Joseph W. Henderson

TLS Con. 380 BTW Papers DLC.

[1] Joseph W. Henderson of Providence, R.I., was a black newspaper editor and president of the Douglass Republican Association.

[2] The New York *Age* accused Henderson of being a faker and grafter who was trying to raise Republican money at one meeting while haranguing President Roosevelt and Secretary Taft at another meeting. The *Age* reported that Henderson was supposedly editor of *The Torchlight*, but could not determine when such a paper was last published. The *Age* also hinted that Henderson might have jumped bail in Philadelphia. (New York *Age*, June 11, 1908, 4.)

From James Jenkins Dossen

New York July 3. 1908

My Dear Doctor Washington This is to say good bye to you and Mrs. Washington. We will sail D. V for Liberia tomorrow morning. I expect to be a fortnight in Hamburg and to reach Liberia about the 12th. Aug. D. V.

I trust I shall hear from you often and that our friendship will become more intimate. On behalf of the Liberian Government I thank you for the very valuable help you have given the Commission which shall be prominently mentioned in our report and I hope some action taken there on to record the nation's appreciation. I just received an English paper this morning in which you are prominently mentioned in relation with the Commission.

I hope to take up the question of sending some Liberians to Truskegee at the meeting of the next Legislature. Yours Sincerely

James J Dossen

ALS Con. 369 BTW Papers DLC.

To William Howard Taft

Tuskegee, Ala., July 7, 1908

Personal and confidential leading men of our race feel Mr. Hitchcock would be proper man to place in charge and hope he will be selected with Mr. Vorys assisting in Chicago or elsewhere very much hope that plan will be carried out having strong colored man on executive committee in New York and one on committee in Chicago if possible.

Booker T. Washington

TWSr William Howard Taft Papers DLC. Addressed to Taft at Hot Springs Va.

To Frederick Randolph Moore

[Tuskegee, Ala.] July 7, 1908

Dear Mr. Moore: There is great danger in having too much political matter in The Age. You ought to bear in mind that the great industrial, educational and moral interests of the race ought not to be neglected. This refers not only to the news column, but to the editorial column.

There is also danger of your editorials becoming cheapened by reason that they contain too much advice dashed off without consideration on the part of the writer. It is the easiest thing in the world for the writer of an editorial to give advice instead of basing the editorial upon facts based upon careful research in careful directions. If you will read the editorial pages of papers like the Times, Sun, etc., you will find that there is at least one editorial nearly every day that deals with some subject that has required deep research and investigation on the part of some one in order to secure the facts upon which the editorial is based. That is the kind of thing that makes a great paper. Yours truly,

B. T. W.

TLpI Con. 6 BTW Papers DLC.

To William Howard Taft

[Tuskegee, Ala.] July 9, 1908

Personal and Confidential.

My dear Judge Taft: In case you plan to make any reference to the Negro in your letter of acceptance, I should like to have the opportunity of seeing what you plan to say before it is given out. I feel rather sure that Mr. Bryan in his letter of acceptance will say something on that subject. Yours truly,

Booker T. Washington

TLpS Con. 7 BTW Papers DLC.

To Wilford H. Smith

[Tuskegee, Ala.] July 9, 1908

Personal and Confidential.
My dear Mr. Smith: What I am writing is in the strictest professional confidence.

I have come to the conclusion that, in justice to myself and family, I ought to place my holdings in the property which you recently attended to when Mr. Scott was in New York, in a more satisfactory and legal condition.[1] The storm regarding the change of hands has now blown over, and in my opinion, there is no reason why the matter cannot be re-organized in a perfectly legitimate way so there will be no question about my interests. Of course, I do not mean that this should be given to the public, for there is no reason for it, but I think I ought to be protected in a perfectly legitimate manner. Of course, I understand that this will require re-organization perhaps all around.

By the time I see you, which will be next week, I wish you would think out some plan by which what I am suggesting can be carried out. I do not want you to speak to anyone about it. Please write me at Huntington, L.I. Yours truly,

Booker T. Washington

TLpS Con. 382 BTW Papers DLC.

[1] A reference to BTW's part-ownership and control of the New York *Age*.

To William Loeb, Jr.

[Tuskegee, Ala.] July 10, 1908

My dear Sir: It is not often that I feel called upon to write such letters as the one which follows, but there seems no way around it.

There is in the Quartermaster's Department at Washington, a colored man, R. W. Thompson, who is seeking to be allowed the maximum compensation for a third grade appointment, namely $840.00 per annum. Thompson's colleague does exactly the same work as he does and gets $840.00, while he receives the salary of $55 per month.

Thompson is an exceptional kind of fellow. He has organized a strong Negro Press Bureau in Washington, and it is through him that considerable work has been done in the direction of sending notes in the months preliminary to the National Convention, to the strongest colored newspapers. It is not too much to say I think that the matter which went through his Bureau was of the most helpful and satisfactory kind. Of course, it is the purpose to keep this Bureau in action straight through till the election.

He has been in the department nearly five years, and practically at a minimum salary; and although classed as a messenger, is on detail as a watchman.

A word from you to the proper officer would bring about this slight change, I am sure. Yours truly,

Booker T. Washington

TLpS Con. 7 BTW Papers DLC.

Ralph Waldo Tyler to Emmett Jay Scott

Washington, D.C. July 10/08

My Dear Friend Scott: Your last received. You ask if the "Eds" referred to provoked any comment in Washington? Well they were simply the talk of the town — in the aristocratic circles, in the holy middle, and in subteranian circles. Our friend the "Eloquent one,"[1] has simply been consumed by a desire to overshaddow the Doctor. He thinks more of being acclaimed our real moses than of anything else. Everyone observes it, and everyone thought the "Eds" were timely, and would, at least, turn the hands on the "Eloquent one's" clock back for thirty minutes, if it did not stop his pendulum from swinging. The chances are that it will break his main spring and stop his clock. One thing sure, he realizes that I am on guard here and that he will never get by the sentinel, on his vain and fruitless, way to eliminate the Doctor, without giving the countersign. And he is neither in possession of the right countersign or pass word.

Well I see the negro Democrats got cold comfort from the Democratic convention. Not a line in their platform to animate the disgruntled Hamites. Understand the Democrats have ordered one million copies of the June Horizon with Du Bois' article on Taft, to use as campaign matter among negroes.

By the way, I sent Moore an article on "Taft and the Negro" Sunday, of about two columns in length. Dont know where he wanted it for The Age or Magazine. Charley Anderson and Will Lewis were here yesterday, on departmental business. The "black cabinet," with the "Dane" left out (W. T. V.) took dinner with them. I see Judge Taft and Hitchcock are working on the Executive and Advisory Committee. We, the race, ought to have representation on both, and especially on the Executive, which is supposed to do the work. An advisory committeeman may mean something or nothing, according to the fancy of the chairman, but a member of the Executive can be a factor. It would not hurt to have representation on both, the Executive and Advisory Committee. I presume the Dr has been consulted. Acting on this presumption, I did not stick in an oar of advice. I know, as a rule, the Doctor never overlooks a play on the checkerboard.

Remember me to the wife and the youthful Scotts, and with high regards for yourself, I am Sincerely

R. W. Tyler

ALS Con. 6 BTW Papers DLC.

[1] William T. Vernon.

From William Howard Taft

Hot Springs, Va., July 11, 1908

My dear Dr. Washington: I have your letter of July 9th, and shall be glad to see you and consult you about my speech or letter of acceptance. I am glad to hear that Bishop Turner has come out for me. Very sincerely yours,

Wm H Taft

TLpS William Howard Taft Papers DLC.

From Melvin Jack Chisum

New York July 11th, 08

My dear Dr Washington: I had an invitation from Bishop Walters to a conference yesterday and attended. It had to do with the forthcoming meeting at Atlantic City.

There is much which I believe you ought to know about it. When and where may I see? Yours faithfully

Chisum

ALS Con. 367 BTW Papers DLC.

Richard W. Thompson to Emmett Jay Scott

Washington, D.C., July 15, '08

My Dear Scott: Your letter came to hand Sunday, and conveyed news that is quite encouraging. I greatly appreciate the interest you are displaying in my behalf. The weather has been very hot here and for several days I have been in bad shape, although have not laid off from work. Your communication came as a welcome tonic, and hopes that had practically vanished into thin air have undergone something of a revival. I can not see how a letter to Mr. Loeb, carrying from you and the Doctor a recital of the circumstances, can fail to bring about some result. Leaving my political efforts out of the equation, I am satisfied that we are not asking for anything not justified by my record in the Department. Trained in the school of "spoils" politics, I am a believer in the theory that political service is a natural corollary of official preferment, and I think the fellow who is "with us" is entitled to consideration, rather than the fellow who is "agin us." The fact remains, however, that those who have been loudest in opposition to the administration, enjoy the best places or secure promotions without apparent effort. I state this, not as a complaint, but as a circumstance; and the "antis" are not slow to boast of what they regard as the timidity of the Rooseveltians about doing anything to them because of their show of "manhood" on the Brownsville, suffrage and other race questions. Among the Foraker element in the Departments there is no enthusiasm for Taft, and not a few are openly declaring their intention of going home to vote for Bryan. The loudest of these, of course, have no vote, and their eloquence is invariably of the benefit of the 14th street claque, being as meek as Mary's little lamb when around their bosses. Nevertheless, they are doing big talk among the Negroes. It will be well for the campaign to begin early, however, and put all forces to work who can bring anything to the ticket, especially in the pivotal states. I hope those who advise with Mr. Hitchcock or Judge Taft will urge a policy of liberality with the Negro workers, emphasizing the Negro newspaper as a moulder of public sentiment. The good a Negro paper can do is an open question; but it is a fact that they can do an immense amount of harm, when disposed to do so. This is not news to you. Money spent among the press gang will be well spent.

The local business league meets tonight at Metropolitan church. Last week's session was quite harmonious. Neither Chase nor Calloway was present. Nobody seems to be kicking over Calloway's removal,[1] and I understand he vouchsafed no explanation or apology for his malfeasance in office. Pittman is disposed to do the best he can and we shall stand by him. Harry Cummings was over Sunday and said things are working well in Baltimore. I arranged with him to introduce me to Gen. Agnew,[2] of the American, and I shall take a run over about the 1st to see what we can do to get a good showing for the League in its columns, etc. The usual arrangement with me, covering personal expenses, and cost of getting out an adequate report, notes, etc., will be satisfactory.

You have doubtless heard all about Cooper's death, his burial by friendly subscription, and the natural comments, etc., upon what might have been. The situation was sad indeed; yet it was the logical outcome of his methods. He had his excellencies, and he had his faults — as all of us have. Requiescat in pace.

You have doubtless noticed the exploitation of your timely intervention in the matter of bandmasters for the Negro regiments. You deserve credit for it and I gave it to you. I usually consult you before going ahead on such matters, but in this case, I remembered your native modesty when your work is to be extolled, and I made up my mind I would shoulder the blame if any came. The columns of the press are open to you for a denial of your criminality in connection with this splendid opening for the talented black musicians of the land. Was anything done finally about the Artillery matter? I have kept the subject in mind, awaiting developments.

I am returning the letter of Elbert Williams, per request.

Am using Bishop Turner's editorial in this week's correspondence. It is a knock-out for the kickers. Bishop Hood has written Dancy that at the proper time he will come out for Taft, and protest in the name of the A.M.E. Zion church against the abuse of the Star of Zion's editorial and news columns by Bishop Walters and Editor Clement[3] in attempting to commit the church to the policy of supporting the democratic ticket.

Let me again thank you for your earnest advocacy of my cause. It is said that it is more difficult to secure promotions for colored men in the War and Navy Departments than anywhere else, largely because of the army and navy's independence of political influence — a matter affecting all civilians, white and colored; and, the general perference in army circles for Negroes in the so-called laboring and serving grades, regarding high-grade clerical positions as the natural property of the white man. Political considerations are supposed to cut less ice in these departments than elsewhere, because the tenure of army and navy people doesn't depend on party victories. However, if Mr. Loeb wants me promoted, my position is not such as will attract any widespread attention, and may not upset any of the time-honored traditions of the Army code. So, I am hopeful that your efforts will not be in vain. It is not likely that I shall know anything about it until the increase is noticed as I go in to sign the pay-roll — where we went that day we made the rounds. If anything is done, it will probably take effect August 1. My anxiety may be overlooked, in view of the fact that the journalistic end of my business is at a dead standstill, and a glaring deficit in my necessary revenues must be made up if I am to escape bankruptcy. The papers that have been paying are in a hole, waiting for the pie to be cut, I suppose; anyhow, they are unable to pay, and those who want fame are also without the wherewithal to pay for such a luxury. I notice the millionaires, even, are complaining of the scarcity of money. Yet our Bureau of Engraving and Printing is running night and day printing greenbacks of every denomination, and the mints are coining it at their full capacity. So long. Faithfully yours,

R. W. Thompson

TLS Con. 42 BTW Papers DLC.

[1] Thomas J. Calloway was removed from the position of corresponding secretary of the Washington, D.C., Negro Business League on July 1, 1908.

[2] Felix Agnus (b. 1839) was born in France and came to the United States in 1860 after fighting in the Franco-Austrian war. He rose in the Union Army to the rank of brigadier general. After the Civil War he became editor and publisher of the Baltimore *American* and the Baltimore *Star*.

[3] George Clinton Clement (1871–1934), an A.M.E. Zion clergyman, edited the *Star of Zion* from 1904 to 1916. He was elevated to bishop in 1916.

To Emmett Jay Scott

Huntington, L.I., July 16, 1908

My dear Mr. Scott: Enclosed I send you a copy of a letter to Mr. Logan which explains itself.

Mr. Hitchcock came to my room at the Manhattan Hotel Monday, and had a talk of some length with me. He seemed to be in good spirits and well pleased. It is evident, however, that he has been told about the feeling among colored people because they could not get in touch with him at Chicago, as he brought up that subject among the first things. He asked me to let all the colored people know — I mean the ones who were at Chicago — that he treated them exactly as he did the white people. He said that many of his best and oldest white friends were treated the same as colored people were, and could not understand how he refused to see them as he had at other times and places. He said the fact was that for a whole week he did not sleep more than two hours during the night; that he had such tremendous responsibilities resting upon him with reference to the whole Convention, that it was a physical and mental impossibility to give more time to his friends than he did. I think you are a little mistaken regarding Vernon's connection with him, for he singled Vernon out of many, as one illustration of a man whom he told that he could not talk with him, that such subjects as he mentioned would have to go over for discussion after the

Convention. He expressed several times his determination to stand by his friends, and expressed his disgust at any man who would forsake his friends. Of course, I do not think it proper to go into any detailed plans at this time; this I shall omit for another occasion. Yours truly,

Booker T. Washington

TLS Con. 582 BTW Papers DLC.

To Melvin Jack Chisum

Huntington, L.I., July 16, 1908

Dear Mr. Chisum: Your letter has been received. I shall be at the Grand Central Station at   o'clock,[1] Saturday afternoon, and shall be glad to see you there. Yours truly,

[Booker T. Washington]

TLc Con. 367 BTW Papers DLC.

[1] The time was not filled in on the carbon copy.

From Melvin Jack Chisum

New York July 17th, 1908

My dear Dr. Washington: I had another conference with Bishop Walters Wednesday evening and succeeded in convincing him that he ought not hold the meeting at Atlantic City.

I got him to write several letters calling it off and I mailed them.

I discussed the matter with Mr Moore both Tuesday and yesterday. There is much which I think you ought to know — which I have not uttered to Mr Moore. Yours faithfully

Chisum

ALS Con. 367 BTW Papers DLC.

To William Howard Taft

Huntington, L.I., July 18, 1908

Dear Secretary Taft: I have your letters of July 10[1] and July 11th.

In regard to the conference with a half dozen colored men, I would state that in my opinion it is hardly possible to get together such a conference as we have in mind by the 29th of July. In the first place, I should like to consider very carefully the names and character of the persons to be invited, and then if possible, to have the invitation to them go directly from you. Of course, in any case it will not be possible to avoid some jealousies in certain quarters by reason of the names selected, but if the names are carefully gotten together, I believe that more good can be done than harm, and this is the reason I want more time for it. I take for granted that you can just as well meet this group of colored men at a later date, or if necessary let it go over until you return to Cincinnati in September.

A committee was appointed during the Chicago Convention to call to see Mr. Hitchcock and yourself, and that committee may appear in Cincinnati. This committee while composed of your friends and all good men, is composed very largely of Federal office holders. In the selection of the names to be invited by you, I have in mind having a very small representation of office holders, and a larger Church representation of men who influence large bodies of people in Church, in politics, and in secular organizations. I shall be able to submit the names to you within a few days, but I do not want to do it hastily.

In regard to your letter of July 11th, it will hardly be possible without my breaking very important engagements for me to see you at Hot Springs about your speech or letter of acceptance. If you intend to touch upon the Negro question in your Cincinnati speech, I wonder if you could send me the extracts here, but in case you are deferring any reference to this subject till your letter of acceptance, there will be ample time for me to see what you plan to say.

Communications sent to me at the above address will reach me during the summer.

Mr. Bryan's recent repudiation of Bishop Walters' utterance

bearing upon his interests in the Negro, simplifies the situation greatly.

If the committee appointed in Chicago calls to see you in Cincinnati, I do not think it will hurt matters at all for the other group of colored men to see you later. The spreading of the fact that you are consulting with colored men the same as with white men will help immensely. Yours truly,

Booker T. Washington

If you want me to send out the invitations I can do so.

TLS William Howard Taft Papers DLC. Postscript in BTW's hand. Addressed to Taft at Hot Springs, Va.

[1] Taft to BTW, July 10, 1908, William Howard Taft Papers, DLC. Taft agreed to a conference with representative black leaders and suggested July 29 as the date for the meeting.

To William Howard Taft

New York, July 20 1908

My Dear Judge: I return herewith the original draft of the passage in your speech referring to the Negro, together with changes and suggestions.[1]

Mr. Charles W. Anderson, Mr. Fred Moore, of the New York Age, and Mr. R. W. Tyler, who came over from Washington especially at my request, have gone over with me every sentence in the speech most carefully.

None of us doubt what you have in mind, and agree fully with the purposes that you seek to carry out.

What you say about the progress of the Negro is strong and will be helpful, but we are all strongly of the opinion that harm will be done if you discuss amendments to Southern constitutions as you have done in this draft.[2]

Since each state's constitution differs in some vital point from the others, and since it is not possible for you to explain yourself fully in detail in so short a document, we all feel it would be safer to leave out all discussion of southern constitutions.

We have watched carefully the Negro newspapers, and the sentiment of that element of Negroes that oppose you, and feel confident that they would misinterpret your meaning, if you used the draft in the form in which you sent it.

All of us feel very strongly the hope that the changes, as near as possible, will be used in the form as indicated in the enclosed new draft.[3] We have reasons which we feel sure you would consider sufficient and satisfactory, if they were explained in detail.

We all thank you for the privilege of reading it, and making suggestions. Very respectfully

Booker T. Washington

Communications sent to Huntington, L.I., N.Y. will reach me.

TLS William Howard Taft Papers DLC. Written on stationery of the Committee for Improving the Industrial Condition of Negroes in New York. Addressed to Taft at Hot Springs, Va.

1 Taft replied: "I have your letter of the 20th of July, and thank you for sending me the draft which you enclosed. I have used it exactly as you sent it." (July 22, 1908, William Howard Taft Papers, DLC.)

2 In his original draft, Taft said: "It is to be taken as a step forward that the States in which there was originally fraud and violence have now sought to base their exclusion of negroes on statutory law, which squares with the Federal Constitution, and this, however much we must deplore the injustice now done to the negro by unfair execution of such laws, I have strong hopes that the wisdom of the equal enforcement of the law will ultimately appeal to the Southern States in such a way as that the rules of ineligibility will be enforced equally against black and white." (Draft enclosed in Taft to BTW, July 19, 1908, William Howard Taft Papers, DLC.)

3 Taft, in his speech of acceptance of the nomination on July 28, 1908, noted the Republican platform's approval of black progress since emancipation and the expansion of black education, and the platform's explicit declaration for the enforcement of the Reconstruction amendments. "It is needless to state," he concluded, "that I stand with my party squarely on that plank in the platform, and believe that equal justice to all men, and the fair and impartial enforcement of these amendments is in keeping with the real American spirit of fair play." (Pamphlet version, William Howard Taft Papers, DLC.)

Ralph Waldo Tyler to Emmett Jay Scott

Washington, D.C. July 21/08

My Dear Mr. Scott: I just returned this morning from New York where I was called Sunday night by the Doctor, he, Charley[,] Fred Moore and I, were in conference, on what the Secretary will say on the Negro in his notification speech. He had sent the Doctor a draft of what he had prepared on the subject. We, however, changed and amended it so that it was not reconizable. What he had prepared was sure of misinterpretation by the Negroes. The Secretary as you know, handles the Negro question in such a broad judicial way that the Negro layman cant just understand. We, who know him so well, can have no reason to doubt the purposes he seeks to carry out, but at this time, there are so many Negro demagogues seeking to put the wrong interpretation on what he says, positiveness is necessary. I received your last letter, with enclosures. I thank you for the compliment you paid me in your note to the Doctor. As you well know, I was a Booker Washington man long before I got office — even long before I knew him personally.

As to the letter written Mr. Loeb in Thompson's behalf, I approve. I myself had written Mr. Loeb asking that he be given Lightfoot's job as messenger at the White House, but he had filled the vacancy before my letter was received. I was rather chagrined over Thompson's failure to pass the clerkship's examination. He, however, can blame no one but himself. He should have prepared himself, and especially so when he knew I was holding a clerkship open for him. The trouble with Dick is he lives too much in the air. Terrell had warned him to get an instructor and make systematic preparation.

I dont know why, but I just have a sneaking suspicion that if H puts a colored man on that advisory committee, it will be the "Eloquent one," I dont think he fancies our bunch.

I see Bryan proposes to try to organize the colored vote.[1] Understand the Democrats propose to subsidize a colored newspaper or two — one in Chicago, to help their cause.

Everything rather quiet. Nobody knows anything, and nobody seems to be doing anything.

Kind regards to all the Scotts. I suppose you will get up to Huntington before the Doctor breaks up his summer home. Sincerely

R. W. Tyler

ALS Con. 6 BTW Papers DLC.

[1] In 1908, largely in protest against the Brownsville dismissal order by Roosevelt, some militant black leaders defected to the Democrats, but there was no large black exodus from the Republican party. William Jennings Bryan, the Democratic presidential candidate, reaffirmed his support of disfranchisement, choosing to strengthen his hold upon southern whites rather than woo the black voters.

To Emmett Jay Scott

Huntington, L.I., July 22, 1908

My dear Mr. Scott: I received the telegram from Secretary Taft asking that I meet him in Hot Springs on Monday. I was in Connecticut when I received the telegram, hence it was impossible for me to reach Hot Springs on Monday, but even had I been here I do not think I should have gone. I telegraphed him to ask him if he could not write what he wanted to see me about in New York; this he did. It was in reference to his Cincinnati speech. Anticipating this, I telegraphed Tyler to come over to New York from Washington, and he, Mr. Anderson, Mr. Moore and I went carefully through the document. It was mighty lucky that I suggested to Secretary Taft to let me see what he was going to say on this subject, otherwise he would have made a great bungle of it. What he proposed to say was in many respects very unhappily put, and his enemies would have simply gloated over his remarks. I feel quite sure that he will accept the changes which we made. In fact, we re-wrote the most of that part of his subject.

Enclosed I send you the old draft and the new draft. Yours truly,

B. T. W.

TLI Con. 582 BTW Papers DLC. No enclosures were found with the letter.

Emmett Jay Scott to Ralph Waldo Tyler

[Tuskegee, Ala.] July 23, 1908

Dear Mr. Tyler: I have your kind letter of July 21st. I knew that the Secretary was to submit the Negro part of his address to the Doctor. I am glad that he had such strong advisors around him as he went over it.

I know you will not believe it, but I am not enamored of Huntington. I have to work too hard when I go there. I am pleased to learn, however, that you enjoyed your trip to the place. It is well worth while for one who can go there for rest, but when I leave

Tuskegee I do not like to undertake again the very thing that I am leaving behind.

With kindest regards, I am, Yours truly,

Emmett J. Scott

I am to go to Huntington after the Business League.

TLpS Con. 6 BTW Papers DLC. Postscript in Scott's hand.

William Wallace Haralson to Emmett Jay Scott

Troy Ala 7/23 1908

Dear Mr Scott, as per our phone conversation, I beg to make the following statement. Aboard the Chicago on June 27th my son in sky larking with a class mate threw some talcum powder on the deck which had been previously swept. A master at arms (petty officer among enlisted men) said "I am going to take a chance at you" meaning put him on the report. My son cursed him and said "you have nothing to do with me." It was reported to the ship commander,[1] and from him to the squadron commander and by him passed on to the Supt of the Naval Academy,[2] the first named recommending dismissal and each concurring in this endorsement and finally reached the Secy of the Navy.[3] At first the Secy was obdurate but through the intervention of Senators Johnson[4] & Bankhead[5] of Ala and Cullom[6] and Culberson[7] together with a number of congressman he relented and agreed to pass it on to the President without any adverse recommendation. Now of course you dont know the boy but you do know me and a word from B. T. Washington to the President stating what I have done for your Institution will go a long way to help my boy out. This case will come up Monday the 27th and I want B. T. to intervene in any way he thinks best to save my boy. Communi[c]ate with him & you will do me a favor I will appreciate all my life and I will show my gratitude some day. With best regards Yours

W W Haralson

ALS Con. 6 BTW Papers DLC. Written on stationery of the City Water Works, Montgomery, Ala., and marked: "Address–Troy Ala."

[1] John Adrian Hoogewerff (b. 1860).

[2] Charles Johnston Badger (1853–1932) was superintendent of the U.S. Naval Academy from 1907 to 1909 and commander of the battleship *Kansas* from 1909 to 1911. In 1911 he was promoted to rear admiral.

[3] Victor Howard Metcalf (1852–1936) was Secretary of the Navy from Dec. 12, 1906, to Nov. 30, 1908.

[4] Joseph Forney Johnston.

[5] John Hollis Bankhead.

[6] Shelby Moore Cullom.

[7] Charles Allen Culberson (1855–1925), a Democrat, was a former attorney general and governor of Texas who served in the U.S. Senate from 1899 to 1923.

From William Calvin Chase

Washington, D.C., July 23 1908

Confidential

My dear Prof: Why don't you arrange it so I can get the *munitions* of war. There is work to be done and it should be done at *once.* Secure me help, that is financial help, and I will show you what can be done with those who are against us. I have a special cartoonist who is fine. Ten thousand Bees ought to be printed weekly and circulated in states where the colored vote is strong. I can't do any business with your friend Hitchcock. In fact no colored *man* can except *yourself.* Let me hear from you at *once.* Confidentially yours

Chase

ALS Con. 367 BTW Papers DLC.

To William Wallace Haralson

Huntington, L.I., July 24, 1908

Will take up the matter tomorrow and will do everything I can in the direction you request. Please telegraph me direct here freely any suggestions or wishes that you may have. Very glad to serve you.

W.

TWIr Con. 6 BTW Papers DLC.

To William Wallace Haralson

Huntington, L.I., July 25, 1908

(Personal and Confidential.)
Case held up until return of Assistant Secretary which will be within three or four days. After Asst. Secretary makes his report, I will then do what I can in the matter. Am keeping in touch with the case.

W.

TWIr Con. 6 BTW Papers DLC.

From Theodore Roosevelt

Oyster Bay, N.Y., July 28, 1908

My dear Dr. Washington: Referring to your letter concerning the case of Midshipman Haralson, I am sorry to say that it is one which it is a little difficult to discuss because of the unspeakably filthy language he used, and which he admits he used. The whole case is set out in the following two letters from Haralson himself, the letter from Captain Hoogewerff, commanding the Chicago, and the letter from Captain Badger, the Superintendent of the Naval Academy:

[To the Commanding Officer of the U.S.S. Chicago, J. A. Hoogewerff]

U.S.S. Chicago, New London, June 26, 1908

Sir: 1. I respectfully state the following in regard to the report against me concerning the master-at-arms. There are two things to which I respectfully call your attention.

2. I did not purposely throw talcum powder on the deck after having been told not to do so. This can be verified by the master-at-arms himself, and Mr. E. W. Spencer.

3. When called up by the Captain and asked exactly what I said I told him everything except "go fuck yourself." I only gave that when pressed for something else that I said. I also stated that I

did not know whether I said that or not and would not swear to it, for I was uncertain. Mr. W. M. Barrett, Mr. E. W. Spencer, Mr. R. W. Bragg, all of whom were standing around, said that they did not hear me say that. The master-at-arms says that he don't remember hearing me say that.

4. As regards the other specifications I said them in a moment of anger when spoken to by the master-at-arms whom I thought had nothing to do with us in that way. Very respectfully,

J. M. Haralson
Midshipman, 2d class.

[TO THE SUPERINTENDENT OF THE U.S. NAVAL ACADEMY, CHARLES J. BADGER]

U. S. S. CHICAGO, New London, Conn., July 12th, 1908

Sir: I respectfully state that the following are my reasons for believing that I should not be dismissed from the Naval Academy.

1. In the report of June 25th against me, it is stated that I purposely threw talcum powder on the deck after being told not to do so. This I did not do.

2. In the same report, it is stated that I told the master-at-arms to go fuck himself. It is doubtful whether or not I said this. Midshipman Bragg, Spencer and Barrett and also the master-at-arms say that they did not hear me say this.

3. The remarks "Go to hell," "I will do as I damn please," and "stick it up your ass" I did say, but these without the remark "Go fuck yourself," are, I think, insufficient to warrant my dismissal.

4. I have not yet reached the age of discretion, at which one is supposed to have complete control over one's self.

5. My remarks to the master-at-arms although entirely improper were said merely to convey to him emphatically the idea that he had overstepped his authority.

6. I spoke in a moment of great haste without realizing what I said.

7. When one is young and has been away from the refining influences of home, one is apt to use highly improper figures of speech merely to emphasize a remark. Very respectfully,

J. M. Haralson
Mid'n, 2d Class

[To the Squadron Commander, W. S. Benson]

U.S.S. Chicago, New London, June 25, 1908

Sir: 1. It is my disagreeable duty to make the following report, which is too serious for me to adjudge punishment, against Midshipman J. M. Haralson, Second Class.

2. This morning about seven o'clock, Midshipman Haralson in throwing talcum powder at another midshipman, with whom he was skylarking, spilled some of the powder on the deck. The acting master-at-arms, who has to keep that part of the deck clean, remonstrated with him and Midshipman Haralson purposely threw more of the powder on deck. From Midshipman Haralson's own story, told in my presence and that of the Executive Officer, Lieutenant Commander C. F. Preston, and practically corroborated by other persons, the enlisted man's language was, "You have been raising quite a great deal of disturbance and I am going to take a chance at you (meaning according to Midshipman Haralson, put him on the report). The decks have been swept down." With no more provocation than the above, which is admitted by Midshipman Haralson, he addressed, according to his own admission, the following language to the enlisted man: "Go to hell; I will do as I damn please, it is none of your damn business; stick it up your ass; you have nothing to do with me at all; go fuck yourself." Fortunately, the enlisted man had sufficient control to turn away without replying, but reported the matter to the Executive Officer. Very respectfully,

J. A. Hoogewerff,
Commander, U.S. Navy, Commanding

[To the Secretary of the Navy, Truman Handy Newberry]

U.S. Naval Academy, Annapolis, Md., July 2, 1908

Sir: I have the honor to forward herewith a report made by Commander J. A. Hoogewerff, U.S.N., commanding U.S.S. Chicago, against Midshipman J. M. Haralson, 2nd Class, for using highly improper, vulgar, and obscene language towards an enlisted man in the Navy.

2. I also enclose Midshipman Haralson's statement in regard to the report, a letter from Commander W. S. Benson, U.S.N., Commanding the Naval Academy Practice Squadron, recommending

the dismissal of Midshipman Haralson; a record of the serious offenses of Midshipman Haralson since his entry into the Naval Academy, and a copy of a letter under date of June 4th from the Superintendent of the Naval Academy to Midshipman Haralson, calling attention to his deficiency in conduct for the Academic year 1907–1908 having received twenty-seven more demerits than permitted by the Regulations, and warning him that this deficiency in conduct would be considered in connection with any subsequent deficiency in his case.

3. The Superintendent fully concurs in the views of Midshipman Haralson's conduct as expressed in Commander Benson's letter. That a young man who after two years at the Naval Academy should use such language, no matter what the provocation, and there seems to have been little or none here, shows such lack of moral fibre and the requirements of an officer and gentleman that I am of the opinion that his connection with the Naval Academy and the Navy should be ended.

4. In accordance with the act of Congress, approved April 9, 1906, I have therefore to state my belief that the continued presence of Midshipman J. M. Haralson, 2nd Class, at the Naval Academy is contrary to the best interests of the service. Very respectfully,

Chas. J. Badger
Captain, U.S. Navy, Sup't.

You will notice that there is no question whatever as to the facts; that Haralson himself stated that he had used the filthy and obscene language of which he was guilty; and that he afterwards merely stated that it was doubtful whether or not he had used the filthiest and most obscene portion of it. This language was used to an enlisted man who was performing his duty, and the midshipman in excuse has practically nothing to say excepting that he has not yet reached the age of discretion and has been away from the refining influences of home! I entirely agree with the statement of Captain Badger that a young man who after two years at the Naval Academy uses such language, no matter what the provocation — and in this case there appears to have been little or none — shows such lack of moral fibre and of all the requirements of an officer and gentleman that it is preeminently in the interest of the United States Navy that his connection with it should be ended. There are plenty of boyish offenses which should be forgiven; but the use of such language to an enlisted man shows a nature of such a character that I would not be justified as Commander-in-Chief of the Navy in longer keeping this man within it.

With regret, believe me, Sincerely yours,

Theodore Roosevelt

TLS Con. 7 BTW Papers DLC.

To William Wallace Haralson

Huntington, L.I., July 30, 1908

I fear that nothing can be done at present. The case is a pretty bad one. Have done my best. Am writing fully.

W.

TWIr Con. 6 BTW Papers DLC.

From James Jenkins Dossen

Hamburg 1 Aug. 1908

Dear Doctor Washington After a very agreeable and successful time in Berlin where we were entertained as the guest of the Government we are sailing today for Liberia. Confidentially I may mention that the Berlin authorities expressed themselves as willing to join in a compact to guarantee the integrity of Liberia and thought that for obvious reasons it should be international as by the United States, England, France and Germany. I don't know what the Washington Government will think of this idea, but perhaps it might allay the jealousy of the other powers better than if England only were invited. We leave this however to the discretion of the United States Government.

I hope I shall hear from you from time to time and shall keep you posted on developments at home. A letter from President Barclay by the last fast mail, expressed deep solicitude in the success of the mission in effecting some arrangement whereby the territorial status quo of Liberia would be secured.

With Kindest regards to you and your circle Yours truly

James J Dossen

ALS Con. 369 BTW Papers DLC.

A Statement on Lynching

Baltimore, August 19, 1908

BOOKER T. WASHINGTON
GIVES FACTS AND CONDEMNS LYNCHINGS IN A STATEMENT
TELEGRAPHED TO THE NEW YORK WORLD[1]

Within the past sixty days twenty-five Negroes have been lynched in different parts of the United States. Of this number only four were even charged with criminal assault upon women. Nine were lynched in one day on the charge of being connected with murder. Four were lynched in one day on the charge that they passed resolutions in a lodge approving the murder of an individual. Three were lynched in one day on the charge that they had taken part in the burning of a gin house. The others were lynched for miscellaneous reasons.

One was publicly burned in open daylight in the presence of women and children, after oil had been poured upon his body, at Greenville, Tex., and reports state that a thousand people witnessed the spectacle in the open square of the town. One other victim was eighty years of age. How long can our Christian civilization stand this? I am making no special plea for the Negro, innocent or guilty, but I am calling attention to the danger that threatens our civilization.

CONDEMNS NEGRO LOAFERS

For the Negro criminal, and especially for the Negro loafer, gambler and drunkard, I have nothing but the severest condemnation, and no legal punishment is too severe for the brute that assaults a woman.

It requires no courage for 500 men to tie the hands of an individual to the stake or to hang or shoot him. But young men and boys who have once witnessed or who have read in the papers of these exciting scenes of burnings and lynchings often get the idea that there is something heroic in attacking some individual in the community who is at least able to defend himself.

No doubt the people who engage in lynchings, and excuse them, believe that they will have the effect of striking terror to the guilty. But who shall say whether the persons lynched are guilty? There is no way of distinguishing the innocent from the guilty except by due process of law. That is what courts are for. Those who have examined into the facts know only too well that in the wild justice of the mob it is frequently the innocent man who is executed.

Terrify the Innocent

These lynchings terrify the innocent, but they embolden the criminal. The criminal knows it is much easier to escape the mad fury of the mob than the deliberate vengeance of the law. But no man is so innocent that he can be safe at all times from the frenzy of the mob.

Statistics show that during the past ten years an average of thirty-two Negroes a year have been lynched on the charge of assaulting women. Granting that thirty-two per year are guilty, is that a just reason for condemning over 3,000,000 adult Negro men who have no part in such crimes? Are we as a nation to allow thirty-two criminals a year out of a race of 10,000,000 of people to throw us into a frenzy and change the complexion of our civilization so that we are held up to foreign nations as an uncivilized people not governed by law or order? Again I would say I am not making any special plea for the Negro, but because I feel that lynching is not only wrong, but a mistake — an awful mistake.

Effect of Mob Justice

Mob justice undermines the very foundation upon which our civilization rests, viz., respect for the law and confidence of its security. There are, in my opinion, two remedies — First of all, let us unite in a determined effort everywhere to see that the law is enforced, that all people at all times and all places see that the man charged with crime is given a fair trial.

Secondly, let all good citizens unite in an effort to rid the communities, especially the large cities, of the idle, vicious and gambling element. And in this connection I would not be just and would not be frank unless I stated that the betters of the black race could use their influence, especially in the cities, to see that the idle element that lives by its wits without permanent or reliable occupation or place of abode is either reformed or gotten rid of in some manner. In most cases it is this element that furnishes the powder for these explosions.

Booker T. Washington

PD Con. 977 BTW Papers DLC.

[1] BTW's statement, coming just a few days after the major race riot in Springfield, Ill., was issued from Baltimore, where he was attending the annual convention of the NNBL. "I want it to have a wide reading," BTW told a reporter from the New York *World*. (BTW to Mr. Sheldon, Aug. 19, 1908, Con. 382, BTW Papers, DLC.) The *World* promised to give the statement to the Associated Press after they had used it exclusively in New York. (*World* to BTW, Aug. 19, 1908, Con. 382, BTW Papers, DLC; the item appeared in the New York *World*, Aug. 20, 1908, 9.) BTW also had it reprinted as a pamphlet.

From William Wallace Haralson

Eufaula, Ala., Aug 24th 1908

Dear Dr Washington. Herewith enclosed please find the Presidents letter for which I thank you for sending me. I am very grateful for the kind things which you have said of me and trust some day to have the opportunity of showing my appreciation. My boy has come home profoundly dejected in spirit and absolutely miserable. I will have a brother in law in Congress this coming term and he is ready to introduce a bill to reinstate the boy but I have not yet dispared of your ultimate success with the President. For your information I want to say that affadavits were forwarded to the Navy Department, but were recd too late for consideration clearly proving that the most obnoxious phrase attributed to him "go ——— yourself" was not said.

The boy was before the Captain who questioned him closely as to what he said. He replied admitting everything save this phrase.

The Capt warned him that deception was a grave offense & to think of everything. Rather than take any chance that in the heat of anger he might have said something else, he foolishly stated "I *might* have said "go ——— yourself." You will bear in mind the official papers did not state this as being conditional but asserted it as a positive fact. The Master at Arms says himself that he heard no such phrase.

I want you to try the Presdt again as my boy's life will be ruined if he dont get back. He has had a lesson he will never forget and he is a good boy at heart. I want him punished but not so severely. Hazing is a worse offense in law than that committed by him yet the West Point boys were reinstated – at least most of them.

Touching on his demerits which during the close of his 3rd class year amounted to 277 or 50 in exces[s] of the allowance, I want to advise you that the last 50 demerits he received was for going to sleep while on duty in one of the corridors for only about 10 minutes. This was an extremely severe penalty for this offense. The boy lost one month in the hospital account of an operation & had to study late every night until 2 and 3 oclock to prepare for his final examinations & was desperately sleepy and worn out.

The President has boys of his own and can appreciate my feelings and the utter misery in which my boy is plunged. I beg of you to intercede with him and ask him to be merciful. Just give the boy one more chance and the Navy will in due season receive a good officer and a gentleman. With best regards Your Friend Truly

W W Haralson

Let me know when you will return.

ALS Con. 6 BTW Papers DLC. Written on stationery of the Bluff City Inn.

To Edgar Gardner Murphy

Huntington, L.I., August 29, 1908

Dear Mr. Murphy: I am in receipt of your kind letter of August 26[1] with copy of letter written to the Outlook enclosed. I thank you very much for writing me. I confess, however, that I do not share this opinion as to the harm that will be done by Mr. Stone's book. Of course, among a certain element it will have an influence for harm, but human nature, as I observe it, is so constructed that it does not take kindly to a description of a failure. It is hard to get up enthusiasm in connection with a funeral procession. No man, in my opinion, could write a history of the Southern Confederacy that would be read generally for the reason that the Southern Confederacy was a failure. I am not saying, of course, that the Negro race is a failure, Mr. Stone writes largely from that point of view, hence there is no rallying point for the general reader.

I agree, however, with you thoroughly that it is most unfortunate and unfair for such a man to have been in charge of the Carnegie work. I entered my earnest protest both to the President of the Carnegie Board and to Mr. Carroll D. Wright. I told them plainly that it was unfair to the race to have such a man in charge of such important work, who really does not believe that the race can succeed. However, I may be mistaken regarding the influence that Mr. Stone's book will have, and I hope that Dr. Houston[2] will write the review.

I am glad to hear that you are preparing two other volumes and I should be glad [to see?] the manuscript which you refer to whenever you send it. I shall be here a week longer when I shall start South.

I am glad to hear that Mr. Ogden has returned very much improved in health. I hope that you are well.

Aside from the strike in the Birmingham district matters seems to be going well in Alabama.

I have just returned from the Session of the National Negro Business League in Baltimore and you will be interested to know that by vote of the City Council, that the streets on which the colored people live in large numbers were illuminated in honor of the meeting of the League. Yours truly,

[Booker T. Washington]

TLc Con. 42 BTW Papers DLC.

1 Con. 42, BTW Papers, DLC, no enclosure attached.

2 David Franklin Houston, born in Monroe, N.C., in 1866, a graduate of South Carolina College with an M.A. from Harvard, was a professor of political science

and dean at the University of Texas, president of Texas A & M College (1902–5), president of the University of Texas (1905–8), chancellor of Washington University (1908–16), and Secretary of Agriculture in Woodrow Wilson's cabinet (1913–21). From 1906 until 1913 he was a member of the Southern Education Board.

To Frederick Randolph Moore

Huntington, L.I., August 29, 1908

Dear Mr. Moore: You will notice that each one of the four leading headlines on the front page of the paper this week refers to the subject of lynching; – this is unfortunate. Not only this, but the first headline on the second page refers to the same thing. In all, you have five headlines given to the same subject.

I meant to have called your attention to the unfortunate article which in some way got into the paper a few weeks ago stating that our people should not celebrate the Emancipation Proclamation. This is entirely against the teachings of the Age and against the teachings of all of your friends. A good many people expressed surprise at such an editorial in the paper.

Just as soon as we can get to it, the thing that the Age most needs is some person who can give a plenty of time to the make-up of the paper; to seeing that all of the news items and editorial items balance and agree with each other. This, however, cannot be done hurriedly. This requires a strong man, one who has the mind to do this kind of thing and one who can devote himself to this kind of work altogether.

As matters are now, every person who writes an editorial for the Age tells somebody else about it and the result is that it is getting noised abroad throughout the country that the Age is edited by anybody who wants to write an editorial. We must as soon as possible bring about a change that will help these matters. Yours truly,

[Booker T. Washington]

TLc Con. 6 BTW Papers DLC.

To James Jenkins Dossen

Huntington, L.I., August 29, 1908

My dear Mr. Vice-President: I wrote to a friend in New York[1] who has for sometime been interested in Liberia and about the visit of the Liberian Envoys to Tuskegee. She has placed in my hands $250.00 to be used for the education of a Liberian student for a year at Tuskegee. Her preference is that this student enter our Phelps Hall Bible Training School, but in case you cannot secure a student who is willing to take this course, she will let the money be used for a student who will take our general course. Of course, she means that the student after graduating from Tuskegee shall return to Liberia for work there. By this mail I am sending you one of our catalogues. You will find the course in Phelps Hall described in it together with the general course. Will you be kind enough to select one of your best men and send him as soon as possible. I should suggest that you choose a man who is between sixteen and twenty-five years of age, one who has some education, and one who is not afraid to work with his hands. Let him understand from the beginning that he must help himself, that he will not have an easy time, and that this lady will be will- . . .[2] willingness to help himself. I do not know how far this money will go in paying for his expenses, but I do not want to ask her for any more money before the end of the year. His expenses at Tuskegee will be at the rate of about $8.50 per month. He ought to work out from $2.00 to $3.00 of this amount each month. Something will have to be allowed, of course, for clothing and books. In the three summer months he ought to be able to earn considerable toward helping himself. Not knowing what the trip from Liberia to Tuskegee will cost I am not sending the money. If you choose you can advance the amount and I will reimburse you or I will send the amount just as soon as I know how much to send. If, when this student lands in New York, he will go to the house of Mr. Fred R. Moore, 14 Douglass Street, Brooklyn, he will give him directions as to reaching Tuskegee.

Mr. Root has not returned to Washington, but will be returning sometime in September, when I shall call at the State Department and shall let you have all the information when I can get hold of it.

Please remember me to all of your fellow Envoys and let the President know how highly I value his good will. Yours truly,

[Booker T. Washington]

TLc Con. 6 BTW Papers DLC.

[1] Olivia Egleston Phelps Stokes sent $500 to Tuskegee in August 1908 for Phelps Hall expenses and those of the Liberian students. Her sister Caroline also took an interest in the support of the Liberian students.

[2] The bottom line of page 1 of the carbon is missing.

To Oswald Garrison Villard

Tuskegee Institute, Alabama September 7, 1908

Personal:

My dear Mr. Villard: I know your hands are full and I hesitate to call upon you for any additional work or sympathy, or means, but there is such flagrant injustice being done to Colored people in Alabama just now, that I thought you might like to assist in the matter.[1]

Colored people, by recent decision of the courts, are being sent to the chain gang in large numbers for violation of contracts. This simply means that any white man, who cares to charge that a Colored man has promised to work for him and has not done so, or who has gotten money from him and not paid it back, can have the Colored man sent to the chain gang. Many of the best lawyers are of the opinion that such practice is wholly unconstitutional, but it will cost about $200 or $300 *now* to have the matter attested before the courts. My own purse has been drawn upon in so many directions, that I can do nothing at present.

The enclosed memorandum was sent me, I might say to you confidentially, by one of the judges. He has done all that he could to break up this terrible practice, but he is compelled to follow the decisions of the higher court — I mean of the State Supreme Court. Please return the memorandum. Yours very truly,

Booker T. Washington

TLS Oswald Garrison Villard Papers MH. A press copy is in Con. 42, BTW Papers, DLC. No enclosure attached.

[1] The Alonzo Bailey case.

To the Editor of the New York *Age*[1]

Washington, D.C., Sept. 7, 1908

If we may judge by the attendance at the recent meeting of the Niagara Movement, from the District of Columbia, we can safely say that the movement is practically dead. So far as can be learned, no one went from Washington to attend this meeting except Mrs. Wm. H. Clifford,[2] the wife of Mr. Clifford, who is an employee in the Treasury Department. We understand that at the meeting of the Niagara Movement, strong resolutions were passed endorsing Mr. Bryan for President. Mrs. Clifford and Dr. Du Bois seem to have been the only people in attendance.

The Lott Carey National Baptist Convention held its annual session in Washington a few days ago, and unanimously passed strong resolutions endorsing Secretary Taft for President. This is the convention of which Rev. Dr. Waldron's church is a member.

TLp Con. 41 BTW Papers DLC.

1 For proof of BTW's authorship of the editorial see BTW to Fred R. Moore, Sept. 8, 1908, Con. 41, BTW Papers, DLC. BTW asked Moore to "leave out of the statement sent you yesterday, the phrase 'only Mrs. Clifford and Mr. Du Bois were present at the recent meeting at Oberlin.'"

2 Carrie W. (Mrs. William H.) Clifford, originally from Ohio, was active in the National Association of Colored Women's Clubs and was founder and president of the Ohio branch from 1901 to 1905. She worked in the anti-lynching crusade and fought against disfranchisement and segregation. In 1905 she urged that the Afro-American Council merge with the Niagara Movement in an attempt to strengthen the role of militant protest. In 1910 she was a member of the NAACP's Committee of One Hundred. Her husband, William H. Clifford, was a prominent black politician in Ohio in the 1890s who served in the state legislature before moving to Washington, D.C.

To William Lukens Ward

[Tuskegee, Ala.] September 8, 1908

Personal and Confidential.

Dear Mr. Ward: On the enclosed slip I send memorandum which I think contains suggestions which ought to be carried out. It can be done, and, as I think you will readily see, it will have a far-reaching effect. Of course, I am taking for granted that Secretary Taft is going to speak at several points outside of Cincinnati. Yours very truly,

Booker T. Washington

[*Enclosure*]

First: At important points where Secretary Taft is to speak during his travels have a delegation of the strongest colored people call upon him, and present him with a short address. Of course, all details of the address should be thoroughly gone over beforehand.

Second: This plan will cost practically nothing and will have a far-reaching effect throughout the country.

Third: I would suggest that Mr. Ralph W. Tyler, of Washington, be placed in charge of the matter of arranging for all details of delegates to call upon Secretary Taft. Of course, he would work through the leaders in the various communities.

Fourth: If Secretary Taft is to speak in Baltimore, twenty-five or thirty of the leading colored men might call to see him and present him with a short address. This effect would be reported throughout Maryland and the country, and would be the best kind of campaigning with practically no cost.

Fifth: Mr. Tyler is a quiet, unobtrusive man who knows how to do things and keep his mouth closed. Of course, if you do not think well of him, I could suggest somebody else to do the same kind of work.

Sixth: I am thinking of having several delegations of colored people call to see Mr. Taft in Cincinnati but this, I presume, ought to be taken up with Mr. Vorys.

TLpS and Enclosure Con. 385 BTW Papers DLC.

From Charles William Anderson

New York, Sept 10 1908

Private & Confidential.

Dear Doctor: I have purposely been remaining away from the National Headquarters as I was informed that Moore & two or three others were in constant attendance, and I thought I would stay away until they sent for me, which they did the other day to talk over my Ohio trip. Learning that Moore & Gov. Pinchback had gone there to see Mr. Ward, I dropped in today after they had left. Ward called me into his private office, where I found Senator Murray Crane in close conference with him. Ward talked out frankly in front of me, and to my surprise, I learned that Crane was talking on the Negro newspaper question. He had a card in his hand bearing these names:

Trotter
Morgan
Alexander.

He was urging Ward to send money to the "Guardian" the "Mirror" and Alexander's magazine. I at once protested. I told them that Trotter and Morgan were both supporting Bryan, but urged Ward to help Alexander. We had quite a session, but at its conclusion Ward agreed to help Alexander, but not Morgan or Trotter. I remained with him after Crane left, and put a quietus on Mr. T. and Mr. M. What do you think of this? It would surely have gone through had I not dropped in. He told me that he was giving Moore $250 per week, which I heartily approved. He said he meant to do something for the "Odd Fellows Journal" which I also approved, but had I not called, both Trotter & Morgan would have gotten by. You see, Ward will not talk these matters over with Moore or any man of that sort. He also told me that he had about concluded to put C. F. Adams in the literary bureau. I did not oppose it, for I didn't know your plans. So I agreed to it. These fellows here are working without me, so I can't be blamed if I checkmate them with a nonentity like Adams.

Ward also told me that Johnson, the colored stenographer to Cannon[1] on the Congressional Committee, had called with Gen. Clarkson, and urged that the General be put in charge of matters concerning the Negro, on the ground that the Negroes of the country all loved him. I put a quietus on this too.

Ward wants the friendly Negro Bishops to meet Hitchcock at The Manhattan Hotel, some time in the near future. I said I would discuss this with him next week after his & my return from the Convention. He also is considering the advisability of sending some influential Negroes through the doubtful states to talk (not to make speeches) to the bretheren. He thinks, and I agree with him, that the right man can do much good. What men do you suggest. I am to see him again next Thursday. I go to the State Convention at Saratoga on Sunday. Will be at United States Hotel, Saratoga on Monday & Tuesday. I am a delegate. If you allow your interests to be played with by men like Moore, your enemies will run off with everything. Boys cant do mens work — especially when they have their hands out for something. He said Moore had brought "old man Pinchback" in and he had patted him on the back. I had to show him that the Governor was an influential man, & capable of good service. So much for being introduced by the wrong man. Vernon has been there and has apparently left a good impression. He offered the services of himself & Adams gratis. This always leaves a good impression. Men who are giving instead of taking are always respected. Had I not been sent for, I should have remained away and these fakirs from Boston would have landed.

This in strictest confidence. Yours Truly,

Anderson

ALS Con. 38 BTW Papers DLC.

[1] Joseph Gurney Cannon (1836–1926), Speaker of the U.S. House of Representatives from 1903 to 1911.

From Oswald Garrison Villard

[New York City] September 10, 1908

Dear Mr. Washington: I am sorry that I cannot, personally, help you in that matter,[1] except by editorial comment in The Evening Post. I am in your same situation of having been squeezed dry, by my John Brown undertaking[2] and other things. I would suggest your writing to Mr. George Foster Peabody and see if he would not advance the money. You see, this is precisely the kind of a case for which I want my endowed "Committee for the Advancement of the Negro Race."[3] With such a body we could instantly handle any similar discrimination against the negro, and carry the case, if necessary, to the higher court. Sooner or later we must get that committee going. Faithfully yours,

[Oswald G. Villard]

TLc Oswald Garrison Villard Papers MH.

1 See BTW to Oswald Garrison Villard, Sept. 7, 1908, above.

2 Oswald Garrison Villard, *John Brown, 1800–1859: A Biography Fifty Years After* (New York, 1910).

3 Later entitled the National Association for the Advancement of Colored People.

To Fred Warner Carpenter[1]

Tuskegee Institute, Alabama September 12, 1908

Personal

My dear Mr. Carpenter: I very much hope you will impress upon Judge Taft that out of all the Negro delegations he may meet during the campaign, none will be more important than the one to visit him September 22d headed by Dr. E. C. Morris. The delegation represents an exceptionally strong and intelligent and far-reaching organization. Yours very truly,

Booker T. Washington

TLS William Howard Taft Papers DLC.

1 Fred Warner Carpenter (b. 1873) was William H. Taft's private secretary from 1901 to 1910. He then held diplomatic posts in Morocco and Siam.

From Archibald Henry Grimké

Boston, Sept. 14 /08

My dear Mr. Washington: I have just rec'd your letter of the 9th addressed to me in Washington & forwarded to me here, & I hasten to send you the information regarding Cedar Hill which you desire.

Mr. Douglass came into possession of Cedar Hill, I think, about 25 years before his death in 1895. The estate comprises a large mansion house, several outbuildings & about 14½ acres of land — located in that part of metropolitan Washington, known as Anacostia. In his last will, the Sage of Anacostia, as he was called, devised this property to his wife, Mrs. Helen Pitts Douglass, who survived him about nine years. Owing to a defect in this instrument by the omission of a third witness, the bequest to his wife became inoperative, & Cedar Hill descended to the widow and children instead of to the widow alone. Mrs. Douglass who had conceived the idea of devoting the property as a perpetual memorial & monument to her illustrious husband, was obliged under these circumstances to purchase of the children of Mr. Douglass their share in Cedar Hill. She paid for their share $15,000. This large payment to the heirs left the widow short of funds to meet the current expenses of maintaining herself & the estate, which was her home to the day of her death — in a suitable manner, including taxes of estate. In order to carry her plans out in respect to Cedar Hill, this noble woman denied herself many of the comforts & sometimes some of the necessities of life. As she did not have the means to support herself & the property she was forced under the circumstances to place a mortgage on it of $5400. Through the initiative of Mr. Washington the trustees have been enabled to reduce the same by $600 — leaving an incumbrance of $4800 on the property today.

Cedar Hill is held by a board of seven trustees under the title of The Frederick Douglass Memorial & Historical Association, which was incorporated by act of Congress in the lifetime of Mrs. Douglass, who was its first president. The act of incorporation exempts the property from the payment of taxes after Mrs. Douglass' death when it came into possession of the trustees.

The trustees desire to maintain Cedar Hill in perpetuity as an anti-slavery museum & of souvenirs connected with the life & labors of Mr. Douglass, & of the history & achievements of the colored race in America.

Trustees:

Archibald H. Grimké, Pres.
Wm. H. Crogman, V. "
Francis J. Grimké, Treas.

Whitefield McKinlay, Sec.
F. A. Clark,[1]
John F. Cook,[2]
J. E. Moorland.[3]

Hoping, my dear Mr. Washington, that the above furnishes the information which you wish to obtain, I am Cordially yours,

Archibald H. Grimké

ALS Con. 887 BTW Papers DLC.

1 Possibly Frank A. Clark, a clerk in the Treasury Department in Washington, D.C.

2 John Francis Cook, wealthy son of the pre-Civil War educator and Presbyterian minister of the same name, was prominent in black life in the nation's capital. He was a D.C. tax collector and served as city alderman beginning in the late 1860s.

3 Jesse Edward Moorland (1863–1938) was for many years the leading black official of the YMCA. Born on a farm in Coldwater, Ohio, he attended Northwestern Normal University in Ada, Ohio. He received an honorary D.D. degree from the Howard University theology school in 1905. After holding Congregational pastorates in Nashville and Cleveland from 1893 to 1898, he became one of the two black secretaries of the International Committee of the Young Men's Christian Association, in charge of segregated institutions for blacks. Moorland held this position until his retirement in 1924, and was instrumental in persuading the Jewish philanthropist Julius Rosenwald to give large sums to this Christian organization for the erection of black YMCA buildings in the leading centers of black urban population. One of the founders of the Association for the Study of Negro Life and History in 1915 and its treasurer for several years, Moorland gave to Howard University in 1914 his personal collection of books and other records of Afro-American history, one of the best in the world. It was the basis for Howard's research collection, the Moorland Room, later named the Moorland-Spingarn Research Center.

From Ernest Lyon

Monrovia, Liberia. September 19, 1908

CONFIDENTIAL.

My dear Doctor: I have just seen a letter, written confidentially from London to the President of the Republic — informing him that Sir Harry Johnston[1] — of West African fame and author of a history of Liberia — has been invited by President Roosevelt to come to the United States for the purpose of studying the Negro question from the American viewpoint as it relates to his emigration to Liberia. The invitation part of the letter may or may not be true. But this is important — Sir Harry has accepted an invitaiton to go to America and thence to Haiti. He will leave England on or about the 14th of October. I have thought that you should know this fact if you have not as yet been made acquainted with it in order that you might be on the look-out for him.

I know Sir Harry. He has been to my place. Bishop Scott knows him and for that reason I am also confidentially acquainting him so that he and you might unite in adopting some plan to aid him if he comes to get the best result — so far as the Negro is concerned out of his visit. He must not study — if we can help it — the Negro from a palace car under the supervision of southern hospitality — He should be made to see our best as well as our worst. It is well that you know, if you do not already know — something of the record of Sir Harry.

The fact that he has lived in West Africa — was instrumental in giving to the British "Uganda Protectorate" — has been President of the Liberian Development Company — has written a history of Liberia and one on the condition of the Congo natives — will give him undoubtedly a standing among men and his findings an authority such as no ordinary individual can gainsay.

Note:

1. Sir Harry is opposed to the American type of Negroes.
2. If he is to have any Negroes at all he prefers the West Indian type of British trained Negroes.
3. He has an unsavory reputation on the West Coast in his treatment of the Negro.
4. I am quite certain that Sir Harry will have nothing good to say of the Liberian Negro — whom he claims is American — but before Sir Harry should be taken seriously — the inside history of the Liberian Development Company and his part in the birth of the organization should be given by some one else.

I know something about it having been on the ground during this trying period in Liberian economic affairs. I am sorry to have to trouble you again — but you have now become diplomatically linked with the future of Liberia. In the capitols of Europe, especially London and Paris — where Liberian matters are discussed in their relations to the United States brought about by the recent commission — your name is mentioned as an important factor.

I plead guilty to having increased your burdens in this new direction but have no apology to make and I am launching out again in this new direction.

Liberia before the going of this Commission misunderstood you — thru the work of designing persons — but the condition has changed and what you have always stood for is now appreciated and admired.

I forgot to say that among the things which form a basis of Sir Harry's coming is the fund of $70,000 or more dollars which are reported to be in the treasury of the Society and of which Dr. Chamberlain[2] is Secretary. In this case Dr. Chamberlain will have much to do with him and as you are yourself connected with the Society you no doubt will understand the matter. Sincerely,

Ernest Lyon

P.S. Please write your publisher to send me forth with 3 copies of "Up From Slavery." If you do not mind—send if you please a copy direct to President Barclay with your Compliments. I am quite sure that he will enjoy and appreciate it.

"L"

TLS Con. 895 BTW Papers DLC. Postscript in Lyon's hand.

1 Sir Harry Hamilton Johnston (1858–1927), the British explorer and writer, visited the United States in 1908 and met with Theodore Roosevelt to discuss East Africa. Johnston then toured the southern United States as a guest of Robert C. Ogden. He visited Hampton Institute, Tuskegee Institute, the steel mills and coal mines of Birmingham, and the all-black town of Mound Bayou, Miss. He then traveled to Central and South America to study blacks there. In 1910 he published *The Negro in the New World,* in which he argued that blacks had made great progress (p. 478). He praised the work of Hampton and Tuskegee and predicted that the race problem would eventually be solved if the Hampton-Tuskegee type of education continued (p. 386). Johnston recalled his visit to Tuskegee in his autobiography. He was impressed by BTW's intelligence and wit and his ability to talk on many subjects. He thought BTW's lack of emotional religion was an asset, since religion did not interfere with his school curriculum. George W. Carver impressed Johnston with his knowledge of North and South American history. Johnston's only negative comment on Tuskegee was the poor quality of the food. He also thought that the school choir should sing Gilbert and Sullivan rather than plantation melodies. (*The Story of My Life and Work,* 390–96.)

2 Leander Trowbridge Chamberlain (1837–1913), a Congregational minister, accompanied Sir Harry Johnston on his tour of the southern United States. It is not clear what society paid the expenses of the trip, but Chamberlain was secretary of the American McCall Association, president of the U.S. Evangelist Alliance, and secretary-treasurer of the American and Foreign Christian Union.

From Charles William Anderson

New York, N.Y., September 29, 1908

(Personal)

My dear Doctor: Henry Lincoln Johnson of Georgia blew in here the other day, and seems to have completely captured Ward. Ward sent for me and spent an half hour in telling me how rich a man, and how great a lawyer Johnson was. I learned that he had taken him to Parsons and convinced Parsons of his greatness, to the end that Parsons ordered two big colored meetings to be arranged, that Johnson might address them. Johnson at once formed a working partnership with Fortune (who, by the way, is on the pay-roll at the National Committee) and Wetmore and Cheshire[1] of New Jersey, to control things generally, around here. They have held two or three meetings at Wetmore's office, and have recommended that Ward put the little "alligator" on the pay-roll. This bunch has also recommended to Mr. Hitchcock the advisability of giving General Clarkson the place made vacant by Du Pont.[2] My man, Sol Johnson, tells me that they are all pretty severe in their criticism of you, and all are trying to hide their work from me. Johnson has not called on me, nor has he called on any of the active colored republicans here, or has he visited the Club. I have said some pretty plain things to Parsons, who is now trying to meet my wishes, but Ward still maintains that H. L. Johnson is the greatest man of the century. He went so far as to say that Johnson prepared all of the Southern cases for the Taft people, which the National Committee passed upon before the Convention, and was in his opinion, the ablest colored lawyer in the country. I mention all of this sickening twaddle to show you how easy it is for a colored blatherskite to fool the average white man. I did not expect much more of Ward, but I confess, I did think better of Parsons' judgment. However, Parsons has seen the light, and will hereafter play ball with his friends. All of this thing came about while I was in Cleveland, making a speech for the cause, and defraying my own expenses, even my own railroad and parlor car fare. I have not asked for, or received a cent for that trip. I forgot to say that Simmons, who is also on the pay-roll, is training along behind Johnson and Wetmore.

When will you be in this section? Yours truly,

Charles W. Anderson

TLS Con. 38 BTW Papers DLC.

[1] John T. Cheshire, of Newark, N.J., was president of the Taft Club.

[2] Presumably the reference is to a Republican party post held by Henry Algernon Dupont (1838–1926), U.S. senator from Delaware (1906–17).

To Theodore Roosevelt

[Tuskegee, Ala.] October 1, 1908

Personal.

My dear Mr. President: I hope you will forgive me for troubling you again about the case of young Haralson, who was dismissed from the Naval Academy.

I have very seldom seen a case where a young man seems to have so completely come to himself as he has. The experience of being dismissed and disgraced, as he was, seems to have made a new individual of him. His one ambition now is to return to the Academy and redeem himself in the eyes of the officers of the Government and his friends.

Having been taught his lesson and received his punishment is there not some way by which he could be reinstated and given a new trial. Would it be of any use for his father to see you or the Secretary of the Navy? Yours very truly,

Booker T. Washington

TLpS Con. 7 BTW Papers DLC.

To James Jenkins Dossen

[Tuskegee, Ala.] October 1, 1908

My dear Vice-President Dossen: Your kind letter of August 21st has just reached me, and I hardly need say that I have read it with the deepest interest. I am very glad to learn that you and your fellow Envoys have reached your homes in good health. I am sure that after so long an absence, it must have been a matter of the greatest satisfaction to be at your home again.

Please let the President and his official family know how very much I appreciate their kind words concerning myself. I sought to do what I thought it was my duty to do. My only regret is that I was not able to do more. I hope to prove of still greater service in the future.

Now, as to the matter in hand, I have had no communication with anyone concerning what should be England's attitude toward Liberia. In fact, the rumor connecting my name with any advice so far as to how Liberia should act in reference to England's claims, is entirely without foundation. I never talk about such matters, outside of official circles, to anyone, and in this particular case I have not discussed the subject with anyone outside of yourself and Secretary Root; and I am sure that Secretary Root made no such suggestion or gave any such advice when we saw him.

I have not attempted to see the Secretary on the subject since we were at the State Department together, for the reason that he and the President, in fact the whole Cabinet, have been out of Washington during the whole of the summer, and it was impossible to get any information, or do any business, except through subordinates, and dealing with subordinates, as you know, is always disagreeable, and besides one cannot get real information.

My present plan is to see the Secretary on the 13th of October and go over the whole matter fully with him, getting all the information that he is willing to give me. I think after a conference with him, I shall be able to write you again more definitely as to how matters stand. Certainly, by that time, he will have had some report from the Agent who visited Liberia. You can depend upon it, that I shall keep you informed if I hear of any new development.

I am glad that you mention in your letter the wish of England to annex Liberia to Sierra Leone. If you hear anything further in that direction, please inform me, as I wish to know how to present the case to the Secretary. My highest ambition is to see Liberia stand for all time on its own feet without being under obligation to any other nation, and whatever I do will be with that in view.

I wish to say, however, for your personal and private information, that this man Downing is a deadly enemy to Liberia, in my opinion, and I think it is through him that many of these reports get scattered. He wrote me a long letter sometime ago in which he made the most damaging statements concerning yourself and fellow Envoys. I paid no attention to the letter, and did not even answer it. He begged me in the letter to put his view of the case before President Roosevelt. Of course, I refused to do it.

I am only making this statement in order to emphasize the necessity of watching this man, as he would not hesitate, in my opinion, to do anything that would denationalize Liberia.

I shall be writing you again soon. Yours very truly,

Booker T. Washington

P.S. I have just written for an engagement with the Secretary of State for October 13th, when I shall take up the matter fully relative to Liberia. Of course, I will write you as soon as I have done so.

TLpS Con. 895 BTW Papers DLC.

H. W. Minster to Emmett Jay Scott

St. Louis, Oct. 1, 1908

Dear Sir: This will introduce to you operative F. E. Miller of the St. Louis office, who goes forward as per Mr. Washington's request to our New York office.

Kindly give him the necessary data in order that he can act intelligently. Yours truly,

Pinkerton's National Detective Agency

TLI Con. 379 BTW Papers DLC. Dictated and initialed by "H. W. M." (H. W. Minster, superintendent of the St. Louis office).

To Charles William Anderson

[Tuskegee, Ala.] October 2, 1908

Personal and Confidential.

My dear Mr. Anderson: I have your letter of September 29th and have read it with deep interest.

I am writing you hastily, as I am just starting on a week's trip through the state of Mississippi.

Your letter reveals some very interesting things. The more I see of the other fellows, the more I am led to admire our friend in the White House. He is one of the few great men, who is not afraid to place power and responsibility in the hands of Colored people. He would not think of doing anything in New York without consulting you and getting your wishes. I believe that our friend, Mr. Taft, is a man of the same type, but of course his hands are tied so far, but they will be loose after November. One compensation, however, is always this. These little Colored men, who bob up and make a noise for a while usually take care of themselves.

I am glad you went to Cleveland, but was surprised that a charge was made at the door. Under the circumstances, I am surprised that you had any audience at all. We can congratulate ourselves, however, that there is only about four weeks more of this kind of thing to endure.

I shall be in New York about the middle of October and shall see you at once. There were several matters which I wanted to take up with you in person before I left New York, but your absence seemed to have made it impossible. What ought to be done is for you to be placed in charge of the whole situation and all matters referred to you. That is what I have urged time and time again. Our friend in the White House and his Secretary, however, would be the only ones who are big enough to carry out such a policy.

You remember Mr. Ward said that some Foraker man had been put at work. The enclosed letter seems to disclose who the man is. I have never heard of him before. Yours very truly,

Booker T. Washington

TLpS Con. 38 BTW Papers DLC. No enclosure found with letter.

From Charles William Anderson

New York, N.Y., Oct 2, 1908

Dear Doctor: I wrote you that Henry Lincoln Johnson had reached here, hypnotized Ward, captured Hitchcock, and formed a close alliance with Roscoe,[1] Fortune, Wetmore & Cheshire. More lately he has added Jim Hayes to the bunch. They have been using Pinchback also, but of course, he does not know that these men spend their time denouncing you. Wetmore's office is their headquarters. They are telling everybody that Hitchcock & Ward have entrusted Lincoln Johnson with the negro end of the campaign. Last night they held their first meeting at Ransome's church. I was not even consulted by Parsons about the meeting. He (Parsons) got up for "Link" Johnson on the recommendation of Ward. Ward has fallen in love with him because Hitchcock is fond of him. Hitchcock is fond of him because he helped to knock out Lyons on the National Committee. You will remember that Johnson put the present white committeeman in nomination in the caucus at Chicago. Hence, Hitchcock's interest in him. Well, they got up the meeting & selected Pinchback as chairman. They put on Johnson, Wetmore, & a white man as speakers. I remained away as did the members of our club. We gave a meeting at the Club the same night, at which the President was defended, and both he and Taft vociferously applauded. At the other meeting, a riot was only narrowly avoided, as Ransome had worked hard to pack the church with his kickers. Fortune tried to speak, but was shouted down. Moore tried also but was jeered at, I am told, but to cap the climax, Wetmore made the last speech of the night, in which he denounced you by name, called you a coward, and accused you of being responsible for the dismissal of the soldiers. As his friend Johnson was handled so roughly by the crowd, for stating that he believed the soldiers guilty, Wetmore changed the tactics, and instead of defending the President, he assailed him, and abused you. Poor Pinchback he had to grin & bear it. He should have consulted me, but he and Moore are sleeping together these days, and are not seeking advice from anybody. Wetmore's speech was the last speech of the night, & therefore didn't get into the newspapers. I gave Parsons a calling down about turning the meeting over to Johnson, Fortune & Wetmore last Monday and told him that an attempt would be made by Ransome & his democratic friends to break it up. Consequently police were sent there. If the police had not been there the democrats and kickers would have thrown the speakers out & captured the meeting. Jim Hayes told me yesterday that he and "Link" Johnson had cooked Booker Washington's goose at The Nat. Com. He said Simmons, Fortune, Wetmore and one or two others had convinced Ward that there was too much Anderson and Washington, but added, "I afterwards found out that you have not been very much consulted." He also said that Hitchcock thought more of Johnson than any other colored man because of his services in defeating Lyons for the National Committee. I sent the information along to Washington D.C. the other day, & predicted that there would be trouble if this crowd of fakirs were allowed to manage things. The trouble came on schedule time. The only sad part of it is, that Roscoe has been working with them with malice prepense, and Pinchback has been used by them, innocently. It is to laugh, as they say on the stage. Yours Truly,

Anderson

ALS Con. 38 BTW Papers DLC.

[1] Roscoe Conkling Simmons.

To Caroline Phelps Stokes

[Tuskegee, Ala.] October 3, 1908

My dear Miss Stokes: In answer to your kind letter of September 28th, I am writing to say that I enclose copies of letters giving at least a portion of the information which I think your last letter calls for.

In reference to the Roberts Memorial Scholarship, I would state that at the time that this scholarship was given, we did not have very perfect methods of filing and caring for our correspondence, such as we now have, and for that reason, the letter which you sent has in some way been misplaced. I have a record, however, of this gift and the following is the official record upon our books:

"April 2d, '98 Roberts Memorial Scholarship,
in memory of the first President of Liberia,
by Miss Caroline Phelps Stokes, New York.
Interest on same to be used yearly to help
some worthy young man. $1,000.00."

Now if these letters put you in possession of the information which you are seeking, I shall be very glad to furnish you detailed information, as far as we can, as to the use of those funds. I am very sorry to prolong the correspondence and to put you to additional trouble, but the loss or misplacing of the letter regarding the Roberts Scholarship is partly the cause.

We have been having a visit this week from Bishop I. B. Scott, who has been located in Liberia for the last four years, and he gave our students a most inspiring talk in the Chapel concerning the Christian development of the Liberian people. You will be, therefore, interested to know that our students and teachers have arranged to support a native worker for the next year, who is to assist Bishop Scott in his work of evangelization in Liberia.

I shall wait to hear from you further before attempting to give detailed information. Yours truly,

Booker T. Washington

TLpS Con. 47 BTW Papers DLC.

A News Item in the *Tuskegee Student*

Tuskegee Institute, Alabama October 3, 1908

TUSKEGEE'S PRINCIPAL AT HIS OLD HOME

Special Correspondence: To the New York Evening Post

Roanoke, Va., October 1 — Booker T. Washington, the noted Negro educator spoke here a few days ago to the white people and the colored people at the Roanoke State Fair. The next day he paid a visit to his old home, at Hale's Ford, in the adjoining county of Franklin.

Several of the descendents of the Burroughs family, who formerly owned Mr. Washington, are living in this city, and met him during his visit here. There are also a number of colored people, who were formerly slaves in the country around Hale's Ford, and knew Mr. Washington as a boy, there. The result of this visit has been to revive a great many stories and reminiscences of Mr. Washington's boyhood, and to give new life to the Washington legend which has been growing up in this region for several years.

Hale's Ford is about twenty-five miles from this city, and a wild and mountainous part of the country. About forty years ago, there was a church and a tobacco factory there. The church still remains, but the tobacco factory is gone. So have most of the people who used to live there. The Negroes began moving out directly after the War. They went off to the mines in West Virginia. A little later the white people began moving out, also. The poor white people moved down into cotton mill centers, at Danville, and other places. The sons of the large planters went to the cities to engage in business. A good many of them are living here in Roanoke. There are miles of territory growing up in timber and underbrush, in Franklin County that were formerly planted in tobacco. The present time, the whole region seems to be inhabited mostly by old people, and others who were not able to get away. Like most other places, where the young people have gone out and left the old people behind, Hale's Ford and the country round it is sad, solitary and neglected.

Among the first colored people to leave this part of the country, after the War, was Jane Burroughs, or perhaps "Aunt Jane" as they called her. "Aunt Jane" was Mr. Washington's mother. Her husband, who lived on a neighboring plantation, had been carried off by a party of "Yankee" raiders a short time before, and, after the surrender, she followed him, taking with her, two sons, Booker and John, and a daughter, Amanda. At that time, Booker Washington, who was then just plain "Booker" was about eight years old, as near as he, and the neighbors who knew him, can make out.

The Old Burroughs homestead contains about two hundred and six acres. No member of the family lives on the old homestead, at present, tho' several of the descendants are living in other parts of Franklin County. Two of them came over to meet Mr. Washington on the day he visited the place. The man who now has the Burroughs place is known as Jack Robertson.

Little of the old home now remains. The old dining room, built of squared logs, where young Washington began his first work as a slave, still stands. This work consisted in moving back and forth a huge fan which hung on hinges over the dining table. This fan swung back and forth served to keep the flies off the table while the family was eating. Mr. Washington, in company with a number of old settlers, was able to locate the kitchen, where Mr. Washington was born; the old weave house, near where "Aunt Sophie," who was an elder sister of Jane Burroughs, lived. The old spring is still there, and willow tree, from which Mr. Washington recalled was cut the switch with which he received his first thrashing.

One of the old settlers, who is something of a wag, remarked that he had read in the newspaper that Mr. Washington was born in a house with a dirt floor. He said he didn't know as they could show him the house, but the floor was still there.

Mr. Washington inquired about Morgan's Mill to which he used to carry corn, and was surprised to find that the Ferguson plantation, which had seemed to him, as a boy, so far away, was actually located within a stone's throw of the Burroughs house. He remembered the mill especially, because he used to have such difficulty in keeping the sack that held the grain, from falling off the mule he rode. When it did fall off, he was too small to put it back, and sometimes had to wait for hours beside the road until some one came along to help him with it.

"I am afraid I wouldn't know the place," said Mr. Washington. "Every thing is changed. But after all, the most remarkable changes that I notice," he continued, laughingly, "is in the size of things. It seems incredible to me that the Ferguson place, where I used to go, as a boy, is now only just across the road. The old dining room too, is not near as large now as it used to be, or at least as it seemed to be, once."

After looking around the Burroughs place, Mr. Washington went back to the front of the house and stood upon the porch, from which he made a little speech, to his old friends and others who had gathered there to meet him. In the meantime an old bell which hangs on a pole at the back of the house, just such a one as was formerly used to summon the slaves from their quarters, was rung to announce the arrival of Mr. Washington. This brought a considerable number of people, white and colored, from the surrounding plantations.

As Mr. Washington stood up to speak, an interesting scene presented itself. What remained of the old aristocracy of the region was gathered directly in front of him. They were mostly grey haired men and women, proud and reserved, they were seated, some of them in chairs, but the most of them upon the lawns. Directly behind him were the remnants and the descendants of their former slaves. Three or four of them were grim fellows, showing in every line and lineament of face and figure, the efforts of continuous and severe labor. They came just as they were directly from the fields. Then there were others, younger people, who came to attend this informal little celebration, as if it were a Sunday school picnic.

In the course of his remarks, Mr. Washington emphasized the fact that he had never been sorry that he was born there, and born as he had been, a slave. He said he had learned a great many things about life, coming up as he had, from that lowly condition in life which he could not have learned if he had been born in any other or higher station. He said he did not regret the fact that he had been born on a farm, and that he had been born poor. He had learned some things from the farm, and some things from poverty that were worth all that they cost. Saying that he thought, now that he had returned after forty years to his birth-place, he owed it to the people who had known him as a boy to tell them something about what had happened to him during the time he had been away, to report, in short, upon his past life; he began telling in a very simple and direct way, the story of what he had achieved, and what were his purposes and motives in all that he had thought to do. He said the most important thing that he had learned was the opportunity that there was in this country for every man, whether he was white or black, if he had the heart and courage to work. He reminded the colored people who were present that it was not too late for them to begin, if they had not already done so, to save a little money to get a little home, and to make something of themselves.

Just before he reached the conclusion of his speech, he noticed in front of him an ancient rose bush, and he made that the theme of a very pretty and touching peroration. He said this old rose bush reminded him of the story of an old Negro who had lived for many years upon an old Virginia plantation. During the time that he was there several generations had had possession of the plantation, but he was always allowed to remain. Finally a new proprietor came to the plantation; he was still allowed to remain as sort of a gardener, working when he was able, but working pretty much as he himself chose. One day his mistress, who was a young woman, and had conceived the idea of fixing up the old house and re-arranging the old garden, called this old man, and pointing to an ancient rose bush, asked him if he felt able to dig it up that morning. The old fellow looked at it for an instant, hesitated, and then bowing politely, as was the custom in the old-fashioned days to which he belonged, said he thought he could. The lady waited a few hours, but nothing had been done to the rose bush, and she called the old man back again. She said to him, "Uncle Joe, aren't you going to dig up that rose bush for me this morning?"

The old man bowed again, politely; his lips trembled a moment as if he wanted to say something, but he didn't.

The next day, when the rose bush still remained untouched, the lady called old Joe to her once again, and with considerable irritation, asked him if he did not intend to dig up the rose bush as she had asked him to do.

The old man bowed again, with the same stately politeness, which he was accustomed to use, and then, tears coming to his eyes, he said: "Missus, let me tell you something. My old Missus planted that rose bush there with her own hands when I was a boy. And Missus, these old hands jest can't dig it up, nohow. I hope you will excuse me."

The point of this story was, there was something precious, and something real in the kindly, and often tender relations which bound master and slave together, in the days before the war. The new generation that has grown up since that time, as a rule, did not understand, and did not value those old relations of kindness, and good-will which had bound the two races together, in the old days.

"But, my friends," he concluded, "we must not dig up the old rose bush, we must preserve the old kindly relations, because, if they are lost, they can never be replaced."

There were a good many interesting incidents that came out in the conversation that occurred during Mr. Washington's visit to the Burroughs' homestead. There are a good many people, white and black, here in Roanoke, who knew Mr. Washington when he was a boy and are able to tell interesting stories about him. The man about here who seems to have known him best is S. C. Burroughs,[1] a Franklin County farmer, and grandson of James Burroughs who was Mr. Washington's master. Mr. Burroughs inquired of Mr. Washington particularly about John Washington, a brother of Mr. Washington, who is now head of the Industrial Department at Tuskegee.

"I knew John better than I did Booker," said Mr. Burroughs, "John and I used to play together a great deal. You know we always thought that John was a good deal cleverer than Booker. Booker was rather slow, but John was as bright as a dollar."

Perhaps the most interesting fact that Mr. Burroughs told, was that he was now in possession of an inventory of his grandfather's estate in which the names of all his slaves and their different values are assessed. James Burroughs, the grandfather, died about 1861. It was when his estate went through the court that this appraisement of his property took place. It is a very interesting fact that Booker T. Washington, upon whom Harvard University recently conferred the honorary degree of Master of Arts, for distinguished service for education and to his country, was valued, at that time, at something like four hundred dollars.

Tuskegee Student, 20 (Oct. 3, 1908), 3–4, reprinted from the New York *Evening Post.*

[1] Silas C. Burroughs (1850–1926) of Davis Mills, Va., was the son of Joseph Nicholas Burroughs, eldest son of BTW's former owners. See his correspondence in Mackintosh, *Burroughs Plantation, 1856–1865,* 33–36.

Reports of Pinkerton Detective F. E. Miller

[Oct. 3–12, 1908]

F. E. M. reports:

St. Louis, Saturday, Oct. 3, 1908

At 9:25 P.M. I left St. Louis via the Illinois Central R. R. for Memphis, Tenn., and at midnight was enroute. Yours respectfully,

Reported 10-6-1908.
St. Louis -B-[1]

F. E. M. reports:

Enroute, Sunday, Oct. 4, 1908

Having been enroute since midnight I arrived in Memphis at 8:35 A.M. and at 7 P.M. called at the residence of Mr. Settle, 421 S. Arlcans St. whose wife informed me that Mr. Settle had gone to the station to meet Mr. Washington and requested me to return at 8:30 P.M.

At that hour I again called at Mr. Settle's residence where I met Messrs. Washington, Scott, and Hunt. Mr. Scott stated threats had been made against Mr. Washington in a letter received by him which reads as follows:

"Cyntha, Miss., Sept. 22, 1908

Dear Friend:

Mr. B. T. Washington,

While sitting alone thinking of the great world and you and that what I have heard of you being a great man and a great help to the colored race of people. Please do not make your visit to Jackson, Miss., on the 4th of October, 1908, and no other month.

It has been said that you will never leave in peace but in corpse or some other way, but not like you came. Take heed in the name of the Lord you may be safe, so good bye.

Yours everly,

J. Matony"

Mr. Scott further stated they had not decided whether they will go to Jackson or not, but may possibly have me go there and look over the situation. This they would decide later. The party will leave Memphis at 7 A.M. tomorrow, Oct. 5, 1908, via the Frisco R. R. in a private car. There will be eighteen in all, including two white newspaper reporters. The first stop will be at Holly Springs. He requested me to be at the station and look the crowd over at 6:30 A.M. and the same when we arrive at Holly Springs, which I am to do throughout the trip. I will ascertain the exact route tomorrow. I then discontinued and returned to the hotel. Yours respectfully,

Reported 10-7-1908.
St. Louis -B-

F. E. M. reports:

Memphis, Tenn., Monday, Oct. 5, 1908

At 6:30 A.M. I arrived at the Union Station in advance of Mr. Washington and party to look over the crowd before their arrival.

At 6:40 A.M. Mr. Washington and party arrived and boarded the train. At 7 A.M. we departed for Holly Springs, arriving there at 8:45 A.M. Mr. Washington was met at the station by a delegation and driven to the Baptist school grounds, then to the Rust Institution, then to Bishop Cottrells'[2] College, and from there to Bishop Cottrells' residence. In the afternoon he made two addresses, one of which was at the Rust Institute and the other at Bishop Cottrells' College. After the addresses he was driven back to the Bishop's residence, where he remained until train time.

At 8:30 P.M. we left Holly Springs via the Illinois Central R. R. for Jackson, Miss. After leaving Holly Springs Mr. Scott informed me that we would arrive in Jackson at 3:06 A.M. and remain there until 6:30 A.M. at which time the party would leave for Utica, Miss. He requested me to be on duty from the time we arrived in Jackson until they left at 6:30 A.M. and then for me to remain in Jackson and learn the sentiment of the people and then to meet them at 12:30 P.M. on the arrival of the train from Utica.

Mr. Washington speaks in Jackson tonight at 8 o'clock, in Natchez, Oct. 7th at 8 P.M., in Vicksburg Oct. 8th at 8 P.M., in Greenville Oct. 9th at 8 P.M., in Mound Bayou Oct. 10, at 8 P.M. and in Helena, Ark., Oct. 11th at 8 P.M.

At midnight we were enroute. Yours respectfully,

Reported 10-8-1908.
St. Louis -B-

F. E. M. reports:

Jackson, Miss., Tuesday, Oct. 6, 1908

At 3:20 A.M. we arrived in Jackson, Miss., and the car occupied by Mr. Washington's party, a tourist sleeper, was side tracked. At 6 A.M. I left car, as per instructions of Mr. Scott, to remain in Jackson and ascertain the feeling of the public in general towards Mr. Washington.

I interviewed both white and colored and found that the colored all were very much pleased to have Mr. Washington visit Jackson. I found some white people who would not express themselves one way or the other, while I found a great many were very anxious to see and hear him. I did not find any one who was opposed to his visit.

At 12:30 P.M. I went to the station and at 1:20 P.M. Mr. Washington and his party arrived. I attended him from the train to his carriage and he was immediately driven away on account of the crowd who were closing in on his carriage to shake hands with him. He was driven to the home of Mr. Risch.[3]

At 2:30 P.M. I called at Mr. Risch's house where I met Mr. Banks, Mr. Howard and Mr. Scott. I advised them how to enter the hall to avoid the crowd. I then went to the hall to meet the party on their arrival. At 4:25 P.M. the party arrived and entered the hall where he addressed about 3000 people, about 300 of whom were white. While he was addressing the audience I had his carriage quietly driven to the back door and sent a note to Mr. Scott to that effect. About three minutes after Mr. Washington closed his address the gallery gave way and fell to the 1st floor. There were about fifteen persons injured. The most serious injuries were two broken limbs. This caused a panic among the people, causing them to jump out windows and break down two doors. We got out without the least inconvenience and Mr. Washington was driven to Mr. Risch's residence.

This evening I called on Mr. Washington to advise him to remain over night at Mr. Risch's residence in place of the car on account of several threats I had heard.

I then discontinued. Yours respectfully,

Reported 10:9-1908.
St. Louis -B-

F. E. M. reports:

Jackson, Miss., Wednesday, Oct. 7, 1908

At 6:30 A.M. I left Jackson via the Y. & M. V. R. R. for Natchez in company with Mr. Booker T. Washington and party and arrived in Natchez at 11:30 A.M. Mr. Washington was later driven to the home of Dr. J. B. Banks. At 3 P.M. he spoke at the laying of the corner stone of the Baptist college[4] and at 8 P.M. at the opera house. At 10:15 P.M. he attended a banquet given in his honor.

I attended Mr. Washington throughout the day. Considerable difficulty was experienced handling the crowd at the college. With the exception of this everything passed off very quietly. Yours respectfully,

Reported 10-12-1908.
St. Louis -B-

F. E. M. reports:

Natchez, Miss., Thursday, Oct. 8, 1908

At 7:30 A.M. I left Natchez via the Y. & M. V. R. R. for Vicksburg in company with Mr. Washington and party. On arriving at Vicksburg at 12:05 P.M. Mr. Washington and party were driven to the Lincoln Bank, then to the hardware store of Mr. Lee Richerson, then to the residence of T. V. McAllister.[5]

At 3 P.M. I accompanied his party in a drive through the National Park. At 8 P.M. he addressed a very large audience of colored and white people at the skating rink. At 10:25 P.M. he was driven to the residence of Mr. Jones[6] where refreshments were served. I attended Mr. Washington throughout the day and evening and made arrangements before the address at the skating rink, thus avoiding any delay. Yours respectfully,

Reported 10-12-1908.
St. Louis -B-

F. E. M. reports:

Vicksburg, Miss., Friday, Oct. 9, 1908

At 8:10 A.M. in company with Mr. Washington and party I left Vicksburg via the Y. & M. V. R. R. for Greenville, Miss., where we arrived at 1 P.M. Mr. Washington was driven to the home of Mr. Wallace.[7] At 3 P.M. he attended a corner stone laying and was driven from there to the court house where he addressed a very large audience of both white and colored, after which he returned to the home of Mr. Wallace.

At 7:30 P.M. I called at Mr. Wallace's house and accompanied Mr. Washington to a reception of the Colored Business Men's League and at 11 P.M. returned to the home of Mr. Wallace.

I then discontinued. Yours respectfully,

Reported 10-13-1908.
St. Louis -B-

F. E. M. reports

Greenville, Miss., Saturday, Oct. 10, 1908

At 9:30 A.M. I left Greenville via the Y. & M. V. R. R. in company with the Washington party for Mound Bayou where we arrived at 12:50 P.M. Mr. Washington was driven to the home of Hon. Chas. Banks, Cashier of the Mound Bayou Bank. At 3 P.M. Mr. Washington was driven to the Oil Mill Grounds where he addressed about 3000 people. After the address he returned to the home of Mr. Banks. At 9 P.M. he went to the M.E. church where he addressed a large audience. He then returned to the home of Chas. Banks.

I discontinued at 11 P.M. Yours respectfully,

Reported 10-13-1908.
St. Louis -B-

F. E. M. reports:

Mound Bayou, Miss., Sunday, Oct. 11, 1908

At 3:20 A.M. I left Mound Bayou via Y. & M. V. R. R. in company with Mr. Washington and party for Helena, Ark. where we arrived at 9 A.M. Mr. Washington was driven to the home of Dr. Morris.[8] At 11:30 A.M. he was driven to the Baptist church where he addressed a very large audience of both white and colored people. After the services he was driven about the city and returned to Dr. Morris' residence. He then decided to leave for St. Louis at 6:15 P.M. and as our baggage had been transferred to the Mississippi side of the river we hired a skiff and accompanied by Mr. Hunt I crossed the river to get the baggage. When we arrived there we found the car locked and porter absent and had to return without the baggage.

At 6:15 P.M. in company with Mr. Washington I left Helena via the St. L. I. M. & S. R. R. for St. Louis, arriving at Winn Jct. at 9:20 P.M. where we had to change cars to the St. Louis and Memphis Division.

At 10:10 P.M. we left Winn Jct. for St. Louis and at midnight was enroute. Yours respectfully,

Reported 10-13-1908.
St. Louis -B-

F. E. M. reports:

Enroute, Monday, October 12, 1908

Having been enroute since midnight we arrived in St. Louis at 8:20 A.M. I purchased a ticket for Mr. Washington to Chicago and saw him aboard the Chicago & Alton train due to leave at 9:05 A.M. I then discontinued. Yours respectfully,

Reported 10-13-1908.
St. Louis -B-

TDIr Con. 379 BTW Papers DLC.

1 Probably George D. Bangs, general manager of the Pinkerton office in New York City.

2 Elias Cottrell (b. 1853) was an A.M.E. clergyman beginning in 1875. In 1894 he was elevated to bishop. He was a trustee, general manager, and the treasurer of Mississippi Industrial College in Holly Springs.

3 H. T. Risher, a successful black baker and restaurateur in Jackson, Miss., and a patron of Campbell College in Jackson, an A.M.E. school.

4 Natchez Baptist College.

5 T. V. McAllister, the black receiver of public monies in Mississippi, served as BTW's escort during the Mississippi tour.

6 Possibly W. B. Jones, a black brickmason.

7 H. C. Wallace.

8 Elias Camp Morris.

From William Loeb, Jr.

Washington October 5, 1908

My dear Dr. Washington: Your letter of the 1st instant, in behalf of young Haralson, has been received and in reply the President directs me to say that there is no possible way in which the young man could be restored to the Naval Academy except thru Congressional action. Sincerely yours,

Wm Loeb, Jr

TLS Con. 7 BTW Papers DLC.

To Seth Low

Vicksburg, Miss. Oct. 8, 1908

My dear Mr. Low: I am still on my tour of Mississippi. Night before last I spoke in Jackson, to at least five thousand people, and a thousand of them were of the best white men and women of that section, the lieutenant governor as well as other state officials being present. In Natchez, where I spoke last night, the entire lower floor of the opera house was filled to overflowing by the leading classes of white men and women and many were kept out, besides there were present in the opera house a good many thousand colored people.

I am making as far as I can a strong appeal to the white people to educate and uplift the Negro, and what I say seems to be having effect. In every way possible the white people show their appreciation. I could not have had a more cordial reception by the white people in Boston than I have had at the hands of the white people in Natchez. If I could spend a week longer in this state I think I could change the Vardaman sentiment regarding Negro education. If I had the time, there is no work that I would prefer doing than this. I speak in Greenville tomorrow, then in Mound Bayou, and then in Helena, Ark.

Last night at the close of my address in Natchez, one of the most wealthy and influential planters in Louisiana came to me and said he would give any reasonable sum of money if I would go to his plantation neighborhood and speak there in the same way I did in the opera house. Yours very truly,

Booker T. Washington

TLS Seth Low Papers NNC.

To Francis Jackson Garrison

Vicksburg, Miss. Oct. 10, 1908

My dear Mr. Garrison: I am spending one of the most profitable and interesting weeks in the state of Mississippi that I have ever spent anywhere. I am speaking two or three times during the day and every night to immense audiences, and you would be surprised to know how largely these audiences are attended by the best white men and women of Mississippi. I am making an especial appeal in every case against Governor Vardaman's idea of leaving the Negro in ignorance, and I am surprised to note how encouragingly many of the white people respond to my appeal. For example, yesterday, when speaking in the court house in Greenville, Miss., I said that the worst enemy of the South was the man who favored keeping the Negro in ignorance, and the sentence was cheered most heartily by practically every white person present. In the same meeting, the county superintendent of education who was present, arose and urged the colored people to send their children to the public schools, saying he would see that all the money necessary was provided for their education; that also was cheered by both white and colored. If I could spend a week longer in this state I believe I could almost wholly change public sentiment. When I went to Jackson, the home of Vardaman, one newspaper there that sympathized with him urged the white people not to attend the meeting, but they came out by hundreds, both men and women. Before going to Jackson I was warned by letter and otherwise not to go there as there would be some demonstration against me or my life would be in danger, but I paid no attention to this. As we were driving to the hall where the meeting was held, Mr. Vardaman, unfortunately for him, happened to meet the procession going to the hall, and you can imagine his embarrassment.

With one or two exceptions, every daily paper in Mississippi has been generous in its treatment of our meetings and has urged the people to attend.

More and more I find that what is needed in the South is something that will bring the best white and colored people together so that each will understand what the other is doing.

I am more and more surprised at the immense progress which the colored people are making in nearly every section of Mississippi. They are determined in spite of the opposition of demagogues like Vardaman and others to let nothing discourage them, and hundreds of white people have told me and pledged me their word that they would stand by the colored people and see that they are educated and receive justice. Yours very truly,

Booker T. Washington

TLSr NN-Sc. The same letter was sent to Oswald Garrison Villard on the same date. (Oswald Garrison Villard Papers, MH.)

From Charles William Anderson

New York, N.Y., October 12, 1908

(Personal)

My dear Doctor: I have a few more facts for you. Henry Lincoln Johnson, so I am informed by a most reliable person who is in his confidence, told Hitchcock that it would not do to have you control the colored end of things — that the colored people of the country were divided into two factions, the majority one being opposed to you, and that Mr. Taft would have every man against him, who is now opposing you, if your close connection with the campaign was not speedily ended. Hitchcock in turn took Johnson to Ward and told Ward to advise with him, and to have Parsons get up some meetings for him, and to remember that he regarded him as the "real thing." He also told Ward that Johnson had prepared all of the Taft contests in the South for the National Committee, and that he was now serving the party without pay. This, of course, made a great impression on Ward. My man now tells me, in confidence, that Hitchcock has instructed Johnson to remain here, and to report to him, privately, all that goes on with reference to the colored people, and that he will be paid by Hitchcock, himself, and not Ward, so that he may appear to be serving through patriotism. Johnson told them that Fortune was the ablest man to do literary work, and ought to have charge of the negro press work.

He said that anything sent out by R. W. Thompson would be known to be inspired by you, and would do much more harm than good. He further told them that the Age really belonged to you, and had no influence among the colored people; that the National Review was much closer to the people than the Age, and Roscoe[1] was therefore put on the pay-roll. In his issue of October 3rd, Roscoe assailed President Roosevelt violently, and opposed the election of Governor Hughes.[2] This reached Mr. Loeb's eye, and Ward was told to cut him off the pay-roll, which he did on schedule time. On Saturday I saw Henry Lincoln Johnson for the second time since he has been in the city, and he at once inquired "what do you think of that editorial in Simmons' paper? Its awful! Well, let *the influences* that put him on the pay-roll of the National Committee shoulder it." This will disclose to you Johnson's methods. First, he has Roscoe put on the pay-roll, on the ground that his paper is more influential than the Age, but as soon as he makes a bad break, he blames you for having placed him. I forgot that he also told my man that you had written a letter in Roscoe's behalf early in the season, but Ward would not place him. He afterwards took the matter up with Hitchcock and had it done at once. Fortune and Wetmore are still his closest advisers. In our two minute talk on last Saturday, Johnson told me that he had charge of getting up a committee of colored men to call on Taft during his visit to this city. Subsequently, Mr. Ward discussed it with me, but before I reached the headquarters, I learned that he (Ward) had been discussing it with Johnson, "Bruce Grit" and Paul Bray. Thus you see, even Ward has been playing the old game. He has discussed this same matter with me two or three times, but has never suggested that I take charge of it, nor has he intimated that he had ever talked the matter over with you.

My informant in all this is Jim Hayes. You will recall that I did him a favor four years ago, in holding up Derrick, and forcing the committee to make Derrick disgorge and divide up with Hayes. He feels somewhat grateful for this and has kept me posted. He is in Johnson's confidence, and brings me all the news. I have been as silent as a clam, and have not disclosed the fact that I am not in sympathy with Mr. Johnson's plans. In this way I have learned it all.

The meeting addressed by Johnson almost provoked a riot, and would have discredited him, but for the fact that Moore went forward and told Ward and the other leaders that the meeting was a big success, and that there were only one or two interruptions, and that Johnson made a good speech, etc., etc. This fool is busy making good for a man who is telling Hitchcock that the "Age" has outlived its usefulness. So much for this heading.

Before I close I think I ought to tell you, that every morning when Ward enters his office he sees the outline of Moore's form on the marble door-step, where the editor of the Age has slept during the night, and has prevented the frost from covering the entire step. This leaves the outline of his figure standing out in bold relief. All of which means that, call when you will, morning, noon or night, you will find Moore just outside of the Ward's door.

These are a few of [the] things you will be able to authenticate when you reach this city. Yours truly,

Charles W. Anderson

TLS Con. 38 BTW Papers DLC.

1 Roscoe Conkling Simmons.

2 Charles Evans Hughes was considered, for a brief time in 1908, the most serious challenge to the Roosevelt-Taft forces for the Republican presidential nomination.

Two News Items on a Lynching in Mississippi

Memphis, Tenn., October 12, 1908

LYNCHING AT
LULA, MISS.

NEGROES SHOOT CONDUCTOR

J. C. KENDALL ASSAULTED ON
TRAIN WITH HIS OWN PISTOL

ANGRY MOB GETS REVENGE

NEGROES ARE CAPTURED AND
SWUNG TO A TREE

KENDALL LIES IN ST. JOSEPH'S HOSPITAL
IN CRITICAL CONDITION — NEGROES
WHO DID SHOOTING WERE RETURNING FROM HELENA, WHERE THEY
HEARD BOOKER T. WASHINGTON

Filled with whisky and cocaine, yesterday afternoon, while returning from Helena, Ark., where they had been to hear Booker T. Washington lecture, two negroes shot down and perhaps fatally wounded Conductor J. C. Kendall, who had charge of the excursion train. The tragedy occurred when a stop was made at Lula at 3:45 o'clock.

Enraged over the deed, a mob of sixty men gathered at the depot and promptly took the two negroes, Jim and Frank Davis, from the custody of Deputy Sheriff W. G. Dickerson and swung them to a tree. Conductor Kendall was brought to Memphis and placed in the city hospital, and at an early hour this morning his life was fast ebbing away. The physicians have little hope for his recovery.

The two negroes were members of a trio, the third one escaping shortly after the shooting. Conductor Kendall, who resides in Memphis, 1003 Kansas avenue, is one of the best known conductors running on the Y. and M. V. railroad. He was in charge of the excursion running between Memphis and Helena when the tragedy occurred.

From the testimony of reliable negroes who witnessed the shooting, the negro who escaped is not considered as directly implicated in the affair, but was present at the time.

Kendall was in charge of an excursion running from Helena, where a large crowd of negroes had gone to hear Booker T. Washington, and his train was just leaving Lula when the shooting occurred. The Davis brothers were standing on the platform of the car, with another negro, whose name is not known. Jim Davis, according to all witnesses, was cursing, and the trio was engaged in loud noises, all being full of mean whisky and cocaine, which they had imbibed during the day. Conductor Kendall remonstrated with the negroes and ordered them into the coach.

Shot with Own Gun

Some of the witnesses stated that Jim Davis replied to the order of the conductor by a vile epithet, whereupon Kendall hit the negro over the head with the butt of a large pistol, which he had. The negro dodged a second blow and darted toward the car door. As he did so Kendall attempted to strike him again, but his pistol slipped from his hand, flying into the car. Davis then grabbed Kendall's revolver and began to fire, one shot taking effect under Kendall's right shoulder and coming out under the left nipple, striking the spinal cord. Kendall attempted to get down the steps, but fell helpless, his lower limbs being paralyzed.

From reliable authority at Lula another story of the affair was that, upon the order of Kendall, Jim Davis applied vile epithets, which Kendall passed unnoticed. He passed through the train, collecting fares, and came back out upon the platform, going into the opposite car, when the negroes opened fire upon him. Five or six shots were fired. Kendall attempted to shoot, but after being struck dropped his pistol, which was picked up by one of the negroes. Immediately after the shooting the Davis brothers and the third negro made their escape. The Davis brothers were soon captured, but the third made a getaway. According to special correspondence of The Commercial Appeal, the gun belonging to Kendall was found on one of the Davis brothers when arrested, and its chambers were full, no indication being shown of its having been fired.

STRUNG UP TO TREE

Deputy Sheriff W. G. Dickerson, who was with the posse when the Davis brothers were captured, took charge of them and locked them in the small local jail until the arrival of the sheriff from Clarksdale. Sheriff J. O. Baugh of Clarksdale was immediately notified and organized a special train to go for the negroes. Upon hearing that the sheriff would shortly arrive for the Davis brothers, the citizens of Lula, about sixty in number, went to the "lock-up" and took them from the deputy, who was powerless to defend. They were then taken quietly to an oak tree about 400 yards west of the depot, where they were strung up. No shots were fired, and the mob was conducted in an orderly manner. When the negroes were finally dead the mob dispersed. When Sheriff Baugh arrived he had nothing to do but look for the third negro, who had made his escape.

Before the negroes were lynched Frank Davis confessed to the shooting. Jim Davis confessed that he had started the trouble, but denied having shot at the conductor. While the two negroes were being "sweated," a number of sober negroes, who witnessed the affair, testified that Jim Davis was the instigator of the trouble and also fired several shots at Kendall.

As soon after the shooting as was possible a special train was secured at Lula by Dr. T. A. Carter, the railroad physician, who reached the side of Kendall almost by the time he fell. A hurried run was made with the wounded man to Memphis, where he was taken to St. Joseph's Hospital. Dr. G. D. Morrow of Lula accompanied him. At the hospital it was found that Kendall's condition was critical. The ball entered under the right shoulder from the rear and came out under the left nipple, striking, if not cutting, the spinal cord. Kendall was able to speak a few words while on the train, but lapsed into unconsciousness when he reached the hospital. Owing to his weakened condition last night no operation was attempted.

KENDALL WELL KNOWN

"Jack" Kendall, as he was familiarly known by a host of friends in Memphis and railroad circles, was one of the most popular men in the employ of the Y. and M. V. railroad. A railroad man said of him last night: "There is scarcely a railroad man on our road and many others that does not know and love 'Jack' Kendall. He was a prominent member of the O. R. C."

Kendall was 30 years of age and had been in the employ of the Y. and M. V. railroad for about fifteen years, leaving the freight service two years ago to become passenger conductor. He had been given the Helena run only two weeks ago. Mr. Kendall has a father and mother, Mr. and Mrs. J. B. Kendall, living at 1003 Kansas avenue, this city, with whom he resides. A sister, Mrs. J. S. Croft, lives at 854 South Lauderdale street. Miss Mamie Kendall, another sister, is at present in St. Louis.

Memphis *Commercial Appeal,* Oct. 12, 1908, 1.

Memphis, Tenn., October 13, 1908

BODIES TAKEN DOWN

Were Not Left Hanging to Be Viewed by Booker T. Washington

LULA, Miss., Oct. 12 — The bodies of the two negroes, Frank and Jim Davis, who were lynched here Sunday night for shooting Conductor J. C. Kendall, were left hanging to the tree where they met their death all night Sunday and were taken down and forwarded to Minter City at 8 o'clock this morning.

The report that the citizens of Lula kept the bodies of the negroes hanging to the tree in order that Booker T. Washington and his party might witness the gruesome sight while en route to Memphis was erroneous. The bodies of the negroes were taken down and turned over to their relatives for burial at 8 o'clock this morning, while the special from Helena passed through the town without stopping at 3 o'clock this afternoon. Booker T. Washington was not a passenger on the tourist sleeper bearing the party, but instead he left Helena for St. Louis over the Iron Mountain road.

The citizens of Lula are very indignant over the report that they kept the negroes hanging to the tree in order that the champion of their race might see their dead bodies dangling from the limbs.

Trouble Long Expected

The people of Lula have been expecting trouble for some time. Every Sunday the railroad runs an excursion train to Helena and negroes from this neighborhood go there to get drunk, returning in an intoxicated condition.

The negroes were left hanging to the tree where they met their death, not to hang there as a sight to greet Washington's eyes, but because no one took the initiative in having them taken down until their relatives called for their bodies.

Some of the best negroes of this place, in speaking to your correspondent today, said that they would have aided in stringing up the negroes for the assault on Conductor Kendall if they had been invited to do so by the white people.

The negro who was also wanted yesterday, and who was thought to have been implicated, was in the city today. He was not arrested, as the citizens believe he was not a party to the crime.

Memphis *Commercial Appeal*, Oct. 13, 1908, 6. Enclosed in William Thornton Montgomery to Emmett Jay Scott, Oct. 14, 1908, below.

William Thornton Montgomery to Emmett Jay Scott

[Mound Bayou, Miss.] Oct 14th 1908

My dear Mr Scott You dont know how bad we felt over the trouble at Lula Miss Especially so when we knew that Mr Washington and party had to pass thro that town. We did not want Mr Washington to witness such a sight. The Evening Scimitar contained a telegram that the Bodies were kept hanging purposely that the Washington party might see them, saying the negroes had been over to hear Mr Washington and intimating that they may have been incited to do the deed on that account. I enclose you a clipping from the Commercial Appeal of Memphis which corrects this impression. I am very glad of it. Well Mississippi maintains her reputation. I hope you are all safely at home and that this little incident will not be allowed to marr pleasant memories of the trip. With best wishes — I am Yours Very Truly & Sincerely

W T Montgomery

ALS Con. 376 BTW Papers DLC.

From Francis Jackson Garrison

Boston Oct. 15, 1908

Dear Mr. Washington: I am just in receipt of your most interesting letter of the 10th inst. from Vicksburg, and am greatly delighted and surprised by what you write me of the success of your Mississippi campaign, and of the extent to which the best white men and women of Mississippi have attended your meetings. I was reading only a day or two ago a shocking telegram from Mississippi telling of the lynching of two poor fellows whose bodies were left dangling by the railroad track that you might see them as you passed, and Vardaman's brutal "warning" that others would be so served if you continued your speeches in the State. If you have been able to evoke such a response and such assurances of sympathy and cooperation as you report, I hope that the way will open for you to do more and more of this missionary work in other Southern States, for it is of incalculable importance to foster and increase the slowly growing sentiment in behalf of justice and fair play to the negro of which we are having increasing evidence. It is an encouraging fact also that with one or two exceptions the daily papers in Mississippi have been fair and generous in their treatment of your meetings. I enclose a clipping about Tuskegee from this morning's Herald, which will interest you, and am, with warm regard, Faithfully yours,

Francis J. Garrison

Thanks for copies of the Vicksburg papers.

TLS Con. 371 BTW Papers DLC.

Emmett Jay Scott to Charles Banks

[Tuskegee, Ala.] October 15, 1908

My dear Friend: I am home again, but not well rested. It seems that I can never get sleep enough to make up for all that I lost on the Doctor's triumphant tour through your imperial state.

I came to Lula last Tuesday afternoon. I was rather amused at the way you scampered home after that lynching happened and as to how Dr. Morris, and the rest of them gave us advice on the Helena side, but did not venture themselves to go across to Lula. Major Moton and I went on the fast train that met our train and did not wait to come in upon the tourist car. We were afraid that we would receive a warm reception from the citizens of Lula. I was rather happy when I found myself in the confine of Memphis.

Seriously speaking, however, the trip through Mississippi was a splendid ovation for the Doctor from beginning to end and I wish in this very formal way to express what I said to you in person, namely, that you more than met every expectation and simply overwhelmed the Doctor with a series of receptions not to be duplicated anywhere else in all the country, I am sure. Every detail seemed to have been worked out and the various incidents occurred with clock-like decision.

Of the trip to Mound Bayou, I cannot speak with too much enthusiasm. It was an eyeopener in every way. I shall never forget the impression made upon me by the progress being wrought there through your and Mr. Francis'[1] aid & assistance. You are a great combination and deserve all praise for what you have done and for what you are doing. I have already promised myself the pleasure of another visit to Mound Bayou whenever I can steal away.

Give me the pleasure of receiving you at Tuskegee whenever the spirit moves you. We shall be very glad indeed to make your visit here both pleasant and profitable.

Please remember me cordially to Mrs. Banks, whom I hope has now recovered, or is recovering, from her illness.

The Doctor went North, as you know. I do not wish to write you in his name a letter of thanks for all you have done for him and shall wait until he comes himself. He will, I am sure, want to express in his usual forceful way his personal appreciation of all that you did for his pleasure and comfort.

With cordial regards always, I am; Very truly yours,

Emmett J. Scott

TLpS Con. 38 BTW Papers DLC.

[1] John W. Francis, president of the Bank of Mound Bayou.

Emmett Jay Scott to William Loeb, Jr.

[Tuskegee, Ala.] October 16, 1908

My dear Mr. Loeb: Some eighteen months ago, Secretary Taft, with the approval of the President, as I understand it, issued an order to the effect that in the future no white man should be enlisted to serve as a band master in Colored regiments.

The Chief Musician of the Tenth Cavalry, Fort McKinley, P.I., it is reported, is white and was re-enlisted to serve with the Tenth Cavalry last August and as the Chief Musician. The Chief Musician of the Twenty-fourth Infantry has not so far been supplanted with a Colored man, although I understand he is at present on furlough.

Would it not be possible for both of these places to be filled by the appointment of suitable Colored men, thus carrying out in letter and in spirit the order issued by Secretary Taft, of which you are of course well advised. Yours very truly,

Emmett J. Scott

TLpS Con. 7 BTW Papers DLC.

To Leo Tolstoi[1]

[Tuskegee, Ala.] October 17, 1908

Honored Sir: It gives me very great pleasure to comply with the suggestion which has come from our mutual friend, Mr. Jerome

H. Raymond[2] of 6217 Madison Avenue, Chicago, Ill., (U.S.A.) in sending you some printed matter giving an account of the work we are trying to do here at Tuskegee Institute. I very much hope that you may find the books in some degree interesting, and the printed matter describing the work of the school equally so.

I need not tell you that I, in common with thoughtful men everywhere, have the deepest sympathy with the efforts constantly being made by you for the amelioration of the condition of your countrymen.

With assurances of my deep interest in your noble work, I am Yours very truly,

Booker T. Washington

TLpS Con. 383 BTW Papers DLC.

[1] Leo Tolstoi (1828–1910), the Russian novelist and social philosopher, was intensely interested in the education of the Russian peasants, and established, at different times, schools on his estate for their education. He believed in developing self-sufficiency for the peasants, whereby all their needs would be supplied by their own labor on their own land. Tolstoi had great respect for manual labor, and disdain for education which made a distinction between the worth of manual and intellectual or higher education.

[2] Jerome Hall Raymond (1869–1928), former private secretary to George Pullman, was an associate professor of sociology at the University of Chicago from 1901 to 1909.

To Fred Warner Carpenter

Tuskegee Institute, Alabama October 19, 1908

Personal

My dear Mr. Carpenter: On the 28th of October, according to the New York program, I understand that Mr. Taft is to deliver an address to the colored people.

In this address I very much hope that you will remind him to make special reference to the work of Charles W. Anderson. He has been doing some heroic work throughout this campaign, and a word from the Secretary would greatly encourage him and strengthen his friends. Yours very truly,

Booker T. Washington

TLS William Howard Taft Papers DLC.

To William Wallace Haralson

[Tuskegee, Ala.] October 19, 1908

Personal.

My dear Mr. Haralson: I have just had a letter from the President to the effect that, after looking into the matter, he says, under the law there is no way by which your son can be reinstated to the Naval Academy except through Congressional action. Now, at first thought this may appear discouraging, but I believe judging from the way the President writes that he would not object to Congressional action in that case. That may be the best course to pursue, especially in view of the fact that your brother-in-law is to be in Congress. I should strongly urge that you decide to try Congressional action and that the whole matter be put before the President. Instead of having his opposition, that course will have his approval. This I think could be arranged for. I am very sorry that under the law the President can do nothing. Yours truly,

Booker T. Washington

TLpS Con. 6 BTW Papers DLC.

From Oswald Garrison Villard

New York October 19, 1908

Dear Mr. Washington: I am very grateful indeed to you for your kind letter of October 10th,[1] which I was able to make prompt use of, as you will see by the enclosed.[2] It is very useful to have something to offset that ghastly story. When you have a moment, will you not tell me the facts in that case, which I presume you ascertained, and if you were actually compelled to see those forms hanging to the pole? Your own Mississippi experience is certainly very gratifying, and I congratulate you upon it. I wish that I might have seen Mr. Vardaman when he met the procession! Very truly yours,

Oswald Garrison Villard

TLS Con. 42 BTW Papers DLC.

[1] See BTW to Frances Jackson Garrison, Oct. 10, 1908, above.

[2] No enclosure was found with the letter.

From Silas C. Burroughs

Davis Mills, Va., Oct 19 1908

Dear Booker Yours of Oct 2nd recd in due time. I guess you think I am a little slow in answering I am kept pretty busy trying to sell a few goods & keeping the Postoffice. Enclosed please find Inventory of Grand Father Burroughs Estate. This is an exact Copy of the Original.

Aunt Laura[1] & Aunt Eliza[2] was sorry they didnt get to see you. If I ever get down South I intend to visit you tell John I would be more than glad to see him.

I think if the Negroes would take your advice they would do well in this Country for all that has been working have done well but the others have done nothing & heap of them wors than nothing. Yours Truly

S. C. Burroughs

N B I havnt recd the Copy of your paper yet

S C B

ALS Con. 365 BTW Papers DLC.

1 Laura Burroughs Holland.

2 Eliza Jane Burroughs Witt (1840–1918).

From Charles Waddell Chesnutt

Cleveland, Ohio, Oct. 19, 1908

My dear Doctor Washington: I was reading yesterday in a copy of the *Boston Transcript* for October 12, I think was the date, an account of a lynching in Mississippi, where the victims were left hanging beside the railroad track where you would pass on your way from one town to another. The statement was coupled with utterances ascribed to Mr. Vardaman and others that if you made half a dozen more speeches in Mississippi there would be a good many more lynchings.

I was very sorry to read this. Things must be in a very bad way down there when even your helpful and hopeful and pacific utterances create such a feeling. I very much fear that the South does not mean, if it can prevent it, to permit education or business or anything else to make of the Negro anything more than an agricultural serf.

I see Georgia has disfranchised the Negro. I wonder how much further the process will go before there is a revival of a liberal spirit. I try to be optimistic about these matters, but conditions are not encouraging. Yours very truly,

Chas. W. Chesnutt

TLS Con. 379 BTW Papers DLC.

To Charles Joseph Bonaparte[1]

[Tuskegee, Ala.] October 20, 1908

Personal and Confidential

My dear Mr. Bonaparte: There has grown up in many portions of the South quite an abuse in the way of imprisoning men for debt. The thing has been rather overdone in some portions of this state.

I beg to enclose herewith a transcript in record of case No. 538.[2] The matter is being handled altogether by philanthropic white men of this state, but I am wondering if it will be possible for the Attorney General's office to interest itself in some way so that the matter may be thoroughly probed. I think you will find the whole statement of the case pretty thoroughly set out in the copy of the record which I am sending to you herewith. Southern white men are behind this case, and it has occurred to me that you may be interested at least to the extent of looking into the matter. Since the cases of Thomas and Vance the Supreme Court has in Harris vs. State of Alabama, 47 Southern Reporter, page 340, shown clearly by dissenting opinion that it is the collection of the debt that is involved. If a supplemental brief could be filed by the Attorney General's office I am sure it would help the whole situation in the most satisfactory way. The Bailey case herein referred to, will be submitted to the Supreme Court of the U.S. sometime next month. Yours truly,

Booker T. Washington

TLpS Con. 365 BTW Papers DLC.

[1] Charles Joseph Bonaparte (1851–1921), a lawyer and municipal reformer from Baltimore, was U.S. Secretary of the Navy (1905–6) and U.S. Attorney General (1906–9). Bonaparte was a champion of black rights from the time he entered law practice in 1874. He fought against Maryland disfranchisement laws in 1905 and 1909 and, as attorney general, supported federal prosecution in peonage cases. offering BTW his aid in the Alonzo Bailey case. Later he served as an attorney for the NAACP in the Pink Franklin case.

[2] For a detailed account of BTW's role in the Alonzo Bailey peonage case, see Daniel, "Up from Slavery and Down to Peonage," 654–70.

From Helen Van Wyck Lockman

Huntington [N.Y.] Oct. 20th '08

My dear Dr. Washington Your letter reached me yesterday. I shall be very glad to see you at West Neck next season under the same terms. Everything is always left in such good order that it does not seem possible that it has been occupied. I have had so much experience in renting that I consider it a great item.

When we are settled I shall certainly send you our address. It will give us much pleasure to hear Secretary Taft speak.

My sister joins me in kindest regards to you all. Very truly Yours

Helen Van Wyck Lockman

ALS Con. 7 BTW Papers DLC.

To Francis Jackson Garrison

Tuskegee Institute, Alabama October 21, 1908

My dear Mr. Garrison: I have yours of October 15th. I am always glad to hear from you. Of course, the matter of the lynching of the two colored men at Lula was a brutal and barbarous affair. I note, however, that the later dispatches from there deny that the bodies were kept waiting, in the way that the first dispatches indicated. The later dispatches state that they simply kept the bodies waiting for the coroner to view them. I was never more convinced than I am at the present that the white people in Mississippi are ashamed of Vardaman and his teachings, and, also, ashamed of the way that the state is held up before the world. If I could spend two additional weeks in the state, I know that I could still further change public sentiment. Every daily newspaper, except one in the state, approved of my addresses.

I am considering the matter of attacking the State of Louisiana sometime in the future; that I consider is the worst state in the Union. I will, of course, have the disadvantage there to begin with of having all the daily papers in New Orleans against me, with the possible exception of one.

Since I left the state, Vardaman has come out in a savage attack, through his paper, on the white people who attended my meetings. This is just what I wanted. This attack on the white people has resulted in a division of white public sentiment; and, of course, in proportion as we can get such a division, why, things will be more hopeful in the future. Many of them did not give much attention to Vardaman so long as he was attacking the colored people, but now, as he has attacked the white people, they are waking up to the harm that he is doing, and are vigorously defending themselves, and disapproving of his course. Yours very truly,

Booker T. Washington

TLS Francis Jackson Garrison Papers NN-Sc. A press copy is in Con. 371, BTW Papers, DLC.

To Mary A. Elliott

[Tuskegee, Ala.] October 21, 1908

My dear Mrs. Elliott: I am planning to be in Columbus next Sunday to speak at two meetings; one in the afternoon, and one at night. The afternoon meeting is to be at some hall, and the night meeting at the A.M.E. Church. I shall hope to see you and other members of the family while I am there.

All are well. Booker is attending school, as I think you know, at Fisk University, and Davidson is teaching here. He is teaching a part of the time and studying a part of the time. Yours very truly,

Booker T. Washington

TLpS Con. 368 BTW Papers DLC.

To Oswald Garrison Villard

[Tuskegee, Ala.] October 21, 1908

My dear Mr. Villard: The enclosed is an extract from a letter written by one of the leading colored lawyers in Jackson, Miss., to Mr. Scott, my secretary. It refers to an article in Vardaman's paper condemning the white people for attending my lecture. Yours truly,

Booker T. Washington

[*Enclosure*]

Extract from Mississippi letter —

I beg to advise that the article has produced quite a sensation here; but it is all resulting in our favor.

I have had any number of Vardaman's political supporters to put themselves to a little trouble to see me and give to Mr. Washington through me their assurance that they have no sympathy with the Governor's article and that their support of the Governor was to break down the "old McLaurin machine"[1] in this state.

Bishop Galloway is walking the streets denouncing Vardaman and openly pronouncing Dr. Washington the greatest living American.

Assure Dr. Washington that his trip to Mississippi has had a wonderful effect for good, for no one could say to these people what he says and with the same effect.

My practice brings me into constant contact with the best, as well as the worst element, of the white citizenry here and I think that I am able to give you the sentiment of this people. They, as a unit, censure Mr. Vardaman and pay tribute to the greatness of our leader.

I told Bishop Galloway how Dr. Washington answered Mr. Vardaman at Greenville when he referred to the "one great big frog"[2] and the Bishop is using that as his weapon.

The "old man" to whom Vardaman refers in one of the articles is Mr. Thos. Helm, one of the wealthiest realty dealers in the South and a devout follower of Bishop Galloway's. Mr. Helm had his arm broken in the crash. He (Mr. Helm) told me that he did not mind his injuries, for, it was worth the suffering from a broken arm to hear the greatest speech of his sixty years of existence.

TLpS and Enclosure Con. 42 BTW Papers DLC.

1 The political machine of Anselm Joseph McLaurin (1848–1909), governor of Mississippi from 1895 to 1900 and U.S. senator from 1901 to 1909.

2 This was a story BTW frequently used to warn his hearers against exaggerated claims of his critics. A farmer living near a resort hotel offered to furnish the hotel dining room with as many frog legs as it could use. The next Saturday he arrived with only one pair of legs and admitted shamefacedly that all summer he thought from the noise that there must be a million frogs in his pond, but when he went to get them he found only "one great big frog." (See A Speech at Hampton Institute, Oct. 13, 1907, above. For another version of the story see above, 1:432.)

To William Loeb, Jr.

Col[umbu]s, Ohio. Oct. 25, 1908

Personal and confidential. Morning papers here state President is preparing to give out statement tonight regarding Brownsville. If this is true unless such statement is very carefully worded fear it will do more harm than good. Matters now in pretty good shape and fear it will not help to stir up Brownsville discussion again.

Booker T. Washington

TWcSr Con. 7 BTW Papers DLC.

From Flavel Sweeten Luther[1]

Hartford, Conn. Oct. 26, 1908

My dear Doctor Washington: I am writing the following letter after some hesitation and with considerable reluctance, and yet from a sincere interest in the advancement of your great work at Tuskegee. I have to say that, so far as I can judge, your agent, Mr. Chisholm,[2] is not likely to increase the reputation of Tuskegee by his work here in Connecticut.[3] My opinion is founded solely on what took place in our own Trinity College Chapel yesterday.

Mr. Chisholm called on me on Saturday and asked permission to address the students, presenting credentials from you. I assented with pleasure, as I wished my young men to be informed as to this work of yours. Mr. Chisholm then asked me if we could take up a collection for him. I explained to him that our collections at our Chapel services are small at best and that we had for some years been devoting them exclusively to missionary work of various sorts, secular and religious, in which our own graduates are employed in various parts of the world, and that I did not think it wise to depart from that policy. Mr. Chisholm then agreed to speak to the students with the view of increasing their interest in Tuskegee.

He came to the service and at the proper time made his address. The students were much interested in his account of the work of the school, as indeed we all were. But Mr. Chisholm diversified his address with a considerable number of ancient and moth-eaten stories, singularly inappropriate at the close of a religious service, although I am not prudish about gleams of humor even in set sermons. He then announced that he should stand outside the door as the students went out and receive contributions and distribute pledge cards. Finally he concluded his remarks by singing very badly what he called a "plantation melody." I was obliged to ask him to abandon his purpose of calling for contributions, and on the whole I was much distressed at the entire episode. I regret to say that the students spoke of it freely as a "vaudeville performance."

It does not seem to me that he is likely to present your claims in such a way as to increase at all the great interest which we all feel in the enterprise at Tuskegee, and I beg you to believe that I write this solely out of good will for Tuskegee and in admiration for yourself. Possibly you will remember me; we have met several times at academic functions.

In case you investigate this matter further, I beg to say that this letter is not intended to be in any sense confidential.

With regards and best wishes, I am Sincerely yours,

F. S. Luther

TLS Con. 375 BTW Papers DLC.

[1] Flavel Sweeten Luther (1850–1928) was president of Trinity College beginning in 1904. He also served in the Connecticut Senate from 1907 to 1911.

[2] Frank P. Chisholm, a Tuskegee graduate in printing in 1902, worked as a printer in Atlanta from 1902 to 1906 while attending college, and began in 1907 as a fund-raiser for Tuskegee in the New England area. This involvement with his alma mater continued for seven decades.

[3] BTW replied that he would "take the matter up at once vigorously." In defense of Chisholm he wrote: "In meeting individuals Chisholm seems to make a good impression, but I presume he is like a good many other people who feel that when they get on the platform they must be unnatural, must not be themselves. While he was in the vicinity of Hartford, one gentleman or firm gave him $250, but that was done by reason of the impression he made upon him in a conversation rather than in a speech." (Oct. 30, 1908, Con. 375, BTW Papers, DLC.) For BTW's remarks to Chisholm see BTW to Chisholm, Oct. 30, 1908, below.

Ralph Waldo Tyler to Emmett Jay Scott

Washington, D.C. Oct 27/08

Dear Mr. Scott: Am sending you our paper, the Ohio State Journal, with matter about Doctor's visit to Columbus. I see he had a great meeting.

Am just passing through Washington enroute west. Spoke at Springfield, Ohio last Saturday, and then jumped to Boston where I spoke Monday. I am now enroute to Toledo Ohio, where I speak Friday.

I understand newspapers had some matter about alleged proposed refusal to accommodate Dr at hotel in Columbus. I reserved the rooms. Some negro "butinsky" preachers, knowing absolutely nothing about the arrangements, butted in. That's all.

Was in New York last evening. Learned that Hitchcock has shipped Lincoln Johnson back home. He had him there, and at once he advised against recognition of all friends of the Doctor's. Like the "eloquent one," he was to assume leadership, management etc. and be Hitchcock's man Friday. But he failed to make good. Charley blanketed him, and Hitchcock sent him to the stable.

Tyler

ALS Con. 8 BTW Papers DLC.

An Item in *Leslie's Illustrated Weekly*

October 29, 1908

LOOK AFTER THE WASTE

If you will study the methods of large business concerns, you will find that business concerns like the great Standard Oil Company, the United States Steel Corporation, and others, who have forged 'way ahead of their competitors, have not gotten ahead by improper or unholy means, but more largely because they have given attention to certain little details which their competitors have neglected. You would be surprised, if you would read carefully and study the history of such concerns as the Standard Oil Company, to see how very careful they are to avoid every little leak in the way of waste. You will find the same thing true in reference to the great pork-packing houses located in Chicago and throughout the great West. Those that have succeeded have succeeded very largely because they have learned not to waste; they have learned how to care for everything. Take the matter of butchering pigs. A large proportion of the pigs a number of years ago used to go to waste. They did not think about caring for the many little portions that now are gathered up and used for food, or used for grease, or for soap. You know they have a saying in the great pork-packing concerns of Chicago that in the killing of the pig they utilize everything except the squeal of the pig, and I think that is very nearly true.

Leslie's Illustrated Weekly, 107 (Oct. 29, 1908), 423.

To Oswald Garrison Villard

Tuskegee Institute, Alabama October 30, 1908

Personal

My dear Mr. Villard: I have your kind letter of October 19th. I thank you for the use which you made of my letter of October 10th.

In regard to the lynching of the men at Lula, Mississippi, I would state that so far as I have been able to get information, there was nothing connected with it, outside of the ordinary disgraceful lynchings that so frequently occur in that state. Another dispatch stated the next day that the dispatch to the effect that the bodies were left, or were to be left hanging until I passed by, was a mistake, that according to the law or custom, that the bodies were only left hanging long enough for the coroner to view them, and that there was nothing upon which to base the first dispatch. My own thought is that an unscrupulous and active Associated Press correspondent saw an opportunity to make his story go, hitching my name on to it, and did so. The only connection that my presence in the state had with the lynching, was the fact that it did occur, and that an excursion train, composed of people who went to Helena, Arkansas to hear me speak, passed through the town. I presume, however, the lynching would have taken place on any occasion, if a difference had arisen between the conductor and the individuals lynched.

During the entire time that I was in the states of Mississippi and Arkansas there was not the slightest discourtesy shown to me or any member of my party, by any persons connected with the train service; without exception so far as I now remember. The train conductor came in and asked for an introduction. In spite of the disgraceful lynching at Lula, I never felt more encouraged over a piece of work than I do now over what I think I accomplished in Mississippi and Arkansas during my ten days work.

As you have seen perhaps, Mr. Vardaman has pitched viciously into me, but that is what I expected. The fact that so many white people attended the meeting had made him pitch into them; this, of course, has divided the white people, just the thing I wanted. They are now defending themselves, and, of course, abusing Vardaman.

It is very, very difficult to get at the real conditions in any of these states, for the reason that there are so many people who are afraid to speak what they think, and so many who say that which they do not believe. I was surprised to find [a] large number of white men and women who, deep down in their hearts, I am sure are all right, but only need encouragement and help to lead them to the point where they will speak out and act more bravely.

Natchez, Mississippi is a place worth visiting. There is a culture and refinement existing among the white people, as well as the colored people there, that was agreeable and surprising.

But the point of all that I am trying to say is this: I believe that a large proportion of the white people in Mississippi are thoroughly tired of Vardaman and his doctrine, and welcome any opportunity to manifest their disapproval aside from speaking out in the open which only a few are as yet prepared to do. Perhaps I did not state in my previous letter that while Vardaman, of course, did not attend the meeting in Jackson, his campaign manager was present and had a prominent seat.

I will try to tell you more of the details when I see you. Yours truly,

Booker T. Washington

TLS Oswald Garrison Villard Papers MH. A press copy is in Con. 42, BTW Papers, DLC.

To Frank P. Chisholm

[Tuskegee, Ala.] October 30, 1908

My dear Mr. Chisholm: I want to urge you in your speechmaking to be just as natural and simple as possible. What would most interest people, in my opinion, would be an account of your own life, showing how you got your education here and in what way you used your education after you had gotten it. Then follow that up with a direct, straightforward account of what our graduates are accomplishing and what progress the race is making by reason of the work of the educated men and women throughout the South, and of course bring in something about the needs of the school. Do not overdo the matter of story telling, especially if the story is not new. Never tell a story for the sake of the story; if it comes in naturally and should be used to illustrate a point, all right, but an audience soon finds out whether a story is simply poked in without a proper fitting point. The minute that becomes true the speaker loses his power.

I would discard singing before audiences. Only very well trained persons can interest an audience. Speaking and singing rarely go well together.

The enclosed letter from Trinity College is the principal reason I am writing you just now. Yours truly,

Booker T. Washington

TLpS Con. 368 BTW Papers DLC.

To Jesse Edward Moorland

[Tuskegee, Ala.] October 30, 1908

My dear Mr. Moorland: I have just had a letter from President Roosevelt in which occurs the following sentence:

"By the way, I have become exceedingly interested in the colored Y.M.C.A. in this city. It seems to me to represent a movement worth having."

I thought you would be interested in it. A little later on, when you get to the point of laying the corner stone, would it not be a good plan to get him to deliver the address? Since he seems so much interested, you might think of some other way in which to use his interest. Yours very truly,

Booker T. Washington

TLpS Con. 376 BTW Papers DLC.

An Article in the *A.M.E. Church Review* by Hightower T. Kealing

Oct. 1908

Booker T. Washington's Tour through Mississippi A New Form of University Extension

"There is no color line in eggs," is the unique way in which Booker T. Washington presented the blessings that await the colored farmer who utilizes the small avenues of profit opening to him in the South; and the roar of applause and rhythm of waving hands told that the philosophy of the epigram had been assimilated by the sixteen hundred people who jammed the chapel of historic old Rust University, Holly Springs, Miss., October 7. A mass of about the same size awaited on the outside, under the promise sent out to them that Dr. Washington would repeat his speech to those who were unable to get in.

This was the beginning of a tour of the State of Mississippi by Dr. Washington and a number of his friends, at the invitation of Mr. Chas. Banks, the noted Negro cashier of Mound Bayou. The movement, whose success can be described by no better term than by the word *tremendous,* seems to be a kind of University Extension in which the eminent industrialist was the teacher, while farmers and their families, even to the uttermost baby, were the pupils; though it must be confessed that no University Extension audience ever before ate so many peanuts or laughed so much out of pure overflowing of gladness.

They were from bottom and hill, in every conceivable mode of conveyance, from the rattle-trap to the carry-all. Think not, however, that grotesque buggies exhausted the transports; there were also phaetons and carriages as glittering, as new, as well kept, as expensive as any you are accustomed to see in a Northern city, and these were drawn by sleek fat horses in new creaking harness.

Among the queer and amusing things that enlivened the tour was a half-grown white boy seated upon a saddled bull yearling, speeding his way, enveloped in a cloud of dust, to the depot as the train pulled in and crying in excited tones, "Where is Booker T.?"

One good old colored lady came out of the chapel where Dr. Washington was speaking, exclaiming to the envy of the others, "I sho' toched 'im!"

The devotion of the Negroes, who regarded him as their Moses, was pathetic; the curiosity of the white people and their efforts to see without seeming was amusing; but the evident desire of all classes, white and black, to hear him speak was not to be masked or mistaken.

Booker T. Washington is an interesting character, perhaps more so as a person in privacy or surrounded by a few friends, than as a public man facing cheering throngs. In his special car, he laughed at ease in a loose gray flannel suit and listened more than he talked. Occasionally he would pass along the aisle and say a pleasant word, but almost before he could receive a response, he seemed to lapse into abstraction or absent-mindedness and passed on. He never worries, but apparently always is thinking about the unfinished or new task rather than that already accomplished.

He is alert without appearing to look about him, and often surprises you by recalling matters which you felt disappointed about because he seemed to pay so little attention to them.

With the honest old awkward farmer or the motherly effusive old ante-bellum woman he is seen at his best, humoring their queer conceits and receiving their home-spun wit with a twinkle and gentle indulgence, yet without stopping for the long rambling talk they expect and desire. His handshakes, when the crowd surges toward him, are greetings warm and dismissals quick in the same grasp. Whoever has shaken hands with President McKinley knows how, in shaking Mr. Washington's hand, he will feel the instant grasp that first draws him to and then drags him by to make room for the next.

A special Pullman had been placed at the service of the party for an itinerary beginning at Memphis, Tennessee, Oct. 5, and ending at Mound Bayou, Miss., the famous Negro town, October 10, including between those dates Holly Springs, where Ex-Governor Vardaman closed the Negro State Normal School; Jackson, the capital of Miss.; Utica, the seat of the Utica Normal and Industrial Institute an important off-shoot of Tuskegee; Natchez, the home of

Southern aristocracy during the war; Vicksburg, of note as the prize of Grant in his struggle against Pemberton; and Greenville, the home of Bishop Lampton.

At all of these places Dr. Washington delivered plain, inspiring and practical talks which the people warmly received. There was an element of hero-worship in the way they dogged his footsteps. One little girl leaned far over the gallery railing as he passed under it, and said with a loving familiarity, "Howdy, Mr. Bookerty!" She got the twinkle out of those gray eyes that look so much like Henry Ward Beecher's; and from thenceforth she will be, I suppose, a heroine among her less venturesome lassie friends.

The gentlemen accompanying Dr. Washington are most of them widely known, and themselves formed a distinguished coterie. They were Dr. Booker T. Washington's Secretary, Emmett J. Scott, and stenographer, Nathan Hunt; Hon. Chas. Banks, cashier of the Bank of Mound Bayou, Mound Bayou, Miss.; Major R. R. Moton, Commandant of the Hampton Institute, Hampton, Va.; H. T. Kealing, editor A.M.E. Church Review, Philadelphia, Pa.; Dr. R. E. Park, Wollaston, Mass.; Dr. Bradley Gilman, Boston, Mass.; R. C. Simmons, editor of the National Review, New York City; Chas. Stewart, newspaper correspondent, Chicago, Ill.; E. P. Simmons,[1] Hollandale, Miss.; W. W. Cox,[2] cashier of the Delta Penny Savings Bank, Indianola, Miss.; Hon. W. E. Mollison, President of the Lincoln Savings Bank, Vicksburg, Miss.; Hon. J. T. Settle, attorney at law, Memphis, Tenn.; Prof. J. A. Martin,[3] Principal Colored City Schools, Jackson, Miss.; Bishop E. Cottrell, C.M.E. Church, Holly Springs, Miss.; A. P. Bedou, photographer, New Orleans, La.

The local Negro Business Leagues in various cities visited elected special committees to accompany Dr. Washington's party from city to city. These various reception committees of course increased the number of persons which went into each of the several cities.

At Holly Springs the party visited the Baptist College, Rust University and the Theological and Industrial Institute founded by Bishop Cottrell, the latter taking the place, as before said, of the State School that died because Governor Vardaman refused to sanction the appropriation for its maintenance. The new college consists of splendid buildings all paid for by the colored people themselves at a cost of some $60,000.

A dinner and evening reception were tendered the visitors by Bishop Cottrell at his mansion which is one of the most spacious and beautiful homes owned by one of our race in all America. It has about three hundred feet of porch extending on three sides of the house and this, with a large lawn covered by trees and flowers, suggests rest and coolness the hottest days.

At Utica was inspected the industrial school plant established by Prof. Holtzclaw, a graduate of Tuskegee, who went out into the woods and made them eloquent with the recitations of girls and boys who, till then, had had no chance. To-day his institution has received and is receiving the support of Northern capital and Southern sympathy. It was here that Dr. Washington declared for all forms of education according to the needs of the individual and the race, boldly declaring that no power on earth could stop the Negro from acquiring an education of some kind, and it was to the interest of all classes to see that he secured a good one.

It is not possible to speak in detail of all the occurrences of the tour, of the enthusiasm, the hospitality and joy of the colored people and of the curiosity mingled with respect shown by the whites. After one of the speeches, a young white bank cashier called upon Dr. Washington in his car and requested a copy of his remarks advising the people to start a bank account, saying, "I am frank to say I want it to advertise my bank, for your words have weight with us all."

Aside from the personnel of the touring party, the addresses, the entertainment accorded and the unusual character of the affair, there was a distinct and characteristic feature or circumstance in the case of each city visited which probably guided Mr. Charles Banks in making out the itinerary. Jotting down a few of these as they came, in order, we reached:

Holly Springs, October the 5th

This was the home and is the last resting place of the late Senator Hiram R. Revels.[4] The late James Hill, ex-Secretary of State and member of the Republican National Committee for Miss., was born and raised here. Holly Springs has three good schools. Rust University, from which Ida B. Wells graduated, is under the auspices of the M.E. Church. Charles Banks also attended Rust. Also the Baptist Academy, under Dr. Teague.[5]

The school of which Bishop Cottrell is head is under the management of the C.M.E. Church. Here is where the State Normal is located that was killed by Gov. Vardaman who vetoed the bill carrying appropriations for that school. Bishop Cottrell's school, which is considerably larger in every way, is in part the result from the Governor's attitude.

Jackson, October the 7th

This, of course, is the Capital. It had a State House costing more than a million dollars, built under Gov. Longino, brother-in-law to Mr. Edgar S. Wilson, U.S. Marshall, and Federal referee up to last year. This is the home of Bishop Galloway. It is the last resting place of Jas. Hill, where his statue is erected, and also of Jas Lynch,[6] who, while not known much outside of the state, in his day was contemporaneous in state affairs with Pinchback, Bruce and John R. Lynch, though the latter was not a relative. There are two colleges here for Negroes. Jackson College, under the auspices of the American Baptist Missionary Society, and Campbell College under the management of the A.M.E. Church. Both have at least two creditable four or five-story brick buildings.

Natchez, October the 7th

This is the home of Hon. John R. Lynch, the last Negro to go to Congress from Miss., and now Paymaster, with rank of Major in the U.S. Army, and, I think, lately retired. Natchez is perhaps the oldest settlement in Mississippi. Six miles east of Natchez, in the same county, Adams, is an old and almost depopulated town, Washington, that was once the capital of Miss., and one of the places to which Aaron Burr fled after his conflict with Alexander Hamilton. There is one college here for Negroes. Natchez Baptist College, the pride of the Negro Baptists of Miss., and one of the first of its kind instituted by the race in the State. They laid the corner stone of their large dormitory during Dr. Washington's visit to Natchez.

Vicksburg, October the 8th

Too much is written in every history of the South and State for me to task you with much about this city. Here was the home and last resting place of Thos. W. Stringer,[7] easily the leader of the State in Church, lodges and politics in his day; he died about 1893 or 1894. The founder of the Masonic order in Miss., as well as the Knights of Pythias, which together now pay out over one quarter of a million dollars to beneficiaries annually, a reference to him is easily a great hit anywhere in Mississippi, and especially at Vicksburg. The National Cemetery Park is here. About twenty miles south of Vicksburg is Davis Bend Island, where is located the plantation owned by Jefferson Davis and his brother Joe Davis, the slave masters and owners of I. T. Montgomery and his father, Benjamin Montgomery.

Greenville, October the 9th

This is the largest Delta town in Washington County, the largest County in the state. It is the home of Bishop Lampton. It has a book store run by a Negro, Granville Carter, that is not excelled by any run by whites in the State, and is the best in Greenville. Here is where Holt Collier lives, the famous Negro bear hunter who was with President Roosevelt when he hunted in Mississippi, a few years ago. Mr. Leroy Percy,[8] commended by the president, and quoted in a New York magazine for the manly stand taken in favor of Negro education, lives in Greenville.

Mound Bayou, October the 10th

Well, I suppose our readers know much about Mound Bayou. In this county, Bolivar, however, the late Hon. Blanche K. Bruce lived, was Sheriff of the county, and elected U.S. Senator while a resident. The Bruce plantation is about ten miles from Mound Bayou. Mr. Chas. Scott,[9] late candidate for Governor on the "Italian emigration" platform, lives here in this county.

As intimated above, this tour is really a form of University extension, since Dr. Washington's purpose is to arouse the people to a fuller appreciation of the economic opportunities right about them.

He eschews politics and sectarian religion and while pleading for a larger measure of friendliness and co-operation between the races, he does not omit to point to the good that is already to be found. Best of all the home-spun country farmers leave these meetings satisfied that good can come out of Nazareth and feeling that farming is as honorable as practicing law. The state of Mississippi holds untold wealth in the fertility of her river bottom lands that, even under present wasteful methods, sometimes produce two bales of cotton to the acre, without fertilization, equivalent to one hundred dollars per acre, with prices at present prevailing.

In my opinion, there is no place where the Southern Negro can do better for himself and battle more effectively for his race than right in the heart of the problem. Where racial estrangement is greatest there is the application of the remedy most needed. It is therefore to be hoped that a great pacificator like the Tuskegeean will continue to spread his optimism by the special car method in addition to all the other means he has hitherto employed.

A trip through Texas, through Arkansas and through Louisiana ought logically to follow Dr. Washington's helpful tour through Mississippi.

H. T. KEALING

A.M.E. Church Review, 25 (Oct. 1908), 20–27.

1 E. P. Simmons, principal for many years of a black school in Hollandale, Miss., was Margaret M. Washington's brother-in-law and the father of Roscoe Conkling Simmons.

2 Wayne Wellington Cox (b.1864), a graduate of Alcorn A & M College, was one of the largest black planters in Mississippi. He later was a postal employee in the railway mail service. Beginning in 1906 he was cashier of the Delta Penny Savings Bank in Indianola. In 1902 Cox's wife, Minnie M. Cox, was postmaster of the Indianola postoffice when James K. Vardaman demanded her removal. Theodore Roosevelt refused to remove her from office but closed the postoffice instead. (Gatewood, "Theodore Roosevelt and the Indianola Affair," 48–69.)

3 J. A. Martin was also president of the Mississippi Colored State Teacher's Association.

4 Hiram Rhodes Revels (1827–1901) was the first black man to serve in the U.S. Senate (1870–71). Born of free parents in Fayetteville, N.C., he attended a Quaker seminary in Indiana and Knox College. After ordination in the A.M.E. Church, he taught, lectured, and preached throughout the Midwest. During the Civil War he assisted in organizing black regiments in Maryland and Missouri. Moving to Mississippi in the wake of the Union Army, he organized black churches and schools and made Natchez his home, serving a term on its city council. Thereafter he served in the state legislature and the U.S. Senate, where he supported a bill to end the disfranchisement of ex-Confederates. Appointed president of Alcorn University, he so ingratiated himself with white Mississippians that he lost the support of blacks, and Governor Adelbert Ames removed him from office. When the white Democrats returned to power in 1875 with Revels's support, he was reappointed president of Alcorn. (Wharton, *The Negro in Mississippi*, 159–60.)

5 Alex Teague, born in Moscow, Tenn., in 1866, was the pastor of the Holly Springs Baptist Church.

6 James D. Lynch was the first black man to hold a major state office in Mississippi, that of secretary of state. A well-educated Pennsylvanian, he moved to Mississippi in 1868 to take charge of the A.M.E. Church in the state. A superb orator and a fluent, graceful conversationalist, he enjoyed the respect of both blacks and whites. When he ran for Congress in 1875 on the Republican ticket, however, white Republican rivals took him into court on a charge of adultery and prevented his nomination. He died soon afterward. (Wharton, *The Negro in Mississippi*, 152, 154–55.)

7 Thomas W. Stringer, a black Ohioan, moved to Mississippi during Reconstruction as superintendent of missions and presiding elder of the A.M.E. Church, a work for which he had been trained in Ohio. He was the chief organizer for his church in the state, and also introduced the Masons and the Knights of Pythias in Mississippi.

He was an influential member of the Mississippi constitutional convention of 1868, where he led the successful movement for a compulsory education provision. He was elected to the Mississippi Senate in 1870. (Wharton, *The Negro in Mississippi*, 148–51, 173–74, 262, 271–72.)

8 Le Roy Percy (1860–1929) was U.S. senator from Mississippi from 1910 to 1913, filling the vacancy left by the death of Anselm J. McLaurin.

9 Charles Scott (1847–1916), a large planter in the Mississippi Delta. Scott fought against the McLaurin machine and ran unsuccessfully for governor in 1907. One of his planks was the promotion of Italian labor to compete with blacks on the plantations.

A Sunday Evening Talk

[Tuskegee, Ala.] November 1, 1908

THE YEARS OF CONCENTRATION

I want to impress upon you as strongly as I can, that, for the most part, during the next two or three years, or four or five years, or whatever length of time you may have to spend here, are years of concentration. I want you to bear in mind that the years immediately before you, in connection with your work here, are to be, or should be, years of concentration. You are going to get hold of habits that are going to help you, or injure you — habits that are going to cling to you all through your life. You must not grow discouraged, or disappointed, if you find yourself leading a very active and strenuous life through the next few months and years. That is what you are here for. That is what the teachers are here for — to help you to put all of your energy, all of your strength in certain directions, so that within a few months, or a few years, at most, there may be such concentration of life, such concentration of activity, that your characters in the larger sense, may be so formed, that what you get here will stay with you and influence you all through your life.

Let me say again, this is the time for concentration, for hard effort and you must not grow discouraged while trying to get hold of things, while trying to crowd into a few months or a few years that which is going to stay with you all of your life. You are going to get habits or should get habits, that should cling to you all through your life.

Many of you should get, for example, the inclination for cleanliness of body, so that you will be unhappy and discontented unless you are absolutely sure that your body is clean. We give a great deal of attention here in all of the departments to the bathing of the body — the cleanliness of the body. We do that because we want to fasten upon you such habits in that direction that you cannot grow away from them. We want to get you so in love with a clean body during the next few months or few years, that you will be unwilling to live with a filthy body the remaining portion of your life. It is for that reason that we give a great deal of attention to careful, systematic bathing while you are here.

We hope you will get certain other habits relating to the cleanliness of the body. If you do not get the habit in school of keeping your finger nails clean, you are likely to go all through life making a mistake in this respect; making yourselves offensive to other people. Learn the value of clean collars and cuffs. Learn to be clean in all things that relate to the body. If a student does not learn here the value of a tooth brush, does not get into the habit of cleaning his teeth at least twice a day, he is not likely to get hold of this habit and make an effort in that direction later in his life. We want that habit to be a part of you, so that it will be a part of your real, every-day life.

Remember, as I said in the beginning, these are years of concentration, when we expect you to get hold of certain fundamental habits that will cling to you. Then these are years of concentration in reference to the strength of the body, in reference to the proper carriage of the body. We give a good deal of attention both among the girls and the boys, to the proper manner of sitting in the class rooms, at the dining room table, the proper method of walking, and of standing. You will get in the next few years habits that will help or hinder you — habits that will cling to you all of your life. If you remain here, you will be taught to sit straight, to stand straight, to walk well, and to hold your body correctly. These are years of preparation when there must be concentration of the most severe nature in order that you may get out of your school life what we plan you should get out of it.

These are years of concentration in reference to your growing in economic worth and power. You are going to get certain habits, certain traits, certain information during the next few months that will make you, or should make you, more valuable from an economic point of view than you were before you came here. In the next few months you will have to concentrate activity of mind and body in order to get this increased economic worth. You will have to give a great deal of attention to getting all you can out of your trade, or your special occupation, whether it happens to be on the farm, or in the shop, or in connection with some of the domestic departments. In all of these directions we want hard, severe, constant concentration, in order that you may equip yourself in these respects within a few months for the life that you are to live when you leave here.

All of this means concentration, severe self-control in the matter of your moral life. We are constantly saying to you: "Cut off this habit; put on that habit." That means we want to help you to so concentrate, to so control all of your inclinations and all of your activities, that within a few months you shall get a certain moral strength, a certain moral tone, a certain moral atmosphere about you that shall cling to you and be a part of you.

In other words, we are trying to help you, from a moral point of view, to drop off and cut off everything that will pull you down, that tends to weaken you, and to put on everything that will strengthen you and enable you to be the absolute master of yourself at all times and under all circumstances. Now is the time for most of you. If you do not make the most of the months and the years that are immediately before you in getting these correct habits of body, correct habits of thought, of work and of moral living, the chances are that you will never get them and you will go through life minus these great qualities needed to make your life a success.

All I am saying to you can be summed up in one sentence and that is, we are trying to teach you to use your bodies, your hands, and your moral force to be of the highest service to yourself. Do not make the mistake that many people make, of feeling that the great object to be obtained by the cultivation of all these powers, to which I have referred, is the gratification of your own desires.

The great object of all education in these respects should be to better fit us to serve somebody else and the individual who begins life with the idea of fitting himself to serve somebody else is always the happiest and most successful individual, whereas, on the other hand, the individual who begins life with the idea of serving himself ends it by being the most miserable and disappointed creature. In other words, the way to be small is to serve yourself; the way to be great, is to use all of your powers of body, of mind and of heart in the service of others.

Tuskegee Student, 20 (Nov. 14, 1908), 1. Stenographically reported.

To Emmett Jay Scott

Tuskegee Institute, Alabama November 2, 1908

Mr. Scott: I wish you would take up as soon as you think wise the following matter and keep it constantly and fully before you.

1 — I want to make the meeting at Spelman on the night of the 20th an unusually successful affair.[1] Begin calling attention to it at once through the Negro papers. Get them in sympathy with it, through two or three Colored papers in Atlanta aside from the Independent. Of course the Independent is the main one.

2 — On Sunday, the 15th, arrange through some individual, sent from here, if necessary, that you can absolutely depend upon, to have an announcement of this meeting made in all the Colored churches in Atlanta.

3 — Begin, say, 5 or 6 days before the Spelman Seminary meeting and have daily reference, if possible, in the white press of Atlanta to that meeting.

4 — In your own way, arrange for the meeting to be advertised in the Colored sections of the city through a reasonable number of lithographs. If you can think of any other method of advertising this meeting, do so. I think Mr. Parks, Principal of Clark University, could be depended upon to render some assistance.

5 — In some way I should like, if possible, to arrange it so that the meeting will not only be packed with Colored people, but with many of the leading white people of Atlanta, so as to teach the Northern white people the folly of being so timid. I think the whole case presents an opportunity to teach a great lesson.

Booker T. Washington

TLS BTW Papers ATT.

[1] One of the sessions of the Society for the Promotion of Industrial Education, which was held at Spelman Seminary on Nov. 20, 1908. The other speakers were Carroll D. Wright and H. B. Frissell.

To Theodore Roosevelt

Tuskegee Institute, Alabama November 2, 1908

My dear Mr. President: I am glad that you are interested in the Y.M.C.A. building in Washington. It is a fine effort in the direction of self-help.

I wonder if you saw the enclosed article, which I published in the Independent,[1] relative to this effort, sometime ago. The plans were drawn by Mr. Pittman, my son-in-law.

In reference to my Mississippi trip; it was a source of constant delight and surprise to find so many really generous and brave white men and women at many points, where I did not expect to find them.

One of the genuine pleasures of life is to find, that there is more good than evil, and that one often finds good where he expects to find evil.

It was a great satisfaction for me to read, a few days ago that you had become connected with the Outlook. The Outlook, I consider in a large degree, is the heart of the nation, and controls the thoughts and activities of more strong people in America than any other one publication. I have had abundant opportunity to test the influence and power of the Outlook. Yours truly,

Booker T. Washington

TLS Lyman Abott Papers MeB. A press copy is in Con. 7, BTW Papers, DLC.

[1] BTW, "How the Colored People of Washington Raised $25,000 in Twenty-six Days," *The Independent*, 63 (Nov. 7, 1907), 1115–16.

To Theodore Roosevelt

[Tuskegee, Ala.] Nov. 3, 1908

Congratulate you most heartily upon great and deserved victory. It is new endorsement of your life and work.

Booker T. Washington

TWSr Con. 7 BTW Papers DLC.

To William Howard Taft

[Tuskegee, Ala.] Nov. 3, 1908

Hearty and sincere congratulations upon your great and deserved victory. Not only for yourself and Mr. Sherman[1] but in the interest of prosperity and justice throughout America.

Booker T. Washington

TWSr Con. 7 BTW Papers DLC.

[1] James Schoolcraft Sherman (1855–1912), Vice-President of the United States from 1909 to 1912.

From Theodore Roosevelt

[White House, Washington, D.C.] November 5, 1908

My dear Dr. Washington: I will read that article with great interest, and I am particularly pleased to know that the plans were drawn by your son-in-law, Mr. Pittman, whom you introduced to me. Is there anything I can do to mark my interest in the building? I am particularly anxious to do so, because it is possible that we may find it necessary to reopen the Brownsville business on account of the discovery of some, at least, of the men who were actively involved in the shooting.[1] I was so pleased with what you said about the Outlook that I took the liberty of sending your letter to Lyman Abbott. Sincerely yours,

[Theodore Roosevelt]

TLp Theodore Roosevelt Papers DLC.

[1] Roosevelt wrote to Charles Banks of Mound Bayou, Miss., two days later and said that "because the Brownsville business may come up again," he wanted "to emphasize the other side of the question—the side typified by Mound Bayou, typified in another way by Tuskegee, and typified by what is being done here in Washington by the colored Y.M.C.A." (Nov. 7, 1908, Theodore Roosevelt Papers, DLC.)

From Walter Hines Page

New York November 5, 1908

My dear Mr. Washington: I am trying to put through here what I regard as one of the most important things that I have ever undertaken, namely, to have a dinner of the Southern men in New York at which a program for the development of the South shall be laid down. The program will be made practically by me and by two or three other men who think as I think. The spokesmen will include men who can speak with authority and breadth about the industrial development and the intellectual development and the whole labor problem. What would be said about politics in a specific way will, I presume, have to be said mainly by me myself for the simple reason that it would not do to get a man who was identified with any narrow view of political activity to do this. I think I can manage to work it in as the presiding officer of the dinner.

Now all this is the mere background and the mere machinery for the real purpose of the dinner and that purpose is to have Mr. Taft follow up his trip to the South and his evident wish to help broad-minded men down there by a speech at this dinner.[1] Just at this time when he has just been elected the Democrats in the crowd will have no bitterness and they will feel as much complimented as the Republicans by his presence and they will listen to him. They will even agree with him, most of them. What he says will, of course, be published in every Southern paper as well as in every Northern one; and I believe, if he will consent to come, he will do a service to his own administration and to the South that is simply incalculable. As I tell you, I believe that this is as important a matter as can be sprung for the building up of a broader sentiment in the Southern States.

Now I am going to send two or three people who are near Mr. Taft to see him in Hot Springs, Virginia, and they will start from here about the time you get this letter. I am bringing every possible pressure upon him that I can to accept. Of course, he will be reluctant to accept, for, of course, he is bombarded by a thousand and one important solicitations; but I am not going to leave any stone unturned.

Now I want you, if you feel so inclined, to sit down and send him at my expense a long, long, earnest telegram. He will be in Hot Springs, Virginia, by the time you receive this. And then I want you to follow it with a letter. If you feel disposed to do this, you will serve your country and you will serve me certainly.

I believe that if he sees that this is a good thing to do from your point of view that this will have a tremendous effect on him. And I assure you that it is a good thing to do. I am going myself to edit in advance every word that is spoken at that dinner, except what he may say if he will come, and I am going to focus every utterance definitely and sharply towards the liberalization of opinion in the South.

The immediate occasion is the annual dinner of the North Carolina Society, but at its annual dinner the North Carolina Society throws down its bars and asks all Southerners to come. It will, therefore, be the most representative Southern gathering that can be got together in the United States. Always heartily yours,

Walter H. Page

TLS Con. 40 BTW Papers DLC.

1 A printed copy of "The South and the National Government," Taft's address before the North Carolina Society of New York, Dec. 7, 1908, is in the William Howard Taft Papers, DLC. Taft spoke amiably of his hope for "a solid, united country" and urged the South to apply its restrictions of the franchise equally to both races. "The Federal Government has nothing to do with social equality," he assured his white audience, and therefore the southern whites should feel free to divide on economic issues. The solution of the race question he found to be "largely a matter of industrial and thorough education," and "the best friend that the Southern Negro can have is the Southern white man."

From Charles Joseph Bonaparte

Washington, D.C. November 5, 1908

My dear Mr. Washington: I am duly in receipt of your letter of the 3d instant,[1] with enclosed proof of brief and argument in the Bailey case, for which I am greatly obliged to you. R. A. Howard, Esq., of this Department, is now preparing a brief to be submitted to the court as *amicus curiae*, and Assistant Attorney General Russell will be associated with him on the brief at a later date. I have taken pleasure in handing the brief sent by you to Col. Howard. Yours very truly,

Charles J. Bonaparte

TLS Con. 365 BTW Papers DLC.

[1] Con. 365, BTW Papers, DLC.

To Richard Watson Gilder

Tuskegee Institute, Alabama November 8, 1908

My dear Mr. Gilder: I wonder if you know that Mr. James W. Johnson, the writer of the poem, "O Black and Unknown Bards," in this month's Century,[1] is a colored man? He is now holding the position, perhaps as you may know, as Consul at Puerto Cabello, Venezuela. He was appointed to this post by President Roosevelt at the recommendation of Hon. Charles W. Anderson of New York. The poem is exciting a great deal of interest among our people, and I am taking measures as far as I can to have it widely circulated and read. It seems to me it is the finest production that has ever come from any member of our race. Yours very truly,

Booker T. Washington

TLS Century Collection NN. A carbon copy is in Con. 371, BTW Papers, DLC.

[1] *Century Magazine*, 77 (Nov. 1908), 66–67.

To William Henry Lewis

New York, Nov. 9, 1908

Personal

My dear Mr. Lewis: Now is the time, in my opinion, for you to begin and get yourself into such intimate and close relations with the masses of the colored people in Boston and Massachusetts that you can become their real leader and guide. There is a great opportunity for you to do this just now; far better than you will ever have in the future, I think. You have this advantage: The people see now the folly of those who have been trying to lead them and deceive them. Further than that, and perhaps the most important in the way of an advantage, is the fact that in organizing and leading the masses now no one can accuse you of having a political or any selfish motive because there is no special political advantage to be accomplished. If you can get hold of the rank and file of the people and keep them thinking and working in the right direction, they will take care of the leaders. The mistake is often made on the part of many of our people in not getting hold of and keeping in close touch with the common people until they want to use these people on some special occasion or accomplish some special purpose, then it is found that those who want to lead them are out of touch with them and have no influence with them. If you can begin quietly, but systematically, a campaign that would bring you into touch with the people in every Negro church and other gatherings during the next four or five months, it would mean much for you and much for the progress of the race. The people are tired of foolishness and are ready for sensible leadership. Now is your time.

I hope you will talk this matter over seriously with Dr. Courtney and others. Yours truly,

Booker T. Washington

Do not let the other fellows get you on the defensive any more. You have them on the run now, and be sure that you keep them in that position. Work from the bottom up, not from the top down. Begin with the scrub women and go up to the college men.

TLSr Copy Con. 375 BTW Papers DLC.

To William Howard Taft

New York, Nov. 9, 1908

I most earnestly suggest that you give serious and if possible favorable consideration to the invitation extended by Mr. Walter H. Page and others to speak at North Carolina Society banquet to be held in New York City December fourth.[1] Mr. Page I consider one of the wisest and most helpful Southern men I have ever met. The occasion can be made one to accomplish great good in liberalizing the South and starting matters off on a new basis. I have written more fully. If you attend this banquet want to have Jeanes Fund Board meeting while you are in city.

Booker T. Washington

TWcSr Con. 7 BTW Papers DLC.

[1] Actually Dec. 7, 1908. See Walter Hines Page to BTW, Nov. 5, 1908, above.

To Walter Hines Page

Hotel Manhattan, New York, Nov. 12, 1908

My dear Mr. Page: Sometime before the banquet I want to go over with you as far as you will permit, some matters in reference to Secretary Taft's address, and also some matters in reference to some of the other addresses.

There is one danger which ought to be guarded against by all, and it is this: A great many Southern white people will fall over themselves in order to gain the friendship and support of Mr. Taft if they get the idea that the Negro is practically to be thrown overboard in his education and political rights. In everything that is said and done it ought to be made clear to the Southern people that the Negro is to be educated and that the same laws which apply to the white race must apply to him with equal certainty and exactness. Yours very truly,

[Booker T. Washington]

TLc Con. 40 BTW Papers DLC.

To Frederick Randolph Moore

New York, Nov. 12, 1908

Personal

My dear Mr. Moore: The Age for this week on the whole is very creditable. There are several improvements which I hope you will make at once. The main one is this: You are not giving enough space by far to local matters, especially New York and Brooklyn. You are to bear in mind that you have some 25,000 or more colored people in Brooklyn and about 40,000 or more in New York and thousands in Jersey City and nearby towns. For example, you give a column of matter on the front page to Chicago where you have very few readers, a city that is many hundreds of miles away. The matter that pertains to New York and vicinity is hid away in the paper so that very few people will read it. You have enough force in your office so that some of them can get out and actually get hold of news in Brooklyn and New York, news that will interest people. I would not depend upon people to send in news for the paper, but the paper that gets in news that has any value has to go for it. Some months ago you used to give considerable space on the front page to local matters which greatly increased readers in New York City and vicinity. That policy ought to be continued and improved upon.

One other matter. I do not believe it helps the paper very much to give so much space to speeches unless they are very important ones. An interesting running account of a meeting is better. I think too much space is given to Bishop Lampton's speech. The same is true of the speech I delivered in Providence. In the case of what is said by Bishop Lampton, the matter needs careful editing. For example, there is nothing in the paper to show where Bishop Lampton is, where this address was delivered or anything about it. It was simply thrown in in the same shape I presume that it came from the Bishop. The head lines speak of it as being delivered in Greenville, but there is a Greenville, Alabama, a Greenville, Tennessee, a Greenville, South Carolina, a Greenville, Mississippi and any other number of Greenvilles, but the main thing is to put your men to work and get some fresh, vigorous New York City news.

Hereafter please suggest to the people in your office that the matter which I send in the form of editorials remain in the same form that I write them. What I wrote about the poem of James W. Johnson is of no value because of the changes that were made in what I said. You only print two verses of the poem, when I said plainly in my editorial that these two verses were only given as a sample of the high character of the poetry.

There are several other little matters that need closer attention as, for instance, there is a communication from Monrovia, Liberia, dated November 9. Your paper is published on November 12. Now everybody knows that there is no possible way by which a communication can reach New York from Monrovia in three days.

Don't you think there is a little danger of advertising Du Bois too much?

The display ad on your front page looks very well. Yours truly,

[Booker T. Washington]

TLc Con. 41 BTW Papers DLC.

To William Loeb, Jr.

Hotel Manhattan, New York. Nov. 12, 1908

Personal

My dear Mr. Loeb: I have just received a letter from the President in which he states that there is a possibility of the Brownsville case being re-opened on account of having found new evidence, or on account of the guilty parties having been discovered.[1]

If this is true, I am very anxious to have a conference with the President before any move is made in this matter. I am qui[te] convinced that the whole matter can be so handled as to not st[ir] up matters to the point where they were before. I am further anxious that there be no basis for the colored people feeling and saying that the matter was kept quiet until after the el[ect]ion and then stirred up again. I am heartily in favor of eve[ry] thing being done that will discover the guilty parties and ha[ve] them punished, but I am simply writing about the method of doing it. I also think it possible through the colored newspapers in a judicious manner to prepare them for what may be done.

Please tell the President that I will write him within a few days concerning the colored Y.M.C.A. matter.

My address after to-day will be at Tuskegee Institute. Yours very truly,

[Booker T. Washington]

Since writing the above I have seen the secretary of the Y.M.C.A.,[2] and he tells me that the President has agreed to speak at the laying of the corner stone of the new building on Thanksgiving. That is fine, and will help much. I shall be sending the President within a few days a memorandum of some points which I think he might emphasize in his speech at the laying of the corner stone.

TLc Con. 7 BTW Papers DLC.

[1] See Roosevelt to BTW, Nov. 5, 1908, above.
[2] Jesse Edward Moorland.

To William Howard Taft

[Tuskegee, Ala.] November 19, 1908

Personal and Confidential.
My dear Mr. Taft: If you will permit me, I want to send you some suggestions, perhaps in the form of sentences, which I hope you can incorporate into your address in New York on the occasion of the North Carolina dinner. I wish it might be possible for me to see you sometime before you deliver this address. There is a large element, as you may know, in the South, who will support you and the Republican party, if they can be made to feel that you are going to throw the Negro overboard in regard to his education and political rights.

My opinion is, and I am sure it agrees with yours, that gradually a strong, helpful Republican party can be built up in the South, and at the same time, complete justice done to the Negro.

I shall keep track of your movements and shall hope to see you in time to be of service to you in this matter. Yours very truly,

Booker T. Washington

TLpS Con. 7 BTW Papers DLC. Addressed to Taft at Hot Springs, Va.

To Archibald Henry Grimké

Tuskegee Institute, Alabama November 19, 1908

Personal

My dear Mr. Grimke: I agree with you thoroughly regarding what you say about Mr. McKinlay,[1] and stand ready to do anything that I can to further his interests. There are very few men anywhere in the country for whom I have a higher regard and a deeper respect. I find myself handicapped, however, even in regard to my best friends when I want to help them. I have taken the position from the beginning, and I think you will agree with me in the wisdom of it, that I would not take the names of candidates for office to the President or any of his Cabinet members. I have told President Roosevelt and members of his Cabinet that at any time if they wished my advice regarding individuals I should be glad to give it. This policy I have pursued from the beginning. I have acted in the same way in this regard that I would act regarding any individual in or out of office who asked my advice concerning the fitness of a man for a public or a private position. Whatever I have been able to do to help my friends has been done in this way. For example, I was asked my opinion concerning the fitness of Mr. Cobb and others for positions, and was glad to tell the President what I knew of them.

Now the thing to do, it seems to me, is for Mr. McKinlay to get his application for some position before the President-elect, and get it to the point where my opinion will be asked regarding him. This will leave me free to give an unbiased, strong endorsement and will not place me in the position of being an office broker. If I go to the President with a candidate for any office, he then simply puts me in the same class that he does scores of others who are taking candidates to him for some office, and my word has no more weight with him than the others, but, on the other hand, if I have not recommended any special candidate but hold myself free, as he has frequently requested that I do, to give an unbiased opinion regarding several candidates, then my influence and word count for something.

Perhaps in the last analysis it might not hurt for an old-fashioned, hard fighting Democrat such as you are, to say frankly to Mr. Taft that you represent an element that opposed his election but favor Mr. McKinlay because of his high personal and moral fitness for some office. I should like to talk the whole matter over with you when I see you.

I sent your brother a check a few days ago covering the matter of the trip down the river in the summer. I am planning to move in a few days further in the direction of getting money for blotting out the debt on the Douglass property. Yours very truly,

Booker T. Washington

TLS Archibald H. Grimké Collection DHU. A press copy is in Con. 371, BTW Papers, DLC.

1 Grimké had written to BTW on Nov. 13, 1908, reminding him of their earlier conversation about Whitefield McKinlay and BTW's promise to secure for him some such office as the recordership of deeds of the District of Columbia. (Con. 371, BTW Papers, DLC.)

From William Howard Taft

Hot Springs, Virginia, November 23, 1908

My dear Dr. Washington: I want to talk with you and have a full and candid discussion of the subject. I should like to see you before the North Carolina dinner on the evening of the 7th, but I don't like to ask you to come so far out of your way as Hot Springs.

In your letter you touch a subject of great delicacy, one upon which I have quite definite ideas, but I am not sure how they conform to what you may deem an appropriate expression of them. I am anxious to cultivate the good will of the South, but I don't wish to do so at the expense of that class of the Republicans in the South who have upheld the banner of Republicanism at great cost to themselves and self-sacrifice.

I should like to hear from you at once on this subject. I shall be at Hot Springs until the night of the 6th of December. Very sincerely yours,

Wm H Taft

TLS Con. 55 BTW Papers DLC.

To William Howard Taft

Hotel Manhattan, New York. Dec. 1, 1908

Personal

My dear Judge Taft: I have taken the liberty of letting Mr. Page see the suggestions which Mr. Scott handed you to be incorporated into your speech at the North Carolina dinner, and Mr. Page approves heartily of all that is contained in the memorandum.

It was very kind of you to send me word through Mr. Scott that you wish to consult with me fully and freely on all racial matters during your administration.[1] I assure you I shall be glad to place myself at your service at all times. I want no office whatever; I simply desire to serve you in any capacity that you desire at any time. The greatest satisfaction that has come to me during the administration of President Roosevelt is the fact that perhaps I have been of some service to him in helping to raise the standard of colored people holding office under him; in helping him to see that they were men of character and ability; in that way I am sure that President Roosevelt has helped the whole race. If I can in any degree serve you in the same manner I shall be most happy. Yours very truly,

Booker T. Washington

TLS William Howard Taft Papers DLC. A draft dated Nov. 30, 1908, is in Con. 6, BTW Papers, DLC.

1 Taft replied: "I need not repeat what I said to Mr. Scott, but I certainly shall expect to call on you at all times to assist me in matters with reference to the colored people in my administration. Of course, I cannot say that I shall always follow your judgment, and you would not exact that promise; but you know I have always valued it." (Dec. 3, 1908, Con. 7, BTW Papers, DLC.)

From Jane Casey[1]

Roanoke City [Va.] December the 1 1908

dear frind I will take pleasure in ansern your kind leter that I receav from you the 28 of Nov. and was glad to receav the money that you send which was $400 dalars. More than glad to receav it for I hav ben very poley my self and my daughter hav ben under the doctor and has ben very sick so she could not help me much but the lord will all wase provide for the pore and the sick Mrs turner was glad to hear from you me and my daughter and Mrs turner allways are glad to her from you I want you to send me your home and familes picture at some convieant time my daughter says that she was sory that she did not get to see you on Sunday morning that you was hear she hav ben thinking about it very much and look like she could see at iny time she want to hear from your brother John and his famly and your sist Mandy also from your dear aunt Yours Respctfull

Jane Casey

ALS Con. 386 BTW Papers DLC.

[1] In a letter three years later Jane Casey wrote BTW again, calling him "Cousian" and mentioning his brother, sister, and cousin Sallie Poe by name. She said she was seventy-six years old and had lived in Roanoke for twenty-seven years. (Feb. 5, 1911, Con. 420, BTW Papers, DLC.) A Jane Casey was reported in the 1900 census as a washerwoman in Roanoke, born in 1850.

To James Jenkins Dossen

Boston, Mass., December 12, 1908

My dear Vice-President Dossen: I have not written you before this for the reason that I have had nothing special to report. I was in Washington this week and had quite an interview with Mr. Root, also with Ambassador Bryce. I think I wrote you some time ago that Ambassador Bryce spent two days recently at Tuskegee in company with Sir Harry Johnston, and we went over Liberian matters pretty thoroughly. I am quite convinced that Secretary Root, Mr. Bryce and Sir Harry Johnston are all friends of Liberia, and in the highest degree favorable to maintaining its independence as a nation. Secretary Root has received the report from the special agent who went to Liberia, but it contains nothing that was not known before and nothing that has not been already covered in discussion.

It is possible that there will be some developments in connection with Liberia within the next few days or weeks. This latter matter I am not permitted to mention just now to anyone. I am to have a conference with President-elect Taft regarding the matter within the next few days. So far as I can get hold of the facts, there seems to be no immediate danger of any interference with Liberia.

Whenever I can serve you, please be kind enough to let me know. I might add that Secretary Root is deeply interested in all that concerns Liberia. Of course what is contained in this letter is confidential. We have many pleasant thoughts of you and your fellow envoys in this country. Very truly yours,

[Booker T. Washington]

TLc Con. 369 BTW Papers DLC.

To Elihu Root

Hotel Manhattan, New York. Dec. 14, 1908

Personal

My dear Secretary Root: I have just had a conference, as you suggested, with Mr. Taft regarding Liberia, and he asks me to say to you that he thinks it will be a good thing to send a commission to Liberia for the purpose that we discussed. He also asks me to say to you that he thinks it might be wise to provide for the expenses of this commission in the diplomatic and consular bill that is to go before the present Congress.

If you wish to see me further regarding this matter, I think I could arrange to call next Monday, December 21st, as I pass through Washington on my way South.

This will be my address until next Monday.

If the sending of this commission is finally decided upon, and if my name is to be seriously considered in connection with the trip, I ought to say that I should have to give very careful consideration to the matter before deciding whether I could go or not.[1] This will be one of the points I should have to discuss with you further.

Since Mr. Taft is to be here until Thursday, if there is need for my seeing him further in connection with the matter, perhaps you will communicate with one of us before Thursday. Yours very truly,

Booker T. Washington

Mr. Taft says that if the commission is to go, it would suit him just as well for it to be arranged for during President Roosevelt's administration as during his own.

TLS Department of State Numerical File, 1906–10, Vol. 794, Case 12083/55 RG59 DNA.

[1] BTW decided not to serve on the U.S. Commission to Liberia (1909–10). At his suggestion E. J. Scott was appointed as the only black member of the three-man commission. The commission recommended and the United States adopted a protectorate over Liberia and a program for reforming its finances and debts. Little was done to implement the commission's recommendations for the promotion of Liberia's economic growth. (Bixler, *Foreign Policy of the United States in Liberia*; Harlan, "BTW and the White Man's Burden," 452–59.)

To Charles Monroe Lincoln[1]

[Tuskegee, Ala.] December Fourteenth, 1908

Dear Sir: Inclosed, please find a statement as to my views on the question of the

WOMAN'S SUFFRAGE MOVEMENT

Thank you very much for your letter. Very truly yours,

Booker T. Washington

[*Enclosure*]

The Woman Suffrage Movement
By Booker T. Washington

I am in favor of every measure that will give to woman, the opportunity to develop to the highest possible extent, her moral, intellectual, and physical nature so that she may make her life as useful to herself and to others as it is possible to make it. I do not, at the present moment, see that this involves the privilege or the duty, as you choose to look upon it, of voting.

The influence of woman is already enormous in this country.

She exerts, not merely in the homes, but through the schools and in the press, a powerful and helpful influence upon affairs. It is not clear to me that she would exercise any greater or more beneficent influence upon the world than she now does, if the duty of taking an active part in party politics were imposed upon her.

But this is a question concerning which, it seems to me, the women know better than men, and I am willing to leave it to their deliberate judgment.

TLpSr and Enclosure Con. 378 BTW Papers DLC. Signature in E. J. Scott's hand. The statement appeared in the New York *Times*, Dec. 20, 1908, pt. 5, p. 4, under the heading "Booker T. Washington Questions the Benefit to Women."

[1] Charles Monroe Lincoln, born in Bath, Me., in 1856, did newspaper work in New Haven and Philadelphia before joining the staff of the New York *Herald* in 1895. He was on the editorial staff of the New York *Times* in 1907–9 and again after 1924.

To Robert A. Franks

Hotel Manhattan, New York, Dec. 16, 1908

My dear Mr. Franks: I thank you very much for your kind letter and for the information which it contains.

I have just seen Mr. Carnegie and Mr. Bertram together, and I think we have got the matter so far as the Business League is concerned straight for the next two years. You will doubtless receive word direct from Mr. Bertram within a few days. The arrangement is, in a word, for Mr. Carnegie to give $2700 for the work of the Business League to extend through a period of two years beginning January 1st, 1909.

If you are not instructed to the contrary by Mr. Carnegie, it would suit our purpose if you could send one half of this amount, say the First of January each year, and the remaining half the first of June each year. Yours very truly,

[Booker T. Washington]

TLc Con. 370 BTW Papers DLC.

From Elihu Root

Washington. December 16, 1908

Dear Mr. Washington: I have your letter of December 14th and I will see that the proper communication is made to Congress asking for an appropriation for the expenses of the Commission to Liberia.

I think it would be a very good thing if you could talk with Mr. Taft and with some other of your friends in New York about the other members of the Commission. I think it would be desirable to have the other members white men and to have them men who have shown an interest in the improvement and welfare of the black race in our Southern States. Perhaps Mr. Ogden could make valuable suggestions on that subject. It would be desirable to have one of them at least a man who has some familiarity with practical government, perhaps some one who has had something to do with the building up of government, either Cuba, Porto Rico or the Philippines. In short, I think now is the time while you are North for you to direct attention to the question of the personnel of the Commission.

If you can come in on your way through Monday the 21st, I shall be very glad to see you. Very sincerely yours,

Elihu Root

TLS Con. 6 BTW Papers DLC.

Seth Low to Elihu Root

New York December 28th, 1908

Confidential.

My dear Mr. Root; As you may know, I am President of the Board of Trustees of the Tuskegee Normal and Industrial Institute, of which Dr. Booker T. Washington is Principal. Dr. Washington has told me of your wish that he should serve upon an important mission to Liberia, and has asked me for my advice. I shall be very much obliged if you will outline to me, as far as you properly may, the matter as you see it, indicating especially, so far as you are free to do so, why it seems to you desirable that Dr. Washington should serve in this way. I feel sure that the Trustees of the Institute will wish him to co-operate with the Government in every proper way, and will give him any necessary leave of absence. On the other hand, it is essential, as you can understand, that I should be able to place the matter before the Board with as much fullness as circumstances permit; and particularly why Dr. Washington appears to be the best man for the purpose.

I should also be glad to know whether it seems to you that, in accepting this particular mission, he would be likely to expose himself to criticism on the part of the white race for mixing in politics; and perhaps, from the black race, as one who may be looking towards Liberia as an important factor in the solution of our problems at home. As George Washington once said, "It is impossible for a man to pursue a course that will escape criticism; but it is always possible to pursue a course that is capable of vindication." The object of my questions is to develop as clearly as may be the precise object of the mission, so that the Trustees may form their own opinion as to the wisdom of Dr. Washington's taking part in it.

I am, my dear Mr. Root, Yours sincerely,

Seth Low

TLS Department of State Numerical File, 1906–10, Vol. 794, Case 12083/60 RG59 DNA.

BIBLIOGRAPHY

This bibliography gives fuller information on works cited in the annotations and endnotes. It is not intended to be comprehensive of works on the subjects dealt with in the volume or of works consulted in the process of annotation.

Addresses in Memory of Carl Schurz. New York: Committee of the Carl Schurz Memorial, 1906.

Baker, Ray Stannard. *Following the Color Line: American Negro Citizenship in the Progressive Era*. New York: Doubleday, Page and Co., 1908; reprint: New York: Harper Torchbooks, 1964.

———. "White Man and Negro in the Black Belt," *American Magazine*, 64 (Aug. 1907), 381–95.

Bixler, Raymond Walter. *The Foreign Policy of the United States in Liberia*. New York: Pageant Press, 1957.

Blakely, Allison. "Richard T. Greener and the 'Talented Tenth's' Dilemma," *Journal of Negro History*, 59 (Oct. 1974), 305–21.

Buckler, Helen. *Doctor Dan, Pioneer in American Surgery*. Boston: Little, Brown and Co., 1954.

Crowe, Charles. "Racial Massacre in Atlanta, September 22, 1906," *Journal of Negro History*, 54 (Apr. 1969), 150–73.

Daniel, Pete. "Up from Slavery and Down to Peonage: The Alonzo Bailey Case," *Journal of American History*, 57 (Dec. 1970), 654–70.

Fleming, William Henry. *Slavery and the Race Problems in the South, with Special Reference to the State of Georgia*. Boston: Dana Estes & Co., [1906].

Fox, Stephen R. *The Guardian of Boston: William Monroe Trotter*. New York: Atheneum Publishers, 1970.

Gatewood, Willard B., Jr. "Theodore Roosevelt and the Indianola Affair," *Journal of Negro History*, 53 (Jan. 1968), 48–69.

Harlan, Louis R. "Booker T. Washington and the White Man's Burden," *American Historical Review*, 71 (Jan. 1966), 441–67.

———. "The Secret Life of Booker T. Washington," *Journal of Southern History*, 37 (Aug. 1971), 393–416.

———. *Separate and Unequal: Public School Campaigns and Racism in the Southern Seaboard States, 1901–1915*. Chapel Hill: University of North Carolina Press, 1958.

Johnston, Harry H. *The Negro in the New World*. London: Methuen, Ltd., 1910; reprint: New York: Johnson Reprint Corp., 1969.

———. *The Story of My Life and Work*. Indianapolis: Bobbs-Merrill Co., 1923.

Kellogg, Charles Flint. *NAACP: A History of the National Association for the Advancement of Colored People, 1909–1920*. Baltimore: Johns Hopkins University Press, 1967.

Link, Arthur S. "The Negro as a Factor in the Campaign of 1912," *Journal of Negro History*, 32 (Jan. 1947), 81–99.

Mackintosh, Barry. *General Background Studies: The Burroughs Plantation 1856–1865*. Washington, D.C.: National Park Service, 1968.

Meier, August. "Booker T. Washington and the Town of Mound Bayou," *Phylon*, 15 (Fourth Quarter, 1954), 396–401.

———. *Negro Thought in America, 1880–1915: Racial Ideologies in the Age of Booker T. Washington*. Ann Arbor: University of Michigan Press, 1963.

Newby, Idus A. *Black Carolinians: A History of Blacks in South Carolina from 1895 to 1968*. Columbia: University of South Carolina Press, 1973.

Ovington, Mary White. *The Walls Came Tumbling Down*. New York: Harcourt, Brace and Co., 1947.

Peck, Elisabeth. *Berea's First Century, 1855–1955*. Lexington, University of Kentucky Press, 1955.

Proceedings of the Twelfth Conference for Education in the South, Atlanta, Ga., April 14–16, 1909. Nashville, 1909.

Render, Sylvia Lyons. "Afro-American Women: The Outstanding and the Obscure," *Quarterly Journal of the Library of Congress*, 32 (Oct. 1975), 306–21.

Semonche, John E. *Ray Stannard Baker, a Quest for Democracy in Modern America, 1870–1918*. Chapel Hill: University of North Carolina Press, 1969.

Sherman, Richard B. *The Republican Party and Black America from McKinley to Hoover, 1896–1933*. Charlottesville: University of Virginia Press, 1973.

Spear, Allan H. *Black Chicago: The Making of a Negro Ghetto, 1890–1920*. Chicago: University of Chicago Press, 1967.

Thornbrough, Emma Lou. *T. Thomas Fortune: Militant Journalist*. Chicago: University of Chicago Press, 1972.

U.S. Congress. *Congressional Record*, 59th Cong., 1st Sess., 1906, 40, pt. 10, App., 83.

Wharton, Vernon Lane. *The Negro in Mississippi, 1865–1890*. Chapel Hill: University of North Carolina Press, 1947; reprint: New York: Harper Torchbooks, 1965.

INDEX

NOTE: The asterisk indicates the location of detailed information. This index, while not cumulative, does include the major identifications of persons annotated in earlier volumes of the series who are mentioned in this volume. References to earlier volumes will appear first and will be preceded by the volume number followed by a colon. Lyman Abbott's annotation, for example, will appear as *3:43-44. Occasionally a name will have more than one entry with an asterisk when new information or further biographical detail is presented.